DATE DUE

			PRINTED IN U.S.A.

SOMETHING ABOUT THE AUTHOR®

Something about
the Author *was named
an "Outstanding
Reference Source"
the highest honor given
by the American
Library Association
Reference and Adult
Services Division.*

ISSN 0276-816X

R

SOMETHING ABOUT THE AUTHOR®

Facts and Pictures about Authors
and Illustrators of Books for Young People

EDITED BY
DIANE TELGEN

VOLUME 74

Gale Research Inc. • *DETROIT* • *WASHINGTON, D.C.* • *LONDON*

STAFF

Editor: Diane Telgen

Associate Editor: Marie Ellavich

Senior Editor: James G. Lesniak

Sketchwriters: Shelly Andrews, Marilyn K. Basel, Sonia Benson, Joanna Brod, Charles D. Brower, Victoria France Charabati, Bruce Ching, Pamela S. Dear, Elizabeth A. Des Chenes, Fran Locher Freiman, David M. Galens, Denise E. Kasincc, Jeanne M. Lesinski, Sharon Malinowski, Thomas F. McMahon, Mark F. Mikula, Michelle M. Motowski, Michael E. Mueller, Tom Pendergast, Nancy Rampson, Susan M. Reicha, Terrie M. Rooney, Jean W. Ross, Michael D. Senecal, Pamela L. Shelton, Kenneth R. Shepherd, Deborah A. Stanley, Roger M. Valade III, Polly Vedder, and Elizabeth Wenning

Research Manager: Victoria B. Cariappa
Research Supervisor: Mary Rose Bonk
Editorial Associates: Reginald A. Carlton, Clare Collins, Andrew Guy Malonis, and Norma Sawaya
Editorial Assistants: Patricia Bowen, Rachel A. Dixon, Eva Marie Felts, Shirley Gates, Sharon McGilvray, and Devra M. Sladics

Picture Permissions Supervisor: Margaret A. Chamberlain
Permissions Associates: Pamela A. Hayes and Keith Reed
Permissions Assistants: Arlene Johnson and Barbara Wallace

Production Director: Mary Beth Trimper
External Production Assistant: Shanna Heilveil
Art Director: Cynthia Baldwin
Desktop Publishers/Typesetters: Sherrell Hobbs, Nick Jakubiak, C. J. Jonik, and Yolanda Y. Latham

∞™ This book is printed on acid-free paper that meets the minimum requirements of American National Standard for Information Sciences—Permanence Paper for Printed Library Materials, ANSI Z39.48-1984.

Library of Congress Catalog Card Number 72-27107

ISBN 0-8103-2284-6 ISSN 0276-816X

Printed in the United States of America

Published simultaneously in the United Kingdom by Gale Research International Limited
(An affiliated company of Gale Research Inc.)

I(T)P™

The trademark **ITP** is used under license.

10 9 8 7 6 5 4 3 2 1

Contents

Introduction

Something about the Author (*SATA*) is an ongoing reference series that deals with the lives and works of authors and illustrators of children's books. *SATA* includes not only well-known authors and illustrators whose books are widely read, but also those less prominent people whose works are just coming to be recognized. This series is often the only readily available information source on emerging writers or artists. You'll find *SATA* informative and entertaining whether you are a student, a librarian, an English teacher, a parent, or simply an adult who enjoys children's literature for its own sake.

What's Inside SATA

SATA provides detailed information about authors and illustrators who span the full time range of children's literature, from early figures like John Newbery and L. Frank Baum to contemporary figures like Judy Blume and Richard Peck. Authors in the series represent primarily English-speaking countries, particularly the United States, Canada, and the United Kingdom. Also included, however, are authors from around the world whose works are available in English translation. The writings represented in *SATA* include those created intentionally for children and young adults as well as those written for a general audience and known to interest younger readers. These writings cover the entire spectrum of children's literature, including picture books, humor, folk and fairy tales, animal stories, mystery and adventure, science fiction and fantasy, historical fiction, poetry and nonsense verse, drama, biography, and nonfiction.

Obituaries are also included in *SATA* and are intended not only as death notices but as concise views of people's lives and work. Additionally, each edition features newly revised and updated entries for a selection of *SATA* listees who remain of interest to today's readers and who have been active enough to require extensive revision of their earlier biographies.

Two Convenient Indexes

In response to suggestions from librarians, *SATA* indexes no longer appear in each volume, but are included in alternate (odd-numbered) volumes of the series, beginning with Volume 57.

SATA continues to include two indexes that cumulate with each alternate volume: the Illustrations Index, arranged by the name of the illustrator, gives the number of the volume and page where the illustrator's work appears in the current volume as well as all preceding volumes in the series; the Author Index gives the number of the volume in which a person's Biographical Sketch or Obituary appears in the current volume as well as all preceding volumes in the series.

These indexes also include references to authors and illustrators who appear in Gale's *Yesterday's Authors of Books for Children, Children's Literature Review,* and the *Something about the Author Autobiography Series.*

Easy-to-Use Entry Format

Whether you're already familiar with the *SATA* series or just getting acquainted, you will want to be aware of the kind of information that an entry provides. In every *SATA* entry the editors attempt to give as complete a picture of the person's life and work as possible. A typical entry in *SATA* includes the following clearly labeled information sections:

- *PERSONAL:* date and place of birth and death, parents' names and occupations, name of spouse, date of marriage, and names of children, educational institutions attended, degrees received, religious and political affiliations, hobbies and other interests.

- *ADDRESSES:* complete home, office, and agent's address.

- *CAREER:* name of employer, position, and dates for each career post; military service.

- *MEMBER:* memberships and offices held in professional and civic organizations.

- *AWARDS, HONORS:* literary and professional awards received.

- *WRITINGS:* title-by-title chronological bibliography of books written and/or illustrated, listed by genre when known; lists of other notable publications, such as plays, screenplays, and periodical contributions.

- *ADAPTATIONS:* a list of films, television programs, plays, and other media which have been adapted from the author's work.

- *WORK IN PROGRESS:* description of projects in progress.

- *SIDELIGHTS:* a biographical portrait of the author's development, either directly from the person—and often written specifically for the *SATA* entry—or gathered from diaries, letters, interviews, or other published sources.

- *FOR MORE INFORMATION SEE:* references for further reading.

- *EXTENSIVE ILLUSTRATIONS:* photographs, movie stills, manuscript samples, book covers, and other interesting visual materials supplement the text.

How a SATA Entry Is Compiled

A *SATA* entry progresses through a series of steps. If the biographee is living, the *SATA* editors try to secure information directly from him or her through a questionnaire. From the information that the biographee supplies, the editors prepare an entry, filling in any essential missing details with research and/or telephone interviews. When necessary, the author or illustrator is sent a copy of the entry to check for accuracy and completeness.

If the biographee is deceased or cannot be reached by questionnaire, the *SATA* editors examine a wide variety of published sources to gather information for an entry. Biographical and bibliographic sources are consulted, as are book reviews, feature articles, published interviews, and material sometimes obtained from the biographee's family, publishers, agent, or other associates. Entries compiled entirely from secondary sources are marked with an asterisk (*).

We Welcome Your Suggestions

We invite you to examine the entire *SATA* series, starting with this volume. Please write and tell us if we can make *SATA* even more helpful to you. Send comments and suggestions to: The Editor, *Something about the Author,* Gale Research Inc., 835 Penobscot Bldg., Detroit, Michigan 48226.

Acknowledgments

Grateful acknowledgment is made to the following publishers, authors, and artists whose works appear in this volume.

CHESTER AARON. Jacket of *Gideon: A Novel,* by Chester Aaron. Copyright © 1982 by Chester Aaron. Reprinted by permission of HarperCollins Publishers, Inc./ Photograph of cougar courtesy of AIMS Media.

KEVIN J. ANDERSON. Photograph courtesy of Kevin J. Anderson.

LAURENCE ANHOLT. Illustration from *What I Like,* by Catherine and Laurence Anholt. Text and illustrations copyright © 1991 by Catherine and Laurence Anholt. Reprinted in the U.S. by permission of G. P. Putnam's Sons. Reprinted in the British Commonwealth and Canada by permission of Walker Books Ltd./ Photograph courtesy of Laurence Anholt.

ISAAC ASIMOV. Cover of *Foundation,* by Isaac Asimov. Ballantine Books, 1983. Copyright © 1951 by Isaac Asimov. Cover art by Darrell K. Sweet. Reprinted by permission of Ballantine Books, a division of Random House, Inc./ Cover of *The Gods Themselves,* by Isaac Asimov. Ballantine Books, 1984. Copyright © 1972 by Isaac Asimov. Cover art by Barclay Shaw. Reprinted by permission of Ballantine Books, a division of Random House, Inc./ Cover of *Mythical Beasties,* edited by Isaac Asimov, Martin H. Greenberg and Charles G. Waugh. Copyright © 1986 by Nightfall, Inc., Martin H. Greenberg, and Charles G. Waugh on author biographies, introductions, selection and compilation. Cover art by Kinuko Craft. Reprinted by permission of New American Library, a division of Penguin Books USA Inc./ Cover of *Foundation and Earth,* by Isaac Asimov. Copyright © 1986 by Nightfall, Inc. Cover art by Michael Whelan. Reprinted by permission of Ballantine Books, a division of Random House, Inc./ Cover of *I, Robot,* by Isaac Asimov. Ballantine Books, 1983. Copyright © 1950 by Isaac Asimov, copyright renewed © 1977 by Isaac Asimov. Cover art by Don Dixon. Ballantine Books, a division of Random House, Inc./ Cover of *The Norby Chronicles,* by Janet and Isaac Asimov. Ace, 1986. Copyright © 1983, 1984 by Janet and Isaac Asimov. Cover art by Barclay Shaw. Reprinted by permission of The Berkley Publishing Group. All Rights Reserved./ Cover of *The Collapsing Universe,* by Isaac Asimov. Copyright © 1977 by Pocket Books. Reprinted by permission of Pocket Books, a division of Simon & Schuster, Inc./ Photograph by Jay Kay Klein.

LYNNE BARASCH. Photograph courtesy of Lynne Barasch.

VALERIE BEALES. Photograph courtesy of Valerie Beales.

IRENE BELTRAN-HERNANDEZ. Cover of *Heartbeat Drumbeat,* by Irene Beltran-Hernandez. Copyright © 1992 by Irene Beltran-Hernandez. Cover design by Mark Piñón. Reprinted by permission of Arte Publico Press.

CARL D. BENANDER. Photograph courtesy of Carl D. Benander.

PAUL BEYER. Illustration by Paul Beyer from *Little Elk,* by Carl D. Benander. Copyright © 1991 by Winston-Derek Publishers, Inc. Reprinted by permission of Winston-Derek Publishers, Inc./ Photograph courtesy of Paul Beyer.

ALLISON LEE BLYER. Photograph by Lee L. Blyer, Jr., courtesy of Allison Lee Blyer.

FRED BORTZ. Photograph courtesy of Fred Bortz.

ROBERT BURCH. Jacket of *Queenie Peavy,* by Robert Burch. Copyright © 1966 by Robert Burch. Illustrations by Jerry Lazare. Reprinted by permission of Penguin Books USA Inc./ Movie still from "The Incredible Ida Early" NBC/Globe Photos, Inc.

PETER DUNCAN BURCHARD. Photograph © Thomas Hoving.

HESTER BURTON. Photograph by Thomas Y. Crowell.

ERNI CABAT. Cover illustration by Erni Cabat from his *Erne Cabat's Magical ABC: Animals around the Farm.* Copyright © 1992 by Erni Cabat. Reprinted by permission of Harbinger House, Tuscon, AZ.

MARY CARAKER. Jacket of *The Faces of Ceti,* by Mary Caraker. Houghton Mifflin Company, 1991. Copyright © 1991 by Mary Caraker. Jacket art copyright © 1991 by Bob Eggleton. Reprinted by permission of Houghton Mifflin Company./ Photograph courtesy of Mary Caraker.

ARTHUR CATHERALL. Jacket of *Last Horse on the Sands,* by Arthur Catherall. Text copyright © 1972 by Arthur Catherall. Illustrations copyright © 1972 by J. M. Dent & Sons Limited. Reprinted in the U.S. by permission of Lothrop, Lee & Shepard Books, a division of William Morrow & Company, Inc. Reprinted in Canada and the British Commonwealth by permission of J. M. Dent & Sons Limited.

PATRICIA CLAPP. Cover of *Constance: A Story of Early Plymouth,* by Patricia Clapp. Copyright © 1968 by Patricia Clapp. Cover illustration copyright © 1991 by Berta Kuznetsova. Reprinted by permission of Lothrop, Lee & Shepard Books, a division of William

Morrow and Company, Inc./ Cover of *The Tamarack Tree*, by Patricia Clapp. Copyright © 1986 by Patricia Clapp. Cover illustration copyright © 1986 by Troy Howell. Reprinted by permission of Lothrop, Lee & Shepard Books, a division of William Morrow & Company, Inc.

MAVIS THORPE CLARK. Photograph © The Herald and Weekly Times Ltd., Melbourne, Australia.

PAT CONNOLLY. Photograph courtesy of Pat Connolly.

ROBIN CORFIELD. Photograph courtesy of Robin Corfield.

CLINTON COX. Cover of *Undying Glory: The Story of the Massachusetts 54th Regiment*, by Clinton Cox. Copyright © 1991 by Clinton Cox. Cover courtesy of the Library of Congress, Collection of F. H. Meserve. Reprinted by permission of Scholastic, Inc.

INGRID CRANFIELD. Photograph courtesy of Ingrid Cranfield.

KEVIN CROSSLEY-HOLLAND. Cover of *Beowulf*, by Kevin Crossley-Holland. Text copyright © 1982 by Kevin Crossley-Holland. Illustrations copyright © 1982 by Charles Keeping. Reprinted by permission of Oxford University Press./ Cover of *Tales from the Mabinogion*, by Gwyn Thomas & Kevin Crossley-Holland. Copyright © 1984 by Welsh Arts Council. Illustrations by Margaret Jones. Reprinted in the U.S. by permission of Overlook Press. Reprinted in the British Commonwealth and Canada by permission of Lund Humphries Publishers Ltd. and Welsh Arts Council./ Photograph courtesy of Kevin Crossley-Holland.

JENNY DAVIS. Cover of *Sex Education*, by Jenny Davis. Copyright © 1988 by Jenny Davis. Reprinted by permission of Dell Publishing, a division of Bantam Doubleday Dell Publishing Group, Inc./ Photograph by Bill Ringle, courtesy of Jenny Davis.

PAUL dePARRIE. Photograph courtesy of Paul deParrie.

HARRY DEVLIN. Illustrations by Harry Devlin from *Old Black Witch*, by Wende and Harry Devlin. Copyright © 1963 by Wende and Harry Devlin. Reprinted by permission of Four Winds Press, an imprint of Macmillan Publishing Company./ Photograph by Fred Keesing.

WENDE DEVLIN. Cover of *Cranberry Valentine*, by Wende and Harry Devlin. Aladdin Books, 1991. Copyright © 1986 by Wende and Harry Devlin. Reprinted by permission of Four Winds Press, an imprint of Macmillan Publishing Company./ Photograph courtesy of Wende Devlin.

EILIS DILLON. Cover of *The Singing Cave*, by Eilis Dillon. Poolbeg Press Ltd., 1991. Copyright © 1959 by Eilis Dillon. Cover design by Carol Betera. Reprinted by permission of Poolbeg Press Ltd./ Photograph courtesy of Eilis Dillon.

RACHEL DIXON. Cover of *The Demon Piano*, by Rachel Dixon. Illustrations copyright © by Jon Riley. Reprinted by permission of Transworld Publishers Ltd./ Photograph courtesy of Rachel Dixon.

NORAH DOOLEY. Photograph by Robert Fairchild, courtesy of Norah Dooley.

ANGELA DRACUP. Jacket of *The Placing*, by Angela Dracup. Copyright © 1991 by Angela Dracup. Jacket illustration by Julie Dodd. Reprinted by permission of Victor Gollancz Ltd./ Photograph by Frank Dracup.

DIANE EBLE. Photograph courtesy of Diane Eble.

PAU ESTRADA. Jacket art by Pau Estrada from *Just Not the Same*, by Addie Lacoe. Jacket art copyright © 1992 by Pablo E. Estrada. Reprinted by permission of Houghton Mifflin Company./ Photograph courtesy of Pau Estrada.

ROBYN EVERSOLE. Photograph by Amanda Saslow Photography, courtesy of Robyn Eversole.

GENE FEHLER. Photograph courtesy of Gene Fehler.

RUSS FLINT. Illustration by Russ Flint from *The Legend of Sleepy Hollow*, adapted from the original by Washington Irving. Copyright © 1991 by Ideals Publishing Corporation. Reprinted by permission of Ideals Children's Books.

LYNNE FOSTER. Photograph courtesy of Lynne Foster.

CHARLES FUGE. Photograph courtesy of Charles Fuge.

SALLIE GOODIN. Photograph courtesy of Sallie Goodin.

ALASTAIR GRAHAM. Photograph courtesy of Alastair Graham.

LORENZ GRAHAM. Jacket of *Whose Town*, by Lorenz Graham. Copyright © 1969 by Lorenz Graham. Jacket by Harold James. Reprinted by permission of HarperCollins Publishers, Inc./ Jacket of *Song of the Boat*, by Lorenz Graham. Copyright © 1975 by Lorenz Graham. Illustrations copyright © 1975 by Leo and Diane Dillon. Reprinted by permission of HarperCollins Publishers, Inc./ Jacket of *Return to South Town*, by Lorenz Graham. Copyright © 1976 by Lorenz Graham. Jacket by Ernest Crichlow. Reprinted by permission of HarperCollins Publishers, Inc./ Photograph courtesy of Lorenz Graham.

SOMETHING ABOUT THE AUTHOR

AARON, Chester 1923-

PERSONAL: Born May 9, 1923, in Butler, PA; son of Albert (a grocer and farmer) and Celia (Charleson) Aaron; married Margaurite Kelly (a jeweler), April 17, 1954 (divorced, 1973); stepchildren: Louis Daniel Segal. *Education:* Attended University of California, Los Angeles; University of California, Berkeley, B.A., 1966; San Francisco State University, M.A., 1972.

ADDRESSES: Home—P.O. Box 388, Occidental, CA 95465. *Office*—Department of English, St. Mary's College of California, Moraga, CA 94575.

CAREER: St. Mary's College of California, Moraga, began as assistant professor, became professor of English, 1980—; writer. Kaiser Permanente, San Francisco, CA, x-ray technician, 1957-58; Alta Bates Hospital, Berkeley, CA, chief x-ray technician, 1957-75; MKI Engineering, San Francisco, technical writer, 1971-72. Also served as a volunteer at the California Marine Mammal Center in Marin County. *Military service:* U.S. Army, 1943-46.

AWARDS, HONORS: Grants from Huntington Hartford Foundation, 1951, the Chapelbrook Foundation, 1970, and the National Endowment for the Arts, 1976; Junior Literary Guild citation, 1979, for *Catch Calico!; Duchess* was named a 1982 notable children's trade book in the field of social studies by a joint committee of the National Council for the Social Studies and the Children's Book Council.

CHESTER AARON

WRITINGS:

YOUNG ADULT FICTION

Better Than Laughter, Harcourt, 1972.
An American Ghost, illustrations by David Lemon, Harcourt, 1973.
Hello to Bodega, Atheneum, 1976.
Spill, Atheneum, 1978.
Catch Calico!, Dutton, 1979.
Gideon, Lippincott, 1982.
Duchess, Lippincott, 1982.
Out of Sight, Out of Mind, Lippincott, 1985.
Lackawanna, Lippincott, 1986.
Alex, Who Won His War, Walker, 1991.

OTHER

The Cowbank (play), produced at University of California, Berkeley, 1955.
About Us (adult novel), McGraw, 1967.

Also author of unpublished novel entitled *Axel.* Contributor of short stories to *Amistad, Coastlines, Highlights for Children, North American Review,* and *Texas Quarterly.*

ADAPTATIONS: Cougar, based on *An American Ghost,* was released by ABC-TV as a weekend special in 1984; *Lackawanna* was optioned for a feature film by Moonlight Productions in association with ITC Productions.

WORK IN PROGRESS: The second book of a trilogy of adult novels; a young adult novel.

SIDELIGHTS: Chester Aaron's desire to become a writer originated in his childhood. An early and avid reader, Aaron remembered an incident that would shape his ultimate career. For his eleventh birthday, he received a copy of Jack London's *White Fang* from one of his brothers. Rushing through the book, the young Aaron rendered an exciting account of it to a spellbound group of children. "But as good as my story was," he recounted in an essay in *Something about the Author Autobiography Series* (*SAAS*), "its impact did not approach the impact the original writing, the words and the sentences Jack London had composed, had had on me.... 'Someday,' I promised the kids as well as myself, 'I'm going to write stories.'" Although he has written throughout his life, it was not until his midforties that he published his first book. Drawing strongly upon the experience of his youth, Aaron crafts realistic fiction primarily for young adults, and earns much praise for its uncompromising honesty. The critical reception of his work has often surpassed its popular success with readers; however, Aaron's "books belong to the sterling old adventure genre, though with more inner subtleties," as Naomi Lewis describes them in *Twentieth-Century Children's Writers.*

Aaron's parents, Jews from Poland and Russia, emigrated at the turn of the twentieth century to settle in the Pennsylvania mining town of North Butler, where they operated a small grocery store. Aaron's five brothers and one sister were nearly adults when he was born in 1923.

The Great Depression of the 1930s threw the region—and the Aaron family—into upheaval. Aaron's parents, generous to those who were unable to pay for their groceries, refused food to no one; and their philanthropy included preparing and delivering packages of meat, vegetables, and bread to the poorest of the unemployed at Christmas. "Before long we were as impoverished as the poorest worker's family," Aaron recalled in *SAAS.* "We had no food. I went, with other kids, to trail along behind the occasional coal trains, gathering fallen lumps of coal for our stove. I hiked many miles with my father to pick wild mushrooms and nuts and berries to supplement the potatoes that composed our meals.... As difficult as it was we never went on welfare, as did almost all of the other families. When our taxes fell due my father insisted on paying them off by working in the hot sun digging ditches, while kids and grown-ups sitting on the porch tried to make sense out of that old Jew's code of morality." With the onset of World War II came a cultural clash and many ethnic slurs to Aaron and his family—insensitive childish remarks and pranks as well as Nazi swastikas painted on their store. "The jokes and curses I received from the kids could no longer be forgiven so easily," Aaron related. "I was driven not just to fight back but to fight and hurt, and even, if

A Jewish boy hides his identity in order to survive Nazi-occupied Poland during World War II in this novel by Aaron. (Cover illustration by Derek James.)

In the television movie *Cougar,* based on Aaron's *An American Ghost,* a young man in the American frontier becomes trapped in a flood with a family of cougars.

necessary, to maim. Driven by a mix of fear and anger I earned the reputation of being a kid it was no longer wise to tease with epithets suggesting Jews were stingy and biblically convicted Christ-killers."

Following high school graduation, Aaron was deferred from the military draft since four of his brothers were already in the service and his parents were both old and ill. He worked in the steel mills for a while but impulsively decided to join the Army. "Fighting ignorant and insensitive kids for their stupid little epithets was no longer enough. I had to kill Germans." Aaron fought in southern Germany; as the war drew to a close, he experienced an event that changed him as a human being. As his military unit approached Dachau, they detected a hovering gray-orange cloud and an increasing stench which they soon realized emanated from burning human flesh. "We stormed the gates of Dachau and overwhelmed the few remaining German troops. I helped open the doors of the various gray wooden barracks that contained the living and the dead, one indistinguishable from the other. We remained at Dachau two days. Those two days changed whatever direction my life, up until then, might have been traveling. I was never the same man. I still dream about those two days at Dachau. I have struggled to convince myself that I am more than a Jew, I am a man, a human

being, like Catholic and Protestant and Moslem men. But it doesn't work. I find myself listening to words of Gentiles, even of those I love, waiting to hear the denunciation that might precede a fist or a rifle butt or knocks at my door in the middle of the night."

Aaron was twenty-two when he returned from the war. For a while, he worked variously at odd jobs while studying creative writing at the University of California, Los Angeles, on the G.I. Bill. He submitted several stories for publication. Although he was generally unsuccessful, Aaron continued to receive encouragement from professors who considered him to have a powerful voice and one that needed to be heard. With the help of a Hartford Foundation grant, he began work on a praised, but ultimately unpublished, novel. Discouraged by this event, Aaron set aside his plans to write full-time and trained instead as an x-ray technician—a profession he worked at for nearly fifteen years while continuing to write part-time. In the late 1960s, Aaron published his first book, a critically acclaimed autobiographical novel, *About Us.*

Calling *About Us* "a beautiful and original book," Donald Fanger praises it in the *Nation* as being "lyrical without mushiness and tough without posing, full of a truth that cannot be abstracted from the words that carry it." Richard G. Lillard describes the book as "a rich cross-section of attitudes and conflicts in America during the Depression and World War II," adding in the *Los Angeles Times Calendar:* "Its radiant insight illuminates a wide circumference of human joy and suffering." "It is a remarkable first novel," Fanger concludes, "able in its authenticity to hear comparison with the best of its kind."

Shortly thereafter, Aaron began teaching at Saint Mary's College in Moraga, California, which gave him more time to pursue writing. When he discovered that his students were ignorant of the Nazi concentration camps, however, he understood that the time had come to write about the Holocaust. The resulting *Gideon* chronicles the story of a brave fourteen-year-old boy who survives the Warsaw ghetto and later the death camp at Treblinka through his own resourcefulness. Lewis labels it a "powerful and important book." And a contributor to *Bulletin of the Center for Children's Books* deems the novel a "moving and terrible story, written with craft and conviction."

Many of Aaron's novels involve animals and their associations, both positive and negative, with humans. *Catch Calico!* presents a young boy who learns some difficult truths after his grandfather contracts rabies from the cat of the title, and is based in part on the author's own experiences after being bitten by a wild cat. A family is brought together trying to save local wildlife after an oil tanker ruptures near their home in *Spill,* while *Duchess* explores the relationship between a boy and his border collie. And in *An American Ghost,* Aaron takes his readers to frontier America to tell the story of a young man who is trapped in a flood with a hungry cougar and her cubs. The boy and the cougar must cooperate to survive; the book was later filmed as an *ABC Weekend Special* under the title *Cougar.*

Aaron explains in his autobiographical essay that in his fiction for adults and young adults alike, "I use the same vocabulary, the same reliance on clear prose, the same insistence on direct narrative (with as little complexity as possible in the structure) that I learned from Jack London." With young adults, however, Aaron discovered a unique and challenging audience—"readers who not merely expressed their enthusiasm for my own work but expressed as well that voracious hunger for literature (stories) that adds depth and color to their world." The author points out that children "admit to an unrestrained thrill, they do not censor or sublimate, they yield to the writer, they willingly suspend disbelief and accept what the writer offers them." Aaron adds that "if the writer stumbles, or deceives, or concocts lies to describe truths, the young readers will quietly but surely turn away, put the book down, shrug off the writer."

WORKS CITED:

Aaron, Chester, essay in *Something about the Author Autobiographical Series,* Volume 12, Gale, 1991, pp. 1-17.

Fanger, Donald, review of *About Us, Nation,* June 26, 1967.
Review of *Gideon, Bulletin of the Center for Children's Books,* June, 1982.
Lewis, Naomi, "Chester Aaron," *Twentieth-Century Children's Writers,* 3rd edition, St. James Press, 1989.
Lillard, Richard G., review of *About Us, Los Angeles Times Calendar,* July 16, 1967.

FOR MORE INFORMATION SEE:

BOOKS

Holtze, Sally Holmes, editor, *Sixth Book of Junior Authors and Illustrators,* H. W. Wilson, 1989.

PERIODICALS

Bulletin of the Center for Children's Books, November, 1977.
Horn Book, December, 1977.
Publishers Weekly, October 28, 1983.

*   *   *

AMES, Gerald 1906-1993

OBITUARY NOTICE—See index for *SATA* sketch: Born Gerald Otto, October 17, 1906, in Rochester, NY; died January 2, 1993, in Manhattan, NY. Painter and author. Ames cowrote over fifty science and magic books for children with his wife, Rose Wyler. Trained in biology and geology, Ames explained complex scientific terms and theories using clear, simple language. He also contributed frequently to scientific journals. Ames had his paintings exhibited with Arts Interaction in New York and the Port Clyde Arts and Crafts Society in Port Clyde, Maine. Among his works were *The Giant Golden Book of Biology, First Days of the World, Magic Secrets,* and *Secrets in Stone.*

OBITUARIES AND OTHER SOURCES:

BOOKS

Authors of Books for Young People, 3rd edition, Scarecrow, 1990.

PERIODICALS

New York Times, January 15, 1993, p. A21.

*   *   *

ANDERSON, Kevin J(ames) 1962-

PERSONAL: Born March 27, 1962, in Racine, WI; son of Andrew James (a banker) and Dorothy Arloah (a homemaker; maiden name, Cooper) Anderson; married Mary Franco Nijhuis, November 17, 1983 (divorced June, 1987); married Rebecca Moesta (a technical editor), September 14, 1991; children: Jonathan Macgregor Cowan (stepson). *Education:* University of Wisconsin—Madison, B.S. (with honors), 1982. *Hobbies and other interests:* Hiking, reading, astronomy.

ADDRESSES: Home—Livermore, CA. *Office*—Lawrence Livermore National Laboratory, P.O. Box 808, L-

KEVIN J. ANDERSON

11, Livermore, CA 94550. *Agent*—Richard Curtis, 171 East Seventy-fourth St., New York, NY 10021.

CAREER: Lawrence Livermore National Laboratory, Livermore, CA, technical writer/editor, 1983—; Materials Research Society, Pittsburgh, PA, columnist, 1988—; International Society for Respiratory Protection, Salem, OR, copy editor, 1989—.

MEMBER: Science Fiction Writers of America, Horror Writers of America.

AWARDS, HONORS: Nominated for best small press writer, Small Press Writers and Artists Organization, 1984; Dale Donaldson Memorial Award for lifetime service to the small press field, 1987; Bram Stoker Award nomination for best first novel, Horror Writers of America, 1988, for *Resurrection, Inc;* "Writers of the Future" honorable mention citations, Bridge Publications, 1985, 1988, and 1989.

WRITINGS:

SCIENCE FICTION

Resurrection, Inc., Signet Books, 1988.
(With Doug Beason) *Lifeline,* Bantam, 1990.
(With Beason) *The Trinity Paradox,* Bantam, 1991.
(With Beason) *Assemblers of Infinity,* Bantam, 1993.

FANTASY

Gamearth, Signet Books, 1989.
Gameplay, Signet Books, 1989.
Game's End, Roc Books, 1990.

(With Kristine Kathryn Rusch) *Afterimage,* Roc Books, 1992.
(With Rusch) *Aftershock,* Roc Books, in press.

OTHER

Work represented in books, including *Full Spectrum,* volumes I, III, and IV, *The Ultimate Dracula,* and *The Ultimate Werewolf.* Contributor of short stories, articles, and reviews to periodicals, including *Analog, Amazing,* and *Fantasy and Science Fiction.*

WORK IN PROGRESS: Three sequel novels to the *Star Wars* movies, for Bantam, to be published beginning in 1994; the text for *The Illustrated Star Wars Universe;* a young adult fantasy novel with John Betancourt, to be published by Atheneum; with others editing *The Star Wars Cantina,* "in which other science fiction authors tell the stories of the aliens in the famous bar-room scene."

SIDELIGHTS: Kevin J. Anderson told *SATA:* "I consider myself a storyteller in a race against time—a dozen ideas usually come to my mind for every one I manage to get written. I seem to be tireless in writing, which is what I would rather be doing than just about anything else. Because of this energy and interest, I am quite prolific. In 1991 alone I wrote nearly 300,000 words— while also working thirty hours a week as a technical editor. Some writers have a muse who speaks in soft, feminine tones; my muse is a gravel-voiced drill sergeant who yells at me to 'Sit down and WRITE!'

"The genres of my writing vary widely, as do my research interests. I have published nearly 150 short stories and about the same number of articles or reviews. From 1987 to 1992 I sold fourteen novels, some of which remain to be written. My fiction ranges from dark horror to high-tech science fiction, high fantasy, and historical adventures.

"I am currently writing three sequel novels to the fantastic *Star Wars* movies, which were a great influence on me when I was younger. I feel honored and intimidated to be given the chance to contribute, in however small a way, to something that has had such an impact on so many people. At the same time, I am writing my first young adult novel, a fantasy, coauthored with John Gregory Betancourt, as well as what will surely be my longest and most complex novel yet, a science fiction disaster novel coauthored with Doug Beason.

"I enjoy exchanging ideas with other people. Often I do this with my wife Rebecca, who handles a lot of the business aspects of my career; she is a very good sounding board for my ideas. Also, I frequently collaborate with other authors, particularly physicist Doug Beason. The collaborative books come out quite different than my solo works, since we have a real synergy in building our story; especially in the complex high-tech novels I write with Doug, two sets of expertise are better than one!"

ANDREWS, Wendy
See SHARMAT, Marjorie Weinman

* * *

ANDREWS, William G. 1930-

PERSONAL: Born August 5, 1930, in Windsor, CO; son of Nathan Edwin (a chiropractor) and Ellen Margarethe (a homemaker; maiden name, Samson) Andrews; married Solange Chandler, September 5, 1954 (divorced, 1966); married Monika Wickert (a nurse), March 22, 1969; children: Donna Ellen Rifken, William G., Jennifer L. Hughes, Edwin B., Christopher Scott, Thomas Nathan. *Education:* Colorado State University, B.A., 1952; University of Bordeaux, C.E.P., 1955; Cornell University, Ph.D., 1959. *Politics:* Republican. *Religion:* Lutheran.

ADDRESSES: Home—46 College St., Brockport, NY 14420. *Office*—Dept. of Political Science, State University of New York, Brockport, NY 14420.

CAREER: Dartmouth College, Hanover, NH, instructor, 1958-59, assistant professor of government, 1959-61; Tufts University, Medford, MA, assistant professor, 1961-64, associate professor of political science, 1964-67; State University of New York, Brockport, NY, professor of political science, 1967—, department chair, 1967-71, dean, 1970-79, and director of social sciences program in Paris, 1983-85 and 1989-91. Chair of Monroe County Special Committee for the Constitution Bicentennial Celebration, 1987-89; member of Rochester Bicentennial Constitutional Convention Commission. *Military service:* Served in the United States Air Force, 1952-54; became first lieutenant.

WRITINGS:

(Editor with Stanley Hoffmann) *The Impact of the Fifth Republic on France,* State University of New York Press, 1981.
(Editor with Hoffmann) *The Fifth Republic at Twenty,* State University of New York Press, 1981.
Presidential Government in Gaullist France, State University of New York Press, 1982.
International Handbook of Political Science, Greenwood, 1982.
The Land and People of the Soviet Union, HarperCollins, 1991.

WORK IN PROGRESS: A textbook on European integration; a study of presidential signing statements.

SIDELIGHTS: William G. Andrews told *SATA:* "Although I have done some journalistic writing, all of my earlier books were for academic audiences. I wrote *The Land and People of the Soviet Union* mainly for my son Thomas, who was thirteen when it was published."

ANHOLT, Catherine 1958-

PERSONAL: Born January 18, 1958, in London, England; daughter of Daniel (an artist) and Diana (a nurse) Hogarty; married Laurence Anholt (a writer and teacher), July, 1984; children: Claire, Tom and Madeline (twins). *Education:* Oxford Falmouth School of Art, B.A. (honors), 1982; Royal College of Art, M.A., 1985.

ADDRESSES: Home and office—Old Woodhouse, Woodhouse Hill, Uplyme, Lyme Regis, Dorset, DT7 3SQ, England.

CAREER: John Radcliffe College, Oxford, training as state registered nurse, 1976; free-lance illustrator of children's books, 1984—.

AWARDS, HONORS: What I Like was named one of the Children's Book Foundation Books of the Year, 1991.

WRITINGS:

CHILDREN'S BOOKS; SELF-ILLUSTRATED

Good Days, Bad Days, Putnam, 1990.
Animal Friends, Orchard, 1991.
Bedtime, Orchard, 1991.
Helping, Orchard, 1991.
Playing, Orchard, 1991.
Make Me Happy, Walker Books, in press.

AND ILLUSTRATOR; WITH HUSBAND, LAURENCE ANHOLT

Truffles' Day in Bed, Methuen, published in U.S. as *Truffles Is Sick,* Little, Brown, 1987.
Truffles in Trouble, Joy Street Books, 1987.
Chaos at Cold Custard Farm, Methuen, 1988.
When I Was a Baby, Joy Street Books, 1988.
Tom's Rainbow Walk, Heinemann, 1989.
The Snow Fairy and the Spaceman, Dell, 1990.
Aren't You Lucky!, Little, Brown, 1990.
What I Like, Putnam, 1991.
Going to the Playground, Orchard Books, 1991.
The Twins: Two by Two, Candlewick Press, 1992.
The Forgotten Forest, Sierra Book Club, 1992.
Can You Guess?, Frances Lincoln, 1992.
All About You, Viking, 1992.
Kids, Candlewick Press, 1992.
Here Come the Babies, Candlewick Press, 1993.

WORK IN PROGRESS: My Toy Bag and *My Shopping Bag,* in a baby board book series.

SIDELIGHTS: Catherine Anholt told *SATA:* "I come from a family of eight children, so have always retained a strong image of childhood. I grew up in a small village in the Cotswold Hills in England, where my father was a potter and artist. Part of our rambling house was given over to this. My mother was a children's nurse at a nearby hospital.

"I have vivid memories of being brought up in a creative household—drawing and making things with clay. For a few years I worked as a nurse myself before

LAURENCE AND CATHERINE ANHOLT

turning to a career in art which seemed better suited to my temperament.

"After the birth of our first child, which coincided with finishing an M.A. at the Royal College of Art, I decided to try to find some way of continuing my interest in art while at the same time being around to see the children grow up.

"Although I had been trained in fine art, illustration was new to me and at first came very slowly. All my drawings are from memory, although I have always intended to work from life. I work very closely with my husband, Laurence, who writes the text of our children's books. We have now produced nearly thirty titles, which are printed in eleven languages. We are looking for universal themes—the daily ups and downs of family life and the development of young children—which is not all that easy. We aim to give a realistic and unsentimental account. We want children to identify with our books and we want them to laugh. Our ultimate aim is to produce that elusive thing—a classic children's story. In the meantime, I never forget how fortunate I am to be able to work from home at something I really enjoy.

"Our house, which overlooks the sea at Lyme Regis, has a very large, very wild garden, just right for our three very large, very wild children. Oh yes—and a dog called 'Jazz.'"

*   *   *

ANHOLT, Laurence 1959-

PERSONAL: Born August 4, 1959, in London, England; son of Gerald Simon (an artist) and Joan (a teacher; maiden name, Pickford) Anholt; married Catherine Hogarty (an illustrator and writer), July, 1984; children: Claire, Tom and Madeline (twins). *Education:* Attended Epsom School of Art and Design, 1976-77; Falmouth School of Art, B.A. (with honors), 1982; Royal Academy of Art, M.A., 1987.

ADDRESSES: Home and office—Old Woodhouse, Woodhouse Hill, Uplyme, Lyme Regis, Dorset, DT7 3SQ, England.

CAREER: Self-employed carpenter/joiner, London, England, 1983-84; free-lance writer and illustrator of children's books, 1987—; art teacher in secondary school, Oxford, England, 1988-89. Part-time education teacher at Swindon School of Art and West Dean College, 1990—.

A group of children express some of their likes and dislikes in *What I Like*, written by Laurence Anholt and illustrated by his wife, Catherine.

AWARDS, HONORS: What I Like was named one of the Children's Book Foundation Books of the Year, 1991.

WRITINGS:

UNDER NAME OF COAUTHOR/ILLUSTRATOR, WIFE CATHERINE ANHOLT

Truffles' Day in Bed, Methuen, published in the U.S. as *Truffles Is Sick,* Little Brown, 1987.
Truffles in Trouble, Joy Street Books, 1987.
Chaos at Cold Custard Farm, Methuen, 1988.
When I Was a Baby, Joy Street Books, 1988.
Tom's Rainbow Walk, Heinemann, 1989.
The Snow Fairy and the Spaceman, Dell, 1990.
Aren't You Lucky!, Little Brown, 1990.

WITH WIFE, CATHERINE ANHOLT UNDER NAME LAURENCE ANHOLT; ILLUSTRATED BY CATHERINE ANHOLT, EXCEPT AS NOTED

What I Like, Putnam, 1991.
Going to Playgroup, Orchard Books, 1991.
The Twins: Two by Two, Candlewick Press, 1992.
The Forgotten Forest, self-illustrated, Sierra Book Club, 1992.
Can You Guess?, Frances Lincoln, 1992.
All About You, Viking, 1992.
Kids, Candlewick Press, 1992.

Here Come the Babies, Candlewick Press, 1993.
Tiddlers, Candlewick Press, 1993.
Bear and Baby, Candlewick Press, 1993.
One, Two, Three, Count with Me, Viking, in press.

SIDELIGHTS: Laurence Anholt told *SATA:* "Almost all the titles listed have been produced with my wife, Catherine. People are often confused about which one of us writes and which one illustrates. In general, Catherine does the illustration and I do the writing, but there are one or two exceptions, for example, *The Forgotten Forest,* which I illustrated and wrote, and *Good Days, Bad Days,* which was written and illustrated by Catherine.

"Just to make things more complicated, I did not use my name as a writer until 1991 because I was still primarily working as a teacher and wanted to keep the writing as a separate activity. Our titles published before this date are therefore in Catherine's name only.

"I was born in London, but spent much of my childhood in Holland as my father's family is Dutch. My father has painted on and off for many years and for me it seemed only natural to follow in his footsteps. I spent eight years at art school and it was not until much later that I began writing seriously. I still spend a lot of time working on my painting and teach painting classes at Adult Education Centers.

"Catherine and I have three children: Claire, who is seven, and twins Tom and Madeline, who are four. All the ideas for our books come from our day-to-day experiences with the family and we often test ideas on the children to see how they respond. In fact one of our recent projects, *The Twins: Two by Two,* is really about our own twins.

"*What I Like* is one of the simplest books that we have worked on. Again, the idea came from listening to our children talking. At first the idea seemed too simple and I had to resist the temptation to complicate it by adding a story or more text. However, in the end it is the simplicity which makes it direct and, in this country, the book was recently selected one of the Children's Book Foundation Books of the Year. I think this lesson on simplicity, or, more to the point, economy, is one of the hardest to learn, but it is there in much of the literature and art that I admire.

"When we work on a book we are always very aware of the responsibility that we have. Books are extremely influential. I was reminded of this recently when I bought an old children's anthology from a second-hand book store. It was a book I had loved as a child, but had not seen for more than twenty-five years. I was amazed to find how intimately I knew each story and illustration. I even found that my favorites and least favorites had remained the same.

"A young child enters into a book completely and, as they read and reread, it shapes the adult they become— and so the society they inhabit. I think it is essential, then, that children's writers and illustrators put a huge amount of care into what they say. I would like to think that our books help children to open their minds to issues of equality—gender and race—to environmental issues, but most of all I want children to get the message that books are fun—it is okay to enjoy yourself, there is plenty to be optimistic about, and the world is a good place to grow up in.

"I think the title which best reflects this sense of fun is *Kids.* I wanted to write a book about what children are *really* like—warts and all. I wanted to break the cliched idea of curly haired little darlings, which any parent knows to be a myth. What are kids like? 'Kids are silly, kids are funny, kids have noses that are runny!'"

*   *   *

ASIMOV, Isaac 1920-1992
(George E. Dale, Dr. A, Paul French)

PERSONAL: Born January 2, 1920, in Petrovichi, U.S.S.R.; died of complications resulting from heart and kidney problems and prostate cancer, April 6, 1992, in New York, NY; brought to the United States in 1923, naturalized citizen in 1928; son of Judah (a candy store owner) and Anna Rachel (Berman) Asimov; married Gertrude Blugerman, July 26, 1942 (divorced, November 16, 1973); married Janet Opal Jeppson (a psychiatrist), November 30, 1973; children: (first marriage) David, Robyn Joan. *Education:* Columbia University, B.S., 1939, M.A., 1941, Ph.D., 1948.

ADDRESSES: Home—10 West 66th St., Apt. 33-A, New York, NY 10023.

CAREER: Writer. Boston University, School of Medicine, Boston, MA, instructor, 1949-51, assistant professor, 1951-55, associate professor, 1955-79, professor of biochemistry, 1979-92. Worked as a civilian chemist at U.S. Navy Air Experimental Station, Philadelphia, 1942-45. *Military service:* U.S. Army, 1945-46.

MEMBER: Authors League of America, Science Fiction Writers of America, National Association of Science Writers, American Chemical Society, Zero Population Growth, Population Institute, National Organization of Non-Parents, Sigma Xi, Mensa.

AWARDS, HONORS: Guest of honor at the Thirteenth World Science Fiction Convention, 1955; Edison Foundation National Mass Media Award, 1958; Blakeslee Award for nonfiction, 1960; special Hugo Award for distinguished contributions to the field, 1963, for science articles in the *Magazine of Fantasy and Science Fiction,* special Hugo Award for best all-time science fiction series, 1966, for *Foundation, Foundation and Empire,* and *Second Foundation,* Hugo Award for best novel, 1973, for *The Gods Themselves,* and 1983, for *Foundation's Edge,* Hugo Award for best short story, 1977, for "The Bicentennial Man," all from World Science Fiction Conventions; James T. Grady Award, American Chemical Society, 1965; American Association for the Advancement of Science-Westinghouse award for science writing, 1967; Nebula Award, Science Fiction Writers of America, 1973, for *The Gods Themselves,* and 1977, for "The Bicentennial Man"; Glenn Seabord Award, International Platform Association, 1979; "Nightfall" was chosen the best science fiction story of all time in a Science Fiction Writers of America poll.

WRITINGS:

"FOUNDATION" SCIENCE FICTION SERIES

Foundation, Gnome Press, 1951, published as *The 1,000 Year Plan* [bound with *No World of Their Own* by Poul Anderson], Ace Books, 1955, reprinted under original title, Ballantine, 1983.
Foundation and Empire, Gnome Press, 1952.
Second Foundation, Gnome Press, 1953.
The Foundation Trilogy: Three Classics of Science Fiction (contains *Foundation, Foundation and Empire,* and *Second Foundation*), Doubleday, 1963, published in England as *An Isaac Asimov Omnibus,* Sidgwick & Jackson, 1966.
Foundation's Edge, Doubleday, 1982.
Foundation and Earth, Doubleday, 1986.
Prelude to Foundation, Doubleday, 1988.
Forward the Foundation, Doubleday, 1993.

ISAAC ASIMOV

"ROBOT" SCIENCE FICTION SERIES

I, Robot (stories), Gnome Press, 1950.
The Caves of Steel, Doubleday, 1954.
The Naked Sun, Doubleday, 1957.
The Robot Novels (contains *The Caves of Steel* and *The Naked Sun*), Doubleday, 1957.
The Rest of the Robots (short stories and novels, including *The Caves of Steel* and *The Naked Sun*), Doubleday, 1964, published as *Eight Stories from the Rest of the Robots,* Pyramid Books, 1966.
The Complete Robot, Doubleday, 1982.
The Robots of Dawn, Doubleday, 1983.
The Robot Collection (contains *The Caves of Steel, The Naked Sun,* and *The Complete Robot*), Doubleday, 1983.
Robots and Empire, Doubleday, 1985.

UNDER PSEUDONYM PAUL FRENCH; JUVENILE SCIENCE FICTION

David Starr, Space Ranger, Doubleday, 1952, reprinted under name Isaac Asimov, Twayne, 1978.
Lucky Starr and the Pirates of the Asteroids, Doubleday, 1953, reprinted under name Isaac Asimov, Twayne, 1978.
Lucky Starr and the Oceans of Venus, Doubleday, 1954, reprinted under name Isaac Asimov, Twayne, 1978.
Lucky Starr and the Big Sun of Mercury, Doubleday, 1956, published under name Isaac Asimov as *The Big Sun of Mercury,* New English Library, 1974, reprinted under name Isaac Asimov under original title, Twayne, 1978.

Lucky Starr and the Moons of Jupiter, Doubleday, 1957, reprinted under name Isaac Asimov, Twayne, 1978.
Lucky Starr and the Rings of Saturn, Doubleday, 1958, reprinted under name Isaac Asimov, Twayne, 1978.

"NORBY" JUVENILE SCIENCE FICTION SERIES; WITH WIFE, JANET ASIMOV

Norby, the Mixed-Up Robot, Walker & Co., 1983.
Norby's Other Secret, Walker & Co., 1984.
Norby and the Invaders, Walker & Co., 1985.
Norby and the Lost Princess, Walker & Co., 1985.
The Norby Chronicles (contains *Norby, the Mixed-Up Robot* and *Norby's Other Secret*), Ace Books, 1986.
Norby and the Queen's Necklace, Walker & Co., 1986.
Norby: Robot for Hire (contains *Norby and the Lost Princess* and *Norby and the Invaders*), Ace Books, 1987.
Norby Finds a Villain, Walker & Co., 1987.
Norby through Time and Space (contains *Norby and the Queen's Necklace* and *Norby Finds a Villain*), Ace Books, 1988.
Norby Down to Earth, Walker & Co., 1989.
Norby and Yobo's Great Adventure, Walker & Co., 1989.
Norby and the Oldest Dragon, Walker & Co., 1990.
Norby and the Court Jester, Walker & Co., 1991.

OTHER SCIENCE FICTION NOVELS

Pebble in the Sky, Doubleday, 1950.
The Stars, Like Dust, Doubleday, 1951, published as *The Rebellious Stars* [bound with *An Earth Gone Mad* by R. D. Aycock], Ace Books, 1954, reprinted under original title, Fawcett, 1972.

The Currents of Space, Doubleday, 1952.
The End of Eternity, Doubleday, 1955.
Fantastic Voyage (novelization of screenplay by Harry Kleiner), Houghton, 1966.
The Gods Themselves, Doubleday, 1972.
Fantastic Voyage II: Destination Brain, Doubleday, 1987.
Azazel, Doubleday, 1988.
Nemesis, Doubleday, 1988.
The Ugly Little Boy [bound with *The Widget, the Wadget, and Boff,* by Theodore Sturgeon], Tor Books, 1989.
Invasions, New American Library, 1990.
(With Robert Silverberg) *Nightfall* (based on Asimov's short story), Doubleday, 1990.

SCIENCE FICTION STORIES

The Martian Way and Other Stories, Doubleday, 1955.
(Contributor) Groff Conklin, editor, *Science Fiction Terror Tales by Isaac Asimov and Others,* Gnome Press, 1955.
Earth Is Room Enough: Science Fiction Tales of Our Own Planet, Doubleday, 1957.
Nine Tomorrows: Tales of the Near Future, Doubleday, 1959.
Through a Glass Clearly, New English Library, 1967.
Asimov's Mysteries, Doubleday, 1968.
Nightfall and Other Stories, Doubleday, 1969, published in England in two volumes, as *Nightfall One* and *Nightfall Two,* Panther Books, 1969, published as *Nightfall: Twenty SF Stories,* Rapp & Whiting, 1971.
The Early Asimov: Or, Eleven Years of Trying, Doubleday, 1972.
(Contributor) Conklin, editor, *Possible Tomorrows by Isaac Asimov and Others,* Sidgwick & Jackson, 1972.
The Best of Isaac Asimov, Doubleday, 1974.
Have You Seen These?, NESFA Press, 1974.
The Heavenly Host (juvenile), Walker & Co., 1975.
Buy Jupiter and Other Stories, Doubleday, 1975.
The Bicentennial Man and Other Stories, Doubleday, 1976.
"The Dream," "Benjamin's Dream," and "Benjamin's Bicentennial Blast": Three Short Stories, Printing Week in New York, 1976.
Good Taste, Apocalypse Press, 1977.
Three by Asimov, limited edition, Targ Editions, 1981.
The Winds of Change and Other Stories, Doubleday, 1983.
The Best Science Fiction of Isaac Asimov, Doubleday, 1986.
Robot Dreams, edited by Bryon Preiss, Berkley, 1987.
Isaac Asimov: The Complete Stories, Doubleday, 1990.
The Asimov Chronicles, 3 volumes, Ace Books, 1990.
Robot Visions, New American Library, 1991.

Also editor or co-editor of over ninety science fiction and fantasy anthologies.

OMNIBUS SCIENCE FICTION VOLUMES

Triangle: "The Currents of Space," "Pebble In the Sky," and "The Stars, Like Dust," Doubleday, 1961,
published in England as *An Isaac Asimov Second Omnibus,* Sidgwick & Jackson, 1969.
An Isaac Asimov Double: "Space Ranger" and "Pirates of the Asteroids", New English Library (London), 1972.
A Second Isaac Asimov Double: "The Big Sun of Mercury" and "The Oceans of Venus", New English Library, 1973.
The Third Isaac Asimov Double, New English Library/Times Mirror, 1973.
The Collected Fiction of Isaac Asimov, Volume 1: *The Far Ends of Time and Earth* (contains *Pebble in the Sky, Earth Is Room Enough,* and *The End of Eternity*), Volume 2: *Prisoners of the Stars* (contains *The Stars, Like Dust, The Martian Way and Other Stories,* and *The Currents of Space*), Doubleday, 1979.
The Alternative Asimovs (contains *The End of Eternity*), Doubleday, 1986.

MYSTERIES

The Death Dealers (novel), Avon Publications, 1958, published as *A Whiff of Death,* Walker & Co., 1968.
Tales of the Black Widowers, Doubleday, 1974.
Murder at the ABA: A Puzzle in Four Days and Sixty Scenes (novel), Doubleday, 1976, published in England as *Authorised Murder: A Puzzle in Four Days and Sixty Scenes,* Gollancz, 1976.
More Tales of the Black Widowers, Doubleday, 1976.
The Key Word and Other Mysteries, Walker & Co., 1977.
Casebook of the Black Widowers, Doubleday, 1980.
The Union Club Mysteries, Doubleday, 1983.
Banquets of the Black Widowers, Doubleday, 1984.
The Disappearing Man and Other Mysteries, Walker & Co., 1985.
The Best Mysteries of Isaac Asimov, Doubleday, 1986.
Puzzles of the Black Widowers, Doubleday, 1990.

Also editor, with others, of many mystery anthologies.

SCIENCE FACT; ADULT

(With William C. Boyd and Burnham S. Walker) *Biochemistry and Human Metabolism,* Williams & Wilkins, 1952, 3rd edition, 1957.
The Chemicals of Life: Enzymes, Vitamins, Hormones, Abelard-Schuman, 1954.
(With Boyd) *Races and People,* Abelard-Schuman, 1955.
(With Walker and Mary K. Nicholas) *Chemistry and Human Health,* McGraw, 1956.
Inside the Atom, Abelard-Schuman, 1956, revised and updated edition, 1966.
Only a Trillion (essays), Abelard-Schuman, 1958, published as *Marvels of Science: Essays of Fact and Fancy on Life, Its Environment, Its Possibilities,* Collier Books, 1962, reprinted under original title, Ace Books, 1976.
The World of Carbon, Abelard-Schuman, 1958, revised edition, Collier Books, 1962.
The World of Nitrogen, Abelard-Schuman, 1958, revised edition, Collier Books, 1962.
The Clock We Live On, Abelard-Schuman, 1959, revised edition, 1965.

Asimov's longtime interest in science fiction included the establishment of *Isaac Asimov's Science Fiction Magazine* and editorship of over ninety collections of short stories. (Cover illustration by Kinuko Craft.)

Words of Science and the History behind Them, Houghton, 1959, revised edition, Harrap, 1974.
Realm of Numbers, Houghton, 1959.
The Living River, Abelard-Schuman, 1959, published as *The Bloodstream: River of Life,* Collier Books, 1961.
The Kingdom of the Sun, Abelard-Schuman, 1960, revised edition, 1963.
Realm of Measure, Houghton, 1960.
The Wellsprings of Life, Abelard-Schuman, (London), 1960, New American Library, 1961.
The Intelligent Man's Guide to Science, two volumes, Basic Books, 1960, Volume 1 published separately as *The Intelligent Man's Guide to the Physical Sciences,* Pocket Books, 1964, Volume 2 published separately as *The Intelligent Man's Guide to the Biological Sciences,* Pocket Books, 1964, revised edition published as *The New Intelligent Man's Guide to Science,* 1965, published as *Asimov's Guide to Science,* 1972, revised edition published as *Asimov's New Guide to Science,* 1984.

The Double Planet, Abelard-Schuman, 1960, revised edition, 1967.
Realm of Algebra, Houghton, 1961.
Life and Energy, Doubleday, 1962.
Fact and Fancy (essays), Doubleday, 1962.
The Search for the Elements, Basic Books, 1962.
The Genetic Code, Orion Press, 1963.
The Human Body: Its Structure and Operation, Houghton, 1963.
View from a Height, Doubleday, 1963.
The Human Brain: Its Capacities and Functions, Houghton, 1964.
A Short History of Biology, Natural History Press for the American Museum of Natural History, 1964.
Quick and Easy Math, Houghton, 1964.
Adding a Dimension: Seventeen Essays on the History of Science, Doubleday, 1964.
(With Stephen H. Dole) *Planets for Man,* Random House, 1964.
Asimov's Biographical Encyclopedia of Science and Technology, Doubleday, 1964, 2nd revised edition, 1982.
A Short History of Chemistry, Doubleday, 1965.
Of Time and Space and Other Things (essays), Doubleday, 1965.
An Easy Introduction to the Slide Rule, Houghton, 1965.
The Noble Gasses, Basic Books, 1966.
The Neutrino: Ghost Particle of the Atom, Doubleday, 1966.
Understanding Physics, three volumes, Walker & Co., 1966.
The Genetic Effects of Radiation, U.S. Atomic Energy Commission, 1966.
The Universe: From Flat Earth to Quasar, Walker & Co., 1966, 3rd edition published as *The Universe: From Flat Earth to Black Holes—and Beyond,* 1980.
From Earth to Heaven (essays), Doubleday, 1966.
Environments out There, Abelard-Schuman, 1967.
Is Anyone There? (essays), Doubleday, 1967.
Science, Numbers and I (essays), Doubleday, 1968.
Photosynthesis, Basic Books, 1968.
Twentieth Century Discovery (essays), Doubleday, 1969, revised edition, Ace Books, 1976.
To the Solar System and Back (essays), Doubleday, 1970.
The Stars in Their Courses (essays), Doubleday, 1971, revised edition, Ace Books, 1976.
The Left Hand of the Electron (essays), Doubleday, 1972.
Electricity and Man, U.S. Atomic Energy Commission, 1972.
Worlds within Worlds: The Story of Nuclear Energy, three volumes, U.S. Atomic Energy Commission, 1972.
Today and Tomorrow and . . ., Doubleday, 1973.
The Tragedy of the Moon, Doubleday, 1973.
Physical Science Today, CRM, 1973.
Asimov on Astronomy (essays), Doubleday, 1974.
Our World in Space, foreword by Edwin E. Aldrin, Jr., New York Graphic Society, 1974.
Asimov on Chemistry (essays), Doubleday, 1974.
Of Matters Great and Small, Doubleday, 1975.
Science Past, Science Future, Doubleday, 1975.

Eyes on the Universe: A History of the Telescope, Houghton, 1975.

The Ends of the Earth: The Polar Regions of the World, Weybright & Talley, 1975.

Birth and Death of the Universe, Walker & Co., 1975.

Asimov on Physics (essays), Doubleday, 1976.

The Planet that Wasn't (essays), Doubleday, 1976.

The Collapsing Universe, Walker & Co., 1977.

Asimov on Numbers (essays), Doubleday, 1977.

The Beginning and the End (essays), Doubleday, 1977.

Quasar, Quasar, Burning Bright (essays), Doubleday, 1978.

Life and Time, Doubleday, 1978.

The Road to Infinity (essays), Doubleday, 1979.

A Choice of Catastrophes: The Disasters that Threaten Our World, Simon & Schuster, 1979.

Visions of the Universe, preface by Carl Sagan, Cosmos Store, 1981.

The Sun Shines Bright (essays), Doubleday, 1981.

Exploring the Earth and the Cosmos: The Growth and Future of Human Knowledge, Crown, 1982.

Counting the Eons, Doubleday, 1983.

The Roving Mind, Prometheus Books, 1983.

The Measure of the Universe, Harper, 1983.

X Stands for Unknown, Doubleday, 1984.

The History of Physics, Walker & Co., 1984.

Isaac Asimov on the Human Body and the Human Brain (contains *The Human Body: Its Structure and Operation* and *The Human Brain: Its Capacities and Functions*), Bonanza Books, 1984.

The Exploding Suns: The Secrets of the Supernovas, Dutton, 1985.

Asimov's Guide to Halley's Comet, Walker & Co., 1985.

The Subatomic Monster, Doubleday, 1985.

(With Karen Frenkel) *Robots: Machines in Man's Image,* Robot Institute of America, 1985.

Isaac Asimov's Wonderful Worldwide Science Bazaar: Seventy-Two Up-to-Date Reports on the State of Everything from Inside the Atom to Outside the Universe, Houghton, 1986.

The Dangers of Intelligence and Other Science Essays, Houghton, 1986.

Far as Human Eye Could See (essays), Doubleday, 1987.

The Relativity of Wrong: Essays on the Solar System and Beyond, Doubleday, 1988.

Asimov on Science: A Thirty Year Retrospective, Doubleday, 1989.

Asimov's Chronology of Science and Technology: How Science Has Shaped the World and How the World Has Affected Science from 4,000,000 B.C. to the Present, Harper, 1989.

The Secret of the Universe, Doubleday, 1989.

The Tyrannosaurus Prescription and One Hundred Other Essays, Prometheus Books, 1989.

Out of the Everywhere, Doubleday, 1990.

Atom: Journey across the Subatomic Cosmos, New American Library, 1991.

Frontiers: New Discoveries about Man and His Planet, Outer Space, and the Universe, New American Library, 1991.

Asimov's Chronology of the World, HarperCollins, 1991.

Asimov's Guide to Earth and Space, Random House, 1991.

(With Frederick Pohl) *Our Angry Earth,* Tor Books, 1991.

SCIENCE FACT; JUVENILE

Building Blocks of the Universe, Abelard-Schuman, 1957, revised and updated edition, 1974.

Breakthroughs in Science, Houghton, 1960.

Satellites in Outer Space, Random House, 1960, revised edition, 1973.

The Moon, Follett, 1966.

To the Ends of the Universe, Walker & Co., 1967, revised edition, 1976.

Mars, Follett, 1967.

Stars, Follett, 1968.

Galaxies, Follett, 1968.

ABC's of Space, Walker & Co., 1969, published as *Space Dictionary,* Scholastic, 1970.

Great Ideas of Science, Houghton, 1969.

ABC's of the Ocean, Walker & Co., 1970.

Light, Follett, 1970.

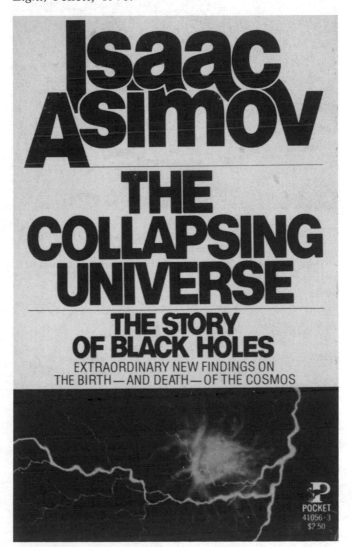

Asimov's clear explanations of complex scientific principles lend themselves to his many volumes of nonfiction as well as his novels.

Asimov won science fiction's highest honors for this tale of two parallel worlds endangered by an invention that bridges the gap between their alternate universes. (Cover illustration by Barclay Shaw.)

What Makes the Sun Shine?, Little, Brown, 1971.
ABC's of the Earth, Walker & Co., 1971.
ABC's of Ecology, Walker & Co., 1972.
Ginn Science Program, Ginn, intermediate levels A, B, and C, 1972, advanced levels A and B, 1973.
Comets and Meteors, Follett, 1972.
The Sun, Follett, 1972.
Jupiter, the Largest Planet, Lothrop, 1973, revised edition, 1976.
Please Explain, Houghton, 1973.
Earth: Our Crowded Spaceship, John Day, 1974.
The Solar System, Follett, 1975.
Alpha Centauri, the Nearest Star, Lothrop, 1976.
Mars, the Red Planet, Lothrop, 1977.
Saturn and Beyond, Lothrop, 1979.
Venus: Near Neighbor of the Sun, Lothrop, 1981.
Those Amazing Electronic Thinking Machines, Watts, 1983.
Beginnings: The Story of Origins—Of Mankind, Life, the Earth, the Universe, Walker & Co., 1987.

Bare Bones: Dinosaur, Holt, 1986.
Franchise, Creative Education, 1988.
All the Troubles of World, Creative Education, 1988.
Think about Space, Walker & Co., 1989.
Little Treasury of Dinosaurs, Crown, 1989.

Also author of 33 volumes in the "How Did We Find Out" series, Walker & Co., 1972-91, 33 volumes in the "Isaac Asimov's Library of the Universe" series, Gareth Stevens, 1987-91, and 41 volumes in the "Ask Isaac Asimov" series, Gareth Stevens, 1991-92.

HISTORY

The Kite That Won the Revolution (juvenile), Houghton, 1963, revised edition, 1973.
The Greeks: A Great Adventure, Houghton, 1965.
The Roman Republic, Houghton, 1966.
The Roman Empire, Houghton, 1967.
The Egyptians, Houghton, 1967.
The Near East: Ten Thousand Years of History, Houghton, 1968.
The Dark Ages, Houghton, 1968.
Words from History, Houghton, 1968.
The Shaping of England, Houghton, 1969.
Constantinople: The Forgotten Empire, Houghton, 1970.
The Land of Canaan, Houghton, 1970.
The Shaping of France, Houghton, 1972.
The Shaping of North America from Earliest Times to 1763, Houghton, 1973.
The Birth of the United States, 1763-1816, Houghton, 1974.
Our Federal Union: The United States from 1816 to 1865, Houghton, 1975.
The Golden Door: The United States from 1865 to 1918, Houghton, 1977.
Futuredays: A Nineteenth-Century Vision of the Year 2000, Holt, 1986.
(With Frank White) *The March of the Millennia: A Key to Looking at History*, Walker & Co., 1990.
Christopher Columbus, Gareth Stevens, 1991.
Henry Hudson, Gareth Stevens, 1991.

OTHER

Words from the Myths, Houghton, 1961.
Words in Genesis, Houghton, 1962.
Words on the Map, Houghton, 1962.
Words from Exodus, Houghton, 1963.
Asimov's Guide to the Bible, Doubleday, Volume 1: *The Old Testament*, 1968, Volume 2: *The New Testament*, 1969.
Opus 100 (selections from author's first one hundred books), Houghton, 1969.
Asimov's Guide to Shakespeare, two volumes, Doubleday, 1970, published as one volume, Avenel Books, 1981.
"Unseen World" (teleplay), American Broadcasting Co. (ABC-TV), 1970.
(Under pseudonym Dr. A) *The Sensuous Dirty Old Man*, Walker & Co., 1971.
Isaac Asimov's Treasury of Humor: A Lifetime Collection of Favorite Jokes, Anecdotes, and Limericks

with Copious Notes on How to Tell Them and Why, Houghton, 1971.

The Best New Thing (juvenile), World Publishing, 1971.

(With James Gunn) "The History of Science Fiction from 1938 to the Present" (filmscript), Extramural Independent Study Center, University of Kansas, 1971.

More Words of Science, Houghton, 1972.

The Story of Ruth, Doubleday, 1972.

Asimov's Annotated "Don Juan," Doubleday, 1972.

Asimov's Annotated "Paradise Lost," Doubleday, 1974.

Lecherous Limericks, Walker & Co., 1975.

More Lecherous Limericks, Walker & Co., 1976.

I, Rabbi (juvenile), Walker & Co., 1976.

Familiar Poems Annotated, Doubleday, 1977.

Still More Lecherous Limericks, Walker & Co., 1977.

Asimov's Sherlockian Limericks, New Mysterious Press, 1978.

Animals of the Bible, Doubleday, 1978.

(With John Ciardi) *Limericks Too Gross,* Norton, 1978.

Opus 200 (selections from the author's second hundred books), Houghton, 1979.

In Memory Yet Green: The Autobiography of Isaac Asimov, 1920-1954, Doubleday, 1979.

Extraterrestrial Civilizations (speculative nonfiction), Crown, 1979.

Isaac Asimov's Book of Facts, Grosset, 1979.

In Joy Still Felt: The Autobiography of Isaac Asimov, 1954-1978, Doubleday, 1980.

The Annotated "Gulliver's Travels," C. N. Potter, 1980.

In the Beginning: Science Faces God in the Book of Genesis, Crown, 1981.

Asimov on Science Fiction, Doubleday, 1981.

Change!: Seventy-One Glimpses of the Future (forecasts), Houghton, 1981.

(With Ciardi) *A Grossery of Limericks,* Norton, 1981.

Would You Believe?, Grosset, 1981.

(With Ken Fisher) *Isaac Asimov Presents Superquiz,* Dembner, 1982.

More—Would You Believe?, Grosset, 1982.

(Editor with George R. Martin) *The Science Fiction Weight-Loss Book,* Crown, 1983.

(With Fisher) *Isaac Asimov Presents Superquiz 2,* Dembner, 1983.

Opus 300 (selections from the author's third hundred books), Houghton, 1984.

Isaac Asimov's Limericks for Children, Caedmon, 1984.

(Editor) *Living in the Future* (forecasts), Beaufort Books, 1985.

The Edge of Tomorrow, T. Doherty, 1985.

(With James Burke and Jules Bergman) *The Impact of Science on Society,* National Aeronautics and Space Administration (NASA), 1985.

Isaac Asimov, Octopus Books, 1986.

Past, Present, and Future, Prometheus Books, 1987.

Other Worlds of Isaac Asimov, edited by Martin H. Greenberg, Avenel, 1986.

(With Janet Asimov) *How to Enjoy Writing: A Book of Aid and Comfort,* Walker & Co., 1987.

Asimov's Annotated Gilbert and Sullivan, Doubleday, 1988.

Asimov's Galaxy: Reflections on Science Fiction, Doubleday, 1989.

Sally (juvenile), Creative Education, 1989.

Robbie (juvenile), Creative Education, 1989.

(Contributor) *The John W. Campbell Letters with Isaac Asimov and A. E. van Vogt,* A. C. Projects, 1991.

Isaac Asimov Laughs Again, HarperCollins, 1991.

Also author of *The Adventures of Science Fiction,* Ameron Ltd.; co-editor of several anthologies on various topics. Author of "Science" column in *Magazine of Fantasy and Science Fiction,* 1958-92. Contributor of stories to numerous science fiction anthologies, and to many science fiction magazines, including *Astounding Science Fiction, Amazing Stories, Fantastic Adventures, Science Fiction,* and *Future Fiction;* contributor of one short story under pseudonym George E. Dale to *Astounding Science Fiction.* Contributor of articles to numerous science journals and popular periodicals. Editorial director, *Isaac Asimov's Science Fiction Magazine.*

A "future history" relating the struggles of an interstellar empire, Asimov's "Foundation" series has been one of the most acclaimed and popular works in science fiction. (Cover illustration by Darrell K. Sweet.)

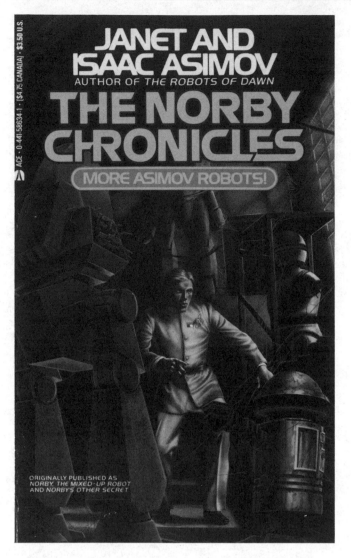

JANET AND ISAAC ASIMOV
AUTHOR OF *THE ROBOTS OF DAWN*
THE NORBY CHRONICLES
MORE ASIMOV ROBOTS!

ORIGINALLY PUBLISHED AS
NORBY, THE MIXED-UP ROBOT
AND *NORBY'S OTHER SECRET*

Together with his wife Janet, Asimov created this series for younger readers about a robot with unusual capabilities. (Cover illustration by Shaw.)

ADAPTATIONS: A sound recording of William Shatner reading the first eight chapters of *Foundation* was produced as *Foundation: The Psychohistorians,* Caedmon, 1976, and of Asimov reading from the same novel was produced as *The Mayors,* Caedmon, 1977; the film, "The Ugly Little Boy," from a short story of the same title, was produced by Learning Corporation of America, 1977.

SIDELIGHTS: Isaac Asimov is "the world's most prolific science writer," according to David N. Samuelson in *Twentieth Century Science-Fiction Writers,* who "has written some of the best-known science fiction ever published." Considered one of the three greatest writers of science fiction in the 1940s (along with Robert Heinlein and A. E. Van Vogt), Asimov has remained a potent force in the genre. Stories such as "Nightfall" and "The Bicentennial Man," and novels such as *The Gods Themselves* and *Foundation's Edge* have received numerous honors and are recognized as among the best science fiction ever written. As one of the world's leading writers on science, explaining everything from nuclear fusion to the theory of numbers, Asimov has illuminated for many the mysteries of science and technology. He is a skilled raconteur as well, who enlivens his writing with incidents from his own life. "In his autobiographical writings and comments," states James Gunn in *Isaac Asimov: The Foundations of Science Fiction,* "Asimov continually invites the reader to share his triumphs, to laugh at his blunders and lack of sophistication, and to wonder, with him, at the rise to prominence of a bright Jewish boy brought to this country from Russia at the age of three and raised in a collection of Brooklyn candy stores."

Asimov's interest in science fiction began when he first noticed several of the early science fiction magazines for sale on the newsstand of his family's candy store. Although as a boy he read and enjoyed numerous volumes of nonfiction as well as many of the literary "classics," Asimov recalls in *In Memory Yet Green,* his first volume of autobiography, he still longed to explore the intriguing magazines with the glossy covers. But his father refused, maintaining that fiction magazines were "junk! ... Not fit to read. The only people who read magazines like that are bums." And bums represented "the dregs of society, apprentice gangsters."

But in August of 1929, a new magazine appeared on the scene called *Science Wonder Stories.* Asimov knew that as long as science fiction magazines had titles like *Amazing Stories,* he would have little chance of convincing his father of their worth. However, the new periodical had the word "science" in its title, and he says, "I had read enough about science to know that it was a mentally nourishing and spiritually wholesome study. What's more, I knew that my father thought so from our occasional talks about my schoolwork." When confronted with this argument, the elder Asimov consented. Soon Isaac began collecting even those periodicals that didn't have "science" in the title. He notes: "I planned to maintain with all the strength at my disposal the legal position that permission for one such magazine implied permission for all the others, regardless of title. No fight was needed, however; my harassed father conceded everything." Asimov rapidly developed into an avid fan.

Asimov first tried writing stories when he was eleven years old. He had for some time been reading stories and then retelling them to his schoolmates, and started a book like some of the popular boys' series volumes of the 1920s: "The Rover Boys," "The Bobbsey Twins," and "Pee Wee Wilson." Asimov's story was called *The Greenville Chums at College,* patterned after *The Darewell Chums at College,* and it grew to eight chapters before he abandoned it. Asimov, in *In Memory Yet Green,* describes the flaw in his initial literary venture: "I was trying to imitate the series books without knowing anything but what I read there. Their characters were small-town boys, so mine were, for I imagined Greenville to be a town in upstate New York. Their characters went to college, so mine did. Unfortunately, a junior-high-school youngster living in a shabby neighborhood in Brooklyn knows very little about small-town life and even less about college. Even I, myself, was forced eventually to recognize the fact that I didn't know what I was talking about."

Despite initial discouragements, Asimov continued to write. His first published piece appeared in his high school's literary semiannual and was accepted, he says, because it was the only funny piece anyone wrote, and the editors needed something funny. In the summer of 1934, Asimov had a letter published in *Astounding Stories* in which he commented on several stories that had appeared in the magazine. His continuing activities as a fan brought him to the decision to attempt a science fiction piece of his own; in 1937, at the age of seventeen, he began a story entitled "Cosmic Corkscrew." The procedure Asimov used to formulate the plot was, he says, "typical of my science fiction. I usually thought of some scientific gimmick and built a story about that."

By the time he finished the story on June 19, 1938, *Astounding Stories* had become *Astounding Science Fiction*. Its editor was John W. Campbell, who was to influence the work of some of the most prominent authors of modern science fiction, including Arthur C. Clarke, Robert Heinlein, Poul Anderson, L. Sprague de Camp, and Theodore Sturgeon. Since Campbell was also one of the best-known science fiction writers of the thirties and *Astounding* one of the most prestigious publications in its field at the time, Asimov was shocked by his father's suggestion that he submit "Cosmic Corkscrew" to the editor in person. But mailing the story would have cost twelve cents while subway fare, round trip, was only ten cents. In the interest of economy, therefore, he agreed to make the trip to the magazine's office, fully expecting to leave the manuscript with a secretary.

Campbell, however, had invited many young writers to discuss their work with him, and when Asimov arrived he was shown into the editor's office. Campbell talked for over an hour and agreed to read the story; two days later Asimov received the manuscript back in the mail. It had been rejected, but Campbell offered extensive suggestions for improvement and encouraged the young man to keep trying. This began a pattern that was to continue for several years with Campbell guiding Asimov through his formative beginnings as a science fiction writer.

Asimov's association with the field of science fiction has been a long and distinguished one. He is credited with the introduction of several innovative concepts into the genre, including the formulation of the "Three Laws of Robotics." Asimov maintains that the idea for the laws was given to him by Campbell; Campbell, on the other hand, said that he had merely picked them out of Asimov's early robot stories. In any case, it was Asimov who first formally stated the three laws: "1. A robot may not injure a human being or, through inaction, allow a human being to come to harm. 2. A robot must obey the orders given it by human beings except where such orders would conflict with the First Law. 3. A robot must protect its own existence as long as such protection does not conflict with the First or Second Laws."

Asimov says that he used these precepts as the basis for "over two dozen short stories and three novels ... about robots," and he feels that he is "probably more famous for them than for anything else I have written, and they are quoted even outside the science-fiction world. The very word 'robotics' was coined by me." The three laws gained general acceptance among readers and among other science fiction writers; Asimov, in his autobiography, writes that they "revolutionized" science fiction and that "no writer could write a *stupid* robot story if he used the Three Laws. The story might be bad on other counts, but it wouldn't be stupid." The laws became so popular, and seemed so logical, that many people believed real robots would eventually be designed according to Asimov's basic principles.

Also notable among Asimov's science fiction works is the "Foundation" series. This group of short stories, published in magazines in the forties and then collected into a trilogy in the early fifties, was inspired by Edward Gibbon's *Decline and Fall of the Roman Empire*. It was

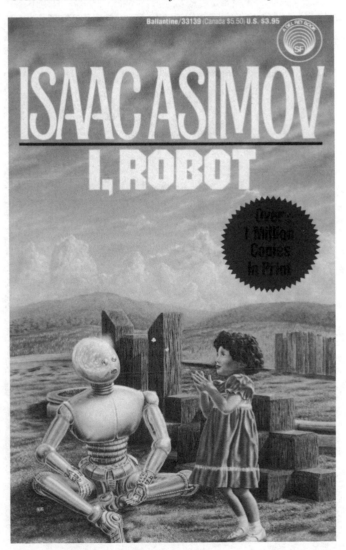

Asimov pioneered the use of robots in science fiction and coined the term for the technology when he articulated the "Three Laws of Robotics" in his early "Robot" stories. (Cover illustration by Don Dixon.)

written as a "future history," a story being told in a society of the distant future which relates events of that society's history. The concept was not invented by Asimov, but there can be little doubt that he became a master of the technique. *Foundation, Foundation and Empire,* and *Second Foundation* have achieved special standing among science fiction enthusiasts. In 1966, the World Science Fiction Convention honored them with a special Hugo Award as the best all-time science fiction series. Even thirty years after their original publication, Asimov's future history series remains popular—in the 1980s, forty years after he began the series, Asimov added a new volume, *Foundation's Edge,* and eventually linked the Foundation stories with his robot novels in *The Robots of Dawn, Robots and Empire, Foundation and Earth,* and *Prelude to Foundation.*

Asimov's first fiction written specifically for a younger audience were his "Lucky Starr" novels. In 1951, at the suggestion of his Doubleday editor, he began working on a series of science-fiction stories that could easily be

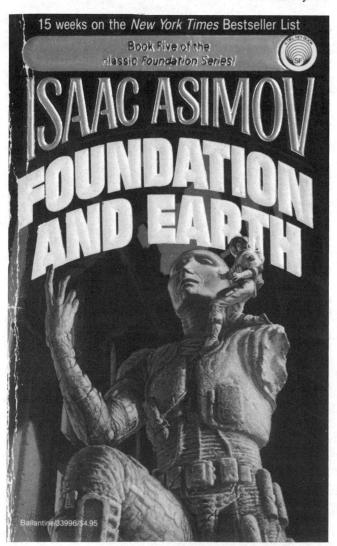

Asimov drew together his "Foundation" and "Robot" universes in this conclusion to his popular "Foundation" series. (Cover illustration by Michael Whelan.)

adapted for television. "Television was here; that was clear," he writes in *In Memory Yet Green.* "Why not take advantage of it, then? Radio had its successful long-running series, 'The Lone Ranger,' so why not a 'Space Ranger' modelled very closely upon that?" *David Starr: Space Ranger,* published under the pseudonym Paul French, introduced David 'Lucky' Starr, agent of the interplanetary law enforcement agency the Council of Science. Accompanying Lucky on his adventures is his sidekick, John Bigman Jones, a short, tough man born and raised on the great agricultural farms of Mars. Together the two of them confront and outwit space pirates, poisoners, mad scientists, and interstellar spies—humans from the Sirian star system, who have become the Earth's worst enemies.

Although the "Lucky Starr" series ran to six volumes, the television deal that Asimov and his editor envisioned never materialized. "None of us dreamed that for some reason ... television series would very rarely last more than two or three years," Asimov writes. "We also didn't know that a juvenile television series to be called 'Rocky Jones: Space Ranger' was already in the works." Another problem the series faced was in the scientific background of the stories. "Unfortunately," state Jean Fiedler and Jim Mele in *Isaac Asimov,* "Asimov had the bad luck to be writing these stories on the threshold of an unprecedented exploration of our solar system's planets, an exploration which has immensely increased our astronomical knowledge. Many of his scientific premises, sound in 1952, were later found to be inaccurate." In recent editions of the books, Asimov has included forewords explaining the situation to new readers.

Asimov has also written science fiction stories aimed at a younger audience in collaboration with his wife Janet. She writes, "I wrote the 'Norby' series because Walker & Co. wanted a children's s-f series. I had started *Norby, the Mixed-up Robot* back in the sixties, before I married Isaac, but didn't get far then. Ultimately I rewrote it, then asked Isaac to rewrite it again on his word processor (I didn't have one then). We put his name on it, too—and on all the other 'Norby' books—because he helps with plotting, although I now write the books alone."

Asimov's first nonfiction book was a medical text entitled *Biochemistry and Human Metabolism,* begun in 1950 and written in collaboration with William Boyd and Burnham Walker, two of his colleagues at the Boston University School of Medicine. He had recognized his ability as an explainer early in life, and he enjoyed clarifying scientific principles for his family and friends. He also discovered that he was a most able and entertaining lecturer who delighted in his work as a teacher. He told *New York Times* interviewer Israel Shenker that his talent lies in the fact that he "can read a dozen dull books and make one interesting book out of them." The result is that Asimov has been phenomenally successful as a writer of science books for the general public. Asimov later added: "I'm on fire to explain, and happiest when it's something reasonably intricate which

I can make clear step by step. It's the easiest way I can clarify things in my own mind."

WORKS CITED:

Asimov, Isaac, *In Memory Yet Green: The Autobiography of Isaac Asimov, 1920-1954,* Doubleday, 1979.

Fiedler, Jean, and Jim Mele, *Isaac Asimov,* Ungar, 1982.

Gunn, James, *Isaac Asimov: The Foundations of Science Fiction,* Oxford University Press, 1982.

Shenker, Israel, "Asimov, 'On Fire to Explain,' Writes 100th Book—about Himself," *New York Times,* October 18, 1969, p. 35.

Twentieth Century Science-Fiction Writers, 2nd edition, St. James Press, 1986.

FOR MORE INFORMATION SEE:

BOOKS

Asimov, Isaac, *The Bicentennial Man and Other Stories,* Doubleday, 1976.

Asimov, Isaac, *In Joy Still Felt: The Autobiography of Isaac Asimov, 1954-1979,* Doubleday, 1980.

Children's Literature Review, Volume 12, Gale, 1987.

Clareson, Thomas D., editor, *Voices for the Future: Essays on Major Science Fiction Writers,* Popular Press, 1976.

Contemporary Literary Criticism, Gale, Volume 1, 1973; Volume 3, 1975; Volume 9, 1978; Volume 19, 1981; Volume 26, 1983.

Dictionary of Literary Biography, Volume 8: *Twentieth-Century American Science Fiction Writers,* Gale, 1981.

Greenberg, Martin H., and Joseph D. Olander, editors, *Isaac Asimov,* Taplinger, 1977.

Miller, Marjorie Mithoff, *Isaac Asimov: A Checklist of Works Published in the United States,* Kent State University Press, 1972.

Patrouch, Joseph F., Jr., *The Science Fiction of Isaac Asimov,* Doubleday, 1974.

Platt, Charles, *Dream Makers: The Uncommon People Who Write Science Fiction,* Berkley Publishing, 1980.

Schweitzer, Darrell, *Science Fiction Voices 5,* Borgo Press, 1981, pp. 7-14.

Slusser, George E., *Isaac Asimov: The Foundations of His Science Fiction,* Borgo Press, 1979.

Wollheim, Donald A., *The Universe Makers,* Harper, 1971.

PERIODICALS

Books and Bookmen, July, 1968; February, 1969; July, 1973.

Chicago Tribune Book World, March 4, 1979; January 19, 1986.

Chicago Tribune Magazine, April 30, 1978.

Fantasy Newsletter, April, 1983.

Fantasy Review, September, 1985.

Globe and Mail (Toronto), August 10, 1985.

Magazine of Fantasy and Science Fiction, October, 1966; September, 1980.

Nation, March 5, 1983.

New York Review of Books, September 12, 1977; October 24, 1985.

New York Times, January 1, 1980; December 17, 1984; February 26, 1985.

New York Times Book Review, November 17, 1968; January 28, 1973; January 12, 1975; May 30, 1976; June 25, 1978; February 25, 1979; December 16, 1979; December 19, 1982; October 20, 1985.

Publishers Weekly, April 17, 1972; September 2, 1983.

Science Fiction and Fantasy Book Review, December, 1982; June, 1983; November, 1983.

Science Fiction Review, winter, 1982; spring, 1984; winter, 1985.

Time, February 26, 1979; November 15, 1982.

Times Literary Supplement, October 5, 1967; December 28, 1967.

Washington Post, April 4, 1979.

Washington Post Book World, April 1, 1979; May 25, 1980; September 26, 1982; September 27, 1983; August 25, 1985.

SOUND RECORDINGS

Isaac Asimov Talks: An Interview, Writer's Voice, 1974.

B

BALTIMORE, J.
See CATHERALL, Arthur

*   *   *

BARASCH, Lynne 1939-

PERSONAL: Born March 23, 1939, in New York, NY; daughter of Robert Julius and Elaine (Haas) Marx; married Kenneth Robert Barasch (an ophthalmologist), June 20, 1958; children: Wendy, Jill (deceased), Nina

LYNNE BARASCH

(deceased), Cassie, Dinah. *Education:* Attended Rhode Island School of Design, 1957-58; Parsons School of Design, B.A., 1976. *Politics:* Democrat. *Religion:* Jewish. *Hobbies and other interests:* Theater, ballet, art.

ADDRESSES: Home and office—320 East Seventy-second St., New York, NY 10021.

CAREER: Children's author and illustrator.

MEMBER: Authors Guild.

WRITINGS:

SELF-ILLUSTRATED PICTURE BOOKS

Rodney's Inside Story, Orchard Books, 1992.
A Winter Walk, Ticknor & Fields, 1993.

SIDELIGHTS: Lynne Barasch told *SATA:* "I have been drawing and painting all my life. Ten years ago, when my daughter Cassie was five years old, she got on the wrong bus the first day of school. That event became my first book (still under construction, revision, etc.).

"The peculiar form of words and pictures called picture books is a very gratifying means of expression. I hope to continue to grow through this medium."

*   *   *

BEALES, Valerie 1915-

PERSONAL: Born July 5, 1915, in Johannesberg, South Africa; daughter of Alfred George Rosenthal and Maude Irene Duval; married Philip Beales (a surgeon), July 22, 1941; children: David, Martin, Julia, Sylvia. *Education:* Attended London School of Economics. *Politics:* Labour Party. *Hobbies and other interests:* Reading, painting.

ADDRESSES: Home—43 Elm Bank Gardens, Barnes, London SW13 ONX, England.

CAREER: Writer. Has worked as a secretary, barrister, and solicitor. Former member of Rossington Parish Council.

VALERIE BEALES

MEMBER: Association of Women Solicitors, Married Women's Association, Amnesty International.

WRITINGS:

Emma and Freckles, Simon & Schuster, 1990.

Also author of "Three Little Bunnies Who Lost Their Mummies," which was originally broadcast on the program *Listen with Mother,* British Broadcasting Corp. (BBC), 1953, and later published in the collection *"Listen with Mother" Stories,* edited by Dorothy Edwards, BBC, 1972.

WORK IN PROGRESS: Emma and Freckles Ride On.

SIDELIGHTS: Valerie Beales told *SATA:* "I live in Barnes at present but spent many years in an old Coaching Inn in Rossington Bridge, near Doncaster, where my children kept ponies in a field across the road. I used to ride myself and have always, until recently, kept ducks and chickens, and I am a great lover of dogs, horses, and all animals.

"I qualified as a solicitor after the last of my four children left school, and practiced both as a barrister and as a solicitor, specializing in matrimonial cases. It was after I came to London, with a more restricted environment, that I started writing seriously, and I greatly enjoyed writing *Emma and Freckles.*"

BELTRAN-HERNANDEZ, Irene 1945-

PERSONAL: Born April 4, 1945, in Waco, TX; daughter of Emmett Tovar (a mechanic) and Isabelle (a nurse; maiden name, Quinones) Beltran; married Gilberto Roland Hernandez (a construction superintendent), June 15, 1983; children: Dominick Frank Navarro, Fatima Rose Hernandez. *Education:* Durham's Business College, certificate of secretarial science, 1963; University of North Texas, B.A., 1970; Institute of Children's Literature, diploma, 1980; attended Baylor University, East Texas State University, and Mountainview Community College. *Religion:* Catholic.

ADDRESSES: Home—506 Shelly Ct., Duncanville, TX 75137; and 7302 Alabonson, Apt. 304, Houston, TX 77088. *Office*—3200 South Lancaster Rd., No. S230A, Dallas, TX 75216.

AWARDS, HONORS: First place, San Antonio Writers Festival Award for juvenile literature, 1982; City of Dallas Service in Excellence Award, 1991; University of Wisconsin—Madison fellowship, 1992.

CAREER: Waco News Tribune-Times Herald, Waco, TX, clerk, 1963-67; Opportunities Industrial Center, vocational counselor, 1970-71; Jaycee-Zaragoza Recreation Center, Dallas, TX, recreation leader, 1971-85; J. Eric Jonsson Library, Dallas, public information assistant, 1985-86; Mayor's Office, Dallas, administrative assistant, 1986-87; West Dallas Multipurpose Center, caseworker, 1987-92; City of Dallas Health and Human Services Department, adolescent health caseworker, 1992—; writer. Chair of the Breast Cancer Mobile Screening Project and the Texas Instruments Christmas Project; cochair for the Women's Center Second Annual Emerging Leaders Conference and the Cinco de Mayo Festival; judge for the Texas Reader/Writers Contest; Dallas County Youth Village speaker; other volunteer work for organizations such as the Stop Measles Project, Hispanic Encuentro Conference, and Channel Eight Toy Project.

WRITINGS:

Across the Great River (novel), Arte Publico, 1989. *Heartbeat-Drumbeat* (novel), Arte Publico, 1992.

WORK IN PROGRESS: The Secret of Two Brothers, a novel about an adolescent ex-convict.

SIDELIGHTS: Irene Beltran-Hernandez told *SATA:* "I was born April 4, 1945, and was one of eight children. It was a poor life lacking many material comforts, but mother made it worthwhile. We all got our high school diplomas. I received my bachelor's degree and went on to graduate school.

"My mother was a smart woman, dedicated to the church and her children. She allowed me to spend Saturday mornings at the city library reading and checking out books. As we lived out in the country, she'd drop me off at the library to check out books while she did the weekly shopping. I stacked myself with a week's worth of reading material. Reading, it turned out, was my only escape from the daily routine of the household and the isolation of the country, as we were not allowed to go anywhere else except church.

"My grandmother Linda Lopez Quinones was the person I loved most. I was raised in her house until I was five and my father returned from Europe. I remember being happy there. By the age of nine I was forever running off to her house. She lived ten blocks away and my mother would trot over to get me. Through my grandparents I learned the secret of keeping locked boxes, locked diaries, locked chests. I remember breaking into a locked drawer that belonged to my grandfather and finding all his secret papers. After I read them all, I put them back as they were, straightened my skirt, and pretended nothing had happened. What I found was fascinating and that's when I started keeping my own secret journal. I think Grandpa knew I'd been in his secret drawer, but he never admonished me for doing so.

"I wrote my first journal on ordinary notebook paper, hiding from the rest of the family. I wrote by flashlight, late at night, so I wouldn't wake my sister; my journal was filled with things about school, my school friends, or important happenings of that day. When I was a teenager I learned shorthand just to keep my episodes private. Keeping a diary was another escape for me. Many more journals followed.

"At Waco High School, I excelled. I worked in the library as an assistant. My grades were very good. My problem was skin color. I was too white for the Chicano kids and too dark for the Anglos. I didn't push the issue, but by the time I finished high school in 1963 I had three dear friends, two Anglo girls and a Mexican girl who was fair like me. To this day we are close friends.

"In my junior year in high school, I drew Mr. Cornelius for English class. He was the toughest English teacher in the town. I remember trembling when I saw his name on my subject card, for all the kids feared him. My friend, JoAnne, who was to be valedictorian, laughed at me. She said I turned 'whiter than normal,' but that I could handle him. Her confidence spurred me on to almost my first subject failure. I struggled in that class and I thought that Mr. Cornelius ignored me until one theme assignment. I can still hear the gasps of receiving an 'F' as the papers were handed back. This is it, I thought! I've flunked! He threw my paper down on my desk, walked about four steps then stopped, came back and picked up the paper before I even had a chance to look at it, saw my name on it and said, 'Well, well.' He looked straight into my eyes, bent down, and said, 'Someday, you'll be somebody important. Mark my words.' I gasped to see he'd given me a 'B' and the theme and then I started to cry into my paper—only one other person received a 'B.' He ignored me for the rest of the semester, but I never forgot his prediction.

"My job after high school was with the *Waco News Tribune-Times Herald* as a copy girl. I was promoted to proofreader for editorials. From there I went to night

school at Baylor University, pursuing a degree in journalism. Then my supervisor talked to me about working part-time and going to school the rest of the day. I accepted his offer and was on my way to my sophomore year when I decided it was time to leave home. I chose North Texas State University. I saved my money and took off the following September. I did not like the journalism teachers and at the beginning of my senior year I changed my major to sociology. I spend the rest of the time writing letters home to friends, my mother, and my grandmother. I was intrigued with human interest stories, but the journalism teacher repeatedly assigned me to cover the business school.

"After college I landed a job as a school counselor. The job involved a lot of paperwork, but the best part was listening to the life stories of the students under my care. During this time I was asked by a professor from Sothern Methodist University to undertake a study dealing with recent illegal aliens from Mexico who had settled in the West Dallas area. I was to locate and

A young girl encounters conflict when she explores her identity as both a Mexican American and a Native American in Beltran-Hernandez's second novel. (Cover illustration by Mark Pinon.)

interview them and help compile the statistics. It was fascinating, long, and tedious, and in the end it landed me a job working for the City of Dallas Park and Recreation Department as a programmer, recreation leader, and social worker.

"I was stationed in a predominately Hispanic neighborhood, which delighted me. It was a dangerous job, and I soon learned why the pay was so great. One's life was on the line every minute of the day, but it was also exciting. I quickly learned how to defend my people as well as to stand my own ground within the city network. The job sprouted gray hairs on my head and I matured at a much faster rate than necessary.

"I turned to writing as my therapy. I wrote about people, often wondering how these people would end up. Ten years later my first book, *Across the Great River,* was published. As with any skill or craft, I took courses during those ten years. I took creative writing, a correspondence course, and also graduated from the Institute of Children's Literature. I attended local writers' groups until I found an English teacher from Richland College who held a workshop Sunday afternoons in his home. I faithfully attended until I felt it was no longer useful and from then on I depended on my own resources.

"For myself, to take away my writing is to take away my spirit. To take away my best-sellers, which I love to read, would render me blind."

*   *   *

BENANDER, Carl D. 1941-

PERSONAL: Born August 15, 1941, in Mullen, ID; son of Carl E. (a pastor) and Beverly (a teacher; maiden name, Brooks) Benander; married Susan Beyerlein (a teacher), July 23, 1988; children: Angela, Carl Eric; stepchildren: Matt, Erin. *Education:* Western Michigan University, B.A., 1965. *Politics:* Democrat. *Religion:* Episcopalian. *Hobbies and other interests:* Travel, golf, hunting, fishing.

ADDRESSES: Home—610 North Bowery, Gladwin, MI 48624. *Office*—1400 Spring St., Gladwin, MI 48624.

CAREER: Teacher of speech, theatre, debate, and literature, 1965—. Also worked as a sports broadcaster and as host of the talk show *Let's Talk,* WGDN. Charter member of Mid-Michigan Community College Committee for Theatre Arts.

WRITINGS:

Little Elk's Miracle, Winston-Derek, 1991.

WORK IN PROGRESS: "Little Elk" sequels; a three-act comedy.

SIDELIGHTS: Carl D. Benander told *SATA:* "I am not a sage or a guru, but being human I can and do create. It has been my experience that many people believe they

CARL D. BENANDER

can somehow learn to be more creative. I believe that quantity has nothing to do with being successfully creative. Tapping into what one knows and what one feels about what he/she knows and funneling it into a specific media is creativity.

"I was raised in Iowa, and early on became aware of some of the legends of the plains Indian. I became a father rather later than others. These two obvious disparate experiences came together to become the story line of *Little Elk's Miracle.* Even if it's the genre of children's literature, or fantasy (or science fiction for that matter), a story still must be based in the reality of experiences and feelings.

"I sincerely believe that all creativity is good. That is not to say what has been created is necessarily good. It is the act of creativity that elevates. The product is indeed secondary to the process. Writing for me is often lonely and frustrating, but it is at the same time compelling. Primarily I write for me, and as the manuscript becomes a 'reality' its merit is based on my interpretation of what it means and how it feels. When readers share the feeling and 'reality' of a story (children included) a writer has his/her reward. A writer doesn't copy writers; a writer lives and recalls—feels and reacts with words. All else is immaterial."

*   *   *

BEYER, Paul J. III 1950-

PERSONAL: Born January 24, 1950, in Omer, MI; son of Paul J. (an engineer) and Lucille Mae Beyer; married

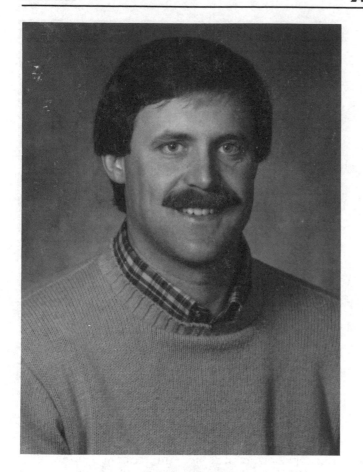

PAUL J. BEYER III

Mary Kathleen Beyer (an elementary school teacher), March 11, 1972; children: Thomas Paul, Bethany Lynn. *Education:* Judson College, B.A., 1972; Central Michigan University, M.A., 1980. *Politics:* Independent. *Religion:* Christian.

ADDRESSES: Home—614 Lennon Lane, Gladwin, MI 48624. *Office*—Gladwin High School, 1400 N. Spring Gladwin, MI 48624.

CAREER: Gladwin High School, Gladwin, MI, visual art instructor, 1974-92, fine arts department chair, school improvement chair; free lance illustrator, 1989—. Has also worked as a watercolorist and calligraphic artist.

MEMBER: National Art Education Association, Michigan Watercolor Society, Phi Delta Kappa.

ILLUSTRATOR:

The Vitamin Parade, Winston Derek, 1989.
Huckleberry Fun, Winston Derek, 1989.
Carl Benander, *Little Elk's Miracle,* Winston Derek, 1991.

WORK IN PROGRESS: Sequels to *Little Elk's Miracle,* tentatively titled *Little Elk's Lost Temper* and *The Gathering of the Crows.*

SIDELIGHTS: Paul J. Beyer told *SATA:* "I began drawing at age two. With encouragement from both parents (who love and appreciate art), I developed drawing skills even before entering kindergarten. We lived in a beautiful area on Lake Huron, and many times entertainment for me was a day spent with paper and pencil.

"It wasn't until college that I discovered that I really wanted to seriously study art. With the support of Professor Janet Hseih at Judson College, I also became interested in the teaching profession. Throughout the twenty years that I have taught art in Gladwin, my students have been a constant inspiration. Over time, I have found that my students give back to me as much as I give to them. For this—and many other reasons—teaching has been a rewarding profession.

"For most of my professional life, I have worked in watercolors. With the birth of our children, I became interested in children's book illustration. I read children's books to my kids every night and became fascinated with the art in each book. After studying the genre, I knew that I wanted to pursue my dream of illustrating children's literature. There was only one problem—I couldn't write! I then enlisted the help of my talented friend and collegue Carl Benander. It wasn't long before he produced a manuscript which we broke down into a page-by-page format. After some months and long nights had passed, *Little Elk's Miracle* was born.

Little Elk

ISBN: 1-55523-294-9

A young boy is visited by the Great White Buffalo in this Native American tale retold by author Carl D. Benander and illustrated by Beyer.

"The greatest challenge lay ahead—getting published. We were an unknown author/illustrator duo with no agent and only a dream. But, we *believed* in our work, and were extremely fortunate to find a publishing company interested in the book. When *Little Elk's Miracle* went into a second printing in just a year's time, we knew that our journey had been worth the effort. Always remember: If you want something badly enough and you believe in yourself and follow your dreams, you can succeed."

*   *   *

BISHOP, Claire Huchet 1899(?)-1993

OBITUARY NOTICE—See index for *SATA* sketch: Born c. 1899, in Geneva, Switzerland (one source says Brittany, France); died of an aortal hemorrhage, March 11, 1993, in Paris, France. Political activist, librarian, and author. Bishop, whose early career was spent as a storyteller in Paris and New York City, created prize-winning books that have been translated into numerous languages. In 1924, Bishop helped open France's first children's library, L'Heure Joyeuse, and she later worked at the New York Public Library. A fable she told to youngsters at that library became her first book, *The Five Chinese Brothers.* In her serious works, like *Twenty and Ten* and *Yeshu, Called Jesus,* Bishop examined war and religion. A leading opponent of anti-Semitism, Bishop served as the president of both the Jewish-Christian Fellowship of France, from 1968 to 1981, and the International Council of Christians and Jews, from 1975 to 1977. Her crusade against racial and religious prejudice led to several significant changes, including the omission of anti-Semitic language in the Catholic catechism. Among Bishop's most popular works are *Pancakes Paris, All Alone,* and *How Catholics Look at Jews.*

OBITUARIES AND OTHER SOURCES:

BOOKS

The Writers Directory: 1990-1992, St. James Press, 1990.

PERIODICALS

New York Times, March 14, 1993, p. 42.

*   *   *

BLYLER, Allison Lee 1966-

PERSONAL: Born August 23, 1966, in Princeton, NJ; daughter of Lee L.(an engineer) and Harriet (a teacher; maiden name, Lillard) Blyler. *Education:* Princeton University, B.A., 1988; University of Virginia, M.A., 1990. *Politics:* Independent. *Religion:* Independent. *Hobbies and other interests:* Reading, photography, cooking, music, movies, pop culture, birds, running, weightlifting, and hiking.

ADDRESSES: Home—1980 East Arlington Blvd., Charlottesville, VA 22903.

CAREER: Writer. University of Virginia, Charlottesville, VA, teaching assistant in literature and composition, 1988-92.

AWARDS, HONORS: Samuel Shellabarger Memorial Prize (best senior thesis), Princeton University, 1988, for poetry.

WRITINGS:

Finding Foxes, illustrated by Robert Blake, Philomel, 1991.

WORK IN PROGRESS: A book of poems entitled *A Natural History;* a dissertation on the elegiac in the poetry of American women entitled *Muses Mournful.*

SIDELIGHTS: Allison Lee Blyler told *SATA:* "I've been writing poems since third grade, but I never had any idea that I would write a children's book. *Finding Foxes* happened because my friend, mentor, and editor, Patricia Lee Gauch, one day picked up an imitation of Wallace Stevens's poem 'Thirteen Ways of Looking at a Blackbird' that I'd written in high school and suggested it might make a good picture book. She found Robert Blake, a fellow New Jerseyan, to illustrate, and my poetic exercise became a Philomel release. I was somewhat bewildered the whole time this was going on, and I'm pleased and surprised and still awestruck by the final results. I'd love to write another children's book now, but I still feel I have a lot to learn about the genre. I learned quite a bit when I worked at Philomel during two college summers, but reading and editing manuscripts for young readers is quite different from penning

ALLISON LEE BLYLER

them. When I do come up with an idea for a new book, I suspect it will be another imagistic piece like *Finding Foxes;* I've never been much on plot! (Or argument for that matter, which is why I'm stalling in getting my dissertation off the ground.)

"I'm in my fifth year of graduate school now, teaching undergraduates, and dreaming about publishing a book of poems and getting a job teaching creative writing at a small and intimate eastern university. I'd love to go back home to New Jersey and teach at Princeton; I've always been a provincial soul with a sometimes unbearable desire to get back the past. I do like Virginia now—my unstructured life as a graduate student, the warm days, the old town of Charlottesville, the closeness of mountains and woods—but since I suspect I'll have to move on soon, I like to think about going back where I came from. I love teaching and immersing myself in the natural world. I always want to live somewhere I can find running space, running water, and birds.

"My favorite poets are W. S. Merwin, Elizabeth Bishop, Emily Dickinson, and my college advisor, Jim Richardson. I admire Elizabeth Bowen and Robert Frost, Amy Clampitt and [William] Wordsworth. I think Jane Yolen (and Pat Gauch, of course) are terrific children's authors. I'm aspiring to publish a book of poems by the time I'm thirty, and maybe another children's book as well."

* * *

BORTZ, Fred 1944-

PERSONAL: Full name Alfred B. Bortz; born November 20, 1944, in Pittsburgh, PA; son of Harry A. ("the best refrigeration/air conditioning serviceman in Pittsburgh") and Rose (an office manager; maiden name, Taksa) Bortz; married Susan G. Grossberger (a teacher and community volunteer), June 17, 1967; children: Brian S., Rosalie E. *Education:* Carnegie Mellon University, B.S., 1966, M.S., 1967, Ph.D., 1971. *Hobbies and other interests:* "Who needs one? My writing started out that way. Now it is consuming me!"

ADDRESSES: Home—1312 Foxboro Dr., Monroeville, PA 15146. *Office*—Center for University Outreach, Carnegie Mellon University, 5000 Forbes Ave., Pittsburgh, PA 15213. *Agent*—Andrea Brown, P.O. Box 429, El Granada, CA 94018.

CAREER: Bowling Green State University, Bowling Green, OH, assistant professor of physics, 1970-73; Yeshiva University, New York City, research associate, 1973-74; Westinghouse Electric, Madison, PA, senior engineer in Advanced Reactors division, 1974-77; Essex Group, Inc., Pittsburgh, PA, staff scientist in Advanced Control Systems, 1977-79; Carnegie Mellon University, Pittsburgh, PA, scientist in Computer Engineering Center, 1979-83, assistant director, Data Storage Systems Center, 1983-90, director of Special Projects for Engineering Education, 1990-92, senior fellow, Sci/Tech Education, 1992—. Consultant to publishers of children's science books.

FRED BORTZ

MEMBER: American Association for the Advancement of Science, American Physical Society, Society of Children's Book Writers and Illustrators, Alfred University Parent's Advisory Council, Sigma Xi.

AWARDS, HONORS: Received special mention from Children's Science Writings Award committee, American Institute of Physics, 1991, for *Superstuff!*

WRITINGS:

Superstuff! Materials That Have Changed Our Lives, F. Watts, 1990.
Mind Tools: The Science of Artificial Intelligence, F. Watts, 1992.

Also contributor to *The New Book of Knowledge,* Grolier, beginning 1988. Contributor of articles on theoretical and applied physics to periodicals, including *Physics Today.* Specialist reviewer for *Appraisal: Science Books for Young People.*

WORK IN PROGRESS: A book on the role of failure in engineering, entitled *Catastrophe! Learning from Spectacular Failure,* expected from Scientific American Books for Children, 1994.

SIDELIGHTS: Fred Bortz writes, "I always connect the dedications of my books to the subject matter. I also use them to make a point about what I value in life. For instance, the dedication of *Superstuff!,* which is about materials science and engineering, begins, 'To my parents, who produced the raw material, to my teachers, who processed it with care, . . .' The dedication of *Mind*

Tools: The Science of Artificial Intelligence honors my wife: 'To Susan, who uses her knowledge base and natural intelligence in an unending quest for wisdom.' The dedication of *Catastrophe! Learning from Spectacular Failure* was written even before the first chapter was completed to my satisfaction, for reasons that are obvious: 'In memory of my father, Harry A. Bortz (1901-1991), who taught me not to fear failure, nor to accept it, but to learn from it in order to succeed.'

"I started to write for children as a diversion from my everyday work, so my first published articles had nothing to do with science. The very first sale resulted from my second assignment in the Institute of Children's Literature correspondence course. It was a classic assignment in which I had to choose five items from a list of ten and weave them into a story.

"I chose parrot, elephant, umbrella, watering can, and mountain, stirred gently, and came up with a story-poem in nonsense verse, *a la* Dr. Seuss, called 'The Mysterious Message.' I didn't intend for the message to be religious, but I recognized that the poem's recurring chorus, 'Though you ask what you want / You will get what you need,' had religious appeal. I sold it to the *Christian Science Monitor* for $50 in 1978, and from then on I was a *writer!*

"Suddenly everything in my life was changing—or so I thought. In my work, I preferred writing about the research to actually carrying it out. But in truth, things have not changed all that much. The most enjoyable part of writing for me is research: struggling to understand new scientific knowledge and technological wonders, then getting so excited about what I learned that I simply have to share it.

"Like any writer, I appreciate good reviews. But I especially like to read reviews in which the reviewer's comments reveal that I accomplished what I had set out to do. In his review of *Superstuff!* for *Science Teacher*, Thomas E. Thompson concluded: 'The strength of this book lies in the relationship between science and technology. The implicit relationship between the science of materials and the resulting technological developments is found throughout the book. High school students interested in the physical sciences would find this worthwhile reading.' Thanks, Mr. Thompson, for the greatest compliment I could have hoped for."

FOR MORE INFORMATION SEE:

PERIODICALS

Science Teacher, October, 1991, pp. 80-81.

*   *   *

BURCH, Robert J(oseph) 1925-

PERSONAL: Born June 26, 1925, in Inman, GA; son of John Ambrose (a bookkeeper) and Nell (Graham) Burch. *Education:* Graduated with a B.S. from University of Georgia; attended Hunter College (now of the City University of New York) and New York University. *Politics:* Democrat. *Religion:* Methodist.

ADDRESSES: Home—2021 Forest Dr., Fayetteville, GA 30214.

CAREER: Civil service employee with Atlanta Ordnance Depot, Atlanta, GA, 1951-53, and with U.S. Army, Yokohama and Tokyo, Japan, 1953-55; Muir & Co. (advertising agency), New York City, clerical worker, 1956-59; Walter E. Heller & Co. (industrial finance company), New York City, clerical worker, 1959-62; writer, 1959—. *Military service:* U.S. Army, 1943-46; served in New Guinea and Australia.

MEMBER: Authors Guild, Authors League of America.

AWARDS, HONORS: Fellowship in juvenile literature, Bread Loaf Writers' Conference, 1960; Child Study Association of America children's book award, and Jane Addams Children's Book Award, both 1967, for *Queenie Peavy;* Georgia Children's Book Award, 1969, for *Skinny,* 1971, for *Queenie Peavy,* and 1974, for *Doodle and the Go-Cart;* Phoenix Award, Children's Literature Association, 1986, for *Queenie Peavy.* Several of Burch's books have been Junior Literary Guild or Weekly Reader Book Club selections.

ROBERT J. BURCH

WRITINGS:

The Traveling Bird, illustrated by Susanne Suba, McDowell, Obolensky, 1959.

(Translator) Egon Mathieson, *A Jungle in the Wheat Field* (Danish picture book), McDowell, Obolensky, 1960.

A Funny Place to Live, illustrated by W. R. Lohse, Viking, 1962.

Tyler, Wilkin, and Skee, illustrated by Don Sibley, Viking, 1963, reissued in hardback by University of Georgia Press, 1990.

Skinny, illustrated by Sibley, Viking, 1964 (published in England with illustrations by Ian Ribbons, Methuen, 1965), reissued in hardback by University of Gergia Press, 1990.

D. J.'s Worst Enemy, illustrated by Emil Weiss, Viking, 1965.

Queenie Peavy, illustrated by Jerry Lazare, Viking, 1966.

Renfroe's Christmas, illustrated by Rocco Negri, Viking, 1968.

Joey's Cat, illustrated by Don Freeman, Viking, 1969.

Simon and the Game of Chance, illustrated by Fermin Rocker, Viking, 1970.

The Hunting Trip, illustrated by Suba, Scribners, 1971.

Doodle and the Go-Cart, illustrated by Alan Tiegreen, Viking, 1972.

Hut School and the Wartime Home-Front Heroes, illustrated by Ronald Himler, Viking, 1974, published as *Home-Front Heroes,* Viking, 1992.

The Jolly Witch, illustrated by Leigh Grant, Dutton, 1975.

Two That Were Tough, illustrated by Richard Cuffari, Viking, 1976.

The Whitman Kick, Dutton, 1977.

Wilkin's Ghost, illustrated by Lloyd Bloom, Viking, 1978.

Ida Early Comes over the Mountain, Viking, 1980.

Christmas with Ida Early, illustrated by Gail Owens, Viking, 1983.

King Kong and Other Poets, Viking, 1986.

ADAPTATIONS: Ida Early Comes over the Mountain was adapted as *The Incredible Ida Early,* for television by the National Broadcasting Corporation (NBC-TV), 1987.

SIDELIGHTS: Robert J. Burch specializes in books for children in the middle grades, such as *Ida Early Comes Over the Mountain* and the award-winning *Queenie Peavy.* But he has also written picture books for younger children, such as *Joey's Cat* and *The Jolly Witch,* in addition to books for young adults like *The Whitman Kick.* Burch's work usually displays his intimate knowledge of rural Georgia and the years surrounding the Great Depression; he has also been praised by critics for his realism and lack of sentimentality.

Burch was born June 26, 1925, in Inman, a farming community in Fayette County, Georgia. Shortly after his birth, his family moved to Fayetteville, the slightly larger, but also rural, county seat. Surrounded by seven siblings and many farm animals that he made into pets, Burch grew to love the country life. He once commented to *SATA:* "When I was a boy, I planned to be a farmer.... In any event, I did not give a thought to writing stories until I was thirty years old."

But after graduating from high school, Burch served in the U.S. Army during the last half of World War II, and was stricken with wanderlust after being stationed in New Guinea and Australia. Though after completing his military stint he returned and obtained a B.S. in agriculture from the University of Georgia, a year spent working in a greenhouse left him with a desire to travel again. Burch did clerical work at the Atlanta Ordnance Department, which led him to similar duty with the U.S. Army that took him to Yokohama and Tokyo, Japan. When he returned from overseas, he settled in New York City for eight years.

There Burch continued his clerical work, but he also began to be interested in writing as a hobby. He took writing classes at Hunter College (now part of the City University of New York) and at New York University. As he once affirmed in *SATA,* Burch considers himself "very much indebted to Dr. William Lipkind," his instructor in a class on writing for children. Lipkind encouraged him "to write stories for young people that

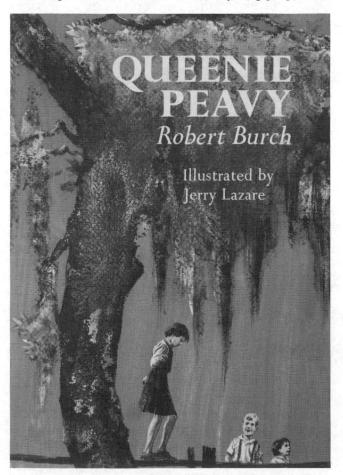

In Burch's award-winning novel, a complex girl struggles against her oppressive environment in the Depression-era South.

are drawn from [his] own background." By 1959, Burch had published his first children's book, *The Traveling Bird*. In it, claimed Hugh T. Keenan in a *Dictionary of Literary Biography* article, "he gives a unique and personal twist to the familiar story of a child and a helpful animal." Young David receives a parakeet from his uncle, when he would have preferred a dog instead. The sympathetic parakeet eventually manages to trade himself for a dog, but by then David has become attached to the bird and regrets the exchange.

After his first effort, Burch did two picture books, including a loose English translation of the Danish book *A Jungle in the Wheat Field*, before abandoning his clerical work and moving back to his beloved Fayetteville to become a full-time writer. With his 1963 publication *Tyler, Wilkin, and Skee*, however, Burch "found his appropriate audience—slightly older children—and his proper milieu: the domestic life of children in the Great Depression in rural Georgia," according to Keenan. Burch himself remarked of these works: "In them I hope to give boys and girls of today a glimpse of what it was like to have lived during the Depression years, when almost everyone was poor. At the same time, I try to show that we sometimes had ourselves a pretty good time back then and that there are lots of things more important than money or material wealth." Burch revisits the characters of *Tyler, Wilkin, and Skee* in his later book, *Wilkin's Ghost*.

In 1964 Burch published *Skinny,* which marked the beginning of his reputation for uncompromising realism. Skinny is an illiterate orphan who plots with spinster Miss Bessie to arrange her marriage to traveling man "Daddy" Rabbit so that the couple will adopt him. Their plot fails, however, and Skinny is sent to the orphanage with the consolations of vacations with Miss Bessie and learning to read and write. *Skinny* later garnered Burch the Georgia Children's Book Award in 1969. Other Burch books noted for their refusal to resolve into perfect happy endings are *Simon and the Game of Chance,* which deals with infant death, mental illness, and the fatal accident of the oldest sister's fiance, and *Queenie Peavy,* one of Burch's most popular works about a troubled tomboy whose father is not changed for the better by a term in prison. The latter story won Burch several honors, including the Jane Addams Children's Book Award in 1967. In 1990 *Skinny* and *Tyler, Wilkin, and Skee* became the first children's books to be reprinted by the University of Georgia Press in the Brown Thrasher series, books of distinction by southern writers.

The Whitman Kick, Burch's 1977 effort, was a departure from his other books in that it was aimed at older adolescents. It concerns two platonic friends, Alan and Amanda, who share a love of Walt Whitman's poetry but gain sexual experience through others. Unfortunately, Amanda becomes pregnant; Alan is not happy with his sexual relationship either, since he initiated it merely for spite after Amanda became interested in another boy. As Keenan put it, "the story is somber and more

An eccentric housekeeper provides lessons about life as well as laughs in the television adaptation of Burch's *Ida Early Comes over the Mountain.* (From *The Incredible Ida Early,* broadcast by NBC.)

bitter than sweet ... but the book does treat serious domestic issues with sensitivity and restraint."

Notable among Burch's later works are his two books about the irrepressible Ida Early, *Ida Early Comes over the Mountain* and *Christmas with Ida Early.* Ida comes to serve as housekeeper for the Sutton family, who have just suffered the death of Mrs. Sutton. With her amusing and unconventional ways, such as wearing overalls and doing rope tricks, Ida manages to distract the Sutton children from their grief and teach them about life. *Ida Early Comes over the Mountain* proved so popular that it served as the basis for a National Broadcasting Corporation (NBC) television special in 1987. The sequel, in which the family's cantankerous Aunt Earnestine comes for an extended holiday visit, was deemed "a blithe and comic tale" by the *Bulletin of the Center for Children's Books.*

Humor "becomes a vehicle for easing the pain and reality of life" in *King Kong and Other Poets,* according to Frances Bradburn of *Wilson Library Bulletin.* A sixth-grade boy's account of how the new girl in school is gradually accepted by her classmates, *King Kong* uses a comic attitude and funny poems to relate serious issues, such as coping with a parent's death. Whether dealing with problems directly or with humor, whether he sets his tale in his native Georgia or not, Burch "universalizes the action, characters, and themes of his fiction," Malcolm Usrey states in *Twentieth-Century Children's Writers.* "His novels speak elemental truths: wealth does not necessarily create happiness; ... poverty is not always degrading; and family and community, good and bad, are usually what people make them."

WORKS CITED:

Bradburn, Frances, "Middle Books," *Wilson Library Bulletin,* February, 1987, pp. 48-49.
Review of *Christmas with Ida Early, Bulletin of the Center for Children's Books,* November, 1983, p. 44.
Keenan, Hugh T., essay in *Dictionary of Literary Biography,* Volume 52: *American Writers for Children since 1960: Fiction,* Gale, 1986.
Usrey, Malcolm, "Robert Burch," *Twentieth-Century Children's Writers,* 3rd edition, St. James Press, 1989, pp. 154-55.

FOR MORE INFORMATION SEE:

BOOKS

Hopkins, Lee Bennett, editor, *More Books by More People,* Citation Press, 1974.

PERIODICALS

Atlanta Journal and Constitution Magazine, November 29, 1964.
Bulletin of the Center for Children's Books, April, 1977; March, 1978; February, 1979; October, 1986.
Horn Book, August, 1966; August, 1972; June, 1974; August, 1974; October, 1978.
Junior Literary Guild, September, 1980.
New York Times Book Review, May 5, 1974; January 18, 1981.

* * *

BURCHARD, Peter Duncan 1921-

PERSONAL: Born March 1, 1921, in Washington, DC; son of Russell Duncan (a lawyer) and Ethel (Brokaw) Burchard; married Elizabeth Chamberlain, March 23, 1945 (marriage ended); married Lucy Edwards (marriage ended); married Linda Wemyss Carman (a journalist), August 29, 1987; children (first marriage): Lee, Peter Jr., Laura. *Education:* Philadelphia Museum School of Art, graduate, 1947. *Politics:* Registered Democrat. *Hobbies and other interests:* Sailing, tennis, and cross-country skiing.

ADDRESSES: Home—18 Water St., Williamstown, MA 01267.

CAREER: Free-lance illustrator, 1947—, writer, 1956—, and photographer, 1975—. Member of panel of advisers, George Polk awards, 1983—. *Military service:* U.S. Army Signal Corps, 1943-46.

MEMBER: Authors Guild, Authors League of America, International PEN.

AWARDS, HONORS: Boys Club of America Award, 1955, for illustrating *Squanto: Friend of the White Man;* Nancy Bloch Award, 1963, and Lewis Carroll Shelf Award, 1964, for illustrating *Roosevelt Grady;* Lewis Carroll Shelf Award, 1966, for *Jed: The Story of a Yankee Soldier and a Southern Boy;* Guggenheim fellowship, 1966-67; *Bimby* named to *Horn Book* honor list, 1968; *Pioneers of Flight* included on Child Study Association book list, 1970; Christopher Award, 1972, for illustrating *Pocahontas and the Strangers;* Western Writers award for illustrations, 1975, for photographs illustrating *Ride 'Em Cowgirl;* Edgar Allan Poe nomination, 1978, for illustrating *Night Spell.*

WRITINGS:

The River Queen, self-illustrated, Macmillan, 1957.
The Carol Moran, self-illustrated, Macmillan, 1958.
Balloons from Paper Bags to Skyhooks, self-illustrated, Macmillan, 1960.
Jed: The Story of a Yankee Soldier and a Southern Boy, self-illustrated, Coward, 1960.
North by Night, Coward, 1962.
One Gallant Rush: Robert Gould Shaw and His Brave Black Regiment, St. Martin's, 1965, published as *Glory,* 1989.
Stranded: A Story of New York in 1875, Coward, 1967.
Bimby, self-illustrated, Coward, 1968.
Chito, illustrated with photographs by Katrina Thomas, Coward, 1969.
Pioneers of Flight, St. Martin's, 1970.
Rat Hell, self-illustrated, Coward, 1971.
A Quiet Place, Coward, 1972.
The Deserter: A Spy Story of the Civil War, Coward, 1973.
Harbor Tug, Putnam, 1974.
Whaleboat Raid, self-illustrated, Coward, 1977.
Ocean Race: A Sea Venture, illustrated with photographs by the author, Putnam, 1978.
Chinwe, self-illustrated, Putnam, 1979.
Digger, Putnam, 1980.
First Affair, Farrar, Straus, 1981.
Sea Change, self-illustrated, Farrar, Straus, 1984.
Venturing: An Introduction to Sailing, illustrated with photographs by the author, Little, Brown, 1986.
We'll Stand by the Union, Facts on File, 1993.

ILLUSTRATOR

Marie McSwigan, *Our Town Has a Circus,* Dutton, 1949.
Virginia Haviland, *William Penn,* Abingdon, 1952.
Hildreth T. Wriston, *Show Lamb,* Abingdon, 1953.
Clyde Robert Bulla, *Down the Mississippi,* Crowell, 1954.
Grace Tracy Johnson and Harold N. Johnson, *Courage Wins,* Dutton, 1954.
Bulla, *Squanto: Friend of the White Man,* Crowell, 1954, published as *Squanto: Friend of the Pilgrims,* 1969.
Margaret Glover Otto, *Tiny Man,* Holt, 1955.
Alf Evers, *Treasure of Watchdog Mountain,* Macmillan, 1955.
Marian Cumming, *Clan Texas,* Harcourt, 1955.

PETER DUNCAN BURCHARD

William L. Brown and Rosalie Moore, *The Boy Who Got Mailed,* Coward, 1957.

Bulla, *Pirate's Promise,* Crowell, 1958.

Wilma Pitchford Hays, *The Fourth of July Raid,* Coward, 1959.

Hays, *Easter Fires,* Coward, 1960.

Louisa R. Shotwell, *Roosevelt Grady,* World Publishing, 1963.

Earl S. Miers, *Pirate Chase,* Holt, 1965.

Peggy Mann, *The Street of Flower Boxes,* Coward, 1966.

Lonzo Anderson, *Zeb,* Knopf, 1966.

Bulla, *Pocahontas and the Strangers,* Crowell, 1971.

Lynn Haney, *Ride 'Em Cowgirl,* Putnam, 1975.

Robert Newman, *Night Spell,* Atheneum, 1977.

Also illustrator of many other books.

OTHER

Contributor of stories, articles, and reviews to magazines, including *Boy's Life, Interplay, Connoisseur,* and *American Heritage.*

ADAPTATIONS: One Gallant Rush, re-released as *Glory,* together with Lincoln Kirstein's *Lay This Laurel,* served as a historical source for the film *Glory,* released by TriStar Pictures in 1989.

SIDELIGHTS: Author and illustrator Peter Burchard has many links with both history and the sea, links that are reflected in his works. He was born in Washington, D.C., where his father was serving as a lawyer with the federal government, but grew up in New Jersey, near New York City. He developed a pronounced stutter which has followed him throughout his life. However,

"difficulties aren't always leaden weights around the necks of sufferers," Burchard declares in his *Something about the Author Autobiography Series (SAAS)* entry. "In compensating for my handicap, I triumphed in other ways." He became a track star and first-string halfback on the football team of the private academy he attended. Later, he explains in his *SAAS* entry, he attended a boarding school in Avon, Connecticut, where "I excelled in almost everything I undertook but my speech impediment kept me from becoming arrogant. It was, as one of my friends chose to put it, 'a great leveller.'"

Burchard demonstrated an interest in art before he started school. His father was an amateur artist. "In our house," Burchard writes in his *SAAS* entry, "my father set aside a room where he put up an easel and sometimes, as he worked on a painting, I sat close to him and did crayon drawings, most of them of fire engines rushing toward a blazing building." Burchard spent his teens at a private boarding school in Avon, Connecticut, where Paul Child—an enthusiastic teacher—taught him to draw and paint. It was at Child's suggestion that Burchard went on to study at the Philadelphia Museum School of Art, now called The University of the Arts.

As the United States became involved in World War II, Burchard was just beginning his sophomore year at the College of Art. At first, his speech impediment kept him out of the military. "In January, 1942, I left school and went to work as a draftsman, doing detail and perspective drawings for designers of a cargo plane to be built for the Navy," he explains in *SAAS.* In 1943, he was accepted by the U.S. Army and, after basic training in New Orleans, he became a Signal Corps maritime radio operator and was assigned to the troop transport *Sea Robin.* "Since childhood, I had loved the seashore—shallow waters, bright beaches, sounding waves," Burchard writes, and his eighteen transatlantic crossings instilled in him a love of deep water voyages.

Burchard was married for the first time in March, 1946—to Betsy Chamberlain—and was discharged from the Army a month later. After spending six months working on perspective drawings for a secret Navy project, he resumed his education at the College of Art. He finished his studies in 1947 and, with his wife and their first child moved to Rockland County, New York, where he worked as a freelance illustrator. Burchard started writing in 1958. After about eleven years illustrating children's books, he writes in *SAAS,* "an editor at Macmillan suggested that I write a text for a children's picture book, something that I might like to illustrate." His first book was called *The River Queen,* about a riverboat like the ones that he had seen in New Orleans.

Burchard's family history played an important role in starting his writing career. "In 1959," Burchard writes in his *SAAS* entry, "my mother gave me a shoebox containing my grandfather's papers. In 1861, at sixteen, my mother's father joined a New York regiment." His grandfather's letters and diaries, written while he served in the Union Army, inspired Burchard to study Civil

War history. *Jed: The Story of a Yankee Soldier and a Southern Boy* was Burchard's first book about the war. It became a minor classic, Burchard explains in *SAAS,* and won recognition from critics—one of whom likened it to Stephen Crane's novel *The Red Badge of Courage.* The book's success, Burchard says, "encouraged me to write other books about the Civil War. The next, inspired by an incident in the life of Betsy's grandfather, was *North by Night,* which begins in the Sea Islands of South Carolina and involves a battle at Fort Wagner."

This family connection led Burchard to write his best-known and most popular book. "A week after Betsy's grandfather took part in an attack on Wagner," Burchard explains in his *SAAS* entry, "a young man named Robert Gould Shaw, leading the first black regiment recruited in the North, charged the fort and was shot in his attempt to capture it. I was touched by Shaw's dedication and the heroism of his men and decided to become his first biographer."

"*One Gallant Rush: Robert Gould Shaw and His Brave Black Regiment,* published in 1965, was a critical success," Burchard continues, "but its universal value went unrecognized until much later when it came to the attention of producer Freddie Fields, who made the motion picture *Glory.*" Released in 1989, *Glory* won three Academy Awards and brought Burchard's book to

public attention. "As things stand now," Burchard writes in *SAAS,* "*One Gallant Rush* has been read by perhaps 100,000 people." "Summing up," he concludes, "I can say that I am happy to have played a minor role in the restructuring of the history of our country, to have helped give Robert Gould Shaw and his officers and men the prominence they deserve."

Six of Burchard's books are about the Civil War, and the others deal with a variety of subjects. *Bimby,* published in 1968, tells the story of a young black boy born into slavery who is driven to ecape. *Rat Hell* is the story of an escape from a Civil War military prison. *Whaleboat Raid,* published in 1977, is about the Revolutionary War, and is based on an episode that took place in 1777. *Chinwe,* published in 1979, is about a young African woman who is captured and put aboard a slave ship bound for Cuba. Chinwe and her fellow captives stage a successful mutiny but, in the end, spend their lives in slavery in America.

Burchard has also written two books about sailing. He started ocean racing in 1976, aboard Danforth Miller's sailboat *Blixtar.* As part of Miller's crew, he sailed several dozen major races. "Out of my experience aboard *Blixtar* came my first book about the sport—*Ocean Race,* published in 1978," Burchard says in his *SAAS* entry. "Later, in *Venturing: An Introduction*

Based in part on Burchard's novel *One Gallant Rush,* the movie *Glory* tells the story of an African American regiment that fought in the American Civil War. (From *Glory,* distributed by Tri-Star.)

to Sailing, published in 1986, I expressed my love for sea and wind and gave beginning sailors tips on sail handling, helmsmanship, and basic navigation." Burchard concludes his *SAAS* entry with a reminiscence of a night spent on a sailboat anchored in a harbor on the eastern shore of Maryland: "I am aware that I have led a checkered life but, that night, I thanked God for my blessings—for my children, for my talents, for the love of many friends."

WORKS CITED:

Burchard, Peter Duncan, essay in *Something about the Author Autobiography Series,* Volume 13, Gale, 1990, pp. 55-70.

*   *   *

BURFORD, Eleanor
See HIBBERT, Eleanor Alice Burford

*   *   *

BURTON, Hester (Wood-Hill) 1913-

PERSONAL: Born December 6, 1913, in Beccles, Suffolk, England; daughter of Henry G. (a surgeon) and Amy (Crowfoot) Wood-Hill; married R. W. B. Burton (a tutor-lecturer in classics at Oxford University), August 7, 1937; children: Catharine Anne, Elizabeth Mary, Janet Hester. *Education:* Oxford University, honors degree in English literature, 1936. *Politics:* Liberal.

ADDRESSES: Home—Mill House, Kidlington, Oxford, England.

CAREER: Writer of historical novels for children, biographer, and editor. Part-time grammar school teacher; examiner in public examination.

AWARDS, HONORS: Carnegie Medal runner-up, c. 1962, for *Castors Away!;* Carnegie Medal, 1963, and Honorable Mention in the New York *Herald Tribune* Children's Spring Book Festival, 1964, for *Time of Trial;* Boston *Globe-Horn Book* Award, 1971.

WRITINGS:

JUVENILE FICTION; EXCEPT WHERE NOTED

(Editor and author of commentary) *Coleridge and the Wordsworths* (nonfiction), Oxford University Press, 1953.
(Editor and author of commentary) *Tennyson* (nonfiction), Oxford University Press, 1954.
(Editor) *Her First Ball: Short Stories,* illustrated by Susan Einzig, Oxford University Press, 1959.
The Great Gale, illustrated by Joan Kiddell-Monroe, Oxford University Press, 1960, published in United States as *The Flood at Reedsmere,* illustrated by Robin Jacques, World, 1968.
Castors Away!, illustrated by Victor Ambrus, Oxford University Press, 1962, World, 1963.
Time of Trial, illustrated by Ambrus, Oxford University Press, 1963, World, 1964.

A Seaman at the Time of Trafalgar (nonfiction), illustrated by Ambrus, Oxford University Press, 1963.
No Beat of Drum, illustrated by Ambrus, Oxford University Press, 1966, World, 1967.
In Spite of All Terror, illustrated by Ambrus, Oxford University Press, 1968, World, 1969.
Otmoor for Ever!, illustrated by Gareth Floyd, Hamish Hamilton, 1968.
Thomas, illustrated by Ambrus, Oxford University Press, 1969, published in America as *Beyond the Weir Bridge,* Crowell, 1970.
Through the Fire, illustrated by Floyd, Hamish Hamilton, 1969.
The Henchmans at Home, illustrated by Ambrus, Oxford University Press, 1970, Crowell, 1972.
The Rebel, illustrated by Ambrus, Oxford University Press, 1971, Crowell, 1972.
Riders of the Storm, illustrated by Ambrus, Oxford University Press, 1972, Crowell, 1973.
Kate Rider, illustrated by Ambrus, Oxford University Press, 1974, published in United States as *Kate Ryder,* Crowell, 1975.
To Ravensrigg, illustrated by Ambrus, Oxford University Press, 1976, Crowell, 1977.
Tim at the Fur Fort, illustrated by Ambrus, Hamish Hamilton, 1977.
A Grenville Goes to Sea, illustrated by Colin McNaughton, Heinemann, 1977.
When the Beacons Blazed, illustrated by Ambrus, Hamish Hamilton, 1978.
Five August Days, illustrated by Trevor Ridley, Oxford University Press, 1981.

Also served as assistant editor for the *Oxford Junior Encyclopaedia,* 1956-61. Burton's books for children have been translated into several languages, including Dutch, Swedish, German, Danish, Polish, Portuguese, Spanish, Afrikaans, and Hebrew.

FOR ADULTS

Barbara Bodichon, 1827-1891 (biography), Murray, 1949.

SIDELIGHTS: English author Hester Burton specializes in writing historical novels for children. "The plot which I most enjoy exploring in my stories," she explained in an essay for *Something about the Author Autobiography Series* (*SAAS*), "is to gather a small group of children together and then plunge them into some terrible danger or misfortune out of which they have to scramble without help from their elders." Because, as Burton put it in the essay, natural disasters are now scarce and "in modern England, children are largely ... protected from the dangers of murder and kidnapping by good parents," she has for the most part relied on historical events to provide these plots rather than setting her stories in contemporary times. Novels such as *Castors Away!* and *Kate Ryder* have won her critical acclaim and fans among readers, and her *Time of Trial* garnered Burton the prestigious Carnegie Medal in 1963.

HESTER BURTON

Burton was born December 6, 1913, in Beccles, Suffolk, England. Her parents encouraged her to use her imagination from an early age, and she and her older sisters would act out plays they had written with a toy theater that their father had built for them. Burton's mother would read classic children's books to them, and made them costumes for their plays. Burton was forced to depend even more on her imagination for entertainment when a series of illnesses—whooping cough, Asian influenza, and double pneumonia—struck her in succession when she was about six years old. As she related in her *SAAS* essay, she was confined to her bed for a long time and "I spent hours and hours, physically languid, but in my imagination putting my heroes through the most fearful trials. My favourite game was to build a fort on my bed table with my toy bricks and fill it with brave British soldiers and to imagine the fort being besieged by a howling tribe of red Indians." But Burton's illnesses, as might be expected, also caused her disadvantages. Unable to attend school for a time, she was late in learning how to read. Nevertheless, "once I had learned to read," Burton recalled for *SAAS*, "a marvellous new world was opened to me and once I realized that grown-ups actually sat down and wrote out the kind of imaginary adventures which had been going on in my own mind, I knew I wanted to be a writer."

Burton's earliest written efforts after that decision were poems, because longer forms at first intimidated her. But she drifted away from writing when she was sent to board at Headington School in Oxford, England, at the age of twelve. As she explained in her *SAAS* essay, "I was not unhappy there. I had friends, I was not stupid, and we were well fed. So what went wrong? First and foremost, I had left my dreamworld behind; I could no longer conjure up characters and adventures for them in my head. I think this was because in a boarding school one always lives in a crowd.... Clearly, my kind of

imagination needs a certain amount of solitude in order to flourish." So Burton concentrated on her studies, but still physically delicate because of her earlier illnesses, she spent much of the time allotted for sports and recreation reading the historical novels of authors such as Robert Louis Stevenson, Alexander Dumas, and James Fenimore Cooper.

When Burton graduated from Headington School, she entered Oxford University. She studied English literature, and had famous fantasy authors C. S. Lewis and J. R. R. Tolkien among her professors. In the year before she earned her degree, she met her husband, R. W. B. Burton, an Oxford tutor and lecturer, and became engaged. They married in August, 1937. While beginning her family, Burton endured the hardships and fears that much of Great Britain knew during World War II. She and her husband were hosts to some of their fellow citizens whose homes were destroyed in the bombing of London, and later Burton used her memories of the experience to help in the writing of her novel, *In Spite of All Terror*.

By 1949, Burton's youngest daughter was ready to attend nursery school, and Burton herself began teaching part-time at a girls' grammar school. The same year also saw the publication of her first book, an adult biography of nineteenth-century British feminist Barbara Bodichon. Burton then edited both *Coleridge and the Wordsworths* and *Tennyson*, which she described in her *SAAS* essay as "introducing the lives and poetry of the great poets to boys and girls of about sixteen." In 1956 she began serving as assistant editor of the *Oxford Junior Encyclopaedia*, and it was in this capacity that she first realized her true calling to write children's novels. "It was an interesting job in many ways," Burton recalled for *SAAS*, "but after five years it suddenly occurred to me that instead of writing *facts* for children, it would be much more fun to write *fiction*."

Burton's first story was based on a real-life flood in East Anglia, England, in 1953. Since it took place only seven years previous to the book's publication, Burton considered *The Flood at Reedsmere* more contemporary than historical. For her second children's novel, *Castors Away!* Burton used the Battle of Trafalgar in 1805 as historical background. She explained her affinity for this time in English history in her *SAAS* essay: "Not only has Lord Nelson always been my favourite national hero, but I have also come to feel a special sympathy for my countrymen living at that time. Then, as in 1940, England was facing an all-conquering European tyrant. Change Hitler for Napoleon and the threat of a German invasion of these islands for the very real threat of a French invasion, and it is not hard to see how I have come to understand the ordeals of that earlier generation." Burton has also explored the period during and after the English Civil War extensively, in her books *Kate Ryder* and *Beyond the Weir Bridge*.

Though most of Burton's books are set in historical times, they have contemporary relevance in that Burton infuses a strong sense of social conscience into her stories. *To Ravensrigg* deals with the issues of personal identity and slavery, *No Beat of Drum* chronicles the British class struggles of the early 1800s, and *Time of Trial* discusses freedom of speech. Despite her love of historical settings, Burton returned to modern times for her 1981 story *Five August Days.*

Burton's novels have been praised for their deft blend of historical fact, social relevance, and solid narrative technique. As Ruth Hill Viguers noted in her review of *Time of Trial* in *Horn Book,* "A recital of incidents or relating of plot can give no idea of the reality of the characters, the appeal of the gentle love story, or the vitality of the book as a whole. It is written with such seeming ease that it sweeps the reader along too fast for him to notice how clear is the picture of the times and how much wider his view has grown." Burton has cited the use of history in her books as a learning tool, drawing parallels to modern society. For example, she has likened the impact of the plague on sixteenth century society to the effects of AIDS on the twentieth century. In her view, the human race is linked to the past and must learn from it. "Whether we were born in the sixteenth century when one wore doublets and hose or in the twentieth when one wears jeans, we are all members of the human race," Burton related in her *SAAS* entry. She continued, "Whether we like it or not, we are inescapably chained to the past . . . surely we can learn from our forbears." Burton feels it is important for young people to be aware of history, to know what was gained or lost so that the modern world may exist as it does. By combining historical fact with interesting stories, she is able to extend this information to young people. She sees a great benefit in possessing this knowledge. She wrote in *SAAS:* "Knowing and understanding the heroism of our forbears surely makes us prouder patriots. We 'walk taller' for knowing our past."

WORKS CITED:

Burton, Hester, essay in *Something about the Author Autobiography Series,* Volume 8, Gale, 1989, pp. 51-64.
Viguers, Ruth Hill, review of *Time of Trial* in *Horn Book,* June, 1964.

FOR MORE INFORMATION SEE:

BOOKS

Children's Literature Review, Volume 1, Gale, 1976.

PERIODICALS

Bulletin of the Center for Children's Books, January, 1974; May, 1976; September, 1977.
Children's Literature in Education, summer, 1977.
Horn Book, August, 1964; February, 1968; June, 1969; February, 1976; August, 1976.

C

CABAT, Erni 1914-

PERSONAL: Born July 1, 1914, in New York, NY; married, wife's name Rose (a ceramicist), October 17, 1936; children: George, Michael, and June. *Education:* Attended Art Student's League, Mechanics (Art) Institute; graduated from Cooper Union Art Institute, 1936; studied ceramics at the Greenwich Settlement House; studied engineering principles at the University of Arizona, c. 1943.

ADDRESSES: Office—The Cabat Studio, 627 North Fourth Ave., Tucson, AZ 85705.

CAREER: Worked for advertising agencies in New York City, including J. Walter Thompson and Young & Rubicam, 1940-42; Time-Life, New York City, art director, 1942. Consolidated-Vultee Aircraft Corp., Tucson, AZ, supervisor of production illustration, 1943-45; Cabat-Gill Advertising Agency, Tucson, co-founder, 1945-1972; taught advertising, design, and marketing at Tucson High School, Iowa State College, 1966, and University of Arizona, 1969. Artist and illustrator, 1967—. Owner, with wife, Cabat Studios, Tucson; lecturer in painting and creativity. *Exhibitions:* Cabat's works have been exhibited in numerous museums and galleries, including Museum of Contemporary Crafts, New York City, 1959; Museum of International Folk Art, Santa Fe, NM, 1969; Smithsonian Institution, Washington, DC, 1969, 1972; American Watercolor Society, Washington, DC, 1972; Tucson Museum of Art, Tucson, 1987; Arizona Commission of the Arts, five-year traveling exhibition, 1990—.

MEMBER: Society of Children's Book Writers and Illustrators.

AWARDS, HONORS: Third place medal, New York City Society for the Prevention of Cruelty to Animals (SPCA), 1927, for poster design; Gold Medal, Cooper Union Institute, 1934; Printers Ink Silver Medal Award, Tucson Advertising Club, 1967; numerous other advertising and painting awards.

ILLUSTRATOR:

CHILDREN'S BOOKS

Lollie Butler, *Erni Cabat's Magical World of Dinosaurs* (verse), Great Impressions, 1989.
Butler, *Erni Cabat's Magical World of Prehistoric Animals* (verse), Great Impressions, 1989.
Constance Andrea Keremes, *Erni Cabat's Magical World of the Carousel* (verse), Harbinger House, 1990.
Daniel Cohen, *Erni Cabat's Magical World of Monsters,* Cobblehill Books, 1992.
Michael J. Rule, *Erni Cabat's Magical ABC, Animals around the Farm* (verse), Harbinger House, 1992.

OTHER

Charles W. Polzer, *Father Eusebio Francisco Kino and His Missions of the Pimeria Alta,* Cabat Studio, Book 1: *The Side Altars,* 1982, Book 2: *The Main Altars,* 1983, Book 3: *Facing the Missions,* 1983.
Charlotte M. Cardon, *Life on the Tanque Verde,* Cabat Studio, 1983.
Rodney G. Engard, *The Flowering Southwest: Wildflowers, Cacti, and Succulents in Arizona, California, Colorado, Nevada, Texas, and Utah,* Great Impressions, 1989.

Also illustrator of notecards and limited-edition prints.

WORK IN PROGRESS: Animals in the Wild; working on several concept books for children.

SIDELIGHTS: Although internationally known as an artist and designer, with work exhibited throughout the world since he began his artistic career in the early 1950s, it took almost forty years before Erni Cabat illustrated his first book for children, *Erni Cabat's Magical World of Dinosaurs.* Since then, he has created more magical worlds, filling the pages of four more books with his brightly colored, intricate animal illustrations. Cabat's books for children have won the admiration of critics, librarians, and, most of all, the children themselves.

ERNI CABAT

Growing up in New York City, Cabat was fascinated by fairy tales, fantasy, dragons, mythology, and heroes. An active child who enjoyed stickball and rough play as much as art, Cabat's boundless energy attracted the attentions of his childhood friend and future wife, Rose. "He was brash and very sure of himself, and he still is. He hasn't changed his character. I didn't care much for him when we were little," she admitted in *Erni and Rose Cabat: Retrospective,* a museum catalog celebrating the couple's successful fifty-year marriage and artistic collaboration.

Romance blossomed between the pair while they were attending different night courses in art at a local high school. "Erni kept coming around," Rose recalled, "and we started going steady." After the Cabats were married in 1936, the problem of making a living arose. During the first few years of their marriage, Cabat completed his formal art training. After graduating from the Cooper Union Art Institute, he embarked on a career in advertising and became successful enough to eventually open his own agency in Tucson, Arizona, with partner Norval Gil in August of 1945. Meanwhile, Rose raised the couple's three children and pursued her interest in

working with clay; artist Rose Cabat has exhibited her ceramic sculptures and porcelain "feelies" throughout the U.S. and internationally.

Cabat found success not only in the advertising field, but as a teacher as well. Having won recognition for his artistic and creative talents, he used his expertise to design courses for students at both local high schools and colleges in the surrounding area. The courses were designed "to make students think, think, think," Cabat told a reporter in the *Tucson Daily Citizen.* Although his advertising career and interest in teaching kept him busy, Cabat never lost sight of the artistic aims of his childhood. He continued to paint and experiment with different art forms, and was fortunate to eventually find an opportunity to combine his love of art with his love of teaching. In 1972, Cabat was asked by the U.S. Information Service to travel throughout Brazil to teach creativity. In the same year, he spent three months in Iran teaching crafts, advertising, marketing and promotion, and creativity for the International Executive Service Corps. Three years later, he was in Peru, teaching once again. Cabat has traveled to over thirty-one countries to both teach and paint on location.

It wasn't until several years later however, at the age of seventy-four, that Cabat tried his hand at illustrating a book for children. "I always thought I could do and would like to do art for children's books," he told *SATA,* "but nobody asked me until the fall of 1989 when I showed a publisher my dinosaur idea." Cabat's concept was to develop what he called a "brand new style." Using gouache (opaque watercolor), he painted dinosaurs that were physically accurate and yet totally unlike the earthen-colored creatures commonly illustrated. With skins of intricate patterning, Cabat created a world of fantastic, magical creatures in vivid, jeweled tones. As the artist told *SATA:* "A sense of joy ... a sense of learning ... trying to stimulate their sense of imagination," is his aim in illustrating for young people.

Cabat's first book for children, *Erni Cabat's Magical World of Dinosaurs,* was followed by his *Magical World of Prehistoric Animals* and the colorful *Erni Cabat's Magical World of the Carousel.* As Peggy Larson notes in the *Tucson Daily Citizen,* the artist's "style is uniquely suited to the animals .... Horses, a lion, camel, swan, elephant, reindeer, unicorn and rooster prance across the bright pages, each wearing a saddle for the child rider for whom it waits." In *Erni Cabat's Magical World of Monsters,* the creatures of myth and legend are illustrated in the artist's unique style. And Cabat's alphabet book for preschoolers, *Animals around the Farm,* translates capital letters of the alphabet into barnyard animals made magical through the artist's vision of the fantastic. In designing the book for very young children, Cabat spent eight weeks seeking advice from librarians, teachers, and, as he told *SATA,* "the experts: the kids themselves."

Cabat believes strongly in the power of creativity to unlock people from the past. As he told *SATA:* "Creative thinking can provide many, many good solutions to

Cabat's colorful illustrations of farm animals provide children with a fun way to learn the alphabet. (Text by Michael Rule.)

any given problem. Young children in particular, should be taught to think independently and have the courage to put their thoughts into creative action. This is a magic key that unlocks the strange and fantastic worlds that are hidden all around us." Cabat added, "I believe in fantasy. I live in a world of WHY . . . ? WHAT IF . . . ? and WHY NOT . . . !"

WORKS CITED:

Larson, Peggy, "Colorful Critters," *Tucson Citizen,* August 4, 1992, p. C1.

Quinn, Robert, *Erni and Rose Cabat: Retrospective,* Tucson Art Museum, 1986.
Tucson Daily Citizen, April 11, 1967, p. 9.

FOR MORE INFORMATION SEE:

PERIODICALS

Arizona Daily Star, June 2, 1992, p. C1.
Arizona Republic, June 21, 1991, p. 8.
Art Voices, March, 1980.
40, July, 1978, p. 50.
Southwest Art, February, 1980.

CARAKER, Mary 1929-

PERSONAL: Born September 19, 1929, in Astoria, OR; daughter of Henry (a farmer) and Hilma (a homemaker; maiden name, Salmon) Lumijarvi; married Emmett Caraker (a naval officer and realtor), March 3, 1957 (deceased); children: Catherine, George, Richard, Elizabeth. *Education:* Willamette University, B.A., 1951; San Francisco State University, M.A., 1968. *Hobbies and other interests:* Wildlife, forestry, gardening, hiking.

ADDRESSES: Home—1879 Chestnut St., San Francisco, CA 94123. *Agent*—Adele Leone Agency, 26 Nantucket Place, Scarsdale, NY 10583.

CAREER: Kamehameha School for Girls, Honolulu, HI, teacher of secondary English, 1952-53; Benjamin Franklin Junior High School, Vallejo, CA, teacher of secondary English, 1955-56; San Francisco Unified School District, San Francisco, CA, teacher of English and substitute teacher, 1968-81; free-lance writer, 1982—.

MEMBER: Science Fiction Writers of America, Greenpeace, Sierra Club.

WRITINGS:

YOUNG ADULT SCIENCE FICTION

Seven Worlds, NAL/Signet, 1986.
Watersong, Warner Questar, 1987.
The Snows of Jaspre, Houghton, 1989.
The Faces of Ceti, Houghton, 1991.

WORK IN PROGRESS: A young adult science fiction novel; an autobiography; research on the Kalevala and the Finnish-American experience.

SIDELIGHTS: A *Publisher's Weekly* reviewer has described Mary Caraker as a "promising [science fiction] writer" for her creation of attractive futuristic worlds filled with complex problems. Two of her books, *Seven Worlds* and *The Snows of Jaspre,* focus on the experiences of Morgan Farraday, an employee of the Space Exploratory Forces, or SEF, who travels from her home planet of Terra to challenging assignments on other worlds. In *Seven Worlds,* Morgan relives seven such journeys as part of a psychological exam required for future service with the SEF. She tells of working as a teacher of the Terran language in places such as Parth, a swampy place inhabited by reptile-like people who inspire a revulsion in Morgan that she must overcome. Another story outlines the difficulties the young teacher has in Roga, the home of a vampire-like race. These two chapters were singled out by *Fantasy Review* critic Constance Ash as "bread-and-butter alien-character and alien-world science fiction." Penny Blubaugh in *Voice of Youth Advocates* appreciated the humanness of the protagonist, stating that "Morgan herself is likeable and real, never shown as a superwoman."

The character of Morgan Farraday reappears in Caraker's 1989 novel, *The Snows of Jaspre.* Jaspre, originally a snow-bound planet inhabited only by the hardy Finnish pioneers known as "snowgrubbers," has been altered with the addition of a satellite, Argus, that increases the amount of sunlight it receives. The greater solar energy has allowed the central portion of the planet to become an agricultural area, and the snowgrubbers now live in the northern glacial land known as Lumisland. Morgan arrives on the planet as a new school administrator and becomes embroiled in the controversy over the SEF's plan to add a second solar source. A new solar satellite would destroy the unique environment of the north where the rays from Argus radiate a rainbow of colors in the snow and sky, creating an effect that promotes health and psychic powers to those in the area. The struggle between Morgan's loyalty to her superiors in the SEF and her sympathies for the snowgrubbers and their breathtaking land are heightened when her daughter Dee runs away to join the clan of the charismatic and powerful snowgrubber leader, Anders Ahlwen. Reviewers praised Caraker's descriptions of the unique landscape of Jaspre. Joel Shoemaker, in a *Voice of Youth Advocates* assessment of *The Snows of Jaspre,* declared that "the book has an interesting premise [and] a beautifully described setting." And a *Horn Book* contributor stated, "The beauty and power of the colored snows is a fascinating, original idea."

Caraker is also the author of *The Faces of Ceti,* a 1991 novel that follows a young woman's trials on a harsh new planet. Soon after her family settles on a colony on Ceti, Maya's father dies from eating the planet's only vegetation—a poisonous jade plant. Desperate in their search for safe food, the settlers are excited by the find

MARY CARAKER

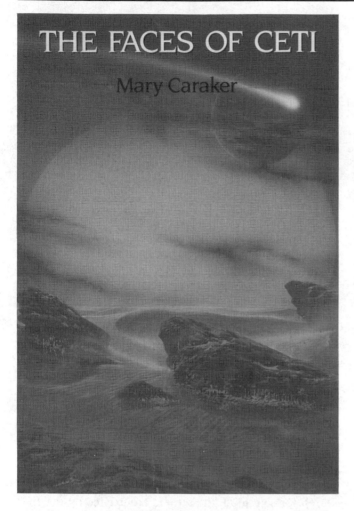

THE FACES OF CETI

Mary Caraker

Maya Gart discovers a creature that could save her people from starvation on their new planet in this science fiction novel by Caraker. (Cover illustration by Bob Eggleton.)

of kangaroo-like animals called hlurs. Maya, however, finds that the hlurs are sentient and telepathic creatures, and with her boyfriend Brock, attempts to convince her people that the animals can teach them how to survive on Ceti and should not be slaughtered for food. "As in ... *The Snows of Jaspre,* the setting is the main character here," noted a critic in the *Bulletin of the Center for Children's Books.* Other reviewers praised Caraker's use of themes such as the balance of ecosystems, political struggle, and the role of young people in decisions that affect civilization.

Caraker told *SATA:* "I have always been interested in science fiction—in the possibility of life on other worlds. Besides being endlessly fascinating, it also gives one the opportunity to speculate on how to fix things. Science fiction can be a sounding board for our present society. Most of all, though, it is great fun. My fictional alter ego, Morgan Farraday, has wonderful adventures that I wish could happen to me. I hope my readers enjoy them too.

"My work has been called 'sociological' science fiction, and I guess that's how I would characterize it as well. I dislike militaristic science fiction. I like to show a future in which the potentials of science are used in a positive manner."

WORKS CITED:

Ash, Constance, "Space Teacher Is Not Jean Brodie," *Fantasy Review,* October, 1986, p. 21.
Blubaugh, Penny, review of *Seven Worlds, Voice of Youth Advocates,* February, 1987, p. 290.
Review of *The Faces of Ceti, Bulletin of the Center for Children's Books,* March, 1991, p. 161.
Shoemaker, Joel, review of *The Snows of Jaspre, Voice of Youth Advocates,* June, 1989, p. 114.
Review of *The Snows of Jaspre, Horn Book,* May/June, 1989, pp. 373-74.
Review of *The Snows of Jaspre, Publisher's Weekly,* February 24, 1989, p. 236.

FOR MORE INFORMATION SEE:

PERIODICALS

Analog, October, 1990, p. 81.
Finnish American Reporter, July, 1991, p. 12.
Language Arts, November, 1991, p. 586.
Publisher's Weekly, July 31, 1987, p. 72.
Voice of Youth Advocates, August, 1991, p. 177.

* * *

CARR, Philippa
See HIBBERT, Eleanor Alice Burford

* * *

CATHERALL, Arthur 1906-1980
(J. Baltimore, A. R. Channel, Dan Corby, Peter Hallard, Trevor Maine, Linda Peters, Margaret Ruthin)

PERSONAL: Born February 6, 1906, in Bolton, Lancashire, England; died January 6, 1980; married Elizabeth Benson, 1936; children: Margaret Ruth (Mrs. F. N. Parker), John Arthur. *Religion:* Congregationalist.

ADDRESSES: Agent—Hope, Leresche & Steele, 11 Jubilee Pl., Chelsea, London, SW3 3TE, England.

CAREER: Worked in cotton-spinning industry before becoming a free-lance writer, mainly of books for children. Founder of a society which maintains a residential school for children with neural disorders. *Military service:* Royal Air Force, 1940-45; served in India, Burma, Ceylon; became flight lieutenant; staff officer to Commander in Chief, Royal Air Force, South East Asia Command.

MEMBER: Society of Authors, North Regional Authors (chairman).

WRITINGS:

FOR CHILDREN

Rod o' the Rail, Pearson, 1935.

The Rival Tugboats, A. & C. Black, 1936.

Adventurer's Ltd., A. & C. Black, 1938.

Black Gold, Pearson, 1939.

Vanished Whaler, illustrations by S. Drigin, Nelson, 1939.

Keepers of the Khyber, Nelson, 1940.

Lost with All Hands, Nelson, 1940.

Raid on Heligoland, Collins, 1940.

The Flying Submarine, Collins, 1942.

The River of Burning Sand, Collins, 1947.

The Bull Patrol, Lutterworth Press, 1949.

Riders of the Black Camel, Venturebooks, 1949.

Cock o' the Town, illustrations by Kenneth Brookes, Boy Scouts Association (London), 1950.

Wings for a Gull, Warne, 1951.

Pirate Sealer, Collins, 1953.

Shanghaied!, Collins, 1954.

Ten Fathoms Deep, illustrations by Geoffrey Whittam, Dent, 1954, Criterion, 1968.

Jackals of the Sea, illustrations by Whittam, Dent, 1955.

The Scuttlers, illustrations by A. Bruce Cornwell and Drake Brookshaw, Nelson, 1955.

Sea Wraith, Lutterworth Press, 1955.

Wild Goose Saboteur, illustrations by Brookes, Dent, 1955.

Forgotten Submarine, illustrations by Whittam, Dent, 1956.

Land under the White Robe, illustrations by Whittam, Dent, 1956.

Jamboree Challenge, illustrations by Brookes, Roy, 1957.

Java Sea Duel, illustrations by Whittam, Dent, 1957.

Java Trap, illustrations by Paul Hogarth, Dent, 1958, Roy, 1967.

Tenderfoot Trapper, illustrations by Edward Osmond, Dent, 1958, Criterion, 1959.

Sea Wolves, illustrations by Whittam, Dent, 1959, Roy, 1960.

Dangerous Cargo, illustrations by Whittam, Dent, 1960, Roy, 1961.

Lapland Outlaw, illustrations by Fred Wood, Dent, 1960, Lothrop, 1966.

(Under pseudonym Trevor Maine) *Blue Veil and Black Gold,* illustrations by Richard Kennedy, Odhams Press, 1961, Roy, 1965.

China Sea Jigsaw, illustrations by Whittam, Dent, 1961, Roy, 1962.

Orphan Otter, illustrations by N. Osten-Sacken, Dent, 1962, Harcourt Brace, 1963.

Vagabond Ape, illustrations by Osten-Sacken, Dent, 1962.

Yugoslav Mystery, illustrations by Stuart Tresilian, Dent, 1962, Lothrop, 1964.

Prisoners under the Sea, illustrations by Whittam, Dent, 1963.

Lone Seal Pup, illustrations by Edward Osmond, Dent, 1964, Dutton, 1965.

The Strange Invader, illustrations by Tresilian, Dent, 1964, also published as *The Strange Intruder,* Lothrop, 1965.

Tanker Trap, illustrations by Whittam, Dent, 1965, Roy, 1966.

(Under pseudonym Linda Peters) *Reindeer Rescue,* illustrations by F. M. Johnson, E. J. Arnold, 1966.

Sicilian Mystery, illustrations by Tresilian, Dent, 1966, Lothrop, 1967.

A Zebra Came to Drink, illustrations by Osmond, Dutton, 1967.

Prisoners in the Snow, illustrations by Victor Ambrus, Lothrop, 1967.

Death of an Oil Rig, illustrations by Whittam, Dent, 1967, Phillips, 1969.

Night of the Black Frost, illustrations by Roger Payne, Lothrop, 1968.

Camel Caravan, illustrations by Joseph Papin, Seabury Press, 1968, published in England as *Desert Caravan,* Macdonald, 1969.

Kidnapped by Accident, illustrations by Ambrus, Dent, 1968, Lothrop, 1969.

Island of Forgotten Men, illustrations by Whittam, Dent, 1968.

Duel in the High Hills, illustrations by Stanley Smith, Dent, 1968, Lothrop, 1969.

Red Sea Rescue, illustrations by Ambrus, Dent, 1969, Lothrop, 1970.

Antlers of the King Moose, illustrations by Edward Mortelmans, Dutton, 1970.

The Big Tusker, illustrations by Douglas Phillips, Lothrop, 1970.

Keepers of the Cattle, illustrations by Bernard Brett, Dent, 1970.

Freedom for a Cheetah, illustrations by Shyam Varma, Lothrop, 1971.

Barracuda Mystery, illustrations by Gavin Rowe, Dent, 1971.

The Unwilling Smuggler, illustrations by Whittam, Dent, 1971.

Last Horse on the Sands, illustrations by David Farris, Dent, 1972, Lothrop, 1973.

Cave of the "Cormorant", Dent, 1973.

A Wolf from the Sky, illustrations by Derek Lucas, Dent, 1974.

Stranger of Wreck Buoy Sands, Dent, 1975.

Twelve Minutes to Disaster and Other Stories, illustrations by Lucas, Dent, 1977.

The Ghost Elephant, Abelard Schuman, 1977.

The Last Run and Other Stories, Dent, 1977.

No Surrender! and Other Stories, Dent, 1979.

The Thirteen Footprints and Other Stories, Dent, 1979.

Smuggler in the Bay, Dent, 1980.

FOR CHILDREN; UNDER PSEUDONYM A. R. CHANNEL

Phantom Patrol, Collins, 1940.

The Tunnel Busters, Collins, 1960.

The Million-Dollar Ice Floe, illustrations by Eric Mudge-Marriott, Dobson, 1961.

Operation V.2., Collins, 1961.

Arctic Spy, illustrations by Horace Gaffron, Collins, 1962.

The Forgotten Patrol, Collins, 1962.

The Rogue Elephant, illustrations by D. J. Watkins-Pitchford, Dobson, 1962, Macrae Smith, 1963.

Mission Accomplished, Collins, 1964.

Red Ivory, illustrations by Watkins-Pitchford, Macrae Smith, 1964.

Jungle Rescue, illustrations by Watkins-Pitchford, Dobson, 1967, Phillips, 1968.

FOR CHILDREN; UNDER PSEUDONYM MARGARET RUTHIN

Kidnapped in Kandy, illustrations by C. Cane, Blackie, 1951.
The Ring of the Prophet, Warne, 1953.
White Horse of Hungary, Warne, 1954.
Strange Safari, Warne, 1955.
The Secret Pagoda, Warne, 1960.
Jungle Nurse, illustrations by Hugh Marshall, Watts, 1960.
Reindeer Girl, illustrations by Marie Whitby, Dobson, 1961, also published as *Elli of the Northland,* Farrar Straus, 1968.
Lapland Nurse, illustrations by Whitby, Dobson, 1962.
Secret of the Shetlands, illustrations by Gwen Gibson, Dobson, 1963.
Katrina of the Lonely Isles, illustrations by Gibson, Dobson, 1964, Farrar Straus, 1965.
Kidnapped on Stromboli, Dobson, 1966.
Hungarian Rebel, Dobson, 1970.

FOR CHILDREN; UNDER PSEUDONYM PETER HALLARD

Coral Reef Castaway, illustrations by Terence Greer, Phoenix House, 1958, Criterion, 1960.
Barrier Reef Bandits, illustrations by Marshall, Criterion, 1960.
Guardian of the Reef, illustrations by Marshall, Dobson, 1961.
Boy on a White Giraffe, illustrations by Shelia Bewley, Seabury Press, 1969, published in England as *White Giraffe,* Macdonald, 1969.
Lost in Lapland, illustrations by Judith Ann Lawrence, Macdonald, 1970, also published as *Puppy Lost in Lapland,* Watts, 1971.
Kalu and the Wild Boar, illustrations by W. T. Mars, Watts, 1973.

FOR CHILDREN; UNDER PSEUDONYM DAN CORBY; U.S. EDITIONS UNDER NAME ARTHUR CATHERALL

A Shark on the Saltings, Parrish, 1959.
The Little Sealer, Parrish, 1960, also published as *The Arctic Sealer,* Criterion, 1961.
Lost Off the Grand Banks, Parrish, 1961, Criterion, 1962.
Man-Eater, illustrations by Richard Lewis, Parrish, 1963, Criterion, 1964.
Thunder Dam, illustrations by Omar Davis, Parrish, 1964, Criterion, 1965.
Conqueror's Gold, Parrish, 1965.

FOR ADULTS

Tomorrow's Hunter, Jenkins, 1950.
Vibrant Brass, Dent, 1954.
(Under pseudonym J. Baltimore) *Singapore Sari,* Fiction House, 1958.
No Bouquets for These, Tempest Press, 1958.
(With David Reade) *Step in My Shoes* (play), produced in Southport, Lancashire, 1958.

OTHER

Camp-Fire Stories and How to Tell Them, Jenkins, 1935.
(With George W. Blow) *The Steam and Steel Omnibus,* illustrations by Blow, Collins, 1950.
The Scout Story Omnibus, Collins, 1954.
The Young Baden-Powell, illustrations by William Randell, Parrish, 1961, Roy, 1962.
Vanishing Lapland, Watts, 1972.

Contributor of over a thousand short stories to numerous publications, including *Boy's Life of America;* regular Boy Scouts columnist for the *Bolton Evening News* for thirty-five years.

ADAPTATIONS: Catherall's adult novel *Vibrant Brass* has been optioned for filming.

SIDELIGHTS: Arthur Catherall set a high standard for himself as a children's writer: he wanted to write realistic stories that contained honest, worthy characters for young boys and girls to emulate. His legacy of nearly a hundred books and over a thousand short stories is a monument to his success in achieving those goals. Throughout his works Catherall presents characters who

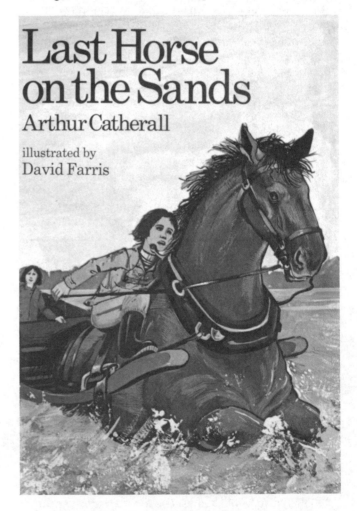

In Catherall's tale, two children put the safety of others first when a dangerous tide threatens a rescue operation.

encounter difficulties in all parts of the world and overcome the difficulties through their resourcefulness and their courage. Gwen Marsh, writing in *Twentieth-Century Children's Writers,* said that Catherall "always held up to his readers an image of a hero or heroine with courage, kindness, loyalty, and spirit."

Catherall was a world traveler who vowed that he went out and searched for material to fill his books. "I have shoveled coal on small fishing vessels off the coast of Iceland and in the north east Atlantic," he once said. "I have traveled on tramp steamers, and gone with members of their crews to the dives on many a waterfront.... My travels have taken me to Algeria, and across the Atlas mountains into the desert. I have camped and climbed in a number of European countries, walked across Lapland and climbed Sweden's highest mountain. I spent some time in the Faroe Islands, pony trekked in Austria—at heights varying from 4 to 6,000 feet. I traveled the length of Finnish Lapland in 1969 and I have walked over Norwegian and Swedish Lapland." His stories have been justly praised for their authenticity and for their attention to the geography of the land in which they are set.

Catherall wrote primarily for boys, he said, because he worked with the Boy Scouts in England for all his life, contributing a regular column on Scout activities to his local newspaper. "You don't find any unnecessary clubbing or shooting in my books," he was quoted as saying in *Twentieth-Century Children's Writers.* "Boys can be little savages without the inspiration of a story to start them off. They look for heroes in a story. I try to give them the right kind of heroes, for boys are great imitators." The author has written for girls as well, under the pseudonym Margaret Ruthin. "The dozen books I have written for girls," he once commented, "were done immediately on my return from service with the Royal Air Force when publishers were stacked up with boys manuscripts, and had very few stories for girls." Catherall also wrote under a number of other pseudonyms.

Catherall once said: "I write because I must. There are so many things I want to write about that the business has become almost a disease. I recently received among my fan mail a letter from a boy in Chicago who said, 'Please keep on writing, I think you are the best writer in the world.' I wish I could believe him, but letters of appreciation from youngsters makes me keep on telling stories I think they like."

WORKS CITED:

Marsh, Gwen, "Arthur Catherall," *Twentieth-Century Children's Writers,* 3rd edition, St. James Press, 1989, pp. 177-179.

FOR MORE INFORMATION SEE:

PERIODICALS

Books and Bookmen, September, 1969.
Library Journal, July, 1970.
Saturday Review, March 22, 1969.

Times (London), July 2, 1980.
Times Literary Supplement, May 25, 1967, p. 459; June 26, 1969; April 16, 1970.*

* * *

CHANNEL, A. R.
See CATHERALL, Arthur

* * *

CLAPP, Patricia 1912-

PERSONAL: Born June 9, 1912, in Boston, MA; daughter of Howard (a dentist) and Elizabeth (Blachford) Clapp; married Edward della Torre Cone (a transportation consultant), March 3, 1933; children: Christopher, Patricia, Pamela. *Education:* Attended Columbia University for two years; various writing courses later. *Religion:* Protestant.

ADDRESSES: Home—83 Beverley Rd., Upper Montclair, NJ 07043.

CAREER: Writer of adult and children's books and plays; many years of involvement with community theater.

AWARDS, HONORS: National Book Award runner-up, and Lewis Carroll Shelf Award, both 1969, both for *Constance: A Story of Early Plymouth;* American Library Association Best Young Adult Book citation, 1982, for *Witches' Children: A Story of Salem.*

WRITINGS:

JUVENILES

Constance: A Story of Early Plymouth, Lothrop, 1968.
Jane-Emily, Lothrop, 1969.
Popsicle Song (verse), Encyclopedia Britannica Education Corp., 1972.
King of the Dollhouse, illustrated by Judith Gwyn Brown, Lothrop, 1974.
Dr. Elizabeth: The Story of the First Woman Doctor (biography), Lothrop, 1974.
I'm Deborah Sampson: A Soldier in the War of the Revolution, Lothrop, 1977.
Witches' Children: A Story of Salem, Lothrop, 1982.
The Tamarack Tree, Lothrop, 1986.

Constance has appeared in French and Danish translation; *Witches' Children* has been translated into Danish.

JUVENILE PLAYS

Peggy's on the Phone (one-act), Dramatic Publishing, 1956.
Smart Enough to Be Dumb (one-act), Dramatic Publishing, 1956.
The Incompleted Pass (three-act), Dramatic Publishing, 1957.
Her Kissin' Cousin (three-act), Heuer Publishing, 1957.
The Girl out Front (three-act), Dramatic Publishing, 1958.

The Ghost of a Chance (three-act), Heuer Publishing, 1958.
The Curley Tale (three-act), Art Craft, 1958.
Inquire Within (three-act), Row, 1959.
The Girl Whose Fortune Sought Her (one-act), published in *Children's Plays from Favorite Stories,* edited by S. E. Kamerman, Plays, 1959.
Edie-across-the-Street (three-act), Baker Co., 1960.
The Honeysuckle Hedge (three-act), Eldridge Publishing, 1960.
Never Keep Him Waiting (three-act), Dramatic Publishing, 1961.
Red Heels and Roses (one-act), McKay, 1961.
If a Body Meets a Body (three-act), Heuer Publishing, 1963.
Now Hear This (one-act), Eldridge Publishing, 1963.
The Magic Bookshelf (one-act), published in *Fifty Plays for Junior Actors,* edited by Kamerman, Plays, 1966.
The Other Side of the Wall (one-act), published in *Fifty Plays for Holidays,* edited by Kamerman, Plays, 1969.
The Do-Nothing Frog (one-act), published in *100 Plays for Children,* edited by A. S. Burack, Plays, 1970.
The Invisible Dragon (one-act with music), Dramatic Publishing, 1971.
A Specially Wonderful Day (one-act), Encyclopedia Britannica Educational Corp., 1972.
The Toys Take over Christmas (one-act), Dramatic Publishing, 1977.
Mudcake Princess (one-act), Dramatic Publishing, 1979.
The Truly Remarkable Puss in Boots (one-act), Dramatic Publishing, 1979.

PATRICIA CLAPP

Also author of several other plays, including *A Feather in His Cap, The Wonderful Door, A Wish Is for Keeping, Susan and Aladdin's Lamp, The Signpost, The Friendship Bracelet, Christmas in Old New England, The Straight Line from Somewhere, Yankee Doodle Came to Cranetown,* and *When Ecstasy Cost a Nickel,* published in *Instructor Magazine, Plays Magazine, Grade Teacher Magazine,* and *Yankee Magazine,* 1958-81.

OTHER

A Candle on the Table (adult one-act play), Baker, 1972.
The Retirement (adult one-act play), Eldridge Publishing, 1972.
(Contributor) Donna E. Norton, editor, *Through the Eyes of a Child* (college textbook), Merrill, 1983.

Also author of published poetry; editor of little theater publications.

SIDELIGHTS: Patricia Clapp is best known for her acclaimed children's novels, such as *Constance: A Story of Early Plymouth, Jane-Emily,* and *The Tamarack Tree.* She has also published many plays for children and adults, as well as verse and biography. Clapp often concentrates on history to provide material for her fiction, but she has also tried her hand at fantasies, such as *King of the Dollhouse.* Her work in novel form has garnered her prestigious honors, such as runner-up for the National Book Award for *Constance,* and the American Library Association Best Young Adult Book citation for *Witches' Children: A Story of Salem.*

Clapp was born June 9, 1912, in Boston, Massachusetts. Her father, a dentist, died when she was only nine months old, and her mother supported the family by continuing his toothbrush-importing business. Mrs. Clapp eventually remarried and moved with her daughter to Montclair, New Jersey. Clapp spent most of her summers with her maternal grandmother in Cape Cod, and enjoyed reading and writing from an early age. Her favorite stories were, as she recalled in an essay for *Something about the Author Autobiography Series (SAAS),* "all the Oz books, of course, and *Five Little Peppers* and *Heidi* and *Little Lord Fauntleroy* and *The Secret Garden*—so many! A bit later there were the Augusta Huiell Seaman mysteries for girls, and *Daddy-Long-legs,* and one about a poor, dear waif who was orphaned and lived in a cold attic room, and a monkey came across the roof tiles and brought her warm clothes and food and the monkey was the trained pet of a wealthy Indian nabob and it was all tremendously satisfying! I remember Mother once urging me to 'go outside, dear! It's such a lovely day.' So I took a book and went out and sat in the car parked in the driveway—and read."

Although Clapp affirmed for *SAAS* that she "had written things ever since I first learned how," and that she wrote some "rather arty poetry," she also enjoyed riding and dancing lessons. In fact, she recalled in her autobiographical essay, her "one dream" as a child "was to be a professional dancer and work in musical comedies." This ambition continued until she graduated from high school, but because of the Great Depression, her mother and stepfather urged her to pursue a more practical profession. So Clapp enrolled at Columbia University to study journalism. While there, she also took classes in poetry and short story writing, but after leaving school for an emergency appendectomy, she never returned. Eventually a childhood friend asked her to help run a nursery school that she was starting. In this setting, Clapp met her friend's older brother, Edward della Torre Cone, whom she married in 1933.

After her marriage, Clapp became involved with a community theater in Montclair. This experience led, after she had children, to her being asked to produce a play for her daughters' Girl Scout troop. As she explained in *SAAS:* "I agreed and started looking for a likely vehicle. I combed the libraries and was unable to find anything I felt was suitable, so I wrote one. It was tailored to fit the number of little girls who wanted to be in it, and asked nothing more of them—either in lines or acting—than I thought they could manage. The result was gratifying for cast and audience alike, and for a few years I was in demand for on-the-spot playwriting. Encouraged by the results I popped one of these plays off to a publisher and lo and behold, back came a check for twenty-five dollars! (You must remember that there was a time when twenty-five dollars was a welcome amount.) That was the start of my quiet career as a playwright."

Clapp began publishing her plays heavily during the late 1950s, and wrote nothing else for over a decade. Some of her titles include *Peggy's on the Phone, The Ghost of a Chance, Never Keep Him Waiting,* and *The Truly Remarkable Puss in Boots.* As she had with plays, she got into writing children's novels by accident. The author recounted in her autobiographical essay: "A cousin of Edward's sent us a genealogical record of their maternal forebears, the Chamberlains. It had been compiled over many years and was huge. Edward suggested I make a legible typed copy, taking my time, and that was the beginning of a whole new part of my life—writing books. It was in those pages that I discovered Constance Hopkins who came to America with her family on the *Mayflower.* The more I copied that mass of material the more I thought about Constance. Fourteen years old, snatched from a familiar, comfortable life in London by an enthusiastic adventurer of a father, carted off to a land of wolves and Indians—how did she feel? I spent a lot of time thinking about her." Despite various family responsibilities, such as her aging mother and new grandchildren, Clapp admitted in *SAAS* that "Constance was still wandering around in my head, and finally something had to be put on paper.... I had, in recent years, written nothing but plays and poetry, so my first reaction was to make a full-length play about Constance Hopkins. It never got off the ground. Too large a cast, too much time to cover, too many sets required to give it a sense of space and movement—it wouldn't work. So then I just started writing and it came out as Constance's journal. I didn't plan it that way, it just took off by itself and happened."

For a first novel, *Constance: A Story of Early Plymouth* met with amazing success. A *Book World* reviewer, for instance, noted that Clapp gives her version of the Plymouth story "such freshness and immediacy that it is certain to be a favorite." C. A. Hough likewise commented in *Library Journal* that *Constance* is "skillfully written" and "historically accurate," with "a fine sense of place." Clapp's use of Constance's journal to tell the story is used "brilliantly," Zena Sutherland wrote in *Twentieth-Century Children's Writers,* making the novel "one of the most outstanding books set in the colonial period of the United States—and there are many." *Constance* was a runner-up for the National Book Award in 1969 and won the Lewis Carroll Shelf Award.

Clapp's next children's novel, *Jane-Emily,* about a little girl who begins to take on the personality of her dead aunt, proved even more popular with readers, though it won no awards. Some of the author's other books include *I'm Deborah Sampson,* a fact-based historical novel about a female soldier in the American Revolutionary War; *Witches' Children,* concerning the young girls who were instrumental in starting the Salem witch hunts during colonial times; and *The Tamarack Tree,* which chronicles the American Civil War as seen

Clapp's interest in history takes her to the colonial period of the United States in this narrative of an enthusiastic girl who arrives in the New World on the *Mayflower.* (Cover illustration by Berta Kuznetsova.)

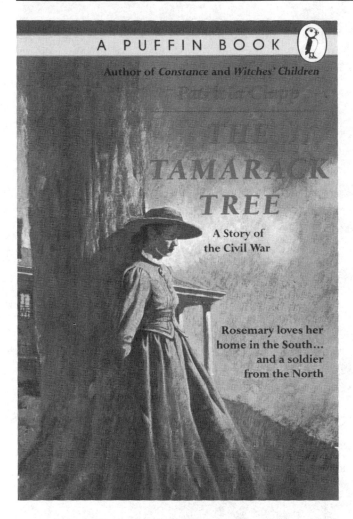

A PUFFIN BOOK

Author of *Constance* and *Witches' Children*

Patricia Clapp

THE TAMARACK TREE

A Story of the Civil War

Rosemary loves her home in the South... and a soldier from the North

A young English woman living in Mississippi is torn between her love of her southern friends and her opposition to the practice of slavery in Clapp's historical novel. (Cover illustration by Troy Howell).

through the eyes of a visiting English girl. Clapp also penned a biography of the first American woman doctor, Elizabeth Blackwell; Sutherland praised the book for its "immediacy" and called it "valuable both as a segment of medical history and as a chapter in the long struggle for women's rights."

Clapp has continued writing plays and novels through the years, though she doesn't consider herself a professional writer. She alternates between writing, her involvement with community theater, and spending time with her family. Currently she is working on a history of her local community theater and an autobiography, neither of which she intends to publish. She explained in *SAAS:* "Writing I can do when I choose to, not because I have to for financial reasons. I can afford to wait for the first flicker of an idea, to spend as long as I like on research, and then to lose myself in another era, living with people I will only know in my imagination, but who will become totally real to me."

WORKS CITED:

Clapp, Patricia, essay in *Something about the Author Autobiography Series,* Volume 4, Gale, 1987, pp. 129-45.
Review of *Constance, Book World,* May 5, 1968, p. 26.
Hough, C. A., review of *Constance, Library Journal,* March 15, 1968, p. 1318.
Sutherland, Zena, "Patricia Clapp," *Twentieth-Century Children's Writers,* 3rd edition, St. James Press, 1989, pp. 200-02.

FOR MORE INFORMATION SEE:

PERIODICALS

Bulletin of the Center for Children's Books, September, 1977; March, 1982; November, 1986.
Horn Book, August, 1977; September/October, 1986.
New York Times Book Review, August 18, 1968, p. 34.
Saturday Review, May 11, 1968, p. 42.

* * *

CLARK, M. R.
See CLARK, Mavis Thorpe

* * *

CLARK, Mavis Thorpe 1909-
(M. R. Clark, Mavis Latham)

PERSONAL: Born in Melbourne, Victoria, Australia, in 1909; daughter of John Thorpe (a building contractor) and Rose Matilda (Stanborough) Clark; married Harold Latham (deceased); children: Beverley Jeanne (Mrs. Ralph Henderson Lewis), Ronda Faye (Mrs. Peter Hall). *Education:* Attended Methodist Ladies' College, Melbourne.

ADDRESSES: Home—1/22 Rochester Rd., Canterbury, Victoria 3126, Australia.

CAREER: Writer.

MEMBER: International PEN (Australia Centre; vice-president of Melbourne branch, 1968, 1971, 1973, 1974; president of Melbourne branch, 1969, 1980, 1981), Australian Society of Authors (member of management committee for fifteen years), National Book Council (member of promotions committee for seven years), Fellowship of Australian Writers (life member, 1990), Children's Book Council of Australia (life member).

AWARDS, HONORS: Children's Book Council of Australia Commendations, 1956, for *The Brown Land Was Green,* and 1968, for *Blue above the Trees,* and Book of the Year Award, 1967, for *The Min-Min; The Min-Min* was chosen as an American Library Association Notable Book, 1969; *Spark of Opal,* 1971, and *Iron Mountain,* 1973, were placed on Deutscher Jugendbuchpreis (German Youth Book Award) list.

WRITINGS:

NOVELS FOR YOUNG TEENS

(Under name M. R. Clark) *Hatherly's First Fifteen,* illustrated by F. E. Hiley, Whitcomb & Tombs, 1930.

Dark Pool Island, Oxford University Press, 1949.

The Twins from Timber Creek, Oxford University Press, 1949.

Home Again at Timber Creek, Oxford University Press, 1950.

Jingaroo, Oxford University Press, 1951.

Missing Gold, Hutchinson, 1951.

The Brown Land Was Green (also see below), illustrated by Harry Hudson, Heinemann, 1956, special school edition, Heinemann, 1957, published with new illustrations, Lansdowne Press, 1967, published as *Kammorra,* Octopus-Heinemann, 1990.

Gully of Gold, illustrated by Anne Graham, Heinemann, 1958, published with new illustrations, Lansdowne Press, 1969.

Pony from Tarella, illustrated by Jean M. Rowe, Heinemann, 1959, published with new illustrations, Lansdowne Press, 1969.

They Came South, illustrated by Joy Murray, Heinemann, 1963, published with new illustrations, Lansdowne Press, 1971.

The Min-Min (also see below), illustrated by Genevieve Melrose, Lansdowne Press, 1966, Macmillan (New York), 1969, published as *Armada Lions,* Collins, 1975.

Blue above the Trees, illustrated by Melrose, Lansdowne Press, 1967, Meredith Press, 1969, published with new illustrations, Hodder & Stoughton, 1975.

Spark of Opal, illustrated by Melrose, Lansdowne Press, 1968, Macmillan (New York), 1973.

Nowhere to Hide, illustrated by Melrose, Lansdowne Press, 1969.

Iron Mountain, illustrated by Ronald Brooks, Lansdowne Press, 1970, Macmillan (New York), 1971, published as *If the Earth Falls In,* Scabury Press, 1975.

New Golden Mountain, Lansdowne Press, 1973.

Wildfire, Hodder & Stoughton, 1973, Macmillan (New York), 1974.

The Sky Is Free, Macmillan, 1976.

The Hundred Islands, illustrated by Astra Lacis, Macmillan, 1977.

The Lilly-Pilly, illustrated by Prue Chammen, Rigby Reading Series, 1979.

A Stranger Came to the Mine, illustrated by Jane Walker, Hutchinson, 1980.

Solomon's Child, Hutchinson, 1981.

The Brown Land Was Green [and] *The Min-Min* (classic edition), John Ferguson, 1982.

Soft Shoe, illustrated by Ziba Westenberg, Bookshelf, 1988.

OTHER

John Batman (adult biography), Oxford University Press, 1962.

(As Mavis Latham) *Fishing* (textbook), illustrated by Joy Murray, Oxford University Press, 1963.

Pastor Doug: The Story of an Aboriginal Leader (adult biography), Lansdowne Press, 1965, revised edition published as *Pastor Doug: The Story of Sir Douglas Nicholls, Aboriginal Leader,* 1972.

The Pack-Tracker (textbook), illustrated by Shirley Turner, Oxford University Press, 1968.

The Opal Miner (textbook), illustrated by Barbara Taylor, Oxford University Press, 1969.

Iron Ore Mining (textbook), illustrated by Jocelyn Bell, Oxford University Press, 1971.

Joan and Betty Rayner: Strolling Players (adult biography), Lansdowne Press, 1972.

Spanish Queen (remedial reader), Hodder & Stoughton, 1977.

The Boy from Cumeroogunga: The Story of Sir Douglas Nicholls, Aboriginal Leader, Hodder & Stoughton, 1979.

Joey (reader), Mount Gravat College of Advanced Education, 1980.

Boo to a Goose (reader), Mount Gravat College of Advanced Education, 1981.

The Thief Who Came Quietly (reader), Mount Gravat College of Advanced Education, 1981.

Young and Brave (collection of true short stories), Hodder & Stoughton, 1984.

No Mean Destiny: The Story of Jessie Mary Vasey and Her Founding of the War Widows' Guild of Australia, Hyland House, 1986.

Also author of radio-script adaptations of *The Brown Land Was Green,* 1961, *Gully of Gold,* 1962, and *They Came South,* 1965, for Australian Broadcasting Commission, each broadcast as fifty-two episode serials. Author of many other radio plays, short stories, and articles. Contributor to anthologies, including *Australian Bushrangers,* Casell (Australia), 1973; *Australians at War,* Casell (Australia), 1974; *Australian Escape Stories,* Casell (Australia), 1976; and *A Handful of Ghosts,* Hodder & Stoughton, 1976. Contributor to *Cricket* (magazine), 1987.

ADAPTATIONS: In 1976, film and television rights for *The Sky Is Free* were purchased by Walt Disney Productions.

WORK IN PROGRESS: A new novel for young adults, set in Australia's Northern Territory; an autobiographical account of the author's wanderings throughout Australia, over many years, with emphasis on people met, places visited and lived-in, and incidents that have figured in her books: "this autobiographical work has taken much longer, with much more travelling involved, than planned. The latter justified in the cause of accuracy of detail but the truth being, of course, that the red earth wields its own drawing power. One trap, too, has been the quantity of material available, and the decision, taken in the initial stage, to put in rather than leave out. Now, at revision level, the pruning hurts."

SIDELIGHTS: Mavis Thorpe Clark is one of Australia's premier young adult novelists. In works such as *The Brown Land Was Green, The Min-Min, Blue above the Trees, The Sky Is Free* and *Spark of Opal,* she portrays

MAVIS THORPE CLARK

Australian life, both modern and pioneer, in the harsh beauty of the Australian landscape—ranging from the opal mines and sheep stations of the Outback to the lush jungles of the north to the bird-life of the seashore. "I have travelled thousands of miles in search of material," Clark commented, "criss-crossing this vast country from east to west and north to south. I've travelled to Europe and Asia, too, but the spell of my own wide red land lures me continually and sets me on the lonely dusty outback track."

Clark was born in a suburb of Melbourne, the youngest child of a Scottish-born building contractor and his Australian wife. She showed a talent for story-telling and writing early in life, entertaining her friends at school with anecdotes. "Those stories I told my friends—a tight, loyal gang of five—were the immediate prelude to the written story," Clark wrote in her *Something about the Author Autobiography Series* (*SAAS*) entry. "In fact, that began almost at the same time, and was nurtured by my oral weavings. I would lie on my stomach in the seclusion of the lounge room floor with half-a-dozen finely sharpened lead pencils, and an exercise book with a shiny plastic-type cover. My eldest sister, Vi, who was a young adult when I was born, was a secretary; she would take my stories to her office, type them out, and bring them back to me set out like small books, the pages fastened together with blue and yellow striped ribbon."

Clark continued her interest in writing throughout her school years. "I wrote my first full-length manuscript when I was fourteen, while studying for my Intermedi-

ate Certificate at the Methodist Ladies' College, Melbourne," she noted in the *Fourth Book of Junior Authors*. "This story was not published in book form, but it did appear in the children's pages of the *Australasian*, an Australian weekly newspaper of that time. My first book in hard covers was published when I was eighteen and was an adventure story of boys." This was *Hatherly's First Fifteen*, a story about blindness and the game of rugby. "For this work I consulted with the local doctor on the subject of blindness, and with a young man, who had played rugby for Scotland, on the fine points of the game," Clark explained in her *SAAS* entry. "The actual games described in the book were played out on the dining-room table using matches for players. This was the beginning, if an unrecognised one, of my interest in the factual background. And an early awareness that I must be familiar with my subject."

Clark married young, but continued writing magazine stories, newspaper articles, radio plays, and children's adventure serials for newspapers. One of these, *Dark Pool Island*, was later published as a book. "It was a typical story of the period; a quick-moving boys' school story—no doubt inspired by my own childhood taste—of a fake headmaster, a treasure of gold in the pool, and four lively teenagers who rescued the real headmaster and saved the treasure," Clark remarked in her *SAAS* entry. "This was followed by *The Twins from Timber Creek, Home Again at Timber Creek, Jingaroo, Missing Gold.* These were for the ten year olds, with emphasis on adventure and story."

The Brown Land Was Green, Clark's next book, marked an important change in her writing: it had a historical background (the frontier of Victoria in 1844); it was based in part on the experiences of her Aunt Martha, who had entertained Clark as a child with her stories of pioneer life; and it featured a heroine named Henrietta Webster, who "was untrammelled by being female," Clark wrote in her *SAAS* entry. Aunt Martha, she continued, "immersed me, the child, in that district. Through her, too, the land ... the earth ... of Australia made its first rendezvous with me, though, at the time, its reaching-out was not recognized.... It was the first book—and the forerunner of all the others—to bear the imprint of the land." *The Brown Land Was Green* was followed by *Gully of Gold* and *They Came South,* both novels set in Victoria during pioneer days.

In *The Min-Min,* her most celebrated novel, Clark moved out of settled Australia into the Outback. The book was based in part on a trip the author took with Harold Darwin, a retired schoolteacher who organized his own travelling library in an old van and spent his days driving from one isolated homestead or sheep station to another, carrying books to people who could not otherwise get them. Clark actually saw the Min-Min on the trip: a bright light, too low for a star, that appeared just above the horizon, changed color, moved back and forth, and vanished as suddenly as it had appeared.

The novel itself is the story of Reg, a troubled young man, and his sister Sylvie, who set off on their own from their isolated camp on the border of the railroad to cross the desert. "The whole of that book—the characters, the setting, the happenings—went home with me," Clark explained in her *SAAS* essay; "and also that pure bright light as a symbolic goal for Sylvie to follow, her walking towards the lure of a better life." As a result, the characters "are real people," a *Junior Bookshelf* reviewer writes, "so that along with them one can feel the heat and the thirst and wonder if one will die a lingering death out in the Australian desert." The *Min-Min* "is undoubtedly Clark's most outstanding work," Barbara Ker Wilson concludes in *Twentieth-Century Children's Writers,* praising the work for its "conviction and compassion."

Other travels throughout Australia brought other books. "Now I began to range wide," Clark stated in her *SAAS* entry. "My whole country—this Australia—was my oyster. I was fascinated by it, awed by its size, its age—one of the oldest land masses in the world—it strength; bound to it by its colour, its scent, its people, most of all by its people. The urge for that further overseas travel which had prickled since I was thirteen, was overlaid and made dormant by this stronger desire to get closer and closer to my own country." *Blue above the Trees,* her next book, was based on the destruction of the Australian rain forest by cattle and sheep ranchers. *Spark of Opal, The Sky Is Free,* and *A Stranger Came to the Mine* are all set in the famous opal fields of Coober Pedy, while *Iron Mountain* evokes the mining towns of Tom Price and Dampier on the very western edge of the continent. In each of these works Clark brings her native land to life; as Virginia Haviland notes in *Horn Book,* in *Iron Mountain* even "the hot, dust-filled iron-mining country ... becomes a protagonist."

The geographical and cultural details found in Clark's novels echo the deep love she feels for her native Australia and give insight into that country to those who have never been there. "Here again is the tremendous reward of friends in out-of-the-way places and glimpses of lives that are lived so simply yet so richly with the earth of the world's oldest continent," Clark commented. "These intangible joys are the real reward of the writer."

WORKS CITED:

Clark, Mavis Thorpe, essay in *Fourth Book of Junior Authors and Illustrators,* edited by Doris de Montreville and Elizabeth D. Crawford, H. W. Wilson, 1978, pp. 84-86.
Clark, Mavis Thorpe, essay in *Something about the Author Autobiography Series,* Volume 5, Gale, 1987, pp. 69-87.
Haviland, Virginia, review of *Iron Mountain, Horn Book,* February, 1972.
Ker Wilson, Barbara, "Mavis Thorpe Clark," *Twentieth-Century Children's Writers,* 3rd edition, St. James Press, 1989, pp. 206-08.
Review of *The Min-Min, Junior Bookshelf,* June, 1967.

FOR MORE INFORMATION SEE:

BOOKS

Contemporary Literary Criticism, Volume 12, Gale, 1980.

PERIODICALS

Junior Bookshelf, August, 1968; August, 1972; October, 1974; August, 1975.
Library Journal, December 15, 1969.
New York Times Book Review, January 25, 1970.
Times Literary Supplement, May 25, 1967; June 6, 1968; July 14, 1972.

*   *   *

COHEN, Barbara 1932-1992

OBITUARY NOTICE—See index for *SATA* sketch: Born March 15, 1932, in New Jersey; died of cancer, November 29, 1992, in Bridgewater, NJ. Educator and author. Cohen, an award-winning writer, penned more than thirty books for children and young adults. She taught in New Jersey from 1955 until 1972, when she published her first book, *The Carp in the Bathtub.* Cohen's best-known work, *Molly's Pilgrim,* tells the story of a Jewish immigrant girl who teaches her classmates the meaning of Thanksgiving; a movie version of that book won the 1986 Academy Award for best short subject. In 1991, Cohen was inducted into the New Jersey Literary Hall of Fame. She also authored such works as *Seven Daughters and Seven Sons, King of the Seventh Grade, Canterbury Tales, The Long Way Home,* and a sequel to *Molly's Pilgrim* entitled *Make a Wish Molly.* At the time of her death, Cohen had several new books slated for publication.

OBITUARIES AND OTHER SOURCES:

BOOKS

The Writers Directory: 1992-1994, St. James Press, 1992.

PERIODICALS

Detroit Free Press, December 2, 1992, p. 7B.
Los Angeles Times, December 5, 1992, p. A26.
New York Times, December 1, 1992, p. B13.
School Library Journal, January, 1993, p. 18.

*   *   *

COLE, Hannah 1954-

PERSONAL: Born February 21, 1954, in London, England; children: Kerry, Leon, Corin. *Education:* Received primary education certificate from Oxford Polytechnic; received M.A. from King's College, Cambridge.

ADDRESSES: Home—36 Old High St., Hedington, Oxford OX3 9HN, England.

CAREER: Children's author. Worked in a day center for mentally handicapped adults and in a nursery school.

MEMBER: National Union of Journalists.

WRITINGS:

On the Night Watch, J. MacRae, 1984.
Our Horrible Friend, illustrated by Julie Stiles, J. MacRae, 1986.
In between Times, illustrated by Kate Rogers, J. MacRae, 1987.
Kick Off, J. MacRae, 1987.
In at the Shallow End, J. MacRae, 1989.
The Pantomime Witch, illustrated by Dawn S. Aldridge, Ideals Publishing, 1990.

Also author of *The Midnight Feast,* illustrated by Kate Aldous.*

*   *   *

CONNOLLY, Pat 1943-

PERSONAL: Born September 1, 1943, in Santa Monica, CA; daughter of Omeara (a teacher; maiden name, Olsen) Daniels; married Jim Winslow, June, 1963 (divorced); married Harold Vincent Connolly, Jr.; children: (first marriage) Bradley, (second marriage) Adam, Shannon C. *Education:* Attended Santa Monica College. *Politics:* Independent.

ADDRESSES: Home—Silver Spring, MD.

CAREER: Woodlake and Oakcreek Spas in California, health and recreation advisor, 1965-70; Beverly Hills High School, Beverly Hills, CA, track and field coach, 1971-72; University of California, Los Angeles, track and field and cross-country coach, 1972-78; Medalist Track Club, Venice, CA, coach and fitness consultant, 1979-84; Puma Track Club, Venice, coach and fitness consultant, 1985-87. Former member of the United States Olympic Committee and U.S. track and field Olympic Team.

MEMBER: Women's Sports Foundation.

AWARDS, HONORS: Named to the *San Mateo Times'* Hall of Fame in 1990.

WRITINGS:

Coaching Evelyn, HarperCollins, 1991.

Contributor to periodicals, including *New York Times.*

WORK IN PROGRESS: Willye-Billee, completion expected in 1994.

SIDELIGHTS: Pat Connolly told *SATA:* "As a youngster, I studied ballet for eight years and dreamed of becoming a ballerina, but in my twelfth summer I grew from five-feet-two to five-feet-ten. The thought of Rudolph Nureyev hoisting me over his head became ludicrous and the dream died. I first heard about the Olympics just a few months before I turned sixteen, and all it took to motivate me was for my mother to tell me I didn't have a chance to make the Olympic team that following summer. I made it! At sixteen, I was the baby of the track and field team and the lone entrant in the

PAT CONNOLLY

800-meter run, considered at the time to be the longest distance 'safe' for a woman to run. I became a pioneer and record setter throughout my career as an athlete and coach probably because my great-grandmother came across the plains with the Mormon pioneers and, as hard and painful as it is to be a pioneer, I just can't stop myself—pioneering is in my blood.

"Sometimes on long training runs at San Gregorio beach in Northern California, I would be trapped by crashing waves at high tide and would climb up into a cave in the high palisades, crawl through a tunnel about fifty meters, feel around for the ledge where I had hidden two books, and then sit by an opening that was a shear drop to the sea and read my two favorite poets, Robert Frost and Emily Dickinson. What would Emily have written about my view and spirit? Someday I hope to write that poem, but until it bursts forth, like sweat on my body, I will continue to work on books about the sports microcosm of life."

*   *   *

COOKE, Jean (Isobel Esther) 1929-

PERSONAL: Born July 11, 1929, in London, England; married A. Theodore H. Rowland-Entwistle (an author and editor).

ADDRESSES: Home and office—West Dene, Stonestile Lane, Hastings, East Sussex TN35 4PE, England.

CAREER: Writer. Teacher at Foote School, New Haven, CT, Windsor Mountain School, Manchester, VT, and at various schools in England. Volunteer editor, recorder, and reader for the Hastings Talking Newspaper for the Blind.

WRITINGS:

WITH HUSBAND, THEODORE ROWLAND-ENTWISTLE

Animal Worlds, Warwick Press, 1974.
Famous Explorers, David & Charles, 1974.
Famous Composers, David & Charles, 1974.
Famous Kings and Emperors, David & Charles, 1976.
(With Ann Kramer) *History Factfinder,* Ward Lock, 1977.
(With Kramer) *History's Timeline: A 40,000-Year Chronology of World Civilization,* Crescent Books, 1981.
(Compiler) *The World Almanac Infopedia: A Visual Encyclopedia for Students,* World Almanac, 1990.
(Compiler) *Factfinder,* Kingfisher Books, 1992.

OTHER

(With others) *Archaeology,* edited by Jennifer Justice, Sampson Low, 1976, Warwick Press, 1977.
(With David Sharp) *The Performing Arts,* Silver Burdett, 1981.
Projects for Easter and Holiday Activities, illustrated by Janos Marffy, Garrett Educational Corp., 1989.

*   *   *

CORBY, Dan
See CATHERALL, Arthur

*   *   *

CORFIELD, Robin Bell 1952-

PERSONAL: Born July 14, 1952, in London, England; son of Peter William David (a surgeon) and Myrra (Coe) Corfield; married; wife's name, Susan (an educational psychologist). *Education:* Norwich School of Art, B.A. (with honors), 1975.

ADDRESSES: Home—"Victoria Cottage", 1 Main Road, Twyford, Melton Mowbray, Leicestershire, England LE14 2HL.

CAREER: Freelance artist, illustrator, and educator. Art lecturer at Weston-Super-Mare Technical College, 1980-83; and Strode College, 1987-88; art teacher at King Alfred Comprehensive School, 1983-84; Sydenham Community School, 1984-86; John Ellis Community College, 1990-91; Leicester Adult Education College, 1991—; and Longfield High School, 1991—; art supply teacher at Blake Comprehensive School, 1988-89; and Rowley Fields Community College, 1989-90. *Exhibitions:* One man exhibitions at Robin Garton Fine Art Gallery, London, 1977, 1978, and 1981; and Silk Top Hat Gallery, Ludlow, Shropshire, England, 1991 and 1993. Group exhibitions at various locations, including Royal West of England Academy, 1980, 1981, and 1982; David A. Cross Fine Art Gallery, Bristol, England, 1981; Bath Contemporary Arts Festival, Bath, England, 1983; and National Trust Exhibition, Attingham Park, Shropshire, 1993.

MEMBER: Association of Illustrators.

AWARDS, HONORS: Reckitt and Coleman Award, 1973; Royal Bath and West County Show awards, first prize, 1981, third prize, 1982.

ILLUSTRATOR:

Paul Rogers, *Tumbledown,* Atheneum, 1987.
Rogers, *Somebody's Sleepy,* Bodley Head, 1988.
Rogers, *Somebody's Awake,* Bodley Head, 1988.
Rogers, *Don't Blame Me,* Bodley Head, 1989.
A. E. Housman, *A Shropshire Lad,* Walker Books, 1990.
Emma Rogers and P. Rogers, *Zoe's Tower,* Simon and Schuster, 1991.
Barbara Willard, *The Farmer's Boy,* Julia Macrae, 1991.
William Trevor, *Juliet's Story,* Bodley Head, 1992.
Beverly Birch, *Marconi: The Battle for Radio,* Mathew Price, in press.

Also contributed illustrations to selected books, including "The Opie Rhyme Book," *Tail Feathers from Mother Goose,* Walker Books, 1988; "The Tree," *The Woodland Trust,* David and Charles, 1990; and "The Sea," *Greenpeace,* David and Charles, 1993.

WORK IN PROGRESS: Writing and illustrating an untitled work of my own design, expected completion in 1994.

ROBIN BELL CORFIELD

SIDELIGHTS: Robin Bell Corfield's work has been influenced by many artists, but especially watercolorists like Samuel Palmer, Thomas Girtin, and Peter DeWint, illustrators such as Gabrielle Vincent, E. H. Shepard, Lizbeth Zwerger, and Errol LeCain, and the etcher Robin Tanner. Corfield told *SATA:* "I started drawing with conviction when I was about twelve. I later went to the Norwich School of Art and spent many hours looking at beautiful watercolors by John Sell Cotman, Miles Edmund Cotman, Henry Bright, and many others." After graduating from Norwich, Corfield taught art in Somerset, England, where he met author Paul Rogers. An appreciation for each other's talents developed into a partnership, and the two collaborated on *Tumbledown,* the story of a dilapidated village whose residents have grown comfortable with its ragged charm. *Tumbledown* earned praise for Corfield; a reviewer for *Publishers Weekly* declared that the artist's "first performance as an illustrator of children's books was that of a virtuoso." The success of *Tumbledown* convinced Corfield to leave teaching and become a full-time illustrator. "It wasn't easy," he recalled, "not only financially, but also because I had a lot to learn. However I was fortunate enough to be doing what I wanted, and the insecurity was balanced against the immense satisfaction I gained."

Corfield has provided the illustrations for several other children's books, and he has explored working in mezzotint, an etching method. Watercolor, however, remains his favorite means of illustration. "Watercolor is a fascinating medium," he said. "I spend days, like a chemist, combining different hues, different overlays—not as experiments in themselves, but normally as part of my work. The combination of the pen line and translucent watercolors is a craft to be learned over a lifetime. It is a special area where I find I can express a part of me that I cannot do in any other way.

"I start generally with simple tonal sketches where I can see the distribution of shapes and tones, and where I can get the feel of the atmosphere. I then draw from models and other references if need be, but I rely on my imagination. I support all this by doing drawings from life and going to drawing classes. I try to take a sketchbook with me when I go out. I find a rich assortment of faces on tube trains in London! In contrast, I love drawing by streams and old farms."

Evaluating his role in the success of a title, Corfield admits, "A strong story is the primary ingredient in a children's book. Without that the illustrations seem indulgent. They must enhance the story, not compensate for it." He added, "Children's books allow this wonderful affection for the subject to come out. I illustrate to please myself, and then I hope it pleases parents and children. When the work is going well, I consider it a privilege to be doing the job I am doing!" Based on his statements, Corfield's involvement with books seems sure to continue. "During my career I have seen the reproduction of watercolor improve to its present high standard," he stated, "and with the good printing techniques and interest shown by the public, books are a natural home for watercolors."

WORKS CITED:

Publishers Weekly, December 23, 1988, p. 31.

*   *   *

COX, Clinton

PERSONAL: Born June 10, in Sumter, SC; son of Lafayette C. (a Baptist minister) and Magdalene E. (a librarian; maiden name Jackson) Cox; married Anita B. Irwin, April 28, 1965. *Education:* Goddard College, B.S., 1970; Columbia University, M.S., 1971.

ADDRESSES: Schenectady, NY.

CAREER: Community News Service, New York City, reporter and city editor, 1972-74; *New York Daily News,* New York City, magazine writer and political reporter, 1974-79; freelance journalist and magazine writer, 1979-89; *City Sun,* Brooklyn, NY, columnist, 1990-92; author.

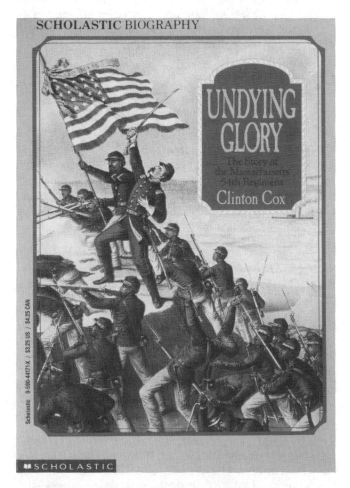

Cox's book tells how a daring raid on Fort Wagner during the Civil War helped earn the mostly black 54th Regiment of Massachusetts, also known as the "Glory" regiment, a place in history.

AWARDS, HONORS: Page One Award, Newspaper Guild of New York, 1976, for best local reporting in a magazine; has been nominated for two Pulitzer Prizes.

WRITINGS:

The Undying Glory, Scholastic, 1991.

WORK IN PROGRESS: A book on the Buffalo Soldiers, the black cavalrymen in the West, to be published by Scholastic in 1993.

SIDELIGHTS: Clinton Cox told *SATA:* "My father, who was a chaplain in World War II, used to tell me about his experiences in an all-black army unit. I was amazed that all the war movies I saw as a child never included black soldiers who were going through the kind of experiences I heard my father and his friends describe. The books I read in school also banished them from the roles they lived in real life. This taught me early on that there was a great need for an honest writing of history of a few decades ago, the history of several centuries ago, or last week's history. This kind of honesty is what I try to bring to my writing, both in the weekly column I write for *The City Sun* in Brooklyn, and in my books.

"My first book, *Undying Glory,* told the story of black soldiers in the Civil War. I thought it was important to show the racial atmosphere they were forced to live in, and how that affected both them and this country. I'm doing the same thing with the book I am currently working on, the story of the Buffalo Soldiers—the black cavalrymen in the West who rode to the rescue of wagon trains, shot it out with the bad guys and did all the other things you see cavalrymen doing in the movies.

"Once again, however, these black men were banished from the history they lived and their deeds are still known by relatively few people. You can find this same white-washing of American history in virtually every field and every era, so I'm trying to use my writing to bring a little more racial reality into the field of historiography for young adults. In this way, young people will have a better knowledge of this society and how it was molded by people of all colors. That increased knowledge in turn will, hopefully, lead to an increased ability to transcend the boundaries of color that too many generations of Americans have lived with."

*   *   *

CRANFIELD, Ingrid 1945-

PERSONAL: Born November 17, 1945, in Melbourne, Australia; daughter of Severin (an importer/wholesaler) and Annette (Philipp) Briar; married Brian Cranfield (a scientist), October 24, 1970 (separated); children: Tim, Adam, Helvi. *Education:* University of Sydney, B.A. *Politics:* Labour. *Religion:* Jewish.

ADDRESSES: Home—16 Myddelton Gardens, Winchmore Hill, London N21 2PA, England. *Office*—c/o The Dictionary of Art, 4 Little Essex St., London WC2R 3LF, England.

CAREER: International Wool Secretariat, London, England, research assistant, 1966-68; Royal Geographical Society, London, England, senior assistant, 1968-72; Map Productions Ltd., London, England, map project coordinator, 1972; free-lance writer, editor, translator, and consultant, 1972—. Endeavour Training Ltd., member of Council, 1978—, member of Executive Board, 1984—, and chair of Chief Executive's Working Group, 1984—. Governor of comprehensive school in London Borough of Barnet, 1988—. Co-organizer of Democracy Day meeting for public and parliamentary candidates, Hornsey, London, April, 1992.

MEMBER: Royal Geographical Society (Life Fellow), WEXAS (travel club; VIP member).

WRITINGS:

(Translator with Peter Adler) Hans Juergen Hansen, *The Ships of the German Fleets, 1848-1945,* Hamlyn, 1974.
The Challengers: British and Commonwealth Adventure since 1945, Weidenfeld & Nicolson, 1976.
(Editor with Richard Harrington) *Off the Beaten Track,* WEXAS/Wilton House Gentry, 1977.
(Editor with Richard Harrington) *The Independent Traveller's Handbook,* WEXAS/Heinemann, 1980.
(Editor with Richard Harrington) *The International Traveler's Handbook,* Dial, 1982, published in England as *The Traveller's Handbook,* WEXAS/Heinemann, 1982.
Skiing Down Everest and Other Crazy Adventures, Severn House, 1983.
Q Challenge Quiz Books, Volume 1: *Know It All,* Volume 2: *Word Wise,* Volume 3: *Trivia I,* Volume 4: *Trivia II,* Price, Stern, Sloan, 1988.

INGRID CRANFIELD

Animal World, Hamlyn, 1990.
(Translator) Michel Hoang, *Genghis Khan,* Saqi Books, 1990.

Contributor of articles and reviews to newspapers and other periodicals, including *Traveller, Observer Magazine, Education and Training, Training Officer, Business Traveller, Personnel Executive, Go Global, English Today, Use of English, Geographical Magazine, Contemporary Review,* and *Geographical Journal.*

WORK IN PROGRESS: Senoir Desk Editor (Japan) for *The Dictionary of Art,* to be published by Macmillan in 1994-95; research on family history.

SIDELIGHTS: Ingrid Cranfield writes: "People and words matter to me, in that order. Words, perhaps because of my bilingual background, when hardly an evening meal passed without a call for a dictionary to settle some contentious point; and of course because words are the principal means of communication between people. I specialized for a while in the field of adventure and exploration, identifying with people who lived dangerously (as I do too in my way). Education and training attract me too, partly because, having three children well spread out in ages, I shall of necessity be involved in that area for some thirty years; and I believe in the long-term development of the whole person, in education in its original sense of 'drawing out' a person's innate capabilities. To instill in children a love of the written word is to introduce them to a world of experience which, in the longest and fullest life, will otherwise be barred to them for lack of time or opportunity, and to give them an intellectual and emotional life that lasts longer than any career and most relationships."

* * *

CROSSLEY-HOLLAND, Kevin (John William) 1941-

PERSONAL: Born February 7, 1941, in Mursley, Buckinghamshire, England; son of Peter Charles (a professor) and Joan Mary (an MBE for services to the arts; maiden name, Cowper) Crossley-Holland; married Caroline Fendall Thompson, 1963; married Ruth Marris, 1972; married Gillian Cook, 1982; children: (first marriage) Kieran, Dominic; (third marriage) Oenone, Eleanor. *Education:* St. Edmund Hall, Oxford, M.A., 1962. *Hobbies and other interests:* Music, archaeology, travel.

ADDRESSES: Home—The Old Vicarage, Walsham-le-Willows, Bury St. Edmunds, Suffolk IP31 3BA, England. *Agent*—Rogers Coleridge and White, 20 Powis Mews, London W11 1JN, England.

CAREER: Writer and translator. Macmillan publishers, London, England, editor, 1962-71; Victor Gollancz Ltd. (publisher), London, editorial director, 1972-77; Andre Deutsch Ltd. (publisher), London, general editor, Mirror of Britain series, 1975—; Boydell and Brewer (publisher), Woodbridge, Suffolk, England, editorial consultant, 1983-91; University of St. Thomas, St. Paul,

MN, professor and endowed chair of humanities and fine arts, 1991—. Visiting lecturer, professor, or fellow at various colleges and universities, including Tufts-in-London Program, 1967-78, University of Leeds (Gregory Fellow), 1969-71, University of Regensburg, 1978-80, Winchester School of Art, 1983-84, and St. Olaf College (Fulbright Scholar), 1987-88; visiting lecturer for British Council in Germany, Iceland, India, and Yugoslavia. Trustee, Wingfield College, 1989—, and chairman of Friends of Wingfield College, 1989-91. British Broadcasting Corp., London, talks producer, 1972; contributor to radio and television dramas, talks, and features, and to musical works by Sir Arthur Bliss, William Mathias, and others.

MEMBER: Poetry Book Society (board of management, 1977-83), Eastern Arts Association (chairman, Literature Panel, 1986-89), Friends, Wingfield College, (trustee and chairman, 1989—).

AWARDS, HONORS: Arts Council award for the best book for children, 1966-68, for *The Green Children;* poetry award, 1972, for *The Rain-Giver;* Poetry Book Society Choice, 1976, for *The Dream-House;* Francis Williams Award, 1977, for *The Wildman;* Carnegie Medal, (British) Library Association, 1985, for *Storm;* Poetry Book Society Recommendation for *Waterslain and Other Poems,* 1986.

WRITINGS:

FOR YOUNG ADULTS

Havelok the Dane, illustrated by Brian Wildsmith, Macmillan, 1964, Dutton, 1965.
King Horn, illustrated by Charles Keeping, Macmillan, 1965, Dutton, 1966.
The Green Children, illustrated by Margaret Gordon, Macmillan, 1966, Seabury, 1968, illustrated by Alan Marks, Oxford University Press, 1994.
(Editor) *Winter's Tales for Children: No. 3,* Macmillan, 1967, St. Martin's, 1968.
The Callow Pit Coffer, illustrated by Gordon, Macmillan, 1968, Seabury, 1969.
(With Jill Paton Walsh) *Wordhoard: Anglo-Saxon Stories,* Farrar, Straus, 1969.
(Translator) *Storm and Other Old English Riddles* (verse), illustrated by Miles Thistlethwaite, Farrar, Straus, 1970.
The Pedlar of Swaffham, illustrated by Gordon, Seabury, 1971.
The Sea Stranger, illustrated by Joanna Troughton, Heinemann, 1973, Seabury, 1974.
The Fire-Brother, illustrated by Troughton, Heinemann, 1974, Seabury, 1975.
Green Blades Rising: The Anglo-Saxons, Deutsch, 1975, Seabury, 1976.
The Earth-Father, illustrated by Troughton, Heinemann, 1976.
The Wildman, illustrated by Keeping, Deutsch, 1976.
(Editor) *The Faber Book of Northern Legends,* illustrated by Alan Howard, Faber, 1977.
(Editor) *The Faber Book of Northern Folk-Tales,* illustrated by Howard, Faber, 1980.

KEVIN CROSSLEY-HOLLAND

(Editor) *The Riddle Book,* illustrated by Bernard Handelsman, Macmillan, 1982.

The Dead Moon and Other Tales from East Anglia and the Fen Country, illustrated by Shirley Felts, Deutsch, 1982, Faber, 1986.

Beowulf, illustrated by Keeping, Oxford University Press, 1982.

(With Gwyn Thomas) *Tales from the Mabinogion,* illustrated by Margaret Jones, Gollancz, 1984, Overlook Press, 1985.

Storm, illustrated by Marks, Heinemann, 1985.

Axe-Age, Wolf-Age: A Selection from the Norse Myths, illustrated by Hannah Firmin, Deutsch, 1985.

(With Susan Varley) *The Fox and the Cat: Animal Tales from Grimm,* illustrated by Varley, Andersen, 1985, Lothrop, 1986.

(Editor) *Northern Lights: Legends, Sagas and Folk-Tales,* illustrated by Howard, Faber, 1987.

British Folk Tales: New Versions, Orchard, 1987.

Boo!, illustrated by Peter Melnyczuk, Orchard, 1988.

Dathera Dad, illustrated by Melnyczuk, Orchard, 1988.

Piper and Pooka, illustrated by Melnyczuk, Orchard, 1988.

Small-Tooth Dog, illustrated by Melnyczuk, Orchard, 1988.

(With Thomas) *The Quest for Olwen,* illustrated by Jones, Lutterworth Press, 1988.

Wulf, Faber, 1988.

Under the Sun and over the Moon (poetry), illustrated by Ian Penney, Putnam, 1989.

Sleeping Nanna, illustrated by Melnyczuk, Orchard, 1989.

(With Thomas) *The Tale of Taliesin,* Gollancz, 1992.

Long Tom and the Dead Hand, illustrated by Felts, Deutsch, 1992.

Norse Myths, illustrated by Gillian McClure, Simon & Schuster, 1993.

The Labours of Hercules, illustrated by Peter Utton, Orion, 1993.

POETRY

The Rain-Giver, Deutsch, 1972.

The Dream-House, Deutsch, 1976.

Time's Oriel, Hutchinson, 1983.

Waterslain and Other Poems, Hutchinson, 1986.

The Painting-Room and Other Poems, Century Hutchinson, 1988.

East Anglian Poems, Jardine, 1988.

New and Selected Poems: 1965-1990, Hutchinson, 1991.

Also author of numerous poetry broadsheets, pamphlets, and limited editions, including *On Approval,* 1961; *My Son,* 1966; *Alderney: The Nunnery,* 1968; *Confessional,* 1969; *Norfolk Poems,* 1970; *A Dream of a Meeting,* 1970; *More Than I Am,* 1971; *The Wake,* 1972; *Petal and Stone,* 1975; *Between My Father and My Son,* 1982; *The Wanderer,* Jardine, 1986; *Oenone in January,* 1988; and *Eleanor's Advent,* 1992.

EDITOR

Running to Paradise: An Introductory Selection of the Poems of W.B. Yeats, Macmillan, 1967.

Winter's Tales 14, Macmillan, 1968.

(With Patricia Beer) *New Poetry 2,* Arts Council of Great Britain, 1976.

The Norse Myths: A Retelling, Pantheon, 1980, Deutsch, 1981.

(And translator) *The Anglo-Saxon World: An Anthology,* Boydell Press, 1982, Barnes and Noble, 1983.

Folk Tales of the British Isles, Folio Society, 1985, Faber, 1986, Pantheon, 1988.

The Oxford Book of Travel Verse, Oxford University Press, 1987.

Medieval Lovers: A Book of Days, Weidenfeld & Nicolson, 1988.

Medieval Gardens: A Book of Days, Rizzoli, 1990.

Peter Grimes: The Poor of the Borough, Folio Society, 1990.

TRANSLATOR

The Battle of Maldon and Other Old English Poems, edited by Bruce Mitchell, St. Martin's, 1965.

Beowulf, Farrar, Straus, 1968.

The Exeter Riddle Book, Penguin, 1969, revised edition, 1993.

The Old English Elegies, Folio Society, 1988.

OTHER

Pieces of Land: Journeys to Eight Islands, Gollancz, 1972.

(With Andrew Rafferty) *The Stones Remain: Megalithic Sites of Britain,* Rider, 1989.

Also author, with Nicola LeFanu, of children's opera *The Green Children,* based on his work of the same title, 1990. A collection of Crossley-Holland's poetry notebooks is housed in the Brotherton Collection at the University of Leeds; the manuscripts of his children's books are housed in The Osborne Collection, Toronto; the Kerlan Collection, Minneapolis, MN, holds material relating to *Under the Sun and over the Moon.*

WORK IN PROGRESS: Writing a second opera with Nicola LeFanu, *The Wildman,* for the 1995 Aldeburgh Festival.

SIDELIGHTS: Kevin Crossley-Holland's books for children focus mainly on the retelling and translating of myths, legends, and folktales, particularly from his native East Anglia, England. He manages to keep the characters and messages in these retellings fresh and timeless, while conveying subtle truths about life which are as pertinent today as they were when these tales were originally told. Crossley-Holland has the unique ability to bring stories of the past sharply into the present, while preserving their mystery, richness, and texture.

Crossley-Holland's youth was spent learning viola, which he described in the *Fourth Book of Junior Authors and Illustrators* as a "purgatory, for me and for others." He was born into a very musical family and, as he related in *The Ronald M. Hubbs and Margaret S. Hubbs Lectures,* "when I think of my early childhood, I hear

A young man must face two powerful monsters in Crossley-Holland's retelling of this famous Anglo-Saxon narrative. (Cover illustration by Charles Keeping.)

sounds. The sound of the music of many cultures, spinning at seventy-eight revolutions per minute on our old gramophone; the sound of my father singing-and-saying traditional tales from north and south, east and west, sometimes accompanying himself on his Welsh harp." The author had little recollection of reading books, claiming to have finished less than fifteen throughout his youth. Somewhat ironically, when he went to Oxford University he studied English, eventually to become an accomplished writer. In college, he learned about the Anglo-Saxons, natives living in Britain before the Norman conquest, and became fascinated with their history and literature. In the early 1960s, he finished his degree and also began earning acclaim as a poet. He took a job in publishing in 1962, while maintaining his own personal writing career.

His first work for young adults was *Havelok the Dane.* This was followed by several books about the Anglo-Saxon world with which Crossley-Holland had fallen in love: *Wordhoard,* a picture of that ancient culture; and *The Sea Stranger, The Fire-Brother,* and *The Earth-Father,* which tell the story of an Anglo-Saxon missionary and a boy named Wulf. Another focus of Crossley-Holland's young adult work has been the folktales of his native East Anglia, England. "They are less well known than they should be; at their best—as in *The Green Children* and *The Wildman*—they are utterly haunting," he reported in *Fourth Book of Junior Authors and Illustrators. The Green Children,* one of his most acclaimed works, contains retellings of several medieval tales. As a testament to Crossley-Holland's ability to bring these age-old stories to life, Charles Causley commented in *Twentieth-Century Children's Writers* that in *The Green Children* "mind and imagination are continuously stimulated and fed as the tales are resolved."

The Dead Moon and Other Tales from East Anglia and the Fen Country is another example of Crossley-Holland's adaptations—this time, focusing on more ghostly tales. Boggarts, will-o'-the-wykes, witches, dead hands, and green children come to life in these pages. In addition to his work collecting East Anglian tales, Crossley-Holland has also spent many hours finding and documenting the age-old stories of other areas in rural England. One of his notable retellings is *Small-Tooth Dog,* which recounts the story of a curious dog who saves the life of a man only to demand the man's only daughter as payment.

As a writer, Crossley-Holland works very carefully on his manuscripts, putting them through many revisions. When writing about the sea, he insists on getting the cadence of the waves into his prose. He claims this need comes from his early exposure to the rhythms of music. In his translations, Crossley-Holland tries to be as faithful as possible to the original work. However, he admits he enjoys trying out new methods to tell his tale. "From time to time I've stepped into a tale and told it, as it were, from the inside out ... by allowing [the protagonist] to tell his or her own story," he related in *Magpies.* "Recently, I've been thinking further about

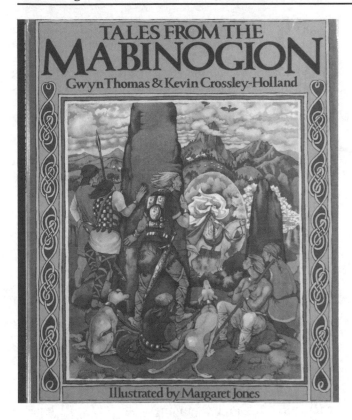

Giant warriors, powerful magicians, and other heroes and heroines populate this ancient Welsh tale told by Crossley-Holland and Gwyn Thomas. (Cover illustration by Margaret Jones.)

the use of monologue, and the possibilities of giving inanimate objects the power of speech."

The real power of Crossley-Holland's folktales lies in his ability to take an ancient story and make it appeal to a modern audience. As he commented in the Hubbs lecture, "A tale names, it expresses what children already instinctively know; it therefore helps them to understand their own thoughts and feelings." In addition, some tales can foster understanding and tolerance for others; these are stories "that relate us—that tell each of us who we are and connect us to one another," Crossley-Holland added. Although it seems a "paradox," this type of tale "makes two apparently opposing points. Firstly it says, 'each one of us is *one*, is singular, completely and utterly different from any other one.' And then, in the same breath, the story says 'we are all the same, all of us, and together we are one, and only together are we one.'" The author also enjoys bringing to his books some of the things he loves—the sea, Anglo-Saxons, and East Anglia. Asked to describe the basis of his work, he once commented that it was lodged in "roots, the sense of past embodied in present, [and] the relationship of person to place."

WORKS CITED:

Causley, Charles, "Kevin Crossley-Holland," *Twentieth-Century Children's Writers,* 3rd edition, St. James, 1989, pp. 248-49.

Crossley-Holland, Kevin, "The Flying Word, The Word of Life: Approaches to Norse Myth and British Folktale, Pt. II," *Magpies,* July, 1991.
Crossley-Holland, Kevin, *The Ronald M. Hubbs and Margaret S. Hubbs Lectures,* number 1, University of St. Paul, 1992.
De Montreville, Doris, and Elizabeth D. Crawford, editors, *Fourth Book of Junior Authors and Illustrators,* Wilson, 1978, pp. 108-09.

FOR MORE INFORMATION SEE:

BOOKS

Dictionary of Literary Biography, Volume 40: *Poets of Great Britain and Ireland since 1940,* Part 1, Gale, 1985.

PERIODICALS

Listener, November 14, 1968.
Observer Review, February 26, 1970.
Punch, October 23, 1968.
Saturday Review, March 15, 1969.
Young Reader's Review, January, 1967; June, 1968; October, 1969.

*   *   *

CRUZ MARTINEZ, Alejandro (?)-1987

CAREER: Political activist and poet.

WRITINGS:

The Woman Who Outshone the Sun: The Legend of Lucia Zenteno, adapted by Rosalma Zubizaretta, Harriet Rohmer, and David Schecter; illustrated by Fernando Olivera, Children's Book Press, 1992.

SIDELIGHTS: Alejandro Cruz Martinez spent much of his career collecting the oral poems and stories of Mexico's Zapotec Indians. Perhaps his most famous story is a verse adaptation of the tale of Lucia Zenteno, a beautiful young woman perfectly in tune with nature. Because she is different, Lucia is scorned by her neighbors and driven out of her village; it is only after nature begins to mourn her loss that the villagers repent. Ann Welton, writing in *School Library Journal,* finds *The Woman Who Outshone the Sun* to be "skillfully told" and "solidly steeped with the imagery of earth and sky," while a *Publishers Weekly* reviewer notes that "much of the imagery is refreshing."

WORKS CITED:

Review of *The Lady Who Outshone the Sun: The Legend of Lucia Zenteno, Publishers Weekly,* January 6, 1992.
Welton, Ann, review of *The Lady Who Outshone the Sun: The Legend of Lucia Zenteno, School Library Journal,* March, 1992.

FOR MORE INFORMATION SEE:

PERIODICALS

Z Magazine, November, 1991.*

CULLIFORD, Pierre 1928-1992 (Peyo)

OBITUARY NOTICE—See index for *SATA* sketch: Born June 25, 1928, in Brussels, Belgium; died December 24, 1992, in Brussels. Cartoonist and author. Culliford, who worked under the name "Peyo," was the creator of the popular blue cartoon dwarfs known as the Smurfs. Culliford spent his early career as a cartoonist for a Brussels animation studio, then began a long association with *Spirou,* a weekly comic magazine, in 1954. The Smurfs first appeared as extras in Culliford's comic strip "Johan et Pirlouit," and by 1957 the cartoonist had created a separate strip starring the tiny trolls. Since then, the Smurfs have appeared in an animated feature film, a highly rated television series, a number of television specials, and a series of recordings. The Smurfs are not only successful as entertainments but as marketable merchandise; their likeness adorns hundreds of products, including toys, games, and clothing. A Smurf theme park was even opened in France, although it closed due to financial difficulty. Among Culliford's other works are *Les Taxis Rouges, Pour faire une flute, The Smurfs and the Toyshop, The Wonderful World of Smurfs,* and *What Do Smurfs Do All Day?* His last work was a Smurfs recording titled *The Money Smurfs.*

OBITUARIES AND OTHER SOURCES:

PERIODICALS

Chicago Tribune, December 25, 1992, section 2, p. 10.
Los Angeles Times, December 25, 1992, p. A30.
New York Times, December 25, 1992, p. A29.
Times (London), January 2, 1993, p. 15.
Washington Post, December 25, 1992, p. D7.

*   *   *

CUMMINGS, Phil 1957-

PERSONAL: Born December 22, 1957, in Port Broughton, South Australia, Australia; son of Cyril Gordon (a carpenter and builder) and Rachel Henrietta Arbon (a homemaker) Cummings; married Susan Chalmers (a teacher), February 1, 1987; children: Benjamin David, Alyssa Claire. *Education:* Received diploma in teaching from Salisbury College of Advanced Education, South Australia. *Hobbies and other interests:* Listening to music, playing guitar, sports, reading, "playing with my kids."

ADDRESSES: Home—7 Robert Road, Hillbank, South Australia 5112, Australia. *Office*—P.O. Box 84, Para Hills, South Australia 5096, Australia.

CAREER: Education Department of South Australia, teacher, 1979—.

WRITINGS:

Goodness Gracious!, Orchard, 1992.

Also author of *Midge Mum and the Neighbors* and *Find My Friends,* both published in Australia.

WORK IN PROGRESS: "Two other books due for release in Australia."

SIDELIGHTS: Phil Cummings told *SATA:* "I love to write. It's great to come up with something that entertains others, particularly 'little' others. Writing books for young children presents numerous rewards for me. Giving them language to play with, use and expand upon is fuel for my creativity. Creating characters, settings and images and moulding them like clay is also exciting.

"I am the youngest child of a family of eight children. I grew up in the dusty town of Peterborough in the mid-North of the state of South Australia. In my most recent works, it is the experiences from those wonderfully adventurous years that I am now calling upon as I write. And, you know, I don't think there are going to be enough years in my life to record them *all* in print, but I'm going to give a real good try."

D

DALE, George E.
See ASIMOV, Isaac

* * *

DAVIS, Jenny 1953-

PERSONAL: Born June 29, 1953, in Louisville, KY; daughter of Marcum Jay (an engineer) and Georgia (a teacher and counselor; maiden name, Ethridge) Schneider; married Dee Davis, August, 1975 (divorced, 1981); children: Boone, Willie. *Education:* Attended Allegheny Community College; University of Kentucky, B.A., 1976, and M.A., 1981. *Politics:* "Active." *Religion:* "Believer." *Hobbies and other interests:* Walking, reading, art museums, looking at the moon, the ocean.

ADDRESSES: Home—723 Melrose, Lexington, KY 40502.

CAREER: Child advocate, Hazard, KY, 1975-77; Health Department, Lexington, KY, sex educator, 1981-83; teacher, Lexington, 1983—.

WRITINGS:

Goodbye and Keep Cold, Orchard, 1987.
Sex Education, Orchard, 1988.
Checking on the Moon, Orchard, 1991.

SIDELIGHTS: Jenny Davis told *SATA:* "I don't know where I get my ideas for plots and characters. It seems to me they come and get me. To write, I pay attention—to my ideas, hunches, dreams, memories, to my experiences, all of them, real and imagined. Writing helps me feel more alive and more aware. It can also make me feel crazy and sad if the story I'm telling is a hard one to get out. Even so, on balance, writing heals me, it amuses me, and most of all—no matter how hard to tell—it makes me wonder. And I love to wonder.

"You asked how old I was when I decided to become a writer. I haven't yet decided, so—not yet. So far, I've decided to write, when and if I can, or when and if I can't help it. I've been doing that since I was eight or

JENNY DAVIS

nine. I decided to become a school teacher eight years ago and have since been teaching reading and writing to 5th and 6th graders. Mostly because I don't like to ask my students to do something I'd be unwilling to do myself, I began writing regularly at that time, but I'd written many stories, essays and poems prior to then.

"I also didn't decide to write for teenagers. Rather selfishly, I try to write books that I would want to read. Other people—conspicuously my editor, and the publishers—determined that the audience was 'Young

LAUREL-LEAF CONTEMPORARY FICTION

An unusual high school class

A life-changing lesson

A novel about loving and caring

SEX EDUCATION

BY JENNY DAVIS

DELL • 20483-6 • U.S. $2.95 CAN $3.50

As part of a class project, two students befriend a troubled pregnant woman in Davis' novel.

Adult.' I assume this means there's still a lot of teenager in my soul, and that's okay by me. There is so much really wonderful writing in the Young Adult category that I feel honored to have a place there.

"What do I do when I'm not writing? Well, besides teaching, I have two teenage sons. I love living with them and being their mother. We squabble a bit about homework, housework, bedtimes, movies, cable TV, politics, and most of the usual things. They would be embarrassed if I said too much about them, but the fact is they are simply marvelous people who are among the dearest, kindest, sweetest, funniest and certainly most patient I've ever known. They are exceedingly good to me, and I doubt I'd be able to write at all without their support and help.

"My grandmother, Willie Snow Ethridge, was a writer, and my grandfather, Mark Ethridge, a newspaperman. They gifted all of us in my family with a love for story and a respect for words. They taught me, too, the difference between fact and fiction. My parents endowed me with a yen for justice and the strength to be

myself. The hardest part about growing up for me has been bearing the ambiguities.

"To teachers who teach writing I would say, be respectful of what your students give you. Writing is very hard work, and often frightening because of what is discovered, or sometimes uncovered. Be full of care in your responses, and when you can, be kind. If you doubt me, try writing something of your own and sharing it with your class. You'll see in a hurry how scary it can be.

"When I was in the 7th grade, I was given my first chance to write creatively. Up until then we'd only diagrammed sentences and copied words out of the spelling book. I worked long and hard on what I thought was a terrific story. I read it to my mother, my neighbors, my sisters, and my dog. I was very proud of this piece which was narrated by a raindrop. My English teacher, Miss Macateer, however, didn't share my enthusiasm. She handed it back with a large D on the front, and the rest of it covered in red ink because I hadn't, apparently, the vaguest notion what to do with commas. Oh well. Miss Macateer didn't stop me from writing, but she certainly set me back a ways. I try not to ever do that to my students. It was humiliating. I hope if you are writing you will keep at it; if you're not you might give it a try. You never know what might come out."

* * *

dePARRIE, Paul 1949-

PERSONAL: Born June 19, 1949, in Teaneck, NJ; son of Edward (an engineer and accountant) and Jeanne (Sirois) deParrie; married Bonnie Vargas (a teacher), May 25, 1969; children: Djinn, Joshua, Jeanne, Yvonne. *Politics:* "Right wing social democrat (apologies to Mort Sahl)." *Religion:* Christian.

ADDRESSES: Home—4211 Southeast 39th, Portland, OR 97202. *Office*—415 Northeast 80th, Portland, OR 97213. *Agent*—Wolgemuth & Hyatt, P.O. Box 2107, Brentwood, TN 37024.

CAREER: Painter in Portland, OR, 1973-87; writer, editor, political activist, and social critic.

WRITINGS:

(With Mary Pride) *Unholy Sacrifices,* Crossway, 1987.
The Rescuers, Wolgemuth & Hyatt, 1988.
(With Pride) *Ancient Empires of the New Age,* Crossway, 1989.
Romanced to Death, Wolgemuth & Hyatt, 1989.
Satan's Seven Schemes: An Overcomer's Guide to Spiritual Warfare, Wolgemuth & Hyatt, 1991.
A Haunt of Jackals (young adult fiction), Crossway, 1991.
Blood upon the Rose (fiction), Crossway, 1992.

Editor of *Life Advocate* magazine, 1989—.

PAUL dePARRIE

WORK IN PROGRESS: A House Divided, a nonfiction work on racism in the American church, 1993; *Self-Help Law,* 1993; *Deliverers of Anara,* a science fiction novel; *Jesus against the Church,* a comparison of the current church and apostate Jews of Jesus' time; *Foster's Night,* "a near future novel of the descent of a new dark age in America following the squelching of 'incorrect' beliefs'"; an untitled fantasy.

SIDELIGHTS: Paul deParrie told *SATA:* "My desire to write is founded on my desire to teach. I feel there are universal truths that are objective, discoverable, and constant. Finding these and applying them to my life is the most important endeavor. Writing helps me to put these beliefs to the test. It allows me to see my thought in writing where errors are more likely to appear. It also presents me with the need to be prepared to defend those beliefs or admit I was wrong. Sometimes being published is scary for that reason.

"I believe the most important right of all persons is the right to life. Without it, all other rights lose significance. Life is given by God and should be taken by no other. Our lives—and thus our bodies—are not our own.

Humanity has a penchant to look for ways to justify mistreating or killing others. The main method is by dehumanizing them. If there is one central theme that has saturated my writing to date, it is that.

"Probably the next most important theme is that of responsibility. I believe every man and woman is responsible for others. It is not enough to believe that all persons are equal, we must all work to make sure that ideal is realized. This is especially true for Christians because the commands of Christ are so clear on this score. Writing helps me to explore the practical applications of the commands of Christ and, I hope, helps me and my readers to begin to put those things into action."

*   *   *

DERMAN, Martha (Winn) 19(?)-

PERSONAL: Born in New York; daughter of Arthur (a brick and lumber yard manager) and Ruth (Collins) Winn; married Cyrus Derman (a professor); children: Adam, Hessy. *Education:* Received B.A. and M.L.S. from Vassar College.

ADDRESSES: Agent—Ann Tobias, A Literary Agency for Children's Books, 307 South Carolina Ave. SE, Washington, DC 20003.

CAREER: Writer of children's books, 1981—. Worked variously as a copywriter for ad agencies and radio stations.

WRITINGS:

The Friendstone, Dial, 1981.
And Philippa Makes Four, Four Winds, 1983; published in the Netherlands as *Met Philippa Als Vierde,* Uitgeverij Clavis, 1984.
Tales from Academy Street, Four Winds, 1992.

WORK IN PROGRESS: No Geraniums in the Park.

SIDELIGHTS: Martha Derman told *SATA:* "When my children were still at the read-to-me stage, I always told them that I was older than God and thus escaped having to bake cakes to celebrate my birthday. Telling this tale is now a habit that I will not change for other people's children.

"I was born in a small Hudson River town where my father managed a brick and lumber yard, and my mother managed various school PTAs. My early experiences included views of brick pyramids built high as houses and set to bake in the kiln shed. I had to study four years of Latin, grammar, Gallic Caesar, Cicero, and Virgil as a teenager and it made a strong impression on me. Writing offered an ideal escape from work. First, of course, came reading. I can remember rising at six in the morning to finish reading a Walter Scott novel before anyone bothered me.

"I am married to a professor in the school of engineering at Columbia University. Prior to starting a family, we travelled abroad for many years and visited other schools, especially Stanford University in California. Then, with children to read to, I picked up an interest in writing for them, from them. My son Adam always insisted I put him into whatever story I read to him. I thought I might as well learn how to write a child's story from scratch. My daughter Hessy wanted to read only about horses. I have not yet done that for her."

*   *   *

DEVLIN, (Dorothy) Wende 1918-

PERSONAL: Born April 27, 1918, in Buffalo, NY; daughter of Bernhardt Philip (a veterinarian) and Elizabeth (Buffington) Wende; married Harry Devlin (an artist and writer), August 30, 1941; children: Harry Noel, Wende Elizabeth (Mrs. Geoffrey Gates), Jeffrey Anthony, Alexandra Gail (Mrs. James Eldridge), Brion Phillip, Nicholas Kirk, David Matthew. *Education:* Syracuse University, B.F.A., 1940. *Politics:* Independent. *Religion:* Congregationalist.

ADDRESSES: Home and office—443 Hillside Ave., Mountainside, NJ 07092. *Agent*—(literature) Dorothy Markinko, McIntosh & Otis, Inc., 475 Fifth Ave., New York, NY 10017; (art) Swain Gallery, 703 Watchung Ave., Plainfield, NJ.

CAREER: Free-lance writer and portrait painter. Member of Rutgers University advisory council on children's

WENDE DEVLIN

literature; New Jersey Literary Hall of Fame, trustee, 1984—. *Exhibitions:* One-person art exhibitions, Schering Plough, Kenilworth, NJ, 1986, City of Trenton Museum, Trenton, NJ, 1987, and Schering Plough, Madison, NJ, 1988. Works represented in permanent collections, including Midlantic Bank, Edison, NJ, and Central Jersey Trust, Freehold, NJ.

MEMBER: Authors Guild, Authors League of America, Woman Days Club, Association of Artists.

AWARDS, HONORS: Special Citation for Husband-Wife Writers of Children's Books, New Jersey Institute of Technology, 1969; New Jersey Teachers of English Award and New Jersey Institute of Technology New Jersey Authors Award, both 1970, both for *How Fletcher Was Hatched!;* Award of Excellence, Chicago Book Fair, 1974, for *Old Witch Rescues Halloween;* Arents Award for Art and Literature, Syracuse University, 1977; inducted into New Jersey Literary Hall of Fame, 1981; New Jersey Institute of Technology New Jersey Authors Award, 1987, for *Cranberry Valentine;* The Michael Award, New Jersey School of Engineering, 1987.

WRITINGS:

JUVENILE; COWRITTEN AND ILLUSTRATED BY HUSBAND, HARRY DEVLIN

Old Black Witch, Encyclopaedia Britannica Press, 1963.
The Knobby Boys to the Rescue, Parents' Magazine Press, 1965.
Aunt Agatha, There's a Lion under the Couch, Van Nostrand, 1968.
How Fletcher Was Hatched!, Parents' Magazine Press, 1969.
A Kiss for a Warthog, Van Nostrand, 1970.
Old Witch and the Polka Dot Ribbon, Parents' Magazine Press, 1970.
Cranberry Thanksgiving, Parents' Magazine Press, 1971.
Old Witch Rescues Halloween, Parents' Magazine Press, 1973.
Cranberry Christmas, Parents' Magazine Press, 1976.
Cranberry Mystery, Four Winds Press, 1978.
Hang on Hester, Lothrop, 1980.
Cranberry Halloween, Four Winds Press, 1982.
Cranberry Valentine, Macmillan, 1986.
Cranberry Birthday, Macmillan, 1988.
Cranberry Easter, Macmillan, 1990.
Cranberry Summer, Macmillan, 1992.

Author of feature page, "Beat Poems for a Beat Mother," *Good Housekeeping,* 1963-71.

ADAPTATIONS: Old Black Witch was filmed by Gerald Herman as *The Winter of the Witch,* starring Hermione Gingold, Parents' Magazine Films, 1972; *How Fletcher Was Hatched!, A Kiss for a Warthog, The Knobby Boys to the Rescue,* and *Aunt Agatha, There's a Lion under the Couch* were adapted as film strips by Spoken Arts, Inc., in 1985; *Cranberry Halloween, Cranberry Thanksgiving, Cranberry Christmas,* and *Cranberry Mystery* were adapted as film strips by Spoken Arts, Inc., in 1986.

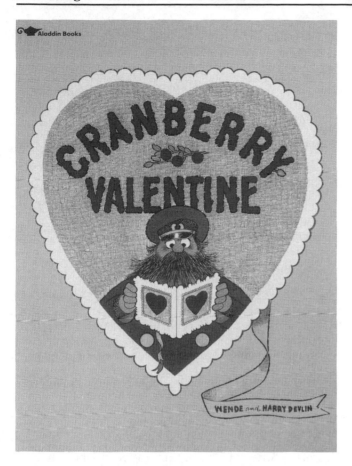

A citizen of Cranberryport is thrilled when he receives a valentine from a secret admirer in this book in Wende and Harry Devlin's Cranberryport series. (Cover illustration by Harry Devlin.)

SIDELIGHTS: Wende Devlin collaborates on children's books with her husband, Harry Devlin. "My husband and I became children's book-oriented," she once told *SATA*, "when we had seven children of our own. We had a built-in sounding board for ideas and I can't think of more worthwhile work than pleasing and developing a child's mind and imagination." The team has won a Special Citation from the New Jersey Institute of Technology for their work in children's literature, and many of their books have been best-sellers.

Particularly popular with children are the Devlins' books set in the town of Cranberryport and featuring a girl named Maggie, her grandmother, the local sewing circle, and Mr. Whiskers. Usually set during a holiday celebration, the Cranberry stories emphasize the value of good friends.

FOR MORE INFORMATION SEE:

PERIODICALS

Elizabeth (NJ) Daily Journal, August 29, 1968.
Library Journal, May 15, 1969; May 15, 1970.
Newark Star Ledger, June 22, 1988.
New York Times, June 19, 1977.
New York Times Book Review, May 9, 1965; January 4, 1970.*

DEVLIN, Harry 1918-

PERSONAL: Born March 22, 1918, in Jersey City, NJ; son of Harry George (a general manager) and Amelia (Crawford) Devlin; married Dorothy Wende (an artist and writer), August 30, 1941; children: Harry Noel, Wende Elizabeth (Mrs. Geoffrey Gates), Jeffrey Anthony, Alexandra Gail (Mrs. James Eldridge), Brion Phillip, Nicholas Kirk, David Matthew. *Education:* Syracuse University, B.F.A., 1939. *Religion:* Congregationalist.

ADDRESSES: Home and office—443 Hillside Ave., Mountainside, NJ 07092.

CAREER: Artist, 1939—. *Collier's,* New York City, editorial cartoonist, 1945-54; Union College, Cranford, NJ, lecturer in history of fine arts and history of American domestic architecture, 1962-64. Mountainside Public Library, president, 1968-69; New Jersey State Council on the Arts, served as grants chair and vice-chair, 1970-79; Advisory Board on the Arts, Union County, NJ, chair of vocational and technical schools, 1972-75; Morris Museum, Morristown, NJ, trustee, 1980—; member of New Jersey Committee for the Humanities, 1984—; founding member of Rutgers University Advisory Council on Children's Literature. *Exhibitions:* One-person art exhibitions, Morris Museum, 1979, World Headquarters, General Electric, Fairfield, CT, 1980, Union League Club, New York City, 1981, World Headquarters, AT&T, 1986, Schering Plough, 1986, and Jane Voorhees Zimmerli Art Museum, Rutgers State University, New Brunswick, NJ, December 9, 1990-February 24, 1991. Works represented in permanent collections, including the Midlantic Bank, Crum & Foster, First Atlantic Bank, and the Corporate Headquarters of City Federal Savings. *Military service:* U.S. Naval Reserve, 1942-46; served as artist; became lieutenant, Office of Naval Intelligence.

MEMBER: Society of Illustrators (life member), National Cartoonists Society (president, 1956-57), Associated Artists of New Jersey (president, 1984-85), Artists Equity Association (New Jersey), Graphic Artists Guild, Dutch Treat Club.

AWARDS, HONORS: Best in Advertising Cartoon Award, National Cartoonists Society, 1956, 1962, 1963, 1977, and 1978; Special Citation for Husband-Wife Writers of Children's Books, New Jersey Institute of Technology, 1969; New Jersey Teachers of English Award and New Jersey Institute of Technology New Jersey Authors Award, both 1970, for *How Fletcher Was Hatched!;* Award of Excellence, Chicago Book Fair, 1974, for *Old Witch Rescues Halloween;* New Jersey Institute of Technology Award, 1976, for *Tales of Thunder and Lightning;* Arents Award for Art and Literature, Syracuse University, 1977; elected to Hall of Fame in Literature, New Jersey Institute of Technology, 1980; Chairman's Award for the painting "House on High Street," Society of Illustrators, 1981; elected to Advertising Hall of Fame, 1983; D.H.L., Kean College, 1985; inducted into New Jersey Literary Hall of Fame, 1987.

HARRY DEVLIN

WRITINGS:

FOR CHILDREN; SELF-ILLUSTRATED

To Grandfather's House We Go, Parents' Magazine Press, 1967.
The Walloping Window Blind, Van Nostrand, 1968.
What Kind of House Is That?, Parents' Magazine Press, 1969.
Tales of Thunder and Lightning, Parents' Magazine Press, 1975.

WITH WIFE, WENDE DEVLIN; FOR CHILDREN; SELF-ILLUSTRATED

Old Black Witch, Encyclopaedia Britannica Press, 1963.
The Knobby Boys to the Rescue, Parents' Magazine Press, 1965.
Aunt Agatha, There's a Lion under the Couch, Van Nostrand, 1968.
How Fletcher Was Hatched!, Parents' Magazine Press, 1969.
A Kiss for a Warthog, Van Nostrand, 1970.
Old Witch and the Polka Dot Ribbon, Parents' Magazine Press, 1970.
Cranberry Thanksgiving, Parents' Magazine Press, 1971.
Old Witch Rescues Halloween, Parents' Magazine Press, 1973.
Cranberry Christmas, Parents' Magazine Press, 1976.
Cranberry Mystery, Four Winds Press, 1978.
Hang on Hester, Lothrop, 1980.
Cranberry Halloween, Four Winds Press, 1982.
Cranberry Valentine, Macmillan, 1986.
Cranberry Birthday, Macmillan, 1988.
Cranberry Easter, Macmillan, 1990.

Cranberry Summer, Macmillan, 1992.

OTHER

Portraits of American Architecture (adult nonfiction), East View Editions, 1982, published as *Portraits of American Architecture: Monuments to a Romantic Mood, 1830-1900,* David Godine, 1989.

Also author and host of four films entitled "Fare You Well, Old House," 1976, 1979, 1980, and 1981, and of films "Houses of the Hackensack," 1976, and "To Grandfather's House We Go," 1981, all for New Jersey Public Broadcasting Corp.

ADAPTATIONS: Old Black Witch was filmed by Gerald Herman as *The Winter of the Witch,* starring Hermione Gingold, Parents' Magazine Films, 1972; *How Fletcher Was Hatched!, A Kiss for a Warthog, The Knobby Boys to the Rescue,* and *Aunt Agatha, There's a Lion under the Couch* were adapted as film strips by Spoken Arts, Inc., 1985; *Cranberry Halloween, Cranberry Thanksgiving, Cranberry Christmas,* and *Cranberry Mystery* were adapted as film strips by Spoken Arts, Inc., 1986.

SIDELIGHTS: Harry Devlin collaborates on children's books with his wife, Wende Devlin. "Our first book," he once told *SATA,* "sold over a million copies, which beguiled us into the belief that we could write." The team has written more than fifteen books together and earned a Special Citation from the New Jersey Institute of Technology for their work in children's literature. Many of their books have been best-sellers.

Although he had been an artist since 1939, Devlin's career took off just after the Second World War when he became an editorial cartoonist for *Collier's* magazine, a position he held for nine years. His cartoons won him acclaim as a shrewd and clear-headed commentator on the current scene. During this time he also created two short-lived comic strips, *Fullhouse* and *Raggmopp,* the latter comic strip being described by Jerry Robinson in *The Comics* as "stylishly drawn with a tasteful use of white space." Devlin has also done artwork for magazine and newspaper advertising. He has won five awards for his advertising work from the National Cartoonists Society.

Because of his stature as an artist, Devlin was asked to become a member of the New Jersey State Council on the Arts in 1970. "While a member...," he tells *Contemporary Graphic Artists* (*CGA*), "I was able to get funding for the founding of the Rutgers University Collection of Children's Art and Literature, now a thriving entity of the Voorhees Zimmerli Museum of Rutgers University."

Devlin says in *CGA* that the variety of his works has enabled him to have a long artistic career: "As I have survived as an artist and writer, I can say that diversity is the key to survival. I have illustrated magazines, novels, children's books, painted portraits and murals, and was an editorial cartoonist." He says that his collaboration with his wife utilizes the strengths that

A witch's arrival adds excitement to the new home of a boy and his mother in the Devlins' *Old Black Witch*.

each one possesses. "Wende writes more and better than I can," Devlin told *SATA*. "I write only about those things that I think may fascinate and pay no heed to trends or styles."

WORKS CITED:

Contemporary Graphic Artists, Volume 1, Gale, 1986.
Robinson, Jerry, *The Comics: An Illustrated History of Comic Strip Art,* Putnam, 1974.

FOR MORE INFORMATION SEE:

BOOKS

Gauley, Sherrie, *Harry Devlin: Illustrations for Children's Literature, Essay and Annotated Catalogue,* Jane Voorhees Zimmerli Art Museum, 1990.

PERIODICALS

Library Journal, May 15, 1969; May 15, 1970.
New York Times Book Review, May 9, 1965; January 4, 1970.*

*   *   *

DICKENS, Monica (Enid) 1915-1992

OBITUARY NOTICE—See index for *SATA* sketch: Born May 10, 1915, in London, England; died of cancer, December 25, 1992, in Reading, England. Humanitarian, columnist, and author. Dickens, a great-granddaughter of famous British novelist Charles Dickens (*Great Expectations, A Tale of Two Cities*), published over fifty books, many of them humorous novels that cast an eye on upper class British society. As a young woman, she rebelled against her cultured upbringing, refusing to become a debutante and instead going to work as a servant and a cook. Dickens later wrote for a local paper and had a column in *Woman's Own* for twenty years. In 1974, she opened the first American branch of The Samaritans, an organization that counsels the depressed and suicidal. Dickens's first book, *One Pair of Hands,* was a fictionalized account of her life as a domestic. She was also the author of *An Open Book, Enchantment,* and *One of the Family,* among other titles, and wrote several children's books, including *The House at World's End.*

OBITUARIES AND OTHER SOURCES:

BOOKS

The Writers Directory: 1990-1992, St. James Press, 1990.

PERIODICALS

Chicago Tribune, December 30, 1992, section 3, p. 11.
Los Angeles Times, December 28, 1992, p. A22.
New York Times, December 27, 1992, p. L41.
Times (London), December 28, 1992, p. 13.
Washington Post, December 28, 1992, p. B6.

*   *   *

DILLON, Eilis 1920-

PERSONAL: Given name is pronounced El-*eesh;* born March 7, 1920, in Galway, Ireland; daughter of Thomas (a university professor) and Geraldine (Plunkett) Dillon; married Cormac O'Cuilleanain (a university professor), March 28, 1940 (died, 1970); married Vivian Mercier (a professor and critic), April 5, 1974 (died, 1989); children: (first marriage) Eilean, Maire (died, 1990), Cormac. *Education:* Educated in Ireland. *Politics:* Irish Nationalist. *Religion:* Roman Catholic. *Hobbies and other interests:* Music, travel, and the theatre.

ADDRESSES: Home—7 Templemore Ave., Rathgar, Dublin 6, Ireland. *Agent*—Georges Borchardt, Inc., 136 East 57th St., New York, NY 10022; and David Bolt Associates, 12 Heath Dr., Send, Surrey, GU23 7EP England.

CAREER: Writer. Lecturer on creative writing, Trinity College, Dublin University, 1971-72, and University College, Dublin, 1988. Lecturer at American universities and colleges on three tours, speaking on writing for children and Anglo-Irish literature, especially poetry.

MEMBER: Societa Dante Alighieri (Cork), Royal Society of Literature (fellow), Irish Writers Center (executive boardmember), Irish Writers Union (chair), Irish Children's Book Trust (chair), Irish Copyright Collection Agency (secretary).

AWARDS, HONORS: Children's Spring Book Festival Honorable Mention citations, *New York Herald Tribune,* 1960, for *The Singing Cave,* 1964, for *The Coriander,* and 1970, for *A Herd of Deer;* German Juvenile Book Prize Honor List citation, 1968, for *A Family of Foxes;* Notable Book citation, American Library Association, and Lewis Carroll Shelf Award, both 1970, for *A Herd of Deer;* Irish Book of the Year Award, 1991, for *The Island of Ghosts;* D.Litt., National University of Ireland, 1992; *Children of Bach* was named to the New York Public Library list of titles for teenage readers, 1993.

WRITINGS:

JUVENILE FICTION

Midsummer Magic, illustrated by Stuart Tresilian, Macmillan, 1949.
The Lost Island, illustrated by Richard Kennedy, Faber & Faber, 1952, Funk, 1954.
The San Sebastian, illustrated by Kennedy, Faber & Faber, 1953, Funk, 1954.
The House on the Shore, illustrated by Kennedy, Faber & Faber, 1955, Funk, 1956.
The Wild Little House, illustrated by V. H. Drummond, Faber & Faber, 1955.
The Island of Horses, illustrated by Kennedy, Faber & Faber, 1956, Funk, 1957.
Plover Hill, illustrated by Prudence Seward, Hamish Hamilton, 1957.
Aunt Bedelia's Cats, illustrated by Christopher Brooker, Hamish Hamilton, 1958.
The Singing Cave, illustrated by Kennedy, Faber & Faber, 1959, Funk, 1960.
The Fort of Gold, illustrated by Kennedy, Faber & Faber, 1961, Funk, 1962.

EILIS DILLON

King Big-Ears, illustrated by Kveta Vanecek, Faber & Faber, 1961, Norton, 1963.
A Pony and a Trap, illustrated by Monica Braisier-Creagh, Hamish Hamilton, 1962.
The Cats' Opera (also see below), illustrated by Vanecek, Faber & Faber, 1962, Bobbs-Merrill, 1963.
The Coriander, illustrated by Kennedy, Faber & Faber, 1963, illustrated by Vic Donahue, Funk, 1964.
A Family of Foxes, illustrated by Kennedy, Faber & Faber, 1964, Funk, 1965.
The Sea Wall, illustrated by Kennedy, Farrar, Straus, 1965.
The Lion Cub, illustrated by Kennedy, Hamish Hamilton, 1966, Duell, Sloan & Pearce, 1967.
The Road to Dunmore (also see below), illustrated by Kennedy, Faber & Faber, 1966.
The Key (also see below), illustrated by Kennedy, Faber & Faber, 1967.
The Cruise of the Santa Maria, illustrated by Kennedy, Funk, 1967, F. M. O'Brien, 1991.
Two Stories: The Road to Dunmore [and] *The Key,* illustrated by Kennedy, Meredith, 1967.
The Seals, illustrated by Kennedy, Faber & Faber, 1968, Funk, 1969.
Under the Orange Grove, illustrated by Kennedy, Faber & Faber, 1968, Meredith, 1969.
A Herd of Deer, illustrated by Kennedy, Faber & Faber, 1969, Funk, 1970.
The Wise Man on the Mountain, illustrated by Gaynor Chapman, Hamish Hamilton, 1969, Atheneum, 1970.
The Voyage of Mael Duin, illustrated by Alan Howard, Faber & Faber, 1969.

The King's Room, illustrated by Kennedy, Hamish Hamilton, 1970.

The Five Hundred, illustrated by Gareth Floyd, Hamish Hamilton, 1972, F. M. O'Brien, 1991.

The Shadow of Vesuvius, Thomas Nelson, 1978.

Down in the World, illustrated by Kennedy, Hodder & Stoughton, 1983.

The Horse Fancier, Macmillan, 1985.

The Seekers, Macmillan, 1986.

The Island of Ghosts, Macmillan, 1989.

Children of Bach, Macmillan, 1992.

ADULT FICTION

Death at Crane's Court (mystery novel), Faber & Faber, 1953, Walker & Co., 1963.

Sent to His Account (mystery novel), Faber & Faber, 1954, Walker & Co., 1969.

Death in the Quadrangle (mystery novel), Faber & Faber, 1956, Walker & Co., 1968.

The Bitter Glass, Faber & Faber, 1958, Appleton-Century-Crofts, 1959.

The Head of the Family, Faber & Faber, 1960.

Bold John Henebry, Faber & Faber, 1965.

Across the Bitter Sea, Simon & Schuster, 1973.

Blood Relations, Simon & Schuster, 1977.

Wild Geese, Simon & Schuster, 1980.

Citizen Burke, Hodder & Stoughton, 1984.

The Interloper, Hodder & Stoughton, 1987.

PLAYS

Manna, produced on Radio Eireann, Dublin, Ireland, 1962.

A Page of History, produced in Dublin at the Abbey Theatre, 1966.

The Cats' Opera (for children; adapted from novel of the same title), produced at the Abbey Theatre, 1981.

IN GAELIC

An Choill bheo (title means "The Living Forest"), Oifig an tSolathair (Government Publications Sale Office), 1948.

Oscar agus an Coiste se nEasog (title means "Oscar and the Six-Weasel Coach"), Oifig an tSolathair, 1952.

Ceol na Coille (title means "The Song of the Forest"), Oifig an tSolathair, 1955.

OTHER

(Editor) *The Hamish Hamilton Book of Wise Animals,* Hamish Hamilton, 1973.

Living in Imperial Rome, Faber & Faber, 1974, Thomas Nelson, 1975, published as *Rome under the Emperors,* Thomas Nelson, 1976.

Inside Ireland (travel), with photographs by Tom Kennedy, Hodder & Stoughton, 1982, Beaufort Books, 1984.

(Author of introduction) Pat Donion, editor, *The Lucky Bag: Classic Irish Children's Stories,* F. M. O'Brien, 1984.

Dillon's books have been translated into French, German, Dutch, Swedish, Czech, Polish, Hebrew, and Norwegian.

WORK IN PROGRESS: A new novel.

SIDELIGHTS: Eilis Dillon "is simply a good writer," a critic for the *Times Literary Supplement* states, "loving and understanding people, and concerned to tell stories that are as exciting as adventure stories should be but in which the events are tied firmly to human possibility." Dillon, who speaks Gaelic, English, French, and Italian, most often sets her adventure stories on the Irish seacoast and writes of the fishermen and farmers who make that region their home. In *Use of English,* Winifred Whitehead emphasizes the sense of community that Dillon creates in her novels: "Her books are remarkable for their distinctive recreation of rural Ireland; the men living close to the land or sea, as farmworkers or fishermen; the women working equally hard in their small houses, caring for their menfolk and their children; and the children themselves, seen essentially as a part of the community with their own place in it and their own chores to carry out at home, having only so much liberty to range the countryside, with its rich wildlife and its possibilities of adventure."

Dillon once explained how she learned about her subject: "My father was professor of chemistry at a university. We lived in a village on the sea coast a few miles west of Galway, where the common language of the people was Irish. From visiting our neighbors, from going to the village school, and mainly from my early knowledge of the Irish language and the old Irish songs, I came gradually to know the mind of these people. Later I spent summers in the Aran Islands and also in the remote parts of Connemara where we used to camp in tents. My school was the Ursuline Convent in Sligo, where William Butler Yeats lived as a boy. It is beautiful country, dominated by two mountains, Benbulben and Knocknarea, whose names are associated with the oldest of the Irish folk tales.

"I never remember a time when I did not want to write. I composed my first story at the age of seven, about a mouse called Harry who got into bad company, committed murder and was hanged. I would not choose such a subject for a children's book now."

Dillon was not fond of Sligo, and she left the school after her first year. She then went to live with her grandparents and attended an Irish-speaking school. She kept busy studying literary classics with her grandfather and attending cello lessons, but she was often alone and relished the time she had to herself. She began to write poetry and at sixteen saw her work published under a pseudonym in a small magazine.

After a year away, Dillon returned to Sligo, where a teacher suggested she try her hand at writing novels. Dillon studied literary theory and found that the prefaces to many classics contained helpful guidelines. She worked at this, "practising every day as I would on a musical instrument," she wrote in the *Contemporary Authors Autobiography Series* (*CAAS*). Her first successful work was written in Irish, the language she had

Finding a Viking tomb in a seaside cave is just the beginning of a boy's adventures in western Ireland in Dillon's novel. (Cover illustration by Carol Betera.)

learned at home and as manager of an Irish language school owned by a friend of her father.

Recalling that effort, Dillon related, "I began to write in Irish, a children's book—not about mice behind the walls but rabbits underground. I used the beautiful old script that was still standard in Ireland. It was all handwritten, of course, since typewriters with that script were rare. The story ran to about 30,000 words and was well-plotted. I sent it to the Government Publications Sale Office, which had a program of publishing as well as distributing official documents. It was accepted at once. By the time I was notified of this, I was one-third the way through the next one."

Dillon added that breaking into print was easy for her, stating, "Publishing was almost an unknown business in Ireland at that time. One or two houses existed, mainly for producing school texts, and occasionally they published a novel of guaranteed respectability. But England, always a great publishing country, was frantically looking for material after the long years of the war when no one had the time or inclination to write. I decided to make one attempt and to stand or fall by that.... I had written a very old-fashioned children's book about a magic loaf of bread that gave animals the power of speech. The river figured in it, and the burned out castle on the opposite bank, and the lovely house that we had left so long ago. Macmillan in London accepted it and published it with black and white drawings by an artist who knew how to give character to animals. Then Macmillan decided against publishing children's books and handed me on to Faber and Faber, who had always had Irish writers on their list."

During her collaboration with Faber and Faber, Dillon produced the award-winning *A Herd of Deer,* which concerns the efforts of a wealthy Argentinian to raise a herd of imported deer in Ireland. The foreigner's ignorance of Irish ways offends his neighbors, who steal some of the herd. The bitter feelings that arise soon escalate into violence; when teenager Peter Regan attempts to mediate the crisis, he finds himself caught in the middle of an increasingly frightening situation.

Critics found Dillon's handling of the characters to be the novel's strength. Reviewing *A Herd of Deer* in *Children's Book News,* D. Huddy asserted, "Miss Dillon brilliantly conveys the men who are a mass of superstitions and contradictions." And Catherine Storr, writing in *New Statesman,* declared that *A Herd of Deer* is "a beautifully paced book which ... is memorable for the appreciation of every human relationship it touches on with surety and warmth."

Dillon's recent work includes *The Seekers,* which follows an Englishman's pursuit of romance across the Atlantic to the Pilgrim settlement at Plymouth and his return to his homeland with his bride, and *Children of Bach.* That book describes the effects of the Holocaust on a group of Hungarian refugees. *Children of Bach* chronicles the adventures of a family of Jewish children and their aunt who flee to Italy to escape German soldiers. The youngsters, whose parents disappeared during a Nazi round-up, must travel across dangerous territory while hidden in a moving van. Despite the hardships, the children still manage to devote time to their great love—classical music—which sustains them on the journey. Joyce Adams Burner, reviewing *Children of Bach* in *School Library Journal,* was impressed with Dillon's attention to detail, judging that the author "shows thorough research and neatly integrates background into the story."

In 1991, Dillon became the first author to receive the Irish Book of the Year award, presented to her for *The Island of Ghosts.* The honor was especially pleasing to her, considering the way the Irish feel about awards. Dillon noted in *CAAS:* "The Irish make sure that no one will become conceited and they slap down any tendency in that direction unhesitatingly. I have a great many admirers there, but I have never been honored in any way.... Still, the Irish do love their writers, though one has an impression that they feel, as [Anton] Chekhov said, that a country which nurtures writers is like a farmer who owns a granary and breeds rats." Even if that feeling does exist, Dillon once admitted, "Coming back to live permanently in Ireland has been enormously stimulating. The company and conversation are so good that I feel my life as a writer has been restarted."

WORKS CITED:

Burner, Joyce Adams, review of *Children of Bach, School Library Journal,* December, 1992, p. 133.
Dillon, Eilis, *Contemporary Authors Autobiography Series,* Volume 3, Gale, 1986, pp. 49-67.
Huddy, D., "Fiction: *A Herd of Deer,*" *Children's Book News,* May-June, 1970, p. 130.
"The Passion and the Glory," *Times Literary Supplement,* March 1, 1974, p. 201.
Storr, Catherine, "Dream Meanings," *New Statesman,* May 15, 1970, p. 704.
Whitehead, Winifred, "Eilis Dillon and the Sense of Community," *Use of English,* spring, 1979, pp. 58-62.

FOR MORE INFORMATION SEE:

BOOKS

Books for Children, 1900-1965, American Library Association, 1966.
Contemporary Literary Criticism, Volume 17, Gale, 1981, pp. 92-102.
Eyre, Frank, *British Children's Books in the Twentieth Century,* Longman, 1971.
Fisher, Margery, *Intent upon Reading: A Critical Appraisal of Modern Fiction for Children,* Hodder & Stoughton, 1961.
Larrick, Nancy, *A Parents' Guide to Children's Reading,* 3rd edition, Doubleday, 1969.

PERIODICALS

Best Sellers, October 1, 1967.
Books and Bookmen, December, 1967; August, 1968; March, 1970; May, 1970.
Book World, December 31, 1967.
Chicago Tribune, November 12, 1960.
Commonweal, August 18, 1978.
Creation, August, 1962.
Listener, November 16, 1967; March 14, 1974.
New Statesman, November 8, 1963; May 15, 1970.
New York Herald Tribune Book Review, June 17, 1956; November 17, 1957.
New York Times Book Review, November 17, 1957; October 4, 1959; April 27, 1969.
Punch, December 19, 1969.
Saturday Review, November 13, 1954.
Spectator, July 8, 1955.
Times Literary Supplement, November 27, 1953; December 9, 1965; May 25, 1967; July 11, 1975; April 7, 1978; November 19, 1987, p. 1248.
Washington Post Book World, January 4, 1981, p. 6.*

DIXON, Rachel 1952-

PERSONAL: Born July 31, 1952, in Bristol, England; daughter of Denzil Nathaniel (a headmaster) and Amy (a social worker; maiden name, Chanter) Underwood; married Anthony Michael John Dixon (died April, 1986); married Martin James Tennant (a music technology consultant), November 3, 1989; children: Emily Jane Tennant. *Education:* Westminster College of Education, Oxford, B.Ed., 1974.

ADDRESSES: Home and office—30 Templar Rd., Oxford OX2 8LT, England. *Agent*—A. P. Watt, Literary Agents, 20 John St., London, WC1N 2DR, England.

CAREER: Bishop Kirk Middle School, Oxford, England, teacher, 1974-82; children's writer, 1986—. Oxford Operatic Society, member, 1989—.

WRITINGS:

Black Nest, Puffin, 1990.
The Demon Piano, illustrated by Jon Riley, Doubleday, 1991.
The Fox of Skelland, illustrated by Neil Reed, Puffin, 1991.
The Marshmallow Experiment (first book in the "Jo and Gemma" series), illustrated by J. Riley, Puffin, 1992.
Max and the Fire Crystals (second book in the "Jo and Gemma" series), Puffin, 1992.

RACHEL DIXON

The Witch's Ring, illustrated by Doffy Weir, Double-day, 1992.
The Genie of the Lamppost, illustrated by D. Weir, Doubleday, 1993.

WORK IN PROGRESS: A book of poems for children.

SIDELIGHTS: A former schoolteacher in Oxford, England, Rachel Dixon has turned to writing for children, producing books that feature such subjects as wizardry and the supernatural. In *The Demon Piano,* for instance, she relates the story of Bella, a young girl who moves in with her grandmother and later finds herself rooming with a haunted piano, which forces its owners to play no matter how fatigued they become. In *The Witch's Ring,* Dixon delves into witchcraft. In the narrative Amy, a main character, finds herself transported many miles from her garden, where she had been deceived into placing a magic ring on her finger. She is imprisoned by an old, disagreeable witch and must save herself. "Children will love all the revolting recipes, spooky spells and ghastly goings-on" in the work, decided a reviewer for the London *Weekend Telegraph.*

Dixon told *SATA:* "I started 'observing' when I was very young, collecting powerful visual images of the world around me. There was always a strong imaginary current, running parallel to my real life. I would spend hours daydreaming either during the day or in bed on light summer evenings, and I played many wonderful 'let's pretend' games with my best friend Helen.

"Later, when I tried to put what I saw and imagined into words, my mother would say, 'write it down,' and, when I was older, I was further encouraged by my English teacher at secondary school. I am afraid I daydreamed my way through numerous other school subjects, which, unless they had a particularly stimulating teacher, held little interest for me. My English teacher noticed this and suggested that I was spending too much time on essay writing, perhaps to the detriment of my other work. He continued to give me great support, however, and I was delighted to have two short stories printed in the national teenage magazine *Elizabethan.*

"On leaving school I was accepted at Westminster College of Education, Oxford, to study English and drama. The drama course was like a dream come true, with plenty of opportunities for make-believe. I also bought a guitar and wrote numerous songs, some funny, but most sad. In 1974 I obtained my B.Ed. degree in drama. I married Tony Dixon, a fellow student, and we both took up teaching posts in Oxford. I taught music and general subjects at a middle school, where I stayed until the birth of my daughter, Emily, in 1982.

"Although I had kept up my writing as a hobby ever since school, it wasn't until the sudden death of Tony in 1986 that I devoted a serious amount of time to it. I bought a word processor, which helped me to be much more critical of my work, and wrote morning and night, when I was not caring for my daughter. I completed my

A mysterious piano seems to control its owner in this suspenseful work by Dixon. (Cover illustration by Jon Riley.)

first children's novel, *Black Nest,* in 1987 and had it accepted for publication.

"I married my second husband, Martin Tennant, in November of 1989. He moved to Oxford to live with my daughter and me. As a family we all enjoy music as a hobby. Martin and I are members of the Oxford Operatic Society and like both the stage productions and singing duets together in smaller concerts. We all play the piano; I play the violin, Martin the guitar, and Emily the clarinet. We also have a Clavinova and various small percussion instruments.

"We like to spend time in our garden, where we have two ponds. The larger pond, which is three meters in diameter, is left fairly wild, with lots of reeds, marigolds, irises, and lilies, and is inhabited by frogs, newts, and numerous other small creatures. I am delighted that the frogs have read the storybooks and like to sit on lily pads. My family also enjoys swimming and country walks.

"I now work during the day, when my daughter is at school. Evenings are normally reserved for family activities."

WORKS CITED:

"Computerised Witchcraft," *Weekend Telegraph* (London), May 30, 1992.

FOR MORE INFORMATION SEE:

PERIODICALS

Books for Keeps, November, 1990, p. 11.
Junior Bookshelf, June, 1991, pp. 110-11; October, 1991, p. 212.

*   *   *

DOLAN, Sean J. 1958-

PERSONAL: Born April 1, 1958, in Schenectady, NY; son of John J. (a teacher) and Frances M. (a nurse; maiden name, Vaillancourt) Dolan; married Anne B. Bianchi (an attorney), October 1, 1988; children: Brian John. *Education:* State University of New York College at Oswego, B.A., 1980. *Politics:* Democrat. *Religion:* Catholic.

ADDRESSES: Home—Mt. Kisco, NY. *Office*—Chelsea House, 95 Madison Ave., New York, NY 10549.

CAREER: Chelsea House, New York City, senior editor, 1986—.

WRITINGS:

Chiang Kai-shek, Chelsea House, 1989.
Robert F. Kennedy, Chelsea House, 1989.
Christopher Columbus: The Intrepid Mariner, Columbine, 1990.
Lewis and Clark, Chelsea House, 1990.
Daniel Boone, Chelsea House, 1990.
Matthew Henson, Chelsea House, 1991.
Junipero Serra, Chelsea House, 1991.
West Germany: On the Road to Reunification, Chelsea House, 1991.
James Beckwourth, Chelsea House, 1992.
The Polish Americans, Chelsea House, 1992.
Roald Amundsen, Chelsea House, 1992.
Gabriel Garcia Marquez, Chelsea House, 1993.
The Irish-American Experience, Millbrook Press, 1993.
Ray Charles, Chelsea House, 1993.
Thurgood Marshall, Millbrook Press, 1993.
W. E. B. DuBois, Millbrook Press, 1993.
Earvin "Magic" Johnson, Chelsea House, 1993.
Michael Jordan, Chelsea House, 1994.

FOR MORE INFORMATION SEE:

PERIODICALS

School Library Journal, November, 1988, p. 136; February, 1992, pp. 112 and 114.
Voice of Youth Advocates, February, 1989, p. 300; June, 1991, p. 121; February, 1992, p. 391.

DOOLEY, Norah 1953-

PERSONAL: Born July 17, 1953, in New York, NY; daughter of Raymond (a ship's master and pilot) and Adelaide (a registered nurse; maiden name, DiBrizzi) Dooley; married Robert Fairchild (a master electrician), February 21, 1981; children: Sira, Julia, Ferron, Rosalie (all daughters). *Education:* School of the Museum of Fine Arts, B.F.A., 1976; Lesley College, M.Ed., 1990. *Religion:* Roman Catholic.

ADDRESSES: Home—Royalston, MA.

CAREER: Kaji Aso Studio (an art gallery and school), Boston, MA, arts administrator, music director, and instructor, 1974-82; writer and storyteller, 1988—. Worked variously as a burglar alarm operator, paste-up/graphic artist, production manager for a printing firm, manager of a print shop, bicycle courier, bookkeeper, booking manager for a classical trio, and a farming apprentice. Active in her Cambridge, MA, neighborhood, where she helped organize block parties, planted gardens, and conducted art projects for children.

AWARDS, HONORS: Grants from the Cambridge Arts Council, 1984, 1985, and 1991.

WRITINGS:

Everybody Cooks Rice (picture book), illustrated by Peter J. Thornton, Carolrhoda, 1991.

NORAH DOOLEY

WORK IN PROGRESS: That's Just Darryl, an urban folktale; *Guani,* a Puerto Rican folktale; *Bouquerin,* a Honduran folktale; and *A Season with Vivaldi,* a chapter book.

SIDELIGHTS: Norah Dooley told *SATA:* "After my first two children were born I became very involved in my neighborhood, an inner-city, racially and ethnically diverse part of Cambridge, Massachusetts. The neighbors on my block, many of whom appear in my book *Everybody Cooks Rice,* taught me a lot about how to be a good neighbor as well as sharing their recipes with me. I have been storytelling for two years now in and around Cambridge and in my new home in the country. I work on an organic farm as the farming apprentice. Our neighbors from the city come to visit often and the farm supplies some of them with vegetables. My next writing projects will reflect my new understanding of stewardship of the land and how this affects the entire planetary ecology."

*   *   *

Dr. A
See ASIMOV, Isaac

*   *   *

DRACUP, Angela 1943-
(Caroline Sibson)

PERSONAL: Born January 31, 1943, in Bradford, Yorkshire, England; daughter of George (a gown manufacturer) and Muriel (a homemaker; maiden name, Reid) Sibson; married Frank Dracup, 1965; children: Anna. *Education:* University of Sheffield, B.A. (with honours), 1964; University of Manchester, educational psychology diploma, 1968. *Politics:* "Leftish—Liberal Democrat." *Religion:* Church of England. *Hobbies and other interests:* Reading, music, drama, fine wines, fast cars.

ADDRESSES: Home—6 Lancaster Rd., Harrogate, North Yorkshire HG2 0EZ, England. *Office*—Education Section, County Hall, Northallerton, Yorkshire DL7 8AE, England. *Agent*—Jane Conway-Gordon, 1 Old Compton St., London W1V 5PH, England.

CAREER: Educational psychologist in Bradford, England, 1964-72, in Leeds, England, 1975-78, and in North Yorkshire, England, 1981—. Senior lecturer at the College of Ripon and York St. John, 1975-78.

MEMBER: British Psychological Society, Authors Society, Romantic Novelists Association, Association of Educational Psychologists, National Canine Defence League.

AWARDS, HONORS: The Placing was shortlisted for the Carnegie Medal and highly commended for the Lancashire Children's Book Prize.

WRITINGS:

(Under pseudonym Carolyn Sibson) *The Chosen One,* Hale, 1988.
(Under pseudonym Carolyn Sibson) *Birds of a Feather,* Hale, 1990.
The Placing, Gollancz, 1991.
The Split, Gollancz, 1993.

"RAINBOW ROMANCE" SERIES

An Independent Spirit, Hale, 1984.
Bavarian Overture, Hale, 1986.
A Tender Ambition, Hale, 1986.
A Man to Trust, Hale, 1987.
Dark Impulse, Hale, 1987.
Star Attraction, Hale, 1988.
Dearest Pretender, Hale, 1989.
Venetian Captive, Hale, 1989.

WORK IN PROGRESS: Let Me Speak, a young adult novel; *The Horse That Danced,* a young adult novel; *Roses for Mozart,* a young adult novel; *Lion on the Loose,* a romantic novel.

SIDELIGHTS: Angela Dracup told *SATA:* "Writing fiction crept up on me. I was in my late thirties before I made the discovery that writing stories was the ideal way to relax after spending the day getting to grips with the problems of children with special educational needs. The first story started out as something short and snappy intended for a women's magazine. Over the course of a summer it grew, eventually ending up as a novel which was accepted by a British publisher to include a newly launched romance series. I fell in love

ANGELA DRACUP

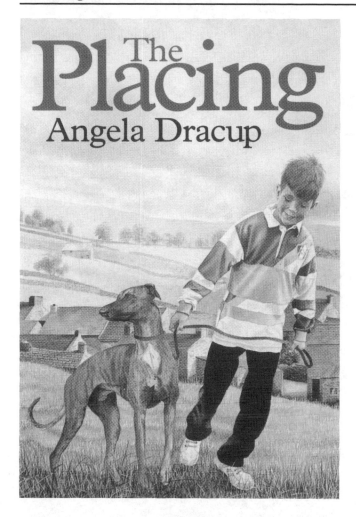

The Placing
Angela Dracup

A boy sent to a succession of foster families searches for a loving home in Dracup's first novel for children. (Cover illustration by Julie Dodd.)

instantly with the notion of being a 'romance novelist' and seven further novels with a love theme followed.

"By this time I'd wrenched myself from my beloved fountain pen and Italic script to a word processor—and was completely hooked on producing books. I felt a need to move on from romance and two mainstream adult novels followed. Then the idea came to me of the story of a young boy which I would tell in the first person. Walking in the woods with my dog later the simple, raw idea developed and expanded rapidly. I started writing on New Year's Day and finished *The Placing* the following July.

"My ideas start with a central character and a sketchy plot. I go straight to the word processor and get something down before I even start to think about researching or a synopsis. The process of writing a novel is both exhilarating and scary—sometimes I get wonderful surprises when I 'discover' something about my characters or events in the plot. And then there are days when everything I write seems about as exciting as a bucket of chicken livers! That's the time to grit the teeth and keep on going at any price, and that would be my only advice to aspiring authors: get out your pen, switch on the word processor and *produce words*. Writing is like sculpting, you've got to throw some clay on the board before you can start the shaping and moulding."

* * *

du BOIS, William (Sherman) Pene 1916-1993

OBITUARY NOTICE—See index for *SATA* sketch: Born May 9, 1916, in Nutley, NJ; died following a stroke, February 5, 1993, in Nice, France. Illustrator, editor, and author. Du Bois, an award-winning author and illustrator of children's books, was known for his whimsical plotlines and imaginative drawings. Du Bois published his first children's book, *The Great Geppy*, at age nineteen, and his success convinced him to make children's literature his life's work. In 1948 he received the Newbery Medal for *The Twenty-One Balloons*, which recounts the remarkable travel adventures of a retired professor. Two other works, *Bear Party* and *Lion*, were named Caldecott honor books. In World War II du Bois edited and illustrated *Yank* and other military publications, and he later served as a founding editor of the *Paris Review*. Du Bois also illustrated *The Rabbit's Umbrella* and *The Owl and the Pussycat*, and he wrote and illustrated *Otto at Sea*, *Bear Circus*, and *Porko von Popbutton*, among other works.

OBITUARIES AND OTHER SOURCES:

BOOKS

The Writers Directory: 1990-1992, St. James Press, 1990.

PERIODICALS

Chicago Tribune, February 8, 1993, section 4, page 8.
New York Times, February, 1993.
School Library Journal, March, 1993, p. 108.

E

EBLE, Diane 1956-
(Cynthia Spence)

PERSONAL: Surname pronounced "*ebb*-lee"; born December 25, 1956, in Bridgeport, CT; daughter of William John (a plumber) and Marie Catherine (a homemaker; maiden name, Boos) Filakovsky; married Gene M. Eble (a sales manager), May 31, 1980; children: David. *Education:* University of Connecticut, B.A., 1978. *Religion:* Christian (Evangelical Presbyterian).

ADDRESSES: Home—0S758 Madison St., Winfield, IL 60190. *Agent*—Curtis Bruce Agency, P.O. Box 967, Plover, WI 54467.

CAREER: InterVarsity Press, Downers Grove, IL, associate producer, campus liaison, and bookclub manager, 1978-85; *Campus Life,* Carol Stream, IL, associate editor, 1985-90, contributing editor, 1990—; *Marriage Partnership,* writer and special projects editor, 1987—; freelance writer, 1990—.

MEMBER: Formerly Employed Mothers At the Leading Edge (F.E.M.A.L.E.).

AWARDS, HONORS: EPA Higher Goals award, second place, 1986, for interviewing; fourth place, 1988, for interview article; third place, general articles category, 1990, (under name Cynthia Spence) for "Men in Search of Work."

WRITINGS:

I.D., Tyndale House, 1987, revised and reissued as *Personal Best,* Zondervan, 1991.
Campus Life Guide to Dating, Zondervan, 1990.
(With Chris Lutes and Kris Bearss) *Welcome to High School,* Zondervan, 1991.
Discover Your Best Possible Future, Zondervan, 1993.

Also author of column "Creative Ways to Work" for F.E.M.A.L.E. newsletter. Contributor to periodicals, including *Today's Christian Woman* and *Christianity Today.*

DIANE EBLE

WORK IN PROGRESS: "So, What Do You Do for a Living?": Coping Strategies for Men in Search of Work and Those Who Love Them, for Zondervan, expected 1994; *Life Designs for Women,* for Zondervan, expected 1994.

SIDELIGHTS: Diane Eble told *SATA:* "I have wanted to be a writer since I can remember. I always kept diaries and journals (though sadly, everything before high school is now lost) and read voraciously. In college I decided I wanted to go into publishing. I majored in English and took courses in publishing at the University of Connecticut. When I got out of college, I began working for a small religious publisher, InterVarsity

Press, writing and editing scripts for the radio show they produced at that time. It was great fun. When it ended I started writing copy for ads, brochures, the bookclub flyer, the campus communications and the like. All during that time I kept journaling, kept writing for myself, and began to think of myself as a writer, though I wasn't published yet.

"Then in 1985 someone I worked with told me that *Campus Life* magazine was looking for a female editor. My friend urged me to apply. At the time I wasn't looking for another job, but I couldn't get it out of my mind that I should check this out. After months went by, I finally said, 'OK, if it's still available, I'll check it out.' It was still open, I checked it out, and was hired. And that's really how I began to realize my dream of becoming a writer, because *Campus Life* was a great place to learn how to write: much of the magazine is staff-written, and over the years I was able to get the training and experience I needed to hone my skills.

"When I began my family in 1990, I had achieved what I set out to do: become good enough that I could make a living at freelance writing. Now I have three books published, with four more on the way, and over 125 articles published in magazines like *Marriage Partnership, Campus Life, Christianity Today, Today's Christian Woman, Discipleship Journal,* and others. I am also writing a regular column for the F.E.M.A.L.E. Forum newsletter as well as editing two columns for *Campus Life* and *Marriage Partnership.*

"All this keeps me pretty busy—too busy at times! Being a freelance writer takes a lot of self-discipline, and it's not for everyone. But for someone who must write, who feels she has something to say to people of all ages, it's a wonderful life. It also allows me to spend the kind of time with my family I want to. Presently I have a son who is almost two. I wouldn't want to miss his growing up years, and although I'm committed to my career and work the equivalent of twenty to twenty-four hours a week, much of it is worked around my family's schedule. That's another good thing about freelance writing— you can be committed and productive at it in less than forty hours a week.

"At this point, most of my writing has a journalistic bent. I love to interview people because I learn so much, and so I have written some books 'with' others who are experts at something. I like helping other people tell their unique stories, and I like helping people who have found solutions to problems many people struggle with to communicate what they've learned to a wider audience. My dream is someday to write fiction as well as nonfiction. I've had an idea for a 'coming of age' type novel for years now."

*   *   *

ESTRADA, Pau 1961-

PERSONAL: Born November 12, 1961, in Barcelona, Spain; son of David (a teacher) and Frances (a teacher; maiden name, Luttikhuizen) Estrada. *Education:* At-tended American College of Barcelona, 1979-81; University of Barcelona, B.A., 1984; Rhode Island School of Design, M.A.E., 1988. *Hobbies and other interests:* Flamenco and classical guitar, hiking, travel, and cinema.

ADDRESSES: Office—Travessera de Dalt 56, 08024 Barcelona, Spain.

CAREER: Illustrator. Teacher of Spanish literature, English, and drama, 1985-92. Radio translator and commentator on Catalan Public Radio, Barcelona, 1991. Set designer and actor at University of Barcelona and Brown University. Performer with flamenco group *ConFuego,* Newport, RI, 1988. *Exhibitions:* Sol Koffler Gallery, Providence, RI, 1987; LIBER '87, Madrid, Spain, 1987; Rhode Island School of Design, 1988; Bologna Children's Book Fair, 1990.

AWARDS, HONORS: Fulbright/La Caiza scholarship for graduate studies in the United States, 1986-88.

ILLUSTRATOR:

La cuca Quica, La Galera, 1986.
Aixo son rates comptades, La Galera, 1986.
Canguelis Pocapor, La Galera, 1986.
Qui canta sos mals espanta, Abadia de Montserrat, 1989.
Boira a les butxaques, La Galera, 1989.
Aquest era en Hirbel, La Galera, 1989.
Marion Markham, *The Birthday Party Mystery,* Houghton, 1989.
Papirot, Onda, 1990.

PAU ESTRADA

Si aixo es una escola jo soc un tigre, La Galera, 1990.

Marion Markham, *The April Fool's Day Mystery,* Houghton, 1991.

El raton y su hijo, Siruela, 1991.

L'Olimpisme i els seus jocs, Generalitat de Catalunya, 1992.

Joan Knight, *Opal in the Closet,* Picture Book Studio, 1992.

Addie Lacoe, *Just Not the Same,* Houghton, 1992.

La caputeta vermilla (title means "Little Red Riding Hood"), La Galera, 1993.

Also illustrator of textbooks.

SIDELIGHTS: Pau Estrada writes: "My mother, a writer of educational textbooks, had me illustrate some of her books when I was barely a teenager. We worked together for several years and eventually I woke up to find myself an illustrator in my own right. I had illustrated more than a dozen books when I walked into my first formal art class at Rhode Island School of Design (RISD).

"My interest in illustration comes from a desire to do figurative art combined with a fondness for story telling. I like to think of the picture book as an art object in itself combining a number of experiences both simultaneous and chronological: the texture of the paper, the sequence of the layout, the interplay between the story narrated through the text and the visual imagery. Ideally, I try to approach each book as an independent project, which sometimes leads to surprising differences in style from one book to the next. That is why my goal

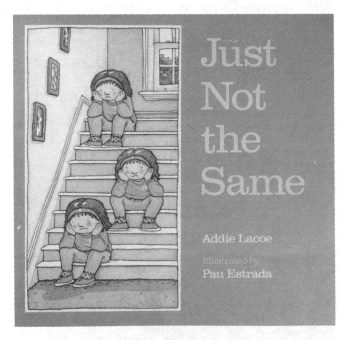

Three selfish sisters, humorously illustrated by Estrada, learn that sharing can be more fun than fighting, especially when they all want the same thing—a new puppy. (From *Just Not the Same,* written by Addie Lacoe.)

is to become both the author and illustrator of my own stories.

"Like most European boys, I grew up reading not picture books but comic books and, in particular, *The Adventures of Tintin.* My admiration for Herge continues to this day. *Tintin* is unique in quality, creation of characters, design, story telling, scope of issues, and ultimately endearment with the audience. To me, Herge is the Walt Disney of comic books: creating a new genre and at the same time becoming the ultimate master at it.

"Being more of a sketcher than a draftsman, I find comic books and animation too laborious as mediums. The picture book is an ideal creative object. Quite often, the style of my illustrations has been labelled 'French.' In Catalonia, one would describe it as *linia clara* (fine line), as it is vaguely reminiscent of my admired *Tintin:* lined contours and more or less flat surfaces. While I avoid 'cuteness' (my characters have simple black dots for eyes!) my artwork on the whole does have an endearing and sympathetic quality. In this sense, my most admired illustrator is my fellow Barcelonian and friend Carme Soler, whose artwork combines artistic quality with simplicity, humor, and human warmth. Among American artists, my admiration goes to Edward Gorey, William Steig, and my friend and former teacher at RISD, David Macaulay.

"Apart from picture books, I have always been very interested in other arts which combine the visual with the verbal, such as the cinema, the theatre, and almost any of the performing arts. Among the fine artists, I must mention my devotion to Rembrandt, Goya, Degas, Matisse, and Picasso—and everything in the permanent collection at the MOMA [Museum of Modern Art]."

           *   *   *

EVERSOLE, Robyn Harbert 1971-

PERSONAL: Born June 23, 1971, in Clarksburg, WV; daughter of George H. and Marilyn (Crawford) Eversole. *Education:* Graduated from Interlochen Arts Academy, 1989; graduated from Trinity University, 1993. *Religion:* Protestant.

ADDRESSES: Home—Route 3, Box 69, Bridgeport, WV 26330. *Agent*—Barbara Kouts, P.O. Box 558, Bellport, NY 11713.

CAREER: Has worked with Refugee Aid Project, Inner City Development, and a Trinity University literacy program in San Antonio, TX. Co-chair of special projects for the Trinity University Voluntary Action Center.

AWARDS, HONORS: West Virginia Governor's Medal for the Arts, 1987; Presidential Scholar in the Arts, 1989; Young Artist Award, Interlochen Arts Academy, 1989; short story awards, West Virginia Writers Inc., 1989 and 1990.

ROBYN HARBERT EVERSOLE

WRITINGS:

The Magic House, Orchard, 1992.

WORK IN PROGRESS: La Tocadora de Flauta / The Flute Player, a bilingual picture book to be published by Orchard.

SIDELIGHTS: Robyn Harbert Eversole told *SATA:* "I have been writing since age eight, but did not begin writing picture books until I spent a few months in Australia at the end of my senior year of high school. I was in Australia as an exchange student, but was living on a cattle station in the outback four hours from town, which made it impossible for me to attend school. I had planned this, of course. However, a zealous study-abroad coordinator insisted that I enroll in correspondence courses. She sent me to enroll in the Adelaide School of Technical and Further Education, and one of the courses I chose was 'Writing for Children.' Chapter two was about writing picture books, and the assignment was to write one. I drew upon a memory of an imaginary waterfall which used to run down the main staircase in a house in West Virginia, and wrote a story which several revisions later became *The Magic House.*

"*La Tocadora de Flauta / The Flute Player* will be my second book, and it also comes indirectly out of an experience abroad. While studying Spanish and anthropology in Cochabamba, Bolivia, in the fall of 1991, I was living in a family with three young grandchildren. One day while I was trying to write a story for Spanish class, the children began playing a recorder out in the garden. I imagined a person who lived on the top floor of a building and did nothing all day but play music. Many, many drafts later, this story became a picture book manuscript, in two languages.

"At present I am twenty-one years old and finishing my undergraduate degree in anthropology. I am interested in Latin American cultures and I want to learn as much as I can about different cultures and then write about them—to bring these people and places alive for young readers, through stories."

F

FAXON, Lavinia
' See RUSS, Lavinia

* * *

FEHLER, Gene 1940-

PERSONAL: Surname is pronounced "*fay*-ler"; born September 30, 1940, in Savanna, IL; son of Franklin and Hazel (Ashpole) Fehler; married Polly Diane Eggert (a nurse educator), December 26, 1964; children: Timothy Gene, Andrew Scott. *Education:* Northern Illinois University, B.S., 1962, M.S., 1968. *Religion:* Protestant. *Hobbies and other interests:* Baseball, golf, tennis, playing board and card games, old movies.

ADDRESSES: Home—106 Laurel Lane, Seneca, SC 29678.

CAREER: Kishwaukee College, Malta, IL, English teacher and writer in residence, 1969-80. Has held teaching positions at Park College, Austin, TX, Austin Community College, Austin, Auburn University at Montgomery, Montgomery, AL, and high schools in Illinois, Texas, and Georgia. Visiting poet at Artist-in-Education programs in Alabama, Texas, and South Carolina.

MEMBER: National Federation of State Poetry Societies, Society for American Baseball Research, Texas Poetry Society, Austin Poetry Society.

AWARDS, HONORS: Jim Harrison Award, *Spitball* magazine, 1984, for outstanding contributions to baseball literature.

WRITINGS:

Center Field Grasses: Poems from Baseball, McFarland & Co., 1991.

POETRY CHAPBOOKS

The Day Willy Missed the Bus, Mailbox Press, 1979.
But Nobody Slam-Dunked, Mailbox Press, 1979.
By Book or by Crook, Mailbox Press, 1985.

GENE FEHLER

Fehler's poems and short stories have appeared in numerous periodicals and anthologies, including *Baseball, I Gave You All the Best Years of My Life,* North Atlantic Books, 1978; *Baseball Diamonds,* Anchor Press, 1980; *From Hide and Horn,* Eakin Press, 1985; *Light Year '86,* Bits Press, 1985; *Light Year '87,* Bits Press, 1986; *The Bedford Introduction to Literature,* St. Martin's, 1987; *Writing Poems,* Little, Brown, 1987; *The Best of Spitball,* Pocket Books, 1988; and *At the Crack of the Bat,* Hyperion, 1992. Fehler's work was also featured in *When It Was a Game II,* a documentary film produced by Home Box Office.

WORK IN PROGRESS: Young adult novels and picture books; research on the 1956 Major League baseball season.

SIDELIGHTS: Gene Fehler told *SATA:* "I grew up in Thomson, Illinois, a town of five hundred people. My wife and sons and I moved to the South in 1980; yet if I have a personal voice as a writer, it is a Midwestern voice, shaped by growing up within sight of Twain's Mississippi; shaped by forty years of having lived and taught in Illinois; shaped by attending a tiny country Methodist church whose yard bordered and joined with ours, a yard where I spent hour upon pleasant hour with my two sons playing baseball and tossing a football. That big backyard in the shadow of a church steeple and surrounded by cornfields was not only 'Our Yankee Stadium,' as I described it in my poem 'Backyard Glory'—it was our own field of dreams.

"Most of my fondest memories of my childhood and teen years are of playing baseball, basketball, and sandlot football. And reading. Our village library was open only a few hours a week, on Wednesday evenings and Saturday afternoons. I loved to browse through the children's and young adult collections. Each visit would excite me with a new discovery, a new book or series with its unique colors and smell and feel and story. In high school, I think I managed to read every sports novel in our public and school libraries.

"I started to write poetry only when I realized it was entirely permissible to enjoy a poem even without being able to decipher its meaning. For a long time I had worried that I wasn't very good at understanding poetry. I was thirty-three years old before I learned that the understanding isn't as important as enjoying the sounds and images and emotions. I like what Dylan Thomas said of poetry: 'All that matters is the enjoyment of it.' The understanding of it is merely a nice bonus.

"I love to give poetry readings, especially in a school setting. I'm in South Carolina's Artist-in-Education program as a visiting poet, as I was in Texas and Alabama. As such, I've had the pleasure of reading my poems to thousands of students. I find that young people are often surprised (and always delighted) to learn that most poetry is written about everyday subjects by 'regular people' just like them. Too many students seem to have the impression that poets are people whose only purpose for writing is to make it easier for English teachers to bore or confuse or frustrate their students.

"Much of what I write has baseball in it. Why? Because I've always loved playing and watching it, and I never tire of trying to find fresh, new ways of writing about it. I believe that a writer should explore a wide range of topics and approaches; I also believe that writing about what one knows and loves most increases the likelihood that a writer will create poems and stories of passion and truth.

"Some say poetry is 'a lie that tells the truth.' That's true of most of my poems, especially those in which I've drawn from my own experiences yet strayed from the truth in order to create a particular effect. I try to write the kind of poems I most like to read: poems about people (almost all of my poems, even my baseball poems, have people in them), poems that tell stories,

poems that stir the emotions, poems with pleasing sounds—yet always poems that illustrate a careful attention to craft. Almost everything I write goes through many drafts as I search for the best words and the best form. I would offer young writers this advice: don't be afraid to revise. You must cross out passages, add details, rethink, reshape. But most of all—write, and write often. You might have to write ten or twenty poems or stories that fail for each one that works. But creating one that works makes the effort worthwhile.

"*Center Field Grasses* is a collection of 204 poems about baseball. Though the poems were written over a fifteen-year period (1976-91), they were a lifetime in the making. Many of the 58 poems that make up the first part of the book, 'Up Close and Personal,' grew out of my own experiences with baseball, both as a child and an adult. The poems are about more than baseball; they are about friendship and death, joy and disappointment, family relationships. They are about lives that just happen to be touched in some way by baseball.

"The fifty-nine poems that make up the second part, 'Parodies from the Classics,' have a dual purpose: to bring pleasure and to lead into a reading of classic poems by Frost, Dickinson, Poe, Shakespeare, Whitman, and thirty-three other famous poets. Each of these poems follows the same form and style of a famous poet while focusing on some baseball happening. Most of these poems were written between 1981 and 1991. For example, in 1984 I wanted to write a poem about the George Brett 'pine tar incident' that had stirred up strong emotions in the baseball world. Frost's opening line from 'Stopping by Woods' popped into my head: 'Whose woods these are I think I know.' It seemed (with a minor change) a perfect way to begin my poem: 'Whose bat this is I think I know./It's caked with pine tar high and low.' Once I had the beginning, it was merely a matter of following Frost's distinctive rhyme scheme and rhythmic pattern while telling the story.

"I'm pleased that so many people who read and enjoy those baseball parodies are inspired to find and read the famous poems that served as the model for my poems. *The Book Report* said of this section of *Center Field Grasses:* 'Our job as educators is to get [these] ... poems into the heads of Fehler's readers in their early years. In effect, Fehler has given us a core poetry list for students.'

"Part Three, 'The Players,' is a collection of eighty-seven poems about individual players, many of them from the '50s (my grade school and high school years). Most players are famous (Nolan Ryan, Sandy Koufax, Mickey Mantle, Willie Mays) but a few are relative unknowns (Gavvy Cravath, Phil Linz, Harry Agganis, Steve Blass). I wrote many of these poems from 1976 to 1979, then added some new ones ten years later when I worked on extensive revisions of the earlier poems.

"While I continue to write poems, much of my writing time is spent working on picture books for children and on young adult novels. And while baseball and other sports play a major role in some of the books, those books are not so much 'sport' books as they are books about the people whose lives just happen to be in some way touched by the world of sport."

WORKS CITED:

Moore, Richard, review of *Center Field Grasses, Book Report,* March/April, 1992, pp. 43-44.

FOR MORE INFORMATION SEE:

PERIODICALS

Spitball, February, 1983, pp. 5-12.

* * *

FISHER, Margery (Turner) 1913-1992

OBITUARY NOTICE—See index for *SATA* sketch: Born March 21, 1913, in Camberwell, London; died December 24, 1992, in Northampton, England. Educator, lecturer, publisher, editor, critic, and author. An expert in the field of children's literature, Fisher wrote informative, analytic guides to children's fiction and nonfiction. She taught English from 1939 to 1945 in England and published her first work, the novel *Field Day,* in 1951. At that point, she turned her attention to children's books by other authors, becoming a prolific book reviewer, and, in 1962, she created her own reviewing journal, *Growing Point,* which she also edited and published. Fisher spoke about the state of children's book publishing at conferences, award ceremonies, and on radio. She was credited with creating books that addressed and examined neglected aspects of children's literature. Among Fisher's titles are *Intent upon Reading, Matters of Fact, Who's Who in Children's Literature,* and *The Bright Face of Danger.*

OBITUARIES AND OTHER SOURCES:

BOOKS

Who's Who, 145th edition, St. Martin's, 1993.

PERIODICALS

Junior Bookshelf, February, 1993, p. 8.
Times (London), January 4, 1993, p. 17.

* * *

FLINT, Russ 1944-

PERSONAL: Born February 15, 1944, in Pasadena, CA. *Education:* Attended Viola College and Art Center College of Design, Pasadena, CA.

CAREER: Founder of Dayspring Card Co., 1971; affiliated with Dayspring Card Co., 1971-78; free-lance illustrator of children's books. Affiliated with Coop Art Gallery and The Quincy Art Works. *Military service:* U.S. Air Force, first airman, served four years as medical technician; became staff sergeant.

Spooky walks through the forest provided the inspiration for Russ Flint's self-illustrated adaptation of Washington Irving's *The Legend of Sleepy Hollow.*

WRITINGS:

FICTION FOR CHILDREN

Let's Build a House: A White Cottage before Winter, Ideals, 1990.

ILLUSTRATOR

Washington Irving, *The Legend of Sleepy Hollow,* Ideals, 1991.

Also illustrator of Charles Dickens's *A Christmas Carol,* Ideals.

SIDELIGHTS: Russ Flint commented: "I'm generally afraid of the dark. While doing *The Legend of Sleepy Hollow,* I went on long walks through the forest at night for inspiration."

* * *

FORD, Elbur
See HIBBERT, Eleanor Alice Burford

* * *

FOSTER, Lynne 1937-

PERSONAL: Born November 4, 1937, in Long Beach, CA; daughter of C. O. (a retired navy officer) and Marie (a homemaker; maiden name, Taylor) Payne; married Lyle Gaston (a professor); children: Lisa Foster. *Education:* San Diego State University, B.A. *Hobbies and other interests:* Nature, environmental issues, sports, the outdoors, languages.

ADDRESSES: Home and office—3648 Mt. Vernon Ave., Riverside, CA 92507.

CAREER: Writer, 1983—. Worked as a medical, linguistics, and textbook editor, 1973-78, and as a freelance editor and workshop leader, 1974-83; has edited Sierra Club environmental publications.

MEMBER: Authors Guild, Society of Children's Book Writers and Illustrators, Southern California Council on Literature for Children and Young People.

AWARDS, HONORS: Best children's book, National Park Service Conference of Cooperating Associations, 1992, for *Exploring the Grand Canyon.*

WRITINGS:

Mountaineering Basics (for adults), Sierra Books/Avant Books, 1983.
Adventuring in the California Desert: The Sierra Club Travel Guide to the Great Basin, Mojave, and Colorado Desert Regions of California (for adults), Sierra Books, 1987.
Exploring the Grand Canyon: Adventures of Yesterday and Today (for children), Grand Canyon Natural History Association, 1990.
Take a Hike! The Sierra Club Kid's Guide to Hiking and Backpacking, Sierra Books, 1991.

WORK IN PROGRESS: Winter at Heron Hall (tentative title), a fantasy novel for children; *Exploring Denali National Park, One People, Many Languages, Alaska's Natural Wonders,* and *Earthviews,* all nonfiction works; researching the planet Mars for a science fiction novel for young people.

SIDELIGHTS: Lynne Foster told *SATA:* "Imagine a medium-sized kid with medium-brown hair. Also imagine a scabby nose, scabby elbows, scabby knees, and general grubbiness. Dress the kid in muddy tennies, ragged blue-jean shorts, and a too-small plaid shirt. Add

LYNNE FOSTER

a big smile. Add a rusty bike with a battered basket piled high with library books. That was me as a kid. That's also me now. My bike isn't as rusty, but I haven't changed much—inside.

"That kid isn't quite what most people think a bookworm looks like. But that's because most people don't know that bookworms can also be crazy about roller skating, ice skating, biking, swinging from Tarzan ropes, horseback riding, hiking, fishing, baseball, swimming, and hanging out. I was crazy about all those things—and books—and lots of other things. I still am.

"I still don't look like a bookworm—but I am. I don't know if I look like a writer—but I am. I started writing when I was about eight. What did I write about? Mostly what my mom and dad didn't want me to write about. Things like what my dad called the car while he was changing a tire. Things like what bulls and cows did when they got together. Things like what I found in fish guts. Of course, no one thought these 'stories' were cute. Of course, no one asked me to write more. But I did.

"I didn't know it then, but I was doing the right thing. I was writing about things I knew something about. When people who teach writing give advice to people who want to become writers, they usually tell them to write about what they know. That's what I did. And I kept on doing it. I didn't think about being a writer, I just wrote about what interested me.

"And I kept on reading. I loved facts and I loved stories. I wanted to know about stories, so I read *The Black Stallion, Thunderhead,* and *National Velvet.* I wanted to know what it was like to live in America before the Declaration of Independence was signed, so I read *Johnny Tremaine.* Living on an island sounded exciting, so I read *The Swiss Family Robinson* and *Robinson Crusoe.* I wanted to know about the weird animals that [nineteenth-century naturalist Charles] Darwin found in the Galapagos Islands, so I read his *Voyage of the Beagle.* I wanted to know if people might ever get to the center of the earth, the moon, and to the planet Mars. So I read Jules Verne's *Voyage to the Center of the Earth* and *First Men in the Moon,* and Robert Heinlein's *Red Planet.* I liked to be scared, so I read Edgar Allan Poe's stories and poems. I liked puzzles and mysteries, so I read Sherlock Holmes stories. I wanted to know what it was like to be stalked by a tiger, so I read Jim Corbett's *Maneaters of Kumaon.*

"Along the way I painted fences with *Tom Sawyer,* floated down the Mississippi with *Huckleberry Finn,* found my way home with *Lassie,* mourned the death of *The Yearling,* flew into the fantastic world of *Mary Poppins,* robbed the rich and gave to the poor with *Robin Hood,* explored the Grand Canyon with *Brighty,* faced Marley's ghost with Scrooge in *A Christmas Carol* and celebrated *A Child's Christmas in Wales* with Dylan Thomas, adventured with Arthur and Merlyn in *The Once and Future King,* spent *Three Years before the Mast,* watched *Marie Curie* discover radium, and with the help of *Microbe Hunters,* saw Alexander Fleming discover penicillin and Louis Pasteur discover a cure for smallpox.

"I also chewed up book after book on ancient history (especially Egypt and Greece), dinosaurs and other fossils, airplanes and rockets, animals, medicine, Indians, the rest of the world (including the oceans), and people from anywhere and any time who had done or were doing something interesting. And I did all this without knowing it was going to help me be a writer someday.

"All the time I was growing older and bigger, I kept reading and writing. I read so much that my folks teased me about being 'brought up by books' instead of by them. Other kids called me a 'walking encyclopedia'—and they usually didn't mean it as a compliment! But I never thought of being 'a writer.'

"By the time I got to high school, some of my teachers thought I was a good writer. I had stopped writing about fish guts and was trying to write about the funny things that happened when my family took trips, which was often (my dad got transferred every year or two). I also started writing poems and stories, and I won some essay contests. But no one ever said anything about my becoming a writer.

"After high school, I went to college to become a biologist. In my courses, I kept on reading and writing, mostly about science. After being a biologist for a long time, I went back to school and became an English teacher so I could help college students learn more about reading and writing. Still later, I became an editor and helped writers make their books better. Still, no one said, 'Why don't *you* become a writer?'

"Then one day, I got bored with helping other people become better writers. I got to thinking—and discovered I had lots of ideas about what I thought made a good book. Almost before I knew it, I'd decided to write a book myself.

"First I chose what to write about. I picked something I already knew something about—hiking, camping, and having fun in the mountains. Then I found a publisher who wanted to do the book. And, finally, I wrote *Mountaineering Basics*. People liked it, so I wrote another. This one was about hiking, camping, and having fun in the desert. It's called *Adventuring in the California Desert*.

"Well, now I was really rolling! One of the places I liked to roll to as often as I could was the Grand Canyon. So I decided to write a book for kids about that. Because many strange, interesting, and funny things had happened at the Canyon in the old days, I put a lot about them in the book. And, of course, I talked about trails and hiking, too. This book's called *Exploring the Grand Canyon*. One of the things that makes this book so special is that a very good artist did lots of drawings for it. The National Park Service liked the book so much, they gave it an award.

"People also started calling me an 'author,' and invited me to come to schools, clubs, conferences, and meetings to talk about writing—and my books. Suddenly, I started feeling like a writer and began planning several more books. While doing this, I got a call from one of my publishers, asking me if I'd like to write a book about hiking and camping for kids. You can imagine what I said! And that's how the idea for *Take a Hike!* got started.

"Once *Take a Hike!* was finished, I decided to write more fact-type books for kids. One I'm working on is called *One People, Many Languages*. It will show how there got to be so many languages all over the world. I'm also writing a book for kids called *Earthviews*. It's the story of how ancient people and modern people have lived on our planet and how they have changed it. Another book I'm writing now is *Alaska's Natural Wonders*. It's about whales, glaciers, grizzlies, the Arctic, the Northern Lights, the highest mountains in North America, and lots more.

"I'm also working on my first novel for kids—*Winter at Heron Hall*. It's the story of a twelve-year-old who goes unwillingly to England to visit elderly relatives. These folks are a very mysterious bunch, and strange things are always happening at Heron Hall. I can hardly wait to find out how the book is going to end!

"Besides writing books, I also keep on reading them. What do I like to read? Well, as you might guess, I like reading about people, languages, the environment, and interesting places. If I didn't, it wouldn't be much fun to write about them."

*   *   *

FRENCH, Paul
See ASIMOV, Isaac

*   *   *

FUGE, Charles 1966-

PERSONAL: Born May 3, 1966, in Winchester, England; son of Charles Alistair (a doctor) and Susan Boulter (a former nurse and homemaker) Fuge. *Education:* Camberwell School of Art, B.A., 1988. *Politics:* Green.

ADDRESSES: Home—16 Eastlake Rd., London SE5 9QL, England. *Agent*—Eunice McMullen, 38 Clewer Hill Rd., Windsor SL4 4BW, England.

CAREER: Author and illustrator.

AWARDS, HONORS: Macmillan Prize, Macmillan Children's Books, 1987, and Mother Goose Award, 1989, both for *Bush Vark's First Day Out*.

WRITINGS:

FOR CHILDREN; SELF-ILLUSTRATED

Bush Vark's First Day Out, Macmillan, 1988.

CHARLES FUGE

(Editor) *Monstrosities* (poetry anthology), Hutchinson, 1989.
So Slow Sloth, Macmillan, 1990.

ILLUSTRATOR

John Rice, *Bears Don't Like Bananas* (poetry), Simon & Schuster, 1991.
Tim Healey, *A Box of Ogres,* Simon & Schuster, 1991.
Paul Rogers, *Funimals,* Bodley Head, 1991.
Rice, *Dreaming of Dinosaurs,* Macmillan, 1992.

Also illustrator of *The Magic Cheese,* Gollancz, 1991.

WORK IN PROGRESS: Whale Is Stuck, to be published in 1993; research on dogs for a picture book about a flea looking for the right home.

SIDELIGHTS: Charles Fuge began his career as a children's book illustrator almost by accident, as the result of an art project he entered in a competition during his last year at England's Camberwell School of Art. He told *SATA:* "We were given a project—to write and illustrate a children's picture book. For the first time at art college, I drew animals (creatures invented, but inspired by living oddities). The best thing I could do, I thought, was to draw what would have pleased me as a child."

Born in 1966, in Winchester, England, Fuge lived near enough to the countryside "to escape by myself and spend the summers looking for snakes and lizards, or to search for dead animals that I could stuff, with the help of a taxidermy book, to create the illusion that I was surrounded by wild animals. I kept many pets: rabbits,

guinea pigs, toads, newts, lizards, hamsters, mice, a rat ... but it was never enough! Being a 'day boy' at a local public school, friends were mostly unavailable, as they were either stuck at school or lived some distance away. So I spent my time learning about animals and drawing them."

Fuge did not expect his childhood interests to become a career, but found his academic education to be repressive. "When I was finally churned out with my university place secured, I knew that I had to change course. With the support of my parents (to my surprise!), I applied for art college where I could explore creative arts instead of just drawing animals."

During his second year at Camberwell School of Art, Fuge wrote and illustrated *Bush Vark's First Day Out* as a class assignment. The book's entrance into a competition resulted in the Macmillan Prize in 1987 and subsequent publication. Two years later Fuge was the recipient of the Mother Goose Award—1,000 and "an authentic gilded goose egg"—for "most exciting newcomer to children's book illustration." Remarking on Fuge's craft, one of the award's judges, Colin McNaughton, told Margaret Carter in *Books for Your Children,* "It's very difficult to simplify images, and this illustration is bold and brave—and risky. There's an individuality about it not normally seen in children's books."

Compared with Maurice Sendak's *Where the Wild Things Are* by *School Librarian* reviewer David Lewis, *Bush Vark* is the story of a young creature who ventures out to explore the world. Carter describes the book as a variety of "weird and wonderful creatures" that "peer, leer, and generally assail the eyes—but do not for one moment disturb the imperturbable bush vark as he dodges, hops, chases, swims, and takes on all comers." Though Fuge admitted to Carter that he's not much of a reader, the reviewer credits him for the successful balance between his artwork and text in *Bush Vark:* "Today's picture books frequently have artwork of an infinitely better standard than the text. This isn't so with this book.... the pace of the sentences matches the pace of the illustrations."

After the publication of *Bush Vark* in 1988, Fuge was approached with requests for his illustrations. "Since I have not refused it, my career seems to have decided itself for me!" he told *SATA.* Among the commissions that followed was the task of illustrating a collection of monster poems appropriately titled *Monstrosities,* complete with the warning, "Only the bravest monsterphiles should read on." He has also illustrated two books of poetry by John Rice, *Bears Don't Like Bananas,* published in 1991, and 1992's *Dreaming of Dinosaurs.*

Fuge explained to Carter that people have an inclination to compare his invented animals to the likes of monsters. "I like to think of them rather as at a different stage of evolution," he noted. For this reason, in *So Slow Sloth,* his latest sole creation, he chose to rely on real South American animals as characters, "some of which are so unfamiliar to us that they look like inventions."

"I have a deep concern about the environment and the rights of animals," Fuge told *SATA*, "and I hope that my picture books are not exploitative, but might inspire children to take further interest in nature."

WORKS CITED:

Carter, Margaret, "Mother Goose Lays Another Golden Egg," *Books for Your Children*, summer, 1989, p. 7.

Lewis, David, review of *Bush Vark's First Day Out*, *School Librarian*, February, 1989, p. 15.

FOR MORE INFORMATION SEE:

PERIODICALS

School Librarian, May, 1990, p. 73; November, 1990, p. 141.

G

GAINER, Cindy 1962-

PERSONAL: Born May 13, 1962; married William C. Matrisch; children: August. *Education:* Received B.F.A. from Seton Hill College.

ADDRESSES: Home—316 Chestnut Lane, Jeannette, PA 15644. *Contact*—c/o Mary Ann Kohl, Bright Ring Publishing, 1900 Northshore Dr., Bellingham, WA 98227.

CAREER: Art teacher in southwestern Pennsylvania, 1984—.

WRITINGS:

(With Mary Ann F. Kohl, and illustrator) *Good Earth Art: Environment Art for Kids,* Bright Ring Publishing, 1991.

* * *

GARD, Robert Edward 1910-1992

OBITUARY NOTICE—See index for *SATA* sketch: Born July 3, 1910, in Iola, KS; died December 7, 1992, in Madison, WI. Educator, folklorist, playwright, and author. Gard began his career as an instructor at several institutions, including Cornell University in Ithaca, New York, before becoming a professor at the University of Wisconsin at Madison, where he taught until his retirement. Active in the community, Gard was a member of several organizations including the Wisconsin Arts Foundation and Council and the Wisconsin Regional Writers Association. The author of more than forty books, Gard was interested in folklore and drama, writing such texts as *The Lake Guns of Seneca and Cayuga, and Eight Other Plays* and *Wisconsin Is My Doorstep: A Dramatists Yarn Book of Wisconsin Lore.* Gard also wrote for children, including *A Horse Named Joe* and *Scotty's Mare.* Among Gard's other publications are *The Big One, The Error of Sexton Jones, Innocence of Prairie,* and with Allen Crafton, *A Woman of No Importance.*

OBITUARIES AND OTHER SOURCES:

BOOKS

Authors of Books for Young People, 3rd edition, Scarecrow, 1990.

PERIODICALS

Chicago Tribune, December 8, 1992, sec. 1, p. 10.

* * *

GOODIN, Sallie (Brown) 1953-

PERSONAL: Born December 14, 1953, in Charleston, MO; daughter of A. S. (a farmer) and Barbara (a bookkeeper; maiden name, Parker) Brown; married Lee Goodin (a farmer), December 29, 1973; children: Charlotte, Lee-Stroud. *Education:* Attended University of Missouri, Columbia, 1972, and Southeast Missouri State University, 1974-75 and 1982-84. *Religion:* United Methodist. *Hobbies and other interests:* Reading, music, hand sewing, art.

ADDRESSES: Home—1309 Warde Rd., Charleston, MO 63834. *Office*—P.O. Box 279, Charleston, MO 63834.

CAREER: Oliver-Goodin and Co., Inc. (design company), Charleston, MO, owner with Cookie Oliver, 1987-92; Simplicity Pattern Co., New York City, free-lance designer with Oliver, 1989-92; Charleston Jr. High School, Charleston, MO, teacher's aide in special education, 1991-92; children's author and illustrator. Methodist Church, Charleston, church organist, 1981-83, children's choir pianist, 1990-92; Charleston swim team, president, 1991-92.

MEMBER: Daughters of the American Revolution; PEO (former corresponding secretary and recording secretary for chapter CV), Parent-Teacher Association.

WRITINGS:

SELF-ILLUSTRATED; WRITTEN WITH COOKIE OLIVER

I Want to Smock, Oliver-Goodin and Co., 1990.

SALLIE GOODIN

Come Comet, Come Cupid, Winston-Derek, 1991.

Also illustrator and coauthor of nine clothing patterns and thirty-one smocking plates, all for Oliver-Goodin and Co., 1987-90. Illustrator and coauthor of twenty-five patterns for Simplicity Pattern Co., 1989-92.

WORK IN PROGRESS: Developing more patterns for the Simplicity Pattern Company.

SIDELIGHTS: Sallie Goodin told *SATA:* "I find that, as I grow older, I am increasingly interested in the pursuit of knowledge. Everything I have learned so far in my design business has helped me immensely in other aspects of my life. My partnership with Cookie Oliver has been a wonderful, inspiring relationship. We are as close as sisters, and I feel very fortunate to be her friend. My family is of the utmost importance to me. I believe in education, communication, effective living, and having fun. Everything is so much nicer when we laugh (sometimes at ourselves!)."

*   *   *

GRAHAM, Alastair 1945-

PERSONAL: Born February 18, 1945, in London, England; son of John Douglas (in business) and Edna May Smith (a secretary; maiden name, Fairweather) Graham; married Diane Randall; children: Gemma Jane, Toby Douglas. *Education:* Attended Trinity College, Glenalmond, Scotland, 1963. *Politics:* None. *Religion:* None. *Hobbies and other interests:* Listening to music, playing conga drums in a modern jazz band, reading, chopping wood.

ADDRESSES: Home—Chapel End, Priors Marston, Near Rugby, Warwickshire CV23 8SA, England.

CAREER: Free-lance animation artist in London, England, 1971-75; T.V. Cartoons (animated film production company), London, producer and designer, 1975-77; free-lance illustrator and writer, 1977—.

WRITINGS:

Full Moon Soup; or, The Fall of the Hotel Splendide (fiction), Dial Books for Young Readers, 1991.
Full Moon Afloat (sequel to *Full Moon Soup*), David Bennett Books, in press.

ILLUSTRATOR

Ellen Weiss, *Pigs in Space: Starring Jim Henson's Muppets,* Muppet Press/Random House, 1983.
P. E. King, *Down on the Funny Farm,* Random House Books for Young Readers, 1986.
(With Allan Curless, Peter Elson, Tom Stimpson, and Martin White) John Foster, editor, *Spaceways: An Anthology of Space Poetry,* Oxford University Press, 1987.
Tim Wood, *Our Planet Earth,* Aladdin, 1992.

WORK IN PROGRESS: Katya and the Mouseking, a screenplay for an animated film.

ALASTAIR GRAHAM

SIDELIGHTS: Alastair Graham told *SATA:* "As an impressionable only child, I was thrilled by the cinema and can remember thinking at a very early age that I would become a film director. However, the single most potent catalyst toward my metamorphosis into an artist was jazz.

"I became enthralled by jazz in my mid-teens and remained so up until a year or so ago when for some reason the magic began to wane. Then 1991 brought the death of my idol and constant inspiration for over thirty years, the great Miles Davis, and my interest began to turn more fully to classical music. Music has always been a crucial factor in my emotional and creative life, supplying the sound track to my imagination and the heroes for me to emulate.

"One of my most permanent dreams is to somehow create a synthesis between my drawing, my storytelling, and the music. To this end I'm working on a film project, an animated version of a retelling of the story of the Nutcracker (music, of course, by Pyotr Ilich Tchaikovsky) for which I've designed the characters."

*   *   *

GRAHAM, Lorenz (Bell) 1902-1989

PERSONAL: Born January 27, 1902, in New Orleans, LA; died of cancer, September 11, 1989, in West Covina, CA; son of David Andrew (a minister) and Etta (Bell) Graham; married Ruth Morris, August 20, 1929; children: Lorenz, Jean (deceased), Joyce (Mrs. Campbell C. Johnson), Ruth (Mrs. Herbert R. May), Charles. *Education:* Attended University of Washington, Seattle, 1921, and University of California, Los Angeles, 1923-24; Virginia Union University, A.B., 1936; Columbia University, M.S.W., 1954; also studied at New York School of Social Work for two years and at New York University. *Politics:* "Liberal, Democratic, sometimes called Left." *Religion:* Disciples of Christ.

CAREER: Monrovia College, Liberia, West Africa, missionary teacher, 1924-28; lecturer and fund-raiser in United States for Foreign Mission Board, National Baptist Convention, 1929-32; teacher in Richmond, VA, 1933-35; U.S. Civilian Conservation Corps, camp educational adviser in Virginia and Pennsylvania, 1936-42; manager of public housing, Newport News, VA, 1943-45; free-lance writer, real estate salesman, and building contractor, Long Island, NY, 1946-49; Queens Federation of Churches, New York City, social worker, 1950-57; Los Angeles County (CA) probation officer, 1958-66. Lecturer at California State Polytechnic College (now University), Pomona, 1970-77.

MEMBER: PEN International, Authors League of America, National Association for the Advancement of Colored People (NAACP), U.S./China People's Friendship Association, U.S.A./Soviet Friendship Society.

AWARDS, HONORS: Thomas Alva Edison Foundation special citation for *The Ten Commandments;* Charles W. Follett Award, 1958, and Child Study Association of

LORENZ GRAHAM

America Award, 1959, both for *South Town;* Association for Study of Negro Life and History award, 1959; Los Angeles City Council award, 1966; Vassie D. Wright Award, 1967; Southern California Council on Literature for Children and Young People award for significant contribution to the field of literature for young people, 1968; first prize from *Book World,* 1969, for *Whose Town?;* California Association of Teachers of English citation, 1973; Martin Luther King Award from Southern California region of Christian Church, 1975; *Boston Globe/Horn Book* Award, and Children's Book Showcase Award, both 1976, both for *South Town;* D.H.L., Virginia University, 1983.

WRITINGS:

JUVENILE

How God Fix Jonah (collection of biblical tales told in Liberian dialect), illustrated by Letterio Calapai, Reynal & Hitchcock, 1946.
Tales of Momolu, illustrated by Calapai, Reynal & Hitchcock, 1946.
(Adapter) *The Story of Jesus* (Classics Illustrated edition), Gilberton, 1955.
(Adapter) *The Ten Commandments* (Classics Illustrated edition), Gilberton, 1956.
I, Momolu, illustrated by John Biggers, Crowell, 1966.
Every Man Heart Lay Down (originally published in *How God Fix Jonah*), illustrated by Gregorio Prestopino, Crowell, 1970.
God Wash the World and Start Again (originally published in *How God Fix Jonah*), illustrated by Clare Romano Ross, Crowell, 1971.

John Brown's Raid: A Picture History of the Attack on Harper's Ferry, Virginia, Scholastic Magazines, 1971.

David He No Fear (originally published in *How God Fix Jonah*), illustrated by Ann Grifalconi, Crowell, 1971.

(Compiler with John Durham and Elsa Graser) *Directions 3-4* (anthology), two volumes, Houghton, 1972.

Carolina Cracker (novelette), Houghton, 1972.

Detention Center (novelette), Houghton, 1972.

Stolen Car (novelette), Houghton, 1972.

Runaway (novelette), Houghton, 1972.

Hongry Catch the Foolish Boy (originally published in *How God Fix Jonah*), illustrated by James Brown, Crowell, 1973.

Song of the Boat (originally published in *Tales of Momolu*), illustrated by Leo Dillon and Diane Dillon, Crowell, 1975.

John Brown: A Cry for Freedom, Crowell, 1980.

"TOWN" SERIES; JUVENILES

South Town, Follett, 1958.
North Town, Crowell, 1965.
Whose Town?, Crowell, 1969.
Return to South Town, Crowell, 1976.

OTHER

Also author of plays for amateur groups, schools, and colleges. Contributor of articles to agency and department publications.

Most of Graham's manuscripts are held in the Kerlan Collection of the University of Minnesota, Minneapolis; other manuscripts are deposited in the North Carolina Central University Library in Durham.

SIDELIGHTS: While he was growing up, Lorenz Graham never imagined he would become an author. Graham's family moved several times during his childhood because his father was a pastor in the African Methodist Episcopal (AME) church and was transferred to different AME churches around the country. This wandering shaped Lorenz Graham in ways that gave him a unique point of view, which was useful when he began to write books.

Graham was born in New Orleans, Louisiana, in 1902. As he related in *Something about the Author Autobiography Series* (*SAAS*): "I was born in the Deep South but I have only vague memories of my life there.... [My] family moved to the North while I was still a baby. [My sister] Shirley taught me to read before I went to school. At the age of six I was enrolled at Doolittle School in Chicago and I was immediately placed in second grade. Soon after that we moved southward again, this time to Nashville, Tennessee, where I first felt the effects of racial segregation."

Having to live apart from the white people he had lived among in the North was a new experience for Graham. "The new way of life did not bother me at first," he disclosed in *SAAS,* "but I was surprised to find that my

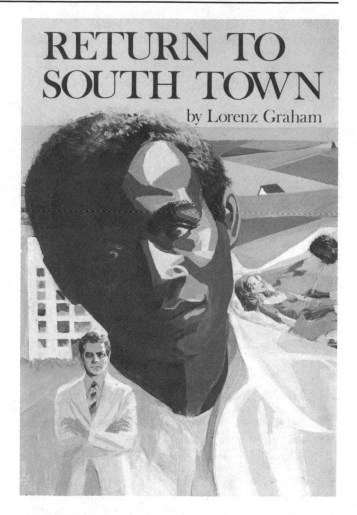

The books in Graham's "Town" series deal with racism in various parts of the United States, as in this tale of a young man who attempts to become a small southern town's first black doctor. (Cover illustration by Ernest Crichlow.)

young friends were actually afraid of white people, all white people. 'They're bad,' they told me. 'You got to keep away from them. They'll hurt you if they get a chance.' To this, I would reply, 'Oh, no. They're not bad. They won't hurt you. We used to go to school with them. They aren't so different.'" But one day some young white boys threw a rock at Graham. The rock hit him in the forehead, and a doctor had to stitch up the wound. Graham's friends came to visit the injured boy. "'I bet that will learn you about white folks,' they said. 'They're bad. They'll hurt you, and there ain't nothing your daddy or anybody else can do about it.' They were right," Graham admitted in *SAAS.* "That did 'learn me' and when I went back to school, I was the first to jump off the sidewalk whenever the bad white people wanted to pass."

Soon Reverend Graham was transferred to Clarksville, another city in the South, where schools for black children only went through the ninth grade. Lorenz recalled in *SAAS* that "there were some conversations in the family regarding the fact that there was but the one school for us, while there were a high school and several neighborhood schools for white children. I remember that my father often said that conditions would improve, and that we as Negroes had to work hard to make them improve. He insisted that as we developed our skills, taking advantage of every opportunity for education, we could more and more increase our income and our ability to serve. Even in those early days, he and our mother talked about 'when you go to college' and sometimes 'when you become well educated.'"

But, as Graham candidly admitted, he did not do well at school. "I was not considered a very bright child," Graham wrote in *Elementary English;* "not one of my teachers observed, or reported, a spark of talent in me." His sister, Shirley, "did brilliantly," Graham remarked in *SAAS;* "brother David, talkative and aggressive, one year ahead of me, received good grades and the praise of teachers. Along came Lorenz, and I did poorly." People also began to notice that he was afraid of white people. Reverend Graham decided he had to transfer to a church outside the South, and he moved his family to Colorado Springs, Colorado, and then to Spokane, Washington. As the author remembered: "The school situation sort of leveled off.... I did get good grades, and showed high proficiency in arithmetic and in composition and grammar. Evidence of fear of white people did not surface ... [and] I discovered the public library."

In the early 1920s Graham first attended college in Washington state, where he heard an AME bishop give a speech asking for people to work as teaching missionaries at a school in Monrovia, Liberia. Graham wanted to go. He explained in *SAAS:* "I had grown up in a Christian home and had been told the rewards of service." The bishop explained that the job was not glamorous, the pay was poor, and health conditions were bad. But he also told Graham that three years of service would leave the young man able to make wise decisions about how he would want to spend his life.

So Graham volunteered to go to Liberia, "believing that I would be able to help the poor benighted Africans, that I could bring light to the dark land, and that I could open the door to a new life for the ignorant people," he related in *Elementary English.* "I was due for a rude awakening." Graham was to discover about the Africans the same thing he had noticed about white people as a child—that they were not so different from himself: "Shortly after I arrived in Liberia I realized that the people of Africa were so very, very much like people in other lands.... In time I realized that I had accepted an image of the African people which had been presented in the [movies] and the books which I had read. I began to wonder about books which described Africans honestly and I wondered why I had not read these books while I was in the United States. When I sought them I found that there were no such books. I found there were no books written about African people as people. There were books describing Africans as wild animals, as anthropophagical mysteries, as poor heathens groping for the light, as savages wandering in primeval darkness. There were no books describing them in the way that I

came to know them, as people living in families and groups, in towns and cities, moving within the bounds of customs and laws which were community recognized and community fashioned."

The author continued: "At that point I began saying that someone should write some decent books and let the world, especially my American world, know that the Africans were people. I talked this to those about me, to other teaching missionaries, to government people.... It seemed that no others had time or inclination to do such writing. It was then that I decided that since it needed to be done and since no one else would do it, I would write. I would write books which would make Americans know that Africans were people. This was my beginning."

During his time in Liberia Graham suffered from malaria. His doctor ordered him to leave Africa for several months to help him recover. Europe in the mid-1920s was between world wars, and Graham chose France in which to recuperate because its economy was depressed and the cost of living was lower there than elsewhere. To learn French, Graham took an apartment where only French-speaking people lived, and in just a few months the young man found he was also thinking in French. But, as he reported in *SAAS,* "the most significant impression that came out of being in France for those months, was that my racial identity was of no importance." Even in Africa Graham had felt that his skin color was a factor in all his relationships. "In France it seemed that no one noticed or cared. In France there were people of color lighter and darker than mine. I was curious about them—from what country? Africa? the Caribbean? South America? However, the French

Rich images of life in an African village accent Graham's story of a boy who accompanies his father on a journey to find the perfect tree for a new canoe. (Cover illustration by Leo and Diane Dillon.)

people did not show any curiosity about me or my origin." So Graham left France to return to his teaching job in Liberia, and, as he noted in *SAAS:* "I was back quite eagerly on duty at Monrovia College. My horizons had widened. Even more than before did it seem that writing would be my life's goal. Writing with the one message, 'People are People'—white, black, and all shades and colors in between, African, American, French, German. The cultures of the world, and the conflicts when we who call ourselves people refuse to recognize that those whom we call enemies are also people, very much like ourselves, with desires and needs and hopes which are quite identical to our own desires and needs and hopes."

When Graham's teaching commitment was over, he returned to the United States to take up his writing career. He wanted to live in New York because the black literary and artistic cultures were flourishing with the Harlem Renaissance. His sister, Shirley, was studying and writing in New York. Graham admitted that his educational background was not geared to writing, but he took additional classes at Columbia University and immersed himself in the thriving black renaissance of the day, lecturing about his African experiences, even acting in the play *Harlem,* based on Wallace Thurman's novel *The Blacker the Berry.* The play performed on Long Island for one week before opening on Broadway for another twenty weeks.

Graham began to think his writing was about to succeed as well. But each time he seemed about to be published, a roadblock would appear: no one could believe the positive picture of the Africans that Graham had developed. The editors informed Graham that Americans understood Africans to be savages and would not buy books that depicted them as intelligent human beings.

Though the response to his writing was extremely frustrating, Graham refused to change his approach. In 1929, just as the Great Depression was starting, he married Ruth Morris, a woman he had met in Liberia who also taught at Monrovia College. Graham continued his interest in publishing his stories but also worked other jobs to support his growing family.

More than fifteen years passed before Graham realized his dream of becoming published. His sister, Shirley, had been too busy to take an assignment a publisher was offering, but she referred her brother for the work, and so *How God Fix Jonah* was released to the book-buying public in 1946. His second book, *Tales of Momolu,* also came out in 1946, and Graham was extremely pleased when a reviewer wrote that the American reader "will recognize Momolu as just another fellow."

Graham went on to publish many books, including the "Town" series—*South Town, North Town, Whose Town?,* and *Return to South Town*—about prejudice and racism in America. But Graham constantly had to deal with delays. Usually it was the same old story: publishers would not believe the characters in his stories could

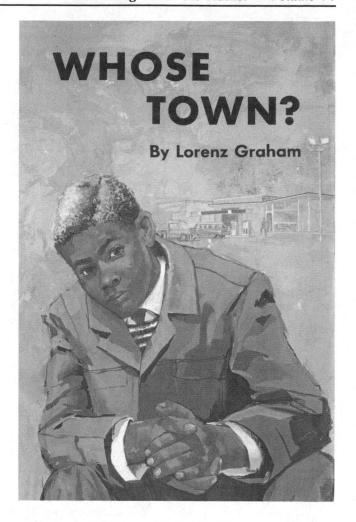

Tension builds between black and white communities in a northern town after a trial for the murder of a black student in Graham's sequel to *North Town*. (Cover illustration by Harold James.)

possibly be real. Nearly ten years lapsed between *Tales of Momolu* and Graham's next works, two adaptations he did for Classics Illustrated—literary classics done in comic-book format—*The Story of Jesus* and *The Ten Commandments.* Graham's stories written in a Liberian pidgin dialect, which originally appeared in *How God Fix Jonah,* were brought out in separate editions in the 1970s. Among these books were *Hongry Catch the Foolish Boy,* retelling the Bible story of the prodigal son, and *Song of the Boat.* Reviewers were once again approving, calling Graham's stories poetic, compelling, and vigorous.

Graham had found his writing life to be very gratifying, and he was proud of the writing tradition being established in his family—his sister, Shirley, and his wife, Ruth, were also published authors. Graham had also remained true to his message in all his books; as he said in *SAAS,* "I am writing for young people and I am trying to establish with them the idea that in every man is potential, and there is need for struggle and courage and movement toward definite goals."

WORKS CITED:

Graham, Lorenz, "An Author Speaks," *Elementary English,* February, 1973, pp. 185-188.
Graham, Lorenz, essay in *Something about the Author Autobiography Series,* Volume 5, Gale, 1988, pp. 111-145.

FOR MORE INFORMATION SEE:

BOOKS

Children's Literature Review, Volume 10, Gale, 1985.
Dictionary of Literary Biography, Volume 76: *Afro-American Writers, 1940-1955,* Gale, 1988.
Twentieth-Century Children's Writers, 3rd edition, St. James Press, 1989.

*   *   *

GREGORY, Kristiana 1951-

PERSONAL: Born June 12, 1951, in Los Angeles, CA; daughter of Harold (an inventor) and Jean (a swim instructor; maiden name, Kern) Gregory; divorced c. 1972; married Kip Rutty (a photographer and editor), 1982; children: Gregory, Cody. *Education:* Alamogordo High School, diploma, 1969. *Religion:* Christian. *Hobbies and other interests:* Reading, swimming, camping, studying Scripture, shopping at thrift shops, listening to music, taking walks on the beach.

ADDRESSES: Home and office—Redlands, CA. *Agent*—Barbara Markowitz, 117 North Mansfield Ave., Los Angeles, CA 90036.

CAREER: Gardena Valley News, Gardena, CA, free-lance feature writer, 1977-79, free-lance reporter, 1978; *Southern California Business,* Los Angeles, CA, associate editor, 1978; *Los Angeles Times,* book reviewer and columnist, 1978-91; *San Luis Obispo County Telegram-Tribune,* reporter, 1980-81; homemaker and writer, 1982—.

MEMBER: Society of Children's Book Writers and Illustrators.

AWARDS, HONORS: Golden Kite Award for fiction, Society of Children's Book Writers, citation for Notable Children's Trade Book in Social Studies, National Council for Social Studies-Children's Book Council (NCSS-CBC), and Book for the Teen Age award, New York Public Library, all 1989, for *Jenny of the Tetons;* best book for young adults citation, American Library Association, and citation from NCSS-CBC, both 1992, for *Earthquake at Dawn.*

WRITINGS:

HISTORICAL FICTION FOR YOUNG ADULTS

Jenny of the Tetons, Harcourt, 1989.
The Legend of Jimmy Spoon, Harcourt, 1990.
Earthquake at Dawn, Harcourt, 1992.
Jimmy Spoon and the Pony Express, Scholastic, in press.

KRISTIANA GREGORY

Contributor of a short story, "The Gift," to *Moody Monthly.*

WORK IN PROGRESS: Research on pirates and California missions.

SIDELIGHTS: Kristiana Gregory transforms historical documents into full-fledged stories of nineteenth- and early-twentieth-century American life. In novels such as *Jenny of the Tetons,* she vividly depicts the days of free-ranging Indians, vast buffalo herds, and westward-moving white settlers. Central to her works are the adventures of young people who, like their modern counterparts, face emotional crises and hard choices. Careful research distinguishes her books, which have received a number of commendations.

Books were always an important part of Gregory's life. As she told *SATA:* "We had books everywhere, and my parents read to me a lot. If we had questions, my father would say, 'Let's look it up in the encyclopedia.' Then we'd get in this long, involved, fun adventure going through an encyclopedia, and I think that's where I got my love for research. All the historical things I write remind me of my childhood and the excitement of exploring something and finding out about it."

Gregory's love of books served her well in school. In her *SATA* interview, she commented: "I was a very good student when I was in elementary school. I loved writing and English and history. I remember I loved doing reports. I would go home and read an encyclopedia—not a whole encyclopedia, but if I was researching apples, I would pick up the *A,* and I would rarely get around to writing my report on apples. I would get so enthralled in the volume *A* that I would end up finding something else I wanted to write about."

One subject Gregory chose to write about as an adult— Native American history and culture—was also part of her upbringing. "When we moved to New Mexico we were very close to the Mescalero Apache Indian reservation," she commented. "My parents were interested in the Native Americans, and they would take us around to the different powwows and pueblos. They had almost a reverent respect for them, and they passed that on to us. Anything that had to do with Native Americans they were interested in. We would go to museums, and we had Navajo rugs in our home and trinkets and that sort of thing."

Gregory's first taste of professional writing came during the 1970s when she became a free-lance writer for newspapers. "I went to the editor of the *Gardena Valley News* and said, 'I don't have any writing experience but I love to write—will you hire me?' I can't believe I did this, because I had no experience. He hired me to write feature stories for ten dollars each, plus they would give me a byline. Eventually that editor became editor of the Los Angeles Chamber of Commerce's weekly tabloid, *Southern California Business,* and asked me to come along. Later I met a *Los Angeles Times* editor through a college course on writing who offered me a job there.

"It was so exciting. I started out as an editorial assistant, and I compiled the best-seller list and did a variety of things around the office, and gradually it evolved into copy editing. I would edit the book reviews that came in, and then I started reviewing books on my own. I got bored with that job and moved to San Luis Obispo, California, where I kept badgering the newspaper editor for a reporter job. Finally, after about six months of my calling him every week and saying, 'Well, do you have an opening yet?,' he hired me. I started out writing weather reports, obituaries, and weddings—those were a real challenge—and then gradually I would give them ideas for feature stories. Finally they let me try some.

"I remember one time having to fill in for a reporter who was sick, and I had to cover a business meeting of the city government. It was boring, and I came back and wrote this very flowery lead that had nothing to do with the story. The editor said, 'Kristi, you should be writing fiction, not this kind of straight bone facts.' That led to the historical fiction, because it was hard for me to stick to the truth. I did when I was reporting, but there was this immense desire to exaggerate. I love writing historical fiction because you can start with facts, and obviously you weren't there in the 1800s, so you do have to invent certain conversations and so on."

Children's books became an increasingly important part of Gregory's life after she married Kip Rutty and started a family in Pocatello, Idaho. "I was invited to write a children's book column for the *Los Angeles Times Book Review,*" she explained. "I was in the middle of nowhere, in very cold weather—it was below zero for weeks at a time, which was difficult for a native Californian, plus I had a toddler and an infant—and the United Parcel Service would deliver these huge boxes of books, brand-new children's books. It was quite a thrill, because the editor said, 'Just write a column, pick eight or so books per column.' The column appeared every other week and I had all these wonderful books to choose from.

"When my children were a little older I started tutoring at the Pocatello High School. I got to know a lot of the Native Americans from Fort Hall, which was seven miles north of Pocatello. That was the real spark of the desire to write, when I saw how hungry these teenagers were to know about their culture. We would try to find books to interest them in reading, and very little is written about their ancestors. That was my main motivation for writing *Jenny of the Tetons.* I found a real Shoshone woman with nothing written about her, and I wanted to honor her and honor the culture.

"I had visited Jenny Lake up in the Tetons, thinking, 'This is a beautiful lake; I wonder who Jenny was?' I asked around at the ranger stations and the gift shops, and all that people could tell me was that Jenny was a Shoshone Indian who had lived with an English fur trapper. Someone showed me a little pamphlet about the Tetons, and in it was a quotation from a journal by the trapper, 'Beaver Dick' Leigh, in the University of Wyoming archives. After I got back home, I called the university and timidly asked for the archive section. This lovely gentleman got on the phone, and I said, 'I'm writing a book about Jenny of the Tetons'—that title just popped into my mind, and I'd never written a book before. I said, 'Is there any way I can get a copy of those journals?' And he said he would photocopy and mail them. In about ten days this huge package of journals and letters was sitting on my desk and I started poring through them.

"I got some geological survey maps of the area and spread them out on our kitchen table. As I read the journals, when Beaver Dick would talk about going up this canyon or traveling through this river or lake, I would highlight that area, and pretty soon I had a visual image of where he had traveled and how many hours a day he traveled to hunt. Because we lived in the area, I would drive up to see what it looked like—the trees and the terrain, and how you could see this mountain range from this point of view. So I was able to put it all in. In *Jenny of the Tetons* all the canyons, lakes, and rivers are real, and the days to travel and the time that it took, all that is real."

In *Jenny of the Tetons* Gregory tells of Jenny and Beaver Dick's lives from the point of view of a fictional immigrant orphan, Carrie Hill, adopted by the Leighs. Grieving for her parents, who were killed in an Indian raid, fifteen-year-old Carrie agrees to help Beaver Dick's wife tend their many children, unaware that his wife is herself an Indian. Once Carrie arrives at the Leighs' rustic home, she struggles to reconcile her hatred and Jenny's kindness. Gradually the family's love eases her

A young girl orphaned by an Indian attack learns to appreciate the beauty of the Tetons and Native American beliefs about nature through a Shoshone woman's example in Gregory's award-winning first novel. (Cover illustration by Wendell Minor.)

grief. When tragedy strikes the Leighs, she shares the sorrow fully. According to Richard Peck, assessing the book in the *Los Angeles Times Book Review,* "The strength of the writing lies in its research and the underplayed description of unqualified sorrow."

The research Gregory did for *Jenny of the Tetons* included getting firsthand information about Shoshone life. "I interviewed some of the elders on the Shoshone reservation and went out to one of their homes. A lovely woman named Emma Dann took me all over the reservation and showed me the little buffalo calves that they have there in the bottoms and the different plants, and she showed me what Jenny would have used to diaper her baby. She pulled off the bark of a sagebrush plant to get this long strip of bark about two feet wide. She rubbed it between her hands to make it real soft and said that this is what the mothers use to diaper their babies. I used that in both *Jenny* and *Jimmy Spoon.*"

Gregory noted that writing *Jenny of the Tetons* while mothering two small children had presented certain challenges. "It was not until my youngest son started

sleeping through the night that I was able to have the energy to write," she said. "I had to get up at four in the morning before the first baby woke up, and sometimes I would only write for half an hour, but it was very exciting seeing this story unfold. It was a lot of fun.

Deciding how to tell the tale was another interesting problem. "I chose first person with *Jenny of the Tetons* because Jenny died. At first I was going to write it from her point of view, but then I realized that if she dies and it's first person that's kind of a bummer of an ending. Also, I did not really know the Indian people well enough to get inside her and present what she might be thinking. I created a white girl, who was myself, who was new to Indians because I had just moved to Idaho and was a little afraid of them because I didn't know them. A lot of the narrator's characteristics were my own, and I was able to describe the emotions of not being sure about the Indians. Also, I was living at the time away from my family in California and was desperately lonely and very depressed, and I could identify with Carrie's not having her family with her. A lot of the heartache she felt was my heartache. As I got to know the Indian students in Pocatello and began to see their genuineness and how wonderful they were, Carrie started warming up to Jenny in the novel. By the end she has a deep love for her. In that situation Carrie the narrator was my own projection.

"After *Jenny of the Tetons* was published," Gregory added, "I arranged my own book signing tour in Idaho and the Tetons. I stopped in Pocatello, and this one Indian woman came up to me with a copy and wanted me to sign it. She was so excited, and it turned out she was Beaver Dick's granddaughter. She said, 'Thank you, thank you so much for telling our story.' Everywhere I went in Idaho those two weeks I would run into people, granddaughters or fifth-generation grandchildren of this man Beaver Dick, who were just thrilled about it."

Gregory stayed with Indian themes for her next book, *The Legend of Jimmy Spoon,* the tale of a young white boy who goes to live among the Shoshone. It was based on the memoirs of a nineteenth-century pony express rider. Twelve-year-old Jimmy is frustrated with both his father's refusal to give him a horse and the boredom of working at the family store. After meeting two Indian youths outside of town, he decides to accept their gift of a horse in return for a visit to their camp. The tribe wants him to stay permanently, however, and for the next three years Jimmy works to learn and understand Shoshone ways as the adopted son of the chief's mother. Eventually Jimmy's father discovers his whereabouts and threatens war if he does not return; to preserve the peace, Jimmy leaves the tribe. *Los Angeles Times Book Review* writer Eileen Heyes found the book "skimpy in the basics of story," but she judged it "rich in its portrait of Indian philosophy and daily life." Paula J. Lacey, reviewing *The Legend of Jimmy Spoon* in *Voice of Youth Advocates,* described it as "well researched" and "exciting."

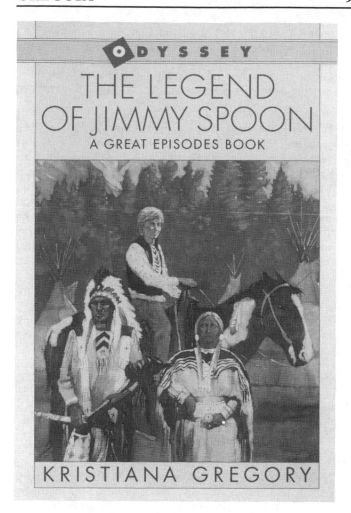

A white boy who lived with a Shoshone tribe in the 1800s provided the inspiration for this coming-of-age story by Gregory. (Cover illustration by Greg Shed.)

Gregory's personal knowledge of the Idaho Shoshone came into play in this book as well. "A boy that I tutored was telling me about how he was going to go with his uncle to get an eagle feather," she related. "He told me the honorable way to do it was not to kill the bird or harm it. He described how they would dig a pit and sit inside it while an elder would cover up the pit with twigs and sticks for camouflage and then put a piece of raw meat on top of a kind of trap door. The boy would sit inside this little hole all night and wait for an eagle to land on the meat, and at that instant he would thrust his hand out and grab a feather. I went home and immediately wrote it all down, and then when Jimmy Spoon goes to get an eagle feather I used that story and those details."

The idea for Gregory's third book came only after some setbacks. "After another book I had been trying to sell was again rejected, I was so depressed I said I was never going to write again," she told *SATA*. "I had kind of an angry conversation with God and said, 'If you want me to write again, you're going to have to show me a character, an event, and an original source document,' which is basically what I've done with the other two books. So I was in my orthodontist's office, and normally I don't get to read the magazines; this time he kept me waiting for forty-five minutes, and I had a chance to go through all the magazines on my lap. The last magazine was a *National Geographic* from 1990, and it was about the 1989 San Francisco earthquake with a sidebar about the 1906 earthquake. There were some never-before-published photographs taken by a young woman, and there was a little photo of her. It told this very tiny story, and there was an excerpt from a letter never before published describing what one woman had seen in the 1906 earthquake. There were incredible details—things that I had never heard or thought about—like looters being shot and babies being born in the parks. A set of triplets had been born after the earthquake. My heart started beating rapidly, and I said, 'Oh, this is a character, it's a young woman, there is a major event—the earthquake—and here's a document.'

"So I went home and called *National Geographic* to see if I could contact these people. They put me in touch with the owner of the letter and told me about Brigham Young University, which had the photos, and the photographer's nephew James Irvine, of the Irvine family of southern California. It was a big California story, not only because of where it happened, but because the Irvine family was one of the first white landowners in California.

"I started doing research. I called James Irvine and told him what I was doing, and he was very helpful. He gave me all kinds of information. He would drive to my house and give me photo albums of the Irvine family, and he left the photo albums at my home. I said, 'You do realize that I have two small children . . . .' He said, 'I trust you.' The story evolved from that and from a lot of research. Again, I did it all from my home, with books about the 1906 earthquake. There is still ongoing research as to the death toll. They believe it was much higher than what was originally reported, so I used a lot of that information."

In *Earthquake at Dawn* Gregory chronicles the experiences of photographer Edith Irvine and her traveling companion, the fictional Daisy Valentine, in San Francisco at the time of the great earthquake of April 18, 1906. The two young women come to the city early on the morning of the quake to board a ship to Australia and, ultimately, Paris, where Edith has been invited to show her photographs. The earthquake shatters their plans. They spend the next several days trying to find Edith's father, from whom they have been separated, and sharing the trials of several residents who become like family to them. One of their new friends is Mary Exa, whose 1906 letter about the earthquake provided revealing quotes for the beginning of each chapter. Despite thirst, hunger, exhaustion, fires, rats, and additional earth tremors, Edith makes time to photograph the devastation. This itself endangers them, for authorities trying to conceal the extent of the catastrophe have been destroying cameras and photographic plates. Mary Hedge, assessing the book for *Voice of Youth Advocates*, wrote, "The emotional impact . . . blends well with the adventure plot, making it an excellent choice for the rare teenage historical fiction lover."

"The theme that I tried to pull through in *Earthquake at Dawn*," Gregory explained to *SATA*, "was that you can survive. No matter how terrible something is that you might dread, often when you actually experience it it is not as bad as you had feared. You do get through it, and there are ways to get water. In the book they got water from the dew that gathered during the night and from melted ice and a lake, and eventually they brought river water over. They were eating frogs, they were making dandelion tea, and most of all they were banding together. Strangers became friends, and within a matter of hours they became family members because of how much they depended on each other. I'm hoping that whatever events kids go through, they see that there is hope in anything."

Gregory, who has lived much of her life in California, has had her own experiences with earthquakes. "Earthquakes are the only reason we would like to move from California," she said in her interview. "We're right on

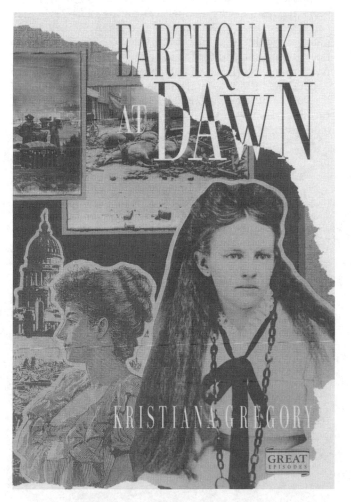

Gregory's tale of a photographer's attempt to record the 1906 earthquake in San Francisco is based on photographs by the real-life Edith Levine, who witnessed the disaster first-hand. (Cover illustration by David Kahl.)

the San Andreas Fault. I remember the one on June 28, 1992, the Big Bear quake. We are just below Big Bear, and at quarter to five in the morning the house started swaying. We're sort of used to them—you just wait for them to stop—but this one did not stop; it got stronger and stronger. It was the first time I actually went and pulled my children out of bed and sat in the hallway, and it was the most eerie feeling because I had just finished writing *Earthquake at Dawn*. It had just been published, and here I was reliving the experiences of my characters in a very intense way. We sat in the hallway and watched the floors of the house heave up and down, and the doors were all swinging on their hinges. There was a tinkling sound from everything in the cupboard that was shaking and moving, and things on the walls were shaking and moving. There were earthquakes all day long, little tremors. We sat outside for hours, and you could feel the grass move underneath you and see trees moving. We slept out in a tent for four nights because it was just too scary in the house.

"The next Monday after the earthquake I flew up to San Francisco for the American Booksellers Association convention and I was terrified to leave my family. It was traumatic for me to leave and then to go up to San Francisco. I stayed in a hotel right by the City Hall that had been destroyed in the 1906 earthquake."

Gregory's readers soon prompted her to write again, returning to an earlier subject. "I got so many letters from children all over the country asking for a sequel to *The Legend of Jimmy Spoon* that I said okay. It was called *Jimmy Spoon and the Pony Express*. I spent months researching the pony express. Because I couldn't get to Nevada, I called bookstores and museums all along the pony express trail and asked them to tell me what titles they had. I had bookstores send me things about Nevada flowers and the terrain and immigrant diaries from that era. One man sent me a videotape of the pony express trail that he had done all the way from Missouri to California so I could see what the terrain was like in Nevada. I would have loved to travel myself, but when you have children in school, you just don't have the time.

"As a mother I never know what my day is going to be like. I don't have high expectations for what I will accomplish, so I get up at about 4:30 in the morning and head out to my desk with some strong coffee. I always read the Bible first and pray, and then I start writing. When I am planning a book I do make outlines, because what's nice about history is I know the beginning, middle, and end. I know historically what happened in these months. With *Jimmy Spoon and the Pony Express*, I knew that the Civil War started here, Abraham Lincoln was inaugurated here; I have a little tiny graph with the real events. As I do research I pencil in things that are interesting that I think a character might have done in this month: what they would have done in the summer or winter, what kind of clothing they may have had to wear to keep warm. I pencil it in and then I start writing; I don't know exactly what I'm going to do.

"I rarely have isolated time to write; my desk is in the family room. What was neat about being a reporter was the training to write under any kind of pressure or deadline or noise. There were teletype machines going, other typewriters, phones ringing; an editor would interrupt you and say, 'Stop this story; go do this one.' That was wonderful training for being a mother trying to write, because that exactly describes what my day is like; it never goes as planned."

Gregory told *SATA* that she is "really thorough" about her research. "I'm really careful, and even so there is the chance that I could make a mistake. It is a challenge. I think that's why I will never write a biography, because you have to be so precise, and there is really no margin for error. If you do make an error, that sort of wipes out your credibility. I like the cover of fiction, historical fiction, because it's already surmised that most of it or a lot of it is fiction. I do try to be as accurate as possible."

One kind of writing she would like to practice is the short story. "I love O. Henry," she said. "I love the idea that there is a surprise at the end and a story written in a very distinct form. I was writing stories before I fell into book writing, and I was always getting rejected. I did have one story published a couple of years ago, but I haven't really pursued it since then. I think it's a real art form to pack all this into a short story."

In all her writing, Gregory tries to convey the need for love and hope. "What I'm gradually learning—I wish I'd learned it younger—is that your family is those you love, and you can have a family anywhere. Our society is very disrupted, full of broken families, and there are a lot of kids, at least here in San Bernardino County, who have lost a parent to murder. The gang population is very high, and the violence is pretty bad, and it's astounding to me the grief that some of these kids must feel. What do you do? Does that mean you have no family anymore? Part of my motivation is I'm hoping that kids, as I said, see that there is hope, there is always hope, and there is always somebody to love, and there is always someone who will love you." Love is paramount in her books, Gregory asserted, "love for your fellow human being regardless of color or circumstances, taking time to try to understand another person and not make snap judgments."

WORKS CITED:

Gregory, Kristiana, telephone interview with Polly A. Vedder for *Something about the Author,* conducted February 4, 1993.

Hedge, Mary, review of *Earthquake at Dawn, Voice of Youth Advocates,* June, 1992, p. 94.

Heyes, Eileen, review of *The Legend of Jimmy Spoon, Los Angeles Times Book Review,* October 28, 1990, p. 12.

Lacey, Paula J., review of *The Legend of Jimmy Spoon, Voice of Youth Advocates,* December, 1990, p. 281.

Peck, Richard, "A Blending of Two Cultures," *Los Angeles Times Book Review,* May 28, 1989, p. 8.

GRIPE, Maria (Kristina) 1923-

PERSONAL: Surname is pronounced "*gree*-puh"; born July 25, 1923, in Vaxholm, Sweden; married Harald Gripe (an artist), 1946; children: Camilla. *Education:* Attended Stockholm University; received General Certificate of Education.

ADDRESSES: Home—Frauengsgatan 5, 61131 Nykoeping, Sweden.

CAREER: Free-lance writer.

AWARDS, HONORS: Nils Holgersson Plaque for the best book of the year, Association of Swedish Libraries, for *Hugo och Josephin;* Lewis Carroll Shelf Award, Wisconsin Book Conference, for *Pappa Pellerin's Daughter;* honor book, *New York Herald Tribune*'s Children's Spring Book Festival, for *Pappa Pellerin's Daughter; Expressen* (Swedish evening newspaper) "Heffaklumpen" Award, 1966, for *Hugo;* Litteraturfraemjandets stipendium, 1968, for *Nattpappan;* Sveriges foerfattarfonds konstnaars stipendium, 1970-71; Astrid Lindgren-priset, 1972; Hans Christian Andersen International Children's Book Award, 1974; Sveriges foerfattarfonds premium foer litteraar foertjaanst, 1974; Hjalmar Bergman-priset, 1977; Doblougska priset, 1979; LO stipendiet, 1980; Metalls Kulturpris, 1981; Premio Nacional, utdelat av Spanska Kulturministeriet, 1982; Litteraturfraemjandets stora barnbokspris tillsammans med Harald Gripe, 1982; Jeremias i Troestloesapriset, 1983; Allmaenna Barnhusets Stora Pris, 1992.

MARIA GRIPE

WRITINGS:

IN ENGLISH TRANSLATION

Pappa Pellerin's Daughter, translated by Kersti French, John Day, 1966 (originally published as *Pappa Pellerins dotter,* Bonniers, 1963).

Hugo and Josephine, translated by Paul Britten Austin, Delacorte, 1969 (originally published as *Hugo och Josefin,* Bonniers, 1962).

Josephine, translated by Austin, Delacorte, 1970 (originally published as *Josefin,* Bonniers, 1961).

Hugo, translated by Austin, Delacorte, 1970 (originally published as *Hugo,* Bonniers, 1966).

The Night Father, translated by Gerry Bothmer, Delacorte, 1971 (originally published as *Nattpappan,* Bonniers, 1968).

The Glassblower's Children, translated by Sheila La Farge, Delacorte, 1974 (originally published as *Glasblaasarns Barn,* Bonniers, 1964).

The Land Beyond, translated by La Farge, Delacorte, 1974 (originally published as *Landet utanfoer,* Bonniers, 1967).

Julia's House, translated by Boethmer, Delacorte, 1975 (originally published as *Julias hus och Nattpappan,* Bonniers, 1971).

In the Time of the Bells, translated by La Farge, Delacorte, 1976 (originally published as *I Klockornas Tid,* Bonniers, 1965).

Elvis and His Secret, translated by La Farge, Delacorte, 1976 (originally published as *Elvis Karlsson,* Bonniers, 1972).

Elvis and His Friends, Delacorte, 1976 (originally published as *Elvis! Elvis!,* Bonniers, 1973).

Agnes Cecilia, translated by Rika Lesser, Harper, 1990 (originally published as *Agnes Cecilia-en saellsam historia,* Bonniers, 1981).

UNTRANSLATED WORKS

I vaar lilla stad, Bonniers, 1954.

Naar det snoeade, illustrated by Harald Gripe, Bonniers, 1955.

Kung Laban Kommer, Bonniers, 1956.

Kvarteret Labyrinten, Bonniers, 1956.

Sebastian och Skuggan, Bonniers, 1957.

Stackars Lilla Q, Bonniers, 1957.

Tappe inte Masken, Bonniers, 1959.

Da smaa roeda, illustrated by Harald Gripe, Bonniers, 1960.

Glastunneln, Bonniers, 1969.

Tanten (based on her radio play *The Aunt*), Bonniers, 1970.

...ellen dellen..., Bonniers, 1972.

Den "riktiga" Elvis, illustrated by Harald Gripe, Bonniers, 1976.

Att vara Elvis, illustrated by Harald Gripe, Bonniers, 1977.

Tordyveln flygeri i skymningen (based on her radio play), Bonniers, 1978.

Bara Elvis, illustrated by Harald Gripe, Bonniers, 1979.

Skuggan oever stenbaenken, Bonniers, 1982.

... och de vita skuggorna i skogen, Bonniers, 1984.

Skuggornas barn, Bonniers, 1986.

Skugg-goemman, Bonniers, 1988.

Hjaertat som ingen ville ha, Bonniers, 1989.

Tre trappor upp med hiss, Bonniers, 1991.

Eget rum (sequel to *Tre trappor upp med hiss*), Bonniers, 1992.

OTHER

Also author of screenplays for film versions of *Hugo and Joesphine,* 1968, the Elvis Karlsson books, 1976, and *Agnes Cecilia,* 1991; author of radio plays *The Night Daddy* and *Elvis Karlsson,* 1973, and *Elvis! Elvis!,* 1974, all based on her books, six-part radio play *The Aunt,* 1969, and 13-part radio play *Tordyveln flyger i skymningen,* 1976; author of teleplays based on *The Night Daddy,* 1971, and *Flickan cid stenbaenken,* a nine-part teleplay based on the books *Skuggan oever Stenbaenken, ... och de vita skuggorna i skogen,* and *Skuggornas barn,* 1989.

SIDELIGHTS: The characters who populate Swedish writer Maria Gripe's novels are children struggling for a sense of their own identity, often in the face of parental opposition or neglect. Like her literary ancestor, Hans Christian Andersen, she uses fantasy and a deceptively simple style to explore psychological complexities. Critics have labeled her work difficult, disturbing, and moody, but have also appreciated the beauty and perceptiveness in her writing.

The author once commented that her father provided her with early guidance as to her future career: "He said that in all the literature of the world there is only one person worthy of being called an *author:* Hans Christian Andersen. After him nobody. Light years behind him come all the poor wretches who were just 'writers.' Do you want to be one of those miserables?" About her own youthful writing her father was just as severe: "'My dear, this is terrible. In order to write you need to (a) have something to write about, and (b) know how to write. While waiting for (a) learn (b).' Such was his judgement."

Throughout her youth Gripe wrote infrequently, and then mostly, following her father's advice, to improve her Swedish. She attended Stockholm University, where she studied philosophy and history of religion but did not earn a degree. When she left school she married Harald Gripe, an artist, and had a daughter, Camilla. It was to satisfy Camilla's appetite for tales that she began making up her own stories, her husband providing illustrations. When she became a mother she fulfilled her father's first requirement for writing: "There was no getting around it—I had something to write about—and somebody to write *for,*" she said.

Her first published effort, *I var lilla stad*—a fantasy about a village inhabited by animals—and the next several works were fairy stories. *Josephine,* published in 1961, was the first novel in which Gripe explored the themes most associated with her subsequent work. Josephine is actually named Anna Gra, but, as Lorraine Stanton notes in *Catholic Library World,* Josephine "refuses to use her real name ... because she cannot accept the role in life she has been born into." There is a tension between Josephine's feelings about herself and her parents' feelings about her, explains Mary Orvig in *Horn Book*: "Josephine knows that she is quite a different person from what her parents imagine, but she is mistaken concerning their expectations of her. She is a child who listens to adults and lets her own imagination and limited experience get to work on what she hears; and the result is a dangerous misunderstanding. But the misunderstanding is cleared up, and the world is put right again for Josephine."

Much of the inspiration for *Josephine* came from Gripe's own childhood, which is still very vivid in the author's mind. As a young girl she had a rich fantasy life and felt herself very different than other children. Nevertheless, she wanted to fit in, and so "I played the wildest games with the rascals in the neighborhood—I changed my personality completely within the shortest time," Gripe recounted in *Bookbird*. "I was deathly afraid that someone might catch a glimpse of my inner life, and whenever I got a hint that it might happen I merely stuck out my tongue. I scoffed at my earlier self and began to speak in a new and more effective way. Undeniably, I was more successful. I became popular and that was a most welcome change.... But I no longer felt so naturally happy, although I behaved as though I did." To help herself cope with this "split" reality, Gripe would read her favorite fairy tales many times over.

Hugo and Josephine reflects the author's own experience, as Josephine enters school and tries to conform to the ways of the other students in order to fit in. She isn't happy, however, being "*nearly* like everyone else," and admires Hugo, who isn't *anything* like anyone else. Hugo and Josephine become friends, and she is inspired by his honesty and courage. This novel continues Gripe's exploration of the theme of identity, as Josephine continues to use her fictitious name, allowing herself to be called Anna Gra only at the end of the book.

Hugo completes the trilogy of novels begun with *Josephine* and continued with *Hugo and Josephine*. Generally considered to be the best novel of the three, *Hugo* elaborates on the life of its title character. Hugo's mother is dead and his father is in prison—"two events," observes Orvig, "which arouse tremendous curiosity among his classmates but which he himself regards with superb equanimity." Hugo, the ultimate nonconformist at age seven, finally leaves school because the world outside the classroom has so much more to offer him.

In addition to the "Hugo" and "Josephine" books, Gripe has written several novels that combine the fantastic elements of her early work with the psychological probing of her later novels. These works include *The Glassblower's Children, In the Time of the Bells,* and *The Land Beyond. The Glassblower's Children* tells the story of a brother and sister's captivity in the house of the Lord of All Wishes Town. The children are turned into puppets, and eventually they vanish completely. They

are saved by a kind old woman, whose twin sister was responsible for the children's transformation.

In the Time of the Bells uses the relationship between an unhappy young king and the peasant boy chosen to receive punishment on the king's behalf as a forum for "discussion of determinism and free will," as noted by Sally Holmes Holtze in *Horn Book*. The presence of court astrologers, an evil dwarf, and a vicious cat add to the fairy-tale quality of the story. *The Land Beyond* is also on the surface a fairy-tale, this one telling the story of a young king, a princess, and an explorer, who each wish to find a place not located on any map. Their quest for that land also leads them within themselves.

Maria Gripe deftly mixes a delicate style, perceptive characterization, and a sense of wonder. While children no doubt find her novels challenging, they just as surely discover within her works their own anxieties and fantasies faithfully rendered. And this, as the author stated in *Bookbird,* is one motivation for her writing: "I write [my books] because I simply believe that they are necessary.... Children differ from one another, immensely.... The child who feels himself different doesn't know why and merely conforms more and more. That is the situation."

An unusual babysitter gains the trust and friendship of a reluctant young ward in Gripe's novel. (Cover illustration by Harald Gripe.)

WORKS CITED:

Gripe, Maria, "A Word and a Shadow," *Bookbird,* March 15, 1974, pp. 4-10.
Holtze, Sally Holmes, *Horn Book,* February, 1977, p. 51.
Orvig, Mary, "A Collage, Eight Women Who Write Books in Swedish for Children," *Horn Book,* April, 1973, pp. 119-26.
Stanton, Lorraine, "Shadows and Motifs: A Review and Analysis of the Works of Maria Gripe," *Catholic Library World,* May-June, 1980, pp. 447-49.

FOR MORE INFORMATION SEE:

BOOKS

Children's Literature Review, Volume 5, Gale, 1983.
Egoff, Sheila A., *Thursday's Child: Trends and Patterns in Contemporary Children's Literature,* American Library Association, 1981.
Twentieth-Century Children's Writers, 3rd edition, St. James Press, 1989.

PERIODICALS

Bulletin of the Center for Children's Books, September, 1966.
Christian Science Monitor, February 20, 1971.
Horn Book, October, 1970.
Junior Bookshelf, April, 1966; April, 1972, pp. 97-98; October, 1978.
New York Times Book Review, September 2, 1973, p. 20.
Times Literary Supplement, April 2, 1971, p. 391.

*   *   *

MORTON GROSSER

GROSSER, Morton 1931-

PERSONAL: Born December 25, 1931, in Philadelphia, PA; son of Albert J. (an industrial realtor) and Esther (Mendel) Grosser; married Janet Zachs (an engineer and calligrapher), June 28, 1953; children: Adam. *Education:* Massachusetts Institute of Technology, B.S., 1953, M.S., 1954; Stanford University, Ph.D., 1961. *Hobbies and other interests:* Transportation, fitness, model-building, dance.

ADDRESSES: Home and office—1016 Lemon St., Menlo Park, CA 94025.

CAREER: Massachusetts Institute of Technology, Cambridge, research associate, 1954-55; Raytheon Corp., Waltham, MA, engineering designer, 1955-56; Clevite Transistor Products, Waltham, head of design for the developmental division, 1956-57; Boeing Corporation, Seattle, WA, director of publication, 1964-66; independent technology and management consultant in Palo Alto and Menlo Park, CA, 1967-83 and 1987-93; L. H. Alton and Co., San Francisco, CA, founding general partner and managing director, 1984-87. Has taught at Stanford University and Massachusetts Institute of Technology; lecturer. Member of Gossamer Albatross Team, 1978-81.

MEMBER: American Institute of Aeronautics and Astronautics, American Society of Mechanical Engineers, Association for Computing Machinery, Astronomical Society of the Pacific, Society of Automotive Engineers, Authors Guild.

AWARDS, HONORS: Coates and Clark graduate fellow, Massachusetts Institute of Technology, 1953-54; Ford Foundation Fellow in Chinese, Stanford University, 1960; postdoctoral fellow at the University of California, Los Angeles Medical Center, National Institutes of Health, 1961-62; Wallace Stegner Creative Writing Fellow, Stanford University, 1963-64; Commonwealth Club medal for literary excellence, 1991, and Golden Sower Award nomination, 1992, both for *The Fabulous Fifty.*

WRITINGS:

NOVELS; FOR YOUNG ADULTS

The Snake Horn, Atheneum, 1973.
The Fabulous Fifty, Macmillan/Atheneum, 1990.

OTHER

The Discovery of Neptune, Harvard University Press, 1962.
The Hobby Shop (novel), Houghton, 1967.
Diesel: The Man and the Engine, Atheneum, 1978.
Gossamer Odyssey: The Triumph of Human-Powered Flight, Houghton, 1981.
On Gossamer Wings, Du Pont/York, 1982.

Contributor of papers, articles, fiction, and poetry to periodicals, including *Atlantic, Harper's, New Yorker,* and *Saturday Evening Post.*

The Discovery of Neptune has been translated into German, Japanese, and Italian.

WORK IN PROGRESS: A mystery/suspense novel set in New York; a nonfiction book on the parenting of gifted children.

* * *

GURAVICH, Dan 1918-

PERSONAL: Born February 22, 1918, in Winnipeg, Manitoba, Canada; immigrated to United States, 1949; son of Joshua (a merchant) and Sarah (Friedman) Guravich; married, 1942; wife's name, Betty; divorced, 1964; children: Martha Weissman, Paula, David. *Education:* University of Manitoba, B.S., 1939; University of Wisconsin, M.S., 1948, Ph.D., 1949. *Politics:* Conservative.

ADDRESSES: Home and office—407 Rebecca Dr., Greenville, MS 38701.

CAREER: Delta Branch Experiment Station, Stoneville, MS, cotton geneticist, 1949-53; free-lance location photographer, Greenville, MS, 1953—. President of Polar Bears Alive, Inc. *Military service:* Served in the Canadian Tank Corps in Italy and Germany, 1942-45; commander of photographic section during last eight months of World War II.

MEMBER: Society of American Travel Writers, American Society of Magazine Photographers, Travel Journalists Guild.

AWARDS, HONORS: Award of merit, Art Director's Club of Metropolitan Washington, 1968, for aerial photography; Image Makers Award, *Professional Photography,* 1970, for arctic moonscape; publication award, Geographic Society of Chicago, 1970, for Mississippi River photography; Cannes Film Festival selection, 1970, for film *In the Path of History;* certificate of merit, Society of Publication Designers, 1973; Gold Quill, International Association of Business, 1975, for "Exxon USA"; achievement in science award, Mississippi Academy of Science, 1985; certificate of excellence, *Parenting,* 1991, for *Polar Bear Cubs.*

Dan Guravich and polar bear friend.

WRITINGS:

TEXT AND PHOTOGRAPHS

The Grand Banks, Rand McNally, 1968.
Man and the River: The Mississippi, Rand McNally, 1970.
The Northwest Passage, Rand McNally, 1970.
The Gulf of Mexico, Viking, 1972.
Inside Passage, Doubleday, 1976.
The Mormon Trek West, Doubleday, 1980.
Yesterday's Wings, Doubleday, 1982.
Lords of the Arctic, Macmillan, 1982.
The Return of the Brown, Louisiana State University Press, 1983.
A Field Guide to Southern Mushrooms, University of Michigan Press, 1984.
Polar Bears, Simon & Schuster, 1988.
Polar Bear Cubs, Simon & Schuster, 1989.
Skimmers, Simon & Schuster, 1990.
An Arctic Summer, Simon & Schuster, 1993.
The Polar Bear, Chronicle Press, 1993.

Contributor to periodicals, including *Life, Town & Country, Outdoor Photography, Boys Life,* and *Health and Safety Review.*

WORK IN PROGRESS: Children's books on wetlands and arctic foxes.

H

HALLARD, Peter
See CATHERALL, Arthur

* * *

HANNA, Jack (Bushnell) 1947-

PERSONAL: Born January 2, 1947, in Knoxville, TN; son of Edwin Ross (in real estate) and Caroline (a homemaker; maiden name, Bushnell) Hanna; married Suzanne Egli, December 20, 1968; children: Kathaleen, Suzanne, Julie. *Education:* Muskingum College, B.A., 1969; postgraduate study at University of Tennessee. *Politics:* Republican. *Religion:* Reformed Church of America.

ADDRESSES: Home—8900 Turin Hill Ct., Dublin, OH 43017. *Office*—P.O. Box 277, Dublin, OH 43017. *Agent*—Nancy Rose, Levine, Thall & Plotkin, 1740 Broadway, New York, NY 10019.

CAREER: Knoxville Zoological Park, Knoxville, TN, head curator, 1970-72; Central Florida Zoo, Sanford, FL, director, 1973-75; Stan Brock Wilderness Adventures, vice-president and associate producer, 1975-78; Columbus Zoological Park, Columbus, OH, executive director, 1978-93, director emeritus, 1993—. Speaker and wildlife conservator. Associate producer, *The Forgotten Wilderness,* 1975; co-host of television programs *Hanna's Ark,* 1981, and *ZooLife with Jack Hanna;* regular guest on *Late Night with David Letterman,* NBC-TV, and *Good Morning America,* ABC-TV; other numerous appearances on *Larry King Live, Nashville Network, Everyday with Joan Lunden, Disney Channel, Discovery Channel,* and PBS programs. Cofounder, Rhino Rescue, Inc. Chairman, Easter Seals, Central Ohio Chapter, 1984-85; president, Leukemia Society, Central Ohio Chapter, 1984-85. Trustee, Muskingum College, 1981-93, International Center for the Preservation of Wild Animals, 1984—, Kiski Preparatory School for Boys, Saltsburg, PA, 1987-93. Member of board of directors of The Digit Fund, Denver, CO. *Military service:* U.S. Army Reserve, 1968-71.

MEMBER: International Wildlife Federation (fellow), American Association of Zoological Parks and Aquariums, Appalachian Zoological Society (honorary director, 1975—), Explorer's Club.

AWARDS, HONORS: Named Outstanding Citizen, Columbus Jaycees, 1979, 1980; Distinguished Alumni Award, Muskingum College, 1980; Citizen of the Year award, Columbus K.C., 1980; distinguished service award, 1980; honorary D.Sc., Otterbein College, 1983, Capital University, 1985.

WRITINGS:

(With John Stravinsky) *Monkeys on the Interstate, and Other Tales from America's Favorite Zookeeper,* New American Library/Dutton, 1990.
Let's Go to the Petting Zoo with Jungle Jack, illustrated by Neil Brennan, Doubleday, 1992.
(With Kelly Anne Tate) *The Lion's Share,* Viking Penguin, 1992.

SIDELIGHTS: "Things happen to me," writes Jack Hanna in his best-selling memoir *Monkeys on the Interstate.* "Sometimes I ask for it, sometimes I'm an innocent bystander. Sometimes it's funny, and sometimes it's not—at least when it's happening." Known to millions of Americans from his frequent appearances on *Late Night with David Letterman* and *Good Morning America,* wildlife conservator and animal advocate "Jungle Jack" Hanna uses almost any means at his disposal to increase public awareness and concern for endangered wildlife. "I can hope," he tells *People* magazine's Toni Schlesinger, "... that I've made someone aware of how important animals are and why wildlife should be preserved."

Jack Hanna grew up on a farm near Knoxville, Tennessee, surrounded by animals. "It was here," he writes in *Monkeys on the Interstate,* "that I first became fascinated by little furry creatures." When Jack was eleven, he began working for Dr. Warren Roberts, the vet that cared for the Hannas' dogs, first simply cleaning up, then moving on to assist with farm births and feeding

In his many television appearances, Jack Hanna
introduces people to different kinds of wildlife and
points out the importance of preserving endangered
species. (From *Monkeys on the Interstate.*)

and watering. "If you can somehow enjoy cleaning out
their cages," Hanna declares, "then you know you
genuinely love animals." At the same time Jack began
his own collection of animals—fish kept in ponds on the
property, lots of rabbits, and even miniature donkeys,
which he bred with much success.

When Jack was fifteen, his poor grades led his parents to
send him off to a boarding school in Pennsylvania. He
maintained his interest in animals, trying to obtain a
cougar for the school mascot and (when that scheme fell
through) trying to trap squirrels for the same purpose.
After graduation, Jack enrolled at Muskingum College, a
small liberal arts school in Ohio, where one of his
donkeys became the school mascot and where he met
Suzi Egli, whom he later married. Suzi, the captain of
the school cheerleading squad, was as enthusiastic about
animals as Jack was. "If I've made it this far through all
the animal craziness over the years," Hanna writes in
Monkeys on the Interstate, "I have to thank Suzi for
going along with everything all the way."

After graduation Jack and Suzi returned to the Knoxville area and opened a pet store specializing in exotic

animals. Sadly, a tragic accident involving a young child
who was mauled by a lioness forced them to close the
business. Jack took a job working with animals in
Georgia, and when a position opened with the Central
Florida Zoo, he moved his family further south. Over
the next two years, with hard work and perseverance—
plus occasional assistance from Stan Brock, veteran of
the *Wild Kingdom* nature television series—Jack expanded the zoo from a single-acre to a 104-acre facility.
In addition, he gained a reputation as a sort of adjunct
animal control officer. When a bear was discovered
wandering through an affluent Orlando suburb, or an
alligator had bitten through the tire of a police cruiser
and couldn't get its teeth unstuck, Jack Hanna was
called in to handle the situation.

Jack left the Central Florida Zoo in 1975 and returned
to Knoxville, where he worked for a time promoting a
wildlife film, *The Forgotten Wilderness*—a project,
states Hanna in *Monkeys on the Interstate,* that "turned
out to be an effort best forgotten." Over the next few
years he worked at a variety of projects, including selling
real estate and releasing captive jaguars into the Vene-
zuelan jungle. None of these activities, however, proved
satisfying for him. When a friend mentioned an adver-
tisement for a position as zoo director in Columbus,
Ohio, Jack jumped at the chance.

"The jump to being director of the Columbus Zoo,"
Hanna writes in *Monkeys on the Interstate,* "was the
biggest thing that had ever happened to me in my life—
like going from dogcatcher to mayor without running for
office." Although honored by zoologists for having bred
and raised the first captive-born gorilla—Colo, born in
1956—in the intervening years the Columbus Zoo had
become run-down, a second-rate facility. Jack Hanna
dedicated himself to improving it. Using his talent for
promotion, Jack brought the zoo's predicament to
public notice, raised funds to supplement its small
budget, and, declares Stephen Whitty in *Cosmopolitan,*
"built Ohio's Columbus Zoo into one of the country's
best—and most popular—menageries."

Jack did this in part by appealing to wealthy citizens and
corporations. Multimillionaire John McConnell donat-
ed funds to revamp the gorilla's quarters, and Colum-
bus-based Nationwide Insurance contributed money for
animals and their care. "You need solid, consistent
attendance and corporate donations to pull through,"
Hanna writes in *Monkeys on the Interstate;* "the only
way to get these is to make people aware of the zoo,
make them feel as though they're contributing to a
necessary part of the community, a part of the community that's just as important as the symphony, libraries
or even the school system."

At the same time Jack built a reputation as a man who
loved animals, who would go to great lengths to insure
that they had proper treatment, and who thrived on
publicity. In 1979, Jack and a colleague rescued a kitten
marooned on a ledge in the middle of a dam near the
zoo. Local authorities often called on him to handle
snake problems: a man who kept cobras in his apart-

ment, for example, or a trio of ladies who discovered a corn snake in their toilet bowl. Also, early in his career, two Japanese snow monkeys escaped from the zoo grounds and led Jack and his staff on a merry chase that lasted over seven months and traveled up Interstate Highway 71 toward Cleveland. Through skillful use of the media, Jack changed what might have been an embarrassment into a comic event—and again brought the zoo into the public eye.

Jack Hanna and the Columbus Zoo became national media stars in 1983, in a segment aired on *Good Morning America* (*GMA*). The show was initially attracted by a very rare event—the birth of twin gorillas at Columbus. After a few more segments, the show invited Jack to make monthly appearances and "adopted" the zoo. The program benefited Jack, the Columbus Zoo, and wildlife in general by bringing them nationwide exposure. "The image *GMA* was trying to project with the zoo segments," Hanna explains in *Monkeys on the Interstate,* "was one where the viewer would learn something (often about threatened or endangered species) and still enjoy the animal as well." In 1985, Jack made his first appearance on *Late Night with David Letterman,* bringing the zoo and its animals to a different, late-night audience. "My philosophy is to entertain and hope people learn," Hanna declares in *Monkeys on the Interstate,* "rather than to teach and hope people are entertained.... People play for laughs on Letterman, which is something we've managed to do for [some time] now without demeaning or hurting any of the animals."

Jack regards public education about animals as one of his most important functions. "I really do the television appearances to reach people—my job as a zoo director would be a lot easier if I *didn't* do them," he tells Whitty. He has directed safaris to Kenya's Serengeti Plain, Rwanda's Great Apes sanctuary to see the rare mountain gorillas, and to the Galapagos Islands. He also helped bring the plight of the black rhinoceros to public notice, forming Rhino Rescue, Inc., to help preserve the species. "What you're doing [in a zoo] is teaching conservation in a fun way," Hanna explains to Whitty. "People need to understand what's happening to the earth's wildlife."

In 1993, Jack retired as active director of the Columbus Zoo to become director emeritus. He has explored other fields, including writing—in addition to his memoir *Monkeys on the Interstate,* he has composed *Let's Go to the Petting Zoo with Jungle Jack,* a touch-and-feel book for very young children that introduces them to exotic animals. It became a best-seller, with more than 115,000 copies sold. He has also coauthored *The Lion's Share,* a mystery novel about a zoo veterinarian who must turn sleuth in order to keep some of his animals from being destroyed. But he will probably not move on to more zoo work. "This is the last zoo Jack Hanna will be director of," he tells Whitty. The director emeritus position, he continues, gives him more free time— "where I wouldn't have the day-to-day operations but

would maybe continue some of my TV appearances, speeches, books, and educational work."

WORKS CITED:

Hanna, Jack, with John Stravinsky, *Monkeys on the Interstate, and Other Tales from America's Favorite Zookeeper,* New American Library/Dutton, 1990.
Schlesinger, Toni, "Jack Hanna Braves Tigers and *Letterman* to Become TV's Favorite Zookeeper," *People,* February 1, 1988, pp. 87-89.
Whitty, Stephen, "Cosmo Talks to Jack Hanna, Director of the Columbus Zoo," *Cosmopolitan,* February, 1991, pp. 110, 118, 120, 142.

FOR MORE INFORMATION SEE:

PERIODICALS

Cosmopolitan, August, 1989, p. 76.
Library Journal, June 1, 1989, p. 114; April 1, 1992, p. 153.
New York Times Book Review, June 7, 1992, p. 19.
Publishers Weekly, May 12, 1989, p. 269; March 2, 1992, p. 50; April 13, 1992, p. 56.

*   *   *

HARLAN, Judith 1949-

PERSONAL: Born February 3, 1949, in Albany, NY; daughter of Jack (a military officer) and Ruth Harlan; married Terry Tintorri (a real estate agent), December 10, 1988. *Education:* University of Arizona, B.A., 1971; San Francisco State University, M.A., 1979.

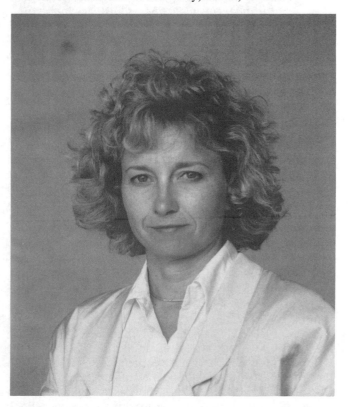

JUDITH HARLAN

ADDRESSES: *Agent*—c/o Publicity Director, Franklin Watts, Inc., 387 Park Ave. South, New York, NY 10016.

CAREER: Free-lance journalist and author. *Harbor Times* (a beach and harbor weekly), editor, 1980-81; Murphy Organization (advertising agency), news copywriter, 1982-83; *Freebies* (magazine), editor, 1984-85; Oxnard College, instructor, 1991—. Has also worked as a feature and news stringer for the *Los Angeles Times.*

MEMBER: Society of Professional Journalists, Society of Children's Book Writers and Illustrators.

AWARDS, HONORS: Notable Book citation, National Council for Social Studies and Children's Book Council, 1987, for *American Indians Today;* Carter G. Woodson Outstanding Merit Award, National Council for Social Studies, 1989, for *Hispanic Voters.*

WRITINGS:

American Indians Today: Issues and Conflicts, Franklin Watts, 1987.
Hispanic Voters: Gaining a Voice in American Politics, Franklin Watts, 1988.
Sounding the Alarm: A Biography of Rachel Carson, Dillon Press, 1989.
Bilingualism in the United States: Conflict and Controversy, Franklin Watts, 1991.

Also West Coast editor and author of monthly column, *Earnshaw's* magazine; contributor to numerous periodicals, including *Alternative Energy Retailer, American Way, Art Business News, Business Travelers International, L.A. Parent,* and *Entree.*

SIDELIGHTS: Judith Harlan told *SATA:* "I have always been a sucker for a good story, always interested in reading, writing, and people. In elementary school, I was an outdoors, rough-and-tumble kind of girl during the day; in the evenings, I was a silent adventurer, discovering the worlds far away inside books.... I read all the adventures and wanted to be just like the heroes in them. When I was a teenager, I noticed that I enjoyed writing stories almost as much as reading them. I've been writing them ever since, from newspaper and magazine articles to advertising copy to children's books. And children's books are what I enjoy most, what takes me back to those faraway places I used to go as a child.

"I hope that the books I have written so far have been helpful and informative for young readers. All four books are approached from a journalist's perspective—I wanted to know all sides of the issues, to present those sides as objectively as is humanly possible. Three of the books involve the study of multiculturalism in the United States, a topic about people, a topic of interest to me; the fourth one is about one of my heroes, Rachel Carson. The work I'm doing now is a departure from these journalistic books. I am working on picture book projects and on a novel for young readers."

HARRIS, Christie (Lucy) Irwin 1907-

PERSONAL: Born November 21, 1907, in Newark, NJ; immigrated to Canada in 1908; daughter of Edward (a farmer) and Matilda (Christie) Irwin; married Thomas Arthur Harris (a Canadian immigration officer), February 13, 1932; children: Michael, Moira (Mrs. Lee Block), Sheilagh (Mrs. Jack Simpson), Brian, Gerald. *Education:* Attended University of British Columbia, 1925. *Religion:* Church of England.

ADDRESSES: *Home*—430 Arnold Ave., Victoria, British Columbia V8S 3M2, Canada.

CAREER: Teacher in British Columbia, 1926-32; free-lance writer for Canadian Broadcasting Corporation Radio, 1936-1963; author, 1957—.

MEMBER: Writers' Union of Canada.

AWARDS, HONORS: First award in educational radio and television competitions in Columbus, OH, for school radio series "Laws for Liberty"; Book of the Year for Children Medal, Canadian Association of Children's Librarians (CACL), 1967, for *Raven's Cry;* Vicky Metcalf Award, 1973; Book of the Year for Children Medal, CACL, 1977, and IBBY honor list citation, both for *Mouse Woman and the Vanished Princesses;* Children's Literature Prize, Canada Council, 1980, and Canadian Library Association book of the year runner-up citation and Amelia Frances Howard-Gibbon Award, both 1981, all for *The Trouble with Princesses;* member of the Order of Canada, 1981.

CHRISTIE IRWIN HARRIS

WRITINGS:

Cariboo Trail, Longmans, Green, 1957.

Once upon a Totem (American Indian legends), illustrated by John Frazer Mills, Atheneum, 1963.

You Have to Draw the Line Somewhere, illustrated by daughter, Moira Johnston, Atheneum, 1964.

West with the White Chiefs, illustrated by Walter Ferro, Atheneum, 1965.

Raven's Cry, illustrated by Bill Reid, Atheneum, 1966.

Confessions of a Toe-Hanger, illustrated by Johnston, Atheneum, 1967.

Forbidden Frontier, illustrated by E. Carey Kenney, Atheneum, 1968.

Let X Be Excitement, Atheneum, 1969.

(With Johnston) *Figleafing through History: The Dynamics of Dress,* illustrated by Johnston, Atheneum, 1971.

Secret in the Stlalakum Wild, illustrated by Douglas Tait, Atheneum, 1972.

(With husband, Thomas Arthur Harris) *Mule Lib,* McClelland and Stewart, 1972.

Once More upon a Totem (American Indian legends), illustrated by Tait, Atheneum, 1973.

Sky Man on the Totem Pole?, illustrated by Tait, Atheneum, 1975.

Mouse Woman and the Vanished Princesses (American Indian legends), illustrated by Tait, Atheneum, 1976.

Mouse Woman and the Mischief-Makers (American Indian legends), illustrated by Tait, Atheneum, 1977.

Mystery at the Edge of Two Worlds, illustrated by Lou Crockett, Atheneum, 1978.

Mouse Woman and the Muddleheads (American Indian legends), illustrated by Tait, Atheneum, 1979.

The Trouble with Princesses (American Indian legends), illustrated by Tait, Atheneum, 1980.

The Trouble with Adventurers (American Indian legends), illustrated by Tait, Atheneum, 1982.

The majority of Harris's juvenile works were published simultaneously in Canada by McClelland and Stewart.

Also author of twelve adult plays, juvenile stories, journal articles, and radio scripts, including several hundred school programs. Women's editor, *A S & M News.*

WORK IN PROGRESS: Three more stories "in the works."

SIDELIGHTS: An award-winning author of novels, short stories, and radio plays, Christie Harris is best known for her fiction for children that is based on the mythology of the Canadian Northwest Indians. Harris has spent many years learning firsthand about the culture that informs her retellings of Indian legends and her historical novels of the Canadian Northwest. While her works often combine mythical, scientific, historical, fantastic, and modern family elements, it is the authenticity of the Indian world view and culture, as well as her sense of humor, that critics applaud.

ONCE MORE UPON A TOTEM

CHRISTIE HARRIS

Illustrated by Douglas Tait

These traditional stories, retold by Harris, were used by Northwest Indian tribes to explain natural and spiritual phenomena and the history of their people. (Cover illustration by Douglas Tait.)

Born in New Jersey in 1907, Harris's family immigrated to western Canada when she was an infant. Her father, a farmer who had come to North America from Ireland, was known in the area for his storytelling, and the family farm was often the site of impromptu gatherings. Thus the young girl grew up knowing that stories were an important part of life, and indeed they were, for at that time she knew nothing of radio or television, and there were few books at the one-room school she attended. While doing her chores she often recited poetry or told stories to an audience of animals. "Stories could lift any old job into another dimension," Harris wrote in an essay for *Something about the Author Autobiography Series* (*SAAS*). "And when I was given a really boring job, like keeping the turkeys out of the garden while the fence was being fixed, I worked on my own stories."

As a high school student Harris wrote and sent the district news to the area's weekly newspaper, but she did not aspire to become a writer and was not encouraged by her teachers to pursue such a career. Instead she enrolled after graduation in a teacher's college and by age nineteen found herself at the front of a class in a Vancouver primary school. Harris was enthusiastic about teaching and especially enjoyed reading and telling stories to children in the lower grades. Suddenly she realized her talent as a storyteller: "[I]t came like a dazzling revelation: *I could tell my own stories.* For two weeks I could scarcely wait for recess and noon and after school and the weekend to get on with those ideas that were keeping me awake at night; I could scarcely wait to read them to my pupils, who *seemed* to love them," the author wrote in *SAAS.* After selling a series of stories to the *Vancouver Daily Province,* Harris became a regular contributor to the children's page.

One day the author found Thomas Harris, an adventurous young man whom she had met a few years earlier at her father's farm, waiting on her doorstep. He had served in the Royal Canadian Mounted Police and recently had returned from visiting his father in Argentina. They rekindled their acquaintance and entered what was to be a long engagement, for Thomas had decided to reenlist—and mounties were not allowed to marry without permission, and then only after serving for seven years. Mounties were also highly mobile and the couple soon parted when Thomas was posted to Prince George, five hundred miles north of Vancouver, leaving his fiancee to teaching and to discovering a new field for writers—radio. After several years of service, Thomas Harris left the Royal Canadian Mounted Police for the Immigration Service, and the couple married early in 1932. Harris was forced to quit teaching because married women were not at that time allowed on school staffs.

While raising their five children, Harris wrote humor for the *Vancouver Daily Province.* She also created a series of fifteen-minute radio programs for children and took her pilot program to the Vancouver affiliate of a national radio network. By the time she had handed in three pilots, she was asked to write a program for children for the official Coronation Day Programme for King George VI in May 1937. This juvenile musical fantasy marked the beginning of a quarter century of writing adult plays and humorous sketches, school broadcasts, women's talks, and a children's adventure serial, all for the Canadian Broadcasting Corporation (CBC). Harris reminisced in *SAAS,* "A friend remembers coming upon me in the back garden one summer afternoon—me with my typewriter on an apple box, a child in the playpen, another up an apple tree, and two more playing in the sandbox. (The fifth had not yet arrived.)"

Radio led Harris to books. In the mid-fifties after she completed a juvenile adventure serial for the CBC, she was invited by Longmans, Green of Toronto to write a historical novel, which turned out to be *Cariboo Trail,* the story of the 1860s gold rush in British Columbia. At this time, her husband was posted to Prince Rupert, and the CBC asked the author to write a final series on the Indian cultures of the area, which were then declining.

Mouse Woman, a small but effective supernatural being, rescues tribal princesses kidnapped by less altruistic spirits in Harris's collection of stories from the native people of the Canadian Northwest. (Cover illustration by Tait.)

She easily managed to write the school series, but it was only after three years of intense research in museums, archives, and among the Indians that she felt comfortable retelling the legends traditionally associated with figures found on totem poles in *Once upon a Totem.* "When I started rewriting them for modern readers," Harris wrote in "The Shift from Feasthouse to Book" in *Canadian Children's Literature,* "I didn't know there were two schools of thought. One holds that every word is sacred as it stands in the collections [written down by ethnologists]. The other maintains that the writer must turn the collected story into *literature,* uninhibited by the demands of authenticity. I find both a little startling. My own instinct and experience dictated that I move to a middle ground. And I still think this is the right approach." Therefore Harris tries to interpret the legends for modern readers by unobtrusively providing the cultural information necessary to understand the tales.

Harris wrote several other historical novels (*West with the White Chiefs,* and *Forbidden Frontier*), but works on Indians flowed the most regularly from her typewriter. While doing research in Prince Rupert, Harris discovered the artwork of Charles Edenshaw, a great Haida Eagle Chief. Although his carvings and jewelry were treasured in the world's great museums, little was known about the artist. Harris set out to fill in the gaps and ended up writing about three generations of chiefs and the effects of Indian and white interactions in the historical novel *Raven's Cry.* For this work Harris won her first major award, the Canadian Association of Children's Librarians' (CACL) Book of the Year for Children Medal. Harris continued re-creating Indian legends in *Once More upon a Totem.* "The Northwest Coast Indians especially interest me; and I've been fortunate enough to get into many remote villages and to make friends with old Indians who will tell me things I can't find out in libraries and archives. I've found it a real challenge to take their tragic history, their magnificent culture, and their fascinating legends; and then make it all real and understandable to today's young people," she once told *SATA.*

Harris also used elements of Indian culture in other fictional works, most notably *Secret in the Stlalakum Wild* and *Sky Man on the Totem Pole?* In these later works Harris combines elements of the scientific world and the mythical world. After a native friend had told the author about *stlalakums,* the unnatural beings that inhabit the Lower Fraser Valley, Harris made them part of an adventure-fantasy in the mountains that she had hiked with her children. The idea for *Sky Man on the Totem Pole?* was sparked by seeing an unidentified flying object and wondering if the legend of the Sky Man of the totem pole was really a visit to the Indians by an extraterrestrial.

The Mouse Woman is the supernatural main character of three of Harris's collections of Indian legends: *Mouse Woman and the Vanished Princesses, Mouse Woman and the Mischief-Makers,* and *Mouse Woman and the Muddleheads.* Mouse Woman, a shape-changing being who can appear as a mouse or as the smallest and most imperious of grandmothers, is known affectionately to the Tsimshian, Nisgha, Haida, and Tlingit peoples and often appears in their tales. So it was natural that Harris should retell her many adventures. For *Mouse Woman and the Vanished Princesses* Harris won her second Book of the Year for Children Medal from the CACL.

Princesses were very important in northwest coast Indian society. Only their sons could become great chiefs, so only they seemed to be sought after to become the wives of supernatural beings. In *The Trouble with Princesses,* the author's Canada Council Children's Literature Prize book, Harris focuses on the problems of Indian storytale princesses and compares them with those of the European tradition. In its companion book, *The Trouble with Adventurers,* she recounts the adventures of both humans and animals.

Much of Harris's work has been widely recognized for its sympathetic portrayals of the Indian culture and for the author's ability to bridge the gap between white and Indian cultures. Harris has received numerous awards for her works and in 1980 she was invested into the Order of Canada, but it is her reputation among the Indian peoples that satisfies her the most. She told Cory Davies of *Canadian Children's Literature,* "[All the] native approval of what I do 'makes my heart sing' so I just keep on writing."

WORKS CITED:

Davies, Cory, "Bridge between Two Realities: An Interview with Christie Harris," *Canadian Children's Literature,* Number 51, 1988, pp. 6-24.
Harris, Christie, "The Shift from Feasthouse to Book," *Canadian Children's Literature,* Number 31/32, 1983, pp. 9-11.
Something about the Author Autobiography Series, Volume 10, Gale, 1990, pp. 103-111.

FOR MORE INFORMATION SEE:

BOOKS

Dictionary of Literary Biography, Volume 88: *Canadian Writers, 1920-1959, Second Series,* Gale, 1989.
Egoff, Sheila, *The Republic of Childhood: A Critical Guide to Canadian Children's Literature in English,* 2nd edition, Oxford University Press, 1975.
McDonough, Irma, *Profiles,* revised edition, Canadian Library Association, Ottawa, 1975.

PERIODICALS

Bookbird, April, 1981.
Canadian Children's Literature, Number 2, 1975; Number 5/6, 1976; Number 7, 1977; Number 15/16, 1980; Number 55, 1989.
Canadian Literature, Number 78, 1978.
Horn Book, April, 1963; June, 1964; August, 1964; June, 1965; October, 1966; April, 1968; August, 1973; June, 1976; October, 1979.
New York Times Book Review, May 12, 1963; April 4, 1965.

*   *   *

HART, Carolyn G(impel) 1936-

PERSONAL: Born August 25, 1936, in Oklahoma City, OK; daughter of Roy William (an organ builder) and Doris (Akin) Gimpel; married Philip Donnell Hart (an attorney), June 10, 1958; children: Philip Donnell, Sarah Ann. *Education:* University of Oklahoma—Norman, B.A., 1958. *Religion:* Protestant.

ADDRESSES: Home—1705 Drakestone Ave., Oklahoma City, OK 73120. *Agent*—Deborah C. Schneider, Gelfman Schneiders Agents Inc., 250 West 57th St., New York, NY 10107.

CAREER: Norman Transcript, Norman, OK, reporter, 1958-59; *Sooner Newsmakers* (University of Oklahoma alumni newsletter), editor, 1959-60; free-lance writer,

CAROLYN G. HART

1961-82; University of Oklahoma, School of Journalism and Mass Communications, assistant professor, 1982-85; full-time writer, 1986—.

MEMBER: Sisters in Crime (president, 1991-92), Mystery Writers of America (past national director), Authors Guild, Phi Beta Kappa, Theta Sigma Phi.

AWARDS, HONORS: Dodd, Mead-*Calling All Girls* Prize, 1964, for *The Secret of the Cellars;* Agatha Award, Malice Domestic, 1989, for *Something Wicked;* Anthony awards, Bouchercon, 1989, for *Something Wicked,* and 1990, for *Honeymoon with Murder;* Macavity Award, Mystery Readers International, 1990, for *A Little Class on Murder.*

WRITINGS:

JUVENILE

The Secret of the Cellars, Dodd, 1964.
Dangerous Summer, Fair Winds, 1968.
Rendezvous in Vera Cruz, M. Evans, 1970.
No Easy Answers, M. Evans, 1970.
Danger! High Explosives!, M. Evans, 1972.

"DEATH ON DEMAND" MYSTERIES

Death on Demand, Bantam, 1987.
Design for Murder, Bantam, 1988.
Something Wicked, Bantam, 1988.
Honeymoon with Murder, Bantam, 1989.
A Little Class on Murder, Doubleday, 1989.
Deadly Valentine, Doubleday, 1990.
The Christie Caper, Bantam, 1991.
Southern Ghost, Bantam, 1992.

OTHER

Flee from the Past, Bantam, 1975.
A Settling of Accounts, Doubleday, 1976.
(With Charles F. Long) *The Sooner Story, 1890-1980,* University of Oklahoma Foundation, 1980.
Escape from Paris, Hale, 1982, St. Martin's, 1983.
The Rich Die Young, Hale, 1983.
Death by Surprise, Hale, 1983.
Castle Rock, Hale, 1983.
Skulduggery, Hale, 1984.
The Devereaux Legacy, Harlequin, 1986.
Brave Hearts, Pocket Books, 1987.
Dead Man's Island, Bantam, 1993.

SIDELIGHTS: Carolyn G. Hart is best known as the award-winning author of the best-selling "Death on Demand" series of mystery novels. Set on fictional Broward's Rock Island, South Carolina, the series features Annie Laurance, proprietor of the mystery bookshop *Death on Demand.* With her handsome blond husband, consultant Max Darling, Laurance both sells and solves mysteries that come her way.

Inspired by a love of reading, Hart began her literary career as a reporter, later becoming an author of young adult novels. "I can't even remember when I started reading," she told *SATA* in a specially conducted interview. "It was always a part of my life. I read very widely when I was young; Robert Louis Stevenson and Charles Dickens were favorites. There were so many—Thomas Chastain, Pearl S. Buck.... And of course I adored Alexandre Dumas's *The Man in the Iron Mask* and *The Count of Monte Cristo* (that was my favorite). My parents were both readers: my father enjoyed Agatha Christie, and my mother was always interested in history. I don't remember ever not being involved with books.

"I always loved mysteries, especially the Nancy Drew stories. A lot of women mystery writers have talked about this at conferences, and to all of us she was a wonderful inspiration. At that time (the forties, before the independent female characters that characterize fiction today appeared) Nancy had her own roadster, and she was free to come and go as she wished. She solved the problems, not her boyfriend Ned. This was one of the few areas in which girls could read about a young woman who was in charge of her own destiny. So I think Nancy Drew had a tremendous effect, not only on me, but on many of the women who are writing mysteries today.

"I enjoyed the Hardy Boys thoroughly as well. I was especially fond of Joe—I thought he was very, very attractive. Another of my great favorites were the Beverly Gray Mysteries, written by Clair Blank. I think it was wonderful that there was reading available for us young girls that truly gave us a feeling of freedom—a feeling that we didn't find in the rest of our society and environment at that time.

"I grew up in Oklahoma during World War II, and the war had a great effect upon my approach to life. We waited so eagerly for the newspaper—of course you did get news on the radio, but this was still in the era of newspaper extras—when something very exciting or important happened in the war. I think my whole perspective as a child was affected by the war: the newspaper was very important, so obviously it was very important to produce newspapers. This formed my ambition to be a newspaper reporter. That's what I worked toward all the way through school and at the University of Oklahoma.

"It never occurred to me that I would write fiction, but as so often happens in life, different things affect the course of our lives. I met a young law student at the university, and we were married. When I had finished being a reporter and was starting to have a family (that was in the period before young women were expected to have full-time careers and full-time families at the same time) I was at home a lot. I wasn't happy not writing, and that was the first time it ever occurred to me to write fiction. I think I first tried juvenile mysteries because of my original love of Nancy Drew. That's the story of my transformation from a newspaper reporter to a writer of fiction."

Hart's first book, titled *The Secret of the Cellars,* appeared in 1964. She followed it with another mystery and several young-adult suspense novels, including *No Easy Answers,* about the Vietnam War, and *Danger! High Explosives!,* about a college torn over the question of a military presence on the campus. "There's a very definite distinction between mystery and suspense," Hart told *SATA.* "In a mystery novel the point of the book is to figure out who committed a crime. When you do that, what you're really exploring (especially in the case of murder, which is what mysteries are usually about) is what went wrong in the lives of these people. How did these relationships become so tortured that violence resulted? A suspense novel, on the other hand, tells the story of a person who is trying to accomplish something. It doesn't matter if it's getting to the top of the mountain, escaping from the Japanese during the war, or whatever—the suspense novel is built around a series of episodes where the character must continue to struggle to achieve a goal. It's a very different kind of story than a mystery.

"The juveniles I wrote are no longer in print, although they are apparently still in libraries, because every so often someone (a librarian usually) will come up to me and ask about the books. In fact, someone once told me that they were ordering some of my early books through interlibrary loan, and that's how they came across the juveniles I had written. When I was president of Sisters in Crime, an organization of mystery readers and writers, I had a phone call from a hopeful author, a young woman out in California who was asking about information to join. Very shyly she asked, 'Did you write *The Secret of the Cellars?*' And I said, 'Oh yes! You have certainly come up with a piece of my past!' It was most exciting, because that was the book she had read as a student that had really attracted her to mysteries. Now she is a grownup who is busy writing mysteries.

This young adult mystery involves the violent events surrounding a college's decision to have ROTC, a military training program, on campus. (Jacket design by Moneta Barrett.)

"I think I stopped writing juveniles for several reasons. One shows how young I was at the time, and the unfortunate power reviewers have over writers. I wrote a book about Vietnam, *No Easy Answers,* during the period when our country was so terribly divided by the war in that country, and I was trying to show both sides of the question. The protagonist's father is a career military officer, his brother was killed in Vietnam, and the young man's very bitter about the whole thing. One of the reviewers said that I'd written so many books (at that point I'd just written four others), and that I was not serious about what I was doing. The reviewer even suggested that I had cynically exploited the Vietnam period. And that was one of the most difficult books I ever wrote. To hear somebody say that I had cynically exploited this period upset me so much that I never wrote another juvenile. As I look back from a more sophisticated and jaded perspective, having seen a lot of reviews in my time, I think that was absurd. Who was this reviewer? What did it matter?

"I rather doubt that I will ever write another juvenile. I believe that to write a successful juvenile you have to have a real understanding of what it is like to look at life without preconceptions—the difference between an

CAROLYN G. HART
author of *A Little Class on Murder*

DEATH on DEMAND

"Hart has a light touch with her characters, a fresh heroine in Annie, and a delightfully different setting!" —Alfred Hitchcock Magazine

$3.50 VALUE
ONLY
$2.25
IN CANADA
$2.75

Mystery bookshop owner and crime solver Annie Laurance becomes the prime suspect when a famous mystery novelist is murdered in her store in this first volume of Hart's "Death on Demand" series. (Cover illustration by Cathy Deeter).

adult and a child. At the point I wrote those books, I was much younger, and I had young children. Now I'm 56, I've just started a new series from the perspective of a retired newspaper woman about ten years older than I am (it's a very sardonic appraisal of life), and I don't think that I could ever go back and find the freshness you have to have to be a successful juvenile author, and that I so admire with Joan Lowery Nixon and George Edward Stanley.

"My sense is that the current boom in the mystery genre will last because the caliber of the writing is so good— there are so many wonderful writers writing mysteries now. So as long as readers are happy I think that they will continue to buy mysteries, and I don't see how the readers could help but be extremely happy right now."

WORKS CITED:

Hart, Carolyn G., interview with Kenneth R. Shepherd for *Something about the Author,* January 8, 1993.

FOR MORE INFORMATION SEE:

PERIODICALS

Chattanooga Times, June 26, 1992, p. C6.
Clarion-Ledger (Jackson, MS), July 5, 1992.
Island Packet (Hilton Head Island, SC), June 14, 1992.
Nashville Banner, June 13, 1992.
Pioneer Press (St. Paul, MN), July 15, 1992.
Wilson Library Journal, March, 1987.

* * *

HATHORN, Libby 1943-

PERSONAL: Full name, Elizabeth Helen Hathorn; surname is pronounced "hay-thorn"; born September 26, 1943, in Newcastle, New South Wales, Australia; daughter of Frederick (a detective) and Phyllis (a fashion boutique owner; maiden name, Krahe) Roache; married John Hathorn (a teacher), 1968; children: Lisa Erin, Keiran John. *Education:* Attended Sydney Technical College, 1960-61, and Balmain Teachers College (now University of Technology, Sydney), 1962-63. *Hobbies and other interests:* "Reading, opera, writing poetry, swimming, and more reading."

ADDRESSES: Home—32 Lang Rd., Centennial Park, Sydney, New South Wales 2021, Australia. *Agent*—Tim Curnow, Curtis Brown, Ltd., 27 Union St., Paddington, New South Wales 2021, Australia.

CAREER: Teacher and librarian in schools in Sydney, Australia, 1965-81; worked as a deputy principal, 1977; consultant and senior education officer for government adult education programs, 1981-86; full-time writer, 1987—. Sydney University, part-time lecturer in English and children's literature, beginning in 1982; writer in residence at the University of Technology, Sydney, 1990, Woollahra Library, 1992, and at Edith Cowan University, 1992. Consultant to the Dorothea Mackellar National Poetry Competition/Festival for children, 1992-93; speaker for student, teacher, and parent groups.

AWARDS, HONORS: The Tram to Bondi Beach was highly commended by the Children's Book Council of Australia, 1982; *Paolo's Secret* was shortlisted for the Children's Book of the Year Award and for the New South Wales Premier's Literary Awards, both 1986; *All about Anna* received an Honour Award from the Children's Book Council of Australia, 1987, and was shortlisted for the Kids Own Australian Literary Award (KOALA), 1988, and for the Young Australians Best Book Award (YABBA), 1989 and 1990; Literature Board of the Australia Council fellowships, 1987 and 1988; *Looking out for Sampson* received an Honour Award from the Children's Book Council of Australia, 1988; *The Extraordinary Magics of Emma McDade* was shortlisted for the Children's Book of the Year Award,

1990; Hathorn was highly commended in 1990 by the Society of Women Writers for the body of her work during 1987-89; *Thunderwith* was named Honour Book of the Year for older readers by the Children's Book Council of Australia, 1990, an American Library Association Best Book for Young Adults, 1991, was shortlisted for the Canberra's Own Outstanding List, KOALA, and YABBA, all 1991, and the Dutch translation received an award from Stichting Collectieve Propaganda van het Nederlands Boek (Foundation for the Promotion of Dutch Books), 1992; *So Who Needs Lotto?* and *Jezza Sez* were both named Children's Book Council of Australia notable books, 1991; New South Wales Children's Week Medal for literature, 1992.

WRITINGS:

FOR CHILDREN AND YOUNG ADULTS

Stephen's Tree (storybook), illustrated by Sandra Laroche, Methuen, 1979.
Lachlan's Walk (picture book), illustrated by Laroche, Heinemann, 1980.
The Tram to Bondi Beach (picture book), illustrated by Julie Vivas, Collins, 1981.
Paolo's Secret (novella), illustrated by Lorraine Hannay, Heinemann, 1985.
All about Anna (novel), Heinemann, 1986.
Looking out for Sampson (storybook), Oxford University Press, 1987.
Freya's Fantastic Surprise (picture book), illustrated by Sharon Thompson, Ashton Scholastic, 1988.

LIBBY HATHORN

The Extraordinary Magics of Emma McDade (storybook), illustrated by Maya, Oxford University Press, 1989.
Stuntumble Monday (picture book), illustrated by Melissa Web, Collins Dove, 1989.
The Garden of the World (picture book), illustrated by Tricia Oktober, Margaret Hamilton Books, 1989.
Thunderwith (novel), Heinemann, 1989.
Jezza Says (novel), illustrated by Donna Rawlins, Angus & Robertson, 1990.
So Who Needs Lotto? (novella), illustrated by Simon Kneebone, Penguin, 1990.
Talks with my Skateboard (poetry), Australian Broadcasting Corp., 1991.
(Editor) *The Blue Dress* (stories), Heinemann, 1991.
Help for Young Writers (nonfiction), Nelson, 1991.
Good to Read (textbook), Nelson, 1991.
Who? (stories), Heinemann, 1992.
Love Me Tender (novel), Oxford University Press, 1992.
The Lenski Kids and Dracula (novella), Penguin, 1992.
Valley under the Rock (novel), Reed Heinemann, 1993.
The Way Home (picture book), illustrated by Greg Rogers, Random House, 1993.
Feral Kid (novel), Hodder & Stoughton, in press.
The Wonder Thing (picture book), illustrated by Peter Gouldthorpe, Penguin, in press.
Grandma's Shoes, illustrated by Elivia Salvadier, Little, Brown, in press.

Some of Hathorn's works have been translated into Greek, Italian, Dutch, German, French, Norwegian, Danish, and Swedish.

FOR ADULTS

(With G. Bates) *Half-Time: Perspectives on Mid-life,* Fontana Collins, 1987.
Better Strangers (stories), Millennium Books, 1989.
Damascus, a Rooming House (libretto), performed by the Australian Opera at Performance Space, Sydney, 1990.
The Maroubra Cycle: A Journey around Childhood (performance poetry), University of Technology, Sydney, 1990.
(And director) *The Blue Dress Suite* (music theatre piece), produced at Melbourne International Festival, 1991.

WORK IN PROGRESS: A libretto for a children's opera based on *Grandma's Shoes; Source of Light* (working title), a novel set in Holland; *A Treasury of Days,* a compilation of poetry in collaboration with Hathorn's sister, Margaret Gilbert.

SIDELIGHTS: "I must have been very young indeed when I decided to become a writer," Libby Hathorn commented in an interview with *Something about the Author (SATA).* "My grandmother always kept my stories in her best black handbag and read them out loud to long-suffering relatives and told me over and over that I'd be a writer when I grew up." Though Hathorn started her career as a teacher and librarian, she did eventually become a writer and has published a variety of books for readers of all ages. The popular Australian author's works for children and young adults include picture books, stories, novels, and poems. Best known in the United States for her critically acclaimed novel *Thunderwith,* Hathorn has penned works ranging from serious stories of troubled youth to lighthearted, fast-paced comedies. "Libby Hathorn knows exactly how today's children think and feel," observed Maurice Saxby in *The Proof of the Puddin': Australian Children's Literature, 1970-1990.* "She has an uncanny ear for the speech nuances of the classroom, playground and home.... [She] is always able to penetrate the facade of her characters and with skill and subtlety reveal what they are really like inside."

Hathorn grew up near Sydney, Australia, and recalled to *SATA* that at the time her parents did not own a car. "In fact, not many people on the street where I lived in the early 1950s owned cars. We had no television, either. We amused ourselves with storytelling and reading out loud and lots of games." Hathorn often read and told stories to her sisters and brother; she was encouraged by her parents, who "loved books" and had bookcases crammed with them. "Books were pretty central in our lives," she told *SATA.* "My father in particular read to us at night when he could get home in time. He was a detective and had long shifts at night that often kept him late. When he read we didn't interrupt, in fact we'd never dream of it as his voice filled the room because it seemed so obviously important to him—the ebb and flow of the language. My mother—who was very proud of her Irish ancestry—told us lots of true stories about the history of our family and also about her own girlhood."

As a child, Hathorn read "adventure books set in the Australian bush, like *Seven Little Australians,* as well as classics like *Black Beauty, The Secret Garden, Little Women,* and books by Emily and Charlotte Bronte," she explained to *SATA.* She read works by Australian authors "with considerable delight at finding Australian settings and people in print." Later, Hathorn would lend her own work an Australian flavor after noticing "the need for more books that told Australian kids about themselves."

Hathorn began writing stories and poems of her own when she was still a young girl. Though she was often shy and quiet, Hathorn told *SATA* that she could keep company "entertained with strings of stories that I made up as I went along." Her family encouraged her, and Hathorn "loved being at center stage—so I couldn't have been altogether a shy little buttercup." At school she enjoyed reading and creative writing, and was disappointed in later years when "we had to write essays and commentaries but never, never stories or poems. I was extremely bored in my final years at school." Hathorn acknowledged to *SATA* that her high school years weren't all bad: "After all, I was introduced to the works of William Shakespeare, and particularly in my later years the poetic nature of his work touched me deeply. And best of all we studied the Romantic poets and I fell in love with John Keats and Samuel Coleridge

Suspenseful ghost stories and mysteries as well as tales of love and friendship are all part of Hathorn's collection of short fiction. (Cover illustration by Carlo Golin.)

as well as Percy Bysshe Shelley, Lord Byron, and William Wordsworth."

After graduating from high school, Hathorn worked in a laboratory and studied at night for a year before attending college full-time. She explained to *SATA* that "although I'd been encouraged to write, there seemed no job other than journalism (which my parents rather disapproved of, saying it was no job for a girl!) where I could actually learn the art and craft of novel writing. Anyway, my parents thought it important that I have a profession where I could earn a reasonable living—writers being notoriously underpaid. I was drawn to teaching; so after a year of broken specimen flasks and test tubes and discovering that my science courses did not enthrall me, I left the laboratory."

Hathorn then attended Balmain Teacher's College (now the University of Technology, Sydney) and told *SATA:* "I must admit that I found the regulations of the place quite hard. Many of the lectures of those days seemed so dull to me that I wondered whether indeed I would last as a teacher for very long." Hathorn did enjoy her literature classes and was surprised to find that "when I came out of the rather dull years at college, I not only liked classroom teaching, but I also discovered that it was the most thrilling, absorbing, rewarding, and wonderful job anyone could have!"

After teaching for several years in Sydney, Hathorn applied for a position as a school librarian. "Although I was sorry to leave the intimacy of family that a classroom teacher has with her own class, the library was a new and exciting chapter for me," Hathorn told *SATA.* "I had books, books, and more books to explore and the amazingly enjoyable job of bringing stories to every child in the school!" Her job as a librarian, the author added, "had a major influence on my decision to seriously try to publish my stories."

Hathorn's first book for children was *Stephen's Tree,* which was published in 1979. She followed her debut volume with *Lachlan's Walk* and *The Tram to Bondi Beach.* In the genre of children's picture books, Hathorn told *SATA* she discovered "such a scarcity of Australian material! I wanted to talk about our place, here and now, and have pictures that Australian children would instantly recognize. *Stephen's Tree* was a breakthrough in publishing. I had to fight with my publisher to have a gumtree on the cover. They wanted an ash or elm or oak so it would sell in England and Europe! Similarly, I was told *The Tram to Bondi Beach* should not mention Bondi. I won those fights and I must say *The Tram to Bondi Beach* has made its way onto the American market and American children didn't seem to have much trouble at all."

The Tram to Bondi Beach is about Keiran, a nine-year-old boy who longs for a job selling newspapers to passengers on the trams traveling through Sydney. Keiran wants to be like Saxon, an older boy and experienced newspaper seller. Reviewers commented on the nostalgic quality of the story, which is set in the 1930s. Marianne Pilla assessed the picture book in *School Library Journal,* pointing out its "smooth" narrative and "vivid" passages. *Times Literary Supplement* contributor Ann Martin called *The Tram to Bondi Beach* "a simple but appealing tale" and Karen Jameyson wrote in *Horn Book* that the book "will undoubtedly hold readers' interest."

Hathorn followed *The Tram to Bondi Beach* with *Paolo's Secret, All about Anna,* and *Looking out for Sampson.* As Hathorn told *SATA, All about Anna* "is based on a wild, naughty cousin I had who drove her mother's car down the road at ten years of age and other wild deeds—a perfect subject to write about." The book details the comic adventures of Lizzie, Harriet, Christopher, and their energetic, imaginative cousin, Anna. Lizzie, the narrator, explains that "I like being with Anna because somehow things always seem fast and furious and funny when she's around—and well, she's just a very unusual person." Like *All about Anna, Looking out for Sampson* touches on family themes. In the book Bronwyn wishes that her younger brother, Sampson, were older so that she could have a friend instead of someone to babysit. And when Cheryl and her

mother come to stay with Bronwyn's family, Bronwyn's situation worsens. A disagreeable girl, Cheryl hints that Bronwyn's parents must care more about Sampson, since they give the toddler so much attention. After Sampson is lost briefly at the beach, however, Cheryl and Bronwyn reconcile and Bronwyn's parents express their appreciation of her.

Around the time *All about Anna* was published in 1986, Hathorn decided to give up her job and become a full-time writer. "I wanted to be a full-time writer secretly all my life but when I began my working life as a teacher this dream seemed to recede," the author explained to *SATA.* "And once I was married and with two children I felt I had to keep up my contribution to our lifestyle. My husband is also a teacher and I thought it would be unfair if he had to work every day while I was home writing. It was as if in the eyes of the world writing was not work! And I'm to blame for allowing myself to think like that too.

"I've changed my mind now and I wish I had had the courage to do so much sooner. While I loved teaching, after some years of it I was ready for change. I was already writing short stories but I was aching to tell longer stories, to produce a novel for older readers. This was very hard when I was working full-time and had young children—so the stories I chose to write at that time were for younger children and were either picture books or junior novels like *All about Anna* and *Looking out for Sampson.*"

Libby Hathorn • Sharon Thompson

Hathorn collaborated with illustrator Sharon Thompson to create this whimsical picture book for younger children.

Among Hathorn's other books for young readers is *The Extraordinary Magics of Emma McDade,* which describes the adventures of the title character, whose superhuman powers include incredible strength, the ability to call thousands of birds by whistling, and the ability to influence the weather. Another of Hathorn's books geared towards beginning readers is *Freya's Fantastic Surprise.* In it Miriam tells the class at news time that her parents bought her a tent, a surprise that Freya attempts to top by making up fantastic stories that her classmates realize are false. Freya eventually has a real surprise to share, however, when her mother announces that Freya will soon have a new sister. Published in the United States as well as Australia, *Freya's Fantastic Surprise* was praised by critics. Louise L. Sherman noted in *School Library Journal* that "Freya's concern about impressing her classmates ... is on target." In a *Horn Book* review, Elizabeth S. Watson called the book "a winner" and commented that "the text and pictures combine to produce a tale that proves truth is best."

Hathorn began writing her first novel for young adults, *Thunderwith,* after receiving an Australia Council grant in 1987. "At home writing for a year, I realized that this was to be my job for the rest of my life," Hathorn told *SATA.* "And since I have been able to give full-time attention to my writing it has certainly flowered in many new directions. I have begun writing longer novels for young adults and I have been able to take on more ambitious projects like libretti and music theatre pieces, which I enjoy tremendously."

Thunderwith, which was published in 1989, is about fourteen-year-old Lara, who begins living with the father she barely knows after her mother dies of cancer. Lara's new home is in the remote, semi-rainforest environment of Wallingat Forest in New South Wales, Australia. Though Lara's relationship with her father develops smoothly, he is often away on business and Lara's stepmother is openly antagonistic towards her. Lonely and grief-stricken, Lara finds solace in her bond with a mysterious dog that appears during a storm. She names the dog Thunderwith and keeps his existence a secret; she only tells the aboriginal storyteller she has befriended at school. Eventually, Lara realizes that Thunderwith has filled the space that her mother's death created, enabling her to come to terms with her loss. She is also able to slowly win over her stepmother and to adjust to her new home and family life.

Thunderwith garnered praise as a sensitive, realistic, and engaging young adult novel. A *Publishers Weekly* reviewer commented that "Hathorn deftly injects a sense of wonderment into this intense, very real story." According to *Horn Book* contributor Watson, *Thunderwith* possesses "a believable plot featuring a shattering climax and a satisfyingly realistic resolution." Robert Strang, writing in *Bulletin of the Center for Children's Books,* commended Hathorn's "especially expert weaving of story and setting." Similarly, *Magpies* contributor Jameyson noted that Hathorn's "control over her complex subject is admirable; her insight into character sure

A dog that Lara befriends helps her find happiness with her father and new stepmother in the harsh Australian outback. (Cover illustration by Peter Catalanotto.)

and true; her ear for dialogue keen." Jameyson added that the author's "nimble detour from the usual route will leave readers surprised, even breathless."

The setting of *Thunderwith* is one that Hathorn is intimately acquainted with. As a child, she had relatives who lived in the Australian bush and was able to spend many holidays in the country. "This was to prove very important to me," Hathorn remarked to *SATA.* "The bush weaves its own magic and it's something you cannot experience from a book or television show in a suburban setting. My holidays, especially those on my grandmother's farm in the Blue Mountains, created in me an enduring love for the Australian bush. As a writer, however, up until a few years ago the settings I chose to write about were in the hub of the family and quite often in suburbia."

Hathorn came upon the idea for *Thunderwith* after her brother bought land in Wallingat Forest. "During the first holiday there a huge storm blew up at about midnight and such was the noise and intensity of it we all rose from our beds to watch it," Hathorn said in her *SATA* interview. "You can imagine how vulnerable you'd feel way out in the bush with thunder booming and lightning raging and trees whipping and bending ... and in the midst of this fury suddenly I saw a dog. A huge dark dog dashed across the place where some hours earlier we'd had a campfire and eaten our evening meal under the stars—a lovely looking half-dingo creature.

"When I lay down again I had the image of the dog in my mind, against the landscape of the bush and storm. Again and again I saw the dog and a line of a poem seemed to fall into my head from the storm clouds above. 'With thunder you'll come—and with thunder you'll go.' What did it mean? What could it mean? By morning I had unravelled the mystery of the lines of poetry and I had a story about a girl called Lara whose mother dies in the first chapter and who comes to live on the farm in a forest with her dad and a new family."

The dog that Hathorn had seen became Thunderwith, "Lara's friend, her escape, and her link to her mother," Hathorn explained to *SATA*. Lara's mother was modeled after Hathorn's friend Cheryl, who died of cancer before the book was finished. Hathorn told *SATA*, "I feel that Cheryl's spirit leaps and bounds all through it." The author continued, "So you see for me there are many emotions through many experiences that weave themselves into my stories and into this story in particular—happiness in being together, the joy one feels in being surrounded by natural beauty, a dark sadness at loss, and the pain in hardships that must be endured. And the way people can change and grow even through dark and mystifyingly sad experiences. But you may be pleased to know that love and hope win out in *Thunderwith*. They have to—as I believe eventually they have to in life itself."

After the success of *Thunderwith*, Hathorn moved beyond novels and picture books to publish poems for children and a story collection for young adults. Her poetry book, *Talks with My Skateboard*, is divided into several sections and includes poems about outdoor activities, school, family life, cats, and nature. The poem "Skateboard" is written from a child's perspective: "My sister has a skateboard / and you should see her go ... She can jump and twirl / Do a twist and turn, / What I want to know / Is why I can't learn?" *Who?*, published in 1992, contains stories about ghosts, love and friendship, and mysteries, some of which are based on tales Hathorn's mother told her. The collection includes "Who?," in which a pitiful ghost awakens a family from their beds; "An Act of Kindness," in which a family mysteriously loses their ability to remember the names of objects; and "Jethro Was My Friend," where a young girl attempts to save her beloved bird from rapidly rising floodwaters.

Hathorn soon published more novels, however, with the young adult book *Love Me Tender* and a comic work for junior readers, *The Lenski Kids and Dracula*. Hathorn commented to *SATA* that "*Love Me Tender* was a story I circled for a few years. It drew on my girlhood experiences although it's about a boy called Alan. It's a gentle story set in the days of rock and roll." In the novel, Alan and his sister and brothers are abandoned by their mother and sent to live with various relatives. Alan is taken in by his bossy, unsmiling Aunt Jessie, and the story chronicles his "interior journey as hope fades that he will ever see his Mum and his family again," Hathorn explained to *SATA*. "Alan changes but more importantly he causes people around him—including his old aunt—to change too. Self-growth is a very important message for young people today—looking inside and finding that strength to go on." *Love Me Tender* is among Hathorn's favorite creations; the book "has a place in my heart," she told *SATA,* because it captures the atmosphere of the author's girlhood in the 1950s.

A common thread in several of Hathorn's works is the author's belief in love, hope, and the resiliency of the human spirit. "With all the faults in the world, the injustices, the suffering, and the sheer violence that I am forced to acknowledge though not accept, I still have a great sense of hope," Hathorn related to *SATA*. "Human beings never cease to surprise me with their unexpectedness, their kindness, their cheerfulness, their will to go on against the odds. That's inspiring. And I feel a sense of hope should be nurtured in young people, for they are the hope of the world. My stories may sometimes have sad endings but they are never without some hope for the future."

Hathorn's imaginative verse was featured as part of the Australian Broadcasting Corporation's "Verse for Kids" series. (Cover by Matt Mawson.)

The arrival of a jukebox at a local gathering spot changes the life of a twelve year old Australian boy who has been separated from his family.

In several books Hathorn combines her interest in young people with her concerns about the environment, poverty, and homelessness. "My picture book *The Wonder Thing,* written after a visit to a rainforest to 'sing' about the beauty of the place, is also a plea for the survival of the earth's riches—trees, forests, mountains, and rivers," the author told *SATA.* "There are only four to five words per page and it is a prose poem; I try to make those words the most delicately beautiful and evocative that I can. Both a recent picture book, *The Way Home,* and a recent novel, *Feral Kid,* take up the theme of the homelessness of young people. I feel strongly that we should *never* accept the fact of homeless children on our streets. A society that allows this sort of thing is not a responsible and caring society to my mind; I very much want people to look closely at stories like mine and begin asking questions about something that is becoming all too common a sight in all cities of the world."

Hathorn acknowledged to *SATA* that though her writings often contain messages, "I don't ever want to write didactic books that berate people, young or old, with messages. I don't think you can really write a successful book by setting out with a 'do-good' or any other kind of message in mind. I can only write what moves me in

some way to laugh or to cry or to wonder. I don't know what I'll be writing about a few years hence. There is a great sense of adventure in this—and a sense of mystery about what will find me."

When asked to give advice to aspiring young writers, Hathorn said to *SATA,* "The more you write the better you write. It's as simple and as difficult as that. To write well you must develop an ease with the pen and paper or the word processor or whatever—but most of all an ease with words. To do this you must be immersed in words; they should be your friends and your playthings as well as your tools. So, young writers, write a lot and love what you write so much that you work over it and shine it up to be the best you can possibly do—and then share it with someone."

WORKS CITED:

Hathorn, Libby, *All about Anna,* Heinemann, 1986.
Hathorn, Libby, "Skateboard," *Talks with My Skateboard,* Australian Broadcasting Corp., 1991.
Hathorn, Libby, written interview with Michelle M. Motowski for *Something about the Author,* March, 1993.
Jameyson, Karen, review of *The Tram to Bondi Beach, Horn Book,* July, 1989, p. 474.
Jameyson, Karen, review of *Thunderwith, Magpies,* March, 1990, p. 4.
Martin, Ann, "Encouraging the Excellent," *Times Literary Supplement,* July 23, 1982, p. 792.
Pilla, Marianne, review of *The Tram to Bondi Beach, School Library Journal,* July, 1989, p. 66.
Saxby, Maurice, *The Proof of the Puddin': Australian Children's Literature, 1970-1990,* Ashton Scholastic, 1993, pp. 219-21.
Sherman, Louise L., review of *Freya's Fantastic Surprise, School Library Journal,* August, 1989, p. 120.
Strang, Robert, review of *Thunderwith, Bulletin of the Center for Children's Books,* April, 1991, p. 194.
Review of *Thunderwith, Publishers Weekly,* May 17, 1991, p. 65.
Watson, Elizabeth S., review of *Freya's Fantastic Surprise, Horn Book,* March/April, 1989, p. 199.
Watson, Elizabeth S., review of *Thunderwith, Horn Book,* July, 1991, p. 462.

FOR MORE INFORMATION SEE:

PERIODICALS

Australian Bookseller and Publisher, March, 1992, p. 26.
Junior Bookshelf, October, 1990, p. 232.
Magpies, March, 1993, p. 31.
School Library Journal, May, 1991, p. 111.
Voice of Youth Advocates, June, 1991.

—Sketch by Michelle M. Motowski

*   *   *

**HAVEL, Jennifer
See HAVILL, Juanita**

JUANITA HAVILL

HAVILL, Juanita 1949-
(Jennifer Havel)

PERSONAL: Born May 11, 1949, in Evansville, IN; daughter of Frank Walden (an oil producer) and Ruth Denise (a homemaker; maiden name, Roberts) Havill; married Pierre Masure (a technical writer), 1976; children: Laurence Aimee, Pierre Gustav. *Education:* Attended Universite de Rouen, Rouen, France, 1969-70; University of Illinois at Urbana-Champaign, B.A., 1971, M.A., 1973. *Politics:* Democrat. *Religion:* Roman Catholic. *Hobbies and other interests:* Theater, cinema, listening to piano music, reading philosophy and biography, walking, and swimming.

ADDRESSES: Home and office—28232 North 58th St., Cave Creek, AZ 85331.

CAREER: Freelance writer, 1981—. Translator for companies in France and United States; instructor at Ecole Bi-Lingue de Fontainebleau, Wabash Valley College, The Loft, and The Writer's Voice Project; lecturer. Worked in personnel department, Organisation for Economic Cooperation and Development, Paris, France.

MEMBER: Authors' Guild, Society of Children's Bookwriters and Illustrators, Children's Reading Roundtable.

AWARDS, HONORS: Child Study Children's Book Award, Bank Street College, Children's Choices award, Children's Trade Books, Children's Book of the Year award, Library of Congress, all 1986, and Ezra Jack Keats New Writer award, 1987, all for *Jamaica's Find;* Child Study Children's Book award, Bank Street College, 1989, and Mrs. Bush's Story Hour selection, 1992-93, both for *Jamaica Tag-Along;* Minnesota Book Award nomination, 1991, for *Leona and Ike.*

WRITINGS:

PICTURE BOOKS

Jamaica's Find, illustrated by Anne Sibley O'Brien, Houghton, 1986.
Leroy and the Clock, illustrated by Janet Wentworth, Houghton, 1988.
Jamaica Tag-Along, illustrated by O'Brien, Houghton, 1989.
The Magic Fort, illustrated by Linda Shute, Houghton, 1991.
Treasure Nap, illustrated by Elivia Savadier, Houghton, 1992.
Sato and the Elephants, illustrated by Jean and Mou-Sien Tseng, Lothrop, 1993.
Jamaica and Brianna, illustrated by O'Brien, Houghton, 1993.

NOVELS

It Always Happens to Leona, Crown, 1989.
Leona and Ike, Crown, 1990.

OTHER

(Under pseudonym Jennifer Havel) *The Wacky Rulebook,* Parker Brothers, 1984.
I Love You More, Western Publishing, 1990.
Kentucky Troll (folktale), illustrated by Bert Dodson, Lothrop, 1993.
Jennifer's Quest, Hyperion, in press.

Also contributor to periodicals, including *Cricket, Jack and Jill, U.S. Kids,* and *Children's Magic Window.*

WORK IN PROGRESS: The Embarcadero Upset, a picture book about skateboarders, for Lothrop.

SIDELIGHTS: Juanita Havill told *SATA:* "In a sense, even before I could print, I began to write. I dictated stories to my mother and she wrote them down for me. I made up poems, too, and repeated the words out loud, day after day. I remember my satisfaction and delight at being able to catch something without catching it, to describe a pigeon and hold the words in my mind as if I held the bird in my two hands.

"When I went to school, I learned to print, then to write in cursive, and I experienced all the frustration of not being able to get the words down as fast as I thought them. I began to write down stories and ideas and poems. When I was eleven, I recorded my daily activities, very briefly because my entries were in a five-year diary which offered only a few lines for ruminations of an entire day.

Kevin's magic fort isn't the same when he is forced to share it with his younger brother in this story by Havill. (Cover illustration by Linda Shute.)

"In high school I wrote articles, editorials, and seasonal poems for the bi-monthly student newspaper. I learned how to be straightforward and factual and how to argue in print, and I loved it. In college I wrote term papers, explication de texte, and reports on psychology, astronomy, philosophy, and the cinema. I can't say that I loved them, but I learned from these assignments. One thing I learned was that my audience was probably not in academia.

"After college I worked as a typist, a teacher, and a translator. I traveled and married, and when my children were born, I settled down to write. When I took a course in Minneapolis taught by Emilie Buchwald, who is now publisher of Milkweed Publications, I discovered my audience: young people, and I have been writing for them ever since.

"I write to find out what I think, to give form to thought. That is why I have stacks of journals on my office floor in the space beneath book-filled shelves. The act of writing helps me to get what is hidden out in the open so that I may examine it, study it, describe it, remember it, perhaps understand it. The act of writing soothes me. It restores me. It reminds me that I am a person, that I have dreams and joy, hurts and anger, and that from all I have done and thought and written comes the meaning of me."

FOR MORE INFORMATION SEE:

PERIODICALS

Booklist, March 15, 1988; June 6, 1989; July, 1989; June 1, 1991.
Hungry Mind Review, Summer, 1992.
Publisher's Weekly, May 30, 1986; February 24, 1989; January 18, 1991, p. 58.

HAWKINS, Laura 1951-

PERSONAL: Born May 22, 1951, in Wichita, KS; daughter of Donald (an electrician and farmer) and Dorothy (a homemaker and art teacher; maiden name, Hall) Mundell; married Daryl Hawkins (a lawyer), January 2, 1971; children: Jennifer, Erin. *Education:* B.S. degree from Pittsburg State University. *Hobbies and other interests:* Photography, reading, sports, animals.

ADDRESSES: Home and office—316 North D Street, Herington, KS 67449.

CAREER: Gridley High School, Gridley, KS, secondary English teacher, 1974-75; Central Heights High School, Richmond, KS, English teacher, 1975-76; Herington High School, Herington, KS, ninth-grade English teacher, 1978-79.

MEMBER: PEN, Society of Children's Book Writers and Illustrators.

WRITINGS:

TEEN ROMANCES

Double Exposure, Silhouette, 1983.
Partners in Love, Cora Verlag, 1989.
Made to Order Love, Cora Verlag, 1990.
Next Door Romance, Cora Verlag, 1992.

LAURA HAWKINS

Love Conquers All, Cora Verlag, 1992.
Summer Charade, Cora Verlag, 1993.
Moonlight Magic, Cora Verlag, in press.

JUVENILE FICTION

Figment, Your Dog, Speaking, Houghton, 1991.
The Cat That Could Spell Mississippi, Houghton, 1992.
Valentine to a Flying Mouse, Houghton, 1993.

OTHER

Precious Moments (adult romance), Silhouette, 1985.

Double Exposure has been translated into German and French.

WORK IN PROGRESS: Waiting for Courage, an "upper-middle grade novel with historical (1943) setting in the South, concerning courage to overcome prejudice."

SIDELIGHTS: Laura Hawkins told *SATA:* "My love of books originated with a mother whose rich reading voice made the stories she read to me as a child come alive. My father, an avid mystery fan, read a book every night. Books were special in our household. They whisked me off to faraway places, taught me things I wanted to know and introduced me to fictional characters so real I would have sworn they actually lived. Growing up on a small farm in Kansas, the youngest of four children with an age gap between myself and my older sisters and brother, I entertained myself by reading books. Isolated by distance from every-day playmates, my dearest companions were dogs, cats, chickens, sheep, cows and a horse.

"Although I had written an occasional story or poem for pleasure as a child and excelled at school writing assignments, it didn't occur to me to seriously pursue a writing career until I was nearly thirty years old. After having taught high school English, the births of my two daughters brought about a decision to stop teaching for a while so that I could be at home with them. It was then, during my children's nap times, that I began to write.

"I chose to write teenage romances because my experience working with adolescents as a high school teacher seemed a likely source of knowledge to tap into for story ideas. After publishing my first book, I received a letter from a reader, urging me to create a series from the characters. The reader also told me how much it meant to her to read about how my main character acted in specific scenes, how she had handled particular problems. Although it did not work out for me to write a series from that first book, in the back of my mind I knew that I would write a series some day, and it would concern the problems of lying, cheating, and stealing that all kids face.

"My 'series' took a form I never expected. It began with a shift from writing teen romances to writing middle-grade children's books. A natural influence of this change was that my own children were growing up and reading middle-grade novels. Oftentimes, we read them

Marcella Starbuckle is known for her tall tales, but when she meets Figment, a talking dog, she becomes interested in finding out the truth about her new friend. (Cover illustration by Jennifer Hewitson.)

together. Also, my children and their friends were a rich source of material to feed my writer's brain. One playmate, a child with a very active imagination and teller-of-tall-tales, inspired me to write *Figment, Your Dog, Speaking,* the first book in the 'Riverview Story' series. The talking dog in the book is a composite of all those dogs and other animals that were my companions growing up on a farm.

"It is true that there is a little bit of the writer in every story he or she writes. But there are many other people, too. Every time I begin a new book, I hear my mother's voice reading to me, remember my father's mystery book pleasure and all the other people, animals and places I have known. Although [writing is] a solitary occupation, a writer never writes alone."

BIOGRAPHICAL/CRITICAL SOURCES:

PERIODICALS

New York Times Book Review, November 10, 1991.

HERBST, Judith 1947-

PERSONAL: Born January 3, 1947, in Baltimore, MD; daughter of Nathaniel (a firefighter) and Sylvia (a homemaker; maiden name, Vlotkofsky) Herbst. *Education:* Long Island University, B.A., 1967, M.S. 1969. *Politics:* "Currently Democratic, liberal leanings." *Religion:* Jewish. *Hobbies and other interests:* Camping, skiing, scuba diving, classical ballet, hiking, swimming.

ADDRESSES: Home—45 Sherman St., Huntington, NY 11743; (summer) Otis, ME.

CAREER: Islip School District, Islip, NY, English teacher, 1969-71; freelance writer and editor, 1971-76; Harcourt Brace Jovanovich, Inc., New York City, associate editor for school department, 1976-79; full-time writer, 1979—.

AWARDS, HONORS: School Library Journal Best Book Selection, 1983, and Reader's Choice Award, Silver Burdett, 1989, both for *Sky above and Worlds Beyond; Bio Amazing* was named a book of the month selection by the Junior Library Guild, 1986; *Animal Amazing* was named a book of the month selection by the Junior Library Guild, 1991, listed as a best book of 1992 by the Child Study Children's Book Committee of Bank Street College, and named a best book by the New York City library system, 1992.

JUDITH HERBST

WRITINGS:

Sky Above and Worlds Beyond, illustrated by Richard Rosenblum, Atheneum, 1982.

Bio Amazing: A Casebook of Unsolved Human Mysteries, Atheneum, 1985, paperback edition published as *Beyond Belief: A Casebook of Unsolved Human Mysteries,* Puffin, 1989.

Stars and Planets, Golden Books for Children, 1988.

Animal Amazing, Atheneum, 1991.

Star Crossing, Atheneum, 1993.

WORK IN PROGRESS: Cosmo Amazing, 1995.

SIDELIGHTS: Judith Herbst told *SATA:* "Once upon a time I wrote educational materials for Harcourt, Scholastic, and other publishing companies. I worked for peanuts, but I certainly learned the business—especially how to mark galleys. I'm glad those days are over, but I wouldn't trade the experience for anything—well, maybe for a nice, fat movie deal. Once, when a coworker had his first book published, I began moaning in a blatantly jealous way about how I had written nothing but workbook lessons. A friend said, 'Hey Herbst! Stop complaining and send something in!'

"She made it sound so easy, but what was I going to write? A wonderful English teacher from high school had told me to 'write what you know'—which was the same thing that Ernest Hemingway used to say to anyone who would listen. In 1973 I had seen a total eclipse of the sun and was truly changed by the experience. 'Okay,' I said. 'I'll write about astronomy.' And the rest, as they say, is history. I now write nonfiction—mostly astronomy, physics, and other science—for kids age ten and up. Maybe someday I'll get brave and try fiction.

"I have the best job in the world and can't imagine doing anything else. Sure, I occasionally type out insults to my word processor during particularly nasty writing blocks, but for the most part, I really love writing. I especially like getting letters from kids. The kids are funny, and they ask some tough, thoughtful questions. It gives me hope for the future. My two cats, Beanie and Spike, often help out when I need it the least, although they did provide some vital input for *Animal Amazing.* (They think they wrote it.)

"I have a swell summer place on a lake in Otis, Maine, where I pretend to write. I tell everybody I'm working on my next book when I'm actually eating lobster and Almond Joy ice cream. Kids should read more—a lot more—especially nonfiction. It's just as much fun as fiction. Honest. Read my books. You'll see ..."

*   *   *

HESSE, Karen 1952-

PERSONAL: Born August 29, 1952, in Baltimore, MD; married Randy Hesse, November 27, 1971; children: Kate, Rachel. *Education:* University of Maryland, B.A., 1975.

KAREN HESSE

ADDRESSES: Home—Star Route, Williamsville, VT 05362. *Agent*—Barbara Kouts, P.O. Box 558, Bellport, NY 11713.

CAREER: Writer, 1969—. Leave benefit coordinator for the University of Maryland, 1975-76; worked variously as a teacher, a librarian, an advertising secretary, a typesetter, and a proofreader. Affiliated with Mental Health Care and Hospice, 1988—; Newfane elementary school board chair, 1989; board member of Moore Free Library, 1989-91.

MEMBER: Society of Children's Book Writers and Illustrators (leader of South Vermont chapter, 1985-92).

AWARDS, HONORS: Wish on A Unicorn was named a 1992 Children's Book of Distinction by the *Hungry Mind Review; Letters from Rifka* was awarded the Christopher Medal and the *Horn Book* Fanfare, and was named a *School Library Journal* Best Book, a New York Public Library Book for Sharing, and a Best Book for Young Adults and a notable book by the American Library Association, all 1992; poetry awards from *Writer's Digest* and Poetry Society of Vermont.

WRITINGS:

Wish on a Unicorn, Holt, 1991.
Letters from Rifka, Holt, 1992.
Poppy's Chair (picture book), illustrated by Kay Life, Macmillan, 1993.
Lester's Dog (picture book), illustrated by Nancy Carpenter, Crown, 1993.

Lavender (early chapter book), illustrated by Andrew Glass, Holt, 1993.
Sable (an early picture book), illustrated by Marcia Sewall, Holt, in press.

SIDELIGHTS: Karen Hesse told *SATA:* "I grew up in a row house in Baltimore, surrounded by people, sights, and sounds, but often I felt alone. Thin and pasty, I looked like I'd drifted in from another world and never quite belonged to this one. I had friends, but always I felt separate, unable to blend, not free enough to trust anyone with my core secrets. I read a lot, though I'd often forget what I'd read within a few months and could read the same book again, experiencing it—so it seemed—for the first time. Until, at age eleven or twelve, I discovered the work of John Hersey. His book *Hiroshima* had a profound effect on me. If more books for children had existed at that time with real issues, if I'd seen characters survive the engulfing engine of reality, I don't think I would have felt so lonely, so isolated. I write now for children like the child I was, to show young readers that they are not alone in this world. My hope is to help them through hard times, to present characters who survive ordeals and grow as a result of them."

*   *   *

HEYER, Carol 1950-

PERSONAL: Born February 2, 1950, in Cuero, TX; daughter of William Jerome (a metallurgist) and Merlyn Mary (a teacher and secretary; maiden name, Hutson) Heyer. *Education:* California Lutheran University, B.A.,

CAROL HEYER

1974. *Hobbies and other interests:* Computers and gardening.

ADDRESSES: Home and office—Touchmark, 925 Avenue de los Arboles, Thousand Oaks, CA 91360.

CAREER: Illustrator and author. Image Resource, Westlake Village, CA, staff artist, 1979-81; Lynn-Davis Productions, Westlake Village, staff artist and writer, 1982-86; Lynn-Wenger Productions, Westlake Village, art director and writer, 1986-88; Northwind Studios International, Camarillo, CA, art director, 1988-89; Touchmark, Thousand Oaks, CA, writer and illustrator, 1988—. Hollywood Film School, staff artist, 1986-88; guest speaker at libraries and universities. Designed poster for *Prancer,* Orion Films; has illustrated cover art, maps, and booklets for fantasy board games.

MEMBER: Society of Illustrators (Los Angeles chapter), Society of Children's Book Writers and Illustrators, Association of Science Fiction and Fantasy Artists, Westlake Village Art Guild.

AWARDS, HONORS: Magazine Merit Award, Society of Children's Book Writers, 1988, for cover of *Dragon* magazine; Boomerang Award (best cover art), 1989, for *Aboriginal Science Fiction* magazine; Certificate of Merit, Society of Illustrators, 1990, 1991, and 1992; Regional Design Award, *Print* Magazine, 1992, for "The Cry of the Seagull," *Aboriginal Science Fiction* magazine; Literature award, Oxnard Cultural Arts commission and Carnegie Art Institute, 1992.

Heyer enjoys illustrating myths and fairy tales because of the opportunity to create fabulous creatures.

WRITINGS:

SELF-ILLUSTRATED

Beauty and the Beast, Ideals, 1989.
The Easter Story, Ideals, 1990.
Excalibur, Ideals, 1990.
The Christmas Story, Ideals, 1991.
Rapunzel, Ideals, 1992.

ILLUSTRATOR

Katherine Zwers and John Tobin, *A Star in the Pasture,* Ideals, 1988.
Zwers and Tobin, *The Golden Easter Egg,* Ideals, 1988.
Stephen Cosgrove, *Prancer,* Graphic Arts, 1989.
Cosgrove, *The Dream Stealer,* Graphic Arts, 1989.
Cecil Alexander, *All Things Bright and Beautiful,* Ideals, 1992.

Also contributor of illustrations to periodicals, including *Dragon, Dungeon,* and *Aboriginal Science Fiction.*

OTHER

(With Charles Davis) *Thunder Run* (film), Cannon, 1986.

WORK IN PROGRESS: A children's picture book entitled *Slugasaurus;* research on ancient myths and fantasy characters for a fantasy novel entitled *The Third Light.*

ADAPTATIONS: Prancer was adapted as a film, produced by Rafaella De Laurentiis for Orion Films, 1989.

SIDELIGHTS: Carol Heyer told *SATA:* "My whole life I have loved art and drawing. My strongest childhood memories are of my mother weaving tales of wonder and spending hours in the back garden, teaching me to build the perfect environment that would entice the magical faerie folk to visit each night.

"I think it is because of these memories that I have specialized in fantasy and science fiction art, especially the retelling and illustrating of the old classic stories I so love. There is also a great feeling of artistic freedom to be able to illustrate these fantasy worlds and the landscapes, characters, and creatures inhabiting them. Because, since they are creations of the imagination and not founded in the real world, I can paint with complete self-assurance and abandon, knowing that no one, anywhere, can tell me my dragon is wrong!"

* * *

HIBBERT, Eleanor Alice Burford 1906-1993
(Eleanor Burford, Philippa Carr, Elbur Ford, Victoria Holt, Kathleen Kellow, Jean Plaidy, Ellalice Tate)

OBITUARY NOTICE—See index for *SATA* sketch: Born in 1906, in Kennington, London, England; died January 18, 1993, on a cruise ship in the Mediterranean. Author. In addition to writing historical, Gothic, and romantic novels, Hibbert was perhaps best known by her pseudonyms Jean Plaidy, Victoria Holt, and Philippa Carr. A prolific author, she produced more than 150 books during her lifetime. Hibbert began her literary career writing short stories and was eventually encouraged to create romance novels by her agent. Writing as Jean Plaidy, she published her first novel, *Beyond the Blue Mountains* in 1947. Under this name, she recreated English history and royalty in over ninety novels, such as *Murder Most Royal, Queen in Waiting,* and *Victoria Victorious.* As Victoria Holt, Hibbert wrote Gothic novels with more adventurous heroines, beginning in 1960 with *Mistress of Mellyn* and including the posthumously published *The Black Opal.* Family sagas, historical backgrounds, and extraordinary romance were the domain of Hibbert's pseudonym Philippa Carr, featuring such novels as *The Miracle at St. Bruno's* and *The Adulteress.* Hibbert also published children's books, including *The Young Elizabeth* and *Meg Roper: Daughter of Sir Thomas More,* both under the pseudonym Jean Plaidy.

OBITUARIES AND OTHER SOURCES:

BOOKS

The Writers Directory: 1992-1994, St. James Press, 1992.

PERIODICALS

Chicago Tribune, January 24, 1993, sec. 2, p. 7.
Los Angeles Times, January 22, 1993, p. A22.
Times (London), January 21, 1993, p. 19.
Washington Post, January 21, 1993, p. B7.

*   *   *

HINES, Gary (Roger) 1944-

PERSONAL: Born August 12, 1944, in Oakland, CA; son of W. Roger (a contractor and realtor) and Helen (a secretary; maiden name, Lassen) Hines; married Anna Grossnickle (a children's author and illustrator), June 19, 1976; children: Beth Carlson, Sarah Stephens, Lassen. *Education:* Attended University of California, Davis, 1962-63, and College of Siskiyous, 1963-64; California State University, Chico, B.S., 1967. *Politics:* Liberal. *Hobbies and other interests:* Reading, theatre, skiing, history.

ADDRESSES: Home—R.R. 4, Box 8057, Milford, PA 18337. *Office*—U.S. Forest Service, Box 188, Milford, PA 18337. *Agent*—Ginger Knowlton, Curtis Brown Ltd., Ten Astor Place, New York, NY 10003.

CAREER: Worked variously in construction and as a fire fighter, 1959-67; U.S. Forest Service, budget analyst in San Francisco, CA, 1968-73, administrative assistant in Pinecrest, CA, 1973-75, public affairs director in Pinecrest, 1976-90; children's writer, 1991—. Composer and musician, San Francisco, 1968-73; Card, Pinkerton, and Hines (acoustic folk group), San Francisco, member, 1969-72; affiliated with Hines Sight and Sound (free-lance audio/visual business), Twain Harte, CA, 1980-90; Sierra Repertory Theatre, Sonora, CA, sound designer, 1980-90; actor, appearing in produc-

GARY HINES

tions including *Something's Afoot, The Secret Affairs of Mildred Wild, The Fantasticks,* and *Gifford Pinchot: From the Other Side* (also see below), 1981—. Grey Towers National Historic Landmark, outreach coordinator, 1991—.

MEMBER: National Arborist Society.

AWARDS, HONORS: Distinguished Service Award, U.S. Department of Agriculture, 1990, for theatrical production on Gifford Pinchot, an early conservationist and America's first forester; recipient of numerous awards for educational programs for the U.S. Forest Service.

WRITINGS:

(And creator) *Gifford Pinchot: From the Other Side* (play), first produced in Sonora, CA, 1988.
A Ride in the Crummy (picture book), illustrated by wife, Anna Grossnickle Hines, Greenwillow, 1991.
Flying Fire Fighters (picture book), illustrated by A. G. Hines, Clarion Books, 1993.
Day of the Highclimber (picture book), illustrated by A. G. Hines, Greenwillow, in press.

Work represented in anthologies, including *Haunted House,* edited by Jane Yolen, HarperCollins, 1993. Composer of music for the 1974 Spokane, Washington, World's Fair promotional film; also composer of jingles for radio advertisements.

WORK IN PROGRESS: Three middle-grade novels: *Crooked Road West, Fire in an August Sky,* and *The*

Lost Higgins Gold; conservation research for non-fiction, middle-grade work.

SIDELIGHTS: Gary Hines told *SATA:* "I grew up in a small community in the Cascade mountains of northern California. Surrounded by beautiful peaks and forests, my hometown was a terrific place for my imagination to run wild. The one part of myself I have always tried to nurture is the ability to see life through the eyes of wonder. Sometimes I do this well, sometimes not. But I continually try to remind myself that life is an incredible (though often difficult) journey and that everything one needs to experience it is magically tucked away inside us already. We are all born with the essentials. The trick is not forgetting where they are and to have the courage to search for them when they've been elusive.

"Of course, throughout my growing up years, and especially in my adult years, there have been and still are numerous barriers to wonder and imagination. We've all bumped up against them from time to time. But if you believe in yourself, the barriers eventually fall away and let you pass.

"At one time or another, I have been an outhouse builder, a fire fighter, a construction worker, a bricklayer's assistant, a musician, a songwriter, a recording engineer, a forest ranger, an actor, and a writer. All of these experiences have shaped who I am today.

"Much of my professional career has dealt with the field of conservation. I know firsthand how precious, limited, and often abused the world's natural resources are. I cannot, however, think of a natural resource more valuable and special than children. This is why I choose

Toby's grandfather reminisces about a boyhood trip in the "crummy" or caboose of a train in the 1930s in *A Ride in the Crummy* by Hines. (Cover illustration by Anna Grossnickle Hines.)

to write for young people. They are the future and deserve the very best we can give."

*   *   *

HISLOP, Julia Rose Catherine 1962-

PERSONAL: Born March 13, 1962, in Winnipeg, Manitoba, Canada; daughter of David Moore Cameron (an obstetrician and gynecologist) and Constance Emma (a psychologist; maiden name, Baker) Hislop. *Education:* University of Michigan, B.A., 1984; California State University, Los Angeles, M.A., 1986; California School of Professional Psychology, doctoral study, 1986—.

ADDRESSES: Agent—c/o Rosen Publishing Group, 29 East 21st St., New York, NY 10010.

CAREER: Devereux Foundation, Devon, PA, residential counselor, 1984-85; Fresno City College, Fresno, CA, instructor in psychology, assertiveness training, and human sexuality, 1989-91; D.C. Commission of Mental Health Services, psychology intern, 1991—. Pacifica House, weekend substance abuse counselor, 1986; 1736 Family Crisis Center, counselor for runaway youth, 1986-87.

AWARDS, HONORS: Coping with Rejection was named one of the New York Public Library's Best Books for the Teen Aged, 1992.

WRITINGS:

Coping with Rejection, Rosen Publishing, 1991.

WORK IN PROGRESS: Doctoral dissertation on the psychosocial histories of women who sexually molest children.

SIDELIGHTS: Julia Rose Catherine Hislop told *SATA:* "Much of my work and training in the field of psychology has been with teenagers and young adults. While working at a youth shelter for runaways just outside of Los Angeles, I found that many of the teenagers had concerns related to the issue of sexual abuse. In my free time, I found myself putting together a manuscript for teens who had experienced this problem. Later, when I was working for a sexual abuse treatment team, I added to this manuscript. Thinking that others might benefit from the book, I decided to send it to several publishers. I received numerous rejection letters. One of the companies from whom I received such a letter was the Rosen Publishing Group. They informed me, as had several other companies, that they had recently published a similar book.

"The Rosen Publishing Group has a series of titles which help youth and young adults cope with various difficulties. They asked if I might be interested in writing a book in this series and suggested the title *Coping with Rejection.* I suspect that they felt I had the proper empathy to undertake the title with a fresh rejection letter in hand! We corresponded briefly concerning ideas for the book, and I was asked to write an

JULIA ROSE CATHERINE HISLOP

outline and a sample chapter. In the end, I was given a contract and a year to produce the book. Editors at the Rosen Publishing Group were very helpful in making suggestions as the book went along. The end result was a book that came out in 1991. The Rosen Publishing Group and I were both very pleased that *Coping with Rejection* was placed on the New York Public Library's Best Books for the Teen Aged list for 1992. One of the premises of the book is that rejection is not always a bad thing. The book itself would not have been published had the original rejection not occurred!"

*   *   *

HOFF, Mary (King) 1956-

PERSONAL: Born August 16, 1956; daughter of Harold and Delores (Reinecke) King; married Paul Hoff; children: Tony, Kate, Daniel. *Education:* University of Wisconsin, B.S., 1978; University of Minnesota, M.A., 1984. *Hobbies and other interests:* Hiking, camping, reading, cooking, canoeing, gardening, knitting.

CAREER: Author. Free-lance communicator specializing in science and medical communication.

WRITINGS:

"OUR ENDANGERED PLANET" SERIES; WITH MARY M. RODGERS

Groundwater, Lerner, c. 1991.
Rivers and Lakes, Lerner, c. 1991.
Oceans, Lerner, 1991.
Population Growth, Lerner, 1991.

Tropical Rain Forests, Lerner, 1991.
Life on Land, Lerner, 1992.
Life in the Sea, Lerner, 1993.

WORK IN PROGRESS: Books on atmospheric change for Lerner Publications.

SIDELIGHTS: Mary Hoff told *SATA:* "First, I am a mother, trying to raise our children to be people who make the world a better place. I focus my writing on science and medicine, two areas that I believe will have great influence on our lives in the future and so deserve our attention and understanding."

*   *   *

HOFSEPIAN, Sylvia A. 1932-

PERSONAL: Born January 7, 1932, in Boston, MA; daughter of Harry (a baker) and Lillian (a homemaker and secretary; maiden name, Krekorian) Hofsepian. *Education:* Received B.S. from North Adams State College. *Hobbies and other interests:* "I enjoy watching the birds and wild animals in my yard, reading, walking in the state park a few minutes away, listening to music, baking, handwork, and flower arranging."

ADDRESSES: Home—296 Groveland St., Abington, MA 02351.

CAREER: Writer. Teacher in Abington, MA, 1953-83.

WRITINGS:

Why Not?, illustrated by Friso Henstra, Four Winds, 1991.

Why Not? has been translated into Dutch.

WORK IN PROGRESS: Three folk tales and some nonfiction articles.

SIDELIGHTS: Sylvia A. Hofsepian told *SATA:* "During the thirty years in which I taught first grade, storytime, following lunch and recess, was a favorite time for the children and for me. They became totally involved in the story, and I delighted in watching their reactions and the expressions on their faces.

"I knew how important storytelling, and later, reading was to children, no matter what their ages. Books opened up the world to them, helped them develop a sense of humor, brought an understanding of the feelings of others, and often helped them cope with problems in their own lives.

"My teaching years were a happy and satisfying time in my life, and when I retired, I felt that it was vital that I continue to work for the benefit and enjoyment of children. I decided to try to learn to write. Perhaps someday, somewhere, a child would take delight in a story of mine.

"Although I have tried writing in other genres, folk and fairy tales were my favorites as a child, and I enjoy

SYLVIA A. HOFSEPIAN

writing them now. I am interested, too, in writing about nature, so that children will understand the importance of preserving the creatures in their world and derive the delight and comfort that this awareness can bring throughout life."

FOR MORE INFORMATION SEE:

PERIODICALS

School Library Journal, December, 1991.

* * *

HOGROGIAN, Nonny 1932-

PERSONAL: Name is pronounced "*nonn*-ee ho-*groh*-gee-an"; born May 7, 1932, in New York, NY; daughter of Mugerdich (a photoengraver) and Rachel (Ansoorian) Hogrogian; married David Kherdian (a poet), March 17, 1971. *Education:* Hunter College (now Hunter College of the City University of New York), B.A., 1953; graduate study, New School for Social Research, 1957.

CAREER: Designer and office worker for William Morrow and Co., New York City; illustrator for Thomas Y. Crowell Co., Holt, Rinehart and Winston, and Charles Scribner's Sons, all New York City; illustrator and writer of children's books.

AWARDS, HONORS: Caldecott awards, 1966, for *Always Room for One More,* and 1972, for *One Fine Day;*

New York Times Outstanding Books citation, 1971, for *About Wise Men and Simpletons;* Caldecott Honor Award, 1977, for *The Contest.*

WRITINGS:

SELF-ILLUSTRATED

One Fine Day, Macmillan, 1971.
Apples, Macmillan, 1972.
Billy Goat and His Well-Fed Friends, Harper, 1972.
The Hermit and Harry and Me, Little, Brown, 1972.
Handmade Secret Hiding Places, Overlook Press, 1975.
Carrot Cake, Greenwillow, 1977.
The Cat Who Loved to Sing, Knopf, 1988.

RETELLER AND ILLUSTRATOR

Rooster Brother (Armenian folk tale), Macmillan, 1974.
The Contest (Armenian folk tale), Greenwillow, 1976.
Jacob Ludwig Karl Grimm, *Cinderella,* Greenwillow, 1981.
Grimm, *The Devil with the Three Golden Hairs,* Knopf, 1983.
Grimm, *The Glass Mountain,* Knopf, 1985.
Noah's Ark, Knopf, 1986.

ILLUSTRATOR

Nicolete Meredith, *King of the Kerry Fair,* Crowell, 1960.
Henrietta Bancroft, *Down Come the Leaves,* Crowell, 1961.
Sorche Nic Leodhas (pseudonym of Leclaire G. Alger), *Gaelic Ghosts,* Holt, 1963.
Leodhas, *Ghosts Go Haunting,* Holt, 1965.
Aileen L. Fisher, *Arbor Day,* Crowell, 1965.
Leodhas, *Always Room for One More,* Holt, 1965.
Robert Burns, *Hand in Hand We'll Go: Ten Poems,* Crowell, 1965.
Barbara Schiller, reteller, *The Kitchen Knight,* Holt, 1965.
William Shakespeare, *Poems,* Crowell, 1966.
Virginia A. Tashjian, reteller, *Once There Was and Was Not,* Little, Brown, 1966.
Mary O'Neill, *The White Palace,* Crowell, 1966.
Julie Whitney, *Bears Are Sleeping,* Scribner, 1967.
Beatrice Schenk De Regniers, *The Day Everybody Cried,* Viking, 1967.
Isaac Bashevis Singer, *The Fearsome Inn,* translated by Elizabeth Shub, Scribner, 1967.
The Renowned History of Little Red Riding Hood, Crowell, 1967.
The Thirteen Days of Yule, Crowell, 1968.
Christian Morgenstern, *The Three Sparrows and Other Nursery Rhymes,* translated by Max Knight, Scribner, 1968.
The Story of Prince Ivan, the Firebird, and the Gray Wolf, translated from the Russian by Thomas P. Whitney, Scribner, 1968.
Theodore Fontane, *Sir Ribbeck of Ribbeck of Havelland,* translated from the German by Shub, Macmillan, 1969.
Virginia Hamilton, *The Time-Ago Tales of Jahdu,* Macmillan, 1969.

NONNY HOGROGIAN

Esther Hautzig, *In School: Learning in Four Languages,* Macmillan, 1969.

Virginia Haviland, reteller, *Favorite Fairy Tales Told in Greece,* Little, Brown, 1970.

James Stephens, *Deirdre,* Macmillan, 1970.

Vasilisa the Beautiful, translated from the Russian by T. P. Whitney, Macmillan, 1970.

Rachel Hogrogian, *The Armenian Cookbook,* Atheneum, 1971.

Grimm, *About Wise Men and Simpletons,* translated by Shub, Macmillan, 1971.

Cheli Duran Ryan, *Paz,* Macmillan, 1971.

Tashjian, *Three Apples Fell from Heaven,* Little, Brown, 1971.

David Kherdian, *Bird in Suet* (broadside), Giligia Press, 1971.

Kherdian, *Of Husbands and Wives* (broadside), privately printed, 1971.

Kherdian, *Hey Nonny* (broadside), privately printed, 1972.

One I Love, Two I Love, and Other Loving Mother Goose Rhymes, Dutton, 1972.

Kherdian, *Looking over Hills,* Giligia Press, 1972.

Kherdian, compiler, *Visions of America: By the Poets of Our Time,* Macmillan, 1973.

Kherdian, *Poem for Nonny* (broadside), Phineas Press, 1973.

Kherdian, *Onions from New Hampshire* (broadside), privately printed, 1973.

Kherdian, *In the Tradition* (broadside), University of Connecticut, 1974.

Kherdian, *16:IV:73* (broadside), Arts Action Press, 1975.

Kherdian, editor, *Poems Here and Now* (broadside), Greenwillow, 1976.

Kherdian, compiler, *The Dog Writes on the Window with His Nose, and Other Poems,* Four Winds, 1977.

Kherdian, *Country Cat, City Cat,* Four Winds, 1978.

Lcila Ward, *I Am Eyes, Ni Macho,* Greenwillow, 1978.

Kherdian, reteller (published anonymously), *The Pearl: Hymn of the Robe of Glory,* Two Rivers Press, 1979.

Pigs Never See the Stars, translated by Kherdian, Two Rivers, 1982.

A. L. Staveley, *Where is Bernardino?,* Two Rivers Press, 1982.

Kherdian, *Right Now* (juvenile), Knopf, 1983.

Count Bobrinskoy, *Peacock from Heaven,* Two Rivers, 1983.

Kherdian, *The Animal* (juvenile), Knopf, 1984.

Kherdian, *Root River Run,* Carolrhoda Books, 1984.

George MacDonald, *The Day Boy and the Night Girl,* Knopf, 1988.

Kherdian, *A Song for Uncle Harry* (juvenile), Philomel, 1989.

Kherdian, *The Cat's Midsummer Jamboree* (juvenile), Putnam, 1990.

Kherdian, *The Great Fishing Contest* (juvenile), Philomel, 1991.

Rumer Godden, *Candy Floss,* Philomel, 1991.

Feathers and Tails: Animal Fables from Around the World (juvenile), retold by Kherdian, Philomel, 1992.

Kherdian, *Juna's Journey* (juvenile), Philomel, 1993.

Kherdian, *By Myself* (juvenile), Holt, 1993.

Two thieves vie for the love of a young girl in *The Contest,* an Armenian folktale retold and illustrated by Hogrogian.

OTHER

(Author of introduction) Walter Lester, *Housebuilding for Children,* Overlook Press, 1977.

SIDELIGHTS: Nonny Hogrogian is the illustrator and designer of many children's books, including two winners of the prestigious Caldecott Medal, *Always Room for One More* and *One Fine Day.* Her critically acclaimed works have been included in many exhibitions of children's books by the American Institute of Graphic Arts.

Three generations of Hogrogian's artistic family simultaneously inhabited their brick and stone house on Kingsbridge Terrace in the Bronx, New York, at the time of her birth in 1932. While her father, Mugerdich, earned a living as a photoengraver, he spent the weekends painting and gardening, and her mother, Rachel, also liked to sketch and do needlework. "My fascination with artwork and fine handwork goes back as far as I can remember," Hogrogian wrote in an essay for *Something about the Author Autobiography Series*

(SAAS). "Love of work itself was strong in the family and whenever there were spare moments someone would start a new project. And so, with these influences, when I was about three or four years old, I began to putter with my father's paints and brushes."

Hogrogian's grandfather occupied a large basement room, which also housed the family library. Although many of the books were in Armenian, Hogrogian would, as she wrote in *SAAS,* "sit in the big chair by the bookcase going through the illustrated books ... dreaming about the possibility of making such beautiful pictures." But it would be some time before Hogrogian was able to realize her dream. During her high school years she studied painting and charcoal drawing with an aunt who had studied art at the Sorbonne in Paris. She also completed an illustrating class for young people at the Pratt Institute in Brooklyn. Hogrogian took advantage of any opportunity available to hone her skills: hand-lettering cards for a high school teacher, making scratchboard illustrations for the high school magazine, and hand-painting greeting cards.

Hogrogian was awarded the Caldecott Medal for *One Fine Day,* her self-illustrated tale of a greedy fox.

Hogrogian attended Hunter College, where she majored in art with an art history minor. After graduation she landed a job with William Morrow and Company, working with book-jacket artists, choosing type, getting the artwork approved, and sometimes even creating jacket art herself. Her three years with Morrow proved to be a useful period of on-the-job training. At this time she also studied woodcutting with Antonio Frasconi at the New School for Social Research. Frasconi urged her to leave her publishing job to work as an artist.

Upon leaving Morrow, Hogrogian free-lanced for a time, then continued her work in woodcutting at the Haystack Mountain School of Crafts in Maine, to which she had won a summer scholarship. She had difficulties with the narrowness of the school's view of art, but it brought to the fore her determination. "I never really understood what my relation to artwork was, but I knew somewhere inside that it was what it was, and that I had a responsibility to work with it as best I could," she wrote in *SAAS*.

In 1958 Hogrogian became a production assistant in the children's book department at Crowell, where she was given her first chance to illustrate a children's book: *King of the Kerry Fair*. Later, while working as the art director at Holt, she was asked to illustrate Leclaire G. Alger's *Gaelic Ghosts*. The combination of Hogrogian and Alger, who wrote under the pseudonym Sorche Nic Leodhas, proved to be fruitful, and culminated with *Always Room for One More*, winner of the 1966 Caldecott Award.

Hogrogian has illustrated a growing list of books, many of them folktales, using black-and-white drawings, colored pencil drawings, woodcuts, and paintings, among other techniques. In 1971 she began a fruitful relationship: she married poet David Kherdian, whom she had met at a reception after agreeing to do a cover drawing for a book of his poems. Since then the couple has worked together on many books, including poetry, prose, and picture books for the very young.

Throughout her career, Hogrogian has garnered praise from critics for her artwork. She is commended in particular for her attention to detail, her ability to capture the personalities of sundry characters, and for her skill in creating drawings that complement the text. A reviewer for *Booklist,* for instance, noted that in *The Day Boy and the Night Girl* Hogrogian "reflect[s] the author's vision, quietly and precisely delineating the scenes and characters as the story unfolds." Critics have also called her illustrations "beautiful" and "distinctive." According to a *Booklist* reviewer in a critique of *The Glass Mountain*, Hogrogian's illustrations are "strong and sensitive line drawings filled with rich, delicate watercolors." The critic added that they "are outstanding." Hogrogian is "an artist who can paint enchantment," concluded *Booklist* contributor Sheila-mae O'Hara, in an assessment of *Candy Floss*.

Despite her readers' obvious enjoyment of her illustrations, Hogrogian continually strives to create better art.

Hogrogian researched Scottish dress and customs to give authenticity to her illustrations for author Sorche Nic Leodhas's *Always Room for One More*.

She often does extensive research in order to portray the features, dress, and customs of the people she draws as authentically as possible. While preparing to illustrate *Always Room for One More,* for example, she viewed slides of Scottish people and villages and even listened to traditional Scottish music. As she wrote in *SAAS*, "I am always dissatisfied with my work, always left with the feeling that I must try harder the next time."

WORKS CITED:

Review of *The Day Boy and the Night Girl, Booklist,* February 1, 1989.

Review of *The Glass Mountain, Booklist,* December 1, 1985, p. 573.

O'Hara, Sheilamae, review of *Candy Floss, Booklist,* November 1, 1991.

Something about the Author Autobiography Series, Volume 1, Gale, 1986, pp. 129-40.

FOR MORE INFORMATION SEE:

BOOKS

Alderson, Brian W., *Children's Book Review,* Five Owls Press, 1973.

Children's Literature in Education, Volume 20, number 1, 1989.

Children's Literature Review, Volume 2, Gale, 1976.

Warren Stewig, John Warren, *Reading Pictures: Exploring Illustrations with Children. Ezra Jack Keats, Marcia Brown, Gerald McDermott, Nonny Hogrogian* (four posters and study guide), Jenson Publications, 1988.

PERIODICALS

Booklist, September 15, 1975, p. 165; April 1, 1988, p. 1348.

Bulletin of the Center for Children's Books, April, 1977; January, 1978; June, 1988, p. 207; February, 1993, pp. 180-81.

Horn Book, August, 1966; August, 1972; December, 1976; August, 1983, pp. 431-32; March/April, 1987, p. 201.

Junior Literary Guild, September, 1978.

Kirkus Reviews, August 15, 1992.

Publishers Weekly, October 26, 1984, p. 105; October 11, 1985, p. 65; August 3, 1992.

School Library Journal, March, 1983, p. 162; February, 1986, p. 74; January, 1987, p. 67; April, 1988, p. 80; December, 1991; October, 1992.

*   *   *

HOLT, Victoria
See HIBBERT, Eleanor Alice Burford

*   *   *

HOUSTON, Dick 1943-

PERSONAL: Born December 18, 1943, in Ashtabula, OH; son of Carroll (a tool and die maker) and Dorothy (a county deputy treasurer; maiden name, Ball) Houston. *Education:* Kent State University, B.A., 1965; Edinboro University of Pennsylvania, M.A., 1969. *Politics:* Independent. *Religion:* Episcopalian. *Hobbies and other interests:* Collecting Africana books about Africa's frontier days; collecting movie memorabilia about African films.

Dick Houston and the late naturalist George Adamson on safari.

ADDRESSES: Home—1725 East 46th Street, Ashtabula, OH 44004.

CAREER: Teacher of English and social studies in public schools in Ohio, Maine, and Florida, and in private schools abroad, including Exxon Oil Corporation school in Venezuela, the International School of Kenya, and the American Embassy School of Lusaka, Zambia. Edited manuscripts in Kenya for the late Joy Adamson. Operated adventure safaris in Kenya and Tanzania; conducted overland trips across the Sahara Desert, into the rain forests of Zaire, and across the East African bush country.

AWARDS, HONORS: Beitler Award, Kent State University, 1992; *Safari Adventure* was cited as one of "Ten Best Adventure Stories" by the New York Public Library, 1992, and was recommended by the Iowa Education Dept. for geography classes in public schools.

WRITINGS:

Safari Adventure, Cobblehill/Dutton, 1991.

Contributor of articles to periodicals, including *Smithsonian, Reader's Digest, Holiday, Los Angeles Times, New York Times, Toronto Star, Adventure-Travel,* and the Cleveland *Plain Dealer.* Houston's stories have been syndicated in major publications around the world.

WORK IN PROGRESS: A Distant Drum, a motion picture screenplay about the pioneer cinematographers, Martin and Osa Johnson.

SIDELIGHTS: Dick Houston told *SATA:* "Have you ever imagined yourself *living* a wild impossible dream? My wild childhood dream was to operate my own safari adventures in Africa. I wanted to see it all and do it all: cross the vast Sahara Desert, explore the jungles of Zaire, climb Mount Kilimanjaro, float down the wild Zambezi River in a canoe, set up tents in the middle of the Serengeti wildebeest migration, come face-to-face with wild elephants, and listen to lions roar in the night from my tent. That was just for starters.

"My first 'safari' took place when I was a teenager in the 1950s. I took weekly treks to the old Bula Theatre in my hometown, Ashtabula, Ohio, to watch lavish Technicolor safari movies, everything from *King Solomon's Mines* and *The African Queen* to *Mogambo* and *The Roots of Heaven.* But one particular type of movie had the most influence on me—a series of creaky black-and-white documentaries about Africa that had been produced in the 1920s and 1930s by Martin and Osa Johnson, a daredevil husband-and-wife film-making team from Kansas. The titles of their movies—*Jungle Adventures, Baboona, Congorilla*—were corny, but the Johnson formula for adventure was irresistible: mount an elaborate safari, improvise various situations as you go along, and film them on the spot.

"It was the gritty authenticity of those old Johnson film re-runs that made them so appealing to me. There were

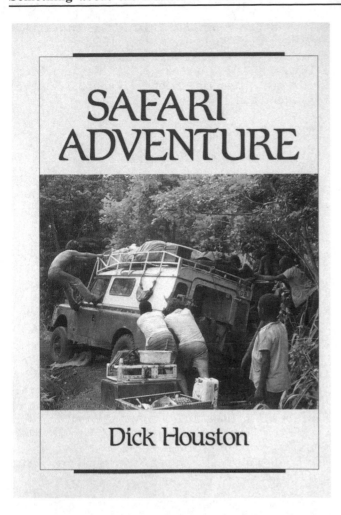

In *Safari Adventure,* Houston tells of how he achieved his childhood dream of a trip to Africa.

always the unexpected dangers of the Johnsons working so close to wild animals. A leopard once crashed through Martin's camera blind and landed on his lap. When Martin provoked a herd of elephants into charging the camera one day, Osa stood there dutifully cranking away until the last possible moment. Then she picked up her rifle and brought the herd leader crashing to the ground only inches from the tripod. It all added up to exciting, authentic movie footage.

"In addition to all the thrills and close calls with wild animals, I was fascinated as to how the Johnsons put their expeditions together. They organized meticulously planned motorized safaris with fleets of trucks that carried boxes and boxes of food, tents, rifles, motion picture equipment, tables, chairs, and even an ice-cream machine. By being self-contained on the road, the Johnsons were able to travel long distances over an extended period of time—and to be in control of when and where *they* wanted to go.

"So there it was. The movies gave me a dream of Africa and also gave me an idea of how to operate authentic, old-fashioned tent safaris. I knew that I just had to get to Africa some day to become a safari leader.

"I had learned through my parents that dreams have to be built on solid foundations. After graduating from college with a master's degree in English, I taught social studies and English in junior and senior high schools. One day, one of my students bluntly asked: 'Hey, if you are so in love with Africa in books and films, why don't you stop talking about it and start doing something about getting there?' Years later, by scrimping pennies, I was eventually able to save up enough to go off to Africa. To take a chance really and see if I could make my dream come true. In my book *Safari Adventure,* I tell how I was able to get my own safari business started.

"And the adventures? Far more exciting than I could ever have imagined. Chased by elephants, nearly bitten by the deadly black mamba, climbing Kilimanjaro, camping amongst hundreds of thousands of wildebeest on the Serengeti Plain, snorkeling in the crystal clear, aquamarine waters of the East African coast, exploring the mysterious Lake Paradise, getting stuck in deserts, and too many adventures to mention here. But most of all, I tell in *Safari Adventure* of what it is like to live completely free under the sun and stars, camping next to elephant watering holes, getting stung by scorpions and safari ants, and experiencing the magic of safari campfires. *Safari Adventure* tells what it is to live like a gypsy, master of one's own fate."

*   *   *

HOUSTON, James A(rchibald) 1921-

PERSONAL: Born June 12, 1921, in Toronto, Ontario, Canada; came to the United States in 1962; son of James Donald (a clothing importer) and Gladys Maud (Barbour) Houston; married Alma G. Bardon, 1950 (divorced, 1966); married Alice Daggett Watson, December 9, 1967; children: John James, Samuel Douglas. *Education:* Attended Ontario College of Art, 1938-40, Ecole Grand Chaumiere, Paris, 1947-48, Unichi-Hiratsuka, Tokyo, 1958-59, and Atelier 17, 1961. *Religion:* Anglican. *Hobbies and other interests:* Fishing, sketching.

ADDRESSES: Home—24 Main St., Stonington, CT 06378 (winter); and P.O. Box 43, Tlell, Queen Charlotte Islands, British Columbia, Canada V0T 1Y0 (summer). *Office*—717 Fifth Ave., New York, NY 10022.

CAREER: Author and illustrator. Canadian Guild of Crafts, Arctic adviser, 1949-52; Government of Canada, West Baffin, Northwest Territories, first civil administrator, 1952-62; Steuben Glass, New York City, associate director of design, 1962-72, master designer, 1972—. Visiting lecturer at Wye Institute and Rhode Island School of Design; honorary fellow, Ontario College of Art. Chair of board of directors of Canadian Arctic Producers, 1976-77, and American Indian Art Center; member of board of directors of Canadian Eskimo Arts Council; president of Indian and Eskimo Art of the Americas; vice-president of West Baffin Eskimo Cooperative and Eskimo Art, Inc. Member of primitive art committee of Metropolitan Museum of

JAMES A. HOUSTON

Art. *Military service:* Canadian Army, Toronto Scottish Regiment, 1940-45; became warrant officer.

EXHIBITIONS: Canadian Guild of Crafts, 1953, 1955, 1957; Robertson Galleries, Ottawa, 1953; Calgary Galleries, 1966; Canadiana Galleries, Edmonton, 1977; Yaneff Gallery, Toronto, 1983, 1986; Steuben Glass, 1987; represented in collections of Glenbow-Alberta Museum of Art, Montreal Museum of Fine Arts, and National Gallery of Art, Ottawa.

MEMBER: Producers Guild of America, Writers' Union of Canada, Canadian Eskimo Arts Council, Canadian Arctic Producers, American Indian Arts Center, Indian and Eskimo Art of the Americas, Royal Society of Art (London; fellow, 1981), Explorers Club, Century Association, Grolier Club, Leash.

AWARDS, HONORS: American Indian and Eskimo Cultural Foundation award, 1966; Canadian Library Association Book of the Year awards, 1966, for *Tikta'liktak: An Eskimo Legend,* 1968, for *The White Archer: An Eskimo Legend,* 1980, for *River Runners: A Tale of Hardship and Bravery,* and runner-up, 1982, for *Long Claws: An Arctic Adventure;* American Library Association Notable Books citations, 1967, for *The White Archer,* 1968, for *Akavak,* and 1971, for *The White Dawn;* decorated officer of Order of Canada, 1972; D.Litt., Carleton University, 1972; Amelia Frances Howard-Gibbon award runner-up, 1973, for *Ghost Paddle;* D.H.L., Rhode Island College, 1975; Vicky Metcalf award, 1977; Inuit Kuavati Award of Merit, 1979; D.F.A., Rhode Island School of Design, 1979; Vicky Metcalf Short Story award, 1980, for "Long

Claws" in *The Winter Fun Book;* Canadian nominee, Hans Christian Andersen Award, 1987; Citation of Merit Award, Royal Canadian Academy of Arts, 1987; D.D.L., Dalhousie University, 1987; Max and Gretta Ebel Award, Canadian Society of Children's Authors, Illustrators, and Performers, 1989.

WRITINGS:

FOR CHILDREN; SELF-ILLUSTRATED

Tikta'liktak: An Eskimo Legend, Harcourt, 1965.
Eagle Mask: A West Coast Indian Tale, Harcourt, 1966.
The White Archer: An Eskimo Legend, Harcourt, 1967.
Akavak: An Eskimo Journey, Harcourt, 1968.
Wolf Run: A Caribou Eskimo Tale, Harcourt, 1971.
Ghost Paddle: A Northwest Coast Indian Tale, Harcourt, 1972.
Kiviok's Magic Journey: An Eskimo Legend, Atheneum, 1973.
Frozen Fire: A Tale of Courage, Atheneum, 1977, 2nd edition, Macmillan, 1992.
River Runners: A Tale of Hardship and Bravery, Atheneum, 1979.
Long Claws: An Arctic Adventure, Atheneum, 1981.
Black Diamonds: A Search for Arctic Treasure, Atheneum, 1982.
Ice Swords: An Undersea Adventure, Atheneum, 1985.
The Falcon Bow: An Arctic Legend, McElderry, 1986.
Whiteout, Key Porter, 1988.
The White Dawn: An Eskimo Saga, Harcourt, 1989.
Drifting Snow: An Arctic Search, McElderry, 1992.

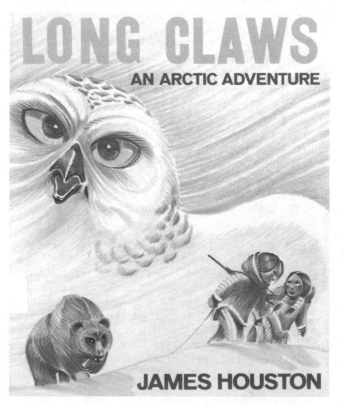

In his self-illustrated *Long Claws,* Houston tells the tale of a brother and sister who set out on an danger-filled trek to recover a buried caribou.

FOR ADULTS

Canadian Eskimo Art, Queen's Printer, 1955.
Eskimo Graphic Art, Queen's Printer, 1960.
Eskimo Prints, Barre Publishing, 1967, 2nd edition, 1971.
The White Dawn: An Eskimo Saga (novel), Harcourt, 1971.
(Editor; self-illustrated) *Songs of the Dream People: Chants and Images from the Indians and Eskimos of North America,* Atheneum, 1972.
Ojibwa Summer, photographs by B. A. King, Barre Publishing, 1972.
Ghost Fox (novel), Harcourt, 1977.
Spirit Wrestler (novel), Harcourt, 1980.
Eagle Song (novel), Harcourt, 1983.
Running West (novel), Crown, 1989.

ILLUSTRATOR

Shoot to Live, 1944.
Alma Houston, *Nuki,* 1955.
Raymond de Coccola and Paul King, *Ayorama,* 1956.
Tuktut/Caribou, 1957.
Elizabeth Pool, *The Unicorn Was There,* Bauhan, 1966.
(And author of introduction) George Francis Lyon, *The Private Journal of Captain G. F. Lyon of H.M.S. Hecla, During the Recent Voyage of Discovery under Captain Parry, 1921-23,* Imprint Society, 1970.
M. J. Wheeler, *First Came the Indians,* Atheneum, 1983.
R. de Coccola and P. King, *The Incredible Eskimo,* Hancock House, 1986.

SCREENPLAYS

The White Dawn, Paramount Pictures, 1973.
The Mask and the Drum, Swannsway Productions, 1975.
So Sings the Wolf, Devonian Group, 1976.
Kalvak, Devonian Group, 1976.

Houston has also adapted *Art of the Arctic Whaleman,* 1978, and *Legends of the Salmon People,* 1978, for the screen.

OTHER

Contributor of short stories to periodicals. Houston's manuscripts are collected at the National Library of Canada, Ottawa.

ADAPTATIONS: Ghost Fox has been recorded on eight cassettes by Crane Memorial Library, 1978.

SIDELIGHTS: James A. Houston is "probably the most popular and influential authority on Arctic culture that Canada has produced," according to T. F. Rigelhof in the Toronto *Globe and Mail.* Houston derives his authority as an author, illustrator, glass designer, and filmmaker from his remarkable experiences living with the Inuit people in the Canadian Arctic. Combining art school training with a life worthy of an adventure movie, he grounds his stories, whether for adults or for children, in the legends and myths of his beloved Inuit. His books explore the challenges of living close to the

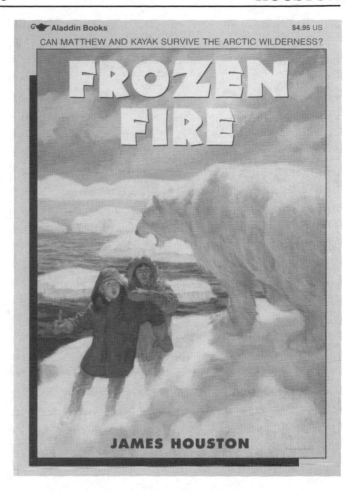

In *Frozen Fire,* Matthew and Kayak struggle to survive in the Canadian Arctic after becoming stranded while searching for Matthew's father. (Cover illustration by Richard Williams.)

land, and detail the changes that an environment can make upon the character of its inhabitants.

Houston was born on June 12, 1921, in Toronto, Ontario, the son of an adventurous clothing importer and an artistic mother. His father took advantage of his traveling salesman status to visit the far reaches of the Canadian wilderness, where he traded with Eskimos and Indians. In "A Primitive View of the World" (his May Hill Arbuthnot lecture delivered at Northern Illinois University and reprinted in *Top of the News*), Houston recalls that his father, on returning home, "would give us each a hug, then produce two pairs of delicious-smelling, smoked, moose-hide moccasins." Houston and his sister would crawl into bed with their parents and their father would tell stories and "draw Sioux pulling toboggans south of Moose Jaw, Saskatchewan, and Sarcee teepees pitched on the plains near Medicine Hat, painted ponies and feathered riders coming to collect their treaty money.... I didn't care what other children's fathers did because I would never have traded theirs for mine."

If his father prepared Houston for a life of adventure, his mother prepared him for life as an artist. When he was eight or nine, Houston was quarantined for three

Houston used an old Arctic legend as the basis for his self-illustrated *The Falcon Bow*.

weeks with a case of scarlet fever, and his mother brought him a book: "I eagerly opened the cover," he recalls in his Arbuthnot lecture, "only to find that it was entirely blank—no words, no pictures. My mother smiled, 'If you want a book, make one yourself.'" He did, writing and illustrating a story about a shipwrecked boy cast away on a small island. When he was nine, he illustrated a poem for a Canadian magazine and was paid three dollars.

Houston's love of drawing continued into his adolescence, and at age twelve he was enrolled in classes at the Toronto Art Gallery (now the Art Gallery of Ontario). Houston recalls that his teacher, Dr. Arthur Lismer, a famous Canadian artist, left for Africa for some time and returned with a surprise for his students: "He arrived on a Saturday morning amidst wild West African drumming and singing. The recorded music resounded through the galleries as he danced among us, his face hidden by a huge Congo mask. I remember thinking who made that mask, who is beating those exciting rhythms on the drums? I was hooked forever on the lives of primitive people. I trembled to think of my own teacher, Dr. Lismer, treading on the soil of Africa, perhaps paddling on the Congo River with big crocodiles around him. I determined at that moment that I,

too, would go to see the wildest corners of the earth." Houston would fulfill his dream, but not before he served in the Canadian Army during World War II and continued his art training in Paris, France.

Houston returned to Toronto via Montreal in 1948, remembering in his Arbuthnot lecture that "after Paris, both cities struck me a being far too proper, with men in gray baggy suits and girls tightly bound in girdles. I asked myself where should I go?" Fueled by his desire to find a "suitable people to draw," Houston hopped aboard a train that would take him as far north as a train would go for nineteen dollars: Moosonee, Ontario, which lay at the south end of James Bay. He lived on an island called Moose Factory, making hundreds of drawings of Cree Indians, who were "dressed in braids, tartan shawls and knee-high moccasins." But Houston longed to explore the vast, nearly uninhabited area that loomed to the north of him, the great Arctic.

When a small plane rushing medical assistance to a village deep in the Arctic landed to refuel, Houston saw his chance. He remembers the co-pilot bursting into his room with this offer: "If you'll help me woggle the gas, you can fly into the Arctic with us—free! We're leaving now! The doctor has an emergency." Houston expected to stay just four days, but when it was clear that the doctor would have to fly the wounded child back to civilization right away, he made a sudden decision: he was staying. As he stood on the shore of the Hudson Bay, surrounded by all he owned—a sleeping bag, a sketch pad, and a can of peaches—and watching the plane disappear, he had no idea that he would live in the Arctic for fourteen years.

At first, Houston knew nothing of the Inuit language, but found that his sketches enabled him to communicate and build the people's confidence in him, for with drawings they shared the same language. The young artist lived with the semi-nomadic tribe in their winter igloos and summer tents, and was astounded by the soapstone carvings crafted by some of the tribesmen. Fascinated by the stories that the carvings told, and by the quality of the workmanship, Houston took a collection of the works to the Canadian Handicraft Guild in Montreal. He has been credited with the "discovery" of this art form, and his discovery led the Canadian government to set up subsidies for Inuit sculptors, which allowed the Inuit to develop a market for their work and made them less dependent on the declining fur trade. Later, Houston taught the Eskimos to make prints from their original stone cuts, further enhancing the spread of their art. Now, many art museums have collections of Eskimo art.

Houston married in 1949, and continued to live in the Hudson Bay area, working for the Canadian Handicraft Guild, and for the Canadian government. In 1955, he became the first federal civil administrator of West Baffin Island, most of which lies within the Arctic Circle. Houston traveled the 65,000-square-mile territory by dog sled, making friends with the 341 Eskimos who earned their living on the desolate island. Camped with these people, he became familiar with their distinctive means of telling stories. These mythic stories commemorated heroic deeds from the Eskimos' shared past, using "that age-old art of oral storytelling which involves the breathtaking excitement of the human voice mixed with animal sounds and shouts often accompanied by dancing and the rhythm of the drum or the howling Arctic winds," Houston told the Arbuthnot lecture audience. "There were, of course, no special stories for children. Every modern story, myth, or legend was told to suit all ages." Houston soon wanted to tell his own tales, for good storytellers were prized in his adopted culture. This desire eventually found its expression in his books for children and adults, which he began to write after leaving the Arctic for the very different world of New York City.

Houston's children's books are known for their sympathetic treatment of native peoples living in the Arctic and the Pacific Northwest, where he maintains a writing and fishing cottage. His early stories have mythic qualities, stressing the importance of human endurance and resourcefulness in the face of overwhelming odds. In *Wolf Run,* for example, a young boy sets out into the Arctic to find food for his starving family. On the point of collapse, the boy is visited by two helpful wolves that

While looking for food to feed his starving family, a young boy gets help from two wolves he believes to be the reincarnation of his dead grandparents. (Illustration by the author from *Wolf Run.*)

he believes to be the spirits of his deceased grandparents, and he then finds food. While the earlier books focus only on native peoples, the later works explore the reaction of primitive cultures to the modern world. In works such as *River Runners, Frozen Fire, Black Diamonds,* and *Ice Swords,* Houston places a white and an Indian boy in a situation that allows them to trust each other and, according to John Robert Sorfleet in *Twentieth-Century Children's Writers,* "the white boys learn respect and affection for the northern environment and native ways, and the native boys learn some practical advantages of modern technology and education." In all of his children's books, Houston's spare yet vivid illustrations set the mood for the story.

Sheila Egoff writes in *The Republic of Childhood: A Critical Guide to Canadian Children's Literature in English* that Houston "has not only been the most prolific spokesman for the Eskimo in children's literature, but also the most artistic writer." Similarly, Alice E. Kane, in *In Review: Canadian Books for Children,* commends Houston's "almost magical power of making the strange, hard world of the Eskimo believable to the city dweller." In his Arbuthnot lecture, Houston states: "I believe having a direct living experience with the culture about which one is writing is invaluable. This has long been my method of relating northern stories, and I believe it would apply to other cultures around the world."

WORKS CITED:

Egoff, Sheila, *The Republic of Childhood: A Critical Guide to Canadian Children's Literature in English,* Oxford University Press, 1975.

Houston, James, "A Primitive View of the World" (May Hill Arbuthnot Honor Lecture delivered at Northern Illinois University, March 13, 1987), *Top of the News,* summer, 1987, pp. 391-402.

Kane, Alice E., review of *Akavak: An Eskimo Journey, In Review: Canadian Books for Children,* winter, 1969, pp. 26-27.

Rigelhof, T. F., "Rites of Passage in the Arctic," *Globe and Mail* (Toronto), November 12, 1988.

Sorfleet, John Robert, "James Houston," *Twentieth-Century Children's Writers,* 3rd edition, St. James Press, 1989, pp. 468-470.

FOR MORE INFORMATION SEE:

BOOKS

Children's Literature Review, Volume 3, Gale, 1978, pp. 83-88.

PERIODICALS

Canadian Children's Literature, Volume 31/32, 1983.
Globe and Mail (Toronto), November 30, 1985.
New York Times Book Review, October 8, 1967; December 13, 1981, p. 39.
Washington Post, April 15, 1983.

HOWARD, Elizabeth Fitzgerald 1927-

PERSONAL: Born December 28, 1927, in Baltimore, MD; daughter of John MacFarland (a teacher and in real estate) and Bertha McKinley (a teacher and clerk; maiden name, James) Fitzgerald; married Lawrence Cabot Howard (a professor), February 14, 1953; children: Jane Elizabeth, Susan Carol, Laura Ligaya. *Education:* Radcliffe College, A.B., 1948; University of Pittsburgh, M.L.S., 1971, Ph.D., 1977. *Politics:* Democrat. *Religion:* Episcopalian. *Hobbies and other interests:* African folklore, French conversation, symphony concerts, grandchildren, family history.

ADDRESSES: Home—919 College Ave., Pittsburgh, PA 15232. *Office*—Library Science Program, West Virginia University, Morgantown, WV 26506. *Agent*—Kendra Marcus, Book Stop Literary Agency, 67 Meadow View Rd., Orinda, CA 94563.

CAREER: Boston Public Library, Boston, MA, cataloging assistant, 1948-51, children's librarian, 1951-56; Hofstra College (now Hofstra University), Hempstead, NY, research assistant in political science, 1956-57; Episcopal Diocese of Pittsburgh, Pittsburgh, PA, resource director, 1972-74; Pittsburgh Theological Seminary, Pittsburgh, reference librarian, 1974-77; University of Pittsburgh, Pittsburgh, visiting lecturer in library science, 1977-78; West Virginia University, Morgantown, assistant professor, 1978-81 and 1982-85, associate professor, 1985-91, professor of library science, 1991—. Member of Radcliffe Alumnae Association Board of Management, 1969-72, Ellis School Board of Trustees, 1969-75, Magee-Women's Hospital Board of Directors, 1980—, QED Communications Board of Directors, 1987—, and Beginning with Books Board of Directors, 1987—; member of vestry, Calvary Church, 1991—.

MEMBER: American Library Association (member of Caldecott committee, 1984), Association for Library Services to Children (board member), Society of Children's Book Writers and Illustrators, National Council of Teachers of English, Beta Phi Mu.

AWARDS, HONORS: American Library Association (ALA) notable book citation, 1990, Hedda Seisler Mason honor book, Enoch Pratt Library, 1991, and *Booklist* Picture Books of the '80s, all for *Chita's Christmas Tree;* Parents' Choice Award, and Teachers' Choice Award, International Reading Association, both 1992, both for *Aunt Flossie's Hats (and Crab Cakes Later).*

WRITINGS:

America as Story: Historical Fiction for Secondary Schools, American Library Association, 1988.
The Train to Lulu's, Bradbury, 1988.
Chita's Christmas Tree, Bradbury, 1989.
Aunt Flossie's Hats (and Crab Cakes Later), Clarion, 1991.
Mac and Marie and the Train Toss Surprise, Four Winds, 1993.
Papa Tells Chita a Story, Four Winds, in press.

SIDELIGHTS: Elizabeth Fitzgerald Howard told *SATA:* "Although I have always been writing something—fat letters from the Philippines Peace Corps days or from Nigeria during a year's leave, newsletters for the Brandeis Faculty Women's Organization and for the Episcopal Society for Cultural Racial Unity, articles for library periodicals, book reviews—it is still new for me to believe that I can be thought of as a writer. It's wonderful! It's really exciting! Why didn't I try writing books for children long ago?

"It was inevitable that I would think back to my own childhood when I began to write stories for children. My sister Babs and I really did take *The Train to Lulu's.* This book was my first effort to try to capture for today's young readers some of the unique and yet universal experiences of children in one African American family mid-century. I hope to write about growing up in Mrs. Ella Ford's rooming house, our quarters in the attic, and sharing the one bathroom with the several black graduate students on the second floor. *Chita's Christmas Tree* tells of old time Christmas as celebrated in my father's family. Chita, my father's first cousin, now age eighty-four, was the daughter of one of Baltimore's first African American doctors. This is a glimpse of a little known facet of African American life. *Aunt Flossie's Hats (and Crab Cakes Later)* celebrates my mother's sister, Aunt Flossie. A teacher in Baltimore schools, she lived to be almost 101, in the same house for sixty-five years, and never threw anything away.

ELIZABETH FITZGERALD HOWARD

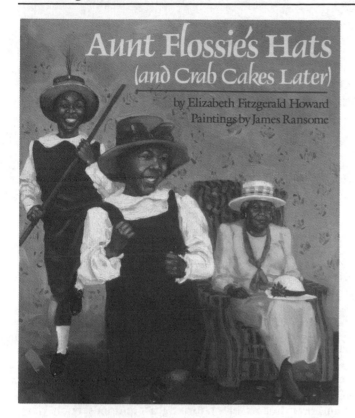

Great-great Aunt Flossie tells stories of long ago to young Sarah and Susan in Howard's tale about family sharing. (Cover illustration by James Ransome.)

There are more stories about Aunt Flossie. And there are stories to be told about my father's father, and his five brothers, who came to Baltimore from Tennessee, and practiced law, medicine, pharmacy and real estate. And great grandfather John Henry Smith and his drydock at Baltimore Harbor. And my mother's uncle Jimmy who owned a grocery store with—to quote Aunt Flossie—'fine terrapins and the best peaches anywhere.'

"This is a time of great richness in children's books. Publishers are interested now in stories that portray the variety of American life so that all children can share in the multicolored experience. Today there are many works by truly distinguished and prolific African American children's authors. But there is so much still to be told. I would like to write more about black American life at the turn of the century, through stories culled from my family's history. I also hope to convey some of the experiences of my sister and me, and of my daughters. There is still a need for more and more books so that children of all colors may discover more and more about growing up black in America—what is different and what is familiar, and how we are all connected."

*   *   *

HUDSON, Wade 1946-

PERSONAL: Born October 23, 1946, in Mansfield, LA; son of Wade and Lurline (Jones) Hudson; married Cheryl Willis (a publisher and writer), June 24, 1972;

children: Katura, Stephan. *Education:* Attended Southern University and Agricultural and Mechanical College, 1964-68. *Politics:* Democrat. *Religion:* Baptist.

ADDRESSES: Home—202 Dodd St., East Orange, NJ 07017. *Office*—301 Main St., Orange, NJ 07050.

CAREER: Writer.

MEMBER: Multicultural Publishers Exchange (board member), African American Publishers, Writers and Booksellers Association.

WRITINGS:

(With Valerie Wilson Wesley) *Afro-Bets Book of Black Heroes from A to Z: An Introduction to Important Black Achievers,* illustrated by Cheryl W. Hudson, Just Us Books, 1988.
Afro-Bets Alphabet Rap Song, Just Us Books, 1990.
Jamal's Busy Day, illustrated by George Ford, Just Us Books, 1991.
Afro-Bets Kids: I'm Gonna Be!, illustrated by Culverson Blair, Just Us Books, 1992.
(With Debbi Chocolate) *NEATE: To the Rescue,* Just Us Books, 1992.
I Love My Family, illustrated by Cal Massey, Scholastic, 1993.
(Editor) *Pass It On: African-American Poetry for Children,* illustrated by Floyd Cooper, Scholastic, 1993.

SIDELIGHTS: In 1988 Wade Hudson and Valerie Wilson Wesley collaborated on *Afro-Bets Book of Black Heroes from A to Z,* which presents biographical information on individuals who have made important contributions to society. Included in the book are entries on such diverse people as boxer Muhammad Ali, activist Martin Luther King, and writer Zora Neal Hurston. Some reviewers noted that the work offers hard-to-find information on individuals such as sculptress Edmonia Lewis and educator Fanny Coppin, who are often overlooked in reference works.

Wade Hudson told *SATA:* "One can never take any image for granted. Images, whether in print, film, television, or on stage, are constantly shaping the way we feel and what we think and believe. This is particularly crucial to the African-American community which has been deliberately given negative images of its history and culture. I find it rewarding to help reshape and change those negative images to reflect truth. I think the struggle to present the correct images, the truth, is the most crucial one facing us all."

*   *   *

HULME, Joy N. 1922-

PERSONAL: Born December 6, 1922, in Cottonwood, UT; daughter of Irvin T. (a landscape architect) and Kathleen (Bagley) Nelson; married Melvin J. Hulme (a bank vice president and real estate broker), May 20, 1944; children: John, David (deceased), Kathy, Douglas, Peggy. *Education:* Utah State Agricultural College, B.S., 1944.

ADDRESSES: Home and office—15941 Viewfield, Monte Sereno, CA 95030. *Agent*—Kendra Marcus, Bookstop, 67 Meadow View Rd., Orinda, CA 94563.

CAREER: Writer. Has worked at a variety of jobs, including newspaper circulation manager and self-employed floral designer.

MEMBER: Society of Children's Book Writers and Illustrators (corresponding secretary, 1989-92; board of directors, NorCal chapter, 1991—).

AWARDS, HONORS: Writing award, *Ensign* (magazine), 1978; Outstanding Science Trade Book citation, 1991, and Children's Choice citation, 1992, both for *Sea Squares;* also recipient of California Writers' Contest award.

WRITINGS:

The Illustrated Story of President Lorenzo Snow, Eagle Systems, 1982.
The Illustrated Story of President George Albert Smith, Eagle Systems, 1982.
The Illustrated Story of President David O. McKay, Eagle Systems, 1982.
A Stable in Bethlehem, Western, 1989.
The Other Side of the Door, Deseret, 1990.

JOY N. HULME

Sea Squares, Hyperion Books, 1991.
Climbing the Rainbow (sequel to *The Other Side of the Door*), Deseret, 1992.
What If? (poems), Boyds Mills, 1993.
The Whistling and Whittling Bridge, Hyperion Books, in press.

Also contributor to periodicals, including *Better Homes and Gardens* and *Good Housekeeping.*

WORK IN PROGRESS: Pilgrims of the Pacific, Downhill All the Way, A Place of Our Own, and *Orange Tree in the Sky* (all historical novels); *Divvy Up* (a division picture book); *Kangaroo Count* (a multiplication picture book); *The A B Sea Book* (a sea-animal alphabet in verse); *The Animal B C Book* (a land-animal alphabet in verse); *The A Bug C Book* (an insect alphabet in verse); *The A Bird C Book* (a bird alphabet in verse); *An Angel's Song* (a Christmas picture book).

SIDELIGHTS: Joy Nelson Hulme has drawn on a wide variety of experience to create picture books that are both instructive and fun. Hulme began her writing career as a magazine contributor; she sold stories, poems, articles, and Christmas crafts to both adult and children's periodicals. For many years, however, the author's dreams of publishing a children's book were frustrated by repeated rejections. Eventually, Hulme became part of a Bay area critique group that included Patricia Polacco and Elisa Klevin. "This was my biggest breakthrough to date," Hulme told *SATA.* "Now I was exposed to many opportunities to learn from and be encouraged by other writers and illustrators." Through this association, Hulme got her first agent, who gave the author "just what I needed to absorb the rejection and heartbreak and resubmit my books instead of stashing them away to mildew in a drawer."

Hulme's first major children's book was *A Stable in Bethlehem.* Since it first appeared in 1989, this counting book has become a Christmas favorite. Hulme followed *Stable* with *The Other Side of the Door* and *Climbing the Rainbow*—middle-grade historical books about a young girl who learns to rise above a disability—and *Sea Squares,* a sea-life counting book that deals with square numbers. *Sea Squares* "combines three of my loves," the author related, "math, biology, and wonderful words."

In describing her career, Hulme noted: "Life as an *author* is much different from life as a *writer!* At last my efforts have been validated.... At an age when most people have retired, my career is just beginning. My part-time-everything life, resulting from a wide range of interests and knowledge, and my child-like fascination with the ingenious intricacy and beauty of nature, is proving very valuable to me as an author of children's books. It is always my goal to encourage the creative awareness that is inborn in youngsters and to keep it alive in them forever.

"No life is long enough to run out of fresh surprises if we watch out for them.... I like to be accurate about facts, fanciful about fiction, and to combine truth and imagination—to make learning as much fun for others as it is for me by creating in a light-hearted manner.... It is my aim that a child of any age can become a little better in some way as a result of reading what I have written."

K

KEITH, Harold (Verne) 1903-

PERSONAL: Born April 8, 1903, in Lambert, Oklahoma Territory; son of Malcolm Arrowwood (a grain buyer) and Arlyn (Kee) Keith; married Virginia Livingston, August 20, 1931; children: John Livingston, Kathleen Ann. *Education:* Attended Northwestern State Teachers College (now Northwestern State College); University of Oklahoma, B.A., 1929, M.A., 1938, special courses in professional writing, 1953-56. *Politics:* Independent. *Religion:* Episcopalian. *Hobbies and other interests:* Quail hunting, trout fishing, singing in a barbershop quartet, long-distance running.

ADDRESSES: Home—2318 Ravenwood Lane, Hall Park, Route 4, Norman, OK 72071.

CAREER: Amorita Consolidated School System, Oklahoma, seventh-grade teacher, 1922-23; *Daily Oklahoman, Tulsa World, Kansas City Star,* and *Omaha World-Herald,* sports correspondent, 1922-29; Red Star Milling Co., Hutchinson, KS, assistant to grain buyer, 1929-30; University of Oklahoma, Norman, sports publicity director, 1930-69.

MEMBER: College Sports Information Directors of America (president, 1964-65), National Collegiate Athletic Association (member of public relations committee, 1960-69), Norman Kiwanis Club (member of board of directors for eleven years).

AWARDS, HONORS: Helms Foundation Sports Publicist of the Year, 1950; Newbery Medal, American Library Association, 1958, and Lewis Carroll Shelf Award, 1964, both for *Rifles for Watie;* Arch Ward Memorial Trophy for outstanding achievement in sports publicity, 1961; Charlie May Simon Award, 1973-74, for *The Runt of Rogers School;* Western Heritage Award, 1975, and Spur Award, both for *Susy's Scoundrel;* Western Heritage Award, 1979, for *The Obstinate Land.*

WRITINGS:

Boys' Life of Will Rogers, illustrated by Karl S. Woerner, Crowell, 1937, revised edition published as *Will Rogers, a Boy's Life: An Indian Territory Childhood,* Levite of Apache Publishing, 1992.
Sports and Games, Crowell, 1941.
Oklahoma Kickoff, privately printed, 1948, University of Oklahoma Press, 1978.
Shotgun Shaw: A Baseball Story, illustrated by Mabel Jones Woodbury, Crowell, 1949.
A Pair of Captains, illustrated by Woodbury, Crowell, 1951.
Rifles for Watie, Crowell, 1957.

HAROLD KEITH

140

THE OBSTINATE LAND by Harold Keith

The Oklahoma land run of 1893 is the backdrop for Keith's 1977 novel about a family trying to homestead in a harsh environment. (Cover illustration by Robert Andrew Parker.)

Komantcia, Crowell, 1965, 2nd edition, Levite of Apache Publishing, 1991.
Brief Garland, Crowell, 1971.
The Runt of Rogers School, Lippincott, 1971.
Go Red, Go!, illustrated by Ned Glattauer, Nelson, 1972.
The Bluejay Boarders, illustrated by Harold Berson, Crowell, 1972.
Susy's Scoundrel, illustrated by John Schoenherr, Crowell, 1974.
The Obstinate Land, Crowell, 1977.
Forty-Seven Straight: The Wilkinson Era at Oklahoma, University of Oklahoma Press, 1984.
The Sound of Strings: Sequel to Komantcia, Levite of Apache Publishing, 1992.

Contributor of sports fiction to *American Boy* and *Bluebook,* and of sports articles to the *Saturday Evening Post* and *Esquire.*

SIDELIGHTS: Harold Keith's books for young people are noted for their accuracy and attention to detail. A thorough researcher, Keith once commented that he drew material for *The Runt of Rogers School* partly from talks with "five runtish Oklahomans who won their spurs as athletes ... and several elementary school football coaches." For *Rifles for Watie,* his Newbery-winning book about the Civil War set in Oklahoma, he interviewed twenty-two veterans of that conflict, all nearly a hundred years old. His material has come primarily from his involvement in sports, both personally and professionally, and his fascination with local history.

Keith grew up in a family that loved books, and in high school he worked as cartoonist, sports editor, and coeditor for the school news magazine. His writing career began at the age of fourteen when a story he wrote, "Dick Moore and His Big Game," was published in *Lone Scout Magazine* and won a few medals. Following high school, Keith attended the University of Oklahoma, where he participated in track, winning the 3,000 meter steeplechase at the Penn Relays, and earned his Bachelor's and Master's degrees in history. During the period between 1922 and 1929 he served as sports correspondent for the *Daily Oklahoman, Tulsa World, Kansas City Star,* and the *Omaha World-Herald.* And from 1930 until his retirement in 1969, he was sports publicity director at the University of Oklahoma at Norman.

Keith's first book, *Boys' Life of Will Rogers,* grew out of his master's thesis on Rogers's father, Clem Rogers, and his influence on Oklahoma history. The inspiration for *Komantcia,* based on the true story of a young Spaniard's captivity by the Comanches in 1865, came from Keith's extensive reading about these "fascinating people," as he once called them, "as well as [from] personally visiting several Comanches still living in Oklahoma, one of them Topay, seventh and last living wife of War Chief Quanah Parker." *Oklahoma Kickoff* is a history of another kind: an account of the first twenty-five years of University of Oklahoma football. And the later book *Forty-Seven Straight* is a biography of Oklahoma football coach Bud Wilkinson as told by his players and by Keith.

In the years before his retirement, Keith wrote at night and on weekends. *Rifles for Watie* was a five-year labor that led him to compare writing to long-distance running: "You had to learn to punish yourself and keep going even after you grew dead tired. But each night I sat down to write, I felt enthusiasm about this story. I never grew tired of it nor doubted for a moment that it would be accepted," he explained in the *Wilson Library Bulletin.* The novel's plot involves a young Union soldier, Jefferson Davis Bussey, who spies behind Confederate lines to find a Cherokee, Stand Watie, who is intercepting rifles intended for the Union Army. Jeff is captured by the Confederates and successfully pretends to be one of them for a time, thus learning, as Zena Sutherland notes in *Twentieth Century Children's Writers,* that "his enemies ... are young men much like himself." In this "substantial historical fiction," as Sutherland and May Hill Arbuthnot call it in *Children and Books,* Keith presents "unforgettable characters ... and all the hunger, dirt, and weariness of war to balance

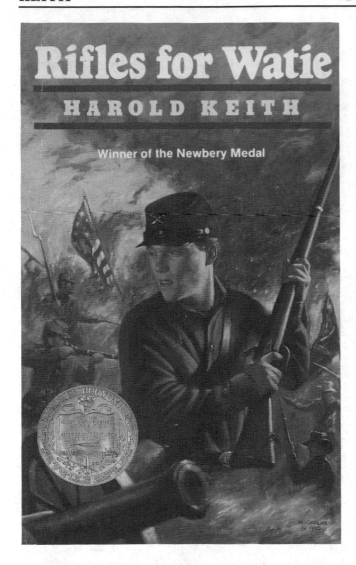

Jeff Bussey learns some hard lessons about the nature of war when he becomes a Union spy behind enemy lines in Keith's Newbery-winning work. (Cover illustration by Michael Garland.)

the heroism." In his Newbery Medal acceptance speech for *Rifles for Watie*, Keith credited his professional writing school experience at the University of Oklahoma for teaching him the skills that critics found so evident in the book.

When he retired from the University of Oklahoma, Keith no longer had to fit his writing into the hours he was away from work. At that time he explained his new writing schedule: "I like to start writing early in the morning and work steadily four hours, then join my friends for a long-distance run, then drive home for a short nap, then return to my library sanctum to work two additional hours in the afternoon.... I compose by hand-writing and triple space on the typewriter and my first drafts are as rough as you'll find anywhere."

Keith lists quail hunting, trout fishing, and singing in a barbershop quartet among his outside interests, in addition to long-distance running. He names Dickens, O. Henry, and Mark Twain as writers he especially

admires. Keith explained in *Twentieth Century Children's Writers* that he finds the hundreds of children's letters he received from all over the United States useful in "telling me what they like or dislike about my books," and that he tries to answer every letter he receives.

WORKS CITED:

Arbuthnot, May Hill and Zena Sutherland, *Children and Books,* 8th edition, HarperCollins, 1991, p. 436.
Keith, Harold, in an interview for *Wilson Library Bulletin,* June, 1958.
Sutherland, Zena, "Harold Keith," *Twentieth Century Children's Writers,* 3rd edition, St. Martin's Press, 1989.

FOR MORE INFORMATION SEE:

BOOKS

Carlson, G. Robert, *Books and the Teen-Age Reader,* Harper, 1967.
Hack, Charlotte S., editor, *Children's Literature in the Elementary School,* Holt, 1961.
Kingman, Lee, editor, *Newbery and Caldecott Medal Books: 1956-1965,* Horn Book, 1965.

PERIODICALS

Horn Book, August, 1958.

*   *   *

KELLOW, Kathleen
See HIBBERT, Eleanor Alice Burford

*   *   *

KENDALL, Carol (Seeger) 1917-

PERSONAL: Born September 13, 1917, in Bucyrus, OH; daughter of John Adam (a cabinetmaker) and Laura (Price) Seeger; married Paul Murray Kendall (a college professor and writer), June 15, 1939 (died November 21, 1973); children: Carol Seeger, Gillian Murray. *Education:* Ohio University, A.B., 1939.

ADDRESSES: Home—928 Holiday Dr., Lawrence, KS 66049.

CAREER: Writer.

MEMBER: Phi Beta Kappa, Phi Mu.

AWARDS, HONORS: Ohioana Award and Newbery Medal Honor Book Award, both 1960, for *The Gammage Cup*; Parents' Choice Award, 1982, and Mythopoeic Society Aslan Award, 1983, both for *The Firelings.*

WRITINGS:

JUVENILE

The Other Side of the Tunnel, Abelard, 1957.
The Gammage Cup, Harcourt, 1959.
The Big Splash, Viking, 1960.

The Whisper of Glocken, Harcourt, 1965, revised edition, Bodley Head, 1967.

(With Yao-wen Li) *Sweet and Sour: Tales from China,* Bodley Head, 1978, Houghton, 1979.

The Firelings, Bodley Head, 1981, Atheneum, 1982.

(Reteller) *Haunting Tales from Japan,* Spencer Museum of Art, University of Kansas, 1985.

The Wedding of the Rat Family (Chinese folktale), illustrated by James Watts, Macmillan, 1988.

Also contributor of folk tales to *Cricket.*

OTHER

The Black Seven, Harper, 1946.

The Baby-Snatcher, Bodley Head, 1952.

WORK IN PROGRESS: (With Li) *Cinnamon Moon: Tales from China*; a fourth fantasy (untitled), 1994.

SIDELIGHTS: Carol Kendall wrote two mysteries for adults before becoming a children's author in 1957. She is best known for her Newbery Award-winning fantasy *The Gammage Cup,* as well as *The Whisper of Glocken* and *The Firelings.* Kendall has also collaborated with Yao-wen Li on translations of Chinese folktales in *Sweet and Sour* and has retold six stories of Japanese origin in *Haunting Tales from Japan.*

CAROL KENDALL

Born Carol Seeger on September 13, 1917, in Bucyrus, Ohio, Kendall was the youngest child in a family of one brother, five half-brothers, and a half-sister. She knew at an early age that she would be a writer. As she said in *Contemporary Authors:* "I don't remember a time I didn't want to write. If there is such a thing as being born a writer, that is what happened to me. I started a diary at six with the first words I learned to spell." Kendall was also influenced by the books left behind by her older brothers; she read about Tom Swift, the Rover Boys, and Joe Strong the Boy Fish. These works inspired her first attempt at a novel when she was in the fourth grade. In it, "Betty Judd, hero, valiantly resisted her father's efforts to 'l'arn' her the art of pickpocketing," Kendall recalled in an essay for *Something about the Author Autobiography Series* (*SAAS*). "By the time I reached page nineteen of this harrowing tale, written large in pencil in a speckly brown composition book, I could no longer keep the thrill of writing to myself. I had to share my glorious work with somebody—and who more worthy of the honor than my fourth-grade teacher?" Kendall did indeed give it to her teacher and asked her how she liked it. The author recorded the result in *SAAS:* "Miss Heinlen, lip curling into a smile of scorn, reached two disdainful fingers into a drawer, plucked out my beloved composition book, and dropped it into my hands with a withering, 'Don't be so silly, Carol.'"

After that, Kendall limited herself to writing in school newspapers, but she continued to plan on a career as an author and gained further inspiration from the writings of others. She remembered a story from the magazine *Child Life* in particular and credited it in her autobiographical essay as helping to create the bias against conformity that is explored in *The Gammage Cup:* "Someone had asked me where I first got the idea of conformity for *The Gammage Cup,* and I found that story—fifty-five years later—still lurking in my head." The magazine story concerned children who follow fads until their mothers trick all of them into coming as sheep for one girl's costume party.

Although her family was poor due to her father's death while she was still a child, Kendall entered Ohio University in Athens, Ohio, upon her graduation from high school. She worked her way through college with a National Youth Administration job that paid thirty cents an hour and by typing dissertations for graduate students. Among the dissertations she typed was a doctoral thesis for Paul Murray Kendall, an instructor at Ohio University; she married him after obtaining her A.B.

Once free of college classes and typing jobs, Kendall began to devote herself to writing. She got many rejections, and an early projected contract to do a children's storybook was canceled because of paper shortages brought on by World War II. She eventually published a mystery for adults, *The Black Seven,* that featured a boy detective. Kendall used the same character in her novel, *The Baby-Snatcher.* While beginning work on a third book with a different set of characters, she realized that she had enjoyed writing about her boy

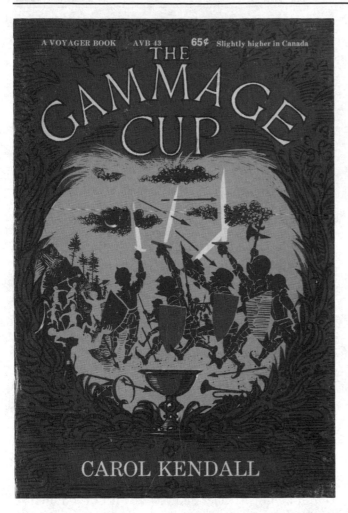

A VOYAGER BOOK   AVB 43   65¢ Slightly higher in Canada

THE GAMMAGE CUP

CAROL KENDALL

The mountaintop home of the exiled Minnipins is threatened by a group of violent invaders in Kendall's novel of magic and mystery.

detective and his friends. She felt that she would be happier writing for and about children than for adults.

Though the Kendalls' homebase was Athens, Ohio, and Ohio University, they spent every third year or so in England where Paul Kendall researched and wrote his biographical works. On the first of these trips, Carol Kendall began writing her first children's book, *The Other Side of the Tunnel.* She recalled in *SAAS:* "It was a cautious passageway into children's books. I still leaned on the mystery format as a prop, and was mildly pleased with the result, though I ached to write a book with meaning, a book that readers would take to their hearts and remember always, the way I remembered the books from my childhood." But her time in England was helping to prepare her to write just such a book. She added in her autobiographical essay: "My own version of a real book was actually already on its way, jolted into being by the people of England. The country itself looked exactly the way I had expected, from chimney pots to village commons. But the people . . . ! No ordinary present-day mortals like Americans, they were characters straight off the pages of a Dickens novel . . . . Think of it: a land full of people out of another time, but living in a quite ordinary, albeit quaint, manner. Like a

sponge, I soaked up the sights and sounds of this strange, yet familiar, country." This sentiment explains the feel of *The Gammage Cup,* a story of a tradition-minded valley people known as Minnipins, who become divided when some of the population question the actions of their leaders. Kendall also drew inspiration for her Minnipin characters from herself and her family. She explained in *SAAS* that Muggles' unorthodox ways of organization are her own, that Curley Green has the flavor of her daughter Carol, and that Walter the Earl resembles her husband: "He inherited Paulish characteristics. Paul's outside was invariably dressed in white shirt, black tie, and dark suit, but his inside . . . . Ah, inside he was an Ideal Knight in a cloak, an embroidered cloak that swept and swirled and could be flung over one shoulder with a flourish."

After the success of *The Gammage Cup,* friends urged Kendall to write a sequel. As she reported in her autobiographical essay, she was reluctant. "Anything more would simply be further action with no growth of character. I groaned a good deal, until my friend Laura Summers jolted me into a new plan of attack." Summers suggested she set the story in the same world as *The Gammage Cup,* but one hundred years later. Kendall "had no intention of going forward one hundred years," as she related in *SAAS,* but she "moved two villages down the Watercress river, set the clock at five years past *The Gammage Cup,* and wrote my tale of how heroes happen, *The Whisper of Glocken.*" In this novel, the character of Silky was inspired by her younger daughter, Gillian.

"When I finished *The Whisper of Glocken* in 1964," Kendall continued in *SAAS,* "the essence of the next book was already more than a shadowy shape in my mind. That summer in Yellowstone National Park *The Firelings* had come bubbling and swirling out of the pink paint pots." But it took her many years to complete *The Firelings,* and in the meantime many changes took place both in her personal life and her work. She learned Chinese, which led to her collaboration with Yao-wen Li on books of Chinese folktales. She and her husband moved to Lawrence, Kansas, where he taught at the University of Kansas before dying of lung cancer in 1973. Her daughters married, and Kendall began traveling several months every year to lands as disparate as Tibet and Easter Island.

The Firelings was finally published in 1981. In the book, Kendall depicts a people, the Firelings, who live on the slopes of an ancient volcano. Legend foretells that an eruption will someday destroy their land. When the volcano threatens to do just that, the Firelings must live out another part of the legend which promises that they will learn the secret path back to their former homeland where they will rejoin their old community. *Voice of Youth Advocates* reviewer Silas Beal declared that in *The Firelings* Kendall "creates good solid characters and makes them as believable as a neighbor." Jennifer Moody, writing in the *Times Literary Supplement,* praised Kendall for creating "a believable and attractive new world." *The Firelings* garnered Kendall both the

The adventures of the Minnipins continue in this tale in which four friends are captured by barbarians while trying to save their flooded village. (Cover illustration by Manuel Garcia.)

Parents' Choice Award and the Mythopoeic Society Aslan Award.

One of Kendall's later projects is a retelling of a Chinese folktale, *The Wedding of the Rat Family,* published in 1988. In the story, a class-conscious rat family seeks to marry their daughter to the most powerful suitor. They first offer the distinction to the sun, who says that the cloud can cover him and is therefore stronger. The cloud insists that the wind controls him, the wind states that the wall can stop him, and the wall admits that the rats can tear him down. The rat family finally decides that a cat, the natural enemy of rats, and therefore strongest, must be their daughter's groom. The cat clan consents to the marriage with the stipulation that all the fattest rats must attend the wedding celebration. The rich rats deny their poor relations the opportunity to go, but are rewarded for their snobbishness by being eaten by the conniving felines. Reviewers lauded Kendall's use of language in her adaptation of *The Wedding of the Rat Family.* Ruth M. McConnell in *School Library Journal* appreciated the book's "lively dialogue and style," while a *Bulletin of the Center for Children's Books* critic noted Kendall's "considerable wit." "Kendall tells her satirical

tale with humor and panache," declared a reviewer in *Kirkus Reviews.*

In addition to *The Wedding of the Rat Family,* Kendall has retold other Asian folktales in *Sweet and Sour: Tales from China* and *Haunting Tales from Japan.* Kendall has also been working on another fantasy in the vein of her three previous, and, as she concluded in her autobiographical essay: "My life and my writing have always been inextricably entangled. When people who don't know me well ask if I'm still writing, I say, 'Am I still breathing?'"

WORKS CITED:

Beal, Silas, review of *The Firelings, Voice of Youth Advocates,* October, 1982, p. 49.

Kendall, Carol, in *Contemporary Authors New Revision Series,* Volume 25, Gale, 1989, p. 250.

Kendall, Carol, essay in *Something about the Author Autobiography Series,* Volume 7, Gale, 1989, pp. 171-89.

McConnell, Ruth M., review of *The Wedding of the Rat Family, School Library Journal,* November, 1988, p. 120.

Moody, Jennifer, "Outlandish Parts," *Times Literary Supplement,* September 18, 1981, p. 1065.

Review of *The Wedding of the Rat Family, Bulletin of the Center for Children's Books,* January, 1989, p. 125.

Review of *The Wedding of the Rat Family, Kirkus Reviews,* August 1, 1988, pp. 1151-52.

Kendall turned to an old Chinese folktale for inspiration when writing this comical tale about the wedding of a well-born rat. (Cover illustration by James Watts.)

FOR MORE INFORMATION SEE:

BOOKS

Twentieth-Century Children's Writers, St. James Press, 1989.

PERIODICALS

Booklist, October 15, 1988.
School Library Journal, February, 1986.

*   *   *

KENNEDY, Dana Forrest 1917-

PERSONAL: Born November 3, 1917, in Milbridge, ME; son of Chester Alexander (a physical education teacher) and Geneva Mae (a homemaker; maiden name, Beal) Kennedy; married Muriel Barbara Hallett (a teacher), May 10, 1941; children: Michael Hallett Kennedy. *Education:* Bangor Maine School of Commerce, Com. Ed., 1938; University of Maine, B.S., 1941; Episcopal Theological School, B.D. and M.D., 1945. *Politics:* Republican. *Religion:* Episcopalian.

ADDRESSES: Home—9 Woodside Ave., Westport, CT 06880. *Office*—K.D.S. Management Co., Inc., 152 Westport Ave., Norwalk, CT 06851.

CAREER: St. Stephen's Memorial Church, Lynn, MA, curate, 1945-47; St. Barnabas Episcopal Church, Springfield, MA, rector, 1947-50; St. James Episcopal Church, Woonsocket, RI, rector, 1951-54; The National Office of the Episcopal Church, New York, NY, radio and television officer, 1954-61; Christ and Holy Trinity Episcopal Church, Westport, CT, rector, 1961-89.

DANA FORREST KENNEDY

King's Daughters and Sons Management Co., president, 1974—. President of Kingsway Apartments, Inc., and Norwalk Town Union of King's Daughters and Sons, Inc.

MEMBER: Masons, Rotary Club.

WRITINGS:

Waterbrooks of the Spirit, Church, 1970.
My Very First Golden Bible (juvenile), Western Publishing, 1991.

Also columnist, "On Your TV Screen," in *Forth,* a national Christian magazine.

SIDELIGHTS: Dana Forrest Kennedy told *SATA:* "I first became aware of my desire to write for children while I was still in seminary school. I was fortunate enough to have a very competent and insightful professor of religious education who scratched the surface of my talent in writing. At about the same time an elderly minister who was renowned locally for his ability to tell children's stories noticed my very special enthusiasm to tell stories to children. As the years went by, I began to pursue this interest and developed some skill in teaching children through the medium of storytelling. Later, I bought a hand puppet and used ventriloquism (of a kind) to tell stories to the children during their church services. By the time I retired years later, in 1989, my leopard puppet, named Tigger, had become more popular than I amongst the children.

"As my interest in telling children stories developed, so did my deeper understanding of the young children themselves. Around 1963 I started a separate day school for pre-school aged children at our church. In the course of administering the school, I learned a great deal about the feelings and driving motivations of pre-school teachers for the children they taught. My association with them as I observed their work at close hand led me to have a much deeper understanding of the importance of this early education in one's life.

"For the last seven or eight years before my retirement, I conducted a weekly chapel service at the school. Between forty to fifty children would gather in a semi-circle before a small altar. I would sit at one side of the altar and lead the service. A major feature would be my telling a story using one or more of my puppets and at times other vehicles of communication. There was much more to the chapel service than this, of course. We would sing together and ask and answer one another's questions. We enjoyed one another. I believe that this young period of a person's life is the most important time in his or her personal growth. And in my opinion, if one had to choose the most valuable and decisive educational experience in a person's life, the pre-school years would be it. It is during this formative period that care, respect, sharing, and personal worth as well as habits of social interaction are best taught and most readily absorbed. This can truly give an individual a head start in life.

Kennedy brings the stories of the Bible to life in this colorful volume written for young readers. (Cover illustration by J. Ellen Dolce.)

"Children, I believe, need adults to share time with them. 'Personal' and 'quality' time are the current catch words for this truth. When adults read to children, they share themselves with the children in the process. I wrote *My Very First Golden Bible* with that very process in mind. What a chance for old and young to share life and outlook with one another. In children's stories that are worth their salt some aspect of truth, heritage, insight, outlook, or new understanding comes bubbling up through. That is fundamentally what makes stories entertaining. There is even something wondrously healthy in those stories that seem to be just for pure fun and nonsense and which children love for their own sake. Such stories add an important ingredient to our psychic nourishment, too.

"Until I wrote *My Very First Golden Bible,* most of my children's stories were told orally. I did not write them first and afterwards read them to the children. I always tried to make them come alive, looking the children in the eyes. I find writing children's stories a sterner discipline, yet very challenging and satisfying. I look ahead to trying my hand at another publication. If Grandma Moses could start late in life and accomplish what she did, perhaps I can do something in a very modest way in the writing of children's stories."

KHERDIAN, David 1931-

PERSONAL: Born December 17, 1931, in Racine, WI; son of Melkon (a chef) and Veron (Dumehjian) Kherdian; married Kato Rozeboom, January 21, 1967 (divorced, 1970); married Nonny Hogrogian (an artist and illustrator), March 17, 1971. *Education:* University of Wisconsin, B.S., 1960.

CAREER: Writer and editor. Salesperson and field manager for Crowell-Collier Publishing Company, 1951-52; worked as shoe salesperson, bartender, day laborer, and factory worker, during 1950s; The Sign of the Tiger (used book store), Racine, WI, owner, 1961-62; The Book House (used book store), Fresno, CA, manager, 1962-63; Northwestern University, Evanston, IL, literary consultant, 1965; Giligia Press, Santa Fe, NM, founder and editor, 1966-73; Santa Fe Theatre Co., Santa Fe, writer and designer of theatre program, 1968; Fresno State College (now California State University, Fresno), Fresno, CA, instructor in poetry, 1969-70; poet-in-the-schools, New Hampshire, 1971-72 and 1972-73; Two Rivers Press, Aurora, OR, founder and editor, 1978-86. Poetry judge, Vincent Price Awards in creative writing, Institute of American Indian Arts, 1968. *Military service:* U.S. Army, 1952-54.

AWARDS, HONORS: Horn Book Award, 1979, Lewis Carroll Shelf Award, 1979, Newbery Honor Book, 1980, Jane Addams Award, 1980, Banta Award, and an American Book Award nomination, all for *The Road from Home: The Story of an Armenian Girl;* Friends of American Writers Award, 1982, for *Beyond Two Rivers.*

MEMBER: PEN.

WRITINGS:

POETRY

(With Gerald Hausman) *Eight Poems,* Giligia Press, 1968.
On the Death of My Father and Other Poems, introduction by William Saroyan, Giligia Press, 1970.
Homage to Adana, Perishable Press, 1970.
Looking over Hills, illustrated by wife, Nonny Hogrogian, Giligia Press, 1972.
A David Kherdian Sampler, edited and with an introduction by Moses Yanes, Community of Friends Press (Boulder Creek, CO), 1974.
The Nonny Poems, Macmillan, 1974.
Any Day of Your Life, Overlook Press/Bookstore Press, 1975.
Country Cat, City Cat (juvenile poems), illustrated by Hogrogian, Four Winds Press, 1978.
I Remember Root River, Overlook Press, 1978.
The Farm, introduction by Brother Jeremy Driscoll, Two Rivers Press, 1979.
Taking the Soundings on Third Avenue, Overlook Press, 1981.
The Farm: Book Two, Two Rivers Press, 1982.
Place of Birth, introduction by Martha Heyneman, Breitenbush Books, 1983.

DAVID KHERDIAN

Threads of Light: The Farm Poems, Books Three and Four, introduction by A. L. Staveley, Two Rivers Press, 1985.
Poems to an Essence Friend, The Press at Butternut Creek, 1987.
The Dividing River/The Meeting Shore, Lotus Press, 1990.
Friends: A Memoir, Globe Press, 1993.

FICTION

It Started with Old Man Bean, Greenwillow, 1980.
Beyond Two Rivers, Greenwillow, 1981.
The Song in the Walnut Grove (juvenile), illustrated by Paul Zelisky, Knopf, 1982.
The Mystery of the Diamond in the Wood (juvenile), illustrated by Paul Geiger, Knopf, 1983.
Right Now (juvenile), illustrated by Hogrogian, Knopf, 1983.
The Animal (juvenile), illustrated by Hogrogian, Knopf, 1984.
A Song for Uncle Harry (juvenile), illustrated by Hogrogian, Philomel, 1989.
The Cat's Midsummer Jamboree (juvenile), illustrated by Hogrogian, Putnam, 1990.
The Great Fishing Contest (juvenile), illustrated by Hogrogian, Philomel Books, 1991.
(Reteller) *Feathers and Tails: Animal Fables from Around the World* (juvenile), illustrated by Hogrogian, Philomel, 1992.
Juna's Journey (juvenile), illustrated by Hogrogian, Philomel, 1993.
By Myself (juvenile), illustrated by Hogrogian, Holt, 1993.

Asking the River (juvenile), Orchard Books, 1993.

NONFICTION

The Road from Home: The Story of an Armenian Girl (juvenile), Greenwillow, 1979.
Finding Home, Greenwillow, 1981.
Root River Run (memoir), illustrated by Hogrogian, Carolrhoda Books, 1984.
Bridger: The Story of a Mountain Man (juvenile), Greenwillow, 1987.
On a Spaceship with Beelzebub: By a Grandson of Gurdjieff (autobiography), Globe Press Books, 1991.

EDITOR

(With James Baloian) *Down at the Santa Fe Depot: Twenty Fresno Poets,* Giligia Press, 1970.
Visions of America: By the Poets of Our Time, illustrated by Hogrogian, Macmillan, 1973.
Settling America: The Ethnic Expression of Fourteen Contemporary Poets, Macmillan, 1974.
Traveling America with Today's Poets, Macmillan, 1976.
Poems Here and Now, illustrated by Hogrogian, Greenwillow, 1976.
The Dog Writes on the Window with His Nose, and Other Poems (juvenile), illustrated by Hogrogian, Four Winds Press, 1977.
If Dragon Flies Made Honey (juvenile poetry), illustrated by Jose Aruego and Ariane Dewey, Greenwillow, 1977.
I Sing the Song of Myself, Greenwillow, 1978.

Editor of *Ararat,* 1971-72.

BROADSIDES

Letter to Virginia in Florence from Larkspur, California, Giligia Press, 1966.
Mother's Day, Gary Chafe and Sanford M. Dorbin, 1967.
Kato's Poem, Giligia Press, 1967.
Christmas, 1968, privately printed, 1968.
My Mother Takes My Wife's Side, illustrated by Judi Russell, Giligia Press, 1969.
O Kentucky, Giligia Press, 1969.
Outside the Library, privately printed, 1969.
Root River, illustrated by Bob Totten, Perishable Press, 1970.
Bird in Suet, illustrated by Hogrogian, Giligia Press, 1971.
Of Husbands and Wives, illustrated by Hogrogian, privately printed, 1971.
Hey Nonny, illustrated by Hogrogian, privately printed, 1972.
Poem for Nonny, illustrated by Hogrogian, Phineas Press, 1973.
Onions from New Hampshire, illustrated by Hogrogian, privately printed, 1973.
In the Tradition, illustrated by Hogrogian, University of Connecticut, 1974.
16:IV:73, illustrated by Hogrogian, Arts Action Press, 1975.
Anniversary Song, Bellevue Press, 1975.
Remembering Mihran, Massachusetts Council for the Arts, 1975.

The Toy Soldier, Bookstore Press, 1975.
Melkon, Isat Pragbhara Press, 1976.
Dafje Vartan, Prescott Street Press, 1978.
October 31, 1980, privately printed, 1980.
Letter to Charles J. Hardy from David Kherdian, privately printed, 1981.
Solstice, Two Rivers Press, 1983.
The Press at Butternut Creek, The Press at Butternut Creek, 1987.

Also author of broadside *Island Park,* Isat Pragbhara Press.

OTHER

A Bibliography of William Saroyan, 1934-1964, Roger Beacham, 1965.
David Meltzer: A Sketch from Memory and Descriptive Checklist, Oyez, 1965.
A Biographical Sketch and Descriptive Checklist of Gary Snyder, Oyez, 1965.
(Compiler) *William Saroyan Collection* (catalog), Fresno County Free Library, 1966.
Six Poets of the San Francisco Renaissance: Portraits and Checklists, introduction by Saroyan, Giligia Press, 1967, new edition, introduction by Kherdian, published as *Six San Francisco Poets,* Giligia Press, 1969.
(Author of introduction) Gerald Hausman, compiler, *The Shivurrus Plant of Mopant,* Giligia Press, 1968.
An Evening with Saroyan, The Ghost of Shah-Mouradian: A Review of 'Short Drive, Sweet Chariot, Monday, May 9, 1966, Giligia Press, 1970.
(Author of introduction) Art Cuelho and Dean Phelps, editors, *Father Me Home, Winds,* Seven Buffaloes Press, 1975.

By David Kherdian and Nonny Hogrogian

The arrival of a visitor from a distant planet causes a group of animals to look at their own world with new insight. (Cover illustration by Nonny Hogrogian.)

(Reteller; published anonymously) *The Pearl: Hymn of the Robe of Glory,* illustrated by Hogrogian, Two Rivers Press, 1979.
(Translator) *Pigs Never See the Stars: Proverbs from the Armenian,* woodcuts by Hogrogian, Two Rivers Press, 1982.
(Author of introduction) Saroyan, *Births,* Creative Arts Book Co., 1983.
(Author of introduction) Staveley, *Themes III,* Two Rivers Press, 1984.
(Reteller) *Monkey: A Journey to the West,* Shambhala Publications, 1992.

SIDELIGHTS: After undertaking a variety of jobs including owning a used book store, tending bar, working in factories, selling shoes, and serving a stint in the U.S. Army, David Kherdian finally found his niche in writing. His first work, a bibliography of American fiction writer William Saroyan, saw publication in 1965, and from there Kherdian embarked on a successful career as an author. By 1970 his first collection of verse, entitled *On the Death of My Father and Other Poems,* had reached publication, and since then he has become a prolific writer, delving into fiction, retellings, biographies, translations, and children's literature.

Although writing interested Kherdian from an early age, he had little hope of making it a career. He was born in 1931 and raised in Racine, Wisconsin, in the midst of many other families that shared his Armenian descent. He felt discriminated against in school for his poor academic performance—by the time he reached sixth grade he had flunked three times—and his overwhelming dislike of classes caused him to turn inward and helped breed a lifelong distrust of all institutions and organizations. He walked out of high school at the age of nineteen, with no thought as to how he would support himself. The next several years saw him laboring at sundry jobs—as a traveling salesman, a busboy, a builder of helicopter propellers. He also served during the Korean War, toured Europe for several months, and periodically attended college. By 1960 (having earned his high school equivalency while in the army) he completed his bachelor's in philosophy. Rather than utilizing the degree, though, he instead traded his home in Wisconsin for a chance to meet Saroyan in California, since Kherdian had been collecting the writer's books for some time and was interested in compiling a bibliography.

After meeting the writer and before deciding to embark on any serious work on the bibliography, Kherdian struggled to find "meaningful work" in California, as he stated in his *Contemporary Authors Autobiography Series* (*CAAS*) essay. Finding little luck, he tried Chicago, where an employment interview changed the course of his life. "I felt degraded by the interview," Kherdian stressed in his *CAAS* article, noting that at one point the interviewer inspected Kherdian's fingernails for dirt and checked his neck to make sure it was clean shaven. "By the time I reached the street I had made an irrevocable decision: I would never again in my life fill out an application form. Instead, I would work at my life until my name itself became what I was and what I would be employed for. It was a bold, desperate decision. It meant, as I knew, that I could never seek regular employment again, that I would have to drift from job to job." By 1965 he had forged a name for himself as the compiler of *A Bibliography of William Saroyan, 1934-1964,* his first published work.

Armed soon thereafter with an offer to amass a bibliography of some of the Beat poets—unconventional American writers of the 1950s—Kherdian produced *Six Poets of the San Francisco Renaissance: Portraits and Checklists.* The volume, for which Kherdian penned sketches of the subjects, reached publication the same year he wed his first wife. Kherdian discussed his marriage in his *CAAS* entry: "The marriage ... was doomed from the start.... While it was on and after it was over, its result for me seemed to be nothing but pain.... it was because of the suffering and because of the remorse that I was able to marry Nonny Hogrogian, a woman my age, who was also an artist, and whose ancestry was the same as mine. It was proof of graduation. My 'failed' marriage had resulted in my making a true and real marriage."

Kherdian recognized, however, that his "failed" marriage had released the poet in him. "There is a reason why poetry, love, and youth are connected in our minds," he wrote in *CAAS.* "Perhaps one has to be mad to write poetry, and being in love makes this madness seem desirable." In between bouts of composing, he founded Giligia Press and worked part time in a bookstore and a library to support himself. In 1970 he edited *Down at the Santa Fe Depot: Twenty Fresno Poets,* a successful compilation of local poetry, and released *On the Death of My Father and Other Poems,* his first collection. "I had arrived," Kherdian exclaimed. "I was a poet, a publisher, and I had made a name in the world—just as I had avowed I would."

A prolific poet who became recognized for drawing upon his surroundings and experiences, Kherdian found himself increasingly pulled toward the subject of his heritage. "There was something calling me," he recalled in *CAAS.* "It had to do with my people, it had to do with my childhood, and it had to do with an understanding of my past—without which I could not inhabit the future." So in the late 1970s, he decided to write his mother's biography, a story he previously had felt too disturbing to explore. The book became the award-winning *Road from Home: The Story of an Armenian Girl* as well as Kherdian's first foray into children's literature.

The recipient of numerous accolades, including an American Book Award nomination, a Lewis Carroll Shelf Award, and a Newbery Honor Award, *The Road from Home* began as a promise that Kherdian had made to his mother, agreeing to tell the story of her life once he had become a writer. As a girl, Kherdian's mother had endured the loss of her entire family when the Turks deported or killed all the Armenians in Turkey around the turn of the century. After escaping to Greece as an orphan and refugee, Kherdian's mother agreed to an

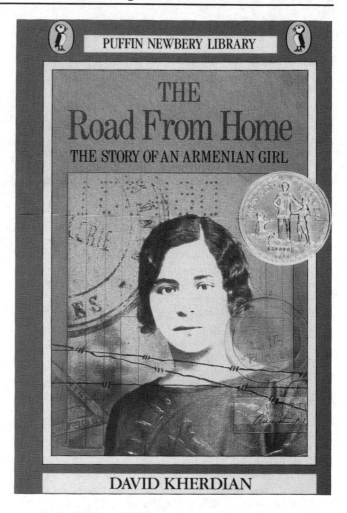

Young Veron tries to cling to memories of happier times while undergoing incredible hardships in Kherdian's true story of his mother. (Cover illustration by Viqui Maggio.)

arranged marriage with a man in America whom she had never met. The couple settled in Wisconsin where, seven years later, Kherdian was born.

"Ever since I was a little boy," Kherdian recalled in his *CAAS* entry, "my mother had said to me, 'Someday you grow up and tell my story.'" Kherdian was more than forty years old by the time he felt himself ready to do so. "For me her story was too painful to listen to; it was a hell she had passed through and that I had no intention of entering. And so here I was, well past the age of forty, never having heard her story of persecution and starvation, but with the promise made at last, that since I was a writer, even though only a poet, I would take it upon myself to bear witness to her life."

Kherdian made a recording of his mother's remembrances and, working from this information, spent a year writing the story of her life. As a reviewer for *Booklist* explained: "Written from the perspective of his mother, Veron Dumehjian, Kherdian retells with simple honesty the story of her childhood.... Deliberately rather than smoothly crafted, with occasionally awkward interweavings of customs and terminology, Kherdian's account provides only a hazy notion of the actual history involved.... Nevertheless, the drama and import of his unusual first-person narrative are unmistakable."

While telling the story of Kherdian's mother, *The Road from Home* also provides a portrait of the Armenian people. The account, Faith McNulty noted in the *New Yorker,* "is more than a record of tragedies, horrors, and escapes. There is also dignity, simplicity, and a haunting view of Veron's people, which reminds us of the strength and the vulnerability of any minority at any place or time." Lillian L. Shapiro wrote in *School Library Journal:* "Interwoven into the telling of this tragic history are warm, intimate details of family life, relationships and customs."

Kherdian continued his mother's story in *Finding Home,* which tells of her new life in America, the adjustments she had to make with her husband and his family, and how she built a family of her own. "*Finding Home* is a plain and honest book," assessed Linda Barrett Osborne in the *Washington Post Book World,* "the style and tone reflecting the condition of its characters. It is not as dramatic, gripping, or glittering with images as *The Road from Home,* but it deals with a different time and situation, and explores the human heart in quieter ways. The two books stand separately, but together they enrich each other greatly. They show the heroism needed to survive violence and catastrophe, and the heroism that helps us face life and rebuild."

In *Root River Run,* illustrated by Hogrogian, Kherdian went on to tell stories of his childhood in Racine, Wisconsin. Together with *The Road from Home* and *Finding Home, Root River Run* completes a loose trilogy concerning his Armenian heritage. The book is a series of connected tales about such subjects as Kherdian's first experience at a dance, his first bicycle, a momentous baseball game in which he makes a major play, and his Uncle Jack's mail order bride.

Kherdian's works for children have grown to number more than a dozen. Among his noted titles is his 1987 nonfiction book, *Bridger: The Story of a Mountain Man.* A biography that elicited particular praise from critics, *Bridger* follows nineteenth-century American pioneer Jim Bridger on an exploratory trek from St. Louis, Missouri, to his 1824 "founding" of Utah's Great Salt Lake. The "joy in living free in a beautiful, uncharted land," judged a *Booklist* reviewer, is "portrayed with dignity." Another acclaimed work is Kherdian's 1989 fictionalized memoir entitled *A Song for Uncle Harry.* Set during the 1930s, the account revolves around twelve-year-old Pete, and his uncle, an Armenian immigrant who has been disabled after being gassed during World War I. "The relationship between Pete and Harry is timeless," decided Denise Wilms in *Booklist.* Yet another title enthusiastically received by critics is *The Animal,* released in 1984 and illustrated by Hogrogian. The story, about an unidentified creature that emerges from a spaceship amidst a variety of animals, explores how different characters perceive beauty. *The Animal* is

The adventurous life of mountain man and explorer James Bridger comes to life in Kherdian's 1987 biography. (Cover illustration by Joseph A. Smith.)

"almost a fable in form," voiced a *Horn Book* reviewer, and "a paean to the peaceable kingdom." *The Great Fishing Contest,* too, illustrated by Hogrogian and published in 1991, was commended by critics for its sensitive look at a close companionship between two schoolmates.

Some critics have also pointed out that Kherdian's poetic nature surfaces in his books for children. At least one reviewer, a contributor to *Publishers Weekly,* praised the "singing lyrics" in *The Animal.* In addition, Patricia Lee Gauch in a *New York Times Book Review* critique of *The Song in the Walnut Grove* wrote: "Because [Kherdian] is a poet, there is a wonderful auditory quality in his writing, particularly in dialogues."

"We are called to the work we do by the gifts bestowed upon us by nature," Kherdian pointed out to young, aspiring writers in a 1983 interview with Jill Lewis for *Writing!* "If you find that you are to be a writer (and can give up imagining that you have chosen to become one), the only thing you can do, really, is to prepare yourself. The question should be, 'What constitutes a writer's apprenticeship?' It will be slightly different for each person but, generally speaking, it would include reading, travel, observation (how things look, how people speak), practice, patience, stubbornness, resolve—and no expectations.

"Keep your writing for yourself. Nurture it in secret, at least in the beginning; that is, until it is good enough to be seen. Be true to yourself. Do not be afraid to live. We grow through suffering. It is more important to live with the intention of becoming a man than it is to achieve the highest goal imaginable, because no imaginable achievement is as valuable as the realization of one's own being."

Kherdian told *SATA:* "Prior to marrying Nonny Hogrogian, I had never thought of the possibility of writing for children. Her own retellings, as well as her original work did not need my help. She had a unique and compelling style that I could not have improved upon, and could only have hurt. It seems an accident still, but when Greenwillow (the first publisher I sent the work to) accepted *The Road from Home,* I knew I could make a living writing fiction for children. I knew because my

Petey and his beloved Uncle Harry share a special relationship that few people understand, a bond that is threatened when Uncle Harry begins making mysterious trips to Chicago. (Cover illustration by Hogrogian.)

mother, upon hearing me read the concluding pages of the book, said: 'Now you can go ahead and write anything.' I believed her. Up until that time I had earned my living—or should I say, I *struggled* to earn my living—as a poet, editor, teacher, anthologist, etc. In recent years I have turned my attention to the picture book, realizing that a poet's sensibility brings to that genre a quality that seems endemic. A picture book should be lyrical, fanciful, poetic, and, because it is so spare in words and rich in picture, the words that *are* used need to be heightened and intensified, and this a poet can do—and perhaps only a poet can do."

WORKS CITED:

Review of *The Animal, Horn Book,* January, 1985, pp. 46-47.

Review of *The Animal, Publishers Weekly,* September 7, 1984, p. 78.

Review of *Bridger: The Story of a Mountain Man, Booklist,* March 15, 1987, p. 1127.

Gauch, Patricia Lee, review of *The Song in the Walnut Grove, New York Times Book Review,* December 19, 1982, p. 26.

Kherdian, David, article, *Contemporary Authors Autobiography Series,* Volume 2, Gale, 1985, pp. 261-77.

Lewis, Jill, "An Interview with David Kherdian," *Writing!,* November, 1983, pp. 11-14.

McNulty, Faith, review of *The Road from Home, New Yorker,* December 3, 1979, p. 212.

Osborne, Linda Barrett, "Mail-Order Bride," *Washington Post Book World,* May 10, 1981.

Review of *The Road from Home, Booklist,* March 1, 1979, p. 1049.

Shapiro, Lillian L., review of *The Road from Home, School Library Journal,* April, 1979, p. 69.

Wilms, Denise, review of *A Song for Uncle Harry, Booklist,* September 15, 1989, p. 184.

FOR MORE INFORMATION SEE:

BOOKS

Bedrosian, Margaret, *The Magical Pine Ring: Culture and Imagination in Armenian-American Literature,* Wayne State University Press, 1991, pp. 168-76.

Children's Literature Review, Volume 24, Gale, 1991.

Contemporary Literary Criticism, Gale, Volume 6, 1976, Volume 9, 1978.

Fifth Book of Junior Authors and Illustrators, edited by Sally Holmes Holtze, H. W. Wilson, 1983, pp. 178-79.

PERIODICALS

Ararat, summer, 1970, number 43, p. 49; summer, 1971, number 47, pp. 39-40.

Armenian Post, January 12, 1978.

Booklist, April 1, 1977, p. 1165; October 1, 1983, p. 297; April 15, 1991, p. 1640.

Book Source Monthly, April, 1988, pp. 6-9.

Bulletin of the Center for Children's Books, January, 1980; January, 1984, p. 90; October, 1984; April, 1987; February, 1993, pp. 180-81.

Dartmouth, May 25, 1972.

Horn Book, June, 1979, p. 318; February, 1980.

Kirkus Reviews, May 15, 1991, p. 673.
Los Angeles Times, June 27, 1987.
New Laurel Review, spring, 1976.
New Mexican, March 29, 1970.
New York Times Book Review, August 11, 1991, p. 1.
Parnassus, spring-summer, 1976, pp. 175-82.
Poet and Critic, Volume 9, number 1, 1975, pp. 39-44;
    Volume 9, number 3, 1976.
Quill and Quire, August, 1992, p. 29.
School Library Journal, December, 1983, p. 83; January, 1984, p. 65; December, 1984, p. 72; January, 1985, p. 86; April, 1987, p. 111; January, 1990, p. 104; July, 1990, p. 61; June, 1991, p. 83.

*   *   *

KOHL, MaryAnn F. 1947-

PERSONAL: Born January 23, 1947, in Seattle, WA; daughter of John Ross (a bookbinder) and Betty Louise (a homemaker) Faubion; married Michael L. Kohl (a builder), July, 1968; children: Hannah, Megan. *Education:* Old Dominion University, B.S.; Western Washington University, certificate in education; attended Linfield College. *Hobbies and other interests:* Skiing, painting, reading.

ADDRESSES: Office—c/o Bright Ring Publishing, 1900 North Shore Dr., P.O. Box 5768, Bellingham, WA 98226.

CAREER: Teacher in Ferndale school district, 1972-80; owner of Bright Ring Publishing, 1985—.

MEMBER: Women's Press Association.

AWARDS, HONORS: M.B.A. Merit Award; twice awarded Ben Franklin Award.

WRITINGS:

Scribble Cookies, Bright Ring, 1985.
Mudworks, Bright Ring, 1989.
Take Part! (television show), YTV/Mudworks Factory, 1990-92.
(With Cindy Gainer) *Good Earth Art,* Bright Ring, 1991.

WORK IN PROGRESS: ScienceArts: Discovering Art through Science.

SIDELIGHTS: MaryAnn F. Kohl told *SATA:* "While my children were very small and I was on leave from elementary school teaching, the drive to write a book of children's creative art ideas propelled me to start my own publishing company. Since 1985 I have published three books, am presently working on the fourth, and have sold quantities rivaling the major publishers. My books have won the Benjamin Franklin Award as well as other honors.

"What an exciting career to be benefiting children, helping people who work with children, and developing a growing business! Each day I spend most of my time on the publishing work that must be done and a small part of the day on research and writing for the new book. Wearing two hats keeps me on my toes. Being the author of children's creative art books has taken me into many interesting areas of promotion such as travel, television guest spots, and radio interviews. I still enjoy going into schools and working with children first hand using the ideas from my books and testing new ideas. We all have such fun and I learn the most from the children, I think. I look forward to many years of publishing and writing and the adventures of where the business leads, and of course, to years of hard work with wonderful rewards."

*   *   *

KORTE, Gene J. 1950-

PERSONAL: Born October 10, 1950, in Dearborn, MI; son of Orville J. (a sheet metal worker) and Edith (Ciarrocchi) Korte; married February 28, 1975; wife's name, Barbara L. (a manager); children: Zachary. *Education:* Eastern Michigan University, B.S., 1972. *Politics:* Independent. *Religion:* "Multi-Planetary Christian."

ADDRESSES: Home—49565 Powell, Plymouth, MI 48170.

CAREER: Society of Manufacturing Engineers, Dearborn, MI, manager, 1978—.

MEMBER: Arbor Day Foundation, Council of Engineering and Scientific Society Executives.

WRITINGS:

Green Pickle Pie (illustrated by Gary Webb), Winston-Derek, 1991.

WORK IN PROGRESS: Too Many Toys.

SIDELIGHTS: "I began looking at writing as sort of a hobby in 1976," Gene J. Korte told *SATA.* "I was unemployed, between interviews, and I was doing a lot of reading. I ran across an article in the local paper about an individual who made a living selling ideas to greeting card companies, cartoonists, and comedians. Without sounding too smug, I figured I could do the same, so I did. I began submitting ideas to card companies and freelance cartoonists and was quite successful. However, numeric success and financial success are two different creatures. I sold scads of ideas and gags, but this usually added up to hundreds of dollars each year, not thousands.

"I began writing articles and short stories a few years ago and have had modest success. Then in 1990 I landed a publishing contract for my first children's book, *Green Pickle Pie.* You hear stories about authors who have an idea in their head for years and they finally put it in words. Well, this wasn't the case. I had no intention of writing *Green Pickle Pie* until the day the idea was given to me and I especially had no intention of writing a book

GENE J. KORTE

for children, since all of my previous work was for adult markets.

"The concept of *Green Pickle Pie* was given to me by my son, Zachary, who at the time was four. He was riding shotgun in the grocery cart when he looked down into the bakery bin. His eyes got real big and as he pointed at a pie he said, 'Dad, there's a green pickle pie.' He said it in a whispered voice like he didn't want anyone else to see the abomination that was being passed off as food. What he actually saw was a key lime pie with a slice of lime on top which he thought was a pickle chip.

"His comment amused me, but it didn't really strike a chord until I got home and started thinking about how a four-year-old must perceive things in a grocery store. If Zachary thought a key lime pie was a green pickle pie, then he could easily imagine other things, like pineapple pasta, grape jelly fish or cauliflower cookies. With this in mind, I began working on the book.

"When I was satisfied with the copy and verse, I asked my wife Barbara to look at it. She liked the draft; however, spouses and friends aren't always the best critics of your work. The next test for the book was my son, Zachary. I read it to him and he enjoyed it enough to request that it be read to him before bedtime. The final test was submitting it to publishers for consideration and I was fortunate enough to hook up with Winston-Derek.

"Even though it was accepted, it went through another editing phase with the publisher. While some of the words were changed, the story-line escaped without injury. With copy ready to go, I still needed artwork. After discussing this with the editor, I realized his vision of illustrations was not the same as mine. So I hired Gary Webb, who proved to be a wise choice.

"My years of experience working with cartoonists served me well during this process. Since *Green Pickle Pie* was geared toward young children, I wanted illustrations that would capture the interest of the adult reader and Gary was able to help me achieve this.

"Even though writing is very enjoyable, I don't find it to be particularly easy. Selecting the right words, placing them in the proper sequence, and proper punctuation are only a portion of what is needed to write a good book, story, or letter. Understanding the difference between the written and spoken word and the nuances of the language are just as important. I view all books as being the same—it's just that the words are in a different order."

L

LaDOUX, Rita C. 1951-

PERSONAL: Born October 26, 1951, in Spirit Lake, IA; daughter of Carlyle C. (in sales) and Edith (a homemaker; maiden name, Marston) LaDoux; married Paul D. Swedenborg (a scientist), 1987; children: Eliza, Britta. *Education:* Attended Universtat Tubingen, Germany, 1972; Washington University, B.A., 1973, M.A., 1977.

ADDRESSES: Home—St. Paul, MN.

CAREER: KTCA-TV, St. Paul, MN, served on production staff of *Newton's Apple,* 1984-89; freelance writer, 1989—. Producer of children's television programs and educational films; producer and director of documentaries. Member of children's theater group.

AWARDS, HONORS: Emmy Award, best daytime children's program, 1989, for *Newton's Apple.*

WRITINGS:

"STATES" SERIES

Georgia, Lerner, 1991.
Missouri, Lerner, 1991.
Iowa, Lerner, 1992.
Montana, Lerner, 1992.
Oklahoma, Lerner, 1992.
Louisiana, Lerner, 1993.

SIDELIGHTS: Rita C. LaDoux told *SATA:* "The focus of all my work has been communication, and generally communication with a younger audience. My first summer out of college I organized a touring children's theater company in St. Louis. We enjoyed bringing stories to life for our audiences. Later I worked on a number of films, including educational films for children, a film about wetland preservation, and another about American Indian religions. From 1981 to 1983 I coproduced and directed *Great Branches, New Roots: The Hmong Family,* an independent documentary telling the story of Hmong refugees from Laos in the United States.

"In the spring of 1984, I was pleased to join the production staff of *Newton's Apple* and begin researching and developing ways to interpret science for general audiences. Writing books for Lerner's 'States' series has been a natural extension of my previous work. When writing about geography, history, lifestyles, or environmental issues for young readers, I focus on making connections and telling a story. (I also like a good joke!)

"Currently I am inspired by the wealth of children's books at my local library—the St. Anthony Park library, a jewel-box Carnegie library—and far more by my two young daughters who derive great joy from exploring the world through books and book-inspired activity."

*   *   *

LAGER, Claude
See LAPP, Christiane (Germain)

*   *   *

LAPP, Christiane (Germain) 1948-
(Claude Lager)

PERSONAL: Born March 17, 1948, in Liege, Belgium; daughter of Christian and Irma Germain; married Jean-Claude Lapp (in Belgian television), March 7, 1970; children: Adrien, Anais.

ADDRESSES: Home—32 ave. Lambeau, B 1200 Brussels, Belgium. *Office*—79 blvd. L. Schmidt, B 1040 Brussels, Belgium.

CAREER: Affliated with Editions J. Duculot, Louvain-la-Neuve, Belgium, 1970-87; Pastel, Brussels, Belgium, founder and publisher, 1987—.

WRITINGS:

Jeanette and Josie, illustrated by Claude K. DuBois, Viking, 1989 (originally published as *Babette et Virginie,* Pastel/L'Ecole des Loisirs, c. 1988).
13 Happy Street, illustrated by Claudia de Weck, Prentice Hall Books for Young Readers, c. 1988.

(Under pseudonym Claude Lager) *A Tale of Two Rats,* Stewart, Tabori & Chang, 1991.

Petit bout tout doux, Pastel, 1992.

Also the author of the story *Tout Rouge,* illustrated by Claude K. Dubois, 1993.

SIDELIGHTS: Christiane Lapp told *SATA:* "I started to work in publishing in 1970 and very soon was responsible for the children's books list. In 1987, I left Duculot where I had worked for seventeen years and started my own imprint (Pastel) of L'Ecole des Loisirs.

"At Pastel I only publish picture books. Many of them have been sold to American publishers. I do not consider myself a writer, as it is not so simple to be involved in a book both as a writer and an editor. So, it happens from time to time that I have an idea for a story which can suit the style of one of my illustrators. This was the case with *A Tale of Two Rats.*"

*   *   *

LATHAM, Mavis
See CLARK, Mavis Thorpe

*   *   *

LAVALLEE, Barbara 1941-

PERSONAL: Born November 6, 1941, in Davenport, IA; daughter of Clarence H. (a Protestant minister) and Dorothy (a teacher; maiden name, Keeler) Koehler; married Thomas H. Lavallee (a teacher and counselor), October 22, 1965 (divorced, 1981); children: Charles, Mark. *Education:* Wesleyan University, B.F.A., 1964. *Hobbies and other interests:* "Travel—anytime—anywhere."

ADDRESSES: Home—P.O. Box 288, Girdwood, AK 99587. *Studio*—1026 West Fourth Ave., Anchorage, AK 99501.

CAREER: United States Army Service Club, Lenggries, Germany, recreational specialist, 1964-65; social worker in hospital for the mentally handicapped, 1965-66, and for an adoption agency, Portland, ME, 1966-67; Job Corps Center for Women, Poland Spring, ME, counselor, 1967-69; art teacher for Bureau of Indian Affairs, on Navajo Reservation, 1969-70, and in Sitka, AK, 1970-75; self-employed artist in Anchorage, AK, 1975—. Vice president of Girdwood Parent Teacher Association (PTA), 1983-84.

MEMBER: Society of Children's Book Writers and Illustrators.

AWARDS, HONORS: Golden Kite Award, 1991, for *Mama, Do You Love Me?*

ILLUSTRATOR:

Freya Littledale, *The Snow Child,* Scholastic, 1989.

Barbara Joosse, *Mama, Do You Love Me?,* Chronicle, 1991.

"IMAGINE LIVING HERE" SERIES BY VICKI COBB

This Place Is Cold, Walker & Co., 1989.
This Place Is Dry, Walker & Co., 1989.
This Place Is Wet, Walker & Co., 1990.
This Place Is High, Walker & Co., 1990.
This Place Is Lonely, Walker & Co., 1991.
This Place Is Crowded, Walker & Co., 1992.

OTHER

Cecilia Nibeck, *Salmon Recipes from Alaska* (cookbook), AK Enterprises, 1987.
Nibeck, *Alaskan Halibut Recipes* (cookbook), AK Enterprises, 1989.

WORK IN PROGRESS: "Planning a trip to Africa for new book by Vicki Cobb for the 'Imagine Living Here' series."

SIDELIGHTS: Barbara Lavallee is an award-winning illustrator who has received praise for her work with various authors. She is the illustrator of Barbara Joosse's *Mama, Do You Love Me?,* in which a young Eskimo girl presents her mother with mischievous situations. The little girl is curious as to whether her mother would still love her if she were to carry out any of these trouble-making propositions. Noted for its attention to the fine

BARBARA LAVALLEE

Lavallee brings a sense of whimsy and fun to her drawings for Freya Littledale's retelling of the Russian folk tale *The Snow Child*.

details of Eskimo life and its portrait of a loving relationship between mother and daughter, the book won the Golden Kite Award in 1991. Lavallee has also teamed with author Vicki Cobb for the "Imagine Living Here" series of books. These books relate what life is like in various countries and climates around the world. Included in the series are books about Australia (*This Place Is Lonely*), Arctic Alaska (*This Place Is Cold*), and the Brazilian rain forests (*This Place Is Wet*).

Lavallee told *SATA:* "I am undeniably the product of my life's experiences: a 1950s midwest childhood with three sisters and a strong courageous mother who put our lives back together after the death of my father; an adventurous husband who encouraged me to sometimes go beyond the limits of comfort; my beloved sons, who shared their childhood with a single parent; and the roller coaster ride of making a living as a free-lance artist. My family remains a strong influence on my life and work."

In describing how she came to her chosen profession, Lavallee related to *SATA:* "I have always known I wanted to 'do' art, but it was only after I moved to Alaska, fell in love with the land, its people, and fascinating native cultures, that I knew I wanted to be an artist. I majored in art in college and had experience teaching art. When it became time to do my first book, I read Uri Schulevitz's book *Writing with Pictures* to get an idea of how to go about illustrating a book. I found it to be a wonderful resource, a worthy recommendation to anyone who is interested in illustrating."

While Lavallee's initial illustrations were for cookbooks, she soon teamed with Cobb to create the "Imagine Living Here" series of books. She credits these books,

and their author, with truly introducing her to the world of book art. "If I were to name a mentor, it would have to be Vicki Cobb, who first opened the door to children's book illustration for me. I have worked closely with her throughout the 'Imagine Living Here' series, and we have developed a working relationship in which we discuss the kinds of things each of us would like to include in our books. I love to travel and have had the opportunity to experience bits of Peru, Bolivia, Brazil, Australia, and Japan while researching books with Vicki."

All of Lavallee's books have been done in watercolors—her primary medium—and she considers her art much more than a part of her job. "Painting is so much a part of my life that it is impossible to separate art from lifestyle," she related. Once she has decided on a project to illustrate, the artist goes through a series of steps to reach the final artwork: "The creative process begins with the first reading of a manuscript. Because that initial reading is so important, I carefully set the stage. I choose a time, place, and circumstances which will allow me to concentrate fully. I read it through and write down any images and thoughts that come to me. Then I let it stew for a while, for work on a book never begins with that first reading. Sometimes this is because it takes awhile to get contracts signed and deadlines set, usually it is because I am busy working on something else when a manuscript arrives. I find a book requires total concentration, so I clear my decks of any other work before starting on a new book. The first piece of

I love you more than the raven loves his treasure,

Lavallee's illustrations for Barbara Joosse's *Mama, Do You Love Me?* emphasize the natural wonders of the Arctic.

work I do on a manuscript is research, so that authentic details can become part of the characters and story. Then a storyboard needs to be done. The storyboard breaks the text down into pages and action concepts that will occur on each page. I never work on pages in sequence—I always do the one with the strongest, most well developed image (consequently, the easiest one) first. One of the aspects of illustrating I like most is the freedom I'm given by both the author and the editor to create the initial sketches without influence to do it the way either of them sees it.

"*Mama, Do You Love Me?* was an illustrator's dream— a universal concept couched in the trappings of a culture and people that continue to fascinate me after over twenty years of living in Alaska. I was both the mother and the little girl. It was only after the book had been published that I learned that the author, Barbara Joosse, had written the book about a mother and a little boy. Barbara and I have discussed several new projects that we would like to work on together. She is a wonderful writer, as well as a person I like very much, and I look forward to working with her again."

While Lavallee has no immediate plans for another book set in Alaska, she stated that she is "always open to the prospect." She described to *SATA* the aspects of her chosen home that appeal to her: "Alaska is a huge place, with a diverse and exotic history. I have lived here for twenty-three years, and I am still overwhelmed by its staggering beauty. Visual overload is commonplace but never boring or plagued with sameness. The Alaskan native cultures are also extremely diverse, with many differences due to geographic placement within the state. The extraordinary arts practiced by each of these native groups symbolize universal concepts as well as the basic human need to decorate those things that surround one's life. Most of all, the idea that a group of people have managed for generations to exist—and flourish—in a harsh and unforgiving environment, speaks of a culture that has conceptualized working together for the survival of the group. Because of modern life, much of these traditional concepts are changing and the dilemma of adapting to these changes is the greatest challenge to Alaska's natives. I believe that although a way of life may be lost, the artforms of these cultures will survive and continue to be practiced."

In summarizing her ethic for book illustration, Lavallee told *SATA:* "I like to do books with a cultural or ethnic influence, because they are projects that frequently require travel and research, which in turn enriches my life and experiences. My work has always reflected my interest in people—how they live, what they do. I prefer to portray the magnificence of man, his joy and humor, his tenacity, and his ability to overcome. I want my work to illustrate without being illustrative, something a viewer can 'get lost in' as well as relate to. By 'illustrative,' I am referring to images that stick so literally to the action of the text that they capture nothing more than a moment in time that has already been described.

I feel it is the role of the illustration to enhance and enrich the text."

*   *   *

LESTER, Julius (Bernard) 1939-

PERSONAL: Born January 27, 1939, in St. Louis, MO; son of W. D. (a minister) and Julia (Smith) Lester; married Joan Steinau (a researcher), 1962 (divorced, 1970); married Alida Carolyn Fechner, March 21, 1979; children: (first marriage) Jody Simone, Malcolm Coltrane; (second marriage) Elena Milad (stepdaughter), David Julius. *Education:* Fisk University, B.A., 1960.

ADDRESSES: Home—600 Station Rd., Amherst, MA 01002. *Office*—University of Massachusetts, Amherst, MA 01002.

CAREER: Professional musician and singer in the 1960s, recorded with Vanguard Records; Newport Folk Festival, Newport, RI, director, 1966-68; WBAI-FM, New York City, producer and host of live radio show, 1968-75; WNET-TV, New York City, host of live television program "Free Time," 1971-73; University of Massachusetts—Amherst, professor of Afro-American studies, 1971-88, professor of Near Eastern and Judaic Studies, 1982—, acting director and associate director of Institute for Advanced Studies in Humanities, 1982-84. Lecturer, New School for Social Research, New York City, 1968-70; writer in residence, Vanderbilt University, 1985.

JULIUS LESTER

AWARDS, HONORS: Newbery Honor Book citation, 1969, and Lewis Carroll Shelf Award, 1970, both for *To Be a Slave;* Lewis Carroll Shelf Award, 1972, and National Book Award finalist, 1973, both for *The Long Journey Home: Stories from Black History;* Lewis Carroll Shelf Award, 1973, for *The Knee-High Man and Other Tales;* honorable mention, Coretta Scott King Award, 1983, for *This Strange New Feeling,* and 1988, for *Tales of Uncle Remus: The Adventures of Brer Rabbit;* Distinguished Teacher's Award, 1983-84; Faculty Fellowship Award for Distinguished Research and Scholarship, 1985; National Professor of the Year Silver Medal Award, Council for Advancement and Support of Education, 1985; Massachusetts State Professor of the Year and Gold Medal Award for National Professor of the Year, both from Council for Advancement and Support of Education, both 1986; Distinguished Faculty Lecturer, 1986-87.

WRITINGS:

(With Pete Seeger) *The 12-String Guitar as Played by Leadbelly: An Instructional Manual,* Oak, 1965.

The Angry Children of Malcolm X, Southern Student Organizing Committee, 1966.

(Editor with Mary Varela) *Our Folk Tales: High John, The Conqueror, and Other Afro-American Tales,* illustrated by Jennifer Lawson, privately printed, 1967.

(Editor with Varela) Fanny Lou Hamer, *To Praise Our Bridges: An Autobiography,* KIPCO, 1967.

The Mud of Vietnam: Photographs and Poems, Folklore Press, 1967.

Look Out Whitey! Black Power's Gon' Get Your Mama!, Dial, 1968.

To Be a Slave, illustrated by Tom Feelings, Dial, 1969.

Black Folktales, illustrated by Feelings, Baron, 1969.

Search for the New Land: History as Subjective Experience, Dial, 1969.

Revolutionary Notes, Baron, 1969.

(Editor) *The Seventh Son: The Thoughts and Writings of W. E. B. DuBois,* two volumes, Random House, 1971.

(Compiler with Rae Pace Alexander) *Young and Black in America,* Random House, 1971.

The Long Journey Home: Stories from Black History, Dial, 1972.

The Knee-High Man and Other Tales, illustrated by Ralph Pinto, Dial, 1972.

Two Love Stories, Dial, 1972.

(Editor) Stanley Couch, *Ain't No Ambulances for No Nigguhs Tonight* (poems), Baron, 1972.

(With David Gahr) *Who I Am* (photopoems), Dial, 1974.

All Is Well: An Autobiography, Morrow, 1976.

This Strange New Feeling (short stories), Dial, 1982, published in England as *A Taste of Freedom: Three Stories from Black History,* Longman, 1983.

Do Lord Remember Me (adult novel), Holt, 1984.

The Tales of Uncle Remus (four-volume series in progress), illustrated by Jerry Pinkney, Dial, Volume 1: *The Adventures of Brer Rabbit,* 1987, Volume 2: *The Further Adventures of Brer Rabbit,* 1988,

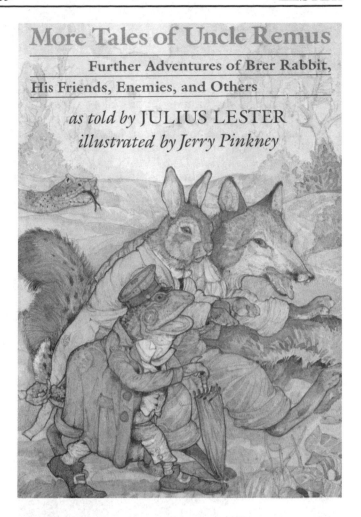

Lester and illustrator Jerry Pinkney received wide critical acclaim for their updated presentation of the "Brer Rabbit" folktales.

Volume 3: *The Misadventures of Brer Rabbit, Brer Fox, Brer Wolf, the Doodang, and Other Creatures,* 1990.

Lovesong: Becoming a Jew (autobiographical), Holt, 1988.

How Many Spots Does a Leopard Have? and Other Tales, illustrated by David Shannon, Scholastic, 1990.

Falling Pieces of the Broken Sky, Arcade, 1990.

Contributor of essays and reviews to numerous magazines and newspapers, including *New York Times Book Review, New York Times, Nation, Katallagete, Democracy,* and *Village Voice.* Associate editor, *Sing Out,* 1964-70; contributing editor, *Broadside of New York,* 1964-70.

Lester's works have been translated into seven languages.

SIDELIGHTS: Julius Lester is the author of acclaimed young adult fiction devoted to preserving the history of black Americans. Though he began his career as a musician and political activist in the 1960s, Lester began writing for children as a way to inform young black people about their African American heritage. As demonstrated in his stories, novels, and retellings of black folktales, Lester often focuses on black experience in the rural Deep South, especially during slavery and the Reconstruction period after the Civil War. Throughout, he has been acclaimed for his blend of realistic detail, dialogue, and storytelling—all contributing to important historical knowledge about African Americans. Quoted in *Twentieth-Century Children's Writers,* Lester upholds history as "the lives of people more than . . . the recording of politics and wars," and describes his work as an effort "to explore and illumine the lives of ordinary men and women, who are history." Moreover, his work aims to illuminate themes central to black history, such as oppression and racism. His ultimate goal, note Eric Foner and Naomi Lewis in the *New York Review of Books,* is to provide readers with "a sense of history which will help shape their lives and politics."

Lester's early years were spent in the segregated South of the 1940s and 1950s. He was born in 1939 in St. Louis,

In these six true stories, Lester looks at black history through the dramatic personal lives of both slaves and freemen.

Missouri, the son of a Methodist minister from whom, as Lester stated in *Fourth Book of Junior Authors and Illustrators,* he "absorbed so much of Southern rural black traditions, particularly music and stories." At the age of two he moved with his family to Kansas City, Kansas, and as a teenager lived in Nashville, Tennessee, spending summers at his grandmother's farm in rural Arkansas. While Lester's memories of the South were not, as he stated in *Fourth Book,* "wholly negative, despite segregation and discrimination," he was profoundly influenced by what he described in *Horn Book* as the South's atmosphere of "deathly spiritual violence." In addition to its "many restrictions on where [blacks] could live, eat, go to school, and go after dark," the segregated South was a dangerous place where there existed "the constant threat of physical death if you looked at a white man in what he considered the wrong way or if he didn't like your attitude."

Lester's early artistic interests were with music, yet he also had aspirations to become a writer. In books he found an outlet from the daily realities of racism, and at a young age became an avid reader. "Although I don't recall any content from my early years of books," he commented in *Horn Book,* "there was the more important emotional content which those books represented—the knowledge that the segregated world in which I was forced to live bounded by the white heat of hatred was not the only reality. Somewhere beyond that world, somewhere my eyes could not then penetrate, were dreams and possibilities, and I knew this was true because the books I read ravenously, desperately, were voices from that world." Lester became especially fond of Westerns and mysteries, which he would read into the early hours of the morning. Through these action stories, as he commented in *Horn Book,* he "found a kind of mirror in which one element of my world—violence—was isolated and, somehow, was made less harmful to me."

Lester graduated in 1960 from Nashville's Fisk University with a degree in English and became politically active in the Civil Rights struggle to desegregate the South and bring about social change. In the mid-1960s he joined the Student Non-Violent Coordinating Committee (SNCC), at a time when the group advocated that blacks assume a more militant stance to fight racism. He became head of the SNCC's photo department and travelled to North Vietnam during the Vietnam War to document the effects of U.S. bombing missions. During the same period, he pursued his music interests and played the guitar and banjo at civil rights rallies. Lester went on to record two albums and performed with such folksingers as Pete Seeger, Phil Ochs, and Judy Collins. His interests in black folk music led to the writing of his first book, *The 12-String Guitar as Played by Leadbelly: An Instructional Manual,* which he coauthored with Seeger in 1965. He then wrote a number of adult books on political themes, including *The Angry Children of Malcolm X* (1966), *Look Out Whitey, Black Power's Gon' Get Your Mama!* (1968), and a book of photographs and poems entitled *The Mud of Vietnam* (1967).

In the late 1960s Lester moved to New York City, where he was the only African American announcer at WBAI-Radio, a noncommercial station featuring alternative programming. He hosted an evening show that featured such diverse music styles as jazz, rock, classical, and experimental, and a morning show entitled "Uncle Tom's Cabin." "Radio is a very intimate medium," he recalled to Barry List in *Publishers Weekly.* "There's the sound of this 'voice' in people's houses and apartments keeping them company. But I didn't make tapes because I felt I was creating in time and space, and that it wasn't supposed to be preserved. If it *was* going to be preserved, it would be preserved in the hearts and souls of people. And that's what happened."

Continuing his varied involvement in black politics, Lester followed the advice of an editor at Dial Press who suggested he branch out into writing children's books. In 1969, he published two books which came to mark his future success as a writer for young people. *To Be a Slave,* a collection of six stories based on historical fact, evolved from an oral history of slaves Lester was compiling. Runner-up for the Newbery Medal, *To Be a Slave* was acclaimed for its contributions to African American history. "Aside from the fact that these are tremendously moving documents in themselves," wrote *Black Like Me* author John Howard Griffin in the *New York Times Book Review,* "they help to destroy the delusion that black men did not suffer as another man would in similar circumstances, a delusion that lies at the base of much racism today." Also in 1969, Lester published his widely praised *Black Folktales,* recasting various human and animal characters from African legends and slave narratives. "Although these tales have been told before, in most of them Lester brings a fresh street-talk language ... and thus breathes new life into them," wrote John A. Williams in the *New York Times Book Review.* "It is a tribute to the universality of these tales—and Lester's ability to see it—that we are thus presented with old truths dressed for today."

During the 1970s and 1980s, Lester followed with a number of similarly acclaimed books that showed his overlapping interests in African American history, folklore, and political themes. *The Knee-High Man and Other Tales* (1972) compiles six black folktales, including those of the famous Brer Rabbit, and brings together humorous, satirical sketches with political overtones. In the story "The Farmer and the Snake," for example, as Ethel Richard noted in the *New York Times Book Review,* "the lesson is that kindness will not change the nature of a thing—in this case, the nature of a poisonous snake to bite." With such books as *Long Journey Home* (1972), *Two Love Stories* (1972), and *This Strange New Feeling* (1982), Lester continued to explore black heritage by writing fiction rooted in African American experience. *Long Journey Home,* a finalist for the National Book Award, was drawn from actual events of everyday blacks during the post-Civil War Reconstruction period. "Abandoning familiar biographical territory," wrote William Loren Katz in *Book World,* "Lester seeks out the lives of footnote people, ordinary men and women who might appear only in a Brady Civil War

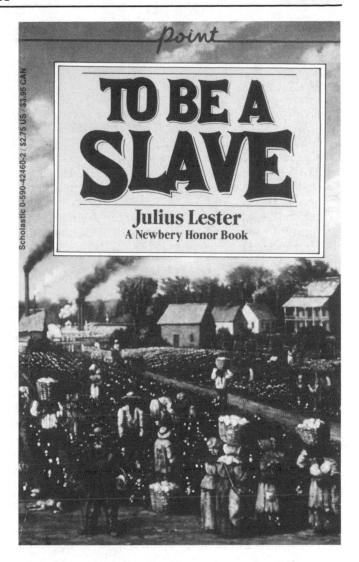

In this 1968 work, Lester used first-person narratives to draw a picture of what it meant to live as a slave.

photograph or a neglected manuscript at the Library of Congress. His tales ... are explorations of the human condition in adversity."

In addition to writing for young readers, Lester has also continued with books for adults, including his 1985 novel *Do Lord Remember Me* and his two-volume compilation *The Seventh Son,* which brings together the writings of the early black political activist W. E. B. Du Bois. He has also authored two autobiographies, *All Is Well* and *Love Song,* the latter which recounts his conversion in the late 1980s to Judaism. In addition to his writing career, Lester has served as professor since the early 1970s at the University of Massachusetts in Amherst, first as a professor of Afro-American studies, and then as a professor Near Eastern and Judaic studies. Writing for children, however, has been a particularly rewarding area to explore aspects of his African American heritage. "Children's literature is the one place where you can tell a story," he told List. "Just, straight, tell a story, and have it received as narrative without any literary garbage. I've done a fair amount of historically based fiction that would be derided as adult literature because it's not 'sophisticated.' I'm just telling a story about people's lives. In children's literature, I can do that."

WORKS CITED:

Foner, Eric, and Naomi Lewis, review of *Long Journey Home: Stories from Black History, New York Review of Books,* April 20, 1972, pp. 41-42.

Griffin, John Howard, review of *To Be a Slave, New York Times Book Review,* November 3, 1968, p. 7.

Katz, William Loren, review of *Long Journey Home, Book World,* September 3, 1972, p. 9.

Lester, Julius, article in *Fourth Book of Junior Authors and Illustrators,* edited by Doris De Montreville and Elizabeth D. Crawford, H. W. Wilson, 1978, pp. 223-24.

Lester, Julius, "The Beechwood Staff," *Horn Book,* April, 1984, pp. 161-69.

List, Barry, "Julius Lester," *Publishers Weekly,* February 12, 1988, pp. 67-68.

MacCann, Donnarae, "Julius Lester," *Twentieth-Century Children's Writers,* 3rd edition, edited by Tracy Chevalier, St. James Press, 1989, pp. 575-76.

Richard, Ethel, review of *The Knee-High Man, and Other Tales, New York Times Book Review,* February 4, 1973, p. 8.

Williams, John A., review of *Black Folktales, New York Times Book Review,* November 9, 1969, pp. 10, 12.

FOR MORE INFORMATION SEE:

BOOKS

Children's Literature Review, Volume 2, Gale, 1976.
Lester, Julius, *All Is Well,* Morrow, 1976.
Lester, Julius, *Lovesong: Becoming a Jew,* Holt, 1988.

PERIODICALS

Bulletin of the Center for Children's Books, May, 1982.
New York Times Book Review, May 17, 1987.*

*   *   *

LEVINE, Evan 1962-

PERSONAL: Born June 15, 1962, in Chicago, IL; daughter of Paul (in consulting) and Phyllis (a museum publicity director; maiden name, Zelkind) Levine; married Robert Levy (an editor and poet), December 2, 1991. *Education:* Swarthmore College, B.A., 1984; New York University, M.A., 1990.

ADDRESSES: Home—New York, NY.

CAREER: Marymount Manhattan College, New York City, instructor in adult education, 1990—. Teacher of private writing workshops, 1991—; administrator of children's writing workshops, 1991—. Metropolitan Museum of Art, developer and writer of children's material.

MEMBER: Society of Children's Book Writers and Illustrators.

AWARDS, HONORS: Not the Piano, Mrs. Medley was a 1991 *Booklist* Editor's Choice.

WRITINGS:

Not the Piano, Mrs. Medley, Orchard, 1991.
What's Black and White and Came to Visit?, Orchard, in press.

Author of column "Guide to Children's Television," syndicated by United Features. Reviewer of videos for children.

WORK IN PROGRESS: A new picture book.

SIDELIGHTS: Evan Levine told *SATA:* "I've always loved children's books, and I still read them—probably more than I read books for adults! I keep notes, journals, funny lines—I write everything down, figuring I'll use it some time. I had a wonderful teacher in graduate school, Paula Fox (who is also a children's book author), who encouraged me to pursue writing. I love to write about small moments, everyday things that somehow get wildly out of control. I also take to heart something that Jim Henson, creator of the Muppets, once told me. I was interviewing him for an article and he told me he worked on things that made *him* laugh—figuring that if he did, then other people, including kids, would too. I always try to remember that when I write; to create what I think is funny, or touching, or wonderful.

"I write, in one sense, to 'give something back,' because I've gotten so much pleasure from reading children's books. I also write because I love the freedom, the pure silliness, and the sense of fun that you have when writing a children's book in combination with the intense need for detail and precision; every word counts.

Evan Levine uses humor and wordplay to describe an adventure-filled day at the beach where getting there is half the fun. (Cover illustration by S. D. Schindler.)

"I also write, as most writers do, from my own experiences; the things that happened to me as a kid. I then mold and shape these elements until they become stories.

"I love books that are quirky and a little offbeat. Some of my favorite children's authors are Russell Hoban, William Steig, and Charlotte Zolotow. When I was young, I considered 'Bread and Jam for Frances' to be up there with Shakespeare. In some ways, I think I still do!"

*   *   *

LINGARD, Joan 1932-

PERSONAL: Born 1932, in Edinburgh, Scotland; married first husband, c. 1954 (divorced, 1970); married second husband, Martin, c. 1972; children: (first marriage) Kersten, Bridget, Jenny. *Education:* Moray House Training College, general teaching diploma, c. 1954.

ADDRESSES: Home—72 Great King St., Edinburgh EH3 6QU, Scotland. *Agent*—c/o David Higham Associates, 5-8 Lower John St., London W1R 4HA, England.

CAREER: Teacher from the mid-1950s to the mid-1960s; writer, 1963—.

WRITINGS:

JUVENILE

Frying as Usual, illustrated by Priscilla Clive, Hamish Hamilton, 1973.
Snake among the Sunflowers, Thomas Nelson, 1977.
The Gooseberry, Hamish Hamilton, 1978, published in United States as *Odd Girl Out,* Elsevier/Nelson Books, 1979.
The File on Fraulein Berg, Elsevier/Nelson Books, 1980.
Strangers in the House, Hamish Hamilton, 1981, Dutton, 1983.
The Winter Visitor, Hamish Hamilton, 1983.
The Freedom Machine, Hamish Hamilton, 1986.
The Guilty Party, Hamish Hamilton, 1987.
Rags and Riches, Hamish Hamilton, 1988.
Tug of War, Dutton, 1990.
Between Two Worlds, Dutton, 1991.
Hands off Our School!, illustrated by Mairi Hedderwick, Hamish Hamilton, 1993.

"SADIE AND KEVIN" SERIES

The Twelfth Day of July, Hamish Hamilton, 1970, Thomas Nelson, 1972.
Across the Barricades, Hamish Hamilton, 1972, Thomas Nelson, 1973.
Into Exile, Thomas Nelson, 1973.
A Proper Place, Thomas Nelson, 1975.
Hostages to Fortune, Hamish Hamilton, 1976, Thomas Nelson, 1977.

"MAGGIE" SERIES

The Clearance, Thomas Nelson, 1974.
The Resettling, Thomas Nelson, 1975.
The Pilgrimage, Thomas Nelson, 1976.

JOAN LINGARD

The Reunion, Hamish Hamilton, 1977, Thomas Nelson, 1978.

FOR ADULTS

Liam's Daughter, Hodder & Stoughton, 1963.
The Prevailing Wind, Hodder & Stoughton, 1964.
The Tide Comes In, Hodder & Stoughton, 1966.
The Headmaster, Hodder & Stoughton, 1967.
A Sort of Freedom, Hodder & Stoughton, 1969.
The Lord on Our Side, Hodder & Stoughton, 1970.
The Second Flowering of Emily Mountjoy, Paul Harris (Edinburgh), 1979, St. Martin's, 1980.
Greenyards, Putnam, 1981.
Sisters by Rite, St. Martin's, 1984.
Reasonable Doubts, Hamish Hamilton, 1986.
The Women's House, St. Martin's, 1989.

Also author of television scripts for Scottish television and British Broadcasting Corp., including "The Sandyford Place Mystery" and "A Kiss, A Fond Embrace," from the novel *Square Mile of Murder* by Jack House, 1980; *Her Mother's House,* 1982.

ADAPTATIONS: The "Maggie" books were adapted as a serial for BBC television.

SIDELIGHTS: Joan Lingard has been writing books for children since 1970. She is perhaps best known for two series of books for young adults—the "Sadie and Kevin" books, centering on the conflict in Northern Ireland, and the "Maggie" books, about a working-class Scottish girl. Lingard explained in her essay for *Something about the Author Autobiography Series (SAAS):* "I am interested in characters caught at a point of social or historical change."

"I was born in a taxi cab in the Royal Mile of Edinburgh," Lingard revealed in *SAAS.* "My mother was a shy woman who didn't like to make a fuss. No doubt she had left it too late to get to the hospital." Early in her life, Lingard moved with her family to Belfast, Northern Ireland, where she lived until she was eighteen. Following her mother's example, the author took a neutral view of the religious conflicts in the city. She recalled in her autobiographical essay that her mother "did not care which religion people were, perhaps because of having been brought up in Edinburgh, and she certainly had no prejudice against Catholics. She believed that one should love thy neighbour.... We ourselves were considered a bit odd though, for we weren't Presbyterian or Church of Ireland or Methodist like most of the other neighbours. We were Christian Scientists, the Mother church of which was in Boston, Massachusetts."

Lingard "was crazy about books as a child," she reminisced in *SAAS*. "I read and read and read—school stories, adventure novels, *Grimms' Fairy Tales, The Wind in the Willows, Alice in Wonderland, Little Women, Anne of Green Gables,* anything I could get my hands on.... One day when I was fed up and had nothing to read and all my friends had gone on madly exciting expeditions (or so I imagined), I moaned loud and long in my mother's ear ... until she turned round and said, 'Why don't you go and write a book of your own?' Write a book of my own? That didn't seem such a bad idea." The story Lingard came up with was about a girl named Gail who helped capture some smugglers while on a visit to her grandmother in southwest England. She admitted in her autobiographical essay: "In this there are strong echoes of an English children's writer called Enid Blyton whose books I was hooked on at that time. She wrote strong stories with lots of action but her characters tended to be like cardboard cutouts."

After that beginning, Lingard became hooked on writing. She declared in *SAAS* that "from then on I wanted to be a writer and nothing else." She continued writing during her teenage years, placing her stories in exotic settings such as Brazil, because she thought that her home in Belfast was too dull to use. Lingard's writing was disrupted, however, by the death of her mother from cancer. After this event, Lingard was shuffled about, living first with her older sister's family in Glasgow, Scotland, then following her father's career move to Portsmouth, England. When she and her father returned to Belfast, she got a teaching job, despite the fact that she was only sixteen. She explained in her autobiographical essay: "In the years following the war, teachers were scarce and almost anyone with a senior school certificate could find employment teaching."

Lingard was assigned to a poor area of Belfast, to an overcrowded school in bad condition. Her pupils were more often than not ragged and sick. She noted wistfully in *SAAS*: "I liked the children but when the school year ended I decided that teaching was not for me. I was too young to cope emotionally with the needs of children such as those." She went to work in a bank until she moved with her father to Edinburgh, where eventually she decided to try teaching again and enrolled in the city's teacher training college.

Shortly after graduating, Lingard married for the first time and began teaching near her husband's home in the Scottish village of Temple; she also began to write again (though her first book was not accepted for publication until 1961). After some time had passed, Lingard quit teaching. She recalled in *SAAS* that when her first marriage broke up in 1970, "it seemed to me that I had two choices: either to go back to teaching or else to try to write for a more lucrative market, like television. I chose the latter. A producer for Scottish Television had approached me and asked if I would like to try writing for a soap opera called *High Living*." Lingard agreed, but also kept working on her own fiction.

Eventually, Lingard began work on *The Twelfth Day of July*. She noted in her autobiographical essay: "I decided to take a Protestant girl, Sadie Jackson, aged thirteen, and give her a brother, Tommy, one year older; and to balance them I created Kevin McCoy, aged fourteen and Catholic, and gave him a sister, Brede, one year younger. I wanted my protagonists to be evenly matched. My aim was to write a book that would show no bias towards one side or the other." The result was very successful, and the sequel, *Across the Barricades,* became Lingard's most popular book. As she concluded in *SAAS*: "In the end I stayed with Sadie and Kevin for five books and for seven years of their lives. They are aged twenty and twenty-one at the end of *Hostages to Fortune.*"

A reviewer for *Times Literary Supplement* called *The Twelfth Day of July* " a good and important book," whose story " is told with admirable impartiality and with a realism children will appreciate." "The family backgrounds are as vivid as ever, and ... the ending is an honest one," noted another *Times Literary Supplement* contributor of *Across the Barricades.* And a *School Library Journal* critic praised *Hostages to Fortune* for rendering "characters and backgrounds economically and well."

Lingard continued to write for a young audience audience for almost a decade. She interspersed books about Sadie and Kevin with books about Maggie, her popular Scottish heroine. In 1979, however, Lingard published an adult novel entitled *The Second Flowering of Emily Mountjoy;* since then she has been alternating between juvenile and adult audiences. Her later books for young people include *The Guilty Party,* inspired in part by her daughter Jenny's activism in the antinuclear movement, and *Between Two Worlds.*

WORKS CITED:

Review of *Hostages to Fortune, School Library Journal,* September, 1977, p. 146.

Lingard, Joan, essay in *Something about the Author Autobiography Series,* Volume 5, Gale, 1988, pp. 223-36.

Review of *Across the Barricades, Times Literary Supplement,* July 14, 1972, p. 803.

Review of *The Twelfth Day of July, Times Literary Supplement,* December 11, 1970, p. 1457.

FOR MORE INFORMATION SEE:

BOOKS

Twentieth-Century Children's Writers, edited by Tracy Chevaliar, 3rd edition, St. James Press, 1989.

PERIODICALS

Library Journal, July, 1973, p. 2202.
Times Educational Supplement, August 12, 1983, p.16.
Times Literary Supplement, December 2, 1977, p. 1415.*

*   *   *

LITTLEDALE, Freya (Lota Brown) 1929-1992

PERSONAL: Born in 1929 in New York, NY; died August 5, 1992; daughter of David Milton (a pianist) and Dorothy (a teacher; maiden name, Passloff) Brown; married Harold Aylmer Littledale (an editor and author; divorced March, 1979); children: Glenn David. *Education:* Ithaca College, B.S., 1951; attended New York University for graduate study, 1952.

ADDRESSES: Agent—Curtis Brown Ltd., 10 Astor Pl., New York, NY 10003.

CAREER: English teacher in Willsboro, New York, public schools, 1952-53; *South Shore Record,* Woodmere, NY, editor, 1953-55; Maco Magazine Corp., New York City, associate editor, 1960-61; Rutledge Books and Ridge Press, New York City, associate editor, 1961-62; Parents' Magazine Press, New York City, juvenile

FREYA LITTLEDALE

book editor, 1962-65; free-lance writer and editor, 1965-1992. Adjunct professor, Fairfield University, 1984 and 1986-91.

MEMBER: PEN, Society of Children's Book Writers and Illustrators, Authors Guild, Authors League of America.

AWARDS, HONORS: The Magic Fish was an International Reading Association (IRA) Children's Choice Selection in 1985; *The Little Mermaid* was named to the Children's Book Council/IRA Liaison Committee's Seventy Favorite Paperbacks of 1986 list.

WRITINGS:

ADAPTER

The Magic Fish: The Fisherman and His Wife (picture book), illustrated by Ed Arno, Scholastic Book Services, 1967, revised edition with cassette, illustrated by Winslow P. Pels, Scholastic, Inc., 1985.
King Fox, and Other Old Tales, illustrated by Robert Andrew Parker, Doubleday, 1971.
The Elves and the Shoemaker (picture book), illustrated by Brinton Turkle, Four Winds, 1975.
The Snow Child (picture book), illustrated by Leon Shtainmets, Scholastic Book Services, 1978, revised edition, Scholastic, Inc., 1989.
Pinocchio, Scholastic Book Services, 1979.
Snow White and the Seven Dwarfs (picture book), illustrated by Susan Jeffers, Four Winds, 1980.
The Magic Plum Tree (picture book; based on a tale from *The Jataka*), illustrated by Enrico Arno, Crown, 1981.
The Wizard of Oz, Scholastic, Inc., 1982.
The Sleeping Beauty (picture book), Scholastic, Inc., 1984.
The Little Mermaid (picture book), illustrated by Daniel San Souci, Scholastic, Inc., 1986.
The Farmer in the Soup (picture book), illustrated by Molly Delaney, Scholastic, Inc., 1987.
The Twelve Dancing Princesses (picture book), Scholastic, Inc., 1988.
Peter and the North Wind (picture book), illustrated by Troy Howell, Scholastic, Inc., 1988.
King Midas and the Golden Touch, Scholastic, Inc., 1989.
Rip Van Winkle, illustrated by Michael Dooling, Scholastic, Inc., 1991.
The Legend of Sleepy Hollow, Scholastic, Inc., 1992.

Also adapter of *Frankenstein* (picture book), 1983.

PICTURE BOOKS

(With husband, Harold Littledale) *Timothy's Forest,* illustrated by Rosalie Lehrman, Lion Press, 1969.
The Magic Tablecloth, the Magic Goat, and the Hitting Stick, Scholastic Book Services, 1972.
The Boy Who Cried Wolf, Scholastic Book Services, 1975.
Seven at One Blow, Scholastic Book Services, 1976, revised edition published as *The Brave Little Tailor,* Scholastic, Inc., 1990.

PLAYS

Stop That Pancake!, Scholastic Book Services, 1975.
The King and Queen Who Wouldn't Speak, Scholastic Book Services, 1975.
The Giant's Garden, Scholastic Book Services, 1975.
The Magic Piper, Scholastic Book Services, 1978.

EDITOR

Grimms' Fairy Tales, Parents' Magazine Press, 1964.
Fairy Tales by Hans Christian Andersen, Parents' Magazine Press, 1964.
A Treasure Chest of Poetry, Parents' Magazine Press, 1964.
Andersen's Fairy Tales, illustrated by John Fernie, Scholastic Book Services, 1966.
Thirteen Ghostly Tales, Scholastic Book Services, 1966.
Ghosts and Spirits of Many Lands, illustrated by Stefan Martin, Doubleday, 1970, illustrated by Alexy Pendle, Deutsch, 1973.
Strange Tales from Many Lands, illustrated by Mila Lazarevich, Doubleday, 1975, illustrated by Pendle, Deutsch, 1977.

Also editor of *Aesop's Fables,* 1964, and *Stories of Ghosts, Witches, and Demons,* 1972.

In this story based on a Buddhist fable, three princes learn about nature by looking at a "magical" plum tree. (Cover illustration by Enrico Arno.)

OTHER

I Was Thinking (poems), illustrated by Leonard Kessler, Greenwillow, 1979.

Contributor to anthologies, including *The Scribner Anthology for Young People,* Scribner, 1976, *This Way to Books,* H. W. Wilson, 1981, and *A New Treasury of Children's Poetry,* Doubleday, 1984. Author of elementary school instructional materials for Silver Burdett. Contributor to Rand McNally's "Look and Do" series, Laidlaw Reading Program, Scott Foresman Reading Systems, and Science Research Associates Reading Laboratory. Contributor to periodicals, including *Humpty Dumpty.* Editorial consultant, Arrow Book Club Division of Scholastic Book Services, 1967.

SIDELIGHTS: Whether writing her own children's books and poems, adapting the stories of other authors, or compiling collections of legend and folklore, Freya Littledale strove to make her writings accessible to beginning readers. Critics often cited her clean, spare writing style and the elegant simplicity of her retellings and acknowledged the faithfulness her versions maintain to the original sources. Littledale selected the material for her adaptations from a wide variety of literature, including tales from Norse legend and Norwegian folklore. Her recasting of a tale from Buddhist literature, *The Magic Plum Tree,* relates the story of three princes whose father takes each of them to see a plum tree several months apart. The appearance of the tree in different seasons makes each of the boys form his own idea of the tree, and their father's point is only discovered upon a fourth, joint trip to see the tree when it is heavy with fruit. In *School Library Journal,* Patricia Dooley recommended the book, feeling that young readers would benefit from the "lesson in the 'magic' of nature, and in the deeper question of identity."

WORKS CITED:

School Library Journal, September, 1981, p. 111.*

*   *   *

LONDON, Jonathan (Paul) 1947-
(Jonathan Sherwood)

PERSONAL: Born March 11, 1947, in Brooklyn, NY; son of Harry and Anne (Sittenreich) London; married first wife, JoAnn (divorced May, 1974); married Maureen Weisenberger (a registered nurse), March 21, 1976; children: (second marriage) Aaron, Sean. *Education:* San Jose State University, B.A., 1969, M.A., 1970; Sonoma State University, teaching certificate for grades K-12, 1985. *Hobbies and other interests:* Hiking, backpacking, kayaking, cross-country skiing.

ADDRESSES: Home and office—P.O. Box 537, Graton, CA 95444. *Agent*—Barbara Kouts, P.O. Box 558, Bellport, NY 11713.

CAREER: Free-lance laborer, dancer, child counselor, display installer, 1979—; children's writer, 1989—.

American Booksellers Association, panelist for the Children's Book Council, 1993.

MEMBER: Amnesty International, Wilderness Society.

AWARDS, HONORS: Ina Coolbrith Circle Award for Poetry, 1979; Parent-Teacher Association (PTA) scholarship, 1984; *Froggy Gets Dressed, The Owl Who Became the Moon,* and *Into This Night We Are Rising* were named Book-of-the-Month Club main selections; *Froggy Gets Dressed* was named a "New Book of Merit" by *Five Owls,* 1993; *Thirteen Moons on Turtle's Back* was named a "Reading Rainbow" book, 1993.

WRITINGS:

(With Joseph Bruchac) *Thirteen Moons on Turtle's Back: A Native American Year of Moons,* illustrated by Thomas Locker, Philomel Books, 1992.

The Lion Who Had Asthma, illustrated by Nadine Bernard Westcott, Albert Whitman, 1992.

Froggy Gets Dressed, illustrated by Frank Remkiewicz, Viking, 1992.

Gray Fox, illustrated by Robert Sauber, Viking, 1993.

(With Lanny Pinola) *Fire Race: A Karuk Coyote Tale,* illustrated by Sylvia Lang, Chronicle Books, 1993.

The Owl Who Became the Moon, illustrated by Ted Rand, Dutton, 1993.

Into This Night We Are Rising, illustrated by G. Brian Karas, Viking, 1993.

Voices of the Wild, illustrated by Wayne McCloughlin, Crown, 1993.

The Eyes of Gray Wolf, illustrated by Jon Van Zyles, Chronicle Books, 1993.

Hip Cat (picture book), illustrated by Woodleigh Hubbard, Chronicle Books, 1993.

Contributor of poems and short stories to periodicals, including *Cricket, Us Kids, Child Life,* and *Short Story International.* Also author of works under the pseudonym Jonathan Sherwood, including *Painting the Fire.*

WORK IN PROGRESS: Where's Home?, a young adult novel for Dutton; *The Lost Cabin,* a middle-grade chapter book; *Lipbad and the Snow Bunny* and *Honey Paw and Lightfoot,* two picture books for Chronicle Books.

SIDELIGHTS: Since embarking on his career as a children's writer in 1989, Jonathan London has penned such works as *The Lion Who Had Asthma, Froggy Gets Dressed,* and *Thirteen Moons on Turtle's Back: A Native American Year of Moons.* The first title revolves around Sean, a youngster who suffers from asthma, a physical condition which causes difficulty in breathing. Using his imagination, Sean pretends he is a lion, until he is beset by a coughing attack. Medicine given by his parents restores his breathing, and he is able to continue his imaginative play. The second story, *Froggy Gets Dressed,* relates a comical tale of a young frog who is so intent on going outside to play in the snow that he forgets to wear necessary clothing like long underwear and a coat. The reader "will surely laugh out loud over this addled amphibian's constant undressing and dress-

JONATHAN LONDON

ing," declared a reviewer for *Publishers Weekly.* The third work, cowritten with Joseph Bruchac and entitled *Thirteen Moons on Turtle's Back,* is based on a Native American legend that states that the thirteen scales Old Turtle carries on his back symbolize the thirteen phases of the moon. In their narrative, the authors offer thirteen chronologically arranged stories that both explain each cycle of the moon and relate its particular Native American tale. *Thirteen Moons* "is an exemplary introduction to Native American culture with its emphasis on the importance of nature," concluded a *Publishers Weekly* critic.

Among London's other works for children is his 1993 title *The Owl Who Became the Moon.* Told in verse, the tale follows a train's nighttime journey as it is imagined by a young boy lying in his bed. As the train travels through a snowy forest, it is joined by an owl, who steals glances at such animals as a cougar, bunnies, and a bear as they prepare for sleep. The work was well received by reviewers, who especially praised London's use of language. "This poet's talent shines through the spare, lyrical text," wrote *School Library Journal* contributor Marianne Saccardi. "With spare elegance," decided a reviewer for *Publishers Weekly,* "London celebrates both the beauty of nighttime ... and the power of the train."

London told *SATA:* "I've been writing for more than twenty years, but I didn't start writing for children until 1989. Though I studied for a master's degree in social sciences, I found that the language of poetry spoke more clearly to my heart, my emotional needs, and what I cared most about. After completing my master's, I spent several years traveling around the world, meeting people of different cultures, and writing poems. Gradually, the goal of become a 'writer' took root and didn't let go.

FIRE RACE
A Karuk Coyote Tale

retold by Jonathan London
illustrated by Sylvia Long

In his adaptation of Kurak legend, London tells the story of Wise Old Coyote and his plan to bring fire to the animal people. (Cover illustration by Sylvia Long.)

"I turned to writing for children late—perhaps because my wife and I waited and had our two sons late (in my late thirties). I told them stories, both to put them to sleep and to wake them up. *The Owl Who Became the Moon,* my first book written for children (though it is my sixth to appear), is a bedtime fantasy I told my younger son, Sean, when he was two. Other book ideas have emerged from experiences I've had, and some are from dreams. *Gray Fox* is based on my own experience finding a fox, dead but still warm and not yet rigid, in the middle of the road, laid out across the median. Such powerful experiences make for powerful literature, when the right words can be found to express the emotions simply, yet evocatively. In the case of *Thirteen Moons on Turtle's Back: A Native American Year of Moons,* coauthored with Joseph Bruchac, the idea for the book

emerged from a dream about 'the moon of joyful roundness' and 'the moon of hazy sorrow.' The dream-moons made me think about some of the traditional Native American names for moons, such as 'The Moon When Wolves Run Together,' a Lakota Sioux moon for the month of December, and their stories.

"But I don't like to be limited by experience or dreams. I catch words and ideas that seem to fly through the air. 'Hip cat,' those two words, became a story because I heard those words as a child might: soon I had a story in mind about a cat who plays the saxophone and wants to become a jazz musician. In much the same way *Froggy Gets Dressed* sprang out of the air when my son Aaron asked me to tell him and Sean a story. The image of a frog dressing in winter clothes so he can play in the snow struck my funny bone—and my kids' funny bones, too! So you see, there are worlds of possibilities living within your imagination from which you can create stories that can make someone want to cry or laugh, play a saxophone, or make a snowman. This act of writing, for me, is a part of my celebration of life, a way to give back a little for all that I have been given."

WORKS CITED:

Review of *Froggy Gets Dressed, Publishers Weekly,* August 3, 1992, p. 70.
Review of *The Owl Who Became the Moon, Publishers Weekly,* December 28, 1992.
Review of *Thirteen Moons on Turtle's Back: A Native American Year of Moons, Publishers Weekly,* February 10, 1992.
Saccardi, Marianne, review of *The Owl Who Became the Moon, School Library Journal,* February, 1993, p. 76.

FOR MORE INFORMATION SEE:

PERIODICALS

Booklist, March 1, 1992; January 15, 1993, p. 922.
Bulletin of the Center for Children's Books, February, 1993, p. 183.
Five Owls, January/February, 1993, p. 59.
Kirkus Reviews, January 15, 1992.

*   *   *

LOWERY, Linda 1949-

PERSONAL: Full name is Linda Lowery Keep; born June 16, 1949, in Chicago, IL; married Richard Cleminson Keep (an artist and teacher), August 12, 1988; children: Kristopher Truelsen. *Education:* DePaul University, B.A. (magna cum laude), 1971. *Politics:* "I vote for candidates sincerely committed to children, equality, and the earth." *Hobbies and other interests:* Hiking, climbing, playing flute, collecting angels, gardening, painting.

ADDRESSES: Home—P.O. Box 1543, Nederland, CO 80466.

CAREER: Worked variously as flight attendant for TransWorld Airlines, French teacher in Williams Bay, WI, assistant in Bozo's Circus, Chicago, IL, and travel consultant; writer, 1983—. Children's Court Advisory Board, chairperson, 1990-91; advocate for crime victims in district attorney's office in Boulder, CO.

MEMBER: Society of Children's Book Writers and Illustrators, Authors Guild.

WRITINGS:

Secret Sorceress, TSR, 1983.
Spell of the Winter Wizard, TSR, 1983.
Moon Dragon Summer, TSR, 1984.
The Star Snatchers, TSR, 1985.
The Maze and the Magic Dragon, TSR, 1985.

Martin Luther King Day (Scholastic Book Club selection), illustrations by Hetty Mitchell, Carolrhoda, 1987.
Earth Day, illustrations by Mary Bergherr, foreword by Gaylord Nelson, Carolrhoda, 1991.
(With Marybeth Lorbiecki) *Earthwise at Play,* illustrations by David Mataya, Carolrhoda, 1992.
(With Lorbiecki) *Earthwise at Home,* illustrations by Mataya, Carolrhoda, 1992.
(With Lorbiecki) *Earthwise at School,* Carolrhoda, 1992.
(With Betty Botts) *Earthwise Teachers' Guide,* Carolrhoda, 1993.
Laurie Tells, Carolrhoda, in press.
Dance Dance Dance (picture book), Ticknor & Fields, in press.

Contributor to periodicals. *Martin Luther King Day* was recorded on audiocassette and released by Live Oak Media, 1987.

WORK IN PROGRESS: Hildegard's Stubborn Garden, a picture book with illustrations by Lowery; "Sky-Bridge Adventures," a star-travel fantasy series for ages ten to twelve.

SIDELIGHTS: Linda Lowery told *SATA:* "Ever since I was in second grade, I wrote my thoughts and feelings in diaries, and I wrote poems. A lot of these writings were about treatment of children. I wanted life to be fair, and I saw very early that life is often unfair, especially for kids. Even when I was growing up, I was extremely aware of kids who were left out because they were a different color from most of us, or because their English wasn't very good, or because they had ideas that were

LINDA LOWERY

Lowery explores the history of Earth Day and gives young readers tips on what they can do to protect the planet in this 1991 book. (Cover illustration by Mary Bergherr.)

considered weird. I also wrote about beautiful things I saw in nature. I had a favorite tree in a prairie near my house, and I sat in that tree and made up poems about the seasons and the wildflowers and the snowflakes, and later I'd go home and write them down. I was very secretive about the things I wrote because it seemed sometimes that my view of life was very different from everybody else's, and I didn't want to be criticized. I wrote in my bedroom closet, I wrote under the dining room table, I wrote in corner chairs of the library.

"Once when I was in fourth grade I had a poem called 'Seasons' published in *Hi* magazine for kids. It was the most exciting thing that had ever happened to me. They paid me a dollar for the poem. Still, I thought you had to be a special kind of person to be an author, very talented and artsy and certainly not like me. I didn't think I was creative at all, so I never even considered trying to work as a writer when I graduated from college. Instead I had a lot of different jobs. All the time I was working these other jobs, I kept writing down poems or thoughts or stories I'd make up. In 1982, after I filled so many notebooks I didn't know what to do with them anymore, I sent some writing to a magazine. It was published. I was as excited as I'd been when my poem was published in fourth grade, so I decided to keep it up. Now I make my living as a writer.

"If there is anything I want to give children through my books, it is hope. There are so many wonderful, powerful people who have worked hard to make this planet a better place. They see prejudice and pain and injustice, and they decide to take steps to make a difference. Change didn't come easily for Martin Luther King, Jr., or for any of those people who have made a difference. It doesn't come easily for any of us, but there is always hope that we will find a way to make it better.

"I believe that children are very powerful. Just look at what kids have done to turn around environmental problems. When I was researching the 'Earthwise' books, the monumental changes I learned that children worldwide have made absolutely staggered me. My coauthor and I would call each other and say: 'Listen to this story about kids who convinced the chairman of the tuna company to stop killing dolphins,' or 'You won't believe this group of fourth graders who actually saved an entire species of wildflower.' We were constantly coming up with stories of amazing and powerful kids.

"I always have several projects going at once—I keep more balanced that way. And I write in my journal every day. I don't write exactly what's going on that particular day. Instead, I try to dig down into my soul and see what's there. It's kind of like taking a flashlight into the deepest place I can find and illuminating it. Doing this makes me see more clearly what I'm feeling inside and often gives me the idea for my next book. I was writing in my notebook in the fall of 1991 when suddenly I started a rhyme: 'Dance with your neighbors, uncles and aunts. Rhumba—if you wanna—in your underpants.' I was tired of being so serious, I realized, and I just wanted to write about something fun—dancing. I kept with it, and after a few weeks I'd written my first picture book: *Dance Dance Dance*.

"I also use my dreams for direction and inspiration. I remember in 1989 when I wanted to write something about caring for the earth. For several weeks I struggled with poems and notes and ideas. I wasn't sure what kind of book would best fit what I wanted to express. Then one morning I woke up and immediately wrote down the first two pages of *Earth Day*. The words had appeared in my dream, spelled out perfectly, just as if they were already in a book. That was it! I wanted to write about how Earth Day got started. Who made it happen? How did it become so successful? Has it made a difference worldwide? So from the seed that started in my dream I began my research and wrote the book."

M

MAGUIRE, Jack 1945-

PERSONAL: Born July 7, 1945, in Columbus, OH; son of John Edward (a carnival worker) and Becky (a teacher; maiden name, Wilson) Maguire. *Education:* Columbia College, B.A., 1967; Boston University, M.A., 1970.

ADDRESSES: Home and office—17 South Chodikee Lake Rd., Highland, NY 12528. *Agent*—Faith Hamlin, Sanford J. Greenburger Associates, 55 Fifth Ave., Fifteenth Floor, New York, NY 10003.

CAREER: Writer and storyteller.

WRITINGS:

"THE MANY LIVES OF UNDERFOOT THE CAT" SERIES

Trouble and More Trouble, Pocket Books, 1990.
Hit the Road and Strike it Rich, Pocket Books, 1991.
Surprise and Double Surprise, Pocket Books, 1991.

OTHER

Creative Storytelling: Choosing, Inventing, and Sharing Tales for Children, McGraw, 1985, revised edition, Yellow Moon, 1991.
What Does Childhood Taste Like?, Morrow, 1986.
Kid's Rooms, HP Books, 1987.
Hopscotch, Hangman, Hot Potato, and Ha Ha Ha: A Rulebook of Children's Games, Prentice-Hall, 1990.
(With Philadelphia Child Guidance Center) *Your Child's Emotional Health,* Macmillan, 1993.

*　　*　　*

MAINE, Trevor
See CATHERALL, Arthur

*　　*　　*

MANTINBAND, Gerda (B.) 1917-

PERSONAL: Born July 19, 1917, in Germany; daughter of Georg Boehm and Helene Weltmann; married James H. Mantinband (a college professor), 1946; children: Susan H. Heffer, Margaret J. *Education:* Brooklyn College of the City University of New York, B.A. (summa cum laude), 1965.

ADDRESSES: Home—2090 Grape Ave., Boulder, CO 80304.

CAREER: Writer. Teacher of early childhood classes; puppeteer performing in schools, nursing homes, and libraries, Boulder, CO, 1981—. Also worked as a nurse in a British children's hospital.

GERDA MANTINBAND

WRITINGS:

FOR CHILDREN

Bing, Bang, Bong, and Fiddle-Dee-Dee, Doubleday, 1979.

Papa and Mama Biederbeek, Houghton Mifflin, 1983.

The Blabbermouths, illustrated by Paul Borovsky, Greenwillow, 1992.

(Editor) *Three Clever Mice,* illustrated by Martine Gourbault, Greenwillow, 1993.

OTHER

Contributor of articles and stories to periodicals.

WORK IN PROGRESS: The Whirling Dervish, a picture book for HarperCollins; a mystery novel for adults; a fantasy story for children; more picture books.

SIDELIGHTS: Gerda Mantinband told *SATA:* "I fell in love with picture books while I was teaching. I wrote a couple of stories and articles that were published in magazines in England when I was a nurse at a children's hospital during World War II. After a long hiatus (because of work and children), I started writing again in the 1970s. I write because I like to write (I love words and language) and I write for children because I like children and hope to amuse them. Also, my writing addresses the child in me."

FOR MORE INFORMATION SEE:

PERIODICALS

Bulletin of the Center for Children's Books, September, 1992.

Horn Book, July/August, 1992.

School Library Journal, August, 1992.

*   *   *

MAZZIO, Joann 1926-

PERSONAL: Born October 3, 1926, in Clarksburg, WV; daughter of Walt G. (a painting contractor) and Lillian (a teacher; maiden name, Dobbins) Berry; children: James, Lee. *Education:* Attended West Virginia Wesleyan College, 1943-45; West Virginia University, B.S., 1948; University of New Mexico, M.A., 1973. *Politics:* Democrat. *Religion:* Atheist. *Hobbies and other interests:* Reading, travel, hiking, and camping.

ADDRESSES: Home and office—P. O. Box 53106, Pinos Altos, NM 88053.

CAREER: Writer. National Advisory Committee for Aeronautics (now known as National Aeronautics and Space Agency [NASA]), Langley Aeronautical Laboratory, Langley, VA, engineer, 1948-50, Washington, DC, 1950-52; Air Force Special Weapons Lab, Kirtland Air Force Base, Albequerque, NM, engineer, 1952-54; Sandia Labs, Albuquerque, NM, engineer, bibliographer, and editor, 1969-72; math teacher for Los Lunas Consolidated Schools, Los Lunas, NM, 1972-74, Las Cruces Public Schools, Las Cruces, NM, 1974-85, and Cobre Consolidated Schools, Bayard, NM, 1985-88.

Consultant to technical libraries, 1960-69. Presenter of educational workshops.

MEMBER: Authors Guild, National Education Association, Society of Children's Book Writers, Southwest Writers Workshop.

AWARDS, HONORS: Educational grants, National Foundation of Science, 1973 and 1980; fellowships, New Mexico Petroleum and Mining Association, 1978-79, and National Endowment for the Humanities, 1985; participant, NASA Summer Teacher Enhancement Program, 1987.

WRITINGS:

YOUNG ADULT NOVELS

The One Who Came Back, Houghton, 1992.

Leaving Eldorado, Houghton, 1993.

WORK IN PROGRESS: A contemporary novel for young adults and a middle-grade chapter book.

SIDELIGHTS: Joann Mazzio told *SATA:* "When I was a kid, it was taken for granted that I would be a writer. 'Here's another story for your book,' my mother would say as we scrambled from the bears that invaded our picnic. When I got to my teens, I had a lot of other things I had to prove first, [before I started writing]. I had to prove that girls were as smart as boys, so I got a degree and worked in engineering. Then I had to prove (even though no one was watching) that I was as good as any other woman, so I married and had two children.

JOANN MAZZIO

"When I was in my forties, I began to realize that my life was finite so I did some summing up. My job was with an agency that dealt in death and destruction. I decided I wanted to work in a field that would be life-affirming and constructive.

"What else but teaching? As I enjoyed fifteen years of teaching math, I learned more and more about young people and the way they looked at the world. A story began to shape in my head. I knew what the characters would look like and what they would say. But I didn't know how to write a book.

"After I studied books about writing, I read thirty to forty contemporary young adult novels and was excited by the excellence of many. They gave me a standard to shoot for. I wrote and rewrote *The One Who Came Back*. My very first full-length book was accepted for publication by Matilda Welty, editor at Houghton Mifflin. I had done it. I had written a book for kids about teenagers who don't fit in, the kind who have to draw on their own resources and depend on each other for support and encouragement.

"My confidence bolstered, I wrote a young adult historical novel set in an old gold-mining town like the one in which I live. My idea came from the grave markers in the old cemetery. Women and children lived short lives. As I began to think how life was for them, I wrote *Leaving Eldorado*.

"I'm now trying to learn how to write a chapter book for middle-grade readers. And I've begun another young adult novel, this one contemporary and dealing with the pressures on young people whose parents want them to aim for careers not compatible with the kids' natures."

*   *   *

McDERMOTT, Gerald (Edward) 1941-

PERSONAL: Born January 31, 1941, in Detroit, MI; married Beverly Brodsky (an artist and illustrator), 1969 (divorced). *Education:* Pratt Institute of Design, B.F.A., 1964.

CAREER: Filmmaker, illustrator, reteller of folktales, author. Graphic designer for public television station, New York City, 1962. Producer and designer of original films, including *The Stonecutter, Anansi the Spider, The Magic Tree,* and *Arrow to the Sun. Exhibitions:* "Film as Art," San Francisco Film Festival, 1966; "Best Short Films," American Film Festival (New York City), 1969; "Contemporary Animated Films," Annecy International Film Festival (France), 1971; "Illustrating Myth and Legend," Everson Museum (Syracuse, NY), 1975; "Illustrating Picture Books," Children's Museum (Indianapolis), 1979; "Best American Animators," Whitney Museum (New York City), 1980.

AWARDS, HONORS: Blue Ribbon, Educational Film Library Association, 1969; Silver Lion, Italian Government, 1970; American Film Festival Blue Ribbon, 1970, for *Anansi the Spider* (film); Caldecott Honor Book,

GERALD McDERMOTT

1973, for *Anansi the Spider;* Honor Book citation, *Boston Globe-Horn Book,* 1973, for *The Magic Tree;* Caldecott Medal, 1975, for *Arrow to the Sun.*

WRITINGS:

RETELLER OF FOLKTALES; SELF-ILLUSTRATED

Anansi the Spider: A Tale from the Ashanti (film adaptation), Holt, 1972.
The Magic Tree: A Tale from the Congo (film adaptation), Holt, 1973.
Arrow to the Sun: A Pueblo Indian Tale, Viking, 1974.
The Stonecutter: A Japanese Folk Tale (film adaptation), Viking, 1975.
The Voyage of Osiris: A Myth of Ancient Egypt, Dutton, 1977.
The Knight of the Lion, Four Winds, 1978.
Papagayo the Mischief Maker, Dutton, 1978.
Sun Flight, Four Winds, 1980.
Daughter of Earth: A Roman Myth, Delacorte, 1984.
Daniel O'Rourke: An Irish Tale, Viking Kestrel, 1986.
Tim O'Toole and the Wee Folk: An Irish Tale, Viking, 1990.
Musicians of the Sun: An Aztec Myth, Delacorte, 1991.
Zomo the Rabbit: A Trickster Tale from West Africa, Harcourt, 1992.
Raven: A Trickster Tale from the Pacific Northwest, Harcourt, 1993.

Arrow to the Sun has been translated into Spanish.

ILLUSTRATOR

Mayer, Marianna, translator and adaptor, *Carlo Collodi's The Adventures of Pinocchio,* Four Winds, 1981.

Mayer, reteller, *Aladdin and the Enchanted Lamp,* Macmillan, 1985.

Mayer, *Alley Oop!,* Holt, 1985.

Mayer, reteller, *The Spirit of the Blue Light,* Macmillan, 1987.

Mayer, *The Brambleberrys Animal Book of Alphabet,* Boyds Mills, 1991.

Mayer, *The Brambleberrys Animal Book of Colors,* Boyds Mills, 1991.

Mayer, *The Brambleberrys Animal Book of Counting,* Boyds Mills, 1991.

Mayer, *The Brambleberrys Animal Book of Shapes,* Boyds Mills, 1991.

Mayer, *Marcel the Pastry Chef,* Bantam, 1991.

SIDELIGHTS: An acclaimed picture-book artist, Gerald McDermott is a noted reteller and illustrator of folktales and myths from around the world. Although he began his career as a successful maker of animated films in the 1960s, McDermott is best known for his innovative picture books, which have earned him prestigious awards such as the Caldecott Medal. Blending modern design techniques, vibrant colors, primitive art traditions, and straightforward narratives, McDermott's books aim to depict complex and archetypal folk symbols of various world cultures. Although some

The folklore and history of the Pueblo Indians of the American Southwest served as the basis for McDermott's self-illustrated work from 1974.

critics describe his work as beyond the scope of children, McDermott believes picture books deserve high artistic standards. "A picture book of artistic integrity will often be the only place where a child can expand his imagination and direct his gaze toward beauty," he remarked in his Caldecott Medal acceptance speech printed in *Horn Book.* "In form and content, the picture book can become an essential element in the child's evolving aesthetic consciousness, and the artist creating a picture book has an opportunity—and a special responsibility—to nurture the development of his young audience's visual perception."

McDermott was born in Detroit, Michigan, where his parents enrolled him at the age of four in classes at the Detroit Institute of Arts. "Every Saturday, from early childhood through early adolescence, was spent in those halls," he stated in *Horn Book.* "I virtually lived in the museum, drawing and painting and coming to know the works of that great collection. I've kept a brush in my hand ever since." McDermott also became interested in films and at the age of nine became a regular actor on "Storytime," a local television program dramatizing folktales and legends. "Working with professional actors and learning how music and sound effects are integrated in a dramatic context were indispensable experiences

Arrow Maker fitted the Boy to his bow and drew it. The Boy flew into the heavens. In this way, the Boy traveled to the sun.

for a future filmmaker," he noted in *Horn Book*. Unable to find suitable film classes, however, McDermott focused his early studies on art and design at Detroit's Cass Technical High School, which offered a special curriculum in Bauhaus principles of design. While in high school, he also experimented with making his own films and gained work experience creating backgrounds for a television animation studio.

After graduating, McDermott received a Scholastic Publications National Scholarship to attend the Pratt Institute in New York City. He also began work as a graphic designer for New York's public television station, Channel 13, and was granted independent credit by Pratt to pursue filmmaking. "I began to experiment with animated films," he stated in *Horn Book*. "My principal goal was to design films that were highly stylized in color and form. I also hoped to touch upon themes not dealt with in conventional cartoons. Instinctively, I turned to folklore as a source for thematic material." McDermott chose the Japanese folktale "The Stonecutter" and developed a method that became his filmmaking trademark. After designing a storyboard, McDermott drew 6,000 frames, each synchronized painstakingly to the notes of a specially composed musical score. "The Stonecutter," as McDermott explained in *Horn Book,* was "an ancient fable of a man's foolish longing for power—a tale of wishes and dreams that can be understood on many levels.... The story contains in microcosm the basic theme of self-transformation that was consciously developed in my later work. While my approach to the graphic design of 'The Stonecutter' was unconventional, traditional animation techniques were used to set the designs in motion."

After completing *The Stonecutter,* McDermott met Joseph Campbell, later the author of *The Power of Myth,* and an authority on the relationship between mythology and psychology. McDermott became profoundly influenced by Campbell's theories of mythology's role in world cultures, and of his view that it functions "to supply the symbols that carry the human spirit forward, 'to waken and give guidance to the energies of life,'" as McDermott summarized in *Horn Book*. With Campbell as his consultant, McDermott began making films that explored the theme of heroic quest in various cultures. From Africa McDermott found material for his next films, *Anansi the Spider* and *The Magic Tree,* and from the Pueblo Indians of the American Southwest, *Arrow to the Sun.* Each tale embodied Campbell's depiction of the classic heroic quest, as restated by McDermott in *Horn Book:* "A hero ventures forth from the world of common day into a region of supernatural wonder: fabulous forces are there encountered and a decisive victory is won: the hero comes back from this mysterious adventure with the power to bestow boons on his fellow man."

In the late 1960s, McDermott moved to southern France to study the techniques of European filmmakers. Before leaving, however, he was offered a multi-volume book contract by American editor George Nicholson to adapt his films into picture books. While in France,

McDermott first focused his energies on producing a book version of his film *Anansi the Spider.* He discovered the difficulties of making the transition from film to the printed page. "This jarring shift from a medium of time to a medium of space posed some special problems," he recounted in *Horn Book*. "There was no longer a captive audience in a darkened room, its gaze fixed upon hypnotic flickering shadows. Gone were the music and sound effects and the ability to guide the viewer through a flow of images with a carefully planned progression. Now the reader was in control. The reader could begin at the end of the book or linger for ten minutes over a page or perhaps merely glance at half a dozen others. As an artist, I was challenged to resolve these problems."

His success was apparent in 1973, when his book version of *Anansi the Spider* was runner-up for the Caldecott Medal. Featuring montage-type illustrations in bold colors, along with native Ashanti art and language patterns, *Anansi the Spider* told the story of a father spider saved from a series of misadventures by his six more responsible sons. "Within each body of the six sons, an abstract symbol represents the individual's particular skill," noted Linda Kauffman Peterson in *Newbery and Caldecott Medal and Honor Books*. "Amid geometric landscapes of magenta, turquoise, emerald, and red, the black figures, readily visible, rock across the pages on angular legs." McDermott followed *Anansi* with a book adaptation of *The Magic Tree: A Tale from the Congo,* and established himself as an innovative, highly stylized illustrator of children's books. "Like the similarly spectacular *Anansi the Spider,*" noted a *Kirkus Reviews* contributor, *The Magic Tree* "is adapted from an animated film and it's difficult not to hear the pulsing jazz music that seems to be visualized on these dynamic, semi-abstract pages, which are distinctly African in patterns and motifs but just as distinctly cinematic in their vibrant color and kinetic energy."

In 1974, McDermott embarked upon his first simultaneous film and book project, *Arrow to the Sun,* which went on to receive the Caldecott Medal. The book adapts the popular legend of a Pueblo Indian boy who journeys to the heavens in pursuit of his cultural heritage. Using limited text and featuring stylized depictions of important Indian symbols—corn, rainbows, and the sun—*Arrow* was an important step in McDermott's own search of the "hero-quest" in world mythologies. "This theme finds its fullest expressions in my book and in my film of *Arrow to the Sun*—with a significant difference," he commented in *Horn Book*. "In previous works, the circle was broken. Through some weakness or failing, or perhaps sheer foolishness, the protagonist fails in his search.... In this Pueblo Indian tale, however, the circle is complete, and the questing hero successfully finishes his journey.... [The Boy's] questing path is the Rainbow Trail—a multihued border motif that appears in the sand paintings, pottery designs, and weaving of the Southwest. It runs through the pages of my book as well; down through the sky to the pueblo, across the earth, blazing up to the sun, framing the drama of the kivas, and bursting forth at the moment of the hero's assimilation to the sun."

Among McDermott's other adaptations of folktales from around the world include a book version of *The Stonecutter; The Voyage of Osiris,* concerning the death and afterlife of an ancient Egyptian god; *Sun Flight,* which retells the ancient Greek myth of Daedalus and Icarus; *Daughter of Earth,* which retells the Roman myth about the origins of spring; *Knight of the Lion,* a black-and-white illustrated adaptation of a King Arthur legend; and two tales from Ireland, *Daniel O'Rourke* and *Tim O'Toole and the Wee Folk.* The illustrations in the 1992 work *Zomo the Rabbit,* a trickster tale adapted from African myth, "masterfully integrate a variety of styles the artist has used in the past," Marilyn Iarusso stated in *School Library Journal.* The critic also lauded the "great good humor" used to create an entertaining story. The result, like the rest of McDermott's works, appeals to adult readers as well as young audiences. "My life and work are inseparably bound up together," McDermott explained to David E. White in *Language Arts.* "If an artist puts himself into his work in the fullest sense—his emotions, his intellect, the symbols from his own psyche—then the work will touch others because it springs directly from the artist's own inner life."

WORKS CITED:

Iarusso, Marilyn, review of *Zomo the Rabbit: A Trickster Tale from West Africa, School Library Journal,* November, 1992, pp. 84-85.
Review of *The Magic Tree: A Tale from the Congo, Kirkus Reviews,* October 15, 1972, p. 1187.
McDermott, Gerald, "On the Rainbow Trail," *Horn Book,* April, 1975, pp. 123-31.
McDermott, Gerald, "Caldecott Award Acceptance," *Horn Book,* August, 1975, pp. 349-54.
Peterson, Linda Kauffman, "Arrow to the Sun," *Newbery and Caldecott Medal and Honor Books: An Annotated Bibliography,* edited by Peterson and Marilyn Leathers Solt, G. K. Hall, 1982, p. 358.
White, David E., "Profile: Gerald McDermott," *Language Arts,* March, 1982, pp. 273-79.

FOR MORE INFORMATION SEE:

BOOKS

Authors in the News, Volume 2, Gale, 1976.
Children's Literature Review, Volume 9, Gale, 1985.

PERIODICALS

Milwaukee Journal, June 1, 1976.
School Library Journal, May, 1993, p. 100.*

*   *   *

McNAIR, Sylvia 1924-

PERSONAL: Born April 13, 1924, in Haiju, Korea; daughter of Victor Hugo (an American missionary and minister) and Sylvia (an American missionary and music teacher; maiden name, Allen) Wachs; married Wilbur F. McNair, 1950 (died, 1974); children: Allen,

Donald, Roger, Patricia. *Education:* Oberlin College, A.B., 1945. *Hobbies and other interests:* "Travel, and learning as much as I can about the United States and the rest of the world."

ADDRESSES: P.O. Box 6196, Evanston, IL.

CAREER: Held various positions in Arizona, Vermont, Rhode Island, Massachusetts, and Illinois, 1945-55; American Hospital Association, Chicago, IL, production editor, 1955-58; Editorial and Research Service, Evanston, IL, partner, 1958—. Herman Smith Associates, research associate, Hinsdale, IL, 1964-68; Rand McNally & Co., senior editor of travel guides and editor in chief of "Mobil Travel Guide," 1968-78; Pick Americana Hotels, director of corporate relations, 1979-81; free-lance writer, 1981—. Member of school board, Niles, IL, 1964-70; Niles Family Service, member of board of trustees, 1971-75, chairman of board, 1973-75.

MEMBER: American Society of Journalists and Authors, Society of American Travel Writers (past member of national board of directors; vice-chair of Freelance Council), Midwest Travel Writers Association (member of board of directors), Chicago Women in Publishing (charter member), Independent Writers of Chicago.

WRITINGS:

JUVENILE

Korea, Children's Press, 1986.
Thailand, Children's Press, 1987.
Kentucky, Children's Press, 1988.
Alabama, Children's Press, 1988.
Virginia, Children's Press, 1989.
Hawaii, Children's Press, 1989.
India, Children's Press, 1990.
Tennessee, Children's Press, 1990.
Vermont, Children's Press, 1991.
New Hampshire, Children's Press, 1991.
Indonesia, Children's Press, in press.

OTHER

Florida and the Southeast, Fisher Travel Guides, 1984.
New England, Fisher Travel Guides, 1985.
Vacation Places Rated, Rand McNally, 1986.

Also contributor to various magazines, including *Home & Away, Rotarian, Travel 50 & Beyond,* and *Vacations.* Travel correspondent for *Elks,* 1987—.

WORK IN PROGRESS: The Caribbean Islands, for Children's Press.

SIDELIGHTS: Sylvia McNair once commented: "I think it is very important for youngsters to learn what other cultures are like. I hope my books are rich in both information and inspiration. If each book gives even one or two young readers an expanded awareness of and enthusiasm for the people of another country, I will be satisfied that I've accomplished something worthwhile."

More recently, McNair told *SATA:* "I first knew I wanted to write books when I was eight or nine years old, and I was past sixty before my first one was published. But ever since, I've been doing exactly what I have always wanted to do. So I never want to retire; I hope to keep writing for the rest of my life. So my advice to anyone is—don't lose sight of your dream!"

*   *   *

MICICH, Paul

PERSONAL: Surname pronounced "*Mish*-ik"; married; children: Ari. *Education:* Attended Drake University and Des Moines Area Community College.

ADDRESSES: Home—1228 42nd Street, Des Moines, IA 50311.

CAREER: Illustrator of children's books and book covers; free-lance commercial artist.

MEMBER: Society of Illustrators.

AWARDS, HONORS: Addy Bronze Award, 1986, and Addy Silver Award, 1989, both from Kansas City Advertising Professionals; Best Illustration Award, 1989, and Best Unpublished Illustration Award, 1990, both from Iowa Art Director's Show; Addy Best of Class Illustration Award, Des Moines Advertising Professionals, 1990; award from Society of Illustrators' 31st Annual Print Regional Design Show, 1990.

ILLUSTRATOR:

Charles Tazewell, *The Littlest Angel,* Ideals, 1991.

Micich has provided book cover art for many children's books, including *A Wrinkle in Time, Sarah Plain and Tall, Bunnicula, Dear Mr. Henshaw, How to Eat Fried Worms, Bridge to Terebithia, Abel's Island, The Best Christmas Pageant Ever, Blue Willow, From the Mixed-up Files of Mrs. Basil E. Frankweiler, Ishi, The House of Dies Drear, James and the Giant Peach, In the Year of the Boar, Jackie Robinson, Mrs. Frisby and the Rats of NIMH, One-Eyed Cat, Queenie Peavey, The Sign of the Beaver, Where the Red Fern Grows, The War with Grandpa, Sounder,* and *Indian in the Cupboard.*

SIDELIGHTS: Artist Paul Micich began his career as a children's book illustrator when he was given the assignment of illustrating several jacket-covers for books about previously-released Newbery Medal winners. "When I read the books I was really impressed by the depth of the material," Micich recalled. "I love the economy and simplicity of children's books. There is so much great storytelling there."

Author Charles Tazewell's retelling of a classic Christmas tale, *The Littlest Angel,* provided Micich with the opportunity to create artwork for an entire book; the project involved not only the artist but his entire family. "There are many gifts in *The Littlest Angel,*" Micich explained. "Tazewell's gift to us all of a beautiful story. The Littlest Angel's gifts—of giving in great humility, of playfulness, and of sincerity, reverence, and hope. My

son Ari's gift of providing inspiration for me, and his hard work, as my model, in finding the littlest angel within himself. I am the recipient of all these gifts."

*   *   *

MILORD, Susan 1954-

PERSONAL: Born August 28, 1954, in Norwalk, CT; daughter of Jerry (a graphic designer, illustrator, and cartoonist) and Anne (an actress; maiden name, Pitoniak) Milord; married Skip Gorman (a folk musician), August 18, 1979; children: Angus Gorman. *Education:* Attended Escuela de Diseno y Artesanias, 1971-72, and University of New Mexico, 1973-74; Kansas City Art Institute, B.F.A., 1977. *Hobbies and other interests:* Gardening, sewing and other needle crafts, cooking, and reading.

ADDRESSES: Office and agent—P.O. Box 307, Sargent Hill Rd., Grafton, NH 03240.

CAREER: Author and illustrator. *Family Circle,* New York City, staff designer, 1977-79; freelance graphic designer, 1977—. Graphic designer for advertising agencies, 1980-83. Instructor, children's after school art program, 1990—; director, Summer Arts Program, 1991-92.

MEMBER: Society of Children's Books Writers and Illustrators, Parent-Teacher Association.

SUSAN MILORD

AWARDS, HONORS: "The One" Award of Excellence, 1983, for graphic design; Parent's Choice Gold Award, 1989, for *Kids' Nature Book.*

WRITINGS:

SELF-ILLUSTRATED

The Kids' Nature Book, Williamson, 1989.
Adventures in Art, Williamson, 1990.
Hands around the World, Williamson, 1992.

WORK IN PROGRESS: Various short fiction pieces.

SIDELIGHTS: Susan Milord told *SATA:* "I suppose I would categorize myself as a 'doer.' Even as a child, I never remember being bored. Although my older brother and I spent a lot of time together, and I had plenty of childhood friends, I always enjoyed being on my own making things. I remember countless hours spent fashioning tiny saddles from leather scraps for my collection of plastic horses, and designing my own paper dolls, complete with extensive wardrobes.

"I also spent a lot of time reading. While I read a lot of fiction, some of my favorite books were those that gave me ideas (and instructions) for doing things with my hands. I never dreamed I would be writing similar books for children when I grew up!

"Not surprisingly, the topics I've covered in my books reflect subjects of lifelong interest. Moving to rural New Mexico when I was seven years old, I quickly cultivated a keen appreciation of nature. It was then, too, that I got my first taste of other cultures, specifically the Hispanic and Native American cultures that are very much alive in that state. As a teenager, I attended schools in both England and Mexico, further broadening my outlook. Coming from an artistic family, it's no wonder my interest in the arts is so strong.

"I started writing children's books quite by accident. I was always tinkering with ways to put my training as a graphic designer to use when I had an idea for a calendar that was inspired by my young son's interest in the natural world. Whereas the color illustrations each month would be eye-catching and appealing, I thought I might include simple suggestions for ways to appreciate nature for each day of each month. It occurred to me that a suggestion such as 'Make a plant press' might take some explaining. At the same time, I realized a collection of suggestions such as these would be valuable from year to year. From that moment, it was just a matter of turning all my thoughts into words.

"I approach my books a little differently than some authors perhaps because I have had the good fortune not only to illustrate my own books (I use some archival spot illustrations in addition to original black and white pen and ink drawings), but I have also designed the books I've written thus far. (As of this writing, I do not work on a computer. I type on a typewriter, and do pencil layouts of each page, which accompany the manuscript when it's time to set type.) 'Doing it all' has

its drawbacks, but thanks to the generosity and encouragement of my publisher and editor, I have a truly special relationship with the books I create."

FOR MORE INFORMATION SEE:

PERIODICALS

American Bookseller, March, 1991.
Booklist, October, 1989.

*   *   *

MUTEL, Cornelia F. 1947-

PERSONAL: Born March 13, 1947, in Madison, WI; daughter of Herbert O. (in forest products research) and Dorothy (a homemaker; maiden name, Groth) Fleischer; married Robert L. Mutel (an astronomy professor), February 7, 1970; children: Christopher, Andrew, Matthew. *Education:* Oberlin College, B.A., 1969; University of Colorado, M.S., 1973. *Religion:* Lutheran. *Hobbies and other interests:* Botanizing, gardening, biking, backpacking, prairie restoration.

ADDRESSES: Home—2345 Sugar Bottom Rd., Solon, IA 52333. *Office*—IIHR, Hydraulics Lab, University of Iowa, Iowa City, IA 52242.

CAREER: Ecological consultant for University of Colorado and private consulting firms in Boulder, CO, 1972-76; University of Iowa, Iowa City, educational resource

CORNELIA F. MUTEL

specialist and medical writer in department of preventative medicine and environmental health, 1976-90, scientific historian in Iowa Institute of Hydraulic Research, 1990—. Free-lance natural history writer and consultant. Zion Lutheran Church Environmental Task Force, chair, 1989—; speaker on Iowa's natural history at local grade schools and museums.

MEMBER: Ecological Society of America, Nature Conservancy (board of directors of Iowa chapter, 1980-86), Iowa Natural History Association, Iowa Academy of Science (board of directors, 1991-94), Johnson County Heritage Trust (board of directors).

AWARDS, HONORS: Staff Achievement Award, University of Iowa, 1986; Shambaugh Award runner-up for best book on Iowa history, 1989, for *Fragile Giants: A Natural History of the Loess Hills.*

WRITINGS:

FOR CHILDREN

(With Mary Rodgers) *Tropical Rain Forests,* Lerner, 1991.

OTHER

From Grassland to Glacier: An Ecology of Boulder County, Colorado, Johnson Publishing Co. (Boulder, CO), 1976.
(With Kelley Donham) *Medical Practice in Rural Communities,* Springer-Verlag, 1983.
Fragile Giants: A Natural History of the Loess Hills, University of Iowa Press, 1989.
(Editor) *Agriculture at Risk: A Report to the Nation,* Pioneer Hybrid International (Johnston, IA), 1989.
(Editor) E. Einstein, *Hans Albert Einstein: Reminiscences of His Life and Our Life Together,* IIHR, University of Iowa, 1991.
(With John Emerick) *From Grassland to Glacier: The Natural History of Colorado and the Surrounding Region,* 2nd edition, Johnson Publishing Co., 1992.

Also author of the "Agricultural Health" series of audiovisual presentations for rural physicians, University of Iowa, 1976-81; and the "Agricultural Respiratory Problems Education" series, American Lung Association (Des Moines, IA), 1986. Contributor of book chapters and articles to journals. Editor of newsletter of Iowa Natural History Association and Johnson County Heritage Trust, both 1987—.

WORK IN PROGRESS: A scientific biography of Hans Albert Einstein, completion expected 1994; research on Iowa's natural history in preparation for additional books for adults and children.

SIDELIGHTS: Cornelia F. Mutel told *SATA:* "Since I was a child, I have focused more on the natural than on the human world. Wild areas and their inhabitants, especially their plants, became not only childhood objects of unlimited fascination, they also were my personal friends with whom I felt most relaxed. So by the time I reached high school, it was natural that I concentrated on the sciences and studied biology as much as was possible, both during the school year and through NSF-sponsored research programs during the summer. My interests in the natural sciences were further fostered by my love of reading about botany and natural history, my father's love of his profession as a forester, and my mother's compassion for all living creatures, large or small. My interest in music was also intense and consuming. These two passions led me through college (with majors in biology and music) and on to graduate school in ecology, where I discovered that to my dismay I was more intent on creating works of art than research projects. That's when I began to write—as a means of combining my need for artistic expression with my sense of unity with the natural world. Thus my present profession—as a writer and scientific historian at the University of Iowa—was totally unpremeditated. Yet I feel comfortable and happy in this life, where I continue to learn and to reach out to others through my writing about topics I think are crucially important.

"I feel happiest when writing natural history, and do so on a free-lance basis whenever possible. Two books for adults, *From Grassland to Glacier* and *Fragile Giants,* have been the result. *Tropical Rain Forests* was my first attempt to write for children. I hope to do much more of this type of writing in the future, possibly by writing regional ecologies of the United States for upper elementary students. In the meantime, I continue my work at the university, where I am presently engaged in preparing a scientific biography of Hans Albert Einstein.

"All of my natural history writing springs from a desire to teach others about the natural regions that I love deeply. I hope that through the understanding I impart, readers will be led to better care for natural areas and their inhabitants. It's my way of trying to save what I love most in this world by practicing what I do well—writing about the intricacies of ecological systems. I feel that my extensive training in the sciences has been especially fortunate, for because of that training, I have become adamant about the need for factual accuracy and straight-forward, clear representation of complex ecological ideas. I definitely am an 'ideas person,' and I constantly work at adding to my base of information through reading and through participating in natural areas preservation and prairie restoration projects here in Iowa."

N-O

NADEL, Laurie 1948-

PERSONAL: Born May 26, 1948, in Brooklyn, NY; daughter of Alfred (a dentist) and Mildred (a home-maker; maiden name, Eismon) Nadel; married Phil Van Dijk (in software management), November 1, 1980; children: Charlene. *Education:* Sarah Lawrence College, B.A., 1969; International Institute for Advanced Studies, M.A., 1989; Greenwich University, Ph.D., 1991; attended American Institute of Hypnotherapy, beginning in 1991.

ADDRESSES: Home—1245 East Twenty-seventh St., Brooklyn, NY 11210. *Office*—11 Waverly Place, New York, NY 10003.

CAREER: Visnews, Ltd., London, England, writer, 1969-70; United Press International and *Newsweek,* South America, reporter, 1973-74; United Nations, New York City, reporter and writer, 1975-77; Diversion Books, New York City, editor and writer, 1977-79; Columbia Broadcasting System (CBS) news department, New York City, writer and producer, 1979-87; self-employed hypnotherapist in New York City, 1989—. Faculty member of New York Open Center, 1991, American Institute of Hypnotherapy, 1992, and Professional Development Institute at the University of North Texas, 1992. Presenter of numerous seminars.

MEMBER: International Association of Counselors and Therapists, International Association of Neurolinguistics Programming, American Society of Journalists and Authors, American Association of Counseling and Development, American Board of Hypnotherapy, American Seminar Leaders Association, National Association of Female Executives, National Board of Hypnotherapy and Hypnotic Anesthesiology.

AWARDS, HONORS: Special Recognition Award, American Board of Hypnotherapy, 1992.

WRITINGS:

Corazon Aquino: Journey to Power, Simon & Schuster, 1987.
Sixth Sense, Prentice-Hall, 1990.
The Great Stream of History: Young Adult Biography of Richard Nixon, Atheneum, 1991.
The Kremlin Coup, Millbrook Press, 1992.

Contributing editor to *Men's Fitness,* 1991-92. Contributor to periodicals, including *Elle, New Woman,* and the *Los Angeles Times Health and Fitness News Service.*

WORK IN PROGRESS: The War Park, a novel about a television reporter covering a Middle East war; *As We Live and Breathe: A Self-Help Guide for People with Asthma.*

SIDELIGHTS: Laurie Nadel told *SATA:* "I have wanted to be a writer since I was twelve years old. There is nothing as rewarding as writing a book and finding it in the library! In recent years, I have become more interested in writing about the mind, instead of writing about politics and people. Writing helps me explore the meaning of why we are here. I love talking to young people about writing, research, and publishing."

*   *   *

OBED, Ellen Bryan 1944-

PERSONAL: Born November 7, 1944, in Orange, NJ; daughter of William Lafrentz (a college administrator) and Margaret (a homemaker; maiden name, Bradley) Bryan; married Enoch Obed, May 26, 1973 (divorced, 1989); children: Keturah, Natan, Seth. *Education:* Bradford College, A.A., 1965; University of Maine at Orono, B.S., 1969; attended Memorial University of Newfoundland, 1971-72, and Prairie Bible Institute, Alberta, Canada, 1972-73. *Religion:* Christian. *Hobbies and other interests:* Canoeing, baking, playing the piano, hiking, running, many other sports.

ELLEN BRYAN OBED

ADDRESSES: Home—154 Stillwater Ave., Old Town, ME 04468.

CAREER: Yale Elementary, North West River, Labrador, school teacher, 1969-71; District No. 26, Fredericton, New Brunswick, music teacher, 1973-74; Jens Haven Memorial School, Nain, Labrador, teacher of English as a Second Language (ESL), 1980-81; Peenamin McKenzie School, Sheshatshit, Labrador, music teacher and librarian, 1986-88; private piano teacher, Old Town, ME, 1989—; free-lance writer, 1989—. Elderhostel Program, Goose Bay, Labrador, coordinator of flora and fauna course, summers, 1985-88.

AWARDS, HONORS: Commendation for poetry, *Scholastic* magazine, 1959; first prize for poetry, *Scholastic* magazine, 1960; poetry award, *American Girl* magazine, 1961; "Our Choice" awards, Canadian Children's Book Center, for *Little Snowshoe*, and 1989, for *Borrowed Black;* Explorations grant, Canada Council, 1984.

WRITINGS:

Borrowed Black: A Labrador Fantasy, illustrated by Hope Yandell, Breakwater Books, 1979, edited by Rhoda Sherwood, Gareth Stevens, 1988, new edition illustrated by Jan Mogensen, Breakwater Books, 1988, Ideals Publishing, 1989.
Little Snowshoe, illustrated by William Ritchie, Breakwater Books, 1984.
Wind in My Pocket (poems), illustrated by Shawn Steffler, Breakwater Books, 1990.

Contributor of poetry to periodicals, including *Chickadee* and *Newfoundland Quarterly.*

Borrowed Black has been translated into six languages. *Little Snowshoe* has been translated into Danish.

ADAPTATIONS: Borrowed Black has been adapted for the stage by the Elysian Theater Student Company and produced at LSPU Hall, St. John's, Newfoundland, 1989.

WORK IN PROGRESS: The Berries of Labrador; The Dilee-Croc Stories; poems about birds.

SIDELIGHTS: A teacher and writer, Ellen Bryan Obed is the author of the award-winning *Borrowed Black: A Labrador Fantasy.* The work is an imaginative, rhyming narrative about the title character, an evil and bizarre creature who "permanently borrows" everything he owns—even the anatomical parts that form his own body. One day he even snatches the moon from the sky and hides it in his sack. The moon breaks into tiny pieces on his journey home, however, and he buries it in the ocean. The remainder of the tale details the adventures of the Curious Crew, personified animals including Mousie Mate and Sinky Sailor, who are intent on finding and restoring the moon to its rightful place, as well as overthrowing the tyrannical Borrowed Black.

Obed told *SATA* that she was born in Orange, New Jersey, and moved to a farm in Waterville, Maine, when she was only thirteen months old. She recalls that it was at the farm that she grew to love the outdoors, since her father often led her and her four siblings on hiking, fishing, swimming, and skating excursions.

Obed first began writing poetry at the age of eleven. "When my father read it, he asked if he could show it to my mother," Obed told *SATA.* "'We have a poet in the family.' he said to her. I still remember that occasion and the significance of it. My heritage and my life experiences were coming together in poetry. My great-grandfather on my father's side was a poet. My great-uncle on my mother's side was a poet. Both of my grandmothers quoted poetry to us. A. A. Milne and Robert Louis Stevenson were favorites. One of the beautiful memories I have of my childhood is of my mother singing poems to us from Stevenson's *Child's Garden of Verses.* My father read to us our favorite books over and over again. One of these was *Charlotte's Web* by E. B. White. Our farm was just like the farm in that book. My father also told us stories. They were usually about pirates and treasures and shipwrecks.

"When I discovered that I could write poetry, I wrote prolifically. I had special places to work on my poetry. My favorite place to write was under an apple tree in the orchard. I would be there so long and so still that warblers would flit within inches of my face. I remember going to my tree one day to find that my dad had put a ring of manure around it. I was very upset. Another place in which I would write was in the crabapple tree—I had made a platform in the crook of its branches. Sometimes I would walk beyond the orchard to where the mayflower patches were. I would sit under a pine on the soft needles and write. I made lots of little books and contributed to the school magazines. I dreamed of the day when I would have a book illustrated and published. When I was fifteen, I went away to Kents Hill, a boarding school. The thing that I dreaded most was not having my own special place in which to think and read and write.

"When I was a senior in high school, I printed my first book. My best friend made the linoleum cuts for the poems. My sister, my closest friends, and I set the type for the book in the Graphic Arts Workshop at nearby Colby College. I titled the book *Wind in my Pocket* and dedicated it to my grandfather for his eightieth birthday.

"My first book, *Borrowed Black,* was published in 1979. The title came to me when I was telling stories with my cousins in a cabin in the Maine woods. It wasn't until I went to the Labrador Coast in 1965 when I was twenty, however, that the story took shape. I used to tell it to the children there but did not write it down until the summer of 1967. On that occasion my uncle and I were flying in his airplane from Maine to Labrador. There was fog over the Gaspe so we spent two days in Tabusintac, New Brunswick, at a fishing lodge. It was there that I wrote the poem. I wrote it in two days with very little revision afterwards. It was as if it were not my own but a gift to me for the children of Labrador.

"Some readers see underlying themes in the story. One is that Humor (represented by the boat that is built in

Obed wrote this multi-themed fantasy over a two-day period while waiting for a fog bank to clear. (Cover illustration by Jan Mogensen.)

Little Snowshoe
Ellen Bryan Obed–William Ritchie

Obed tried to capture the beauty of the Northern woods with words in this 1984 selection. (Cover illustration by William Ritchie.)

the back of the whale) overcomes the Sullen Spirit (represented by Borrowed Black). Another is that Borrowed Black represents the greed in human nature that borrows and borrows from the environment without giving back. Though these ideas surface in the story, they were not my original intention. I wrote *Borrowed Black* for the pure delight of a story. What it says beyond what I originally told intrigues me as much as it does the reader!

"The story *Little Snowshoe* had its beginnings at bedtime when my son Natan, who was then two years old, asked for a story. He liked the story so much that he asked to have it told again and again for many nights. I wrote it down and saved it, thinking that one day I would find an illustrator who could put it in a northern setting. When we were living in Nain, Labrador, I met William Ritchie, an artist who did studies of animals in the subarctic. His illustrations bring the reader to the northern coast of Labrador in winter—the 'endless' snow, the stunted trees in a crowded wood, the white partridge (willow ptarmigan).

"When my publisher asked me for a collection of poems for a book, I gathered together poems I had written over a number of years which have themes of nature and the seasons. For more than a year I searched in my mind for a title. Finally, I decided on the same title I had for the book I printed in high school! Since there were so many references to wind in the poems, I thought it was a fitting title. Most of the poems in this book have their setting in Labrador. 'Sky Carver' talks about the coming of spring in the Inuit (or Eskimo) village where we once lived. The Inuit people are superb carvers. This poem speaks of their culture as well as of the landscape. There are four poems in the book which have the *ch, th, wh,* and *sh* sounds. I wrote these to teach my students the sounds. The limerick 'There Once Was a Man Down the Bay' is a true story. There was a storekeeper in a village in Labrador early in this century who actually dyed his hair with blackberry juice.

"My favorite kind of writing is poetry. I can say something intensely and deeply and clearly in poetry that I cannot do in prose. I like using the metaphor for this purpose. In my poem 'Winter Journey' I call the sunset a 'red fox sleeping on the side of day.' In the poem 'The Robin Sang' I call the sunset a robin's breast. In the poem 'We'll Sing of Strawberries' I call the sunset a strawberry staining the sky.

"I'm working now at writing poems about birds. I am also working on a story about the snowbird and its migratory flight through Labrador to its arctic breeding ground. I have also studied and written a manuscript about the berries of Labrador. For this I have traveled extensively along the Labrador Coast.

"The themes in my writing are about nature and the seasons. I get my ideas when I am outdoors. This is why I love to climb mountains and be on the lakes and rivers. I thought of the poem 'Great Blue' when I was kayaking on a river at dusk. The great blue heron rose silently 'on the shore of night.' I thought of the poem 'The Spittlebug' when I was walking through a dry hayfield in summer. Wet 'spit' from the spittlebugs was all over my legs.

"The most important elements in writing to me are imagination and word choice. Word choice is important for a powerful and successful image. I work very hard on word choice. I carve my poems. Extra words drop to the floor like shavings. I sweep them up and throw them away. That's how one gets a beautiful poem."

FOR MORE INFORMATION SEE:

PERIODICALS

Evening Telegram (St. John's, Newfoundland), March 23, 1989, p. 43.
School Library Journal, September, 1989, p. 256.
Sunday Express (St. John's), March 26, 1989, p. 25.

*   *   *

OLIVER, Shirley (Louise Dawkins) 1958-

PERSONAL: Born December 8, 1958, in Macon, MS; daughter of Meredith Preston Dawkins (a retail owner) and Sarah Louise Dawkins Temkovits (a homemaker; maiden name, Williams); married Ted Emerson Oliver (a retail manager), July 8, 1978; children: Emerson,

Meredith, Joe-David. *Education:* Attended Mississippi University for Women, 1976-78; Murray State University, B.S.B., 1980. *Politics:* Independent. *Religion:* Methodist.

ADDRESSES: Home—243 Point Clear, Conroe, TX 77304. *Office*—Oliver-Goodin and Co., Inc., P.O. Box 279, Charleston, MO 63834.

CAREER: Northaven Elementary School, Memphis, TN, substitute teacher, 1981; Marion Senior High School, Marion, AR, math teacher, 1983-85; Charleston High School, Charleston, MO, substitute teacher, 1986-87; Willis High School, Willis, TX, math teacher, 1992—. Kelly's Kids, Inc., Ferriday, LA, area representative for in-home line of children's applique clothing, 1986-91; Cookie's Heirloom Shop, Sikeston, MO, owner, 1986-87; Oliver-Goodin and Co., Inc. (design firm specializing in children's patterns and smocking plates), Charleston, MO, co-owner, 1987-91; Capitol Imports, Inc., Tallahassee, FL, distributor of imported laces and fabrics, 1990-91. Has done free-lance work for Simplicity Pattern Company and Vive La Fete (a children's clothing company). Has exhibited needlework at the Southeastern Yarncrafters Guild and Smocking Arts Guild of America, both 1989.

MEMBER: Philanthropic and Educational Organization (PEO).

SHIRLEY OLIVER

WRITINGS:

(With Sallie Goodin) *I Want to Smock,* Oliver-Goodin and Co., Inc., 1990.
(With Goodin) *Come Comet, Come Cupid,* Winston-Derek, 1992.

Contributor to magazines, including *Creative Needle.*

SIDELIGHTS: Shirley Oliver told *SATA:* "At a very young age, I loved to read and write. I loved storytelling, making doll clothes, designing book covers, and writing.

It is not that I am extremely talented in one area or the other. The most valuable characteristic I possess is my imagination and being able to use that imagination to create.

"My fascination is not necessarily with books or clothes, but with children. Because of this, I have made many accomplishments. Presently, I am a school teacher, heirloom clothes designer for children, writer of instructional articles, and a book author. The most important lesson for all of us to learn is to take our best characteristic and use it."

P

PEPPE, Rodney (Darrell) 1934-

PERSONAL: Surname is pronounced "*Pep*-py," and accented over the last "e"; born June 24, 1934, in Eastbourne, Sussex, England; son of Lionel Hill (a lieutenant commander in the Royal Navy) and Winifred Vivienne (Parry) Peppe; married Tordis Tatjana Tekkel, July 16, 1960; children: Christen Rodney, Jonathan Noel. *Education:* Attended Eastbourne School of Art, National Diploma in Design, 1958; London County Council Central School of Art and Crafts, Diploma in Illustration, 1959. *Religion:* Church of England. *Hobbies and other interests:* Making automata and moving toys; movies; swimming.

ADDRESSES: Home and studio—Barnwood House, Whiteway, Stroud, Gloucester GL6 7ER, England.

CAREER: S. H. Benson Ltd. (advertising agency), London, England, art director, 1960-64; J. Walter Thompson Co. Ltd. (advertising agency), London, art director for television accounts, 1964-65; Ross Foods Ltd., design consultant, London, 1965-72, Syon Park, Brentford, Middlesex, 1972-73; design consultant to other firms and groups. *Military service:* British Army, Intelligence Corps, 1953-55; served in Malaya.

WRITINGS:

SELF-ILLUSTRATED CHILDREN'S BOOKS

The Alphabet Book, Viking (UK), 1968, Four Winds, 1968.

Circus Numbers: A Counting Book, Viking (UK), 1969, Delacorte, 1969.

The House That Jack Built, Viking (UK), 1970, Delacorte, 1970.

Hey Riddle Diddle! A Book of Traditional Riddles, Viking (UK), 1971, Holt, 1971.

Simple Simon, Viking (UK), 1972, Holt, 1973.

Cat and Mouse: A Book of Rhymes, Viking (UK), 1973, Holt, 1973.

Humpty Dumpty, Viking/Puffin Books, 1974, Viking, 1986.

Odd One Out, Viking (UK), 1974, Viking, 1974.

RODNEY PEPPE

Picture Stories, Viking, 1976.

Rodney Peppe's Puzzle Book, Viking (UK), 1977, Viking, 1977.

Humphrey the Number Horse, Methuen, 1978, Viking, 1979.

Ten Little Bad Boys, Viking (UK), 1978, Viking, 1978.

Three Little Pigs, Viking (UK), 1979, Lothrop, 1979.

My Surprise Pull-Out Word Book: Indoors, Methuen, 1980, F. Watts, 1980.

My Surprise Pull-Out Word Book: Outdoors, Methuen, 1980, F. Watts, 1980.

Run Rabbit, Run!: A Pop-Up Book, Methuen, 1982, Delacorte, 1982.

Make Your Own Paper Toys, Patrick Hardy, 1984.

Press-Out Circus Book, Methuen, 1986.

Press-Out Train Book, Methuen, 1986.

Tell the Time with Mortimer, Methuen, 1986.

Open House, Methuen, 1987, Oxford University Press, 1987.

First Nursery Rhymes, Methuen, 1988, Oxford University Press, 1988.

Thumbprint Circus, Viking (UK), 1988, Delacorte, 1989.

The Animal Directory, Blackie, 1989.

Rodney Peppe's Noah's Ark Frieze, Campbell, 1989.

Alphabet Frieze, Campbell, 1990.

Summer Days, Campbell, 1991.

Winter Days, Campbell, 1991.

ABC Index, Blackie, 1990, Bedrick Blackie, 1991.

The Shapes Finder, Blackie, 1991.

The Color Catalog, Blackie, 1992, Peter Bedrick, 1992.

"HENRY" SERIES; SELF-ILLUSTRATED

Henry's Exercises, Methuen, 1975, enlarged edition, 1978.

Henry's Garden, Methuen, 1975, enlarged edition, 1978.

Henry's Present, Methuen, 1975.

Henry's Sunbathe, Methuen, 1975, enlarged edition, 1978.

Henry's Aeroplane, Methuen, 1978.

Henry Eats Out, Methuen, 1978.

Henry's Toy Cupboard, Methuen, 1978.

Hello Henry, Methuen, 1984.

Hurrah for Henry!, Methuen, 1984.

"MICE" SERIES; SELF-ILLUSTRATED

The Mice Who Lived in a Shoe, Viking (UK), 1981, Lothrop, 1981.

The Kettleship Pirates, Viking (UK), 1983, Lothrop, 1983.

The Mice and the Flying Basket, Viking (UK), 1985, Lothrop, 1985.

The Mice and the Clockwork Bus, Viking (UK), 1986, Lothrop, 1987.

The Mice on the Moon, Viking (UK), 1992, Delacorte, 1993.

The Mice and the Travel Machine, Viking (UK), 1993.

"LITTLE TOY BOARD BOOKS" SERIES; SELF-ILLUSTRATED

Little Circus, Methuen, 1983, Viking, 1983.

Little Dolls, Methuen, 1983, Viking, 1983.

Little Games, Methuen, 1983, Viking, 1983.

Little Numbers, Methuen, 1983, Viking, 1983.

Little Wheels, Methuen, 1983, Viking, 1983.

"RODNEY PEPPE'S BLOCK BOOKS" SERIES; SELF-ILLUSTRATED

Animals, Methuen, 1985.

Colours, Methuen, 1985.

Numbers, Methuen, 1985.

People, Methuen, 1985.

"HUXLEY PIG" SERIES; SELF-ILLUSTRATED

Here Comes Huxley Pig, Warne, 1989, Delacorte, 1989.

Huxley Pig at the Circus, Fantail, 1989.

Huxley Pig in the Haunted House, Fantail, 1989.

Huxley Pig the Clown, Warne, 1989, Delacorte, 1989.

Huxley Pig's Airplane, Warne, 1990, Delacorte, 1990.

Huxley Pig at the Beach, Fantail, 1990.

Huxley Pig at the Restaurant, Fantail, 1990.

Huxley Pig's Dressing-up Book, Warne, 1991.

Huxley Pig's Model Car, Warne, 1991, Delacorte, 1991.

OTHER

(Illustrator) Jill Marchant and Ralph Marchant, *The Little Painter,* Nelson, 1971, Carolrhoda Books, 1971.

Rodney Peppe's Moving Toys (adult nonfiction), Evans Bros., 1980, Sterling, 1980.

ADAPTATIONS: Peppe's "Huxley Pig" books have been adapted as a television series in Great Britain.

SIDELIGHTS: Since publishing his first book in 1968, Rodney Peppe has been the prolific author-illustrator of over seventy picture books for young children. He is best-known for lively character drawings based on his original wooden model toy-figures, including those for his books in the "Henry the Elephant," "The Mice Who Lived in a Shoe," and "Huxley Pig" series. Although Peppe began his career as a designer in advertising during the late 1950s, he ventured into children's

"Help the *Trapeze Artistes,*"
said the Trick Riders.
"They need a net."

Little Thumbkin helps different performers, including the ringmaster and trapeze artists, in Peppe's cleverly designed picturebook. (Illustration by the author from *Thumbprint Circus.*)

picture books nearly a decade later, finding them a particularly rewarding endeavor. As he once commented: "Picture book artists find themselves in rather a privileged position. They are the first communicators of still images to the very young, who as yet cannot read. Their pictures convey ideas which can stimulate the child's visual imagination and prepare him for the wonders to come."

Born in Eastbourne, England, in 1934, Peppe spent his early years near the Himalaya Mountains in India, where his father managed the Peppe family estates and also served in the British and Indian Royal navies. Lionel Peppe's naval duties kept him away from his family for long periods of time, and eventually Peppe's mother Vivienne—wanting her sons to have a standard British education—returned with Rodney and his twin brother, Mark, to Eastbourne. The year was 1942, during the height of the Second World War and the German bombing of England. "From the peacefulness of India, through the excitement of being at sea, we came now to bombs and boarding school," Peppe recounted in the *Something about the Author Autobiography Series (SAAS)*.

Peppe and his brother were enrolled in St. Bede's School, which during the war was relocated to St. Edward's School in Oxford. As a youth, Peppe became interested in model construction, influenced by one of his instructors who had built a model cathedral. Another early interest was the cinema, and at a young age he began drawing cowboys and pirates from films he had seen, as well as caricatures of his favorite cinema stars. Later, when he was a student at the strict St. Edward's School, Peppe was often disciplined for stealing away to view films at Oxford's movie houses. "Much of my free time was spent . . . in going with fellow transgressors to see films which I thought then, and think now, were an important part of my education," he recounted in *SAAS*. Although St. Edward's was a restrictive school, the students found various creative ways to express their individuality. "You could see colourful personalities emerging from this insular society with its petty rules, for they eschewed conformity for its own sake, thereby making a statement to the tiny world we lived in, that they were different—special. Of course they paid for it with the rod!"

Peppe had aspirations to one day become an actor, yet eventually decided to pursue art studies. "I can't remember how I decided to train to be an artist rather than an actor, but there certainly wasn't much soul-searching," he wrote in *SAAS*. His parents were persuaded to allow Peppe and his brother to leave St. Edward's early and enroll at the Eastbourne School of Art, where Peppe went on to pursue painting as his major and wood-engraving as a craft. He continued with his studies until 1953 when he began two years of mandatory military service. Peppe was assigned to British Foreign Intelligence and sent to the Asian country of Malaya. There, as he noted in *SAAS*, he "made friends with the country and its people," and also became fascinated by the country's exotic bazaars and lively cabarets. "I

haunted the dance halls with my sketchbook" and made "notes and sketches wherever I went and worked on them later to make finished drawings and paintings."

When his military service concluded, Peppe resumed his art studies at Eastbourne. He then attended London's Central School of Art and Crafts, choosing illustration as his major, graduating with a diploma in 1959. He studied under the famous illustrator and designer Laurence Scarfe, as well as continuing with wood-engraving under noted craftswoman Gertrude Hermes. "At the time I was a film extra during the holidays, which was a pleasant way to eke out my father's allowance," he added in *SAAS*. Peppe completed a three-year illustration study course in two years, eager "to get *on*," as he wrote in *SAAS*. "Armed with my diploma and a portfolio I walked the streets of London visiting publishers."

Peppe began searching for free-lance illustration work, but instead obtained a job with an advertising agency. "My work at the Central School had been illustrating poems by Keats with detailed wood engravings, or designing programme covers for ballets," he noted in *SAAS*. ". . . Now I had to contend with press advertisements extolling the virtues of smoking cigarettes, drinking beer, or buying oil-fired central heating. There was no point of contact." Although the work was initially frustrating, Peppe came to be proficient at it, and still found room for his own creative endeavors. One of his hobbies became cartoon-making, and during his spare time he began filming self-made cartoon figures in the one-room apartment he shared with his wife Tatjana and newly-born son. "My method was to use translucent coloured celluloid cutouts, which I made into jointed characters," he related in *SAAS*. "I photographed these

Peter ate his breakfast.

The success of *Odd One Out*, which invites the reader to find the deliberate mistake on each page, encouraged Peppe to create more original stories for children.

flat puppets on a light box, with single shots, moving them frame by frame."

The demands of his new family prompted Peppe to focus on his advertising career, however, and eventually he landed a job as a designer with a frozen-foods company in London. "It was for three days a week, working at home two days and visiting their offices every Tuesday—and for the same money I was getting for five days a week.... This was the break I had been waiting for." Undaunted by an earlier, unsuccessful try at producing a children's picture book, Peppe began working on what would become *The Alphabet Book,* published in 1968. "Because words play little or no part in alphabet and counting books, these are often the type of books to which graphic designers turn," he observed in *SAAS.* "I was no exception and appreciated especially the self-working themes of these visual primers, which would give me artistic freedom, unfettered by text and yet supported by the solid structure of the alphabet." In a similar manner, Peppe's second book, *Circus Numbers,* was a children's counting primer featuring images of the circus. "I used the ring graphically to contain the circus acts," Peppe noted in *SAAS,* " ... while outside the ring I place large black cardinal numbers, with captions for each act."

Finding success with his illustration work, Peppe went on to produce pictorial renditions of such children's standards as *The House That Jack Built, Hey Riddle Diddle!,* and *Simple Simon.* "I was ducking the issue of writing my own stories," he said in *SAAS.* "I was an artist, not a writer, and I usefully employed what was in the public domain: Nursery Rhymes." This changed with his 1974 book *Odd One Out,* which tells the story of a day in the life of a small boy. "In each picture the young reader can find an 'odd one out,' one deliberate mistake that turns the simple story into an exciting and colourful game," Peppe noted in *SAAS.* "The book was very successful for me and gave me the confidence to invent my own stories and not rely upon traditional rhymes." Peppe soon discovered that his earlier love of making models could also serve his picture books. He constructed a wooden model elephant named Henry and "would position him in various poses and use him as a lay figure from which to draw." Peppe's elephant became the basis for a series of nine "Henry" books. "Apart from finding a new method of producing picture books, Henry started me off on writing simple stories for the very young," he commented in *SAAS.* "I developed his character as a rather incompetent young elephant whose adventures had a habit of going wrong."

One of Peppe's best-received books has been *The Mice Who Lived in a Shoe* which, along with its sequels, recounts the adventures of a mouse family who live in a weathered, lace-up boot. In addition to garnering favorable reviews from critics, Peppe received requests from children "for instructions on how to build the shoe-house and letters and drawings showing me ingenious examples, using my book as a springboard for ideas," as he noted in *SAAS.* Another successful series for Peppe includes his "Huxley Pig" books, featuring another

The ingenious creatures of Peppe's "Mice" series entertain children while inspiring curiosity about the way things work. (Illustration by Peppe from *The Mice and the Clockwork Bus.*)

character drawn from a wooden figure designed by Peppe. The Huxley books also led to a television series which aired in Great Britain in 1989. "To see my words turn into model animation, my drawn characters brought to life, with voices, was a particular joy to me," Peppe wrote in *SAAS.* "... There are three animators and three Huxleys, jointed, so that they can move by stop-frame animation."

In addition to his picture books, Peppe has produced a number of "pop-up" books, including *Run Rabbit, Run!,* published in 1982. He has also written an adult manual for toy-making, entitled *Rodney Peppe's Moving Toys.* "The results of working on this book," Peppe noted in *SAAS,* "with instructions, diagrams, and photographs for making twenty-two moving toys, many based on Victorian mechanisms (though my own designs), has been one of the greatest influences on my work." Peppe hopes that his own interest in toy-making, illustrations, and model construction not only sparks his readers' interest, but also provides an incentive. He once remarked: "As a picture book artist I like to think of my books being treated like favourite toys.... It's important too that an adult reading aloud to the child should not be bored or irritated by text and pictures. If, while satisfying these requirements I can foster aesthetic appreciation and encourage the child to make his own pictures, so much the better."

WORKS CITED:

Peppe, Rodney, essay in *Fifth Book of Junior Authors,* edited by Sally Holmes Holtze, H. W. Wilson, 1983, pp. 243-45.

Peppe, Rodney, essay in *Something about the Author Autobiography Series,* Volume 10, Gale, 1990, pp. 201-17.

* * *

PETERS, Linda
See CATHERALL, Arthur

* * *

PETERS, Lisa Westberg 1951-

PERSONAL: Born October 19, 1951, in Minneapolis, MN; daughter of Walter M. (an inventor) and Naomi (a nurse; maiden name, Balstad) Westberg; married David G. Peters (a journalist), August 16, 1975; children: Emily, Anna. *Education:* University of Minnesota, B.A., 1974. *Hobbies and other interests:* Hiking, canoeing, swimming, reading, gardening, travel.

ADDRESSES: Home and office—915 West California Ave., St. Paul, MN 55117. *Agent*—Susan Cohen, Writers House, 21 West 26th St., New York, NY 10010.

CAREER: Writer. The Loft, instructor in children's book writing; speaker at conferences; junior great books leader. Science Museum of Minnesota, member. Como Ordway Japanese Garden, volunteer.

LISA WESTBERG PETERS

Spending her childhood vacations by a river gave Peters the appreciation for nature she tries to communicate in her books. (Cover illustration by Ted Rand.)

MEMBER: Society of Children's Book Writers and Illustrators, Geological Society of Minnesota, Minnesota State Historical Society.

AWARDS, HONORS: The Sun, the Wind and the Rain was named an outstanding science trade book, National Science Teachers Association, and was nominated for a Minnesota Book Award, both 1988; *Good Morning, River!* was named a notable children's trade book in social studies, Children's Book Council, 1990; *Water's Way* was named a Children's Choice book, Children's Book Council, and a Children's Book of the Year, Child Study Children's Book Committee, both 1992.

WRITINGS:

The Sun, the Wind and the Rain, illustrations by Ted Rand, Holt, 1988.
Serengeti, Macmillan, 1989.
Tania's Trolls, Arcade, 1989.
The Condor, Macmillan, 1990.
Good Morning, River!, illustrations by Deborah Kogan Ray, Arcade, 1990.
Water's Way, illustrations by Rand, Arcade, 1991.
Purple Delicious Blackberry Jam, Arcade, 1992.
This Way Home, Holt, 1993.
The Room, Dial, in press.

WORK IN PROGRESS: October Smiled Back, for Holt, 1995; *The Hayloft,* for Dial, 1995; picture books on fossils and evolution.

SIDELIGHTS: Lisa Westberg Peters told *SATA:* "Perhaps because I spent childhood summers on a river, I especially like to write picture books involving nature or the natural sciences. The woods and rivers of Minnesota and Wisconsin left a strong impression on me as a child, and my writing career started with poetry on the beach on lazy summer afternoons. Eventually I chose the more practical field of journalism, but after my children were born, I wandered away from newspapering in order to linger over the sounds, patterns, and rhythms found in children's books.

"Because I'm not a scientist, I recognize the need to make scientific subjects appealing and understandable. For the sake of young minds, I blend the facts of science with the pull of story. I also try to use simple and expressive language. My ideas come from my own experiences as a mountain climber, a bird watcher, a fossil finder, and from what I hope is a lifelong curiosity about the earth and its creatures. I'm simply trying to gather kids around and help them discover what I am discovering for myself.

"Besides picture book science, I also write children's fiction. My ideas for those stories come from my childhood, my children, my travels, and from a place in my mind where ideas simmer until they're ready. My inspiration to write often comes from a different source—reading great books or listening to great music."

*   *   *

PEYO
See CULLIFORD, Pierre

*   *   *

PINKNEY, (Jerry) Brian 1961-
(J. Brian Pinkney)

PERSONAL: Born August 28, 1961, in Boston, MA; son of Jerry (an illustrator) and Gloria Jean (a writer) Pinkney; married Andrea R. Davis (an editor and writer), October 12, 1991. *Education:* Philadelphia College of Art, B.F.A., 1983; School of Visual Arts, M.F.A., 1990. *Hobbies and other interests:* Tae kwon do, playing drums.

ADDRESSES: Home—444 Henry St., Brooklyn, NY 11231.

CAREER: Illustrator. Taught at the Children's Art Carnival in Harlem, NY, and the School of Visual Arts in New York City. *Exhibitions:* Pinkney's works have been displayed at the Original Art Show at the Society of Illustrators, 1990, 1991, and 1992, in a solo exhibition at the School of Visual Arts Student Galleries, and at the Society of Illustrators Annual Show.

MEMBER: Society of Illustrators, Society of Children's Book Writers and Illustrators.

AWARDS, HONORS: National Arts Club Award of Distinction, 1990; Parents' Choice Honor Award for Illustration, 1990, for *The Boy and the Ghost;* Parents' Choice Honor Award for Story Books, 1990, for *The Ballad of Belle Dorcus;* Parents' Choice Picture Book awards, both 1991, for *Where Does This Trail Lead?* and

A Wave in Her Pocket; Golden Kite Honor Award, 1991, for *Where Does This Trail Lead?;* Coretta Scott King Honor Book award for illustration, American Library Association, 1993, for *Sukey and the Mermaid.*

WRITINGS:

SELF-ILLUSTRATED

Max Found Two Sticks, Simon & Schuster, in press.

ILLUSTRATOR

(As J. Brian Pinkney) Roy Wandelmaier, *Shipwrecked on Mystery Island,* Troll, 1985.
(As J. Brian Pinkney) R. Rozanne Knudson, *Julie Brown: Racing with the World* (biography), Viking Kestrel, 1988.
(As J. Brian Pinkney) Robert D. San Souci, *The Boy and the Ghost,* Simon & Schuster, 1989.
William H. Hooks, *The Ballad of Belle Dorcus,* Knopf, 1990.
Polly Carter, *Harriet Tubman and Black History Month,* Silver Press, 1990.
Burton Albert, *Where Does This Trail Lead?,* Simon & Schuster, 1991.
Lynn Joseph, *A Wave in Her Pocket: Stories from Trinidad,* Clarion, 1991.
Christopher Cat and Countee Cullin, *The Lost Zoo,* Silver Burdett, 1992.
San Souci, *Sukey and the Mermaid,* Four Winds, 1992.

BRIAN PINKNEY

Pinkney uses scratchboard techniques to "sculpt" images for his illustrations, such as this portrait from Robert D. San Souci's *Sukey and the Mermaid*.

Patricia C. McKissack, *The Dark-Thirty: Southern Tales of the Supernatural,* Knopf, 1992.
Judy Sierra, *The Elephant's Wrestling Match,* Lodestar, 1992.
Andrea Davis Pinkney, *Alvin,* Hyperion, 1993.
San Souci, *Cut from the Same Cloth,* Philomel Books, 1993.
Andrea Davis Pinkney, *Seven Candles for Kwanzza,* Dial, 1993.
(As J. Brian Pinkney) Jean Marzollo, *Happy Birthday, Martin Luther King,* Scholastic, 1993.

Also provided the cover art for Myra C. Livingston's *I Never Told: And Other Poems,* Macmillan, 1992. Work has appeared in *New York Times Magazine, Women's Day, Business Tokyo, Ebony Man,* and *Instructor.*

WORK IN PROGRESS: Illustrations for Maxine Schur's *Day of Delight,* Dial, 1994, and Andrea Davis Pinkney's *Benjamin Banaker,* Harcourt, 1994.

SIDELIGHTS: Brian Pinkney told *SATA:* "Working in scratchboard [a technique, much like engraving, in which the artist 'scratches' away the board's black coating to reveal the white clay beneath it] was an important turning point in my career. I started experimenting in scratchboard when I was at the School of Visual Arts getting my master's degree in illustration. I went back to school because I was looking for something. I wanted the next step in my artistic vision. Working in scratchboard became what I found. I like working in scratchboard because it allows me to sculpt the image. When I etch the drawing out of the board, I get a rhythm going with my lines which feels like sculpture to me.

"When I illustrate stories, I like to be personally involved. I like illustrating stories about African American subject matter because I learn about my culture and heritage. I also like stories I can get involved with like *Where Does This Trail Lead?* I illustrated my experiences growing up on Cape Cod during the summer when I was young. When I illustrated the book *Alvin,* which my wife wrote, I got to act out Alvin's life as a dancer. My wife and I took dance lessons, which was a lot of fun. I modeled for Alvin in the book. The book I wrote, *Max Found Two Sticks,* is based on my experience playing the drums."

FOR MORE INFORMATION SEE:

PERIODICALS

Bulletin for the Center of Children's Books, December, 1992, p. 117.
Publishers Weekly, December 22, 1989, pp. 26-27.
School Library Journal, March, 1991, p. 181.

* * *

PINKNEY, J. Brian
See PINKNEY, (Jerry) Brian

PLAIDY, Jean
See HIBBERT, Eleanor Alice Burford

* * *

POLACCO, Patricia 1944-

PERSONAL: Born July 11, 1944, in Lansing, MI; daughter of William F. (a television talk show host) and Mary Ellen (a teacher; maiden name, Gaw) Barber; married Enzo Mario Polacco (a chef and cooking instructor), August 19, 1979; children: Traci Denise, Steven John. *Education:* Attended California College of Arts and Crafts and Laney College; Monash University, B.A., 1974; University of Melbourne, M.A, Ph.D., 1978.

ADDRESSES: Agent—Edythea Selman, 14 Washington Pl., New York, NY 10003.

CAREER: Author and illustrator, 1986—. Worked previously as an art historian consultant for local museums; speaker at schools and reading organizations. Member of Center for US/USSR Initiatives, 1984—, and Citizens Exchange Council, 1988-91.

MEMBER: Society of Children's Book Writers and Illustrators.

AWARDS, HONORS: International Reading Association best picture book award, 1989, for *Rechenka's Eggs;* Sydney Taylor Award, 1989, for *The Keeping Quilt;* Educators for Social Responsibility Award, 1991; Golden Kite Award for Illustration, Society of Children's Book Writers and Illustrators, 1992, for *Chicken Sunday.*

WRITINGS:

SELF-ILLUSTRATED PICTURE BOOKS

Meteor!, Dodd, 1987.
Rechenka's Eggs, Philomel, 1988.
Boatride with Lillian Two Blossom, Philomel, 1988.
(Adaptor) *Casey at the Bat,* Putnam, 1988.
The Keeping Quilt, Simon & Schuster, 1988.
Uncle Vova's Tree, Philomel, 1989.
Babushka's Doll, Simon & Schuster, 1990.
Just Plain Fancy, Bantam, 1990.
Thunder Cake, Philomel, 1990.
Some Birthday!, Simon & Schuster, 1991.
Appelemundo's Dreams, Philomel, 1991.
Chicken Sunday, Philomel, 1992.
Mrs. Katz and Tush, Bantam, 1992.
Picnic at Mudsock Meadow, Putnam, 1992.
The Bee Tree, Putnam, 1993.

WORK IN PROGRESS: Babushka Ba Ba Ya Ga.

SIDELIGHTS: Patricia Polacco draws on her rich Russian and Irish heritage, as well as her fondly remembered childhood, to create unique and lavishly illustrated picture books. A number of her creations, such as *The Keeping Quilt* and *Uncle Vova's Tree,* relate Russian family customs and folklore, while others, such

PATRICIA POLACCO

as *Meteor!* and *Some Birthday!*, recall incidents that occurred during the many summers Polacco spent on her family's Michigan farm. All of Polacco's works, however, reflect her storytelling background and give a strong sense of the importance of family ties and traditions. Recognizing her various voices, Polacco describes her works in an interview with *Something about the Author* (*SATA*): "From my Russian background my stories are kind of ethnic, primitive, Eastern European—that's one type of voice I write in. Another is my mid-western American farm voice. I also write in a Jewish voice—my family was part Jewish and part Christian, which is an amazing thing. I write in all of the above, all of those voices because they more or less have been the places that I've lived."

Born in Lansing, Michigan, Polacco spent her childhood in a assortment of places. She remained in Michigan until she was close to six, at which point her grandmother died and her mother got a teaching job in Coral Gables, Florida (her parents had divorced when she was three). Staying in Florida for three years, Polacco then moved with her mother to Oakland, California, but she always returned home to Michigan for her summers. "I never really left Michigan, no matter where I lived," she explains in her *SATA* interview. This travelling allowed Polacco to spend time with both her parents, who were able to offer her two equally rich cultural backgrounds.

Her mother's family came from the Ukraine and the republic of Georgia, and her father's family were "shanty Irish." Polacco points out in her *SATA* interview that her parents "have very rich imaginations, and I think what both of them gave me was a feeling of sovereignty as far as being able to dream and think about all the 'what ifs.' They never pooh-poohed any kind of crazy ideas, they always sat and listened and would give their input."

In addition to her parents, Polacco was also "lucky enough" to live with both sets of her grandparents as a child. Her Russian grandparents "were people who made perfectly ordinary events into miracles," relates Polacco in her interview. "They were very lyrical and saw things that most people don't. They spent an awful lot of time building our imaginations. My father's people also have a great oral tradition," continues Polacco, "but theirs was more a passing on of the family history and telling over and over again how everybody got here—little family anecdotes. So I got a sense of history from my father's side and a sense of magic from my mother's."

Surrounded by so much creativity and storytelling, Polacco began drawing at an early age. She remembers herself as being a very shy and introspective child. "One might even describe me as almost disturbing, I was so quiet," she recalls in her *SATA* interview. "I spent an awful lot of time in my imagination because that's where I was safe and I felt good. I also drew all of the time—as long as I can remember, that is something that made me feel good." The objects of Polacco's many drawings varied, but in the beginning she drew a number of houses and environments. Another favorite subject was horses; her father owned some and Polacco grew up with them. "Even then I used to like to draw members of the family and home," Polacco tells *SATA*. "I also used to love especially to do overhead scenes where you'd have entire communities—the kind that you could invent."

In addition to her drawing, Polacco spent her childhood building things, taking ballet classes, and listening to family stories. Her drawing ability was encouraged from the beginning by her family, who used to honor her by hanging up her art. As she grew older, this became especially important to Polacco when she started having difficulty reading and writing. It was not until she was fourteen that she was finally diagnosed as dyslexic. In the meantime, she suffered a great deal of teasing and self-doubt. "Reading out loud for me was a nightmare because I would mispronounce words or reconstruct things that weren't even there," explains Polacco in her *SATA* interview. "So when I would draw, that's when kids would get out of their seats and stand behind me and go, 'Wow, you can really draw.'"

As she moved into her teenage years, Polacco's shyness receded and she became the "class comedian." She spent her high school years like most other youths of the time. "If you've ever watched the movie *American Graffiti,* that was my teenage years," Polacco remarks in her interview. "We used to cruise—two or three of my friends had cars. It was a very innocent thing to do; you kind of drove up and down the roads and talked to your friends. It was an innocent great time. I used to love to go to dance concerts—they used to call them rock and roll shows—where you could dance and that sort of thing."

From high school, Polacco began her jagged college career, which ended up spanning several years. She received a scholarship for school, but then promptly got married at the age of eighteen. She did attend school for a couple of semesters, but soon had to drop out and go to work; she was not able to return and finish her degree until after her two children were born. At this time, and as she was growing up, Polacco never thought she would actually do anything career-oriented with her art. When she was very young she dreamed of being a veterinarian, but when she started having problems with math it became evident that this would not be possible. A dancing career became her aspiration for a while, but through it all she continued with her art.

Polacco's writing, however, was a different story. She did not begin this aspect of her current career until she was forty-one. It was becoming a member of the Society of Children's Book Writers and Illustrators that first prompted Polacco to begin writing. "The first book I did was *Meteor!*, which is based on a family event that happened in Michigan," comments Polacco in her *SATA* interview. "I had told the story for years, as I have with a lot of my other stories; because of my storytelling background I have always been very vocal. When I joined this group, they showed me how to put it into a thirty-two page format, what publishers expect as far as presentation, and all that sort of thing." Soon afterwards, Polacco's mother financed her daughter's first trip to New York, and because of her careful planning, Polacco was able to visit sixteen publishers in one week. "It was grueling," she states in her interview. "A Michigan farm girl, I was too stupid to know that I should be frightened, but I wasn't. My mouth was hanging open, and I thought, 'Gee, what a great place.'" *Meteor!* was among the many rough dummies Polacco took to New York, and she knew within a week that it had been sold to Dodd, Mead. Since then, she has been successful in selling every book she has created.

Meteor! is based on a real event that happened during one of the many summers that Polacco and her brother stayed with their grandparents in Michigan. The family is spending a quiet evening at home when a meteor that is careening toward earth lands on Gramma and Grampa's front lawn. The news buzzes quickly through town the next morning, and a whole slew of activities erupt because of the meteor. The farm literally becomes a carnival, with hot air balloons, the Union City band, a

A small town comes to life with the arrival of a meteor in Polacco's first self-illustrated book.

Polacco reaches into her own family's history for *The Keeping Quilt,* a tender story of an heirloom that connects four generations of Russian Jews.

circus, and meteor basket lunches. And the meteor itself seems to have some kind of magical power—when people touch it they feel different, almost inspired. The meteor continues to be a source of wonder for the townspeople many years after it lands, and it stays in the same spot until it is moved to a green hillside to become Polacco's grandmother's headstone. "There is a nostalgic, homey feeling to this book, and small-town America comes to life in its pages," asserts Barbara S. McGinn in *School Library Journal.* And a *Publishers Weekly* reviewer maintains that *Meteor!* "expresses the magic" brought to the town "from the funny folksy way the story is told to the imaginative ... illustrations."

Since her first published book, a number Polacco's works seem to fall into three categories: those that deal with her Irish background, those that deal with her Russian background, and those that deal with minority groups (blacks, Jews, and the Amish). Among the first group are *Some Birthday!* and *Picnic at Mudsock Meadow.* Those that fall into the Russian category include *Uncle Vova's Tree, The Keeping Quilt,* and *Thunder Cake.* And the last group consists of such works as *Just Plain Fancy, Chicken Sunday,* and *Mrs. Katz and*

Tush. In addition to presenting children with a multicultural view of the world, all contain Polacco's familiar artwork, in which detailed facial expressions and cultural environments are depicted with pencil, colored markers, and acrylic paints. "If you walked into my living room you would see where my drawings come from; there are a lot of oriental persian-looking rugs and lots of pattern on pattern," describes Polacco in her *SATA* interview. "Nothing really matches, but it blends—it's very, very visual. So I guess this is who I am, and my mother's house is the same way—if you're surrounded by it you're almost doomed to create your art that way."

The pictures in *Some Birthday!* contrast a gloomy moonlit night with the homey details of a birthday celebration. Polacco is once again on her family's farm in Michigan, and this time it appears that everyone has forgotten her birthday. Her father comes home from work and suggests a trip to Clay Pit Bottoms at the edge of town (there is rumored to be a monster living in the water). When her father wanders off to investigate a rustling noise, Polacco, her brother, and her cousin are convinced that they see the monster. Running home screaming, they soon discover that it was only Polacco's

father falling into the water—he was the monster. What follows is a traditional birthday celebration, including a cake with a monster on top and presents. "Polacco's inimitable illustrations perfectly accompany this playful tale," remarks Susan Scheps in *School Library Journal*. *Some Birthday!* is "a delicious slice of family life," concludes a *Publishers Weekly* contributor.

Picnic at Mudsock Meadow, published in 1992, also takes place at the Michigan farm. During the course of the annual Halloween picnic, know-it-all Hester spends most of her time pointing out shy William's failures. Finally deciding to get even, William jumps into the eerie and glowing nearby swamp, emerging in his spooky disguise to win the costume contest without much competition. "A cast of clamorous children and colorful adults vivifies Polacco's latest childhood memory," points out a *Publishers Weekly* reviewer, concluding that "there are just enough chills here for Halloween, but this picnic offers year-round cheer."

Among Polacco's many descriptions of Russian customs is *Uncle Vova's Tree,* which is full of fond memories of the family celebrations of Epiphany in the tradition of their Russian homeland. As a child Polacco would

gather with the rest of her family at Uncle Vova's, where they would sing and dance, take part in a feast full of rituals, enjoy sleigh rides, and open presents. The most important part of the day, though, was decorating the outside tree planted by Uncle Vova upon his arrival in the United States as a symbol of his and his family's roots. The year after one of these glorious celebrations, Christmas seems to have lost its magic because of Uncle Vova's death, and the family even forgets to decorate his tree. The children run outside to discover a miracle— the animals from the farm and a nearby forest are dressing the tree. "Full of love and warmth for a time remembered, the story pulses with life even though a death has saddened the family," comments Ellen Fader in *Horn Book*. In *Uncle Vova's Tree,* Polacco "spins the fine threads of family lore into an intricately patterned cloth," concludes a *Los Angeles Times Book Review* contributor.

In *The Keeping Quilt* Polacco presents another aspect of her Russian family's heritage. The quilt, which was made from Polacco's Great-Gramma Anna's old dress and babushka, serves as a link between the women of the family. Throughout the years, the quilt is used at births, weddings, birthdays, and deaths, always a re-

Friendships between people of different ages, races, and religions play a prominent role in Polacco's work. (Illustration by the author from *Mrs. Katz and Tush.*)

minder of the family's Russian heritage. And as the years pass, the changes in Jewish customs and traditions are also portrayed. "Children will be fascinated by the various uses to which the quilt is put," asserts *School Library Journal* contributor Lee Bock. "Useful for the sense of history it presents to young viewers," states a *Booklist* reviewer, "[*The Keeping Quilt*] also carries a warm message on the meaning of family."

Thunder Cake has young Polacco overcoming her fear of thunderstorms. Hiding under the bed at the first crack of thunder, Polacco is drawn out by her Russian grandma, who distracts her from her fears with the making of a thunder cake. The cake is made from scratch, and Polacco and her grandma must gather the ingredients from the farm before the storm actually starts. During the course of their activities, Polacco overcomes many fears, including taking an egg from Nellie Peck Hen, milking Kick Cow, and walking through Tangleweed Woods. The two finish the cake just as the storm hits, and celebrate Polacco's new-found bravery. The recipe is even included on the last page. "What ... Polacco excels at in *Thunder Cake* is depicting the color and light of an approaching storm and the animated hustle and bustle of an old-fashioned farm," maintains Jane Smiley in the *New York Times Book Review*. Megan McDonald, writing in *Five Owls*, points out that "every picture possesses inherent movement to match the story's breathless pacing.... In a perfect blending of story and illustration, this is picture-book artistry at its finest."

One of the minority groups Polacco presents in her works, the Amish, can be found in *Just Plain Fancy*, published in 1990. Naomi tells her younger sister Ruth that she wants something fancy in her otherwise plain life. The very same day, the two girls find an odd looking egg and add it to the other eggs of the family hen. When it hatches, it becomes evident to Naomi and Ruth that this is no ordinary bird, especially when it spreads its magnificent peacock's tail. Fearful that the bird will be shunned because it is too fancy, the two sisters manage to hide it until the day of the summer working bee. Receiving the traditional Amish white cap for her responsible care of the chickens, Naomi also discovers that Fancy is a work of God and therefore acceptable in her community. "Brimming with details of Amish farm life, the illustrations in [*Just Plain Fancy*] are bound to inform as they entertain," relates Carey Ayres in *School Library Journal*. And a *Publishers Weekly* contributor concludes: "Polacco's warm story and sensitive illustrations offer a fresh, balanced perspective on Amish life."

Polacco presents similar stories in two more of her cross-cultural books—*Chicken Sunday* and *Mrs. Katz and Tush*. *Chicken Sunday* recalls another incident from Polacco's childhood. Growing up next door to an African American family, Polacco often attends Baptist services with the Washingtons and enjoys Miss Eula's Sunday dinner of fried chicken, collard greens with bacon, and corn on the cob. She and Miss Eula's two grandsons, Winston and Stewart Washington, hope to earn enough money to buy Miss Eula a new Easter hat. Along the way, they manage to first offend, and then befriend a Russian Jewish shopkeeper. "Without being heavy-handed, Polacco's text conveys a tremendous pride of heritage as it brims with rich images from ... African American and Russian Jewish cultures," describes a *Publishers Weekly* reviewer. *Mrs. Katz and Tush* follows the developing friendship between an elderly Polish-Jewish woman and a neighborhood black child who presents her with the gift of a cat. As they each learn about the other's culture, they discover that blacks and Jews have a lot in common and form a lasting bond. In both *Chicken Sunday* and *Mrs. Katz and Tush* "Polacco blends African-American culture with Russian and Polish Jewish culture and makes a point to show some similarities," observes Maryln Schwartz in the *New York Times Book Review*.

Polacco's many multicultural tales and childhood remembrances make their way to the pages of her books in an unusual manner. "I don't sit at a typewriter and compose like most people do," explains Polacco in her *SATA* interview. "To get back to how I was as a kid—I was a very kinetic child. I had to move all of the time, so I rocked a lot. That translated over into my adulthood, because I love to rock in a rocking chair, and I take this very seriously. I have about thirteen rockers in my house, so my process of doing stories includes a couple hours of rocking in the morning and about an hour at night. You might call this meditation, although I don't; I just call it rocking and dreaming. I will see stories in my head almost like a movie, and I'll run them over and over again until they're the way I want them to be. Sometimes I'll hear the words, sometimes I see the pictures—I don't know how to describe it. I have a little pad and pencil next to these chairs and I jot down a kind of outline while I'm thinking of it, put the outline in a folder, and come back to it when I'm ready to. There is almost like an inspiration, like birth, where you know it's time to work on the story."

More often than not, the story that Polacco ends up working on concerns the multicultural aspects of American society. She believes it is very important for children to learn about and understand the differences among various people. "Not all kids, and I've learned this now by traveling all over the country, are lucky enough to live in neighborhoods where they can experience people of different backgrounds and ideas and skin colors. Their exposure to other cultures, in other words, is only what they read or study in school or what they see on television—they don't have a firsthand experience. That is why multiculturalism in literature is important: we need to get true ethnic people writing about their own. I, as a white person, for instance, cannot write in a black voice because I'm not black, I have no idea what it's like to be in their skin and in their culture. For children to be demystified about each other authentic material, loving material, things that talk about tradition and face and background and beliefs need to be written. I think children need to see this so they can know how absolutely alike we all are. We have different names for things, different religions, but we're very much the same."

WORKS CITED:

Ayres, Carey, review of *Just Plain Fancy, School Library Journal,* December, 1990, p. 86.

Bock, Lee, review of *The Keeping Quilt, School Library Journal,* October, 1988, p. 136.

Review of *Chicken Sunday, Publishers Weekly,* January 27, 1992, p. 96.

Fader, Ellen, review of *Uncle Vova's Tree, Horn Book,* November, 1989, p. 753.

Review of *Just Plain Fancy, Publishers Weekly,* October 12, 1990, p. 62.

Review of *The Keeping Quilt, Booklist,* December 1, 1988, p. 654.

McDonald, Megan, review of *Thunder Cake, Five Owls,* May/June, 1990, p. 83.

McGinn, Barbara S., review of *Meteor!, School Library Journal,* August, 1987, pp. 73-74.

Review of *Meteor!, Publishers Weekly,* April 10, 1987, p. 95.

Review of *Picnic at Mudsock Meadow, Publishers Weekly,* August 17, 1992, p. 499.

Polacco, Patricia, in an interview with Susan M. Reicha for *Something about the Author,* January 11, 1993.

Scheps, Susan, review of *Some Birthday!, School Library Journal,* October, 1991, p. 103.

Schwartz, Maryln, "A Gramma and a Bubee," *New York Times Book Review,* May 17, 1992, p. 24.

Smiley, Jane, "Recipe for Riding Out a Storm," *New York Times Book Review,* May 20, 1990, p. 38.

Review of *Some Birthday!, Publishers Weekly,* August 30, 1991, p. 82.

Review of *Uncle Vova's Tree, Los Angeles Times Book Review,* November 26, 1989.

FOR MORE INFORMATION SEE:

PERIODICALS

Horn Book, March, 1990, p. 194; November, 1990, pp. 732-33; January/February, 1991, p. 59.

Los Angeles Times Book Review, February 25, 1990, p. 8.

New Advocate, spring, 1990, pp. 142-43.

Newsweek, December 28, 1992, p. 54.

New York Times Book Review, April 3, 1988, p. 16.

Publishers Weekly, May 12, 1989, p. 290; October 13, 1989, pp. 52-53; August 10, 1990, p. 443; June 21, 1991, p. 64.

School Library Journal, May, 1988, p. 86; April, 1989, p. 89; March, 1990, p. 199; November, 1990, p. 98; September, 1991, p. 239; May, 1992, p. 92; July, 1992, p. 63.

Tribune Books (Chicago), May 29, 1988.

—Sketch by Susan M. Reicha

R

RANEY, Ken 1953-

PERSONAL: Born December 30, 1953, in Ellsworth, KS; son of Kenneth William Jr. (an antiques dealer) and Shirley (an antiques dealer; maiden name, Turner) Raney; married Deborah Teeter (a homemaker), August 11, 1974; children: Tarl Adam, Tobi Anne, Trey Andrew, Tavia Amber. *Education:* Attended Butler County Junior College and Kansas State University. *Religion:* Christian.

ADDRESSES: Home—P.O. Box 699, Hesston, KS 67062. *Office*—Excel Industries, P.O. Box 7000, Hesston, KS 67062.

KEN RANEY

CAREER: Excel Industries, Hesston, KS, advertising manager, 1984—; author and illustrator of books for children. Member of Ellsworth, KS, school board, 1983-84. *Exhibitions:* Art has been featured in numerous exhibitions and solo shows, including "A Rose by Any Other Name," 1988; "Art with a Heart," 1992; and Kansas Artists Postcard Series VIII, XIII, and XV.

MEMBER: American Institute of Graphic Arts, Wichita Chapter.

AWARDS, HONORS: Named illustrator of the year by the Small Press Writers and Artists Organization; received ADDY award for excellence from American Advertising Federation.

WRITINGS:

FOR CHILDREN; SELF-ILLUSTRATED

Stick Horse, Medlicott Press, 1991.
It's Probably Good That Dinosaurs Are Extinct, Green Tiger Books, 1993.

OTHER

Contributor of illustrations to books and periodicals, including *National Geographic Traveler, Artist's Magazine, Highlights for Children, Campus Life, Christianity Today,* and *The Complete Colored Pencil Book,* North Light Books, 1992.

SIDELIGHTS: Ken Raney told *SATA:* "I'm just a big kid myself—I write and illustrate the things that would have fascinated me as a child. As a Christian, I believe that guiding and entertaining children are very noble things to do. I also believe that books for children need to be imaginative—something that will spark their imagination and creativity."

*   *   *

REEDER, Colin (Dawson) 1938-

PERSONAL: Born September 30, 1938, in Sheringham, Norfolk, England; son of Donald Herbert (a minister)

COLIN REEDER

and Marian (Smith) Reeder. *Education:* National College for Youth and Community Workers, youth community work diploma, 1961.

ADDRESSES: Home—3 Charles Rash Close, Felmingham, North Walsham, Norfolk NR28 0PA, England. *Agent*—Eunice McMullen, 38 Clewer Hill Rd., Windsor, Berkshire SL4 4BW, England.

CAREER: G.J. Galloway (publishers), London, England, artist and designer, 1957-59; Cambridge Education Department, youth and community worker, 1961-64; Hertfordshire Education Department, youth and community worker, 1964-70; Essex Education Department, principal of adult education centre and youth and community worker, 1972-78. Member of advisory government committee on juvenile delinquency, 1962-64. Has exhibited paintings with the Royal Institute of Oil Painters and in Norfolk and other parts of England.

WRITINGS:

ILLUSTRATOR; "LITTLE RED TRACTOR" SERIES

Elizabeth Laird, *The Day Patch Stood Guard,* Collins, 1990, Morrow, 1991, new edition, Picture Lions, 1992.
Laird, *The Day Sidney Was Lost,* Collins, 1990, published as *The Day Sidney Ran Off,* Morrow, 1991, new edition, Picture Lions, 1992.
Laird, *The Day the Ducks Went Skating,* Collins, 1990, Morrow, 1991, new edition, Picture Lions, 1992.
Laird, *The Day Veronica Was Nosy,* Collins, 1990, Morrow, 1991, new edition, Picture Lions, 1992.

SELF-ILLUSTRATED; "WEST MEADOW" SERIES

The Great Flood, Silent Books, 1989.
Moving Day, Silent Books, 1989.
Billy's Mistake, Silent Books, 1989.
Ronnie's Finest Hour, Silent Books, 1989.

Gerald's Saturday, Silent Books, 1989.
Plastered for Christmas, Silent Books, 1989.

SELF-ILLUSTRATED; "THE ADVENTURES OF DUNLOP" SERIES

Dunlop and the Eggs, HarperCollins, 1992.
Dunlop Catches Cold, HarperCollins, 1992.
Dunlop Gives Chase, HarperCollins, 1992.
Dunlop to the Rescue, HarperCollins, 1992.

OTHER

Reeder's work has been published in Sweden, Denmark, and France.

WORK IN PROGRESS: Four "Little Red Tractor" books, and four "Adventures of Dunlop" books, all for Orion; *Benjamin's Creek,* an adventure story for older children, concerning a wildlife area of Norfolk and pollution, for Orion.

ADAPTATIONS: The books in the "Little Red Tractor" series have all been adapted for audio cassette and released with paperback books, HarperCollins.

SIDELIGHTS: Colin Reeder told *SATA:* "My painting and my writing spring from concern for the earth and the people and creatures that inhabit it. Most of my work is at present for younger people. Action takes place in rural settings and the stories carry a level of educational information. I left school in the mid-fifties and began work in a studio in London. At eighteen I exhibited with the Royal Institute of Oil Painters and my work was reviewed in a French art publication. I became disenchanted with the art world and took up full-time college education. Following this I worked until 1978 as a youth and community worker. I worked

Reeder's illustrations for Elizabeth Laird's "The Little Red Tractor" series, set on a simple farm, express his concern for nature. (Illustration by Reeder from *The Day Sidney Ran Off.*)

with many states of teenage life, including drugs and delinquency. I moved to Norfolk in 1978 and have worked since then as a full-time artist and writer. As a Norfolk landscape watercolorist I exhibit regularly in Norfolk and elsewhere. I am at present, in conjunction with a television director, developing one of my current projects (about an animal sanctuary) for television animation, together with four 'Little Red Tractor' stories for television video."

*   *   *

REISGIES, Teresa (Maria) 1966-

PERSONAL: Born December 3, 1966; daughter of Fritz Wilhelm (a jeweler) and Anna Elfriede Reisgies. *Education:* Georgetown University, B.S., 1989; Columbia University, M.S., 1993.

ADDRESSES: Home—P.O. Box 244, Alpine, NJ 07620. *Agent*—c/o Publicity Director, Peterson's Guides, Inc., 202 Carnegie Center, P.O. Box 2123, Princeton, NJ 08543-2123.

CAREER: BKG Youth (a marketing and editorial service), New York City, senior associate editor, 1990-92.

WRITINGS:

(With Marian Salzman) *Greetings from High School,* Peterson's Guides, 1991.
(With Salzman) *150 Ways Teens Can Make a Difference,* Peterson's Guides, 1991.
(Contributor) M. Salzman and Ann O'Reilly, editors, *War and Peace in the Persian Gulf: What Teenagers Really Want to Know,* Peterson's Guides, 1991.
Watcha Gonna Do about Hate?, Simon & Shuster, 1992.

WORK IN PROGRESS: A book of quotes about hatred, racism, and discrimination in America.

SIDELIGHTS: Teresa Reisgies tells *SATA:* "My writing career began one year after my graduation from Georgetown University, when Marian Salzman—an established author of eight books and former magazine editor in chief—took me on as her coauthor for a series of books for high school students. My role was to integrate myself into the lives of New York-area teenagers and to report from the high school front. Working hand-in-hand with five teenage contributing editors, I relived the life of a high school teenager for six months in order to write *Greetings from High School,* a teenage survival guide.

"My next challenge was to interview six hundred teenage activists for *150 Ways Teens Can Make a Difference.* This required extensive travel throughout America's high schools just before war broke out in the Persian Gulf. Marian and I were able to gauge just how concerned America's youth was about the political situation, and I subsequently served as contributing editor for *War and Peace in the Persian Gulf.* In the wake of the Los Angeles riots, I am currently compiling

TERESA REISGIES

a book of quotes by people young and old who feel the need to speak out about the problem of hate in America.

"Writing for teenagers has been rewarding in many ways. Having spent the good part of the last two years in rural, inner-city, suburban, urban, and private schools, I strongly believe that the power of America's youth has been grossly underestimated. The media has represented youth as entirely apathetic and schools as nothing more than breeding grounds for drugs and crime. This is simply not the case. As a journalist I strive to shed a more realistic light on these and other issues I feel are misrepresented to the public."

*   *   *

RIDDLE, Tohby 1965-

PERSONAL: Born May 31, 1965, in Sydney, Australia; son of Edgerton Harold (an engineer) and Jasmine (a psychologist; maiden name, Beck) Riddle. *Education:* Sydney College of the Arts, Bachelor of Visual Arts degree, 1985; Sydney University, Bachelor of Architectural Science degree, 1991, Bachelor of Architecture degree, 1992.

ADDRESSES: c/o Orchard Books, 95 Madison Ave., New York, NY 10016.

CAREER: Freelance cartoonist and illustrator, 1986—; writer/illustrator of picture books, 1988—.

WRITINGS:

SELF-ILLUSTRATED

Careful with That Ball, Eugene!, Pan Books, 1989, Orchard, 1991.
A Most Unusual Dog, Macmillan, 1992.

WORK IN PROGRESS: Arnold Z. Jones Could Really Play the Trumpet, a picture book; *The Tap-Dancer,* a book of cartoons.

SIDELIGHTS: "From an early age I was encouraged to draw," Tohby Riddle told *SATA.* "In the sunniest room in the house I would sit on the floor where my mother would provide me with reams of butcher's paper and a box of crayons. Then I would claim, crayon in hand, that the next drawing would be a masterpiece. Very soon I learned that masterpieces don't come so easily, but although the crayon in my hand is now a pen, I continue to try.

"I was schooled until the age of eleven at a Rudolf Steiner school where again painting, drawing, and other forms of creativity were actively encouraged. This entailed illustrating everything you learned from mythology to mathematics. I suppose the idea was to stimulate both the left and the right hemispheres of the brain during learning.

"Later I studied painting at Sydney College of the Arts. I enjoyed painting, but as a medium to communicate ideas I began to wonder if it could compete in the face of such media as television, film, magazines, and books. I felt painting was tending to reach an increasingly smaller audience in contemporary culture and wondered about my options. I think I was also too lazy to make stretchers for my canvases. After graduating from art

TOHBY RIDDLE

Riddle captures the childhood fear of the consequences of naughty behavior in his self-illustrated *Careful with That Ball, Eugene!*

college, I found myself moving toward the immediacy and accessibility of illustrating and decided that a picture book would be the ideal vehicle for an illustrator. As an unknown, I figured that the best opportunity to illustrate a picture book would be to write the story as well. So far this has worked for me and since I tend to conceive picture book ideas in words and pictures simultaneously (which I find creates special opportunities for the relationship between image and text), I can now think of no better way of working.

"My concerns as a picture book creator are based on the premise that one can never overestimate the natural intelligence of children. I target this intelligence with ideas that I hope neither patronize nor moralize, but stimulate the child's mind. In *Careful with That Ball, Eugene!,* I was drawing very much on my own childhood experiences. My friend next door and I used to spend endless days playing games that involved kicking or throwing a ball and inevitably the ball would get out of control. I particularly remember how scary my friend's father was and seriously thought that if he ever caught us breaking something with the ball an inconceivably horrible fate would await us. Such childhood fears are incredibly real in a child's rich, unfettered imagination and in a sense this book pays homage to those fears."

ROGERS, Emma 1951-

PERSONAL: Born February 17, 1951, in Preston, Lancashire, England; daughter of Ainslite (a hotelier) and Margaret (a chef; maiden name, Hammond) Rothwell-Evans; married Paul Rogers (a writer), August 15, 1977; children: Toby, Thea, Joshua, Ruppert. *Education:* B.A. (with honors) from University of Wales; postgraduate certificate in education from Barts Hospital, London. *Politics:* "Left of center." *Religion:* "Searching."

ADDRESSES: Home— Puech Gaubil, Bournazel, 81170 Cordes, France.

CAREER: Writer; previously worked as a teacher.

MEMBER: Friends of Earth, Action Aid.

WRITINGS:

WITH HUSBAND, PAUL ROGERS

Forget-me-not, illustrated by Celia Berridge, Viking Kestrel, 1984.
Sheepchase, illustrated by Berridge, Viking Kestrel, 1986.
Tumbledown, illustrated by Robin Bell Corfield, Walker, 1987.
From Me to You, illustrated by Jane Johnson, Orchard, 1987.
Rain and Shine (short stories), illustrated by Chris Burke, Orchard, 1987.
Lily's Picnic, illustrated by John Prater, Bodley Head, 1988.
Somebody's Sleepy, illustrated by Corfield, Bodley Head, 1988.
Somebody's Awake, illustrated by Corfield, Bodley Head, 1988.
The Get Better Book, illustrated by Jo Burroughes, Orchard, 1988.
What's Wrong, Tom?, illustrated by Colin Robinson, Viking Kestrel, 1989.
Me and Alice Go to the Museum, illustrated by Prater, Bodley Head, 1989.
Me and Alice Go to the Gallery, illustrated by Prater, Bodley Head, 1989.
What Will the Weather Be Like Today?, illustrated by Kazuko, Orchard, 1989.
Boneshaker (short stories), illustrated by Maureen Bradley, Kestrel Kites, 1989.
The Shapes Game, illustrated by Sian Tucker, Orchard, 1989.
Don't Blame Me!, illustrated by Corfield, Bodley Head, 1990.
Amazing Babies (short stories), illustrated by Dee Shulman, Dent, 1990, printed as *Billy Buzoni and Friends,* 1991.
Surprise, Surprise!, illustrated by Tucker, Orchard, 1990.
Boneshaker Rides Again (short stories), illustrated by Maureen Bradley, Viking, 1990.
Do You Dare?, illustrated by Sonia Holleyman, Orchard, 1991.

EMMA ROGERS

Funimals, illustrated by Charles Fuge, Bodley Head, 1991.
Our House, illustrated by Priscilla Lamont, Walker, 1991.
Zoe's Tower, illustrated by Corfield, Walker, 1991.
Bat Boy, illustrated by Toni Goffe, Dent, 1991.

WORK IN PROGRESS: "We've just completed a longer story about a mischievous and courageous billy goat, to be published by Dent, together with a pair of picture books called *Little Boat* and *Little Train,* and something else called *Ten Terrible Pirates.*"

SIDELIGHTS: Emma Rogers told *SATA:* "Writing stories has a part in my life, along with brushing my teeth, changing a nappy and cooking supper for the family. That is not to say that it isn't something very special to me. Rather it is a natural and integrated part of every day. It doesn't stop when I'm on holiday, or digging the garden, or taking children to school in the car. The truth is there is always some kind of story rattling around and gathering shape inside my head. And there is almost always a piece of paper and a pencil waiting on the kitchen dresser.

"I was not brought up in an especially bookish family. But like many children, I had Peter Rabbit, Winnie the Pooh and the toad from Toad Hall as childhood companions. At the age of ten, I was considering being a teacher. By fifteen years, I had no idea at all where the future might lead. But one thing remained constant throughout—and that was my inclination to tell stories. I told them to myself and to my sister (we lived in a remote bit of North country). I told them to my toys—and made them into miniature books. I told them at school, where I came to love the subject that was known as 'creative English'—and got into many a scrape with my teachers when I filled the back pages of exercise books with stories, where there should have been lists of definitions for physics or French verbs.

"It was at school from around the age of sixteen, and then at university, that I wrapped myself almost exclusively in the most glorious world of stories. I studied English literature with drama and had a go at writing a full-length novel—before hiding it away in a chest of drawers, from where it still might peep if I dig too deeply for a sweater or T-shirt.

"After university, I taught for a while and enjoyed sharing books with young people (age 11 to 18). But I also discovered that for some of them there was little joy—and in some cases something like misery—to be found in books. There were the people who get labeled 'slow learners' or 'learning disabled.' And ... I found that the kind of books they were offered were those which were used to introduce five-year-olds to the skills of reading!

"So my first published work turned out to be a series of books for older readers (age 11 onwards), with a sophisticated cartoon approach and a simple, controlled vocabulary. The cartoons were brilliantly executed by an artist, Jeremy Long, who was then also a fellow teacher.

"Married life and children has led me on to working with many different artists to produce picture books for five-year-olds and under, as well as longer stories for readers aged seven to nine years. It has also brought with it the experience of 'shared' story-telling, as my husband Paul is also a writer. We have now produced lots of books together, working on the principle of fierce mutual criticism. It is not often that we sit at the same table and write on the same piece of paper (though that has happened). Rather, we take turns in refining something that might have begun in Paul's study or on the scrap of paper on the kitchen dresser.

"In between these 'literary exchanges' and 'collaborations,' we get on with life here in rural France, where we have recently settled with our four children and assorted pets. There is the challenge of another language, new places to discover, new friends to be made. And already there is some new story beginning to take shape on that piece of paper."

*   *   *

ROSENBERG, Amye 1950–

CAREER: Born April 27, 1950, in Brooklyn, NY; daughter of Samuel and Martha (Hodes) Rosenberg. *Education:* Hartford Art School, B.F.A., 1971. *Politics:*

AMYE ROSENBERG

Humanist. *Hobbies and other interests:* "I love to travel, read, and climb things. I love old musical instruments and try to play them once in a while. I have an old mandolin which I'm not at all good at! I have also kept bees—a hobby one cannot practice in New York!"

ADDRESSES: Office—245 East 25th St., Apt. 14H, New York, NY 10010-3047; or Intervisual Books, 152 Madison Ave., Suite 2400, New York, NY 10016.

CAREER: Author and illustrator, 1977—. Has also worked as shop clerk, window display artist, and in advertising.

MEMBER: Children's Aid Society, National Organization for Women, Cousteau Society.

WRITINGS:

SELF-ILLUSTRATED

Pop-Up Alphabet Soup, Intervisual Communications, Inc., 1979.
Sam the Detective and The Alef Bet Mystery, Behrman House, 1980.
Sam's Reading Rediness, Behrman House, 1982.
My Calendar, Behrman House, 1984.
Piggy's Playground, Golden Books, 1984.
School Mouse, Golden Books, 1984.
Hedgehog Helps Out, Golden Books, 1984.

Kitty's Clothes, Golden Books, 1984.
Pudge Pig's Counting Book, Golden Books, 1985.
The Biggest, Most Beautiful Christmas Tree, Golden Books, 1985.
Teddy's Toys, Golden Books, 1985.
Sleepy Squirrel, Golden Books, 1985.
Rupert Penguin, Golden Books, 1985.
Pup's Numbers, Golden Books, 1986.
Animals Naughty and Nice, Golden Books, 1986.
Animals Wild and Wooly, Golden Books, 1987.
A-Z Busy Word Book, Golden Books, 1988.
1-100 Busy Counting Book, Golden Books, 1988.
Pinky's First Spring Day, Golden Books, 1989.
Rabbit's Rainy Day, Golden Books, 1989.
The Lucky Fisherman, Golden Books, 1989.
Two-Minute Animal Stories, Golden Books, 1990.
Is It Christmas Yet?, Golden Books, 1990.
Melly's Menorah, Simon & Schuster, 1991.
Good Job, Jelly Bean, Simon & Schuster, 1992.
Ten Treats for Ginger, Simon & Schuster, 1992.
Out of Bed and Back Again, Simon & Schuster, 1992.
Jewels for Josephine, Grosset, 1993.

ILLUSTRATOR

Once upon a Mouse, Dutton, 1979.
4 Little Cloth Books, Dutton, 1979.
My Cash Register, Simon & Schuster, 1980.
My Telephone, Simon & Schuster, 1980.
One, Two, Buckle My Shoe, Simon & Schuster, 1980.
My Clock Book, Simon & Schuster, 1981.
Pig Newton's Plaid Pants, Simon & Schuster, 1981.
Gophers Loafers, Simon & Schuster, 1981.
Baby Seal, Simon & Schuster, 1982.
Look in the Yard, Grosset, 1982.
Play with Me, Grosset, 1982.
My First Little Mother Goose, Golden Books, 1982.
The Tale of Peter Rabbit, Golden Books, 1982.
The Hedgehog's Christmas Tree, Golden Books, 1982.
The Store Book, Golden Books, 1983.
We Wish You a Merry Christmas, Golden Books, 1983.
Cat-A-Log, Grosset, 1983.
Pudgy Peek-A-Boo, Grosset, 1983.
The Little Red Hen, Golden Books, 1984.
Polly's Pet, Golden Books, 1984.
Story-A-Night, Random House, 1985.
Peter Rabbit and Other Tales (video), Golden Video, 1985.
Nursery Rhymes, Ladybird Books, 1987.
Animal Rhymes, Ladybird Books, 1987.
I Don't Want To Go!, Golden Books, 1989.

WORK IN PROGRESS: Collaborating with composer/mandolin player Bill Walach on a musical project for children.

SIDELIGHTS: Amye Rosenberg's fascination with art and stories began as a child. "Ever since I was old enough to hold a crayon, I've been drawing and telling tales," she told *SATA*. "I had a huge curiosity about the physical world and an equally huge imagination. I believed that animals talked to me. I could lie on a sun-warmed rock and hear the earth breathe. I studied the stars and swore they were different colors."

Born in Brooklyn, but raised in rural Connecticut, Rosenberg spent a great deal of her childhood exploring the woods and fields near her home and imagining the people and animals that had lived in those settings. "I tried to recreate all those worlds in my drawings," Rosenberg stated. "Once I even tried to get a frog to pose for a portrait. Silly but true!" During a return trip to Brooklyn, Rosenberg was exposed to the sights and sounds of New York City for the first time, and she was captivated by the experience. The streets of New York "pulsated with energy, roared with noise, and swirled with motion," she recalled. While there, Rosenberg took her first visit to an art museum, an event which changed her life. As she tells it: "When I saw the paintings for the first time, I was electrified by the stories pictures could tell. There, at age five, I glimpsed my future!"

Before her trip was over, Rosenberg had completed dozens of sketches of New York. "I took all those vivid impressions and drawings back to Connecticut with me," Rosenberg continued. "I was obsessed with drawing and covered every surface I could find—scraps, envelopes, bits of cardboard. I devoured anything about art and loved history, archaeology, and adventure tales like *Ivanhoe* and *Treasure Island.* I loved music and developed an awareness of sound, including the sound of words, and I began writing little poems."

Rosenberg's interest in art deepened as she grew older, and during high school, she worked at her local museum and historical society, handling art works, giving tours, and teaching art to children. At Hartford Art School, she gained inspiration from a teacher who recognized and supported her talent. Rosenberg stated that the teacher "told me something that I now tell to kids. He said that

As a youngster with an active imagination, Rosenberg believed that animals could talk, and she recreated their world in her drawings. (Illustration by the author from *The Lucky Fisherman.*)

A love for children as well as a love for storytelling and art led Rosenberg to a career as an author-illustrator.

what I lacked in refined skills, I made up for with sheer determination and the will to succeed. I learned that it is the passion for art that ultimately makes the artist."

Later, Rosenberg decided on a course for her life while staying in London, England. "I began to amuse the children of friends with stories of my own childhood far away," she said. "I made pictures and stories for them. That's how I found my passion for writing and illustrating children's books. It was not just the love for art and storytelling, but, as I discovered, the love of children as well."

Rosenberg gets ideas for her work from many sources, including her travel experiences, but "more often it is the little things, the details of daily life at home and abroad that find their way into my books. Intelligent pictures and good storytelling are things I strive for in my work. I like to encourage creative thinking and participation. I'm always looking for ways to involve children, especially those too young to read, with books. That has attracted me to unusual and innovative formats like pop-ups and sticker books. I like to be challenged to go beyond story and pictures to communicate ideas. I enjoy finding (and teaching) creative ways to solve problems, preferably in a way that is fun, different, and challenging."

FOR MORE INFORMATION SEE:

PERIODICALS

Flair, November 28, 1991, p. B-6.

ROY, Jacqueline 1954-

PERSONAL: Born January 2, 1954, in London, England; daughter of Namba (a painter, sculptor, and novelist) and Yvonne (an actress and teacher; maiden name, Shelly) Roy. *Education:* University of North London, B.A., 1989; University of Leeds, M.A., 1990. *Politics:* Labour.

ADDRESSES: Home—49 Salford Rd., London SW2 4BL, England. *Office*—Manchester Metropolitan University, Lower Ormond St., Manchester M15, England. *Agent*—Rosemary Sandberg, 44 Bowerdean St., London SW6 3TW, England.

CAREER: Manchester Metropolitan University, Manchester, England, lecturer, 1992—; writer.

MEMBER: Society of Authors.

WRITINGS:

(Editor) Namba Roy, *No Black Sparrows: A Vivid Portrait of Jamaica in the 1930s,* Heinemann, 1989.
Soul Daddy, HarperCollins, 1990.
King Sugar, HarperCollins, 1993.

Also author of the short stories "A Family Likeness" and "Joshua's Friend."

WORK IN PROGRESS: Fat Chance, a novel; research in black British women's writing.

JACQUELINE ROY

SIDELIGHTS: Jacqueline Roy told *SATA:* "I was born in London of an English mother and a Jamaican father, and this inevitably raises questions of cultural identity, which I try to explore in my fiction. My late father, Namba Roy, was also a writer. He was a Maroon, a people originally composed of escaped slaves who fled to the mountains in Jamaica and established a community there, which tried to hold on to African traditions. In Africa, the oral tradition is of great importance, and histories, both personal and public, were usually passed on by word of mouth. For this reason, the storyteller has always been a valued member of the community, and the role was passed down through the generations. My father was the storyteller for the Maroons, and although he had settled in England, when he died it was hoped that at least one of his children would succeed him. Therefore, writing is particularly important in my family; my brother and sister are writers too. In addition to producing my own fiction, I edited my father's novel, *No Black Sparrows.* This increased my sense that writing was a family tradition.

"At school, I was very aware of the lack of interest in Afro-Caribbean history and culture, and partly for this reason, I left without taking A-levels; like many young people, I was not sure what an all-white curriculum could say to me and much of the teaching seemed irrelevant. I worked in various places. At one point I cut cheese in a local supermarket—a job I really wasn't too good at. Customers asking for a quarter pound usually ended up with at least twice that! Working in a bookshop was a lot more interesting than this, but my real ambition was still to write, and I spent my spare time writing stories for all age groups from small children to adults.

"Eventually, bored with shop work, I decided to take a degree in English at the Polytechnic of North London (now the University of North London). The course included studies of African, West Indian, and Indian literature, and I found it exciting and stimulating. On graduating, I went on to do an M.A. in Commonwealth Literature at Leeds University. While at the poly, I wrote *Soul Daddy,* which explored identity on two levels: firstly, the need for a racial and/or cultural identity, and secondly, the wish to create an identity within the family. Twinship featured strongly and was a device for looking at the way in which we see ourselves and how this often changes and develops as other people come into our lives. I wanted to show that the family structure is not stable or fixed but fluctuates, just as the social structure does.

"*King Sugar,* my second book for teenagers, concerns Alex, a young actress who gets a part in a West End production. She plays Poll, a young slave, and as she gets into the role, Poll seems to appear to her. Poll says that the way she is presented in the play is inaccurate, and she wants to tell her story. As Alex listens, she is forced to question versions of history and to ask herself whose story the play is telling—that of the masters, or that of the slaves? Just as sugar is central to the life of a Caribbean slave, it is also central to Alex's life—she has

diabetes and is not sure if Poll is a ghost or a symptom of her illness. Alex has a friend called Denise, who becomes the target of the right wing extremists who operate in the area in which the girls live. Denise's victimization, as well as her resilience, show Alex that life is still a struggle for Afro-Caribbeans, but that courage and the will to survive are part of her inheritance.

"*Fat Chance* is for a slightly younger age group (ten to thirteen). It is about the friendship between two misfits, Jasper and Tessa, who are despised and disliked at school and who offer hope to each other. Tessa is overweight and believes slimness is the key to popularity. As she diets and gets thinner, her friendship with Jasper suffers, but he stands by her and helps to prevent her from slipping into anorexia nervosa.

"My books are mainly about young women and the expectations they believe they must meet, whether these are social or personal or relating to the family. For black youngsters, the problems are particularly intense because expectations of them are either very low and negative, or very high, by way of compensation."

The biracial daughter of a famous musician, Hannah must learn to shape her own identity in the face of sudden changes in her life. (Cover illustration by Karen Barbour.)

"My particular interests are Caribbean and Afro-American women's fiction and the role of women in society in general. Toni Morrison is my favorite writer for adults, and for young people's authors I like Rosa Guy and Marlene Phillip. I also like music—everything from soul and reggae to jazz and classical. Aretha Franklin and Laura Nyro are my favorite singers. I enjoy walking and wish I had a dog, as they're so much fun to take out, but that's difficult in British cities—there aren't enough places for them to run. I also love street markets; the bustle, the color, and the variety make them exciting places to be. I have a large collection of teddy bears, which have virtually taken over the house, and more books than I've got space for. My favorite foods arc chocolate and ice cream, though I'm trying to cut back on the chocolate!

"I have just begun to teach in higher education. I had such a good experience of degree work as a mature student that I'd like to be able to pass on some of the skills and interests I developed. Education is an invaluable tool in voicing social and political concerns, and it is something which is often denied to the black and/or underprivileged communities. It is therefore vital to ensure that it does not remain in the hands of the privileged few."

*   *   *

RUSS, Lavinia 1904-1992
(Lavinia Faxon)

PERSONAL: Born July 30, 1904, in Kansas City, MO; died of pneumonia, May 30, 1992, in Manhattan, NY; daughter of Henry Darlington (a wholesale druggist) and Sarah Peake (Askew) Faxon; married Carroll Dunne (divorced); married Hugh Russ (divorced); children: Martin Russ, Sarah Kate Dunne, Margaret Geiger Turner. *Education:* Attended private schools in Wellesley, MA, Greenwich, CT, Piedmont, CA, and Washington, DC. *Politics:* Democrat.

ADDRESSES: Home—50 East Eighth St., New York, NY.

CAREER: Publishers Weekly, New York City, juvenile editor, 1965-72; writer. Also worked as a book buyer for Scribners Book Store, New York City, hosted a children's television show, lectured, and read manuscripts for publishing houses.

WRITINGS:

(Under name Lavinia Faxon) *Young Explorers' New York,* New York Graphic Society, 1963.
Over the Hills and Far Away, Harcourt, 1968.
The Girl on the Floor Will Help You (collection of Russ's articles), illustrated by Mircea Vasilu, Doubleday, 1969.
(Editor with Liza Russ) *Forever England: Poetry and Prose about England and the English,* illustrated by Victor G. Ambrus, Harcourt, 1969.
And Peakie Lived Happily Ever After, Bodley Head, 1969.

Alec's Sand Castle, illustrated by James Stevenson, Harper, 1972.
A High Old Time, or How to Enjoy Being a Woman over Sixty (adult), Saturday Review Press, 1972.
The April Age, Atheneum, 1975.
What Is a Good Children's Book?, Dantree Press, 1977.

Contributor of articles and reviews to periodicals, including *Publishers Weekly.*

SIDELIGHTS: Although she did not begin writing children's books until the age of fifty-seven, Lavinia Russ was a popular and critically acclaimed children's writer. At one time a children's book buyer for Scribners book store and a juvenile editor for *Publishers Weekly,* Russ was described by many of her compatriots as exuberant, funny, and imaginative—traits that critics also attribute to her frequently autobiographical writing. Albert Johnston, writing for *Publishers Weekly,* described Russ as "a lover of people and good books. She has spent a lifetime with both and emerged smiling, wise and ever young in spirit."

Russ was perhaps best known as the author of an autobiographical trilogy of novels—*Over the Hills and Far Away, And Peakie Lived Happily Ever After,* and *The April Age*—that follows the adolescent years of its precocious protagonist, Peakie Maston, through young womanhood. In Russ's 1968 novel, *Over the Hills and Far Away,* set during World War I, Peakie is between the ages of twelve and fourteen and living, variously, at her home in Kansas City and at three different boarding schools. The book presents Peakie's often humorous account of the tribulations of growing up, moving from boarding school to boarding school, and enduring life with her particular family. A *Horn Book* reviewer, commending the novel as a "rare, wholly engrossing story," described it as a set of "autobiographical experiences that will be remembered for their vividness and humor.... They reveal a wit, a lovable precocity, and an intensity that make Peakie herself an unforgettable adolescent." *New York Times Book Review* contributor Polly Longsworth summarized Peakie and her creator: "Fresh and independent minded, Peakie reflects the keen, imaginative insight of a long-time critic of juvenile books and is an original friend girl readers will greet joyfully."

The story of Peakie's high school years continues in *And Peakie Lived Happily Ever After,* a novel that represents the emotional world of an adolescent "with humour and good sense," according to a reviewer for the *Times Literary Supplement.* In *The April Age,* set in 1925, Peakie is eighteen, naive and romantic, and owes her understanding of the world more to novels and poems than to experience. She therefore embarks on a trip to Europe with a group of young women and a chaperone, entering into romantic attachments, albeit brief and misguided ones, as soon as the ship sails. "Only a writer as good as Lavinia Russ could make the roaring twenties purr," Jean Mercier said in her *Publishers Weekly* review. "This story is as exquisite and welcome as the flowers that come only in 'The April Age.'" *New York*

Times Book Review contributor Marion Bell noted the clarity of Russ's depiction of youth. "*April Age* describes growing up with warmth, humor and respect," Bell commented. "Nothing here is contrived or phony because the author vividly remembers what it was to be young."

Russ published several other books in her lifetime, including *Forever England: Poetry and Prose about England and the English,* a collection of writings about England that she, a self-proclaimed Anglophile, compiled and edited in 1969. She also wrote a popular children's picture book, *Alec's Sand Castle,* about a young boy building a sand castle on a beach. When his parents and other adults begin to "help" him with the castle, Alec grows bored and wanders off. Rather than physically building another castle, he uses his imagination to build a much superior one with all the accoutrements of the castles of legend. His imaginary castle does not wash away in the rain, as will the one his parents took over. A reviewer for the *Bulletin of the Center for Children's Books* called *Alec's Sand Castle* "both a song in praise of the imagination and an amusing realistic anecdote about adult participation—or intervention, depending on the viewpoint."

In 1972 Russ, who did not start writing children's books until the age of fifty-seven, wrote an adult nonfiction work called *A High Old Time, or How to Enjoy Being a Woman over Sixty,* in which she offers a personal account of how she gracefully and happily came to terms with being sixty-seven years old. Although *Library Journal* contributor Signe L. Steen commented that "there is not much here that has not already been said," she, along with other reviewers, noted that the warmth and humor of Russ's tone make the book worthwhile reading. *Publishers Weekly* contributor Albert Johnston praised the book and its author, saying Russ's "humor is irrepressible. She believes life and money are to be *spent.* Life to her is a roller-coaster, and death—'When

Death comes for me, I hope I'll be so busy working and laughing, I won't hear his knock.'"

WORKS CITED:

Review of *Alec's Sand Castle, Bulletin of the Center for Children's Books,* February, 1973, p. 96.
Bell, Marion, review of *The April Age, New York Times Book Review,* June 22, 1975, p. 8.
Johnston, Albert, review of *The Girl on the Floor Will Help You,* January 27, 1969, p. 96.
Johnston, Albert, review of *A High Old Time, or How to Enjoy Being a Woman over Sixty, Publishers Weekly,* February 21, 1972, p. 113.
Longsworth, Polly, *New York Times Book Review,* March 24, 1968, p. 38.
Mercier, Jean, *Publishers Weekly,* February 17, 1975, p. 79.
Review of *Over the Hills and Far Away, Horn Book,* June, 1968, p. 331.
Steen, Signe L., review of *A High Old Time, or How to Enjoy Being a Woman over Sixty, Library Journal,* March 15, 1972, p. 1030.
"Themes for the Salad Days," *Times Literary Supplement,* April 3, 1969, p. 354.

FOR MORE INFORMATION SEE:

PERIODICALS

Booklist, March 15, 1973, p. 717.
Horn Book, August, 1975, p. 389.
Library Journal, April 15, 1969, p. 1635; April 15, 1970, p. 1642; April 15, 1973, p. 1379.
Publishers Weekly, November 10, 1964, p. 49.
School Library Journal, September, 1975, p. 126.*

*   *   *

RUTHIN, Margaret
See CATHERALL, Arthur

S

SATTLER, Helen Roney 1921-1992

PERSONAL: Born March 2, 1921, in Newton, IA; died June 2, 1992; daughter of Louie Earl (a farmer) and Hazel (Cure) Roney; married Robert E. Sattler (a chemical engineer), September 30, 1950; children: Richard, Kathryn. *Education:* Southwest Missouri State College (now University), B.S., 1946; Famous Artist's School, Certificate in Commercial Art, 1960. *Politics:* Democrat. *Religion:* Christian. *Hobbies and other interests:* Painting, drawing, cooking, crafts, puzzle solving, and travel.

ADDRESSES: Home—Bartlesville, OK.

CAREER: Author and illustrator. Elementary teacher in Aldrich, MO, 1941-42, Norwood, MO, 1942-45, and Marshfield, MO, 1945-48; Kansas City Public Library, Kansas City, MO, children's librarian, 1948-49; Standard Oil of New Jersey, elementary teacher at company school on Aruba, 1949-50.

MEMBER: Authors League of America, Authors Guild, Society of Children's Book Writers and Illustrators, Oklahoma Writers Federation, Bartlesville Writer's Association (chair, 1967-68 and 1981-82).

AWARDS, HONORS: American Library Association Book of Interest, 1973, for *Recipes for Art and Craft Materials;* Oklahoma Cherubim Award, 1978, for *Nature's Weather Forecasters;* Golden Kite Award nonfiction honor, 1981, and *Boston Globe-Horn Book* honor citation, 1982, both for *Dinosaurs of North America;* Children's Choice Award, 1982, for *No Place for a Goat;* Golden Kite Award (nonfiction), 1983, for *The Illustrated Dinosaur Dictionary;* Oklahoma Book Award, 1989, for *Tyrannosaurus Rex and Its Kin: The Mesozoic Monsters;* numerous outstanding children's book citations from many organizations.

WRITINGS:

CRAFT BOOKS; SELF-ILLUSTRATED

Kitchen Carton Crafts, Lothrop, 1970.

HELEN RONEY SATTLER

Holiday Gifts, Favors and Decorations That You Can Make, Lothrop, 1971.
Sockcraft: Toys, Gifts and Other Things To Make, Lothrop, 1972.
Jewelry from Junk, Lothrop, 1973.
Recipes for Art and Craft Materials, Lothrop, 1973, revised edition, illustrated by Marti Shohet, 1987.
Jar and Bottle Craft, Lothrop, 1974.

PUZZLE BOOKS

A Beginning to Read Book of Puzzles (self-illustrated), Denison, 1971.
Bible Puzzle Collection, Baker Book, 1977.
Bible Puzzle Pack, Baker Book, 1977.
Bible Puzzles for Teens, Concordia, 1979.
Brain Busters, Scholastic Services, 1980.

FICTION

No Place for a Goat, illustrated by Bari Weissman, Dutton, 1981.
The Smallest Witch, illustrated by June Goldsborough, Dutton, 1981.
Charley le mulet, Harlequin, 1981, translation published as *Morgan the Mule,* Ideals Publishing, 1982.

NONFICTION

The Eggless Cookbook, A. S. Barnes, 1972.
Train Whistles: A Language in Code, illustrated by Tom Funk, Lothrop, 1977, revised edition, illustrated by Giulio Maestro, 1985.
Nature's Weather Forecasters (self-illustrated), Dutton, 1978.
Dollars from Dandelions: 101 Ways to Earn Money, illustrated by Rita Floden Leydon, Lothrop, 1979.
(With introduction by John H. Ostrom) *Dinosaurs of North America,* illustrated by Anthony Rao, Lothrop, 1981.
Noses Are Special, illustrated by Charles Cox, Abingdon, 1982.
(With introduction by Ostrom) *The Illustrated Dinosaur Dictionary,* illustrated by Pamela Carroll with a color insert by Rao and Christopher Santoro, Lothrop, 1983, revised edition published as *The New Illustrated Dinosaur Dictionary,* illustrated by Joyce Powzyk, with an introduction by Ostrom, Lothrop, 1990.
Fish Facts and Bird Brains: Animal Intelligence, illustrated by Maestro, Dutton, 1984.
Baby Dinosaurs, illustrated by Jean Day Zallinger, Lothrop, 1984.
Sharks, the Super Fish, illustrated by Zallinger, Lothrop, 1985.
Pterosaurs, the Flying Reptiles, illustrated by Santoro, Lothrop, 1985.
Whales, the Nomads of the Sea, illustrated by Zallinger, Lothrop, 1987.
Hominids: A Look Back at Our Ancestors, illustrated by Santoro, Lothrop, 1988.
Tyrannosaurus Rex and Its Kin: The Mesozoic Monsters, illustrated by Joyce Powzyk, Lothrop, 1989.
The Book of Eagles, illustrated by Zallinger, Lothrop, 1989.
Giraffes, the Sentinels of the Savannas, illustrated by Santoro, Lothrop, 1990.
Our Patchwork Planet: The Story of Plate Tectonics, illustrated by Maestro, Lothrop, 1991.
Stegosaurs: The Solar-Powered Dinosaurs, illustrated by Turi MacCombie, Lothrop, 1992.
The Earliest Americans, illustrated by Zallinger, Clarion, 1993.
The Book of North American Owls, illustrated by Zallinger, Clarion, 1994.

Also contributor of puzzles, how-to articles, stories, and verse to periodicals, including *Child Life, Junior Discoveries, Jack and Jill, Boy's Life, Cricket,* and *Highlights for Children.*

SIDELIGHTS: Helen Roney Sattler was a respected author of lively, informative nonfiction books. Throughout her career, Sattler sought to provide readers with accurate, interesting information about the subjects she covered. Sattler wrote popular craft and nature books but is probably best remembered for her reference works about dinosaurs that clarify the mysteries surrounding those great creatures. Cathryn A. Camper, writing in *School Library Journal,* echoed the opinions of many reviewers when she stated, "Sattler does a superb job of presenting factual material in an appealing and accessible manner."

Before she started writing, Sattler taught elementary school for several years, the last of which was spent on a Dutch island off the coast of Venezuela. The decision to change professions was a simple one, Sattler once said: "I love books and I love children, a perfect combination for either writing or teaching. When I retired from

Writing nonfiction for children was a natural shift for former teacher Sattler, who outlines natural signs of weather changes in this volume. (Cover illustration by Deborah M. Daly.)

teaching to raise my family, I turned to writing as a natural second career."

Sattler's early efforts showed children how to make inexpensive games, gifts, and toys from everyday objects. "Creative work need not be expensive," Sattler commented. "I believe that ... most children can be taught to work with their hands and be creative if shown a few basic designs to get them started." One of her books, *Kitchen Carton Crafts,* contains instructions for preparing masks, ornaments, and party decorations from materials like cereal boxes and egg cartons. Described by Barbara Sherrard-Smith in *Children's Book Review* as a work "that instantly appeals to the eye," *Kitchen Carton Crafts* was Sattler's first in a succession of "how-to" books for children.

After penning a number of puzzle books and fictional stories, Sattler turned exclusively to writing nonfiction, primarily for middle-grade and junior high students. She concentrated on the natural world, covering subjects such as animal intelligence, dinosaurs, the formation of the continents, prehistoric man, eagles, and the American Indian. *Dinosaurs of North America,* Sattler's lengthy volume that offers descriptions of all known dinosaurs native to that continent, is "more meticulous,

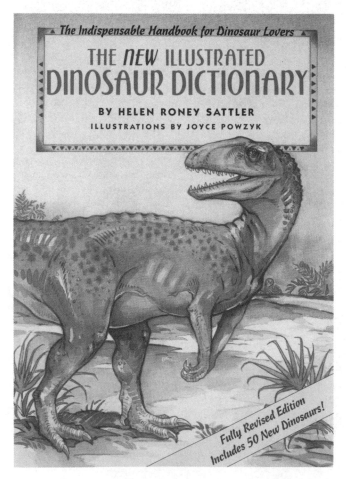

Sattler wrote this landmark children's reference book in response to her grandson's request for dinosaur book "without any mistakes in it." (Cover illustration by Joyce Powzyk.)

more complete, and more elaborate" than other books of its kind, according to Georgess McHargue of the *New York Times Book Review.* The idea for *Dinosaurs of North America* came to Sattler when her grandson asked her to write a book about dinosaurs that "didn't have any mistakes in it," the author recalled. Not wanting to disappoint her grandchild, she produced a comprehensive study about the animals, one that examines the dinosaurs' lifestyles and habitats. Along with information about each dinosaur's physical characteristics and the geographic location in which it was discovered, Sattler includes a review of dinosaur extinction theories. Sarah Gagne, writing in *Horn Book,* stated that *Dinosaurs of North America* "is an outstanding reference work for those who want more technical information than is often available on specific dinosaurs."

While writing *Dinosaurs of North America,* Sattler discovered that the number of accurate reference sources about these creatures was limited. She felt there was a need "for a book that would define all of those words that I could not find in a regular dictionary. A book that would give the pronunciation of each dinosaur and one that would distinguish between dinosaurs and non-dinosaurian Mesozoic animals. So I wrote one." That book, *The Illustrated Dinosaur Dictionary,* took five years to research, during which time Sattler traveled across North America, talking to paleontologists and visiting excavation sites. Sattler's efforts paid off; she collected a considerable amount of information for the book. Included in *The Illustrated Dinosaur Dictionary* are dozens of terms that relate to dinosaurs, as well as entries about dinosaurs discovered throughout the world, each with a pronunciation guide, a passage telling how the dinosaur was named, and a description of its appearance. Bertrand Gary Hoyle, reviewing the work in *Appraisal: Science Books for Young People,* declared that "*The Illustrated Dinosaur Dictionary* is a fascinating mini-encyclopedia for any dinosaur buff." In his critique in the *New York Times Book Review,* McHargue asserted, "From 'Acanthopholis' to 'Zigongosaurus,' this present volume is likely to become the premier reference work on the subject."

Sattler continued her study of dinosaurs in books like *Tyrannosaurus Rex and Its Kin: The Mesozoic Monsters* and *Stegosaurs: The Solar-Powered Dinosaurs.* In *Stegosaurs,* Sattler presents ideas that contradict commonly held beliefs about these plant-eaters. For example, some theories state that the Stegosaurs were slow-witted creatures, possessing brains the size of ping-pong balls; Sattler offers evidence that they were more intelligent than previously believed. She also discusses the idea that the armored plates along the dinosaurs' backs absorbed sunlight, thus helping to control their body temperature. Camper, reviewing *Stegosaurs* in the *School Library Journal,* called it "superior science writing." She added, "It's everything anyone could want in a dinosaur book."

Sattler also collaborated with illustrators Jean Day Zallinger and Christopher Santoro on a number of wildlife books, including *Sharks, the Super Fish, Wha-*

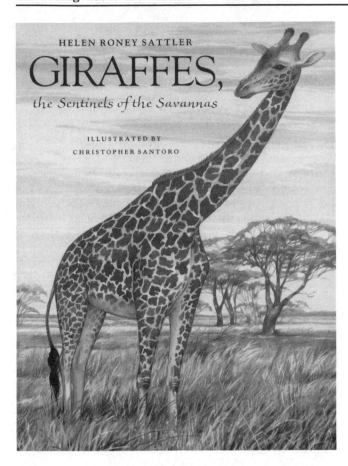

A trip to Kenya to investigate the evolution, habits, and behavior of these tall mammals typified Sattler's attention to research. (Cover illustration by Christopher Santoro.)

les, the Nomads of the Sea, and *Giraffes: Sentinels of the Savannah.* Sattler was able to combine her interests in animals and travel while compiling her material for the books: she visited aquariums in the United States and Canada to gather information for *Sharks,* joined a whale watch off the coast of California while researching *Whales,* and journeyed to Kenya to view wild giraffes in their native habitat for *Giraffes.* Discussing the need for her African trip, Sattler declared, "I had to go to Kenya to get first hand experience with wild giraffes .... It was a totally different experience than seeing these magnificent animals in a zoo." Critics praised Sattler's work on the nature books. Ellen Fader, reviewing *Whales* in *Horn Book,* stated that "the text is packed with accurate and intriguing information." Margaret A. Bush, in a review of *The Book of Eagles* in *Horn Book,* asserted that "Sattler continues to be unerring in her choice of subject and reliably thorough in her arrangement and treatment of information."

Discussing her penchant for hard work, Sattler once remarked, "I know that all children, like my grandson, want the facts in their books to be accurate, so I take great pains to research my books carefully." Summing up her feelings about her career, Sattler added, "Writing nonfiction for children is almost as much fun as reading

[it]. I strive to write books that will capture the interest of all children, especially the reluctant readers."

WORKS CITED:

Bush, Margaret A., review of *The Book of Eagles, Horn Book,* September-October, 1989, pp. 643-44.

Camper, Cathryn A., review of *Tyrannosaurus Rex and Its Kin: The Mesozoic Monsters, School Library Journal,* March, 1989, p. 196.

Camper, review of *Stegosaurs: The Solar-Powered Dinosaurs, School Library Journal,* October, 1992, p. 110.

Fader, Ellen, review of *Whales, the Nomads of the Sea, Horn Book,* January-February, 1988, p. 88.

Gagne, Sarah, review of *Dinosaurs of North America, Horn Book,* February, 1982, p. 77.

Hoyle, Bertrand Gary, review of *The Illustrated Dinosaur Dictionary, Appraisal: Science Books for Young People,* Spring-Summer, 1984, p. 41.

McHargue, Georgess, "Giants of the Earth," *New York Times Book Review,* November 15, 1981, p. 64.

McHargue, Georgess, "Dinosaurs Galore," *New York Times Book Review,* November 13, 1983, p. 46.

Sherrard-Smith, Barbara, review of *Kitchen Carton Crafts, Children's Book Review,* February, 1972, p. 21.

FOR MORE INFORMATION SEE:

BOOKS

Children's Literature Review, Volume 24, Gale, 1991, pp. 212-24.

PERIODICALS

Book World, February 12, 1984.

Horn Book, June, 1974; June, 1984; September-October, 1988; May-June, 1990; January-February, 1991.

New York Times Book Review, June 7, 1970; December 3, 1972.

Publishers Weekly, June 15, 1970; January 16, 1981; July 3, 1981; January 13, 1984; October 19, 1984; May 30, 1986; December 25, 1987; May 19, 1989.

School Library Journal, November, 1977; September, 1978; November, 1981; January, 1982; December, 1983; May, 1984; December, 1987; June-July, 1988; December, 1990; May, 1991.

Tribune Books (Chicago), May 14, 1989.*

*   *   *

SELWAY, Martina 1940-

PERSONAL: Born June 20, 1940, in Worcestershire, England; married John Aston (a graphic designer for television); children: Sophie, Gemma. *Education:* Degree in printmaking and design from Shrewsbury College of Art, 1962. *Hobbies and other interests:* Travel in Europe, watercolors, sailing, hillwalking.

ADDRESSES: Home—Surrey, England; Southern France.

MARTINA SELWAY

CAREER: Author and illustrator, Surrey, England, 1982—. Stylist for still photographer in London, England, 1963-64; artist for ad agency, 1964-66; free-lance illustrator, 1966—. Background illustrator for the animated film *Beatles Yellow Submarine*, King Features, 1967.

MEMBER: Ariel Sailing Club, London.

AWARDS, HONORS: National Diploma in Design.

WRITINGS:

SELF-ILLUSTRATED

The Grunts—What a Day!, World's Work, 1982.
The Grunts Go on a Picnic, World's Work, 1982.
Greedyguts, Hutchinson, 1990.
Don't Forget to Write, Hutchinson, 1991; Ideals Publishing, 1992.
Dear Grandad, I Hate Roland Roberts (sequel to *Don't Forget to Write*), Hutchinson, 1993.
Dear Grandad, Wish You Were Here (tentative title; sequel to *Don't Forget to Write*), Hutchinson, in press.

ILLUSTRATOR

Pat Edwards, *Ahchoo!*, Longman Group USA, 1989.
Edwards, *Fred's Friends*, Longman Group USA, 1989.

Colorist for *Gulliver's Travels: My Adventures in Lilliput, by Lemuel Gulliver, Retold by Jonathan Swift*, by Jonathan Swift, illustrations by Charles E. Brock, Castle Books, 1979. Illustrator of seventeen titles for Longman Reading World, 1988; illustrator of nine titles for

"Maths Storybooks" series published by Longman Cheshire Australia, 1991.

WORK IN PROGRESS: "I am collaborating with a friend who lives on a tiny 'unknown' Greek island. The book will be an account of her adventures (some of which I have shared)."

SIDELIGHTS: Martina Selway told *SATA:* "I left art college and came to London, where I initially found work as a stylist for a well-known stills photographer at the beginning of the swinging 1960s. I quickly moved on to work as a visualiser with one of the big advertising agencies. While there, I began to specialise, with the encouragement of creative director James Fitton, in illustration jobs. During this time, free-lance commissions started to roll in and soon I had to quit my full-time job. I did a series of posters for the National Savings Bank and the London Transport Authority. I also began work on a major commission for the British Broadcasting Corporation (BBC) to produce nearly five hundred drawings for a series of French language teaching programs.

"Educational publishing was expanding rapidly during this period, and I worked with many of the well-known publishers, including Cambridge University Press, Oxford University Press, Macmillan, Collins, and the Longman Group. These publishers are still some of my biggest clients.

"In 1967 my work was seen by John Coates, the director of Television Cartoons, Ltd., who invited me to join a small team of background artists for the animated feature film *Beatles Yellow Submarine*, produced by King Features, USA. This was a great experience. I got to work with many talented people, including the great Canadian animator George Dunning and the German designer Heinz Edelmann, whose work in the pages of *Twen* magazine greatly influenced the London scene at the time.

"My first daughter, Sophie, was born in 1970, and Gemma followed in 1973. Children and homebuilding had to take precedence over my career for a while. The film experience, however, led to other commissions for more manageable children's programmes by BBC-TV and Thames Television. The work was fun and was seen by millions of children. My own kids soon became my severest critics. The Longman Group began to publish 'tie-in' books that corresponded to the television programs. My involvement with books for small children grew when they asked me to illustrate a number of books by their own authors.

"My first books as an author/illustrator are two volumes about a family of pigs, the Grunts, that are published by Worlds Work. Little did I know that my pigs would become the role model for 'Fred Pig,' the central character in a reading scheme. Fred appears in a series of thirty-four books (so far) published by Longman Group. I took my next idea to Hutchinsons Children's Books and they published *Greedyguts*, the story of a greedy, bullying giant defeated by a clever little boy who get his village to work together as a team."

* * *

SHARMAT, Marjorie Weinman 1928-
(Wendy Andrews)

PERSONAL: Born November 12, 1928, in Portland, ME; daughter of Nathan (a wholesaler and manufacturer of dry goods and men's furnishings) and Anna (Richardson) Weinman; married Mitchell Brenner Sharmat (an author and investor), February 24, 1957; children: Craig Lynden, Andrew Richard. *Education:* Attended Lasell Junior College, 1946-47; graduate of Westbrook Junior College, 1948. *Politics:* "Keep changing." *Religion:* Jewish.

Hobbies and other interests: "Desperately seeking spare time and marveling at its elusiveness."

ADDRESSES: Home—Arizona. *Office*—c/o Dell Publishing Co., 666 Fifth Ave., New York, NY 10103. *Agent*—Harold Ober Associates, Inc., 425 Madison Ave., New York, NY 10017.

CAREER: Writer. Yale University, New Haven, CT, circulation staff member of university library, 1951-54, circulation staff member of law library, 1954-55; author of books for children and young adults, 1967—. Writer of greeting card verse and advertising copy; contributor to trade and textbook anthologies; writer of TV and movie novelizations.

AWARDS, HONORS: Book of the Year citations, Library of Congress, 1967, for *Rex*, 1976, for *Mooch the Messy*, 1979, for *Griselda's New Year*, from the Child Study Association, 1971, 1973-76, 1978, 1979, 1980, 1982, and 1988, and from *Saturday Review, Newsweek, Ladies Home Journal*, and *Ms.*; Best Book of the Season citations from the *Today Show*, 1972, for *Nate the Great*, 1975, for *Maggie Marmelstein for President*, and from *House and Garden;* Classroom Choices citations, International Reading Association and Childrens' Book Council, 1976-88; Tower Award, Westbrook College, 1975; Arizona Young Readers' Award first runner-up, 1978-79; Parents' Choice Award, 1980, for *Taking Care of Melvin;* Irma Simonton Black Honor Book Award, 1981, for *Gila Monsters Meet You at the Airport;* Garden State Children's Book Awards, 1984, for *Nate the Great and the Missing Key*, and 1985, for *Nate the Great and the Snowy Trail;* Alabama Young Readers' Choice Award, 1988, for *My Mother Never Listens to Me;* Notable Trade Book in the Field of Social Studies citations, National Council for the Social Studies, 1977, for *Edgemont* and *Frizzy the Fearful;* more than twenty of Sharmat's books have been Junior Literary Guild selections; she has received numerous other awards and award nominations, including the Los Angeles International Children's Film Festival Award for the adaptation of *Nate the Great Goes Undercover.*

WRITINGS:

JUVENILE

Rex, illustrations by Emily McCully, Harper, 1967.
Goodnight, Andrew, Goodnight, Craig, illustrations by Mary Chalmers, Harper, 1969.
Gladys Told Me to Meet Her Here, illustrations by Edward Frascino, Harper, 1970.
A Hot Thirsty Day, illustrations by Rosemary Wells, Macmillan, 1971.
51 Sycamore Lane, illustrations by Lisl Weil, Macmillan, 1971, published as *The Spy in the Neighborhood,* Collier, 1974.
Getting Something on Maggie Marmelstein, illustrations by Ben Shecter, Harper, 1971.
A Visit with Rosalind, illustrations by Weil, Macmillan, 1972.
Sophie and Gussie, illustrations by Lillian Hoban, Macmillan, 1973.
Morris Brookside, a Dog, illustrations by Ronald Himler, Holiday House, 1973.
Morris Brookside Is Missing, illustrations by Himler, Holiday House, 1974.
I Want Mama, illustrations by McCully, Harper, 1974.
I'm Not Oscar's Friend Anymore, illustrations by Tony DeLuna, Dutton, 1975.
Walter the Wolf, illustrations by Kelly Oechsli, Holiday House, 1975.
Burton and Dudley, illustrations by Barbara Cooney, Holiday House, 1975.
Maggie Marmelstein for President, illustrations by Shecter, Harper, 1975.
The Lancelot Closes at Five, illustrations by Weil, Macmillan, 1976.
The Trip, and Other Sophie and Gussie Stories, illustrations by Hoban, Macmillan, 1976.
Mooch the Messy, illustrations by Shecter, Harper, 1976.

MARJORIE WEINMAN SHARMAT

Edgemont, illustrations by Cyndy Szekeres, Coward, 1977.

I'm Terrific, illustrations by Kay Chorao, Holiday House, 1977.

I Don't Care, illustrations by Hoban, Macmillan, 1977.

A Big Fat Enormous Lie, illustrations by David McPhail, Dutton, 1978.

Thornton the Worrier, illustrations by Chorao, Holiday House, 1978.

Mitchell Is Moving, illustrations by Jose Aruego and Ariane Dewey, Macmillan, 1978.

Mooch the Messy Meets Prudence the Neat, illustrations by Shecter, Coward, 1979.

Scarlet Monster Lives Here, illustrations by Dennis Kendrick, Harper, 1979.

Mr. Jameson and Mr. Phillips, illustrations by Bruce Degen, Harper, 1979.

The 329th Friend, illustrations by Szekeres, Four Winds, 1979.

(With husband, Mitchell Sharmat) *I Am Not a Pest,* illustrations by Diane Dawson, Dutton, 1979.

Uncle Boris and Maude, illustrations by Sammis McLean, Doubleday, 1979.

Octavia Told Me a Secret, illustrations by Roseanne Litzinger, Four Winds, 1979.

Say Hello, Vanessa, illustrations by Hoban, Holiday House, 1979.

Griselda's New Year, illustrations by Norman Chartier, Macmillan, 1979.

The Trolls of 12th Street, illustrations by Shecter, Coward, 1979.

Little Devil Gets Sick, illustrations by Marilyn Hafner, Doubleday, 1980.

What Are We Going to Do about Andrew?, illustrations by Ray Cruz, Macmillan, 1980.

Taking Care of Melvin, illustrations by Victoria Chess, Holiday House, 1980.

Sometimes Mama and Papa Fight, illustrations by Chorao, Harper, 1980.

(With M. Sharmat) *The Day I Was Born,* illustrations by Dawson, Dutton, 1980.

Grumley the Grouch, illustrations by Chorao, Holiday House, 1980.

Gila Monsters Meet You at the Airport, illustrations by Byron Barton, Macmillan, 1980.

Twitchell the Wishful, illustrations by Janet Stevens, Holiday House, 1981.

Chasing after Annie, illustrations by Simont, Harper, 1981.

Rollo and Juliet, Forever!, illustrations by Hafner, Doubleday, 1981.

the **329**th friend

by Marjorie Weinman Sharmat
illustrations by Cyndy Szekeres

Emery Raccoon invites 328 strangers to lunch in the hope that one of them will become his friend in Sharmat's story about friendship and growing up. (Cover illustration by Cyndy Szekeres.)

The Sign, illustrations by Pat Wong, Houghton, 1981.

Lucretia the Unbearable, illustrations by Janet Stevens, Holiday House, 1981.

The Best Valentine in the World, illustrations by Lillian Obligado, Holiday House, 1982.

Two Ghosts on a Bench, illustrations by Nola Langner, Harper, 1982.

Mysteriously Yours, Maggie Marmelstein, illustrations by Shecter, Harper, 1982.

Frizzy the Fearful, illustrations by John Wallner, Holiday House, 1983.

Rich Mitch, illustrations by Loretta Lustig, Morrow, 1983.

The Story of Bentley Beaver, illustrations by Hoban, Harper, 1984.

Bartholomew the Bossy, illustrations by Normand Chartier, Macmillan, 1984.

Sasha the Silly, illustrations by Stevens, Holiday House, 1984.

My Mother Never Listens to Me, illustrations by Lynn Munsinger, A. Whitman, 1984.

Attila the Angry, illustrations by Hoban, Holiday House, 1985.

Get Rich Mitch!, illustrations by Loretta Lustig, Morrow, 1985.

The Son of the Slime Who Ate Cleveland, illustrations by Rodney Pate, Dell, 1985.

One Terrific Thanksgiving, illustrations by Obligado, Holiday House, 1985.

Who's Afraid of Ernestine?, illustrations by Chambliss, Putnam, 1986.

Hooray for Mother's Day!, illustrations by Wallner, Holiday House, 1986.

Helga High-Up, illustrations by David Neuhaus, Scholastic, 1987.

Hooray for Father's Day!, illustrations by Wallner, Holiday House, 1987.

Go to Sleep, Nicholas Joe, illustrations by Himmelman, Harper, 1988.

(With M. Sharmat) *Surprises* (reader), Holt, 1989.

(With M. Sharmat) *Treasures* (reader), Holt, 1989.

(With M. Sharmat) *Kingdoms* (reader), Holt, 1989.

Griselda's New Year, illustrations by Normand Chartier, Macmillan Children's Book Group, 1989.

I'm Santa Claus and I'm Famous, Holiday House, 1990.

I'm the Best!, Holiday House, 1991.

"NATE THE GREAT" SERIES; ILLUSTRATIONS BY MARC SIMONT

Nate the Great, Coward, 1972.

Nate the Great Goes Undercover, Coward, 1974.

Nate the Great and the Lost List, Coward, 1975.

Nate the Great and the Phony Clue, Coward, 1977.

Nate the Great and the Sticky Case, Coward, 1978.

Nate the Great and the Missing Key, Coward, 1981.

Nate the Great and the Snowy Trail, Coward, 1982.

Nate the Great and the Fishy Prize, Coward, 1985.

Nate the Great Stalks Stupidweed, Coward, 1986.

Nate the Great and the Boring Beach Bag, Coward, 1987.

Nate the Great Goes down in the Dumps, Coward, 1989.

Nate the Great and the Halloween Hunt, Coward, 1989.

(With son, Craig Sharmat) *Nate the Great and the Musical Note,* Coward, 1990.

Nate the Great and the Stolen Base, Coward, 1992.

"OLIVIA SHARP, AGENT FOR SECRETS" SERIES; WITH HUSBAND, MITCHELL SHARMAT

The Pizza Monster, illustrations by Denise Brunkus, Delacorte, 1989.

The Princess of the Fillmore Street School, Delacorte, 1989.

The Sly Spy, Delacorte, 1990.

The Green Toenails Gang, Delacorte, 1991.

"THE KIDS ON THE BUS" SERIES; WITH SON, ANDREW SHARMAT

School Bus Cat, HarperCollins, 1990.

The Cooking Class, HarperCollins, 1990.

The Haunted Bus, HarperCollins, 1991.

Bully on the Bus, HarperCollins, 1991.

The Secret Notebook, HarperCollins, 1991.

The Field Day Mix-up, HarperCollins, 1991.

YOUNG ADULT

Square Pegs (novelization of television program), Dell, 1982.

I Saw Him First, Dell, 1983.

How to Meet a Gorgeous Guy, Dell, 1983.

How to Meet a Gorgeous Girl, Dell, 1984.

He Noticed I'm Alive ... and Other Hopeful Signs, Delacorte, 1984.

Two Guys Noticed Me ... and Other Miracles, Delacorte, 1985.

How to Have a Gorgeous Wedding, Dell, 1985.

YOUNG ADULT; UNDER PSEUDONYM WENDY ANDREWS

Vacation Fever! (also see below), Putnam, 1984.

The Supergirl Storybook (novelization of motion picture), Putnam, 1984.

Are We There Yet? (also see below), Putnam, 1985.

(Under name Marjorie Weinman Sharmat) *Vacation Fever!* [and] *Are We There Yet?,* Dell, 1990.

"SORORITY SISTERS" SERIES

For Members Only, Dell, 1986.

Snobs, Beware, Dell, 1986.

I Think I'm Falling in Love, Dell, 1986.

Fighting over Me, Dell, 1986.

Nobody Knows How Scared I Am, Dell, 1987.

Here Comes Mr. Right, Dell, 1987.

Getting Closer, Dell, 1987.

I'm Going to Get Your Boyfriend, Dell, 1987.

OTHER

Contributor to books, including *Just for Fun,* edited by Ann Durell, Dutton, 1977; *Sixteen,* edited by Donald Gallo, Dell, 1984; *Visions,* Delacorte, 1987; and *Funny You Should Ask,* Delacorte, 1992. Also contributor to magazines, newspapers, and textbooks. Sharmat's books have been published in England, Japan, Israel, Canada, the Netherlands, Spain, China, Australia, New Zealand, Denmark, France, Germany, and Sweden. Some of her manuscripts are kept in the Maine Women's Writers

Collection, Westbrook College, Portland, ME, and the de Grummond Collection, University of Southern Mississippi, Hattiesburg.

ADAPTATIONS: I'm Not Oscar's Friend Any More was made into a television film and presented as part of the CBS-TV Library Special, *The Wrong Way Kid; Gila Monsters Meet You at the Airport* was made into the pilot film for the PBS-TV *Reading Rainbow* series; *Nate the Great Goes Undercover* and *Nate the Great and the Sticky Case* were adapted for film; Sharmat's work has also been made into videocassettes and numerous recordings. An excerpt from *Nate the Great* was adapted and is on permanent display in an exhibit on the brain and learning at the Museum of Science and Industry, Chicago, IL. A dramatization of *Scarlet Monster Lives Here* was performed April 1990 at the White House Easter Egg Roll for 30,000 guests. The stage production of *The Adventures of Nate the Great* premiered July 1990.

WORK IN PROGRESS: Nate the Great and the Pillowcase, with sister Rosalind Weinman.

SIDELIGHTS: In a *Cricket* article, American children's author Marjorie Weinman Sharmat wrote about her writing process: "I suppose that very few, if any, writers would care to have their brains even remotely compared to litter baskets, but stories do represent the coming together of the diverse and often disparate experiences, emotions, and people that are part of the life of the writer. The writer sorts them out and gives them shape and substance and meaning. Most writers have an almost relentless desire to communicate. It is, perhaps like a sore tooth or a nagging headache, conspicuously unremittingly *there.* I have felt this compulsion ever since I can remember.... The down side of having 110 published books is that I can no longer handle the

thousands of letters that the books generate. Regretfully I have stopped responding."

Sharmat was born to Anna and Nathan Weinman in Portland, Maine. She recalls she was a shy, introspective child who enjoyed solitary activities such as piano playing, reading, and drawing. "My earliest ambition was to become a writer or a detective or a lion tamer," she once commented. "I began writing when I was eight. A friend and I 'published' a newspaper called *The Snooper's Gazette,* which we filled with news we obtained by spying on grown-ups for our detective agency. It achieved a circulation of about four—her parents and mine. At that time I also wrote my first poem. It was about a neighborhood dog, and I still have the memory of my mother supplying the last line when I was stuck.... [This] poem appeared years and years later in my book *The Lancelot Closes at Five.*"

She continued to write—"diaries, music, more poems, stories, and one chapter of a mystery novel"—and to draw, sometimes adding illustrations to her writing. Eventually she wrote for school magazines and newspapers. Her parents encouraged her to keep writing, and even after having many stories rejected by publishers during her high school years, she continued to send stories out to editors. "I couldn't break the habit of unreasonable optimism," she explained.

In college she studied marketing because she thought it was practical. After graduating, her first job was in a department store. Later she worked at Yale University Library. "My first commercially published 'work' was a national advertising slogan for the W. T. Grant Company for their spring promotion. It consisted of four words. I used to enjoy walking into Grant stores and reading my four words. Eventually I had my first story—a short story for adults—published while I was

Bartholomew learns that a bossy attitude makes it hard to make and keep new friends in this tale. (Cover illustration by Normand Chartier.)

working at the Yale Library. This unfortunately caused me to break out in hives. I have since regarded a collection of red spots on the skin as a hallmark of literary achievement, and never the result of eating too much chocolate. My second published story, an article about Yale, became a part of the Yale Memorabilia Collection. (More hives.)"

During the 1960s and 1970s, Sharmat wrote only for children, producing many picture books, readers, and novels. Her own children often provided her with inspiration. Her first published book, the story of a runaway boy who pretends to be an elderly neighbor's dog, came out of the two facts that her son Craig often visited older neighbors and her son Andrew pretended to be a dog. "*Goodnight, Andrew, Goodnight, Craig* came about when my two boys were going to sleep, and Craig wished Andrew 'Pleasant nightmares'," she recalled.

The hero of her mysteries for young children, "Nate the Great," is named after the author's father Nathan Weinman. The small detective solves cases as much by perseverance as by deductive reasoning, but never without a plate of pancakes to get him started. Ideas for some of the mysteries also come from her children's experiences. She wrote, for example, that "*Nate the Great Goes Undercover* had its beginnings when my son, Craig, thought I was the ideal person to effect the rescue of a skunk that he saw in a sewer down the street. I made several phone calls, but I found there was a dearth of people and agencies willing to attempt the removal of a skunk from a sewer. The trail finally led to the game warden whose wife complained (understandably) that she was always being called about such matters, but could offer only advice, not action. Meanwhile, in a related or unrelated incident (never quite determined), garbage cans had been knocked over in my neighborhood. And so the idea for *Nate the Great Goes Undercover* took hold. Nate investigates the mystery of the knocked-over garbage cans and the chief suspect is . . . . By the way, the police finally rescued the skunk."

Sharmat's topic in a number of books is the emotional life of her characters and her readers. *I'm Terrific* looks at Jason Bear's growing understanding that the perfection he believes he represents is not necessarily evident to the people around him, particularly not to his peers. *I Don't Care* was inspired by a television show in which a group of characters were trying to persuade an old man to stop crying. "They were obviously well-intentioned and it did not occur to them that the man should be allowed to cry. I found myself rooting for the man: 'Cry! Cry!'," she said. She continued, "Although there has been an increasing awareness that it's all right to cry, the stigma of crying remains, especially, I think, for men and boys. A child senses that keeping a stiff upper lip and being cool are desirable. Jonathan in *I Don't Care* holds back his true feelings when his balloon floats away. 'I don't care,' he tells himself and his parents and his friend. But he does care. And finally he lets go and cries. And he cries until he is cried out and satisfied."

Diminutive detective Nate uses his wits and perseverence—both fueled by a hearty breakfast of pancakes—to solve a wide variety of mysteries. (Cover illustration by Marc Simont.)

In 1975, the Sharmat family moved across the country from New York City to Arizona. For the author, this relocation was an imaginative as well as a physical challenge. Comments by children from the east and west about what they thought might be waiting for them on the other side of the country helped her to write *Gila Monsters Meet You at the Airport*. After moving west, Sharmat has found that both sides of the country have much in common. The book tries to express both the anxieties about moving and the comforts of finding that life is not so different in faraway places.

When stuck for a particular plot solution or phrase, Sharmat has often found her husband Mitchell has the exactly right words. Eventually, she encouraged him to begin writing his own children's books, and he has become the second published children's and young adults' writer in the family with numerous titles including the classic, *Gregory, the Terrible Eater*. Together the Sharmats have produced the series "Olivia Sharp, Agent for Secrets" and several other books. Sharmat has also collaborated with her son Andrew on a number of books called "The Kids on the Bus" series, and with son Craig on the book *Nate the Great and the Musical Note*.

BURTON and DUDLEY

by Marjorie Weinman Sharmat

illustrated by Barbara Cooney

While out on a long hike, Dudley Possum and Burton Possum learn some lessons that test the limits of their friendship. (Cover illustration by Barbara Cooney.)

In 1982, Sharmat started writing novels for young adults. Her romances are "intelligent and witty," according Diane Roback in *Publishers Weekly,* and *School Library Journal* critic Kathy Fritts calls them "far more literate and graceful than the usual." In *How to Meet a Gorgeous Girl,* a teen just about ruins his chances for a good relationship with the girl of his dreams by trying to follow the advice in a "How To" book on dating. Two girls make a similar mistake in *How to Meet a Gorgeous Guy* by making a cute guy the subject of an article on dating. Sharmat's teens learn about the value of direct and honest communication and develop self-confidence. The author's "flair for dialogue and realistic characterization" enhances her entertaining and plausible books about teen romance and social life, Kim Carter Sands claims in the *Voice of Youth Advocates.*

Critics and readers of all ages have enjoyed Sharmat's books for many years. The author's ability to entertain while developing the reader's thinking skills and emotional growth has been rewarded with many awards and honors, including the Irma Simonton Black Honor Book Award in 1981 for *Gila Monsters Meet You at the Airport* and the Garden State Children's Book Award two years in a row (1984-1985) for "Nate the Great" titles. A *Books of Wonder News* reviewer calls the "Nate the Great" books "the finest mysteries we know of for beginning readers," adding that they are also suitable for reading aloud to children as young as three years old. Sharmat believes the humor in her books is an essential ingredient. She wrote, "I like to write funny books

because I think that life is basically a serious business and needs a humorous counterbalance."

WORKS CITED:

Books of Wonder News, March, 1988, p. 1.
Fritts, Kathy, "Paperback Romance Series Roundup," *School Library Journal,* October, 1987, p. 149.
Roback, Diane, "Forecasts: Children's Books," *Publishers Weekly,* June 27, 1986, p. 94.
Sands, Kim Carter, "Sorority Sisters," *Voice of Youth Advocates,* April, 1988, p. 35.
Sharmat, Marjorie Weinman, "Meet Your Author," *Cricket,* October, 1975.

FOR MORE INFORMATION SEE:

BOOKS

Fifth Book of Junior Authors and Illustrators, H. W. Wilson, 1987, pp. 282-283.
For Love of Reading, Consumer Reports, Consumer Union, 1988.
Larrick, Nancy, *A Parents' Guide to Children's Reading,* 4th edition, Doubleday, 1982.
The New York Times Parents' Guide to the Best Books for Children, Times Books, 1988.
Raphael, Frederick, and Kenneth McLeish, *The List of Books,* Harmony Books, 1981.
Sutherland, Zena, editor, *The Best in Children's Books, 1966-1972, University of Chicago Guide to Children's Literature,* University of Chicago Press, 1973, p. 6.
Twentieth Century Children's Writers, 3rd edition, St. Martin's, 1989, pp. 881-882.

PERIODICALS

Bulletin of the Center for Children's Books, November, 1984.
Chicago Tribune, February 2, 1975; June 8, 1975; April 3, 1977; March 8, 1991.
Christian Science Monitor, November 2, 1977; July 6, 1984.
Horn Book, December, 1980, p. 638; June, 1981, pp. 304-305; August, 1983, p. 436.
Los Angeles Times, November 25, 1990.
New York Times Book Review, October 23, 1981; April 9, 1982; September 27, 1985; June 27, 1986; February 26, 1988; April 6, 1991.
School Library Journal, May, 1984, pp. 94, 100; May, 1985, p. 83; September, 1986; December, 1990; September, 1991; September, 1992, p. 210.
Washington Post Book World, March 13, 1988; March 11, 1990, pp. 8-9.

* * *

SHERWOOD, Jonathan
See LONDON, Jonathan (Paul)

* * *

SIBSON, Caroline
See DRACUP, Angela

SILL, Cathryn 1953-

PERSONAL: Born February 8, 1953, in Asheville, NC; daughter of Jack Howard (an accountant) and Mary (a homemaker; maiden name, Jarvis) Powell; married John Sill (an author and illustrator), March 16, 1975. *Education:* Western Carolina University, B.S.Ed., 1975. *Religion:* Christian.

ADDRESSES: Home—105 Wilkie St., Franklin, NC 28734.

CAREER: Macon County Board of Education, Franklin, NC, elementary schoolteacher, 1976—; children's writer, 1988—.

WRITINGS:

(With husband, John Sill, and Ben Sill) *A Field Guide to Little Known and Seldom Seen Birds of North America,* illustrated by J. Sill, Peachtree Pubs., 1988.

(With B. Sill and J. Sill) *Another Field Guide to Little Known and Seldom Seen Birds of North America,* illustrated by J. Sill, Peachtree Pubs., 1990.

About Birds: A Guide for Children, illustrated by J. Sill, Peachtree Pubs., 1991.

WORK IN PROGRESS: Ideas for natural history books for young children.

SIDELIGHTS: Cathryn Sill told *SATA:* "I enjoy natural history and particularly birds. I am also very fond of teaching. I wanted a simple, informative book about birds to use in my kindergarten classroom. The illustrations needed to be accurate as well as beautiful. Since my husband, John, is an artist and illustrator, we enjoyed working together on *About Birds.*"

*   *   *

SILL, John 1947-

PERSONAL: Born November 22, 1947, in St. Pauls, NC; son of Charles Frank (an artist) and Mary Louise (a homemaker; maiden name, McGoogan) Sill; married Cathryn Powell (a teacher and author), March 16, 1975. *Education:* Received B.S. from North Carolina State University. *Religion:* Christian.

ADDRESSES: Home—105 Wilkie St., Franklin, NC 28734.

CAREER: Viking Penguin, New York City, bird calendar artist, 1978—; *South Carolina Wildlife* magazine, Columbia, SC, illustrator, 1991—; author and illustrator, 1987—.

AWARDS, HONORS: Recipient of first-place awards in North Carolina and Georgia art shows.

WRITINGS:

(Illustrator) *A Guide to Bird Behavior,* Volume 2, Little, Brown, 1983.

(With wife, Cathryn Sill, and Ben Sill; and illustrator) *A Field Guide to Little Known and Seldom Seen Birds of North America,* Peachtree Pubs., 1988.

CATHRYN SILL

JOHN SILL

(With B. Sill and C. Sill; and illustrator) *Another Field Guide to Little Known and Seldom Seen Birds of North America,* Peachtree Pubs., 1990.

(Illustrator) C. Sill, *About Birds: A Guide for Children,* Peachtree Pubs., 1991.

WORK IN PROGRESS: So You Want to Be a Birder, a humorous book about bird-watching.

SIDELIGHTS: John Sill told *SATA:* "I truly enjoy birds. Their beauty, their songs, and their behavior are a continual source of both pleasure and inspiration." Sill added: "I was very fortunate to have been able to learn a great deal from my father, whose main love was watercolor."

* * *

SKURZYNSKI, Gloria (Joan) 1930-

PERSONAL: Surname pronounced "skur-*zin*-ski"; born July 6, 1930, in Duquesne, PA; daughter of Aylmer Kearney (a steelworker) and Serena (a telegraph operator; maiden name, Decker) Flister; married Edward Joseph Skurzynski (an aerospace engineer), December 1, 1951; children: Serena Rose, Janine, Joan, Alane, Lauren. *Education:* Attended Mount Mercy College (now Carlow College), 1948-50. *Religion:* Roman Catholic. *Hobbies and other interests:* Science, technology.

ADDRESSES: Home—2559 Spring Haven Dr., Salt Lake City, UT 84109. *Agent*—Edite Kroll Literary Agency, 12 Grayhurst Pk., Portland, ME 04102.

CAREER: Author. U.S. Steel Corp., statistical clerk, 1950-52.

MEMBER: Society of Children's Book Writers and Illustrators, Utah Women's Forum.

AWARDS, HONORS: Golden Kite Honor Book Award for nonfiction, Society of Children's Book Writers, 1978, for *Bionic Parts for People: The Real Story of Artificial Organs and Replacement Parts; Horn Book* Honor Book, and *Booklist* Reviewer's Choice Award, American Library Association (ALA), both 1979, and Christopher Award, 1980, all for *What Happened in Hamelin;* Best Books for Young Adults Award, ALA, and Notable Children's Trade Book in the Field of Social Studies, National Council for the Social Studies and the Children's Book Council, both 1981, and *Booklist* Reviewer's Choice Award, ALA, 1982, all for *Manwolf;* Golden Kite Award for fiction, *School Library Journal* Best Books of 1983 Award, and Best Books for Young Adults Award, ALA, all 1983, all for *The Tempering;* Utah Children's Choice Book Award, 1984, for *Lost in the Devil's Desert;* Golden Spur Award, Western Writers of America, 1985, for *Trapped in the Slickrock Canyon;* Science Writing Award, American Institute of Physics, 1992, for *Almost the Real Thing: Simulation in Your High-Tech World; School Library Journal* Best Books of 1992 Award, for *Good-bye, Billy Radish.*

GLORIA SKURZYNSKI

WRITINGS:

The Magic Pumpkin, illustrated by Rocco Negri, Four Winds, 1971.

The Remarkable Journey of Gustavus Bell, illustrated by Tim and Greg Hildebrandt, Abingdon, 1973.

The Poltergeist of Jason Morey, Dodd, 1975.

In a Bottle with a Cork on Top, illustrated by Glo Coalson, Dodd, 1976.

(Adapter) *Two Fools and a Faker: Three Lebanese Folk Tales,* illustrated by William Papas, Lothrop, 1977.

Martin by Himself, illustrated by Lynn Munsinger, Houghton, 1979.

What Happened in Hamelin (novel; also known as *Rattenfanger von Hameln*), Four Winds, 1979.

Honest Andrew, illustrated by David Wiesner, Harcourt, 1980.

Manwolf, Clarion Books, 1981.

(Contributor) *Three Folktales,* Houghton, 1981.

The Tempering (novel), Clarion Books, 1983.

The Minstrel in the Tower, illustrated by Julek Heller, Random House, 1988.

Dangerous Ground, Bradbury, 1989.

Good-bye, Billy Radish (novel), Bradbury, 1992.

Here Comes the Mail, Bradbury, 1992.

"THE MOUNTAIN WEST ADVENTURE" SERIES

Lost in the Devil's Desert, illustrated by Joseph M. Scrofani, Lothrop, 1982.

Trapped in the Slickrock Canyon (Junior Literary Guild selection), illustrated by Daniel San Souci, Lothrop, 1984.

Caught in the Moving Mountains, illustrated by Ellen Thompson, Lothrop, 1984.

Swept in the Wave of Terror, Lothrop, 1985.

"YOUR HIGH-TECH WORLD" SERIES

Robots: Your High-Tech World, Bradbury, 1990.

Almost the Real Thing: Simulation in Your High-Tech World, Bradbury, 1991.

Get the Message: Telecommunications in Your High-Tech World, Bradbury, 1993.

Know the Score: Video Games in Your High-Tech World, Bradbury, in press.

NONFICTION

Bionic Parts for People: The Real Story of Artificial Organs and Replacement Parts (Junior Literary Guild selection), illustrated by Frank Schwartz, Four Winds, 1978.

Safeguarding the Land: Women at Work in Parks, Forests, and Rangelands, foreword by Cecil D. Andrus, Harcourt, 1981.

Contributor of articles and short stories to periodicals, including *'Teen* and *School Library Journal.*

ADAPTATIONS: What Happened in Hamelin was adapted for film and telecast by the Columbia Broadcasting System on "Storybreak" in 1987.

WORK IN PROGRESS: Zero Gravity, for Bradbury.

SIDELIGHTS: "Perhaps if I'd known how long it would take me to acquire satisfactory writing skills," wrote author Gloria Skurzynski in the *Fifth Book of Junior Authors and Illustrators,* "I would have been too intimidated to try. But with the innocence of ignorance, I began putting words on paper." Skurzynski, who had been a busy wife and mother, started writing children's books after the last of her five daughters began school, a time when she realized she would need something other than bringing up her children to fill her life. She was also encouraged by the Pulitzer prize-winning poet Phyllis McGinley, whose verse Skurzynski had read after seeing McGinley on the cover of *Time.* When Skurzynski posted a fan letter, McGinley replied, and a correspondence began which lasted until the poet died in 1978. Reacting to Skurzynski's observation-filled letters, McGinley told her that she had talent and should consider writing professionally. Now, Skurzynski is the author of over twenty-five popular and acclaimed children's books.

Skurzynski was born at the beginning of the Great Depression in Duquesne, Pennsylvania, a small town built around the steel mill in which her father, Aylmer (Al) Flister, worked. Her family was fortunate because her father's job allowed them to weather the Depression with relative ease. Mr. Flister had held dreams of succeeding in Hollywood as a producer or director—he was offered a job in the production department of

Metro-Goldwyn-Mayer—but finally decided that he would actually be happier staying in Duquesne and working in the mill. To pursue his interest in acting and theatre on the side, Mr. Flister staged amateur theatrical productions, a total of ninety before he died. Serena Flister, Skurzynski's mother, worked as a telegraph operator at Western Union; of her four children, only Gloria survived infancy.

As a girl, Skurzynski was a devoted library patron and often attended movies. "The books I checked out of the library and the movies I saw each week made me believe in romance," she wrote in an essay for the *Something about the Author Autobiography Series* (*SAAS*). The glamorous, hero-filled world she was admitted to through movies and books was one unlike her own hometown, which was inhabited by hard-working citizens representing a rich diversity of ethnicities. In *SAAS,* Skurzynski described the conversations she would overhear while riding around Duquesne in the daytime: "The bus would buzz with the clicking consonants and sibilant syllables of Polish, Russian, and Slovak words, underscored by liquid Italian vowels."

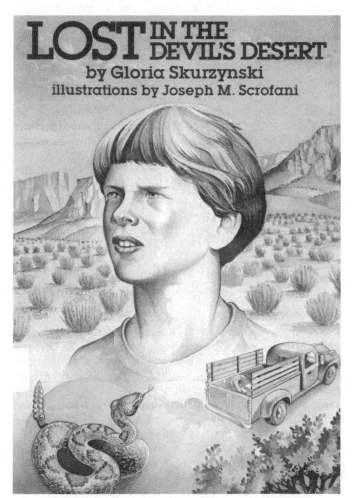

Skurzynski echoes the adventures of her favorite childhood books in this exciting tale of a kidnapped boy left to survive in the deadly desert alone. (Cover illustration by Joseph M. Scrofani.)

After graduating first in her high school class, Skurzynski received scholarships from several colleges. She decided to attend Mount Mercy, a Catholic college whose students were exclusively women, because she had been charmed by a group of nuns she had seen playing in the college's yard during her visit. Unfortunately, her delight wouldn't last; the nuns were strict and had little tolerance. This oppressive atmosphere and her own inability to choose a field to major in made Skurzynski quit after her sophomore year and get a job at U.S. Steel Corporation in Pittsburgh. She married Edward Skurzynski on December 1, 1951, as he was finishing his senior year of college. Before the end of the decade, she and her husband were the parents of five children, all daughters, who immediately became the center of their lives. In *SAAS,* Skurzynski wrote: "The playpen became a permanent fixture in the living room and the high chair stood rooted to the dining room floor, cemented in place by spilled baby food. All my tablecloths were plastic. By the time our oldest daughter reached six, she'd become expert at folding diapers. Had I yet thought about being a writer? Ha! I wrote nothing longer than grocery lists."

By the time her youngest daughter was about to enter school, though, Skurzynski had begun to think that she should go back to college and become a history teacher. Her plans were broken when her husband, an aerospace engineer, was transferred to Utah. Once in her new home, Skurzynski postponed her plans for college so she could have time to adjust to her new surroundings. "Then ... pure chance, the element that controls so much of our lives, took over and changed my direction for good," she wrote in *SAAS.* That was when Skurzynski began to correspond with Phyllis McGinley. As she noted in *SAAS,* she filled her letters with observations such as, "There's something hypnotic about a pot of boiling macaroni." She began to write stories, but for a year and a half she received nothing but rejections from magazines. Finally, on her fifty-eighth submission, Skurzynski sold a short story to *'Teen.*

The difficulties Skurzynski had in making her first sale did not disappear once she became a published writer. She struggled, but managed to have several picture books published. She enjoyed writing children's novels more, however, and her interest in history made her lean naturally toward historical fiction. Just as being a mother had absorbed all of Skurzynski's time, now writing was her passion. In the *Fifth Book of Junior Authors and Illustrators,* Skurzynski wrote, ":While I write a novel, I'm only half aware of what's happening in my family, my house, and the world." Her ability to immerse herself in her created worlds began to pay off: she received a Christopher Award for her historical novel *What Happened in Hamelin.* Skurzynski's retelling of the Pied Piper story is based on actual documents from the town of Hamelin, Germany, which indicate that, in 1284, a relative stranger led 130 children from the town into the surrounding mountains. Neither the Piper nor the children ever returned. Skurzynski's narrator, Geist, is a thirteen-year-old orphan who works in a bakery and is despondent because of the baker's

harshness toward him and the drudgery of his medieval life. He becomes excited, though, when the Piper comes to town and promises to rid it of the rats that trouble the inhabitants. When he successfully does so (manipulating the children to do his work for him) and is then cheated out of his payment, he stays in Hamelin as a musician, loved by the children both for his music and the sweets he gives them. What no one suspects is that the sweets contain a drug which gives the children hallucinations, enabling the Piper to ensnare them with his piping and lead them away from their home into slavery. A *Horn Book* reviewer wrote that "the pompous councilman, the simple-minded priest, and the children are realistically and convincingly depicted," and a contributor to the *Bulletin of the Center for Children's Books* stated that the story "builds nicely toward the tense final tragedy." In the *New York Times Book Review,* Natalie Babbitt noted that "the reader is left with a strong, lingering awareness of mankind's ever-present corruptibility."

History more recent than that of thirteenth-century Europe fills Skurzynski's 1983 novel *The Tempering,* which is concerned with her father's past. In *SAAS,* Skurzynski wrote, "For a long while I'd wanted to write about my father's boyhood, about his decision to drop

The steel mills of the author's native Pennsylvania form the backdrop for this absorbing story of a young man's coming of age. (Cover illustration by Ted Lewin.)

out of school to be a steelworker, his first job in the steel mill when he was only fourteen, his love of music and stage shows." Luckily, Skurzynski was able to read sections of the book to her father just before he passed away in 1982. Canaan, a fictionalized Duquesne, serves as the setting for *The Tempering,* the story of a fifteen-year-old boy living in 1912 Pennsylvania. Karl Kerner is eager to quit school so he can work in the steel mill, even though his teacher, Yulyona, encourages him to continue attending class. Because Karl is in love with Yulyona he considers taking her advice, but ultimately goes to work in the mill only to lose his job on his first day when another man pulls a stunt and gets both himself and Karl fired. The metaphor that gives the novel its title compares the process of tempering steel, during which it is melted and formed into shape, with Karl's development into a man throughout the pages of the book. Outside of Karl's struggles, Skurzynski evokes the atmosphere of an early twentieth-century mill town. According to a *Bulletin for the Center for Children's Books* contributor, Skurzynski paints "a vivid picture of the way in which poverty and life-style are shaped by the environment." In the *New York Times Book Review,* Martha Bennett Stiles praised *The Tempering* for its "satisfying portrayals of love, friendship and neighborly decency."

Skurzynski's multiethnic hometown also served as an inspiration for the setting of her novel *Good-bye, Billy Radish,* which tells the story of Hank Kerner and Bazyli Radichevych, a Ukrainian boy whom Hank calls "Billy Radish." Billy, much like Karl in *The Tempering,* looks forward to his fourteenth birthday when he can go to work in the steel mill. The coming-of-age story shows how the two boys, despite their different backgrounds and languages, create a friendship that overcomes those superficial boundaries. "To me," Skurzynski wrote in *SAAS,* "humankind's most pervasive and deadly failing is to see the otherness of people rather than the sameness. Wistfully, I hope that in some future century, goodwill and tolerance for everyone's differences will become a universal virtue." A *School Library Journal* contributor called *Good-bye, Billy Radish* a "richly textured, lovingly crafted historical novel."

Aside from crafting successful and acclaimed fiction, Skurzynski has also written several nonfiction books. *Bionic Parts for People: The Real Story of Artificial Organs and Replacement Parts,* which received a Golden Kite Honor Book Award, was inspired by family members in the same way some of her fiction has been. This time, two of Skurzynski's daughters served as her motivation: one had worked for the Division of Artificial Organs at the University of Utah, and another had studied in a building in which organ research was conducted. *Bionic Parts* examines the medical field's attempts to create machinery based on the functioning of normal, healthy body organs that can replace dysfunctional or injured organs. A reviewer for the *Bulletin of the Center for Children's Books* called *Bionic Parts* "an excellent survey of the subject."

In one of her many nonfiction books, Skurzynski examines medical and mechanical sciences in investigating the drive to create artificial organs and body parts.

Another of Skurzynski's nonfiction books, *Almost the Real Thing: Simulation in Your High-Tech World,* the second in a series, details some of the techniques scientists use to simulate real-world situations in order to test ideas or products and improve upon them in the early stages of development. A *School Library Journal* reviewer called *Almost the Real Thing* "an excellent and lively book on an offbeat topic," and the American Institute of Physics awarded the book its Science Writing Award in 1992.

Now the author of over twenty-five children's books, Skurzynski told *SATA:* "When I work on a book like *Good-bye, Billy Radish,* I find my way back home to the smoky, sooty, western Pennsylvania town where flames from smokestacks set fire to the night. Today the smoke is gone, and so are the steel mills, but in my own memory, and through the stories my parents told me, I can recreate that time and place. It's important that I do that, because if I don't, no one will remember the rumbles and shrieks of the mills, the smell of the smoke, the blaze of the furnaces, and the enormous power of the steel mills over the townspeople.

"Then, after I've relived that past, I can flash forward. On computer screens, I can enter virtual worlds where I touch things that aren't real, and move around in them, and move them around to wherever I please. In laboratories, designers have shared with me the secrets of their work, giving me breath-stopping previews of the twenty-first century for my books *Robots, Almost the Real Thing, Get the Message,* and *Know the Score.*

"Caught up in the wonderment of the world to come, and infused with equal wonderment over the world long past, I think how lucky I am to be a writer, to be the channel through which this knowledge flows. As much as I admire the work of scientists and engineers and historians and archaeologists, I think my job is the best. I get to have it all. I only wish I could live forever, so I could see how the future turns out."

WORKS CITED:

Babbitt, Natalie, review of *What Happened in Hamelin, New York Times Book Review,* March 30, 1980, p. 16.

Review of *Bionic Parts for People: The Real Story of Artificial Organs and Replacement Parts, Bulletin of the Center for Children's Books,* April, 1979.

Hupp, Marcia, review of *Good-bye, Billy Radish, School Library Journal,* December, 1992, p. 114.

Newman, Alan, review of *Almost the Real Thing: Simulation in Your High-Tech World, School Library Journal,* October, 1991, p. 141.

Skurzynski, Gloria, autobiographical essay in *Fifth Book of Junior Authors and Illustrators,* H. W. Wilson, 1983, pp. 294-95.

Skurzynski, autobiographical essay in *Something about the Author Autobiography Series,* Volume 9, Gale, 1990, pp. 319-34.

Stiles, Martha Bennett, review of *The Tempering, New York Times Book Review,* May 22, 1983, p. 40.

Review of *The Tempering, Bulletin of the Center for Children's Books,* June, 1983.

Review of *What Happened in Hamelin, Bulletin of the Center for Children's Books,* February, 1980.

Review of *What Happened in Hamelin, Horn Book,* February, 1980.

FOR MORE INFORMATION SEE:

PERIODICALS

Bulletin of the Center for Children's Books, October, 1975; April, 1982; June, 1984; December, 1984; March, 1986.

Horn Book, December, 1971; October, 1978; August, 1981.

Junior Literary Guild, September, 1978; March, 1984.

Publishers Weekly, April 1, 1983.

School Library Journal, October, 1992, pp. 46-47.

—*Sketch by Roger M. Valade III*

* * *

SPENCE, Cynthia
See EBLE, Diane

STRONG, Stacie 1965-

PERSONAL: Born April 15, 1965, in Palos Verdes, CA; daughter of Kenneth Donald (a physical therapist) and Sharon Elaine (a dean of students; maiden name, Retter) Strong. *Education:* University of California, Davis, B.A. (cum laude), 1986; University of Southern California, master of professional writing, 1990; attended Duke University, 1991—.

ADDRESSES: Home—13 G Riverbirch Rd., Durham, NC 27705.

CAREER: Free-lance writer, 1986-87; Intervisual Communications, Inc. (children's book packager), Los Angeles, CA, assistant editorial director, 1987-91; writing instructor in Los Angeles and Durham, NC, 1990-92; free-lance writer, 1991—. *Southern California Anthology,* editor in chief, 1989-90; Duke University, founder and director of law mentor program and researcher in prisoner rights program, 1991—.

MEMBER: Women Law Students Association.

AWARDS, HONORS: Chautauqua Creative Writing fellowship, 1988; Elisabeth Kempthorne Creative Writing fellowship, 1989.

WRITINGS:

Noah's Ark, Starlight, 1990.

STACIE STRONG

A Pop-up Look at Animals in Motion

RUNNERS, SLIDERS, BOUNCERS, CLIMBERS

Strong and coauthor Nick Bantock use fun-filled pop-ups to present scientific facts in this book on movement. (Cover illustration by Nick Bantock.)

Ernest Nister's Book of Christmas, Philomel, 1991.
Farmyard Pets, Philomel, 1991.
Going to the Doctor, Simon & Schuster, 1991.
Little Dolls, Philomel, 1991.
My Little Pets, Philomel, 1991.
Our Baby, Philomel, 1991.
Our Picture Puzzle Book, Philomel, 1991.
(Adapter) *Over in the Meadow,* Simon & Schuster, 1991.
Tiny Tots, Philomel, 1991.
The Voyage of Christopher Columbus, Sears, Roebuck, 1991.
Christmas Toys, Philomel, 1992.
Here Comes Santa, Philomel, 1992.
Holiday Delights, Philomel, 1992.
Let's Take a Trip around the Zoo, Price, Stern, 1992.
My Anytime Activity Book, Discovery Toys, 1992.
(With Nick Bantock) *Runners, Sliders, Bouncers, Climbers,* Hyperion, 1992.
What Goes Inside?, Price, Stern, 1992.
Where Does It Come From?, Price, Stern, 1992.
Who Makes This?, Price, Stern, 1992.

Whose Footprints Are These?, Price, Stern, 1992.
Winter Frolics, Philomel, 1992.
Animal Families, Price, Stern, 1993.

Also author of plays *Depths* and *A Mother's Love,* both produced at University of Southern California, 1989.

WORK IN PROGRESS: An adult novel, completion expected in 1993.

SIDELIGHTS: Stacie Strong told *SATA:* "I began reading at an early age (three) and was surrounded by books throughout my childhood. I always knew I wanted to write; I felt I should give something back to the library world which had given me so much.

"I began my writing career very optimistically at the age of eleven and haven't stopped yet. My early attempts included a fantasy novel a la J. R. R. Tolkien's *Hobbit,* a pirate adventure, and anything concerning horses. Surprisingly, my first publications were not middle-reader or young-adult novels, which is what I'd always seen myself doing, but pop-up books. I kind of fell into editing pop-ups when I was living in Los Angeles, pursuing my master's degree. Although I hadn't read many such books as a child, I soon found myself writing them. Sometimes the words get lost behind the pop-up images (figuratively and literally!), but it takes a certain discipline to write condensed but lively copy.

"I've also had the opportunity to teach writing through various college extension classes, an experience which has been a great education for me. It's wonderful to see the eagerness and enthusiasm of prospective writers, and the untapped talent is truly encouraging. Being around so much energy inspires me to work harder; by the time class is halfway through I want to run back home to my computer and write, write, write!

"With the clamor of everyday life, it's sometimes easy to lose sight of your dreams. Sitting down to a blank page or a blank computer screen can be frustrating and lonely, but the end product is always worth the pain."

T

TANNER, Jane 1946-

PERSONAL: Born October 29, 1946, in Melbourne, Australia; daughter of Lionel Stephen (a police officer) and Cecelia Helen (a nurse; maiden name, McCulloch) Tanner; married Joseph Macdermott-Mallin (an artist); marriage ended; children: Mishka Eve. *Education:* Victorian College of the Arts, associateship diploma, 1970, diploma of education, 1977. *Politics:* "Apolitical." *Religion:* Agnostic. *Hobbies and other interests:* Gardening (particularly old-fashioned roses), beach walking, poetry.

ADDRESSES: Home and office—Hawthorn, Victoria, Australia. *Contact*—Penguin Books, P.O. Box 257, Ringwood, Victoria 3134, Australia.

CAREER: Penguin Books, Ringwood, Victoria, Australia, illustrator, 1984—. Has lectured in drawing and printmaking and has served as a judge for both the Macmillan Prize and the Creighton Award in 1990 and 1991. *Exhibitions:* Tanner's works have been displayed in many exhibitions, including a retrospective at Victorian Art Centre in 1992.

AWARDS, HONORS: Shortlisted for the Kate Greenaway Award and the Australian Picture Book of the Year, both 1985, both for *There's a Sea in My Bedroom;* Australian Picture Book of the Year, and shortlisted for the Victoria Premier's Award, both 1989, both for *Drac and the Gremlin;* Australian Government's Human Rights Award for Children's Literature, and shortlisted for the South Australia Literary Awards and the Australian Junior Book of the Year, all 1992, and highly commended for the Joyce Nicholson Award for the best designed book of the year, Australian Book Publishers Association, all for *The Wolf.*

ILLUSTRATOR:

(Contributor) *Time for a Rhyme,* Thomas Nelson, 1983.
Margaret Wild, *There's a Sea in My Bedroom,* Puffin, 1984.
Niki's Walk, Macmillan, 1985.
Allan Baillie, *Drac and the Gremlin,* Viking Kestrel, 1988, Dial, 1989.
Margaret Barbalet, *The Wolf,* Penguin, 1991.
Paul Jennings, *Mischild,* Penguin, 1993.

Has also illustrated many book covers and educational publications.

WORK IN PROGRESS: Writing and illustrating a book for three-year-olds.

SIDELIGHTS: Jane Tanner told *SATA:* "My major concern is with pictorial storytelling, including the use of metaphor, light and dark, texture, and rhythms. Currently, an underwater book necessitates that I study

JANE TANNER

underwater light and work from clay models in order to achieve a realistic style."

* * *

TATE, Ellalice
See HIBBERT, Eleanor Alice Burford

* * *

TAZEWELL, Charles 1900-1972

PERSONAL: Born June 2, 1900, in Des Moines, IA; died June 26, 1972, in Chesterfield, NH; married Louise Skinner.

CAREER: Writer. Actor in Broadway productions, including *They Knew What They Wanted,* 1924, *Lucky Sam McCarver,* 1925, and *Sugar Hill,* 1931. Cofounder and operator of Little Theater in Brattleboro, VT.

AWARDS, HONORS: Thomas A. Edison Prize for best children's story of the year, 1956, for *The Littlest Snowman.*

WRITINGS:

FOR CHILDREN

The Littlest Angel, illustrated by Katherine Evans, Childrens Press, 1946, illustrated by Sergio Leone, Grosset & Dunlap, 1962, illustrated by Paul Micich, Ideals Children's Books, 1991.
The Littlest Stork, illustrated by Katherine Evans, Childrens Press, 1953.
The Littlest Snowman, illustrated by George De Santis, Grosset & Dunlap, 1956.
The Small One: A Story for Those Who Like Christmas and Small Donkeys, illustrated by Marian Ebert, Franklin Press (Primos, PA), 1958.
Littlest Stories, illustrated by Joyce Langelier, Rolton House, 1962.
I'm a Fridgit!, illustrated by Langelier, Rolton House, 1963.

OTHER

Long Engagement (radio play), American Forces Radio and Television Service, 1977.

Also author of scripts for television.

ADAPTATIONS: The Littlest Angel was adapted by Patricia Gray as a play titled *The Littlest Angel: A Christmas Play in One Act,* Dramatic Publishing, 1964, as a television musical broadcast on NBC, 1969, and was recorded as *The Littlest Angel* [and] *The Bells of Christmas,* Caedmon, 1973.

FOR MORE INFORMATION SEE:

PERIODICALS

New York Times, June 28, 1972.*

TENNIEL, John 1820-1914

PERSONAL: Born February 28, 1820, in Kensington, London, England; died February 25, 1914, in Kensington, London, England; son of John Baptist Tenniel; married Julia Giani, 1854 (died, 1856). *Education:* Studied at the Royal Academy Schools.

CAREER: Illustrator, artist, and cartoonist. *Punch,* London, England, illustrator, primarily of political cartoons, 1850-1901. Works exhibited at the Suffolk Street Galleries, London, 1836, and at the Royal Academy, London.

AWARDS, HONORS: Knight of the British Empire, 1893.

ILLUSTRATOR:

F. H. C. de La Motte Fouque, *Undine,* James Burns, 1845.
Thomas James, editor, *Aesop's Fables,* John Murray, 1848.
Shirley Brooks, *The Gordian Knot,* Bentley, 1860.
Thomas Moore, *Lalla Rookh,* Longman, Green, Longman & Roberts, 1860.
(Frontispiece) F. W. Robinson, *Grandmother's Money,* Hurst & Blackett, 1862.
(Frontispiece) Robinson, *No Church,* Hurst & Blackett, 1862.
Lewis Carroll, *Alice's Adventures in Wonderland,* Macmillan, 1865 (recalled), reissued, 1866.
W. H. Miller, *The Mirage of Life,* Religious Tract Society, 1867.

JOHN TENNIEL

(Frontispiece) Dinah Mullock, *A Noble Life,* Hurst & Blackett, 1869.

Carroll, *Through the Looking-Glass,* Macmillan, 1872.

CONTRIBUTOR OF ILLUSTRATIONS

S. C. Hall, editor, *The Book of British Ballads,* Jeremiah How, 1842.

Poems and Pictures, James Burns, 1846.

L'Allegro and Il Penseroso, Art-Union of London, 1848.

The Juvenile Verse and Picture Book, James Burns, 1848.

Charles Dickens, *The Haunted Man,* Chapman & Hall, 1848.

Martin F. Tupper, *Proverbial Philosophy,* Thomas Hatchard, 1854.

Lord Byron, *Childe Harold,* Art-Union of London, 1855.

Barry Cornwall, *Dramatic Scenes,* Chapman & Hall, 1857.

R. Pollock, *The Course of Time,* Blackwood, 1857.

R. A. Willmott, editor, *The Poets of the Nineteenth Century,* Routledge, 1857.

William Cullen Bryant, *Poems,* Appleton Davies, 1857.

Robert Blair, *The Grave,* A. & C. Black, 1858.

The Home Affections Portrayed by the Poets, Routledge, 1858.

Lays of the Holy Land from Ancient and Modern Poets, Nisbet, 1858.

Edgar Allan Poe, *The Poetical Works of Edgar Allan Poe,* Sampson Low, Son & Co., 1858.

H. Cholmondeley-Pennell, *Puck on Pegasus,* J. C. Hotten, 1861.

Mrs. Gatty, *Parables from Nature,* Bell & Daldy, 1861.

R. H. Barnham, *The Ingoldsby Legends,* Bentley, 1864.

English Sacred Poetry of the Olden Time, Religious Tract Society, 1864.

Dalziel's Arabian Nights Entertainments, Ward, Lock & Co., 1865.

Theodore Hersart La Villemarque, *Ballads and Songs of Brittany,* translated by Tom Taylor, Macmillan, 1865.

Adelaide Ann Proctor, *Legends and Lyrics,* Bell & Daldy, 1866.

Touches of Nature by Eminent Artists, Straham, 1866.

Henry Wadsworth Longfellow, *Tales of a Wayside Inn,* Bell & Daldy, 1867.

Charles Mackey, editor, *A Thousand and One Gems of English Poetry,* Routledge, 1872.

Hall, *The Trial of Sir Jasper,* Virtue, 1873.

Walter Thornbury, *Historical and Legendary Ballads and Songs,* Chatto & Windus, 1876.

Also contributor of illustrations to Thomas Hood's *Passages from the Poems of Thomas Hood,* 1858, and *Passages from Modern English Poets,* 1862. Contributor of illustrations to English periodicals, including *Once a Week, Good Words,* and the *Illustrated London News.*

SIDELIGHTS: Sir John Tenniel is remembered chiefly for his illustration of Lewis Carroll's *Alice in Wonderland* (1865) and *Through the Looking-Glass* (1872), works that have won near universal approval from critics and from readers of all ages around the world.

The Tenniel images of Alice and her friends are nearly as important to the lasting success of the works as Carroll's stories, and few subsequent illustrators of *Alice* and *Through the Looking-Glass* have measured up to the master artist who came before. In his own time, though, Tenniel enjoyed more attention for his work as a political cartoonist for the magazine *Punch,* where more than two thousand of his cartoons were published between 1850 and his retirement in 1901. Tenniel was also a life-long artist and art lover who staged his first exhibition when he was sixteen, and by the time he took the commission from Carroll he had already illustrated nearly thirty books either in whole or in part.

Tenniel was born in 1820 in the Kensington section of London to John Baptist Tenniel; his mother died when he was young. By the time he was old enough to go to school he had taught himself to draw. Tenniel's father, a military instructor, taught his son to fence and hoped that Tenniel would lead a military life. During his fencing lessons Tenniel lost an eye, though, and, as Frances Sarzano wrote in *Sir John Tenniel,* "It was soon clear that his career was to be more aesthetic and less athletic than the father, perhaps, had hoped." Tenniel briefly attended the Royal Academy Schools, but he withdrew when he became unhappy with his course of study.

While still a boy, Tenniel joined the Clipstone Street Art Society and honed his talents by sketching live models (a practice he disdained as a professional), studying anatomy, and copying great works in the British Museum. Most of his early work was done in oils; in 1836 he exhibited a work at the Suffolk Street Galleries in London, and the next year the Royal Academy accepted one of his works for exhibition. He exhibited various works at the Academy for the next five years. In 1845 he received his first commission: the British government announced a contest for the solicitation of frescos to patriotic subjects to decorate the houses of Parliament. As Tenniel remembered in a conversation with M. H. Spielmann, quoted in the *Magazine of Art,* "I had a great idea of High Art.... I sent in a 16-foot-high cartoon for Westminster Palace" entitled "The Spirit of Justice." Tenniel was compensated for the ambitious work and invited ("tactfully," said Sarzano) to produce a more acceptable piece: a portrait of the English poet laureate John Dryden's St. Cecilia.

Both these works were exhibited with the other contest submissions in Westminster Palace, and that exhibition brought Tenniel his first contact with *Punch.* "Mr. Punch," the nom-de-plume of the magazine's cartoonists, produced a group of what Sarzano called "ironic" commemorations of Tenniel's austere work.

In the meantime Tenniel had begun illustrating books. His first published book illustrations appeared in *The Book of British Ballads* in 1842; he was the sole contributor of illustrations for the 1845 edition of F. H. C. de La Motte Fouque's *Undine.* Four more partial credits followed between 1846 and 1848, including *The Haunted Man* by Charles Dickens. Tenniel's work on

Aesop's Fables (1848) attracted the attention of the staffers at *Punch,* who invited him in 1850 to take the place of a retiring cartoonist. He quickly became a fixture in English literary, artistic, and political circles through cartoons that "have appealed to all that is best in us in relation to the political and social questions of the day, and if they have not, in the opinion of some, been always in the right, they have erred on the side of generosity and sympathy, and in defense of those principles which *Punch* imagined to be the noblest and the best," related Spielmann.

Tenniel himself once stated, "As for political opinions, I have none; at least, if I have my own little policies I keep them to myself, and profess only those of my paper." The cartoons generally endorsed the conservative and imperialist social philosophy of Victorian Britain and were, at least by subsequent standards, deferential to the politicians and statesmen who were their subjects. Sarzano remarked that if Tenniel dealt "gently" with the politicians, "it may be noted that he also dealt gently

with everyone else with whom he made contact in his life and work. There was no trace of virulence in Tenniel's nature and he counterfeited none in his cartoons." He worked steadily for *Punch* for more than thirty years, and more sporadically for another twenty. The *Junior Books of Authors* quoted him as saying that during the steady period of his work for the magazine he "hardly left London for more than a week."

While at *Punch* Tenniel continued his work as a book illustrator. In 1854, the year he married Julia Giani, some of his work appeared in Martin F. Tupper's *Proverbial Philosophy,* and in 1855 Tenniel illustrations appeared in Lord Byron's *Childe Harold.* Tenniel's wife died in 1856; they had no children and he never married again. In 1861 Thomas Moore's *Lalla Rookh* appeared to widespread critical and popular acclaim. And when it came time to choose an artist to illustrate *Alice in Wonderland,* Lewis Carroll remembered Tenniel's exotic illustrations for this work, as well as those he did for *Aesop's Fables.* Carroll and Tenniel were introduced in

Although he was a noted political cartoonist in his day, Tenniel was to become most famous for his unforgettable illustrations for Lewis Carroll's *Alice's Adventures in Wonderland.* (Illustration of "The Duchess's Lullaby" by Tenniel.)

1864, when the manuscript was already in the process of being set in type; upon reviewing Carroll's work Tenniel agreed to submit forty-two illustrations according to Carroll's detailed instructions and guidelines.

During the production of *Alice in Wonderland* Tenniel and Carroll suffered through more than a few creative conflicts. The strained relationship between Tenniel and Carroll was due primarily to the fact that Carroll—an amateur artist himself who produced the drawings for the initial handwritten version of *Alice*—wanted to produce the drawings for the book himself. As critic Susan E. Meyer noted in *A Treasury of the Great Children's Book Illustrators,* "Rankled that he was unable to execute his own illustrations, Carroll demanded the artist execute his vision precisely. He was adamant that the artist not introduce any alien elements into the story; there was only one truthful portrayal possible." But Tenniel was as much of a perfectionist as Carroll, and even succeeded in convincing the author to "improve" elements of the plot of *Alice.* Neither Tenniel nor Carroll approved of the first printing of the book, in which the illustrations were too faint; the publisher, Macmillan, withdrew the printing and re-engraved the drawings. The refurbished volume appeared in November of 1865.

Carroll was, as Meyer put it, "forced to admit" that Tenniel was the appropriate choice to illustrate the sequel to *Alice, Through the Looking-Glass,* which appeared in 1872. Relations between the two continued much as before; it has been said that of the seventy-two drawings Tenniel submitted for the two books, Carroll accepted only one, a drawing of Humpty Dumpty, upon first examination. After *Through the Looking-Glass,* Tenniel stopped illustrating children's books, claiming that his inspiration was gone. He was, Meyer wrote, "probably the only one who was surprised ... when the Gladstone government announced in 1893 that they had conferred John Tenniel's knighthood." Tenniel was eighty and his eyesight was failing when he retired from *Punch;* he continued to paint, mostly in watercolors, until his sight failed completely. He died three days before his ninety-fourth birthday in 1914. Tenniel's "memory will live, not only because his level of achievement was so uniformly high," concluded a London *Times* contributor, "but also because he had the courage to revolutionize political caricature."

WORKS CITED:

"Death of Sir John Tenniel: The Art of Caricature," *Times* (London), February 27, 1914, p. 11.
Kunitz, Stanley, and Howard Haycraft, editors, *The Junior Book of Authors,* 2nd edition, H. W. Wilson, 1951.
Meyer, Susan E., *A Treasury of the Great Children's Book Illustrators,* Abrams, 1983, pp. 65-77.
Sarzano, Frances, *Sir John Tenniel,* Pellegrini & Cudahy, 1948.
Spielmann, M. H., "Our Graphic Humourists: Sir John Tenniel," *Magazine of Art,* May, 1895, pp. 201-07.

Tenniel's exotic drawings brought him to the attention of Lewis Carroll, who brought him back to work on *Alice*'s sequel, *Through the Looking Glass.* (Illustration of "Jabberwocky" by Tenniel.)

FOR MORE INFORMATION SEE:

BOOKS

Children's Literature Review, Volume 18, Gale, 1989.
Cohen, Jane R., *Charles Dickens and His Original Illustrators,* Ohio State University Press, 1980, pp. 155-58.
Feaver, William, *Masters of Caricature,* Knopf, 1981, pp. 82-83.
Mahony, B. E., and others, editors, *Illustrators of Children's Books, 1744-1945,* Horn Book, 1947, pp. 49-51, 441-42.
Ovendon, Graham, and John Davis, *The Illustrators of Alice in Wonderland,* St. Martin's, 1979.
Price, R. G. G., *A History of Punch,* Collins, 1957.
Reid, Forrest, *Illustrators of the Eighteen Sixties,* Dover, 1975.

PERIODICALS

Design, October, 1951.
Rhode Island School of Design Bulletin, April, 1979, pp. 94-95.*

THAYER, Marjorie 1908-1992

PERSONAL: Born 1908; died of cancer, April 27, 1992, in Los Angeles, CA. *Education:* University of California at Berkley, graduate.

CAREER: Editor, novelist, and playwright. Funk & Wagnalls (publishing firm), New York City, editor, 1939-43; Alfred Knopf (publishing firm), promotion director of juvenile book department, 1951-55. Director of juvenile book department, Pentice-Hall, and editor, Golden Gate Junior Books. Has also worked as a bookseller and bookstore manger.

WRITINGS:

PLAYS; ILLUSTRATED BY MARJORIE BURGESON

The Halloween Witch, Children's Press, 1976.
The First Day of School, Children's Press, 1977.
The Valentine Box, Children's Press, 1977.
The April Foolers, Children's Press, 1978.
A Mother for Mother's Day, Children's Press, 1980.

NOVELS

The Christmas Strangers, illustrated by Don Freeman, Children's Press, 1976.
(With Elizabeth Emanuel) *Climbing Sun: The Story of a Hopi Indian Boy,* illustrated with woodcuts by Anne Siberall, Dodd, 1980.
The Youngest, illustrated by Dale Payson, Dodd, 1982.

OTHER

Editor of Doubleday's "New Home Library" series.

SIDELIGHTS: Marjorie Thayer's career encompassed many facets of book production and publishing. She began as a bookseller, later moving on to editorial positions at a number of publishing firms. In addition to her professional duties, Thayer wrote both juvenile theme plays, such as *The Valentine Box,* and novels such as *Climbing Sun. Climbing Sun* tells the story of Hubert Honanie, a young Hopi Indian sent to the Sherman Institution for "reeducation." While at the school, Hubert must learn to deal with both a hostile environment and feelings of inadequecy. Gale Eaton, writing in *School Library Journal,* called the novel "informative and simply written." In *The Youngest,* Thayer again presents a young protagonist struggling with growing pains in the figure of Maggie Thornton, a nine-year-old living on a California ranch in 1919. In a *Publishers Weekly* review, Jean F. Mercier labeled the novel "breezy amusement."

WORKS CITED:

Eaton, Gale, review of *Climbing Sun: The Story of a Hopi Indian Boy, School Library Journal,* November, 1980, p. 80.
Mercier, Jean F., review of *The Youngest, Publishers Weekly,* June 11, 1982, p. 62.

FOR MORE INFORMATION SEE:

PERIODICALS

Bulletin of the Center for Children's Books, November, 1977.
Publishers Weekly, May 18, 1992, p. 35.*

*   *   *

THESMAN, Jean

PERSONAL: Married; children: two daughters, one son.

ADDRESSES: Home—Washington State. *Agent*—c/o Houghton Mifflin Co., Children's Books Division, 1 Beacon St., Boston, MA 02108.

CAREER: Writer.

AWARDS, HONORS: American Library Association (ALA) Recommended Book for the Reluctant Young Adult Reader, Children's Choices Book, and Young Adult Choices Book, all for *Who Said Life is Fair?;* ALA Recommended Book for Reluctant Readers, for *Running Scared;* ALA Best Book for Young Adults, Recommended Book for the Reluctant Young Adult Reader, Children's Choices Book, Young Adult Choice Book, and Pick of the List, all for *The Last April Dancers;* Children's Choices Book and Young Adult Choices Book, both for *Was It Something I Said?;* Sequoyah Young Adult Award, ALA Recommended Book for the Reluctant Young Adult Reader, and IRA Young Adult Choice Book, all for *Appointment with a Stranger;* ALA Notable Children's Book and ALA Best Book for Young

JEAN THESMAN

Adults, both for *Rachel Chance;* ALA Recommended Book for the Reluctant Young Adult Reader and Phantom's Choice Award, both for *Erin;* Golden Kite Award, Society of Children's Book Writers and Illustrators, 1991, ALA Best Book for Young Adults, *School Library Journal* best book, and *Booklist* Editors Choice, all for *The Rain Catchers;* ALA Notable Book, for *When the Road Ends.*

WRITINGS:

JUVENILE NOVELS

Who Said Life Is Fair?, Avon, 1987.
Running Scared, Avon/Flare, 1987.
The Last April Dancers, Houghton, 1987.
Was It Something I Said?, Avon/Flare, 1988.
Appointment with a Stranger, Houghton, 1989.
Couldn't I Start Over?, Avon/Flare, 1989.
Rachel Chance, Houghton, 1990.
The Rain Catchers, Houghton, 1991.
When Does the Fun Start?, Avon/Flare, 1991.
When the Road Ends, Houghton, 1992.
Molly Donnelly, Houghton, 1993.
Cattail Moon, Houghton, in press.

"THE WHITNEY COUSINS" SERIES

Heather, Avon, 1990.
Amelia, Avon, 1990.
Erin, Avon, 1990.
Triple Trouble, Avon, 1992.

"THE BIRTHDAY GIRLS" SERIES

I'm Not Telling, Avon/Camelot, 1992.
Mirror, Mirror, Avon/Camelot, 1992.
Who Am I, Anyway?, Avon/Camelot, 1992.

SIDELIGHTS: The young adult novels of Jean Thesman are distinguished by their realistic and yet sensitive approach to the difficult issues her teenage protagonists encounter, including suicide, old age, life inside dysfunctional families, and the numerous social pains and problems of school-age people. Reviewers frequently point to the author's lyrical use of language as adding to the emotional power and depth of her characters. In a review of Thesman's "Whitney Cousins" series, a *Publishers Weekly* contributor stated that "it is the author's perceptive characterizations and keen explorations of social issues that make her books notable." Among the books that have earned Thesman a reputation as an engaging children's author are *The Last April Dancers, Appointment with a Stranger, Rachel Chance,* and the Golden Kite Award-winning novel, *The Rain Catchers.*

Thesman's talents became widely recognized in 1987, a year in which she published three books: *Who Said Life is Fair?, Running Scared,* and *The Last April Dancers.* Containing many of the familiar elements of a teen romance novel, *Who Said Life is Fair?* focuses on its sixteen-year-old main character, Teddy. While Teddy is infatuated with one boy at school, she is also the object of admiration by another—her childhood friend, Bill. In addition to this problem, as editor of the school newspaper, she questions her role in the school adminis-

Even with lighter novels such as the "Whitney Cousins" series, Thesman has established a reputation as a writer with a gift for keen characterization and sensitive exploration of social issues.

tration's plan to use the paper for its own purposes rather than the students'. The result is a story that is "better than your average teen romance," according to Margaret Mary Ptacek in *Voice of Youth Advocates. School Library Journal* reviewer Anne Saidman asserted that "Teddy is a likable heroine who's not afraid to speak up for herself." *Running Scared* follows the adventures of fifteen-year-old Caroline Cartwright, whose bus trip to visit her grandmother is complicated not only by the presence of her bug-loving younger cousin Jasper but more seriously by the contents of a mysterious box they come across. The cousins find themselves the prisoners of a group of militant survivalists who want the box and its contents. "There is enough suspense here to keep pages turning," noted Susan Ackler in her *Voice of Youth Advocates* assessment of *Running Scared.* A *Kliatt* contributor pronounced the book "a Y[oung] A[dult] adventure that is a cut above the usual."

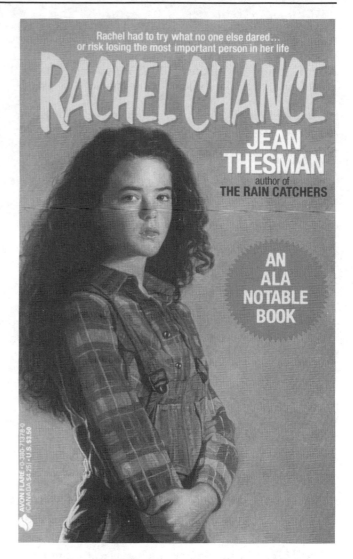

Cat's sixteenth birthday brings only grief and guilt in Thesman's tale of a young girl dealing with her father's mental illness.

Set in rural Washington of the 1940s, this 1990 novel portrays Rachel's attempts to retrieve her little brother, kidnapped from her "nontraditional" family.

In *The Last April Dancers,* Thesman again uses themes of troubled romance and responsibility, weaving them in with the somber topic of death. Catherine St. John, better known as Cat, privately decides to limit her school activities in order to spend more time with her father when his behavior becomes increasingly erratic. Frustrated by her mother's and grandmother's lack of concern for her father and their emotional distance from herself, Cat turns to her friend and neighbor, Cam, for support. Cat's patience with her father slips, however, when he forgets to take her to her driver's test on her sixteenth birthday. Later that night, Mr. St. John commits suicide, and Cat cannot escape the feeling that her harsh words were the cause of his actions. With the help of Cam and her Aunt Leah, Cat overcomes her grief and guilt and determines to take control of her future. Reviewers applauded Thesman's ability to convey a wide range of emotion in *The Last April Dancers.* Blair Christolon in *School Library Journal* suggested that "readers will share Cat's bewilderment, frustration, humiliation, anger, and pain." A *Bulletin of the Center*

for Children's Books writer stated that "the perception with which the author develops Cat's ambivalence, her courage, and her resolution of sorrow, is impressive." "This powerful, disturbing novel is not for those who want easy answers," concluded a *Publishers Weekly* reviewer.

After publishing *Was It Something I Said?* in 1988, Thesman wrote 1989's *Appointment with a Stranger.* The protagonist of this novel also has some difficult obstacles to overcome. The reclusive habits that Keller has developed to hide her severe asthma condition from her classmates in her new hometown, however, is only one part of the plot that Thesman creates. When Keller is saved from drowning in a pond by a boy, Tom, she falls in love with her rescuer. He is unlike other boys, Keller realizes, and she wonders why she only sees him in the woods. Her admirer at school, Drew, is suspicious of Keller's story, and finds in an old newspaper clipping that Tom drowned in the pond forty years earlier and is a ghost. While calling *Appointment with a Stranger* an "unabashedly romantic tale," a *Publishers Weekly* contributor pointed out that the novel embodies "a contemporary message about conquering self-pity and forming realistic relationships." A critic in *Kirkus Reviews* complemented Thesman for her "sympathetic portrait of an asthmatic" and "an engaging narrative style."

Many of Thesman's later books deal with the dynamics of the family. While *Couldn't I Start Over?* is mostly concerned with the trouble between high-school student Shiloh and her devious new acquaintance, Lovey Sullivan, the book is also a story of how the members of Shiloh's family help each other through their personal problems. Patricia Braun in *Booklist* appreciated Thesman's narrative of "a family and its friends working together ... yet maintaining individuality." 1990's *Rachel Chance* concerns a more untraditional family in its struggle to stay to together. The Chance family is a collection of eccentric characters, including Rachel Chance's bad tempered grandfather, his psychic companion Druid Annie, a mentally disabled cousin, and Rachel's widowed mother, who has an illegitimate second child by a migrant worker. They all live together on a farm in Washington State in the 1940s, the objects of gossip and scorn in the nearby town of Rider's Dock. When Rachel's illegitimate baby brother, Rider, is stolen, the townspeople refuse to help and Rachel devises her own plan to save the boy. Accompanied by others from the farm, Rachel eventually finds and rescues Rider, becoming romantically involved with a farmhand, Hank, in the process. *School Library Journal* reviewer Barbara Chatton lauded the way Rachel's powerful loyalty to her family allows her to overcome the weaknesses of others: "The fiercely loving Rachel ... who fights to protect [her family] against all odds, is a character to be remembered." A *Horn Book* critic declared, "The underlying theme, which pits the irresistible force of rugged individualism against the immovable nature of local mores, has seldom been more entertainingly explored."

Published in 1990, the first three books of the "Whitney Cousins" series by Thesman describe the unique situations and challenges of each of three family members, the fifteen-year-old cousins, Amelia, Erin, and Heather. The heroine of Thesman's award-winning novel, *The Rain Catchers,* finds strength through the family-like circle of women who gather at her grandmother's suburban Seattle home each afternoon for tea and talk. The older women's ability to weave every painful life experience into a story with a full history—beginning, middle, and end—inspires young Grayling to get to know more about her own history. She journeys to San Francisco to get to know her unemotional mother better and to learn more about the death of her father. The reunion with her mother is less than satisfying, however, and Grayling returns to the comfort of her grandmother's house. "This is a gracefully written novel, full of exquisite turns of phrase," stated a *Horn Book* reviewer. Barbara Chatton, in her assessment of *The Rain Catchers* in *School Library Journal* maintained, "It is a beautiful story, with elderly characters who exhibit a loving and gracious reaction to life." And a *Publishers Weekly* contributor noted the novel's "characters who

are as memorable as they are quietly eccentric" and Thesman's "lucid, sensual writing."

Thesman's 1992 work, *When the Road Ends,* is the story of three foster children who attempt to forge a lasting family tie despite difficult circumstances. Mary Jack, a twelve-year old veteran of foster homes, Adam, an angry adolescent, and Jane, a physically abused child who refuses to speak, are all under the care of a well-meaning minister, Father Matt Percy and his wife. His wife is unable to cope with the needs of the three children, and the burden is increased by the arrival of Father Matt's adult sister Cecile, who has sustained brain trauma in a car accident. Mrs. Percy sends all four off to Cecile's riverside cottage under the care of a housekeeper who immediately runs off with all the money for the vacation, leaving the children and Cecile on their own. Rather than return to the negative household of Mrs. Percy, the children, under the leadership of Mary Jack, decide to fend for themselves and stay at the cabin. The pressures of taking on all the "adult" responsibilities for the renegade family eventually takes its toll on Mary Jack. She finally learns to ask for help, both from the recovering Cecile and from some trustworthy adult

In Thesman's Golden Kite-winning novel *The Rain Catchers,* Grayling is inspired to seek her own family history by her grandmother's storytelling circle of friends.

neighbors. A *Wilson Library Bulletin* reviewer praised *When the Road Ends* as "an unusual story, full of warmth and quiet humor." A *Horn Book* contributor also enjoyed "the book's weighty theme of children forced before their time to behave like adults." "The small adventure is impelled by a rare and powerful momentum," commented a *Publishers Weekly* critic, who deemed *When the Road Ends*, "Thesman at her best."

Thesman commented: "I grew up in a house full of books, around people who were accomplished storytellers. It didn't take me long to see that bookworms, storytellers, and people who laugh easily are never bored. There is only one logical occupation for a storytelling bookworm with a sense of humor, so I write books for young people. It's the best job in the world."

WORKS CITED:

Ackler, Susan, review of *Running Scared, Voice of Youth Advocates,* December, 1987, pp. 238-39.
Review of *Appointment with a Stranger, Kirkus Reviews,* March 15, 1989, p. 470.
Review of *Appointment with a Stranger, Publishers Weekly,* March 10, 1989, p. 90.
Braun, Patricia, review of *Couldn't I Start Over?, Booklist,* November 15, 1989, pp. 653-54.
Chatton, Barbara, review of *Rachel Chance, School Library Journal,* April, 1990, pp. 145-46.
Chatton, Barbara, review of *The Rain Catchers, School Library Journal,* March, 1991, p. 218.
Christolon, Blair, review of *The Last April Dancers, School Library Journal,* October, 1987, p. 142.
Review of *The Last April Dancers, Bulletin of the Center for Children's Books,* September, 1987.
Review of *The Last April Dancers, Publishers Weekly,* September 25, 1987, p. 112.
Ptacek, Margaret Mary, review of *Who Said Life Is Fair?, Voice of Youth Advocates,* August, 1987, p. 123.
Review of *Rachel Chance, Horn Book,* September/October, 1990, p. 610.
Review of *The Rain Catchers, Horn Book,* July/August, 1991, p. 465.
Review of *The Rain Catchers, Publishers Weekly,* February 22, 1991, p. 219.
Review of *Running Scared, Kliatt,* September, 1987, p. 20.
Saidman, Anne, review of *Who Said Life Is Fair?, School Library Journal,* May, 1987, p. 118.
Review of *When the Road Ends, Horn Book,* May/June, 1992, p. 342.
Review of *When the Road Ends, Publishers Weekly,* February 17, 1992, p. 64.
Review of *When the Road Ends, Wilson Library Journal,* September, 1992, p. 94.
Review of *The Whitney Cousins: Heather, Amelia, and Erin, Publishers Weekly,* April 27, 1990, p. 63.

FOR MORE INFORMATION SEE:

PERIODICALS

Kirkus Reviews, October 15, 1987, p. 1523; February 15, 1991, pp. 252-53; March 15, 1992, p. 400.
Publishers Weekly, September 8, 1989, p. 71; June 22, 1992, p. 62.
School Library Journal, February, 1989, p. 103; April, 1992, p. 126.
Voice of Youth Advocates, February, 1990, p. 348.
Wilson Library Journal, January, 1991, p. 13.

—Sketch by Marie Ellavich

W

WATSON, Wendy (McLeod) 1942-

PERSONAL: Born July 7, 1942, in Paterson, NJ; daughter of Aldren Auld (an art editor, illustrator, and writer) and Nancy (a writer; maiden name, Dingman) Watson; married Michael Donald Harrah (an actor and opera singer), December 19, 1970; children: Mary Cameron Harrah, one other child. *Education:* Bryn Mawr College, B.A. (magna cum laude with honors in Latin literature), 1964; studied painting with Jerry Farnsworth, Cape Cod, MA, summers, 1961 and 1962, and drawing and painting at National Academy of Design, 1966 and 1967. *Religion:* Society of Friends (Quaker). *Hobbies and other interests:* Theater, music (plays the piano and cello), reading, gardening.

ADDRESSES: Home—RFD 2, Box 79, Groton, VT 05046.

CAREER: Hanover Press, Hanover, NH, compositor and designer, 1965-66; free-lance illustrator of books, 1966—.

MEMBER: Authors Guild, Authors League of America.

AWARDS, HONORS: Fisherman Lullabies was included in the American Institute of Graphic Arts Children's Book Show, 1967-68; *When Noodlehead Went to the Fair* was included in the Printing Industries of America Graphic Arts Awards Competition, 1969; *New York Times* Outstanding Books citation, 1971, Children's Book Showcase award, Children's Book Council, 1972, and National Book Award finalist citation, Association of American Publishers, 1972, all for *Father Fox's Pennyrhymes*, which was also included in the American Institute of Graphic Arts Children's Book Show, 1972, and the Biennial of Illustrations, Bratislava, 1973.

WRITINGS:

FOR CHILDREN; SELF-ILLUSTRATED

Very Important Cat, Dodd, 1958.
(Editor) *Fisherman Lullabies*, music by sister, Clyde Watson, World Publishing, 1968.
(Adapter) Jacob Grimm and Wilhelm Grimm, *The Hedgehog and the Hare*, World Publishing, 1969.
Lollipop, Crowell, 1976.
Moving, Crowell, 1978.
Has Winter Come?, Collins & World, 1978.
Jamie's Story, Philomel, 1981.
The Bunnies' Christmas Eve, Philomel, 1983.
Little Brown Bear, Western Publishing, 1985.
Tales for a Winter's Eve (short stories), Farrar, Straus, 1988.
Wendy Watson's Mother Goose, Lothrop, 1989.
Wendy Watson's Frog Went A-Courting, Lothrop, 1990.
Thanksgiving at Our House, Houghton, 1991.
A Valentine for You, Houghton, 1991.
Happy Easter Day!, Clarion, 1993.

ILLUSTRATOR

Yeta Speevach, *The Spider Plant*, Atheneum, 1965.
A Comic Primer, Peter Pauper, 1966.
Love Is a Laugh, Peter Pauper, 1967.
The Country Mouse and the City Mouse, Stinehour Press (Lunenburg, VT), 1967.
Alice E. Christgau, *Rosabel's Secret*, W. R. Scott, 1967.
Paul Tripp, *The Strawman Who Smiled by Mistake*, Doubleday, 1967.
Edna Boutwell, *Daughter of Liberty*, World Publishing, 1967.
Ogden Nash, *The Cruise of the Aardvark*, M. Evans, 1967.
Miska Miles, *Uncle Fonzo's Ford*, Atlantic/Little, Brown, 1968.
The Best in Offbeat Humor, Peter Pauper, 1968.
Kathryn Hitte, *When Noodlehead Went to the Fair*, Parents Magazine Press, 1968.
Nancy Dingman Watson (mother), *Carol to a Child*, music by C. Watson, World Publishing, 1969.
Louise Bachelder, compiler, *God Bless Us Everyone*, Peter Pauper, 1969.
The Jack Book, Macmillan, 1969.
Helen Keller, Scholastic Book Services, 1970.
Nash, *The Animal Garden*, Deutsch, 1970.
Mary H. Calhoun, *Magic in the Alley*, Atheneum, 1970.

Mabel Harmer, *Lizzie, the Lost Toys Witch,* Macrae Smith, 1970.

How Dear to My Heart, Peter Pauper, 1970.

C. Watson, *Father Fox's Pennyrhymes* (verse; also see below), Crowell, 1971.

Life's Wondrous Ways, Peter Pauper, 1971.

America! America!, Peter Pauper, 1971.

A Gift of Mistletoe, Peter Pauper, 1971.

Charles Linn, *Probability,* Crowell, 1972.

C. Watson, *Tom Fox and the Apple Pie,* Crowell, 1972.

Clyde R. Bulla, *Open the Door and See All the People,* Crowell, 1972.

Bobbie Katz, *Upside Down and Inside Out,* F. Watts, 1973.

N. D. Watson, *The Birthday Goat,* Crowell, 1974.

Paul Showers, *Sleep Is for Everyone,* Crowell, 1974.

N. D. Watson, *Muncus Agruncus: A Bad Little Mouse,* Golden Press, 1975.

C. Watson, *Quips and Quirks,* Crowell, 1975.

C. Watson, *Hickory Stick Rag* (verse), Crowell, 1976.

Florence Pettit, *Christmas All around the House,* Crowell, 1976.

Michael Holt, *Maps, Tracks, and the Bridges of Konigsberg,* Crowell, 1976.

C. Watson, *Binary Numbers* (nonfiction), Crowell, 1977.

C. Watson, *Catch Me and Kiss Me and Say It Again* (verse; also see below), Collins & World, 1978.

Miles, *Jenny's Cat,* Dutton, 1979.

C. Watson, *How Brown Mouse Kept Christmas,* Farrar, Straus, 1980.

Jan Wahl, *Button Eye's Orange,* Warne, 1980.

After Freddie Fox takes a tumble, he is comforted by his friends, who tell him *Tales for a Winter's Eve* in Wendy Watson's self-illustrated book.

C. Watson, *Applebet: An ABC,* Farrar, Straus, 1980.

Anne Pellowski, *Stairstep Farm: Anna Rose's Story,* Philomel, 1981.

Pellowski, *Willow Wind Farm: Betsy's Story,* Philomel, 1981.

Pellowski, *Winding Valley Farm: Annie's Story,* Philomel, 1982.

Rebecca C. Jones, *The Biggest, Meanest, Ugliest Dog in the Whole Wide World,* Macmillan, 1982.

C. Watson, *Father Fox's Feast of Songs* (musical adaptations of poems from *Father Fox's Pennyrhymes* and *Catch Me and Kiss Me and Say It Again*), Philomel, 1983.

Pellowski, *Betsy's Up-and-Down Year,* Philomel, 1983.

Carolyn Haywood, *Happy Birthday from Carolyn Haywood,* Morrow, 1984.

Elaine Edelman, *I Love My Baby Sister (Most of the Time),* Lothrop, 1984.

Elizabeth Winthrop, *Belinda's Hurricane,* Dutton, 1984.

John Bierhorst, *Doctor Coyote,* Macmillan, 1987.

Marcia Leonard, *Angry,* Bantam, 1988.

Leonard, *Happy,* Bantam, 1988.

Leonard, *Scared,* Bantam, 1988.

Leonard, *Silly,* Bantam, 1988.

C. Watson, *Valentine Foxes,* Orchard Books, 1989.

B. G. Hennessy, *A, B, C, D, Tummy, Toes, Hands, Knees,* Viking Kestrel, 1989.

Clement Clarke Moore, *The Night before Christmas,* Clarion, 1990.

C. Watson, *Love's a Sweet,* Viking Penguin, in press.

OTHER

(With Alan Dawe and David Harrison) *Assessing English Skills: Writing; a Resource Book for Adult Basic Education,* Ministry of Education (Victoria, BC), 1984.

SIDELIGHTS: An author and illustrator of books for children under the age of ten, Wendy Watson is most often recognized for her artistic work, especially when it accompanies stories written by her sister, Clyde Watson. The sisters' award-winning collaboration, *Father Fox's Pennyrhymes,* was widely praised by critics like *New York Times Book Review* contributor George A. Woods, who calls the book "an American original."

The daughter of a writer and a writer/illustrator, Watson told *SATA,* "My parents provided, indirectly, a great deal of my basic training in drawing and books in general." The drawings for *Father Fox's Pennyrhymes* are typical of the artist's style. Having spent most of her life in Vermont, Watson creates illustrations that exude a New England country charm—"cheerful, old-fashioned illustrations," as one *Publishers Weekly* contributor characterizes them in a review of *A Valentine for You.* "Her colors have a real integrity that seems to derive from the New England light," Christina Olson observes of *Wendy Watson's Mother Goose* in a *New York Times Book Review* article.

Another quality of many of Watson's illustrations is their attention to small details. A picture by Watson is often filled with objects and bustling with activity that

Many tiny details complement Frog's proposal to Miss Mousie in *Wendy Watson's Frog Went a-Courting*, the author's rendition of the traditional song.

catches the reader's eye. This aspect of her work is especially evident in books like *Wendy Watson's Frog Went A-Courting*. But while a *Publishers Weekly* reviewer remarks that "youngsters will enjoy seeking out the many droll details" in the illustrations, Olson feels in this case that the "frenetic" nature of the pictures does not mesh well with the "rhythms of the text." But, for Olson, this is a small complaint when compared to the quality of the artist's work in general. "Wendy Watson is, after all," the critic concludes, "an illustrator who knows what she is doing. There is a sweetness in her work that is unfailingly appealing, and she produces thoughtful and well-made books."

WORKS CITED:

Olson, Christina, "Children's Books," *New York Times Book Review*, May 27, 1990, p. 18.
Review of *A Valentine for You*, *Publishers Weekly*, January 25, 1991, p. 56.
Review of *Wendy Watson's Frog Went A-Courting*, *Publishers Weekly*, April 27, 1990, p. 60.
Woods, George A., review of *Father Fox's Penny-rhymes*, *New York Times Book Review*, August 15, 1971, p. 8.

FOR MORE INFORMATION SEE:

PERIODICALS

Horn Book, October, 1971, p. 474; January, 1989, p. 64.*

*   *   *

WILLARD, Barbara (Mary) 1909-

PERSONAL: Born in 1909, in Hove, Sussex, England; daughter of an actor. *Education:* Attended the Convent of La Sainte Union, Southampton.

ADDRESSES: Home—Stable Cottage, Clockhouse Lane, Nutley, Uckfield, East Sussex TN22 3PA, England.

CAREER: Novelist and writer for children. Worked variously as an actress, bookshop clerk, and script reader.

MEMBER: Society of Authors.

AWARDS, HONORS: Guardian Awards for children's fiction, 1972, for *The Sprig of Broom*, 1973, for *A Cold Wind Blowing*, and 1974, for *The Iron Lily; The Iron*

Lily was also named an American Library Association notable book; Whitbread Award, 1984, for *The Queen of the Pharisees' Children.*

WRITINGS:

FOR CHILDREN

Portrait of Philip, Macmillan, 1950.
Brother Ass and Brother Lion (play; based on the story of *St. Jerome, the Lion and the Donkey,* by Helen J. Waddell), J.G. Miller, 1951.
The House with Roots, illustrated by Robert Hodgson, Constable, 1959, F. Watts, 1960.
Son of Charlemagne, illustrated by Emil Weiss, Doubleday, 1959.
The Dippers and Jo, illustrated by Jean Harper, Hamish Hamilton, 1960.
Eight for a Secret, illustrated by Lewis Hart, Constable, 1960, F. Watts, 1961.
The Penny Pony, illustrated by Juliette Palmer, Hamish Hamilton, 1961, Penguin, 1967.
The Summer with Spike, illustrated by Anne Linton, Constable, 1961, F. Watts, 1962.
If All the Swords in England, illustrated by Robert M. Sax, Doubleday, 1961.
Stop the Train!, illustrated by Harper, Hamish Hamilton, 1961.
Hetty, illustrated by Pamela Mara, Constable, 1962, Harcourt, 1963.
Duck on a Pond, illustrated by Mary Rose Hardy, F. Watts, 1962.

BARBARA WILLARD

The Battle of Wednesday Week, illustrated by Douglas Hall, Constable, 1963, published in United States as *Storm from the West,* Harcourt, 1964.
The Suddenly Gang, illustrated by Lynette Hemmant, Hamish Hamilton, 1963.
Augustine Came to Kent, illustrated by Hans Guggenheim, Doubleday, 1963.
The Dippers and the High-Flying Kite, illustrated by Maureen Eckersley, Hamish Hamilton, 1963.
Three and One to Carry, illustrated by Hall, Constable, 1964, Harcourt, 1965.
A Dog and a Half, illustrated by Jane Paton, Hamish Hamilton, 1964, Thomas Nelson, 1971.
The Pram Race, illustrated by Constance Marshall, Hamish Hamilton, 1964.
The Wild Idea, illustrated by Douglas Bissett, Hamish Hamilton, 1965.
Charity at Home, illustrated by Hall, Constable, 1965, Harcourt, 1966.
Surprise Island, illustrated by Paton, Hamish Hamilton, 1966, Meredith Press, 1969.
The Richleighs of Tantamount, illustrated by C. Walter Hodges, Constable, 1966, Harcourt, 1967.
Flight to the Forest, illustrated by Gareth Floyd, Doubleday, 1967, published in England as *The Grove of Green Holly,* Constable, 1967.
To London! To London!, illustrated by Antony Maitland, Weybright & Talley, 1968.
The Family Tower, Harcourt, 1968.
(With Frances Howell) *Junior Motorist: The Driver's Apprentice,* illustrated by Ionicus, Collins, 1969.
The Toppling Towers, Harcourt, 1969.
The Pocket Mouse, illustrated by Mary Russon, Knopf, 1969, illustrated by M. Harford-Cross, Julia MacRae, 1981.
(Compiler) *Hullabaloo! About Naughty Boys and Girls,* illustrated by Fritz Wegner, 1969.
The Reindeer Slippers, illustrated by Tessa Jordan, Hamish Hamilton, 1970.
Chichester and Lewes, illustrated by Graham Humphreys, Longman, 1970.
Priscilla Pentecost, illustrated by Doreen Roberts, Hamish Hamilton, 1970.
Jubilee!, illustrated by Hilary Abrahams, Heinemann, 1973.
(Compiler) *Happy Families,* illustrated by Krystyna Turska, Macmillan, 1974.
(Editor) *Field and Forest,* illustrated by Faith Jaques, Penguin, 1975.
(Author of English text) Bunshu Iguchi, *Convent Cat,* Hamish Hamilton, 1975, McGraw, 1976.
Bridesmaid, illustrated by Paton, Hamish Hamilton, 1976.
The Miller's Boy, illustrated by Floyd, Dutton, 1976.
The Gardener's Grandchildren, Kestrel, 1978, McGraw, 1979.
The Country Maid, Hamish Hamilton, 1978, Greenwillow, 1980.
Summer Season, Julia MacRae, 1981.
Spell Me a Witch, Harcourt, 1981.
Famous Rowena Lamont, Patrick Hardy Books, 1983.
The Queen of the Pharisees' Children, Julia MacRae, 1984.

Ned Only, Julia MacRae, 1985.
The Farmer's Boy, Julia MacRae, 1991.
The Ranger's Daughers, Julia MacRae, 1992.

"MANTLEMASS" SERIES

The Lark and the Laurel, Harcourt, 1970.
The Sprig of Broom, illustrated by Paul Shardlow, Longman, 1971, Dutton, 1972.
A Cold Wind Blowing, Longman, 1972, Dutton, 1973.
The Iron Lily, Longman, 1973, Dutton, 1974.
Harrow and Harvest, Penguin, 1974.
The Eldest Son, Kestrel, 1977.
A Flight of Swans, Kestrel, 1980.
The Keys of Mantlemass, Kestrel, 1981.

FOR ADULTS

(With Elizabeth H. Devas) *Love in Ambush,* G. Howe, 1930.
Ballerina, G. Howe, 1932.
Candle Flame, G. Howe, 1932.
Name of Gentleman, G. Howe, 1933.
Joy Befall Thee, G. Howe, 1934.
As Far as in Me Lies, Thomas Nelson, 1936.
Set Piece, Thomas Nelson, 1938.
Personal Effects, Macmillan, 1939.
The Dogs Do Bark, Macmillan, 1948.
Proposed and Seconded, Macmillan, 1951.
Celia Scarfe, Appleton-Century, 1951.
Echo Answers, Macmillan, 1952.
One of the Twelve (one-act play), Samuel French, 1954.
He Fought for His Queen: The Pennithornes, illustrated by Geoffrey Fletcher, Epworth, 1957.
Winter in Disguise, M. Joseph, 1958.
Sussex, Batsford, 1965, Hastings House, 1966.
(Editor) *"I . . .": An Anthology of Diarists,* Chatto & Windus, 1972.
The Forest: Ashdown in East Sussex, Sweethaws Press, 1989.

SIDELIGHTS: Although Barbara Willard has written many books for adults, she considers writing for children her true calling. Since introducing the "Mantlemass" series in 1970, Willard has won critical acclaim in both Europe and the United States. Because of her ability to weave universal relationships and issues into historical settings, Willard was dubbed the "Louisa Alcott of our time" by Margery Fisher in the *School Librarian.* "As a novelist for the young she has made a special place for herself as a reliable craftsman and a sound judge of human affairs," asserted Fisher.

Because her father made his living as an actor, Willard was first exposed to the theatre as a young child. "Before he made it to the West End of London, my father toured endlessly, and more often than not my mother and I went with him," Willard commented in an essay for *Something about the Author Autobiography Series* (SAAS). In the same essay, she also recollected a production of *Macbeth* at Stratford-on-Avon in which she played the part of a boy named Macduff: "I had spent the spring and summer holidays at Stratford-upon-Avon, where my father was working with the theatre company. I was eleven then. I have never

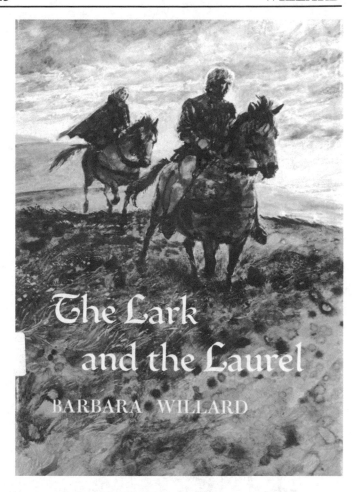

The 1485 ascension of Henry (VII) Tudor to England's throne sets the stage for Willard's first novel in her acclaimed "Mantlemass" series. (Cover illustration by Gareth Floyd.)

recovered from that time. It remains for me the root of all experience." A variation of the experience eventually grew into Willard's book called *Summer Season.*

Both sets of grandparents provided roots for Willard in her native region of Sussex, where she later returned permanently. The writer was an only child until the age of twelve, when her brother Christopher was born. "I doted on the child," Willard admitted in *SAAS,* "perhaps being old enough by then to have quasi-maternal feelings." Christopher was tragically killed while serving in the Royal Air Force, but Willard credits her brother with having influenced her career in the *Fourth Book of Junior Authors and Illustrators.* She wrote: "No doubt at all that it was going over all the old stories with him, finding new ones and making up others that implanted a desire to write for the young."

By the time Willard was ready for formal schooling, the family had set up house in London. She began her education at a school "run by two sisters whose father had been a distinguished journalist. This meant that they were intensely interested in current affairs, particularly in the arts and the theatre—so I was in luck from the start," observed Willard in *SAAS.* There she was able to indulge her love of Shakespeare's plays. A similar school eventually made its way into one of Willard's novels, entitled *Famous Rowena Lamont.* A convent boarding school followed when Willard reached the age of fifteen. While at the convent, she decided to give up dreams of an acting profession, choosing instead to focus on a future career in writing. "Again I struck lucky," reflected Willard in her *SAAS* essay. "Just as I had had the right people to encourage me at my first school, so now I reaped the benefit of a head mistress who also taught us English, who was a member of a distinguished family of scholars."

The teen-aged Willard wrote reams of poetry and fiction. She recalled in *SAAS:* "I filled exercise books with stories, often of a fantastic nature, sometimes straight romance—always, of course, with a tragic ending; and eventually my great historical novel called, challengingly, *Put Not Thy Faith in Princes,* about a devoted young courier in the royal service, and how he was eventually let down by his noble employer and left to cynical reassessment of his own worth." Willard also observed that "one probably needs a bit of loneliness to get deeply involved with writing at an early age."

When Willard left the convent school, she did give acting a try. She related in *SAAS* how her father helped

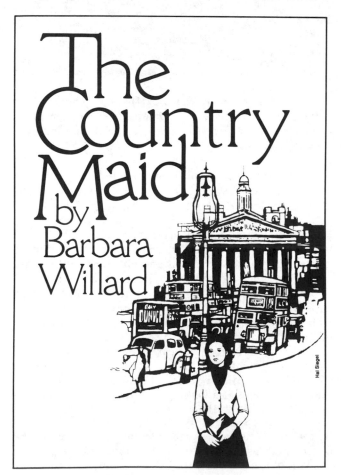

Willard's experiences as a touring actress are reflected in this tale of two young women who become friends despite having very different backgrounds. (Cover illustration by Hal Siegel.)

her get started: "He found me a job in a rather prestigious company touring Shakespeare, where I enjoyed the dressing up, the bits of excitable crowd work, the feeling of being 'in it.' 'I am a player,' I told myself, walking unfamiliar cities from digs to stage door." In her novel *The Country Maid,* Willard mirrors some of her experiences as an actress playing small parts for the first few years following high school. While Willard did once play the part of a heroine in what she termed a "fringe theatre" production, she realized her career wasn't going very far.

Willard's writing career began when she purchased an old typewriter at the age of twenty and set to work on her first serious novel. She relentlessly sent it to one publisher after another until it was finally accepted. But to make enough money to live on, the budding author took odd jobs related to books and the film industry. After working as a clerk in a bookstore, Willard began reading scripts for some American film companies in London. One of the prerequisites of that job was to attend the theatre several times a week. "I greatly enjoyed those years," Willard remarked in *SAAS,* adding: "For good or ill, they confirmed me as a person . . . . I doubt if I ever met the man I felt I really wanted to marry, but I was crazy for a family of some kind." Willard went on to observe that "no doubt that is why I turned eventually to writing for and about children."

While Willard's first book for children was turned down by what she estimated to be about fifty publishers, she persevered. The novel and sequels did see print, but Willard deemed them "old-fashioned" in *SAAS.* She colorfully went on to exclaim, "They are the ones I would dearly love to put in a bag alongside a goodly charge of explosives." Her first success in this genre was *The House with Roots,* published in 1959. "I hit on a story that suited a new mood in writing for children," Willard pointed out in her autobiographical essay. "Since then I have been unable to stop."

But before she began writing children's stories, Willard left London to return to the region of her birth. World War II had ended, and she and a journalist named Frances moved into a small house in Sussex. There Willard was able to adopt the pets she couldn't have in the city, and her menagerie soon grew to include four cats and one dog. *A Dog and a Half* and *Surprise Island* are the two books she wrote featuring animals. Willard explained in *SAAS* how the atmosphere during this period of her life was especially conducive to writing for children, pointing out how her stories about animals "grew out of a time when I was in touch with a good many young children and was keyed in to their particular voice." However, she noted, "My informants grew up like all the rest of us, and their children speak a different language, best handled by younger writers."

Eventually Willard discovered a home in Ashdown Forest that she could not resist. The move proved a fortuitous one for the author, who observed in the *Fourth Book of Junior Authors and Illustrators:* "Practically everything I have written for years and years has its

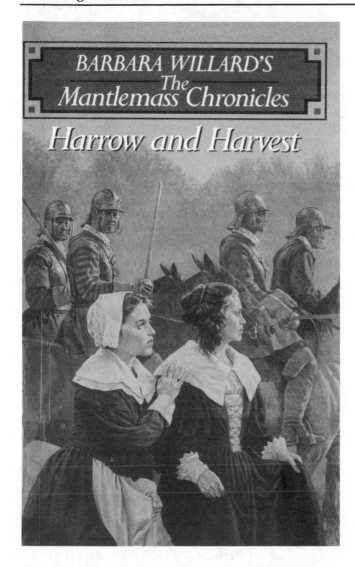

The future of Mantlemass and the Medley family is endangered by the conflict between King and Parliament in this installment of Willard's "remarkable, unique" series.

roots in this place, a development I could not for one moment have envisaged." The area resonated for Willard to such an extent that, as she revealed in her autobiographical essay, "I felt I was returning to my native heath."

About a decade later, Willard brainstormed the beginning of the "Mantlemass" series, for which she is most noted. A fictitious tudor manor in Ashdown Forest, Mantlemass houses families from the end of the War of the Roses in 1485 until Britain's Civil War in the 1640s. In seven volumes, Willard chronicles the lives of the

Medley and Mallory families. *Harrow and Harvest* was meant to conclude the series, but, like Sir Arthur Conan Doyle and his "Sherlock Holmes" series, Willard couldn't resist spinning several more tales about Mantlemass. Calling the series a "remarkable, unique, achievement" in *Times Literary Supplement*, Margaret Meeks stated: "It is a richly varied tapestry of vivid characters and social change; the texture is woven from the cumulative detail that the time span makes possible. Each volume has its own harmony, its own significance, and at the same time reverberates through the others, creating a kind of memory for the reader, who, like the author, lives within the pastoral illusion."

"None of the rich layers of detail in [Willard's] stories has got there by accident," maintained Fisher, adding that Willard is "a good story-teller and a fine technician, well aware that each book must have its own shape and style." Pamela Cleaver, writing in *Twentieth-Century Children's Writers,* similarly observed: "One feels that every person in her books has a full, rounded existence inside and outside the novel." Elizabeth McCallum likewise praised the author in the Toronto *Globe and Mail,* concluding that Willard "expects the best of her readers ... and rewards them with intelligent, riveting prose."

WORKS CITED:

Cleaver, Pamela, *Twentieth-Century Children's Writers,* 3rd edition, St. James Press, 1989, pp. 1046-48.
Fisher, Margery, "Barbara Willard," *School Librarian,* December, 1969, pp. 343-48.
MacCallum, Elizabeth, review of *The Queen of the Pharisees' Children, Globe and Mail* (Toronto), January 13, 1990.
Meek, Margaret, "The Fortunes of Mantlemass," *Times Literary Supplement,* July 18, 1980, p. 805.
Willard, Barbara, essay in *Something about the Author Autobiography Series,* Volume 5, Gale, 1973, pp. 327-41.
Willard, essay in *Fourth Book of Junior Authors and Illustrators,* edited by Doris de Montreville and Elizabeth D. Crawford, H.W. Wilson, 1978, pp. 350-52.

FOR MORE INFORMATION SEE:

BOOKS

Children's Literature Review, Volume 2, Gale, 1976.

PERIODICALS

Growing Point, September, 1978; January, 1988.
Times Literary Supplement, July 15, 1977, p. 859; July 24, 1981, p. 842; July 22, 1983; February 10, 1984; April 12, 1985, p. 418.*

Y

YATES, John 1939-

PERSONAL: Born September 7, 1939, in Brighton, England; son of John Edward (a sales director) and Isabel (a homemaker; maiden name, Cochrane) Yates; married Patricia Margaret Attfield (a secretary), September 15, 1972; children: Sarah Elisabeth, Daniel John. *Education:* West Sussex College of Art and Craft, Worthing, England, 1955-58. *Politics:* Conservative. *Religion:* Church of England.

ADDRESSES: Home and office—4 Mariners Close, Shoreham-by-Sea, West Sussex BN43 5LU, England.

CAREER: Illustrator. McClelland and Stewart, Ltd., Toronto, Canada, chief illustrator, 1967-68; Mercury House Publications, London, England, designer and illustrator, 1968-73; Secura Private, Ltd., Singapore, chief designer and artist, 1973-76; British Council and

JOHN YATES

King Abdul Aziz University, Jeddah, Saudi Arabia, designer and illustrator, 1977-80; Hatlehols Trykkeri A/S, Brattvag, Norway, art director and illustrator, 1984-86. Teacher of graphics and illustration. *Military service:* British Royal Air Force, 1958-61, became corporal.

MEMBER: Chartered Society of Designers.

ILLUSTRATOR:

"YOUNG EXPLORERS" SERIES

Maps and Map Making, Wayland Publishers, Ltd., 1983.
Rivers and Streams, Wayland Publishers, Ltd., 1983.
Hills and Mountains, Wayland Publishers, Ltd., 1983.
Roads, Railways, and Canals, Wayland Publishers, Ltd., 1983.
Where Plants Grow, Wayland Publishers, Ltd., 1983.
Where People Live, Wayland Publishers, Ltd., 1984.
Farms and Farming, Wayland Publishers, Ltd., 1984.
Rocks and Fossils, Wayland Publishers, Ltd., 1984.
Climate and Weather, Wayland Publishers, Ltd., 1984.

"FOOD" SERIES

Potatoes, Wayland Publishers, Ltd., 1988.
Bread, Wayland Publishers, Ltd., 1988.
Milk, Wayland Publishers, Ltd., 1988.
Eggs, Wayland Publishers, Ltd., 1989.
Rice, Wayland Publishers, Ltd., 1989.
Fish, Wayland Publishers, Ltd., 1989.
Citrus Fruit, Wayland Publishers, Ltd., 1989.
Beans and Pulses, Wayland Publishers, Ltd., 1989.
Sugar, Wayland Publishers, Ltd., 1989.
Butter, Wayland Publishers, Ltd., 1989.
Vegetables, Wayland Publishers, Ltd., 1989.
Meat, Wayland Publishers, Ltd., 1990.
Tea, Wayland Publishers, Ltd., 1990.
Apples, Wayland Publishers, Ltd., 1990.
Coffee, Wayland Publishers, Ltd., 1990.
Chocolate, Wayland Publishers, Ltd., 1990.
Pasta, Wayland Publishers, Ltd., 1990.
Herbs and Spices, Wayland Publishers, Ltd., 1990.
Cheese, Wayland Publishers, Ltd., 1990.

"UNDERSTANDING MATH" SERIES

Shape, Wayland Publishers, Ltd., 1991.
Numbers, Wayland Publishers, Ltd., 1991.
Multiplying and Dividing, Wayland Publishers, Ltd., 1991.
Adding and Subtracting, Wayland Publishers, Ltd., 1991.
Graphs and Charts, Wayland Publishers, Ltd., 1992.
Measurement, Wayland Publishers, Ltd., 1992.

"FOOD FACTS" SERIES

Vitamins, Wayland Publishers, Ltd., 1992.
Additives, Wayland Publishers, Ltd., 1992.
Proteins, Wayland Publishers, Ltd., 1992.
Fats, Wayland Publishers, Ltd., 1992.
Sugar, Wayland Publishers, Ltd., 1992.
Fibre, Wayland Publishers, Ltd., 1992.

"HOW MY BODY WORKS" SERIES

Breathing, Wayland Publishers, Ltd., 1992.
Staying Healthy, Wayland Publishers, Ltd., 1992.
Growing, Wayland Publishers, Ltd., 1992.
Eating, Wayland Publishers, Ltd., 1992.
Sleeping, Wayland Publishers, Ltd., 1992.
Moving, Wayland Publishers, Ltd., 1992.

"MY PET" SERIES

Rabbit, Wayland Publishers, Ltd., 1992.
Hamster, Wayland Publishers, Ltd., 1992.
Dog, Wayland Publishers, Ltd., 1992.
Cat, Wayland Publishers, Ltd., 1992.
Fish, Wayland Publishers, Ltd., 1992.
Mini-Pets, Wayland Publishers, Ltd., 1992.
Pony and Horse, Wayland Publishers, Ltd., 1992.
Guinea Pig, Wayland Publishers, Ltd., 1992.

OTHER

The Food Chain, Wayland Publishers, Ltd., 1987.
Our World/Grasslands, Wayland Publishers, Ltd., 1987.
Our World/Temperate Forests, Wayland Publishers, Ltd., 1988.

CO-ILLUSTRATOR

(With Vlasta van Kampen, Jerry Kozoriz, and Gordon McLean) *The Great Lakes,* Natural Science of Canada, 1970.
(With Patricia Lenander, Malcolm McGregor, and Robert Gillmor) *The Life of Birds,,* MacDonald and Co., 1972.
(With Lenander, McGregor, and Peter Harverson) *The Life of Fishes,* MacDonald and Co., 1972.
(With Lenander, McGregor, and Marion Mills) *The Life of Insects,* MacDonald and Co., 1972.
(With Lenander, McGregor, John Barber, Shireen Faircloth, Carol Lawson, Peter Connolly, and Krystyna Rolands) *The Life of Meat Eaters,* MacDonald and Co., 1972.
(With Barber, Joyce Bee, Hilary Burn, Don Forrest, Christine Howes, Annabel Milne, Peter Stebbing, Richard Orr, and Phil Weare) *The Nature Trail of Ponds and Streams,* Usborne Publishing, 1977.

Carnivores provide the subject for Yates' illustrations in the 1973 study *Meat Eaters.*

(With Bruno Elletori, Colin Wilson, and Eugene Fleury) *Discovering the Origins of Mankind,* Trewin Copplestone Books, 1982.
(With Gerard Browne, Carol McCleeve, and Richard Phipps) *Discovering Ecology,* Sceptre Books, 1982.

WORK IN PROGRESS: Research for a children's story book, featuring conservation and green issues.

SIDELIGHTS: John Yates told *SATA:* "I was born in Brighton, a seaside town on the south coast of England. From my earliest memories, drawing, painting, and model-making were my chief hobbies. I can recall as a small boy the excitement and pleasure of planning in my head the big projects I intended to create. I loved pictures and books, and was a very impressionable child, being influenced especially by the cinema."

Yates left school at fifteen to pursue his interests in art, aircraft, and travel. He worked as a technical illustrator at an aircraft construction company and attended art school for three years before joining the Royal Air Force, where he continued his studies in illustration. Later, while working as a technical artist, Yates found himself "drawn more and more to animal and plant drawing. Most surprisingly of all, my love of aircraft was fading." Those feelings were confirmed during a stint as the editorial artist for a gardening magazine. It was during this time, Yates recalls, that it became "my

Yates turned from technical illustrations of aircraft to focus on the portrayal of animals and plants; he has illustrated over sixty books on the natural sciences.

ambition to be involved continually with natural history and the study of plants and animals. The work from the scientific side enthralled me, and as an illustrator of these subjects I was convinced I had found my forte."

The urge to travel has taken Yates to such places as Canada, Singapore, Saudi Arabia, and Norway, yet he has always returned to his native England. Yates believes that he has learned much from his work abroad; for example, he describes his work in Saudi Arabia as "a great experience. The contrast of the empty colorless desert to the vivid color and beauty of scuba-diving in the Red Sea was a complete inspiration. I felt compelled to draw and paint from that environment." The sights of Norway also proved inspirational. Yates remembers that "the light, form, and color of the mountains, fjords, and beautiful snowy landscapes, and a very special natural life, made this a memorable two years. My illustrative work during this time progressed, and I was able to achieve some new techniques."

Yates is currently involved in illustrating children's educational books, "drawing from my past experiences where possible." He adds, "I feel very concerned about the future of the Earth. I am particularly concerned with conservation and all green issues. Through my work I feel I am helping to educate our future generations through children's book publishing. I have a personal goal at some time in the future to write and illustrate my own children's story book concentrating on conservation and animals."

YOUNG, Ed (Tse-chun) 1931-

PERSONAL: Born November 28, 1931, in Tientsin, China; immigrated to United States, 1951, naturalized citizen; son of Qua-Ling (an engineer) and Yuen Teng Young; married, 1962 (divorced, 1969); married Natasha Gorky, June 1, 1971 (marriage ended); married third wife, Filomena. *Education:* Attended City College of San Francisco, 1952, and University of Illinois at Urbana-Champaign, 1952-54; Art Center College of Design, Los Angeles, B.P.A., 1957; graduate study at Pratt Institute, 1958-59.

ADDRESSES: Home—Hastings-on-Hudson, NY.

CAREER: Children's book illustrator and author, 1962—. Mel Richman Studio, New York City, illustrator and designer, 1957-62; Pratt Institute, Brooklyn, NY, instructor in visual communications, 1960-66; Shr Jung T'ai Chi Ch'uan School, New York City, secretary and instructor, 1964-73, director, 1973; Sarah Lawrence College, instructor, Bronxville, NY, 1975—.

AWARDS, HONORS: Award from American Institute of Graphic Arts, 1962, for *The Mean Mouse and Other Mean Stories;* runner-up for Caldecott Medal, 1968, for *The Emperor and the Kite; Horn Book* Honor List and Child Study Association Book Award, both 1969, both

In Ed Young's self-illustrated, wordless picture book *The Other Bone,* a dog loses his bone while trying to catch its reflection.

for *Chinese Mother Goose Rhymes; The Girl Who Loved the Wind* was named a Children's Book Showcase Title in 1973; *New York Times* Best Illustrated Children's Book Award, and Parents' Choice Award, both 1983, both for *Up a Tree; Horn Book* Honor List, 1986, for *Foolish Rabbit's Big Mistake; New York Times* Best Illustrated Children's Book Award, 1988, for *Cats Are Cats;* Caldecott Medal, and *Boston Globe/Horn Book* Award, both 1990, both for *Lon Po Po; Boston Globe/Horn Book* Award, 1992, for *Seven Blind Mice;* U.S. nominee for Hans Christian Andersen Award, 1992.

WRITINGS:

FOR CHILDREN; SELF-ILLUSTRATED

(With Hilary Beckett) *The Rooster's Horns: A Chinese Puppet Play to Make and Perform,* Collins, 1978.
The Terrible Nung Gwama: A Chinese Folktale, Collins, 1978.
High on a Hill: A Book of Chinese Riddles, Collins, 1980.
Up a Tree, Harper, 1983.
The Other Bone, Harper, 1984.
(Translator) *Lon Po Po: A Red Riding Hood Story from China,* Putnam, 1989.
Seven Blind Mice, Philomel, 1992.
Red Thread, Philomel, 1993.

ILLUSTRATOR

Janice M. Udry, *The Mean Mouse and Other Mean Stories,* Harper, 1962.
Leland B. Jacobs and Sally Nohelty, editors, *Poetry for Young Scientists,* Holt, 1964.
Margaret Hillert, *The Yellow Boat,* Follett, 1966.
Jane Yolen, editor, *The Emperor and the Kite,* World Publishing, 1968.
Robert Wyndham, editor, *Chinese Mother Goose Rhymes,* World Publishing, 1968.
Kermit Krueger, *The Golden Swans: A Picture Story from Thailand,* World Publishing, 1969.
Mel Evans, *The Tiniest Sound,* Doubleday, 1969.
Yolen, *The Seventh Mandarin,* Seabury, 1970.
Renee K. Weiss, *The Bird from the Sea,* Crowell, 1970.
Diane Wolkstein, *Eight Thousand Stones: A Chinese Folktale,* Doubleday, 1972.
Yolen, *The Girl Who Loved the Wind,* Crowell, 1972.
L. C. Hunt, editor, *The Horse from Nowhere,* Holt, 1973.
Elizabeth F. Lewis, *Young Fu of the Upper Yangtze,* new edition, Holt, 1973.
Wolkstein, *The Red Lion: A Tale of Ancient Persia,* Crowell, 1977.
Feenie Ziner, *Cricket Boy: A Chinese Tale,* Doubleday, 1977.
N. J. Dawood, *Tales from the Arabian Nights,* Doubleday, 1978.
Wolkstein, *White Wave: A Chinese Tale,* Crowell, 1979.
The Lion and the Mouse: An Aesop Fable, Doubleday, 1979.
Priscilla Jaquith, *Bo Rabbit Smart for True: Folktales from the Gullah,* Philomel, 1981.

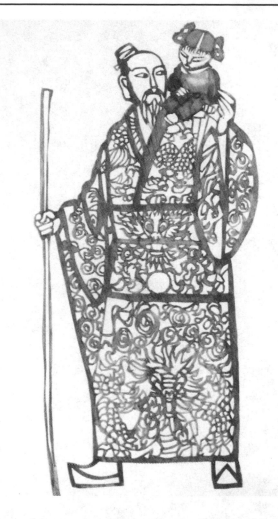

Young was named a runner-up for the Caldecott Medal for his illustrations in Jane Yolan's *The Emperor and the Kite.*

Al-Ling Louie (reteller), *Yeh-Shen: A Cinderella Story from China,* Putnam, 1982.
Mary Scioscia, *Bicycle Rider,* Harper, 1983.
Rafe Martin, editor, *Foolish Rabbit's Big Mistake,* Putnam, 1985.
Jean Fritz, *The Double Life of Pocahontas,* Putnam, 1985.
Phyllis Root, *Moon Tiger,* Holt, 1985.
Margaret Leaf, *Eyes of the Dragon,* Lothrop, 1987.
James Howe, *I Wish I Were a Butterfly,* Harcourt, 1987.
Tony Johnston, *Whale Song,* Putnam, 1987.
Richard Lewis, *In the Night, Still Dark,* Atheneum, 1988.
Nancy Larrick, editor, *Cats Are Cats,* Philomel, 1988.
Robert Frost, *Birches,* Holt, 1988.
Oscar Wilde, *The Happy Prince,* Simon & Schuster, 1989.
Hearn, Lafcadio, *The Voice of the Great Bell,* retold by Margaret Hodges, Little, Brown, 1989.
Ruth Y. Radin, *High in the Mountains,* Macmillan, 1989.
Larrick, editor, *Mice Are Nice,* Putnam, 1990.
R. Lewis, *All of You Was Singing,* Macmillan, 1991.
Nancy White Carlstrom, *Goodbye, Geese,* Philmel, 1991.

Young used soft colors to create the images for Phyllis Root's *Moon Tiger*.

Barbara Savadge Horton, *What Comes in Spring?,* Knopf, 1992.

Mary Calhoun, *While I Sleep,* Morrow, 1992.

Audrey Osofsky, *Dreamcatcher,* Orchard, 1992.

Laura Krauss Melmed, *The First Song Ever Sung,* Lothrop, 1993.

Also illustrator of *The Child's First Books,* by Donnarae MacCann and Olga Richard, 1973, and of film *Sadako and the Thousand Paper Cranes,* based on the story by Eleanor Coerr.

SIDELIGHTS: Ed Young has been illustrating children's books for other authors since the early 1960s; he began writing and illustrating his own in the early 1970s. He often works on projects featuring the folklore of his native China, such as Robert Wyndham's *Chinese Mother Goose Rhymes,* Diane Wolkstein's *Eight Thousand Stones,* and his own Caldecott Medal-winning translation *Lon Po Po: A Red Riding Hood Story from China.* But he has also illustrated editions of great works in the Western tradition, such as Robert Frost's *Birches* and Oscar Wilde's fairy tale *The Happy Prince.*

Young was born November 28, 1931, in Tientsin, China. When he was a boy, his family moved around a lot to escape the wartime invasions of the Japanese. They settled for a time in Shanghai, where Young had a happy childhood, playing with his siblings and friends. As the author recalled in the *Third Book of Junior Authors,* "The war restricted many material things, but my family learned to develop great tenacity and flexibility so as to enjoy life under the most adverse circumstances." From an early age, he made up plays and created many drawings. He did not put as much effort into his schoolwork, because as a child he was determined to do something artistic with the rest of his life; "my formal schooling was secondary to my dreams and everything would be all right in the end," the author recounted.

When the communists took the city of Shanghai during the Chinese civil war, the high-school-age Young moved with his family to Hong Kong. Afterwards, he immigrated to the United States to attend first the City College of San Francisco, then the University of Illinois at Urbana-Champaign. At these schools he studied architecture, trying to put his artistic talents to more practical use, but after enrolling in as many art classes as possible for his architecture program, he decided to try a summer program focusing specifically on art. After that course at the Art Center College of Design, Young stopped fighting his inclinations and enrolled there as a full-time student.

After obtaining his bachelor's degree from the Art Center College of Design, Young moved to New York City to seek his fortune. He recalled in an interview with *Publishers Weekly*'s Dulcy Brainard: "I came with $25 in my pocket. I wanted to try my hand, see how good I was, so it had to be New York. Advertising agencies, magazines, everything was there, and everything seemed possible." Young landed a job with an advertising agency, where one of his assignments was the U.S. Army's recruiting campaign. His designs were successful, appearing on posters and billboards all over the area.

While working in advertising, Young continued his artistic education by attending lectures, visiting museums, and taking graduate courses at Pratt Institute. He also served as an instructor in visual communications there. He recalled for Brainard that while "taking a course at Pratt in industrial design, I ran across a person who thought a designer must have social responsibility. I started rethinking a lot of things." Advertising work, while lucrative, was not as satisfying to him. In 1961, when the agency for which he worked had failed, Young tried his hand at a new field. For years he had spent his lunch hours sketching the animals at New York City's Central Park Zoo; friends who saw these sketches suggested that he illustrate children's books.

"The first name given to me was Ursula Nordstrom at Harper & Row," Young recounted to Brainard. "I didn't know who she was, I just called up, made an appointment and went over with a bunch of drawings stuffed in a shopping bag.... I got into her office, took out this stack of drawings on rice paper with brush, and she looked. She was quiet for a while and then she said, 'As a matter of fact I have something here.' She opened a drawer and brought out the manuscript for *The Mean Mouse and Other Mean Stories.* It was very short so I read it right there. It featured animals in a kind of slapstick [format]. I didn't want to do it, but she said I should take it home and think about it. I showed it to my roommate, complaining that I didn't want to do cartoons. He said, 'Then don't. Do what you think it *should* be.' So that's what I did."

Even though Young followed his own inclinations illustrating *The Mean Mouse,* he didn't think illustrating children's books would provide a decent living. But *The Mean Mouse* won an award from the American Institute of Graphic Arts, and brought Young to the attention of Elizabeth Armstrong, an artists' agent who encouraged

him to continue his illustration work. As Young told Brainard: "She was *good* and kept me busy doing everything. As she got to know me, she offered things that challenged me, that were exciting and made me grow."

Since that time, Young has illustrated over forty books, including a few of his own. *Up a Tree* and *The Other Bone,* two of his own creations, have no text but tell their stories—one of a cat who gets stuck in a tree, the other of a dog who loses his bone trying to get at its reflection in water—solely through pictures. In addition to his many Chinese-oriented projects, he has illustrated stories from cultures such as the Gullah people and the Persians, and stories from history. One of Young's favorite projects was illustrating Jean Fritz's *The Double Life of Pocahontas,* "not just because she's a friend and lives nearby," he explained to Brainard, "but she does her own research thoroughly and supplies me with everything I want. Though, the funny thing is, I found a descendant of Pocahontas living here in town and used her for a model."

A runner-up for the Caldecott Medal in 1968 for illustrating Jane Yolen's *The Emperor and the Kite,* Young won that prestigious award in 1990 for his self-illustrated translation, *Lon Po Po: A Red Riding Hood Story from China.* The story of three sisters who outwit

Three sisters outwit an evil wolf who sneaks into their home in Young's self-illustrated *Lon Po Po: A Red Riding Hoood Story from China.*

an evil wolf who sneaks into their home, *Lon Po Po* is a "gripping" story that "possesses that matter-of-fact veracity that charaterizes the best fairy tales," John Philbrook comments in *School Library Journal.* In *Lon Po Po,* Young uses the technique of dividing his illustrations into sections in order to suggest the form of old Chinese decorative screens. The illustrations "often serve to direct the reader's attention across the page, like a movie camera filming a scene," George Shannon asserts in the *Los Angeles Times Book Review.* The pictures add to the story's mystery, the critic continues: "Rather than illustrating only the words of his tale, ... Young has given new life to its metaphoric essence and created a book to savor."

Writing in the *Bulletin of the Center for Children's Books,* Betsy Hearne also praises Young's evocative artwork, observing that "the wolf makes an eerie appearance in Young's art, with white staring eyes, a long sinister muzzle, and shadowy textured fur." The psychological use of the villainous wolf is noted by Carolyn Phelan in her review for *Booklist:* "Recalling an Indian prayer to the spirit of a deer before releasing the arrow to kill it, Young dedicates the book 'To all the wolves of the world for lending their good name as a tangible symbol for our darkness.'" Hearne concludes that *Lon Po Po* is "a must for folklore and storytelling collections."

WORKS CITED:

Brainard, Dulcy, "Ed Young," *Publishers Weekly,* February 24, 1989, pp. 208-209.
Hearn, Betsy, review of *Lon Po Po: A Red-Riding Hood Story from China, Bulletin of the Center for Children's Books,* November, 1989, p. 74.
Phelan, Carolyn, review of *Lon Po Po: A Red-Riding Hood Story from China, Booklist,* November 15, 1989, p. 672.
Philbrook, John, review of *Lon Po Po: A Red-Riding Hood Story from China, School Library Journal,* December, 1989, p. 97.
Shannon, George, "Of Metaphors and a Boy Flat as a Page," *Los Angeles Times Book Review,* December 10, 1989, p. 9.
Young, Ed, *Third Book of Junior Authors,* edited by Doris de Montreville and Donna Hill, Wilson, 1972.

FOR MORE INFORMATION SEE:

BOOKS

Children's Literature Review, Volume 27, Gale, 1992.

PERIODICALS

Bulletin of the Center for Children's Books, July/August, 1980, October, 1983, June, 1984.
Horn Book, April, 1984.
School Library Journal, January, 1990.
Tribune Books (Chicago), January 14, 1990.

YOUNT, Lisa 1944-

PERSONAL: Born July 28, 1944, in Los Angeles, CA; daughter of Stanley George (founder and chief executive officer of an industrial paper company) and Agnes (an assistant sales manager of a paper company; maiden name, Pratt) Yount; married Charles Siegfried, January 11, 1969 (divorced October, 1970); married Alec Hamilton, October, 1970 (divorced, January, 1980); married Harry Richard Henderson (a writer and editor of computer books), September 23, 1982. *Education:* Stanford University, B.A. (cum laude), 1966. *Politics:* "As little as possible." *Hobbies and other interests:* Photography, poetry, storytelling, songwriting, singing, nature, medicine and biology, environmental issues.

ADDRESSES: Home and office—2631 Mira Vista Dr., El Cerrito, CA 94530.

CAREER: Free-lance textbook writer in San Francisco Bay area, 1967—; free-lance author of books for children and editor, 1980—. Nature guide, Terwilliger Nature Education Center, Corte Madera, CA; volunteer for San Francisco Society for the Prevention of Cruelty to Animals, Sierra Club Save the Bay, and other organizations.

MEMBER: Berkeley Camera Club (field trip chair, 1990-91).

AWARDS, HONORS: Outstanding Science Trade Books for Children citations from Committee of National Science Teachers Association and Children's Book Council, 1981, for *Too Hot, Too Cold, Just Right,* and 1983, for *The Telescope;* Pelican Award, Terwilliger Nature Education Center, 1991, for nature guiding and other activities.

LISA YOUNT

AMERICAN PROFILES

BLACK SCIENTISTS

LISA YOUNT

Yount profiles the lives and achievements of African American inventors, doctors, and scholars in this volume.

WRITINGS:

Too Hot, Too Cold, Just Right, Walker & Co., 1981.
The Telescope, Walker & Co., 1983.
Lore of Our Land, J. Weston Walch, 1984.
Black Scientists, Facts on File, 1991.
Cancer, Lucent/Greenhaven, 1991.
True Adventure Readers, J. Weston Walch, 1992.

Contributor of articles to *International Wildlife, National Wildlife, Cobblestone, Ranger Rick's Nature Magazine, Jack and Jill, Highlights for Children;* contributor of poetry to many small press magazines.

WORK IN PROGRESS: Biographies of contemporary women scientists.

SIDELIGHTS: Lisa Yount writes: "I grew up in San Marino, a small town near Pasadena in southern California. My mother read to me often, and soon I could 'read' my favorite books back to her by reciting them from memory. (I once 'read' one while holding it upside down!). I also tried to read her extensive collection of murder mysteries, a kind of book I still like. My father and I loved to sing folk-songs together. Neither of us was a good singer, but we had fun. He also told stories from the Bible and from his own life.

"I soon began telling and then writing stories, songs, and poems of my own. One of the first stories I wrote down was a fantasy serial, 'Mary the Magic Cat.' I told Mary's adventures to my fellow riders in a day-camp car-pool when I was in fourth grade, and each day they asked to hear more.

"I didn't plan to be a writer, though. I was going to be a scientist, doing medical research. Somewhere in the middle of college chemistry I finally faced the fact that I was too much of a klutz in the lab to be successful in this career. I didn't lose my interest in medical and biological research, but I decided I had better write about it rather than try to do it.

"After college I found a job editing and writing material for textbooks, and I have continued to work in this field ever since. I'm a 'free-lancer,' so I've done work for many different publishers. I've worked on books that teach reading, science, social studies, and other subjects to students between grade 3 and high school. Many people work on a textbook, and their names are not always mentioned in the book. You may have read something of mine in school, even though you didn't know it!

"I wanted to have more control over what I wrote than I could have in textbooks, so I also began writing articles for children's magazines. One of these was expanded into my first book. Both the article (which appeared in *Ranger Rick's Nature Magazine*) and the book were called *Too Hot, Too Cold, Just Right.* They explained some of the unusual ways that animals keep their body temperature 'just right,' no matter how hot or cold it is outside.

"All my books so far have been nonfiction. I like to tell people, especially young people, about the strange and fascinating things that exist in nature. I agree with the British poet Robert Louis Stevenson that 'the world is so full of a number of things / I'm sure we should all be as happy as kings.'

"I live with my husband, who is also a writer, and our four cats in a big house in the San Francisco Bay area. I love writing while sitting in my armchair, typing on my laptop computer (which the cats try to sit on) and looking at the Monterey pines out my window."